T0418570

ST ANTONINUS OF FLORENCE ON TRADE, MERCHANTS, AND WORKERS

St Antoninus of Florence on Trade, Merchants, and Workers

JASON AARON BROWN

UNIVERSITY OF TORONTO PRESS
Toronto Buffalo London

Toronto Buffalo London
utorontopress.com

ISBN 978-1-4875-4594-9 (cloth)
ISBN 978-1-4875-4599-4 (EPUB)
ISBN 978-1-4875-4600-7 (PDF)

Library and Archives Canada Cataloguing in Publication

Title: St Antoninus of Florence on trade, merchants, and workers / Jason Aaron Brown.

Names: Brown, Jason Aaron, author. | Container of (work): Antoninus, Saint, Archbishop of Florence, 1389–1459. Summa theologica. | Container of (expression): Antoninus, Saint, Archbishop of Florence, 1389–1459. Summa theologica. English.

Series: Toronto studies in medieval law; 5.

Description: Series statement: Toronto studies in medieval law ; 5 | Includes bibliographical references and index. | Text in English; some text in Latin.

Identifiers: Canadiana (print) 20230525679 | Canadiana (ebook) 20230525709 | ISBN 9781487545949 (cloth) | ISBN 9781487545994 (EPUB) | ISBN 9781487546007 (PDF)

Subjects: LCSH: Antoninus, Saint, Archbishop of Florence, 1389–1459. Summa theologica. | LCSH: Economics – Moral and ethical aspects – Italy – Early works to 1800. | LCSH: Italy – Commerce – Early works to 1800. | LCSH: Merchants – Italy – Early works to 1800. | LCSH: Employees – Italy – Early works to 1800.

Classification: LCC BX1749.T6 B76 2024 | DDC 330.945/05–dc23

Jacket illustration: Cloister Artworks, San Marco Museum, Florence, Italy, Neil Setchfield / Alamy Stock Photo

Jacket design: Liz Harasymczuk

We wish to acknowledge the land on which the University of Toronto Press operates. This land is the traditional territory of the Wendat, the Anishnaabeg, the Haudenosaunee, the Métis, and the Mississaugas of the Credit First Nation.

University of Toronto Press gratefully acknowledges the financial assistance of the Centre for Medieval Studies, University of Toronto in the publication of this book.

This book has been published with the help of a grant from the Federation for the Humanities and Social Sciences, through the Awards to Scholarly Publications Program, using funds provided by the Social Sciences and Humanities Research Council of Canada.

University of Toronto Press acknowledges the financial support of the Government of Canada, the Canada Council for the Arts, and the Ontario Arts Council, an agency of the Government of Ontario, for its publishing activities.

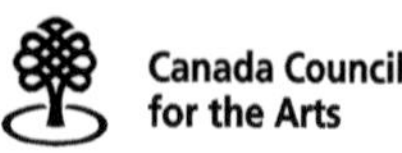

Funded by the Government of Canada
Financé par le gouvernement du Canada

Dedicated to Jacqueline

Contents

Tables, Plates, and Figures

Tables

Plates

Figures

Photos

Photos

Photo of St Antoninus's relics is by Sailko. Photo of the "Duomo" of Florence is by Bruce Stokes. Both are available freely under Creative Commons Licences, https://creativecommons.org/.
Photo of F_3 fol. 1 was taken by the staff of the Biblioteca Nazionale Centrale di Firenze.
All other photos taken by Jason Aaron Brown.

Acknowledgments

I could not have completed this book without the support of many people and institutions. Though I want to name and thank everyone who has helped me or been a friend since I began graduate studies ten years ago, I will confine myself here to those who have supported this particular project in some way.

I wish to thank the director, Magnolia Scudieri, and staff of the Museo di San Marco and Luciano Cinelli, OP, of Santa Maria Novella, who permitted me to consult and photograph the precious autograph manuscripts of St Antoninus's *Summa*, and allowed me generous time and freedom in working with them while I was in Florence in June of 2016. I am also grateful for the assistance of librarians at the Pontifical Institute of Mediaeval Studies Library, Kelly Library, and Robarts Library at the University of Toronto, as well as at St Paul's College and Elizabeth Dafoe libraries, University of Manitoba, and the University of Winnipeg Library. The Department of History at the University of Manitoba has been my professional home for the past five years, providing me not only with office space but with a congenial faculty to teach in. I have also benefited from being, for several periods, part of the Department of Classics at the University of Winnipeg and the Institute for the Humanities at the University of Manitoba.

The research for this book has been supported with funding from many sources since I began it as a PhD student in 2016. I am grateful for the following grants and scholarships: Open Fellowship from the University of Toronto; Ontario Graduate Scholarship from the Government of Ontario; Canada Graduate Scholarship from the Social Sciences and Humanities Research Council of Canada; Research Travel Grant from the School of Graduate Studies; John Munro Doctoral Fellowship in Medieval Economic History from the Munro family; research stipends from the Institute for the Humanities, University of Manitoba; Calihan Academic Grant from the Acton Institute; Anniversary Bursary in Moral Theology from the Redemptorists in English Canada. Finally, the publication of this book has been made possible by funding from the Centre for Medieval Studies, University of Toronto, and the Awards to Scholarly Publications Program, Federation for the Humanities and Social Sciences.

I extend my thanks to the two anonymous readers retained by the University of Toronto Press, who read a very long manuscript with care and whose reviews gave me much encouragement and many useful suggestions. In particular, thanks to their advice this book is quite a bit more accessible to non-specialists than it would have been otherwise, and chapters 1 and 4 (specifically the preamble) have been revised, expanded, and, I believe, made more useful and effective. I have made a serious attempt to apply their thoughts on how to revise the translation, whose clarity has been improved by them. Donna Brown also devoted a lot of time and care to reading through the translation and adding comments, for which I thank her.

I wish to thank in a special way the series editor, Lawrin Armstrong. It was he and Giulio Silano who suggested that I take a look at St Antoninus's writing as a possible editorial project – a suggestion which has proved very fruitful. He was a superb doctoral supervisor and has continued to be a great mentor to me. He has read every chapter of this book at least twice, some three times or more. I am honoured that my book will be the final entry in this series. I extend thanks also to Suzanne Rancourt and Barbara Porter at University of Toronto Press for steering this book through the publication process, and likewise Stephanie Mazza, Judy Williams, Jolanta Komornicka, and Joel Kalvesmaki for their assistance.

I also want to thank the teachers, advisors, and colleagues who have encouraged me in my work on this book and contributed to the intellectual formation which has made it possible: Roisin Cossar, David Watt, Atria Larson, David Peterson, William Caferro, the Rev. Michael Eades, CO, David Foley, Giulio Silano, Alexander Andrée, Joseph Goering, John Magee, Alexander Callander Murray, John Finlay, and Mark Gabbert. My work on St Antoninus has benefited enormously from my friendship with Samuel Klumpenhouwer. I learn something new about medieval canon law, pastoral literature, and biblical studies every time we speak.

I offer heartfelt thanks to my parents Brian and Kelly, my parents-in-law Gabriel and Louise, and my aunt Donna, who have all supported and encouraged me while working on this book these last several years. My children Rosalie, Gabrielle, Elisabeth, Michaël, and Catherine have also been very encouraging, though doubtless they would have liked me to spend less time on the book and more time playing with them. I appreciate their patience.

Finally, in thanks for more than I can express, I dedicate this book to my wife Jacqueline.

Winnipeg
24 August 2022

Preface

St Antoninus or Sant'Antonino, OP, is a moderately well known figure in medieval and Renaissance history. As archbishop of Florence from 1446 until his death in 1459, he governed the Florentine church and was a major figure in civic politics during the height of the Renaissance and the early years of the Medici regime. He was a popular preacher and had a reputation as a model bishop. He has a place in art history as the founder of the Dominican monastery of San Marco in Florence, under whose supervision San Marco was decorated by the celebrated painter Fra Angelico, one of the Dominican friars there. Antoninus's house of San Marco was a spiritual home nourishing such later figures as Girolamo Savonarola and St Philip Neri. Through his prolific writings, Antoninus's influence extended yet more widely; and finally, his canonization in 1523 held him up to the whole Catholic Church as a model to follow and as an intercessor to invoke.

Of St Antoninus's writings, his four-volume *Summa* holds pride of place. It is one of the most comprehensive medieval works of moral theology. It has been read and studied ever since it was completed circa 1454, and for scholars of more recent centuries has held interest for the investigation of both doctrinal and socio-historical questions. For scholars of the history of economic analysis and business ethics, the *Summa* of St Antoninus has long been counted among the more copious, influential, and rewarding medieval sources. It is to this field of inquiry that this book primarily contributes.

The purpose of this book is twofold. Its first purpose is to make available, for scholars and interested lay readers alike, St Antoninus of Florence's teaching on trade, merchants, and workers in as accessible and useful a form as possible. The successful reading of an author depends upon possessing an accurate text, understanding the language, and being able to make sense of the author's doctrinal, historical, and literary references. This book aims to meet these needs through providing a newly edited Latin text accompanied by an English translation, as well as an extensive introduction to Antoninus's teaching.

The foundation is a critical edition of the Latin text of six chapters from Antoninus's *Summa*: 2.1.16 (*De fraudulentia* / On fraud); 2.1.17 (*De variis fraudibus que commictuntur in negotiando* / On the various frauds which are committed in trading); 3.8.1 (*De merchatoribus et artificibus* / On merchants and workers); 3.8.2 (*De diversis generibus contractuum* / On the various kinds of contracts); 3.8.3 (*De negotiatoribus et campsoribus* / On traders and bankers); 3.8.4 (*De diversis generibus artificum* / On the various kinds of workers). The Latin text of these six chapters has been established and critically edited from the original autograph manuscripts. This edition furnishes a more accurate text of these chapters than any other edition currently available. It also provides two *apparatus* which should prove useful to readers and scholars. The *apparatus criticus*, in addition to flagging editorial interventions, indicates the traces of the author's process of composition which remain in the manuscript. The *apparatus fontium* not only completes Antoninus's own citations in modern format, but also provides quotations from the texts Antoninus cites, and indicates other probable or certain sources which Antoninus draws upon for his teaching insofar as the editor has been able to discover them. Finally, an English translation of each chapter has been included, again with the goal of making Antoninus's teaching as accessible as possible. The edition and translation make up part two of this book.

The introduction, which makes up part one, is aimed at explaining Antoninus's teaching on trade, merchants, and workers. Chapter 1 introduces the author St Antoninus of Florence, providing a biography which focuses on outlining his formative influences and the most important historical events which impacted his life, including the Great Schism, the Observant reform movement, and the reign of the Medici in Florence. Chapter 2 provides an overview of Antoninus's *Summa* as a whole, with a particularly detailed study of what the evidence of the autograph manuscripts reveals about the process of composition; this is the most thorough study of the autograph manuscripts that has yet been produced. Chapter 3 provides an introduction to the scholastic tradition of teaching on justice in buying and selling, from which Antoninus acquired his basic moral and economic doctrines; this chapter shows the origins of the principles of economic ethics which Antoninus employs and which were common staples of the scholastic tradition, with a particular focus on the "just price" doctrine. Chapter 4 provides an overview of Antoninus's teaching: it begins by examining historians' arguments about Italian business culture in the wake of the medieval "Commercial Revolution," and whether this culture can be considered capitalistic; then it provides an explanation and analysis of each of the six chapters edited herein; it concludes by proposing an interpretation of the intended purpose of Antoninus's teaching.

The second purpose of this book is to show why a new edition of St Antoninus's *Summa* is desirable, and to illustrate how such an edition can be produced. As an author, St Antoninus is singularly fortunate in that his autograph manuscripts survive, and can be used to recover the text as the author intended it. This has yet to be done, however; scholars continue to rely primarily on Ballerini's edition as the standard reference text, or other early printed editions which did not have recourse to the autograph manuscripts, instead reproducing some version of the received "vulgate" text of Antoninus's *Summa*. My new edition of the six chapters herein, and my work exploring the autograph manuscripts as a whole, shows that these early printed editions cannot be relied upon as consistently transmitting the text Antoninus actually wrote. For ease of reference, Ballerini's edition can be used, but arguments about what Antoninus taught should be based on the text contained in the autograph manuscripts. In my edition and occasionally in my introduction (for example chapter 4, section 5), I give examples of passages printed in Ballerini's edition which do not exist in the autograph manuscripts: they were added to Antoninus's *Summa* by a later copyist or editor at some point between the fifteenth and eighteenth centuries. I have tried in this book to provide as much help as possible to enable scholars to consult the autograph manuscripts successfully, through explanations of their makeup and organization (chapter 2), which are by no means simple, and illustrations of Antoninus's handwriting (appendix 3). I have also tried to show, in chapter 2, section 3, as well as in appendix 1, some of the possibilities for discovering Antoninus's process of composition through the codicology of the autograph manuscripts. Until a complete critical edition of Antoninus's *Summa* is produced, however, it will be in practice difficult for scholars to know if a given passage printed by Ballerini was really written by Antoninus. I hope to produce this edition myself, but the task is immense, and I welcome the forays of other scholars into this field.

A note on citing Antoninus's *Summa*: as I explain below in chapter 2, Antoninus organized his *Summa* in four parts, each part being divided into numbered titles, and each title subdivided into chapters. For clarity and consistency, scholars should adopt the method of citing Antoninus's *Summa* by part, title, and chapter, followed by the page, folio, or column number of the edition they are using. For example, the first chapter I have edited herein is chapter 16 of title 1 in part 2. I suggest that a scholar reading it in Ballerini's edition should cite it thus: Antoninus Florentinus, *Summa*, 2.1.16 (Ballerini 2:247–61). A scholar using my edition and translation in this book could cite it this way: Antoninus Florentinus, *Summa*, 2.1.16, in Jason Aaron Brown, *St Antoninus of Florence on Trade, Merchants, and Workers*, page or section number, line number.

Abbreviations

AL	Aristoteles Latinus.
Ballerini	Antoninus Florentinus. *Sancti Antonini archiepiscopi Florentini ordinis praedicatorum Summa theologica in quattuor partes distributa …* Edited by Pietro Ballerini. 4 vols. Verona, 1740. Facsimile reprint with prologue by Innocenzo Colosio. Graz: Akademische Druck- U. Verlagsanstalt, 1959.
BISLAM	*Bibliotheca Scriptorum Latinorum Medii Recentiorisque Aevi.* Edited by Roberto Gamberini. Florence: SISMEL, Edizioni del Galluzzo, 2003.
BNC	Biblioteca Nazionale Centrale.
CALMA	*Compendium auctorum latinorum medii aevi (CALMA).* Edited by Michael Lapidge, Silvia Nocentini, Francesco Santi, and Claudio Leonardi. Bottai: SISMEL, Edizioni del Galluzzo, 2000–.
DMLBS	R.E. Latham, D.R. Howlett, and R.K. Ashdowne, eds. *Dictionary of Medieval Latin from British Sources.* Oxford: British Academy, 1975–2013.
Du Cange	Du Cange et al. *Glossarium mediae et infimae latinitatis.* Niort: L. Favre, 1883–7.
Friedberg	*Corpus iuris canonici.* Edited by Emil Friedberg. 2 vols. Leipzig, 1879; repr. Graz: Akademische Druck und Verlaganstalt, 1959.
GDLI	*Grande dizionario della lingua italiana.* 21 vols. Turin: Unione tipografico-editrice torinese, 1961–2002.
LCL	Loeb Classical Library.
LS	Charlton T. Lewis and Charles Short, eds. *A Latin Dictionary.* Oxford: Clarendon Press, 1879.
Mamachi	Antoninus Florentinus. *Sancti Antonini archiepiscopi Florentini ordinis praedicatorum Opera omnia ad autographorum fidem nunc primum exacta, vita illius, variis dissertationibus, et adnotationibus aucta.* Edited by Tommaso Maria Mamachi and Dionisio Remedelli. *Summa* parts 1 and 2 in 4 vols. Florence, 1741–56.

McKeon	*The Basic Works of Aristotle*. Edited by Richard McKeon. Introduction by C.D.C. Reeve. New York: Modern Library, 2001.
Ochoa-Diez	*Universa Bibliotheca Iuris*. Edited by Xaviero Ochoa and Aloisio Diez. Rome: Instituto Iuridico Claretiano, 1964–78.
PL	Patrologia cursus completus, series Latina. Paris: J.-P. Migne.
SOPMA	Thomas Kaeppeli and Emilio Panella. *Scriptores ordinis praedicatorum medii aevi*. 4 vols. Rome: Istituto Storico Domenicano, 1970–93.
TUI	*Tractatus Universi Iuris*. 25 vols. Venice, 1584–6.

When citing sources published before 1600, reference will be provided to internal divisions of the text (e.g., book, title, chapter, paragraph) followed by the page number, within parentheses, of the edition consulted. The edition can be found under the author's name in the bibliography.

The *Decretum* of Gratian is cited using the following abbreviations:

c.	*Capitulum.*
C.	*Causa.*
D.	*Distinctio.*
q.	*Quaestio.*
De cons.	*Tractatus de consecratione ecclesiae*, i.e., part 3 of the *Decretum.*
De pen.	*Tractatus de penitentia*, in part 2 of the *Decretum* (C. 33 q. 3).

The canon-law decretal collections (*Corpus iuris canonici*) and civil-law texts (*Corpus iuris civilis*) are cited by book, title, and chapter number, preceded by one of the following identifiers:

X	*Liber Extra*, the book of decretals of Gregory IX.
VI	*Liber Sext* of Boniface VIII.
Extrav.Jo.	*Extravagantes* of John XXII.
Clem.	*Constitutiones* of Clement V.
Extrav.Comm.	*Extravagantes Communes.*
Cod.	*Codex Iustiniani.*
Dig.	*Digesta Iustiniani.*
Nov.	*Novellae constitutiones Iustiniani.*

For further explanation of legal citations, see James A. Brundage, "The Romano-Canonical Citation System," appendix 1 in *Medieval Canon Law* (London: Longman, 1995), 190–205.

English quotations of the Holy Bible are from the Douay-Rheims translation. Latin quotations are from the Vulgate: *Biblia Sacra iuxta Vulgatam versionem*, ed. Robert Weber. Abbreviations for books of the Holy Bible follow those employed in *Vulgate Bible: Douay-Rheims Translation*, Dumbarton Oaks Medieval Library.

Chronology of St Antoninus's Life

Year	Age	Events
1378		Ciompi Revolt in Florence; the Great Schism begins; St Catherine of Siena in Rome
1389		Antoninus (Antonio Pierozzi) is born in late March or early April (after 25 March)
1395	6	Antoninus's mother dies
1399	10	The Bianchi sweep Italy; Giovanni Dominici is exiled from Venice
1404	15	Antoninus asks Giovanni Dominici to allow him to become a Dominican friar
1405	16	Antoninus admitted to novitiate (Cortona); Dominici founds San Domenico of Fiesole
1406	17	Antoninus makes his profession; becomes a friar at San Domenico of Fiesole
1409	20	Observant friars of San Domenico expelled from Fiesole; Antoninus goes to Foligno
1413	24	Antoninus ordained to the priesthood in Cortona
1414	25	Antoninus's father dies
1417	28	Great Schism comes to an end at Council of Constance
1418	29	Antoninus prior in Cortona
1421	32	Antoninus prior of San Domenico of Fiesole
1424	35	Antoninus sent to Naples as visitator then prior; he begins to write
1429	40	Antoninus prior of Santa Maria sopra Minerva in Rome
1430	41	Antoninus oversees translation of relics of St Catherine of Siena in Rome

Year	Age	Events
1431	42	Eugenius IV elected pope while Antoninus resides in Rome; Council of Basel begins
1432	43	Antoninus is appointed as auditor general of the Roman Rota at roughly this time
1434	45	Eugenius IV moves to Florence; Cosimo de' Medici returns from exile
1435	46	Antoninus returns to Florence and resides there for most of the rest of his life
1436	47	San Marco granted to the Observant Dominicans of San Domenico by Eugenius IV
1437	48	Antoninus is vicar general of Observant Dominicans in Italy
1439	50	Antoninus is prior of San Domenico and San Marco; Council of Florence begins
1440	51	Antoninus writes many treatises and replies to questions in roughly these years
1442	53	Antoninus founds *Buonomini* di San Martino
1443	54	Eugenius IV returns to Rome
1444	55	Library of San Marco completed; Antoninus writes very productively for next five years
1445	56	Antoninus is vicar general of Observants; the archbishop of Florence dies
1446	57	Antoninus is consecrated archbishop of Florence
1447	58	Eugenius IV dies; Council of Basel ends
1449	60	Antoninus has finished writing most of parts 2 and 3 of the *Summa*
1450	61	Antoninus condemns Giovanni de Montecatini, who is burned at the stake
1454	65	Antoninus completes the *Summa*; he continues writing the *Chronicles*
1455	66	Antoninus issues a constitution for his diocese
1458	69	Antoninus rebukes the Medici attempt at open balloting, threatens excommunication
1459	70	Antoninus dies on 2 May 1459
1516		Canonization process opened for Antoninus
1523		St Antoninus canonized

PART ONE

Introduction

Photo 1. St Antoninus's relics, Basilica di San Marco, Florence

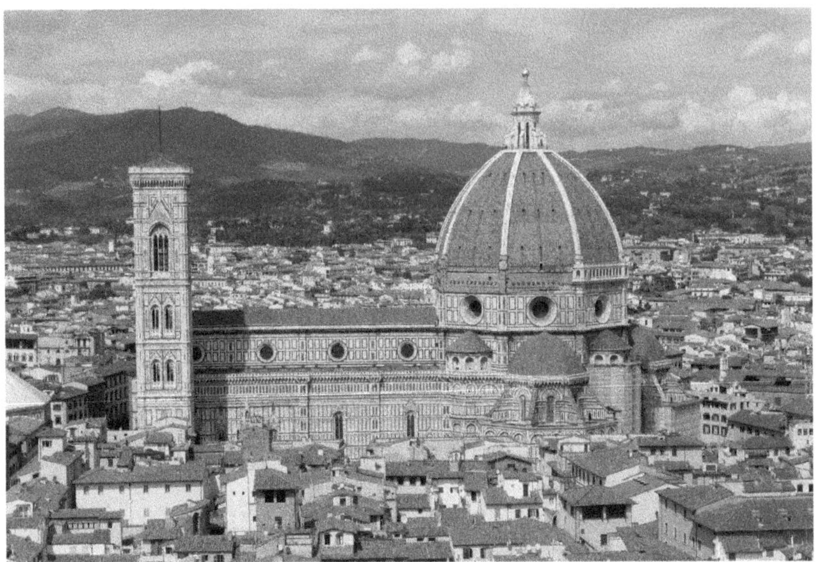

Photo 2. The "Duomo" of Florence, Cattedrale di Santa Maria del Fiore

Photo 3 Statue of St Antoninus by Giovanni Dupré (1854) located in the Loggiato degli Uffizi, Florence

1 St Antoninus of Florence

Preamble. St Antoninus Today

If you visit the city of Florence, you will very likely wish to take a tour of the Museo di San Marco, a former monastery of the Dominican friars, where you can see many of the painter Fra Angelico's masterpieces. A few steps away from the entrance to the museum are the large wooden doors of the church attached to the monastery. Entering, you will find a high-roofed square neoclassical church, beautifully decorated with sculpted stone and carved wood painted with gold. Approaching the altar and turning left, you will be looking into a side chapel filled with pillars, carvings, paintings, and busts, all lit up by a high window in the wall opposite you. If your eyes move up past the window you will see a statue standing over the archway into this side chapel, high above you: a thin man in the dress of a Catholic bishop, mitre on his head, cradling a staff topped with a cross in his left arm, his right hand raised in blessing. Look down now to ground level and you will see that man in the flesh, lying in a glass coffin at the centre of the chapel. He lies dressed in gold vestments, his mitred head resting on a pillow, his body emaciated but still preserved over 560 years after his death. To Italians he is Sant'Antonino, to the French Saint Antonin, to English speakers St Antoninus.

Once you become aware of him, you'll start to notice that Florence is full of artistic representations of St Antoninus. Taking the tour through San Marco, the cloister where you first enter the museum has twenty-two scenes from his life depicted on its four walls. Beginning at his youth, you will see a small boy praying before the crucifix in the church of Orsanmichele; then a teen asking Friar Giovanni Dominici to let him enter the Dominican order. You will see Antoninus, having become a Dominican and been raised to a position of high rank within the order, supervising the construction of San Marco itself and consecrating it while a pope looks on; from there, you will see him entering the city of Florence as its new archbishop in the year 1446, preaching in the cathedral, founding a charitable society for the shamefaced poor, performing miracles, confronting scammers and gamblers, and ministering to the sick during a plague. Finally you will see his funeral, which another pope presided over in 1459. Continuing into the monastery, on the second floor you can look into Antoninus's own cell, where he resided during his years in charge of the monastery and where he returned whenever he could in his later years, to retreat from his activity as archbishop and recollect himself in prayer.

Walk a few streets southwest from San Marco, and you can follow the Via Sant'Antonino to the other Dominican monastery in Florence at the church of Santa Maria Novella. Within the church you will see a bust of St Antoninus on a wall beside the altar. Passing on to the heart of the city, there stands the great "Duomo" of Florence, the Cathedral of Santa Maria del Fiore with its peerless red-brick dome. Above the great bronze doors is a painting of Christ seated and receiving homage from saints; at the same height at the right-hand end of the façade is St Antoninus again, in his familiar mitre and cope, making the sign of the cross with two fingers in his first blessing of the people of Florence as their archbishop. Just around a corner from the Duomo, on the Via dello Studio, is an ancient tower house five storeys tall called the Torre dei Pierozzi; above the door is a bust of a haloed Antoninus, with an inscription identifying this as the house where he was born in AD 1389 and lived his early years. Finally, walking down the Via dei Calzaiuoli (street of hosiers), you will reach the Piazza della Signoria and the Uffizi, the oldest art gallery with the greatest collection of Renaissance art in the world. Before entering the Uffizi you will find yourself standing in the Loggiato, a long unroofed courtyard between the two wings of the gallery, stretching from the Piazza at one end to the river Arno at the other. Between the pillars of this courtyard there are twenty-eight niches, each occupied by a marble statue of a famous Tuscan. Beginning with the Medici statesmen who were the great patrons of Renaissance art, Cosimo "Pater Patriae" and Lorenzo "il Magnifico," the series continues with such artists as Giotto, Donatello, Leon Battista Alberti, Leonardo da Vinci, and Michelangelo Buonarotti, the writers Dante Alighieri, Francesco Petrarcha, Giovanni Boccaccio, and Niccolò Macchiavelli, the explorer Amerigo Vespucci, warriors like Farinata degli Uberti and Giovanni delle Bande Nere, scientists including Galileo Galilei, and finally two scholars and two musicians. One of the scholars is the medieval lawyer Accursius, the other is Sant'Antonino. This time he wears no mitre; he is dressed in the simple hooded cloak of a friar, with only a cloth strip draped across his chest and over his shoulders – the *pallium* – marking him as a bishop. He holds in his left hand a book, and beside his sandalled feet three more volumes are stacked.

There are some common features in these and in most artistic representations of Antoninus. He is a short, thin man, head tonsured (bald on top), with somewhat hollow cheeks and small eyes, and a noticeable Roman nose. Over and over again in busts and portraits of Antoninus, the same expression predominates: one of pity and kindness.

Today, Antoninus is known well in Florence, known across Italy, and little known outside Italy. As a canonized saint his feast day is on 10 May, but since 1969 it is not included in the Roman Catholic liturgical calendar; it continues to be observed by Dominicans and by Catholics who worship at the traditional Latin Mass, which still follows the older calendar. To historians of the Italian Renaissance, of the late medieval Church, and of the history of Catholic theology, Antoninus is better known. In addition to being archbishop of the city at the heart of the Renaissance, Antoninus was involved in civic politics during the early years of the reign of the Medici; he supervised the design and building of San Marco, including its decoration by Fra Angelico, one of the friars there; and he was one of the major theological writers of the fifteenth century, especially known for his writing on moral and pastoral matters. His most famous work is his four-volume *Summa* ("Summary" or "Compendium"), in which he covered a prodigious range of subjects, including the human soul, the moral law, the deadly vices, the different vocations and their special duties and pitfalls, the Church's sacraments, and the cardinal virtues.

The topic of this book is St Antoninus's teaching on trade, merchants, and workers, contained in his *Summa*. The next chapter will give an orientation to the *Summa* as a whole. First, however, a bit of biography is in order. This chapter will provide a basic introduction to the author whose teaching is the subject of this book, with bibliographical indications for further reading. Its additional aim is to point out some aspects of Antoninus's life which are of particular relevance for understanding his writing. It begins with an overview of the most important sources which provide evidence about Antoninus's life. It then outlines the most important formative influences on Antoninus and his writing: his father, the Dominican religious order, the Church's canon law, and the Observant reform movement. It then transitions to the decades when Antoninus was most in the public eye, when he helped found the monastery of San Marco and was archbishop of Florence from 1446 until his death in 1459. It concludes by discussing his canonization and highlights some examples of Antoninus's influence since his death, particularly on Catholic moral theology.

1. Sources for the Biography of Antoninus

The most important primary sources about Antoninus were written in the decades immediately following his death in 1459. Three men who knew him personally and were employed by him during the years when he was archbishop of Florence wrote biographies of Antoninus: his secretary Francesco da Castiglione, his bookseller Vespasiano da Bisticci, and his notary Baldovino Baldovini. Castiglione's Latin *Vita Antonini* (*Life of Antoninus*), written in the years 1460–1, was the first, and it provides the most thorough narrative of his life.[1] Castiglione was intimately

1 Francesco da Castiglione, *Vita Beati Antonini Archiepiscopi Florentini*, 313–25. Following Castiglione's *Vita* in that volume are Leonardo di ser Uberto Martini Berti's *Additiones ad Vitam, intra annum decimum a sancti obitu scriptae*, ibid., 326–35.

acquainted with the archbishop's affairs – as secretary he lived and worked in the archiepiscopal residence – and was also a skilled writer, being highly educated in both humanistic and scholastic learning. Vespasiano and Baldovini wrote about twenty years after Antoninus died, both in Italian. Vespasiano provides a lively portrait of the man.[2] He had him as a client, selling him the paper on which he wrote his *Summa* and having copies made of it; he also knew the Dominicans of San Marco and conversed with Antoninus there. Vespasiano is the closest Antoninus had to a Boswell; from him come snatches of conversation which reveal Antoninus's personality. Baldovini, notary to the archbishop, produced another *Vita* by compiling and translating from Castiglione into Italian, adding some of his own personal recollections; these original portions by Baldovini contribute to our knowledge of certain events in the life of Antoninus not described as fully in the other two biographies.[3] The most important difference between these three sources, besides individual style, is of genre. Castiglione and Baldovini wrote hagiographically, offering firsthand testimony about the life of a saint. They both relate Antoninus performing miracles – Castiglione actually testifies to one that he witnessed within his own family – which is in keeping with the expectations of hagiography; yet the number of miracles they report is small in comparison to what one finds in the later embellished biographies. Vespasiano's account comes from his memoirs, a gossipy work recounting the famous and learned people whom he met while running his business as bookseller and manuscript dealer to humanists, prelates, and statesmen. Beyond these three biographies, there are also contemporary and posthumous mentions, recollections, and shorter *vitae*. For example, there is a brief note in the diary of Luca Landucci on "Archbishop Antonino" as one of the "noble and valiant" men alive at the time (1450), and a posthumous encomium of the archbishop written by Pope Pius II in his memoirs, the *Commentaries*.[4]

These biographical sources tell us mainly about the final thirteen years of Antoninus's life: from his appointment as archbishop of Florence at about age fifty-seven in 1446 to his death at age seventy in 1459. They say little about him as a youth or during the decades when he was a simple friar in the Dominican order. For those decades, the main narrative source is a brief chapter at the beginning of Castiglione's *Vita*. The light which can be shone upon these dark years must be kindled from a diverse array of widely scattered sources: documents from archives,

2 Vespasiano da Bisticci, "Arcivescovo Antonino, Fiorentino."
An English translation is available by William George and Emily Waters, *The Vespasiano Memoirs*. I quote from this translation frequently herein; however, as it is not a consistently reliable translation and silently abbreviates the original, I have always checked it against Vespasiano's Italian, and sometimes eschewed it.

3 Baldovino de Baldovini, *Vita di S. Antonino*.

4 Luca Landucci, *A Florentine Diary from 1450 to 1516*, 2; Pius II, *Commentaries*, 2.29 (1:318–21).

especially notarial and ecclesiastical archives; chronicles of Dominican houses; extant letters and sermons of Antoninus predating his elevation to the episcopacy; and autobiographical comments in the author's own writings.[5] Archival documents, letters, and other evidence are naturally more abundant for the years when Antoninus was archbishop of Florence and heavily involved in ecclesiastical and communal affairs. From the biographies and documentary sources, a relatively firm chronology of Antoninus's life has been established.[6]

The last witness testimony of Antoninus's life was collected during the canonization proceedings, which were opened in 1516. A compendium of these testimonies was assembled in 1519 by the procurator of the cause, Roberto Ubaldini da Gagliano, OP, who at the same time wrote his own abbreviated *Vita* summarizing earlier biographies. From the canonization of Antoninus in 1523, there commenced a new era of hagiographical literature written to edify pious readers and increase the fame of the newly canonized saint; these later biographies of the sixteenth, seventeenth, and eighteenth centuries do not add to our historical knowledge.[7]

In the past two centuries an abundance of scholarship has been produced on St Antoninus.[8] The greatest scholarly biography of Antoninus was produced by the Rev. Raoul Morçay, canon of Tours and professor at the Institut Catholique de Paris († 3 October 1939): *Saint Antonin: fondateur du couvent de Saint-Marc, archevêque de Florence, 1389–1459* (Tours: Mame et Fils, 1914).[9] This is still "the fundamental biography."[10] All scholars of St Antoninus owe a tremendous debt to Morçay for bringing to bear an enormous amount of archival and documentary material as well as information and inferences drawn from Antoninus's own writings, to greatly extend the limited picture of Antoninus drawn by the original *Vitae*.[11] Further progress in bibliographical and archival research was made by Stefano Orlandi, OP, in his *S. Antonino* and *Bibliografia antoniniana*. Biographical

5 Morçay prints a selection of these documents: "Autres documents," appendix 3–2 in *Saint Antonin*, 432–500. An extensive collection of documents of this sort is printed by Orlandi in his 2-vol. *S. Antonino, Arcivescovo di Firenze, Dottore della Chiesa*.

6 A summary, though without bibliographical references, is provided by Marchetti, "Cronologia della vita e delle opere."

7 See Morçay, *Saint Antonin*, xi–xiii.

8 For a sampling of recent scholarship, see the essays in Cinelli and Paoli, *Antonino Pierozzi*. See also Comitato per le onoranze a S. Antonino nel 5. centenario della morte, *Settimana di studio sulla vita e le opere di S. Antonino Pierozzi*; *Supplemento alla posizione per il dottorato di Sant'Antonino*; *S. Antonino e la sua epoca*.

9 Marichal, "Nécrologie: Raoul Morçay."

10 Peterson, "Antoninus."

11 In addition to the sources edited and printed in the appendices of *Saint Antonin*, Morçay also edited Antoninus Florentinus, *Chroniques de Saint Antonin: Fragments originaux du titre XXII (1378–1459)*, and Giuliano Lapaccini, *Annalia conventus sancti Marci de Florentia*.

articles and books have been published since 1900 in many European languages, as a rule relying primarily on Morçay and Orlandi's research.[12] The most helpful narratives of Antoninus's life in the English language are well-referenced book chapters by Ronald Finucane and Sally J. Cornelison.[13]

Let us turn to the life of Antoninus, as it can be reconstructed from the sources I have just outlined. Our focus at the beginning is on Antoninus's formative influences in his early years.

2. First Influences: Niccolò Pierozzi and the Dominican Friars

Antoninus was born in his family home in Florence in the last week of March, 1389.[14] His given name was Antonio (Anthony), and in the style of the time his full name would have been Antonio di ser Niccolò Pierozzi. Throughout his life he always referred to himself by his given name (in Italian Antonio, in Latin Antonius). But early in his life he acquired the diminutive nickname Antonino (Antoninus). The origin of the nickname is customarily said to be his small stature. Today he is known by the nickname.[15] His parents were Ser Niccolò Pierozzi and Madonna Tommasa di Cenni di Nuccio.[16] Antoninus was one of seven children born of Niccolò's three marriages – four daughters and three sons, of whom only

---

12 The standard hagiographical account of St Antoninus in English is Butler, "St. Antoninus (May 10)." A recent popular book on St Antoninus, with colour photo illustrations, is Calzolari and Giordano, *Antonino Pierozzi*. The classic biography in Italian is Calzolai, *Frate Antonino Pierozzi dei domenicani*.

Short articles with bibliographies of varying depth are available in reference works, e.g., *Encyclopedia of Renaissance Philosophy*; *The Oxford Dictionary of the Christian Church*; *New Catholic Encyclopedia*; *Dictionnaire d'histoire et de géographie ecclésiastiques*; *Dictionnaire de théologie catholique*; *Dictionnaire de droit canonique*; Kaeppeli and Panella, *SOPMA*, 1:80–100, 4:27–31; *Dizionario biografico degli italiani*; *Lexikon des Mittelalters*; von Schulte, *Die Geschichte der Quellen und Literatur des Canonischen Rechts von Gratian bis auf die Gegenwart*, 2:444–5.

13 Finucane, "The Reforming Friar-Archbishop"; Cornelison, *Art and the Relic Cult of St. Antoninus in Renaissance Florence*, esp. ch. 1, "The Humblest of Men."

14 Morçay, *Saint Antonin*, 13. For readers not familiar with medieval calendars, the following should be borne in mind. In medieval Europe there were a variety of local customs regarding when a new year began. In Florence, 25 March was considered the first day of the new year. Hence when a Florentine writer refers to any dates between 1 January and 24 March, we must add a year to the date he or she uses: for example, 1 March 1388 Florentine style would be 1 March 1389 to us, or "modern style." We are told by Antoninus's sixteenth-century biographer Frosino Lapini that he was born in 1389 (Florentine style), which requires his birthday to be on or after 25 March 1389 in our calendar. Francesco da Castiglione tells us that Antoninus was seventy years old in April 1459. Therefore the most likely date for Antoninus's birth is between 25 and 31 March 1389, or possibly early April.

15 Vespasiano always calls him Antonino. Vespasiano, "Arcivescovo Antonino," para. 1 (1:171).

16 Morçay, *Saint Antonin*, 16. "Antonius, Florentina urbe oriundus, honestissimis parentibus, patre Nicolao, matre Thomasia natus est." Castiglione, *Vita Beati Antonini*, c. 1 para. 1 (314).

Antoninus and two older sisters outlived their father, who died in 1414. We know little about Antoninus's mother. Since she died in 1395, when he was only about six years old, she could have little influence on his upbringing. Antoninus's father must be counted as his first formative influence.

Niccolò Pierozzi, a Florentine, was a member of the prestigious guild of jurists and notaries (*Arte dei giudici e notai*), in which he had a long career.[17] Guild membership in Florence was not just a matter of occupation; it was also the means by which citizens participated in the city's communal government, the *Signoria*. The principle of representation by guild was established in the Ordinances of Justice (1293), and remained operative at least in theory until the sixteenth century.[18] Positions on the city council or magistracy were assigned by lot: eligible guild members who met the property requirements and passed scrutiny by an electoral committee would have their names placed in a bag. Those whose names were drawn took office, for short terms: priors two months, most other magistrates six months. Many citizens were excluded: the *popolo minuto* (little people) of wage-labourers and members of lesser guilds, and the *magnati* (greats) of the traditional landed aristocracy.[19] Jurists (legal scholars) and notaries like Niccolò Pierozzi were prominent as political leaders in republican Florence and in the humanist movement. This guild had the special function of supplying the city government with notary-administrators.[20] Niccolò Pierozzi held the office of proconsul, the guild's executive head, in 1388, 1396, and 1408, as well as other public offices.[21]

It seems clear, considering Antoninus's life and writings, how much both tangible and intangible he inherited from his father: "the methodical character, conscience, spirit of order, and the meticulousness of a notary," as Morçay puts it.[22] On the basis of Niccolò's testament, Morçay describes him as "an honest man, methodical and pious. While conducting the affairs of others with conscientiousness, he did not at all neglect his own."[23] He held a small property in the area of Siena which he increased bit by bit throughout his career, as his fortune permitted, until at the end of his life the manor was large enough for two families. He was in the habit of writing memoirs in a *ricordanza* in his leisure hours; sadly, these have

17 Finucane, "Friar-Archbishop," 168; Morçay, *Saint Antonin*, 13.

18 Weinstein, *Savonarola*, 45. See ch. 4, "Florence and the Medici," for an overview of Florence's political history.

19 Ibid.

20 Faibisoff, "Chancery Officials and the Business of Communal Administration in Republican Florence," 32–3. For further information see the references therein.

21 Morçay, *Saint Antonin*, 14.

22 "Vivante image de son père, au contraire, il héritera de lui le caractère méthodique, la conscience, l'esprit d'ordre et la minutie d'un notaire." Ibid., 16. All English quotations from Morçay are my translations from the French.

23 "… un honnête homme, méthodique et pieux. Tout en faisant avec conscience les affaires des autres, il ne négligeait point les siennes." Ibid., 14.

perished. The Pierozzi family was both prosperous and pious.[24] One of Niccolò's sisters entered a convent, which one of his daughters later entered as well; two of his sons embraced the religious life; another of his daughters, a married woman, became a member of the Dominican third order (discussed below). Niccolò himself did pious works, contributing to the construction of the Duomo and giving alms to hospitals.[25] Antoninus's oft-remarked qualities as an administrator put one in mind of Ser Niccolò, who carefully stewarded and built up the family property over the years. There is also a discernible resemblance in Antoninus's handwriting to Italian notarial and curial scripts (handwriting styles), which may well show another relic of paternal influence.[26]

He was also a sickly child, suffering from a hernia and fevers which sometimes put his survival in doubt.[27] As an introduction to Antoninus's character as a boy, the description given by Francesco da Castiglione may suffice:

> He was gifted with much intelligence and abundant memory; of a serious disposition, extremely meek and quiet, not large in bodily stature, built up more of bones and nerves than flesh. As a boy he was studious in religion, frequenting church and hearing the Divine Word: he began already then to devote time assiduously to prayer and contemplation. The boy is said also to have formed the habit of going to the figure of the crucifix located in the church of Orsanmichele, as it is called, for a long time each day, and praying there suppliant on bended knees for so long that many people beholding this were astonished that in a mere boy there should be such tolerance in prayer and such constant perseverance. And when there were litanies and public processions, he would follow the Friars Preachers, to whom he was already attracted, with much gravity and modesty. In elementary school, in which he excelled his contemporaries to a remarkable degree, his companions who are still alive in our city do not recollect him ever doing anything immature: for there was already then, in his conduct, speech, and carriage, precocious age and immense gravity.[28]

---

24 "As his kinsfolk were well-to-do, he gave them nought from the archbishopric, saying that these goods were not his, but belonged to the poor." George and Waters, *Vespasiano Memoirs*, 163; Vespasiano, "Arcivescovo Antonino," para. 15 (1:189). Antoninus did make an exception to provide for his nephews, who had been in his service as archbishop: "On 30 April the notary Ser Soletto di Filippo di Teo drew up a testament in which Antoninus willed 350 florins to his nephews on the condition that they donate a portion of that sum to the poor." Cornelison, *Art and the Relic Cult*, 16–17.

25 The foregoing from Morçay, *Saint Antonin*, 14–15.

26 Antoninus's handwriting is discussed below, ch. 2. Compare figure 1 in that chapter with tav. 105 (Italian "littera minuta cursiva") and 109 ("mercantesca diritta") in Cherubini and Pratesi, *Palaeografia Latina: Tavole.*

27 Finucane, "Friar-Archbishop," 169; see Castiglione, *Vita Beati Antonini*, c. 1 para. 4 (315).

28 "Is multa solertia, plus memoria valuit; ingenio gravis, mitisque admodum ac taciturnus, statura corporis non magnus, ossibus ac nervis magis quam carne suffultus. In ipsa pueritia religionis

We know from the foregoing that Antoninus was sent to school – *ludus litterarius*, "elementary" or perhaps "grammar school" – but beyond that the specifics of his childhood education are conjectural.[29] Antoninus gives us a brief, self-deprecating remark in the *proemium* (preamble) of the *Summa* about his early education:

> I confess that I had no guide in grammar except in my boyhood, and he was a poor teacher. I had no one in any other faculty, except for part of dialectic, and that rather intermittent. But I had no master directing my studies after my entrance.[30]

Castiglione said that as a boy Antoninus was already attracted to the Friars Preachers, that is, the Dominicans. Officially called the Order of Preachers (hence the abbreviation OP after the name of a member), this religious order was founded by St Dominic Guzmán in AD 1216.[31] Along with the Franciscans (Order of Friars Minor, OFM), it is one of the two principal orders of mendicant friars, that is, begging brothers. The members are called "friars" from the Latin word *frater*, "brother" (French *frère*, Italian *frate* commonly abbreviated *fra*). As mendicants, Dominicans and Franciscans own no property individually: today, they are generally supported by the assets owned by the order collectively, but in the Middle Ages they were expected to live from alms or work to earn their living. They take

---

studiosus, ecclesiam et auditionem divini verbi frequentabat: coepitque jam tum orationi assidue contemplationique vacare: Ferturque adhuc puer ad figuram Crucifixi, quae in ecclesia S. Michaelis in horto, sic enim appellatur, sita est, longo tempore singulis diebus accedere consuevisse, ibique supplex ac genibus flexis diutius orare; adeo ut plurimi id cernentes admirarentur tantam esse in puero tolerantiam in orando, et in perseverando constantiam. Cum vero letaniae ac processiones publicae fierent, Fratres Praedicatores, quibus jam tum afficiebatur, multa cum gravitate ac modestia sequebatur. Numquam in ludo litterario, in quo supra coaetaneos suos mirum in modum proficiebat, quidquam puerile a sociis, qui adhuc superstites sunt, in nostra civitate fecisse memoratur: erat enim jam tum in ejus moribus, sermoneque ac gestu corporis, praematura senectus gravitasque immensa." Castiglione, *Vita Beati Antonini*, c. 1 para. 1 (314). All translations from Latin sources are my own unless otherwise noted.

29 Finucane, "Friar-Archbishop," 169.

30 "Ducem fateor me non habuisse in grammaticalibus nisi in pueritia et debilem preceptorem. Nullum habui in alia facultate excepta parte dialectice et satis interrupte. Sed nec principem mihi studium imperantem ex prelatione." Antoninus Florentinus, *Summa*, 1 *proemium* (*N* fol. 3v–4r; Ballerini col. 3–4). When I cite Antoninus's *Summa* herein, I refer to manuscripts by the sigla *N*, M_I, F_I, etc., and to printed editions by the editor's name, i.e., Ballerini or Mamachi. See the explanation of abbreviations above and the bibliography. I explain these textual witnesses in the next chapter.
The slightly obscure phrase *ex prelatione* has been variously interpretated by different scholars. I have followed J.B. Walker: "Antonius confessed … that after his entrance he was dependent almost wholly upon his own industry." Walker, *The "Chronicles" of Saint Antoninus*, 6. Cfr Howard, *Beyond the Written Word*, 35 n67.

31 For a brief overview of the Dominican order and its history, see Hinnebusch, Philibert, and Williams, "Dominicans."

monastic vows of poverty, chastity, and obedience (to superiors and to the rules of the order itself); many are ordained to the priesthood, and therefore are members of the Catholic clergy, "clerics." Friars live together in communities called priories, each being ruled by a prior (though these communities are often referred to by the generic terms "houses" or "monasteries"). The friars were a new institution of the thirteenth century, pioneered by St Dominic and St Francis of Assisi. They differed from monks and nuns in that, while monks and nuns sought to retreat from the world into the solitude of a monastery, convent, or hermitage, usually in the countryside or wilderness, the friars' lives were oriented towards activity and mission in the world, especially in the cities. Their founders sought to combine contemplation with service: to make the friars into men of prayer who go out into the world as apostles and workers in God's vineyard, as expressed in the Dominican motto: "To contemplate and to give others the fruits of contemplation."[32] The focus of the Dominicans was, as their official name suggests, preaching. Dominic formed the first groups with the mission of preaching to the Albigensians of southern France, also known as Cathars, a community of Christians who rejected the structures of the Catholic Church and its hierarchy and were condemned as heretics. Pursuing heresy and combating it were Dominican specialties; inquisitional activities were led and staffed to a great extent by Dominicans. Two of the most famous inquisitors, Bernard Gui and Tomás de Torquemada, were Dominicans. We will see Antoninus combating heresy in his diocese as archbishop.

To prepare for their preaching mission, Dominicans had to study. The basic education for "common brothers" (*fratres communes*) occurred in the priory.[33] Every priory was expected to maintain at least one professor to provide schooling for its members. Regional units of the order (provinces) maintained larger provincial schools. The order also established general houses of studies: the first *studium generale* was in Paris, the site of the greatest university faculty of theology in Europe, and later all the major provinces established general houses. The other mendicant orders also tended to be studious, each with their own emphasis; by the end of the thirteenth century, mendicants – including Dominicans, Franciscans, and Hermits of St Augustine – had come to dominate many faculties in the universities of Europe. Some Franciscans became exceptional theologians, such as St Bonaventure, but the medieval Franciscans are most known today for their contributions to philosophy, science, and mathematics, through such men as Roger Bacon, John Duns Scotus, and William of Ockham. It was the Dominican order which produced the greatest theologian of the Middle Ages, St Thomas Aquinas. Many Dominican scholars produced works of synthesis, such as the philosopher St Albert the Great, the compiler of saints' lives James of Voragine, and

32 Ibid.; Van Engen, "The Church in the Fifteenth Century," 322.

33 On the Dominican education system, see Mulchahey, *"First the Bow is Bent in Study…."*.

the encyclopedist Vincent of Beauvais. Dominicans had a special predilection for moral and legal studies: the patron saint of canon law today is the Dominican friar St Raymond of Peñafort, who compiled the first official collection of the law of the Catholic Church, the *Liber Extra*, issued in 1234. In the sixteenth century, the Dominicans Francisco de Vitoria and Bartolomé de las Casas drew on this medieval lineage in moral theology and jurisprudence to advocate for the rights of the Indigenous peoples of the Americas.

A genre which both Dominicans and Franciscans came to specialize in was handbooks for preaching and hearing confessions. Hearing confessions naturally went together with the preaching mission. Though many Dominicans went afield to preach against heresy or to evangelize non-Christians, the majority preached to the Catholic population in the cities of Europe.[34] When preaching to Christians, the goals were to instruct, edify, and convert. Preaching was about educating in sound Christian doctrine, but also persuading and stirring up the passions of the hearers, both to strive after the virtues and ideals of the Christian life and to repent for sins and shun the vices. Hence it was hoped that good preaching would bear fruit in moving people to confess their sins and amend their ways. It was common for a Dominican preacher to give a series of sermons in a particular town, for example a cycle of daily sermons during Lent, followed by opportunities for confession heard by the preacher himself and one or more friars accompanying him. It so happened that, at precisely the same time the Dominican order was being officially established, the whole college of Catholic bishops gathered in the Fourth Lateran Council was elevating pastoral care, called in the Middle Ages the *cura animarum* (care of souls), to the highest of priorities, describing it as the *ars artium* (art of arts).[35] Through their ministries of preaching and confession the Dominican order thus accumulated vast corporate experience in pastoral care. This is the genre to which Antoninus primarily contributed in his writings.

It is worth noting here that the two societies to which Antoninus belonged since his youth were both committed to democracy. Florence's government was in principal a popular republic, with citizens represented through their guilds and some city officials chosen by lottery. In the context of Florentine politics, notaries like Antoninus's father tended to support the guild-corporatism of the *popolo* (people), rather than the elite-directed consensus politics of the urban patricians.[36] The government of the Dominican order was also democratic. The clerics of each priory elected their prior, and priories also sent delegates to sit in the provincial chapter, which represented all houses of the province and was led by a provincial prior. Supreme authority over the whole order resided in the general chapter, an

34 An illuminating book on the urban religious culture in medieval Italy is Thompson, *Cities of God*.

35 Lateran IV, canon 27, in *Decrees of the Ecumenical Councils*, 1:248.

36 Faibisoff, "Chancery Officials," 33. See Najemy, *Corporatism and Consensus in Florentine Electoral Politics, 1280–1400*.

assembly of all provinces held annually until 1370 and every two to three years in Antoninus's time. The general chapter elected the master general of the order, and only the general chapter could modify the order's constitutions (a vote in three successive general chapters was necessary for this).[37]

3. Giovanni Dominici and Canon Law

All of the major mendicant orders established themselves in Florence in the thirteenth century, but the Dominicans were most influential there.[38] The Dominicans whose processions Antoninus followed in his boyhood would have been the brothers of Santa Maria Novella, a prestigious monastery.[39] At that time, Fra Giovanni Dominici was residing there, "the religious man most in the public eye in Florence in the first years of the fifteenth century."[40] Giovanni Dominici was a great popular preacher, famous in the years when Antoninus was an early teen for his part in stirring up a great wave of popular devotion which culminated in 1399 with the summer of the *Bianchi*, "Whites," when people from across Italy joined in prayerful white-robed processions.[41] It was Giovanni Dominici who drew Antoninus to joining the Dominican religious order, as Castiglione relates:

> But when he had reached the age of puberty, he turned his soul to pursuing a religious life; moved, as he would often tell us, by the preaching of that most outstanding man Brother Giovanni Dominici, who out of the Order of Preachers was later, his virtues so demanding it, made a cardinal of the Holy Roman Church. The singular virtues and doctrine of this man, and above all his intelligence and acute nature, Antonio would praise to the skies in highest terms.[42]

Antoninus himself, in his *Chronicles*, confirms the role Dominici played in his own life:

> I could be convicted of ingratitude if I were found to have forgotten that magnificent man, praiseworthy in everything, who attracted me to religious life … I speak of Dom. Br. Giovanni Dominici of Florence, cardinal of Ragusa, who, beyond

37 Hinnebusch, Philibert, and Williams, "Dominicans," 849. On Antoninus in relation to the politics of church and state in Italy, see Peterson, "Archbishop Antoninus"; Peterson, "Out of the Margins."

38 Sullivan, "Antonino Pierozzi," 345.

39 Brucker, *Renaissance Florence*, 199–200.

40 "Là [à Sainte-Marie-Nouvelle] justement résidait le religieux le plus en vue à Florence aux premières années du XVe siècle, fra Giovanni Dominici." Morçay, *Saint Antonin*, 17.

41 Forte, "Dominici, John, Bl." On the *bianchi*, see Bornstein, *The Bianchi of 1399*.

42 "Cum autem ad pubertatis annos pervenisset, animum ad religiosam vitam capessendam convertit; motus, ut saepius nobis narrabat, praedicationibus praestantissimi viri Fratris Joannis

> exceptional dignity in the Church of God, shone in his speech with learning and wisdom and in holiness of life.[43]

Antoninus most likely heard Dominici preach in Florence during Lent.[44] Antoninus records the powerful impression made by his preaching:

> He exhibited in matter and method of evangelizing great gravity and a kind of majesty: his voice resonant like a trumpet, he did not raise it or lower it but applied it strongly, not only teaching clearly and delighting the listeners; but also touching them, softening even hard hearts.[45]

When he was fifteen years old, Antoninus approached Dominici at Santa Maria Novella asking to be allowed to join the Dominican order. This episode is recounted by Castiglione:

> When Antonio had approached him wishing to take up the habit … that most prudent man perceived a boy, sharp indeed of mind and of good character, but of tender age: he directed him to wait some years yet, until he be capable of bearing the austerity of religion. And when the boy, asked to what branch of learning or faculty he devoted his labour, replied that he took great pleasure in reading the *Decretum*, the man said, "Go: when you have committed the whole *Decretum* to memory, then you shall be admitted."[46]

Dominici, qui ex Ordine Praedicatorum postea, ejus virtutibus ita postulantibus, sanctae Romanae Ecclesiae Cardinalis effectus est: cujus viri singulares virtutes atque doctrinam, in primisque solertiam et acumen ingenii summis in caelum laudibus extollebat Antonius." Castiglione, *Vita Beati Antonini*, c. 1 para. 2 (314).

43 "Ingratitudinis argui possem, si oblitus inuenirer illius magnifici et per omnia laudabilis viri, qui me sua doctrina predicationis ad religionem, de qua sermo extat, attraxit, dominum dico fratrem Ioannem Dominici de Florentia, cardinalem Ragusinum, qui ultra dignitatem eximiam in ecclesia Dei, scientie et sapientie sermone ac morum sanctitate effulsit." Antoninus, *Chroniques*, tit. 23 c. 11 §. 3 (106).

44 "Predicavit eximie quadragesimis multis, Venetiis, Florentie permaxime et in aliis civitatibus de diversis materiis. … Unum solum quadragesimale vidi eius recollectum, ubi cum themate occurenti proponebat versus psalmorum, …" Ibid. (107).

45 "Exhibebat autem in materia et modo evangelizandi magnam gravitatem et quasi maiestatem: vox eius sonora quasi tuba; nec extollebat [eam] nec supprimebat, sed valde imprimebat, non solum aperte docens et delectans, sed et flectens, corda eciam obdurata emolliens." Ibid. (108). This passage is also translated in Howard, *Beyond the Written Word*, 232–3 n36.

46 "Ad hunc cum suscipiendi habitus causa accessisset Antonius (ille enim tunc Fesulis ecclesiam B. Dominici ac eum Conventum, qui nunc extat, a fundamentis condebat [*Vita 2 & 3:* dum regularem Ordinis observantiam reformaret.]) visus est homini prudentissimo puer, acutus quidem ingenio ac bonae indolis, sed aetate tenellus: jubet illum adhuc aliquot annis exspectare, donec ad perferendam religionis austeritatem sufficiat. Et quoniam interrogatus ab eo, cuinam scientiae aut

Gratian's *Decretum* is a textbook of canon law, that is, the legal system of the Catholic Church. Gratian was a canonist (a legal scholar who studied the Church's law, or "canons") who lived in the middle of the twelfth century and produced the first academic textbook of canon law, originally titled the *Concordia discordantium canonum* (*The Harmony of Discordant Canons*), but which came to be called the *Decretum* (*Decree*).[47] In the *Decretum* he compiled texts from the Bible, the writings of the Church Fathers, Church councils and synods, and letters of popes, especially decretal letters in which the popes sent authoritative answers to questions of law submitted to them. Gratian designed the work as a casebook, leading the student on an exploration of legal, moral, and theological issues.[48] It was a pioneering work of pedagogy – indeed, I think Gratian should be counted as one of the most brilliant professors ever – and its usefulness as a teaching text led to it being adopted as the foundational textbook of the faculties of canon law in European universities. Gratian's *Decretum* is a deep well of Christian reflection on law, morality, and theology, and a rewarding book to study. Yet it is surprising to find a teenage boy with a taste for reading it. It may be that his interest sprang out of his father's involvement in the legal profession. It could also have been prompted by the preaching of Giovanni Dominici. Antoninus reports (though he was not present for it) that Dominici once took as the subject of a Lenten cycle of sermons the legal maxims contained in the title *De regulis iuris* (*On the rules of law*) in the compilation of papal decretals called the *Liber Sext*, drawing a great crowd of admiring listeners, "expounding them with a theme from a fitting Gospel or Epistle."[49] The influence of canon law in general and Gratian's *Decretum* in particular is very evident in Antoninus's writing.[50] In the chapters from his *Summa* edited below, Antoninus draws on the *Decretum* more frequently than any other source except for the Bible. Even when he is not making an argument from canon law, he often quotes patristic writers (Church Fathers) – such as Ambrose, Jerome, Augustine of Hippo, and Gregory the Great – from passages compiled in the

---

facultati operam daret, respondit, se Decreti lectione plurimum delectari: Vade, inquit, cum totum Decretum memoriae mandaveris, tunc in ordine admitteris. [*Vita 2:* Nos, inquit Joannes, scholares Canonistas in Ordinem nostrum non admittimus, nisi universo Decreto memorato: tu ergo, fili, ita facito: deinde poteris ad nos securior redire.]" Castiglione, *Vita Beati Antonini*, c. 1 para. 2–3 (314), with annotations supplied from Ubaldini and Mainardi by Papebroch on page 315.

47 Winroth, *The Making of Gratian's Decretum*, 5.

48 On Gratian's *Decretum* as a casebook, we await the publication of Giulio Silano's illuminating introduction to his translation of the *Decretum*.

49 "Et inter alia una quadragesima Florentie in ecclesia cathedrali omnes regulas iuris, que habentur in lib. VIo, bis dietim predicavit cum magno concursu audientium, unam de mane, aliam de sero, proponendo cum themate evangelii vel epistole concurrentis, admirantibus cunctis." Antoninus, *Chroniques*, tit. 23 c. 11 §. 3 (107).

50 The contributions of Gratian's *Decretum* to medieval teaching on trade and Antoninus's use of it are discussed more fully below in ch. 3 and ch. 4.

Decretum. Antoninus similarly made use of the *Decretum* as a patristic *florilegium* in his *Chronicles*, as observed by J.B. Walker.[51] Antoninus was not totally unique in this: we know of at least one other medieval writer who used the *Decretum* in this way.[52] Yet the *Decretum* is not designed to be easily accessible as a compendium of texts on various topics. It proceeds discursively, as a slowly unfolding conversation, and the organization of its three parts is famously convoluted.[53] Antoninus's wide acquaintance with canon law texts, including not only the *Decretum* but also the later-compiled *Liber Extra* and *Liber Sext*, is remarkable considering that he never studied law in a university. One of the witnesses in his canonization process was a *doctor decretorum*, i.e., a canonist specializing in Gratian's *Decretum* and its commentaries, who submitted that the extent of Antoninus's learning in jurisprudence and theology without any formal studies had to be the result of a divine gift.[54] That Antoninus could readily quote passages from throughout the *Decretum* in his writings, often apparently from memory (this aspect of his writing process is discussed below in chapter 2), lends some credence to the story that the test of his religious vocation was to memorize it.[55] Antoninus apparently succeeded in this challenge, memorizing the *Decretum* – "which, because of its bulk, could hardly even be read by someone in so short a space of time"[56] – within one year. Castiglione himself, in reporting it, acknowledges this feat as incredible:

> I should not dare to assert definitely what I am about to tell – for Antonio never directly told us such things about himself – but, as evidence of his singular memory, this report was generally circulated about him: the youth is said then to have left the man, and when a year had passed to have returned to him, having made the *Decretum*

51 Walker, *"Chronicles" of Saint Antoninus*, 75–6.

52 Beattie, "A Lawyer's Florilegium."

53 Winroth, *Making of Gratian's Decretum*, 3–4.

54 "Sacrum Praedicatorum Ordinem fuerit ingressus praecedente miraculo quodam, ut scilicet brevissimo tempore et infra annum memoriae mandaverit totum Decretum. … Unde vere concludi potest, quod pro majori parte hujus praeclarissimi viri sana, catholica, vera, et famosissima doctrina, fuerit desuper illi ex divino dono infusa, licet etiam aliqualiter acquisita, quod est inter miracula computandum." Roberto Ubaldini da Gagliano, *Analecta ex summario Processuum impresso*, c. 1 para. 3, in Papebroch, *Acta Sanctorum*, 335.

55 "Extracts from the writings of the Fathers and ecclesiastical writers were drawn, not only from Vincent, but in two instances (in the case of St. Augustine) probably direct from the works of the author, and in two others (in the cases of Sts. Hilary and Augustine) through the *Book of Sentences* of Peter Lombard, and, what appears most extraordinary, a large number through the *Decretum* of Gratian … It proves quite conclusively that Antoninus, the canonist, had mastered his subject, and appears to offer some evidence that he had memorized the *Decretum* (the test of his religious vocation) …" Walker, *"Chronicles" of Saint Antoninus*, 75–6; see also 5 n4.

56 "Ejusdem anni spatio Decretum integrum memoriae mandaverat, quod propter sui magnitudinem tam brevi temporis spatio a quoquam vix legi posset." Clement VII, bull of canonization *Rationi congruit*, 419–20.

> so familiar that, being questioned on any part of the book, he would satisfy him in an astonishing manner.[57]

Antoninus's wish was granted:

> Then indeed no longer repelled, but very eagerly received, in the sixteenth year of his life, taking up the habit of Blessed Dominic and of the Preachers, he *put on the new man, who is created according to God.*[58]

For the rest of his life, even once he had been consecrated as archbishop, he wore the black and white habit of the Dominican friars.

As Antoninus inherited much of his character from his biological father Niccolò Pierozzi, so he seems to have inherited much from his spiritual father Giovanni Dominici. Writing late in his life, Antoninus described Dominici this way: he became highly learned in various fields, including theology and canon law, through his own industry without ever having taken a doctorate; he firmly but uprightly rebuked vice; he prayed devoutly, and carried out the liturgical offices fervently; in his dignity of rank he yet maintained humility in dress, abstinence in food and drink, constancy in work, friendliness to the lowly and the poor, and reverence for the great; he was a great counsellor in every kind of issue; he was cheerful of face yet chaste, circumspect, and carried himself with gravity; he supported the poor generously and lived in poverty, not possessing books of his own either for reading or for preaching, not even a Bible.[59] These virtues which Antoninus noted of Dominici are those he tried to put into practice himself. Indeed, Vespasiano da Bisticci and Pope Pius II described Antoninus's qualities as archbishop in similar terms.[60] Finally, Dominici considered the pastoral care of souls to be foremost among his duties, in obedience to which, Antoninus writes, "he was unwearied in many labours: in lecturing to others, in preaching to the people, and in hearing

---

57 "Non ausim affirmare quid loquar (nam ipse Antonius numquam de se talia nobis narrasset) sed in signum singularis memoriae, vulgo haec de illo fama ferebatur. Dicitur enim adolescens tunc ab homine discessisse, transactoque anno ad eumdem, ita Decreto familiari effecto, rediisse, ut, in quacumque ejus libri parte illum interrogasset, mirum in modum homini satisfaceret." Castiglione, *Vita Beati Antonini*, c. 1 para. 3 (314).
This episode is represented in iconography of St Antoninus, e.g., Cornelison, *Art and the Relic Cult*, plate 5.16: soffit fresco by Alessandro Allori, 1583–8, in the Sant'Antonino (Salviati) Chapel, San Marco, Florence.

58 "Tum vero non jam repulsus, sed avidissime susceptus, sextodecimo aetatis suae anno, assumpto B. Dominici ac Praedicatorum habitu, *novum induit hominem qui secundum Deum creatus est* [Ephesians 4:24]." Castiglione, *Vita Beati Antonini*, c. 1 para. 3 (314).

59 Antoninus, *Chroniques*, tit. 23 c. 11 §. 3 (106–8).

60 Vespasiano, "Arcivescovo Antonino," para. 1, 3–6, 14 (1:171–90); Pius II, *Commentaries*, 2.29 (1:318–21), quoted in note 206 below.

confessions."[61] The expected Dominican devotion to preaching and confession Antoninus received in double measure from his mentor Giovanni Dominici. Thus the main tracks which Antoninus would follow in his life seem to have been laid down quite early: more or less by the time he was sixteen.

4. The Observant Reform Movement and the Founding of San Marco

So far we have covered Antoninus's youth up to his entry into the Order of Preachers. He was admitted to the novitiate at age sixteen in 1405, and one year later made his profession and became a Dominican friar, joining the newly founded Observant house of San Domenico in Fiesole at age seventeen, in the year 1406. The next two sections of this chapter will cover the middle decades of Antoninus's life, a span of roughly forty years: from his profession as a Dominican friar in 1406 to his consecration as archbishop of Florence in 1446. The context for these years of Antoninus's life was shaped by the unfolding of events set in motion in the late fourteenth century. To set the stage, let us look back to eleven years before Antoninus was born. Three events took place in the year 1378 which initiated some of the determining factors in Antoninus's life.

In 1378, textile workers in the wool industry launched a revolution in Florence known as the Ciompi Revolt, named after the wool carders (*ciompi*) who took the leading part.[62] Formerly excluded from participation in the guilds and thus from enfranchisement in the republic, they staged an armed insurrection in July 1378, imposed a friendly government led by a wool carder, created a new guild of Wool Carders, Dyers, and Doublet Makers, and got their wages increased. However, this workers' regime lasted only six weeks; the owners of the wool workshops shut down wool production, causing a grave economic situation, and twenty-three other guilds joined forces to crush the Ciompi.[63] This new guild coalition ruled for four years, until in 1382 Florence's wealthy elite, the bankers and international merchants, were able to gain control of the city under the leadership of Maso Albizzi. The oligarchy of the Albizzi paved the way for the Medici family to later take over the city.[64] The Medici takeover of Florence began in 1434, during Antoninus's adulthood, and became closely intertwined with his life and career from roughly 1436 on, as we will see.

Likewise in 1378, the Great Schism began. Pope Gregory XI died on 27 March 1378, fourteen months after bringing the papacy and curia back to Rome after its multi-generational sojourn in the French city of Avignon (1309–77, the so-called

61 "In laboribus plurimis indefessus, in legendo aliis, in predicando populis, in audiendis confessionibus." Antoninus, *Chroniques*, tit. 23 c. 11 §. 3 (108).

62 See Stella, *La révolte des Ciompi.*

63 Weinstein, *Savonarola*, 47.

64 "Albizzi family," in *The Oxford Dictionary of the Renaissance.*

Babylonian Captivity of the papacy, a term coined by Petrarch). The cardinals, many of them French, gathered in a conclave in Rome to elect the next pope, in the midst of rioting and with mobs outside demanding that they elect an Italian. On 8 April 1378, Urban VI, an Italian, emerged as the newly elected pope. The sixteen cardinals, however, soon became discontented with Urban's governance and behaviour. They repudiated the validity of his election on grounds of duress and held a new conclave, electing Clement VII as pope on 20 September 1378. However, Urban insisted that he was the only valid and true pope, excommunicating Clement VII and the defected cardinals. As Urban was able to hold Rome, Clement and his cardinals retreated to Avignon, where the court system and financial machinery of papal government was still in full operation, beginning a new lineage of Avignon-based papal claimants.[65] Meanwhile Urban remained in Rome and appointed a new college of cardinals of his own. When these two men eventually died, each one's college of cardinals elected a new would-be pope of its own, and thus the existence of two rival papal claimants became self-perpetuating. Each rival had his own body of followers, called an "obedience," who viewed him as the true pope and shepherd of the Christian fold. "For the next thirty-seven years Latin Christendom knew two – for a time, three – 'obediences,' each allied with kings and princes, each enthroned with symbols of sacred authority, each claiming to hold the keys to the kingdom of heaven."[66] The religious orders were divided as well; within the Dominican order itself there was a Roman obedience and an Avignon obedience. This schism (split) lasted from 1378 to 1417. Until 1409 there were two rival papal claimants. In that year, representatives from across Christendom, including cardinals from both sides, gathered at the Council of Pisa and elected Alexander V, proclaiming him the true pope. Although some followers of the Avignon and Roman obediences defected to Alexander V, nevertheless many stood firm, and so from that time there were not two but three rival "popes" until the schism was resolved with the universal acceptance of Pope Martin V, elected at the Council of Constance in 1417.[67]

Finally, again in 1378, a devout Italian woman named Caterina Benincasa, known today as St Catherine of Siena, left Florence and went to Rome along with her spiritual family (*famiglia*) to support Pope Urban VI and help him end the Great Schism. She remained there, unswervingly loyal to Urban VI, until she died at the age of thirty-three in 1380.[68] St Catherine was extraordinarily famous across Europe at this time, considered a living saint. In her youth she had begun a severe penitential regimen of fasting and mortifying her body, and throughout her life she received visions from God and had mystical experiences in prayer; glimpses of

65 Van Engen, "The Church in the Fifteenth Century," 305.

66 Ibid.

67 Ibid., 315.

68 Muessig, Ferzoco, and Kienzle, eds., *A Companion to Catherine of Siena*, xv–xvi.

her spiritual life were passed on to posterity in the *Dialogo*, which she wrote, and the *Orazioni* (prayers), which were set down by others. Since 1368 Catherine carried out a public ministry of serving the poor and needy and trying to make peace between urban families and warring cities in Italy.[69] She was in Florence in 1377–8 trying to end a conflict between the city and the pope, and was nearly assassinated during the Ciompi Revolt.[70] Her greatest success in public life was convincing Pope Gregory XI to leave Avignon and bring the papacy back to Rome, which he did in 1377. Living in Rome after the Great Schism had begun, she wrote letters to political and religious leaders across Europe urging a return to unity behind Pope Urban VI and "prophetically exhorting and denouncing her fellow Christians, not least the male hierarchy," calling for conversion and reform in the Church.[71]

The relevance of Catherine of Siena to Antoninus's life is twofold. First, during her life Catherine was closely associated with the Dominicans. Although not an official member of the Dominican order, she received spiritual care from Dominican friars, as did many devout women who were not nuns.[72] Her closest confidante was Bl. Raymond of Capua, OP, who had been appointed as her confessor in 1374. Some of her final letters were written to Raymond in 1380, the same year he was elected as master general in the Roman obedience of the Dominican order.[73] Her model of sanctity led to the official creation of a Dominican "order of penitents" following a rule inspired by her way of life in 1405, known as the Dominican "third order" (the first order is the Dominican friars, the second order is contemplative Dominican nuns).[74] During Antoninus's life, Catherine was "by far the most popular saint affiliated with the Dominican order," and he himself would oversee the translation (ritual transference) of her relics at Santa Maria sopra Minerva, Rome in 1430.[75] She was canonized in 1461, with testimony of many miracles after her death. Second, Catherine was the inspiration for the Observant movement, which drove forward an internal reform of the Dominican order in the late fourteenth and early fifteenth centuries, according to the key protagonists of the movement (including Raymond of Capua, Tommaso Caffarini of Siena, and Giovanni Dominici).[76] However, as this Dominican reform was but one particular instance of a widespread phenomenon, a brief overview of the Observant movement in general is warranted.

69 Zarri, "Ecclesiastical Institutions and Religious Life in the Observant Century," 51.

70 Muessig, Ferzoco, and Kienzle, *Companion to Catherine of Siena*, xv–xvi.

71 Van Engen, "The Church in the Fifteenth Century," 305.

72 More, "Dynamics of Regulation, Innovation, and Invention," 104.

73 Anne Huijbers, "'Observance' as Paradigm in Mendicant and Monastic Order Chronicles," 124; Muessig, Ferzoco, and Kienzle, *Companion to Catherine of Siena*, xv–xvi.

74 More, "Dynamics of Regulation," 101; Zarri, "Ecclesiastical Institutions and Religious Life," 51.

75 Huijbers, "'Observance' as Paradigm," 124.

76 Ibid., 123–4.

The Observant movement is central to the religious history of Catholic Europe from the late fourteenth century into the sixteenth century. A movement for the reform of religious life that touched nearly every major religious order, its fundamental goal was *observantia regulae* (observance of the rule): "to return to the rules and the lifestyle of their pristine beginnings."[77] The reformers in each of the particular orders were convinced that decadence and corruption had crept in – that loyalty to the rule had been discarded and spiritual ardour had been lost. They pointed to symptoms like the accumulation of private wealth by monks, nuns, or friars, luxurious clothing, private rooms, neglect of the recitation of the Office (daily prayer) and of meals in common, and even monks, nuns, and friars leading totally independent lives.[78] Though the sweeping narratives of disciplinary decline followed by much-needed reform which were put forward in Observants' polemics and chronicles have been called into question in recent scholarship on the late medieval Church,[79] it is still clear that in the fourteenth and fifteenth centuries there was a great desire for change and in particular a dissatisfaction with the personnel and privileges of the existing religious orders.[80] Each order had its own Observant movement which proceeded in its own unique way, but some common features characterized the movement as a whole. Beyond pursuing the primary goal of restoring traditional observance and spiritual zeal within the orders themselves, the Observants also launched new efforts at religious education and pastoral care among the laity, especially through preaching and writing; I will discuss this more below. This drive to restore pristine traditions led to "a veritable renaissance" in many religious orders.[81] Nearly all of the leading religious teachers and popular preachers in the fifteenth and early sixteenth centuries came out of the Observant movement, including Martin Luther (a friar of the Observant Hermits of St Augustine).[82]

Within the Dominican order, the first generation of Observants looked to Catherine of Siena "as the personification of 'Observant' virtues" and "the standardbearer for the Observant reform," as did Antoninus himself.[83] Her confessor,

77 Roest, "Observant Reform in Religious Orders," 446. See also Mixson, "Introduction," in Roest and Mixson, *Companion to Observant Reform*, 1–20, esp. 1–8, 13–15; Van Engen, "The Church in the Fifteenth Century," 323–4.

78 Roest, "Observant Reform in Religious Orders," 446; Hinnebusch, Philibert, and Williams, "Dominicans," 851; Edelheit, "Introduction," 16.

79 In addition to the essays already cited in Roest and Mixson, *Companion to Observant Reform*, see Mixson, "Observant Reform's Conceptual Frameworks between Principle and Practice," and Vargas, *Taming a Brood of Vipers*, esp. 6–12, and the additional references therein.

80 Vargas, *Taming a Brood of Vipers*, 21; Van Engen, "The Church in the Fifteenth Century," 310.

81 Roest, "Observant Reform in Religious Orders," 446.

82 Van Engen, "The Church in the Fifteenth Century," 323.

83 Huijbers, "'Observance' as Paradigm," 123–4. See also von Heusinger, "Catherine of Siena and the Dominican Order."

Raymond of Capua, was elected as master general in the Roman obedience of the order in 1380. The Observant movement was launched in 1388, according to Dominican narratives, when the friars who were gathered at the general chapter of the Roman obedience under the leadership of Raymond of Capua granted permission to friar Conrad of Prussia to start a priory devoted to strictly observing the rule and constitutions of the order.[84] This was the first Dominican Observant community. In 1390 Raymond issued a call to the order to recover its original ideals, and subsequent general chapters decreed that there should be at least one Observant priory in each province of the order, to serve as an example to others.[85] The first Observant Dominican community in Italy was actually a monastery of nuns (of the second order), rather than of friars (of the first order); it was founded by Chiara Gambacorta, a friend and correspondent of Catherine of Siena.[86] Catherine also inspired the Florentine friar Giovanni Dominici, who heard her speak in Florence and Pisa in the 1370s. He was prior of Santa Maria Novella from 1385 to 1387 and brought the Observant movement to Italian priories in the 1390s, beginning with a preaching and reform campaign in Venice. In 1391 he began restoring the observance of traditional discipline in three Dominican houses there.[87] Dominici and later Observant reformers often encountered resistance from friars or whole houses who refused to go along with the reform program. Some communities became bitterly divided; at times friars reacted violently towards reformers, at times reformers were hostile or violent towards their unreformed brethren.[88] Until the mid-fifteenth century there was more success in setting up new Observant houses than in upending the established way of life in existing non-Observant houses; thereafter, however, the Observants increasingly became the leading force across the Dominican order.[89] Beginning in the 1390s, reformed or newly founded Observant houses came to be grouped together into congregations, with each Observant congregation led by a vicar of the observance. Giovanni Dominici was made the first vicar of the observance in Italy in 1393.[90] In the year of the Whites, 1399, the Venetian authorities condemned Dominici to five years of exile for his encouragement of processions of penitents. It was during this exile that he settled

84 The story goes that Conrad dramatically placed a rope around his neck and said that he deserved death for not living in accordance with the rule and constitutions of the order. Huijbers, "'Observance' as Paradigm," 128.

85 Roest, "Observant Reform in Religious Orders," 449.

86 Zarri, "Ecclesiastical Institutions and Religious Life," 54.

87 Huijbers, "'Observance' as Paradigm," 124, 126; Dessì, "John Dominici."

88 Vargas, *Taming a Brood of Vipers*, 20–1. Giovanni Caroli (Iohannes Caroli) gives a firsthand description of the conflict sparked by efforts to bring the Observant movement to Santa Maria Novella in 1459–60 in his *Liber dierum*, 3, 65 and 67–9, quoted and discussed in Edelheit, "Introduction," 17–18.

89 Mixson, "Introduction," 5; Roest, "Observant Reform in Religious Orders," 449–50.

90 Vargas, *Taming a Brood of Vipers*, 8; Edelheit, "Introduction," 12–13.

in Florence and Antoninus heard him preach.[91] Antoninus's awe at Dominici was not atypical. Despite how polarizing their activities could be, Observant preachers were often very popular with the laity in the cities of Italy. The Florentine notary Ser Lapo Mazzei wrote in 1400 to his friend Francesco Datini about Dominici:

> I tell you that I have never heard such a sermon, nor such preaching. It really looks as though the friends of God are on the rise again, to reform the clerics and laity. And he's supposed to preach here at Lent; he's coming from Venice, where everyone follows him about. You'll think you're hearing a disciple of St. Francis and be revived. All of us either wept or stood stupefied at the clear truth he showed to the people, as St Bridget did.[92]

Observants like the Dominicans Giovanni Dominici, Vincent Ferrer, and Antoninus and the Franciscans Bernardino of Siena and John of Capistrano drew huge crowds in the piazzas of the cities of Italy during their preaching tours,[93] giving sermons in the vernacular in which they "attacked avarice and luxury, fostered peace among warring elites, and promoted civic virtue among ordinary townsfolk."[94]

While in Florence, Dominici founded the new Observant priory of San Domenico of Fiesole, overlooking Florence from the nearby hills, which Antoninus entered in 1406 after making his profession. It was during his first years as a friar that the Great Schism directly impacted the trajectory of his life. In 1409, cardinals from both obediences met at Pisa in an attempt to resolve the schism, inviting participants from across Europe to join them there. The council announced that it was deposing the two rival papal claimants, at this time Benedict XIII and Gregory XII, and then elected Alexander V. However, this only exacerbated the schism, with Christendom now divided into the three obediences of Rome, Avignon, and Pisa, with France, England, Bohemia, Prussia, and the majority of the Dominican order going over to the Pisan obedience.[95] Tuscany, including Florence and Fiesole, supported Alexander V, along with the master general of the Dominicans, but the Observant Dominicans broke ranks and remained firmly loyal to Gregory XII of the Roman line.[96] Antoninus and the brothers of Fiesole were expelled and forced to relocate to Foligno.[97] Something of the interpersonal strife and torment of conscience which Christians endured during the Great Schism

---

91 Dessì, "John Dominici."

92 Lapo Mazzei, *Lettere d'un notaro a un mercante del secolo xiv*, 1:228, quoted in Muessig, "Bernardino da Siena and Observant Preaching as a Vehicle for Religious Transformation," 191–2.

93 Van Engen, "The Church in the Fifteenth Century," 321

94 Mixson, "Introduction," 1.

95 "Alexander V," in Kelly and Walsh, eds., *A Dictionary of Popes.*

96 Peterson, "Archbishop Antoninus," 76n.

97 Cornelison, *Art and the Relic Cult*, 12.

may be inferred from this note, which Antoninus appended to his account of the events in his *Chronicles*:

> Many disputations were argued over this matter, many booklets were written to make the argument for either side. Each side or obedience possessed, the whole time this schism lasted, men as learned as can be in Sacred Scripture and canon law, and also very religious men, and, what is more, even shining with miracles; and the question could not ever be settled without leaving most people with lingering doubts. Now although it is necessary to believe that, just as the Catholic Church is one not plural, so also its pastor, the Vicar of Christ, is unique, according to that text of John 10, "there shall be one fold and one shepherd"; nevertheless if it should happen that through a schism more than one supreme pontiff is created or nominated at one and the same time, it does not seem to be necessary for salvation to believe that it is this one or that one, but rather one or the other of them, that is, whoever was canonically admitted to the office. But which of the two was in fact canonically elected, one is not bound to know, just as one is not bound to know canon law; but in this the people may follow their elders or prelates.[98]

During the next thirty years Antoninus moved often among Dominican houses. After Foligno in 1409, he was at Cortona in 1413, where he was ordained to the priesthood, and five years later he was made prior there. In these years the Great Schism was finally brought to an end at the Council of Constance: "The scandal of the schism had affected all Christendom, and to the south German city of Constance there came, eventually, thousands to help end it."[99] The council was initially presided over by John XXIII, the successor of Alexander V in the Pisan line; though he expected to be confirmed as heir to the cardinals from both sides, instead he was pressured to resign, captured by the instigator and protector of the council, King Sigismund of Germany, when he attempted to flee, and then deposed. Gregory XII of the Roman line sent representatives to officially convoke the council on his behalf and then resigned. Benedict XIII held out and never

98 "Multe disputationes facte sunt circa istam materiam, multi libelli editi pro utriusque partis defensione. Peritissimos viros in sacra pagina et iure canonico habuit toto tempore illo quo duravit hoc scisma utraque pars seu obedientia, ac eciam religiosissimos viros; et, quod maius est, eciam miraculis fulgentes, nec unquam sic potuit questio illa decidi, quin semper remaneret apud plurimos dubia. Nam etsi necessarium sit credere, sicut unam esse catholicam ecclesiam non plures, ita et unicum eius pastorem, vicarium Xpisti, juxta illud Ioannis, X: "Fiet unum ovile et unus pastor," tamen [si] contigit plures per scisma creari seu nominari pontifices summos uno et eodem tempore, non videtur saluti necessarium credere istum esse vel illum, sed alterum eorum, qui scilicet fuerit canonice assumptus; quis autem fuerit canonice electus, non tenetur quis scire, sicut nec ius canonicum, sed in hoc populi sequi possunt maiores suos seu prelatos." Antoninus, *Chroniques*, tit. 22 c. 2 (8).

99 Van Engen, "The Church in the Fifteenth Century," 314.

conceded, but was abandoned by most of his following and then deposed by the council. On 11 November 1417, the people who were gathered at the council, including not just cardinals but also representatives from across Europe organized into "nations," elected Pope Martin V, bringing the schism to an end. The tension, however, between "a drive for conciliar involvement and an expectation of papal leadership" continued during the rest of the fifteenth century and into the sixteenth.[100] As for Antoninus, he remained prior in Cortona until 1421, then returned to San Domenico of Fiesole as prior from 1421 to 1424. He was then called upon by the vicar general of the Observants of Tuscany and Naples, who sent him to Naples as visitator and then prior of San Pietro Martire there. He remained in Naples until 1428 or 1429.[101]

Antoninus's writing career begins to be known to us during his time in Naples. Indeed, as will be discussed below in chapter 2, Antoninus wrote that he began the writing of his *Summa* "when I was poised between the summer and autumn of my life."[102] If we take this metaphor literally and assume he was using a "biblical lifespan" of seventy years (which is in fact the age Antoninus attained), it points to the year 1424, when Antoninus was thirty-five years old and just sent to Naples. It may be, and I will suggest this again in chapter 2, that Antoninus considered the *Summa* a repository which comprised all of his literary production, and hence that he viewed all of his earlier writing activity as part of the process of composing it. His first surviving written works do date from this period: a cycle of sermons for the Lent either of 1427 or 1430 and an instruction manual for the sacrament of confession (*Confessionale*), called from its incipit (opening words) "Omnis mortalium cura." It was intended for the use of lay men and women and therefore written in the vernacular Italian, not Latin; Antoninus dedicated it to a Neapolitan nobleman.[103] He later revised and expanded it into two more developed manuals directed to the clergy, the first in Italian, the second in Latin.[104] This first surviving extant composition is in keeping with all of Antoninus's other known writing: he is exclusively a writer of literature dedicated to and serving the *cura animarum* (pastoral care of souls). An overview of Antoninus's written works will be provided below as a preamble to chapter 2; their dates and occasions of composition are omitted, with a few exceptions, in the present chapter.

---

100 Ibid., 315–16.

101 Cornelison, *Art and the Relic Cult*, 12; Finucane, "Friar-Archbishop," 169; Morçay, *Saint Antonin*, 13–46.

102 "Inter estatem et autumpnum etatis constitutus ..." Antoninus, *Summa*, 1 *prohemium* (*N* fol. 3v).

103 Vespasiano, "Arcivescovo Antonino," para. 1 (1:172).

104 Antoninus's manuals for confession are often confounded together under the single title *Confessionale*. They are distinguished by their incipits: "Omnis mortalium cura," "Curam illius habe," and "Defecerunt." These works will be discussed below, ch. 2.

In 1429, Leonardo Bruni wrote on behalf of the city of Florence to the vicar general of the Observant Dominicans asking that Antoninus be brought back to his homeland on account of his popularity there. Instead, after Naples Antoninus was sent to be prior of the important Dominican community of Santa Maria sopra Minerva in Rome.[105] There, in 1430, Antoninus oversaw the translation of the remains of St Catherine of Siena to a sculpted white marble tomb in the basilica.[106] Antoninus was in Rome when Pope Eugenius IV was elected in 1431. Antoninus became close to Eugenius; it was he who ultimately selected Antoninus to be archbishop of Florence. Antoninus states in his *Summa* that during this time he was appointed by Eugenius IV as auditor general of the tribunal of the Rota, the pope's court with final jurisdiction over all ecclesiastical cases – a noteworthy appointment, since Antoninus was not formally trained in law.[107] Eugenius may have also felt kindly disposed because of Antoninus's durable support for the popes when in conflict with councils. We have already seen that Antoninus and his brothers supported the Roman pope Gregory XII, not accepting the validity of the Council of Pisa's attempted deposition. Eugenius himself was soon in need of support. In 1431 a new council had been called at Basel to continue the agenda of constitutional reform in the Church which had been laid out at Constance, but Eugenius was suspicious of the council's intentions and declared it dissolved in December 1431. The members of the council refused to disperse, and over the next two years they asserted the supremacy of the council over the pope with increasing force. In 1434 Eugenius's position was weakened further by the occupation of the papal states by the mercenary captain Francesco Sforza and by an insurrection which forced him to flee Rome. Eugenius took refuge in Florence with the Dominicans of Santa Maria Novella and spent most of the next nine years there or in Bologna, not returning to Rome until September 1443. Eugenius eventually called a new council with himself firmly at the helm, commencing in Ferrara in 1438 and then moving to Florence in 1439, where Antoninus attended it.[108] The council's greatest success was achieved with the negotiation of a decree of union with the Greek Orthodox churches, though in the end it was repudiated by the Greek population. During this time the remaining members of the continuing Council of Basel declared Eugenius deposed and elected an antipope,

105 Finucane, "Friar-Archbishop," 169; Peterson, "Archbishop Antoninus," 75.

106 Cornelison, *Art and the Relic Cult*, 12.

107 Finucane, "Friar-Archbishop," 169. "This is an interesting claim, given the constitution of Eugenius's predecessor Martin V (1417–31), which directed that only well-known doctors of law who'd taught for at least three years after the doctorate were to appointed to the Rota." Ibid., 170, citing Brundage, *The Medieval Origins of the Legal Profession*, 376–7. See also Peterson, "Archbishop Antoninus," 71.

108 Cornelison, *Art and the Relic Cult*, 12. For Antoninus's presence at the Council of Florence and related bibliography, see Cornelison, "Tales of Two Bishop Saints," 635.

Felix V.[109] Antoninus supported Eugenius's authority through all of this: in his *Summa*, Antoninus described the members of the Council of Basel as schismatic,[110] and in his *Chronicles* he denounced it as a "synagogue of satanic authority."[111]

This brings us to a final key event in this part of Antoninus's life: the founding of the Observant Dominican house of San Marco in Florence with the patronage of Cosimo de' Medici. The Medici family ran the richest banking company of the century, bringing in enormous profits from branches across Europe and especially from their role as the pope's own bankers. Cosimo "il Vecchio" de' Medici (1389–1464), the leader of the family and Antoninus's exact contemporary in age, was exiled as a dangerous rival by the Albizzi faction in 1433, but the next year his party in Florence gained ascendancy and welcomed him back to the city triumphant. Cosimo de' Medici exploited his political network, wealth, and popularity in order to become effectively the ruler of Florence, though he maintained the appearance that republican institutions were still functioning. Elections were supervised so that only Medici-approved names were placed in the electoral bags, Medici loyalists were appointed to the most important offices, and Medici partisans directed the councils of the people and the commune.[112] Pope Pius II wrote about Cosimo's reign in Florence:

> After thus disposing of his rivals, Cosimo proceeded to govern the state as he saw fit, amassing a fortune such as even Croesus could scarcely have owned. The palace he built for himself in Florence was fit for a king; he restored a number of churches and erected others; he established the splendid monastery of San Marco and stocked its library with Greek and Latin manuscripts; he decorated his villas in magnificent style. … In matters of war and peace his decisions were final and his word was regarded as law, not so much a citizen as the master of his city. Government meetings were held at his house; his candidates were elected to public office; he enjoyed every semblance of royal power except a title and a court.[113]

As Pius indicated, Cosimo sumptuously patronized the arts, learning, and the Church. It was the founding of San Marco that brought him into close association, and even friendship, with Antoninus. The Observant Dominicans had long wanted to establish a community in Florence. Giovanni Dominici himself had tried to bring the Observant reform to Santa Maria Novella, but did not

---

109 "Eugenius IV," in *Oxford Dictionary of the Renaissance.*

110 Antoninus, *Summa,* 2.3.11.10 (M_1 fol. 169r).

111 "Synagoga satane auctoritate." Morçay, *Chroniques,* tit. 22 c. 10 §. 4 (49), quoted in Peterson, "Archbishop Antoninus," 76n.

112 Weinstein, *Savonarola,* 51.

113 Pius II, *Commentaries,* 2.28 (1:316–17).

succeed, and so had instead founded San Domenico in nearby Fiesole.[114] Cosimo de' Medici also supported the goal of bringing the Observants there from at least 1418–19. There was a Silvestrine congregation of Benedictine monks housed in what is now the monastery of San Marco, and the Dominicans of Fiesole petitioned Pope Martin V to remove them and turn the site into a priory of Observant Dominicans.[115] They claimed that the Silvestrines had become corrupt and were living "without poverty and without chastity," which the monks themselves denied; certainly, however, the community was in decline, with only nine monks in residence at the time.[116] Pope Martin V ordered an inquiry but did not find evidence to support the charges against the monks, and so did not accede to the request. It was the next pope, Eugenius IV, then residing in Florence, who granted the monastery of San Marco to the friars of San Domenico in Fiesole by papal decree in January 1436.[117]

There were several reasons why leading citizens of Florence might have had an interest in bringing the Observant Dominicans into the city. One of the general trends which John Van Engen identified in the fifteenth-century Church was a drive for local control: local lay powers, including kings, princes, and town governments, wished to gain oversight over ecclesiastical institutions.[118] "Urban historians … have documented the ever more active intervention of patrician authorities in the work and life of city churches."[119] This was not necessarily or primarily a matter of exploitation, either financial or political. Lay Christians took religion very seriously, and thought it important that the clergy perform their religious duties, present examples of good living, and uphold the values and reputations of their communities, especially since the laity supported them with alms and other benefits.[120] The Observant movement in the religious orders was thus appealing for multiple reasons. The Observants proclaimed their commitment to the traditional way of life of their orders, including at least a moderate rule of poverty. But founding new communities, or replacing old ones as in the case of San Marco, also meant those new foundations were free of an accretion of privileges, exemptions, and customs which put them beyond the reach of local oversight. The Observants were expected to be "leaner" and more economical – a better use of resources.[121] Moreover, the Observants were committed to pastoral engagement. Through preaching, religious education, hearing confessions, and ministry

114 Ullman and Stadter, *The Public Library of Renaissance Florence*, 3.
115 Ibid., 4; Peterson, "Archbishop Antoninus," 72.
116 Weinstein, *Savonarola*, 28–9.
117 For more about the ejection, see Peterson, "Archbishop Antoninus," 72–3 and nn117–18.
118 Van Engen, "The Church in the Fifteenth Century," 318.
119 Ibid., 313.
120 Ibid., 319; Roest, "Observant Reform in Religious Orders," 457.
121 Mixson, "Introduction," 6.

they provided valued spiritual services to their communities.[122] All these factors, as well as prestige, motivated many towns and wealthy laypeople to sponsor new Observant houses.

Cosimo de' Medici expressed an additional motivation: the need to atone for his sins, particularly those related to his taking power in Florence and to some money "di non molto buono acquisto," not very well acquired.[123] He asked Pope Eugenius IV how he could gain God's pardon for these sins and the pope replied that he should spend 10,000 florins to rebuild San Marco for the newly relocated Observants.[124] The buildings were falling down so that the friars had to live in wooden shacks. Cosimo and his brother Lorenzo thus assumed the role of founding patrons and in the end spent far more than 10,000 florins. They hired their favourite architect, Michelozzo Michelozzi, to build an almost totally new monastery, which he constructed over eight years (1437–44).[125] The painter Fra Angelico was one of the Dominican friars of Fiesole, Bl. Guido or Giovanni da Fiesole by name, and he and his brother the miniaturist Fra Benedetto (da Fiesole) came to decorate the new monastery. Fra Angelico painted the famous San Marco altarpiece for the church, depicting in it the patron saints of the Medici, Cosmas (Cosimo's namesake) and Damian. He also painted in each of the individual monks' cells a scene from the life of Christ to inspire meditation.[126] In 1437 Antoninus was made vicar general of the Observant Dominicans *citra alpes* – "this side of the Alps," i.e., in Italy – and from that time or slightly earlier he resided at San Marco. Cornelison writes:

> Antoninus worked closely with Cosimo and Lorenzo de' Medici as Michelozzo and Fra Angelico renovated the church, rebuilt the convent, added the library to house Niccolò Niccoli's humanist book collection, and carried out its famous fresco and panel paintings. The style of Michelozzo's designs for San Marco's choir, first cloister, and dormitory and that of Fra Angelico's cell frescoes conform closely to Antoninus' preference for piety and simplicity in art and architecture. Antoninus sought to enforce the same artistic ideals elsewhere.[127]

Ullman and Stadter describe the new building complex as expressing "both the religious fervor and austerity of the friars and the rational proportions of the new [Renaissance] architecture."[128] The library was the last part to be

---

122 Ibid.; Roest, "Observant Reform in Religious Orders," 457.
123 Quoted in Ullman and Stadter, *Public Library*, 4n.
124 Weinstein, *Savonarola*, 28.
125 Ullman and Stadter, *Public Library*, 5.
126 Weinstein, *Savonarola*, 29.
127 Cornelison, *Art and the Relic Cult*, 15–16.
128 Ullman and Stadter, *Public Library*, 5.

constructed, completed in 1444. It became the architectural model of the Renaissance library: a long narrow hall divided into three by two rows of columns, with sixty-four benches along the two sides of the central aisle.[129] This was, by the design of Cosimo, to be the home of the first public library in modern times. The library was founded on the estate of the humanist Niccolò Niccoli, who had spent a small fortune amassing an extraordinary collection of manuscripts of classical and patristic authors in both Greek and Latin. In his testament of 1437, two weeks before he died, Niccoli tried to ensure that his collection would be kept together and be made open to the public. He created a committee of sixteen trustees to whom he committed the care and disposition of his books. These trustees included Cosimo and Lorenzo de' Medici, Leonardo Bruni and Poggio Bracciolini (both chancellors of Florence at different times), and, among others, Francesco and Loisio Lapaccini, relatives of friar Giuliano Lapaccini of San Domenico and San Marco, who would become prior of both in 1444.[130] Cosimo de' Medici was the most influential trustee, and as the committee had difficulty finding a permanent site for the book collection, they readily agreed when in 1441 Cosimo proposed placing the books in the library of San Marco, which was just beginning to be constructed.[131] Cosimo paid for all of the expenses involved, including binding the books and attaching chains to them. When the library was ready in 1444, it represented an ideal humanist collection of both secular and religious manuscripts, made up of the more than four hundred volumes from Niccoli's collection with patristic and classical authors very well represented, especially St Augustine, Niccoli's favourite.[132] Cosimo, however, wished this to be not just a collection of ancient literature but a complete library, and so began to supplement Niccoli's collection. He asked Tommaso da Sarzana, later Pope Nicholas V, to draw up a bibliographical canon as a guide to stocking the library, and over the next decade Giuliano Lapaccini, the prior and librarian, as well as Cosimo's book dealer Vespasiano da Bisticci, went periodically to booksellers in nearby towns to add to the collection. Their priority seems to have been to equip the library with "modern" scholastic texts: the first acquisitions were a set of canon-law books, commentaries on the Scriptures, and works of Thomas Aquinas.[133] All was at Cosimo's expense, and indeed, "Cosimo paid for almost everything connected with San Marco: the buildings, furniture and sacred vessels; the clothes, food and daily necessities of the friars; books for the library, sacristy and choir."[134]

129 Ibid., 5, 16.
130 Ibid., 6–9.
131 Ibid., 10–12.
132 Ibid., 12–15.
133 Ibid., 15–23.
134 Ibid., 20.

Hence the cliché was current that "the friars of San Marco ate the bread of the Medici."[135]

The monastery of San Marco and its library became central to the religious and cultural life of Florence. The library was open to all qualified readers and it was even possible to borrow books from it. Humanists and religious alike visited to make use of the treasure trove of manuscripts. The friars preached and ministered in the city. Indeed, from San Marco came the apocalyptic preacher Girolamo Savonarola, who would lead a revolution to establish Florence as a Christian republic at the end of the fifteenth century before being burned at the stake for heresy. The friars also supported the charitable activities of confraternities.[136] In 1442, Antoninus founded a lay confraternity called the *Buonomini* ("Good Men") of San Martino. Its twelve members dedicated themselves to charitable ministry to *poveri vergognosi* ("shamefaced poor"): those who had fallen on hard times and were ashamed to beg. The confraternity came to the aid mainly of the working poor, especially textile workers, as well as aristocratic families.[137] The Medici family were generous contributors to the *Buonomini*. This confraternity still exists today.

Both Cosimo and Antoninus were devoted to San Marco for the rest of their lives. Cosimo kept a personal cell there where he could make retreats, and remained a friend and patron of the friars.[138] Antoninus resided mainly at San Marco until he moved into the archbishop's residence in 1446. In 1439 he became prior of San Domenico of Fiesole, to which San Marco was subordinate, remaining in that post until 1444 when he handed it off to Giuliano Lapaccini. San Marco remained under the prior of the house of Fiesole until July of 1445, when, with Giuliano Lapaccini as prior and Antoninus as vicar of the Observants in Italy, it was separated and gained its own prior.[139] Antoninus certainly benefited from his ready access to the collection of books in San Marco. Speaking of Antoninus after his death, Vespasiano notes that "He had no books of his own, not even a breviary … The books he needed he borrowed from S. Marco or S. Domenico."[140] San Marco's library provided an enormous amount of literature that Antoninus could digest and make use of in his *Summa* and *Chronicles*, which

135 Weinstein, *Savonarola*, 28.

136 Ibid., 29–30.

137 Cornelison, *Art and the Relic Cult*, 15.

138 Finucane, "Friar-Archbishop," 170.

139 The Latin separation document is reproduced and transcribed with an Italian translation in *Gli autografi di S. Antonino Pierozzi e del B. Angelico nell'atto della separazione del convento di S. Marco in Firenze dal convento di S. Domenico di Fiesole concluso nel iuglio del 1445*. See plates 3–5 below, ch. 2, where the document is discussed as a sample of Antoninus's handwriting.

140 George and Waters, *Vespasiano Memoirs*, 163; Vespasiano, "Arcivescovo Antonino," para. 14 (1:189). Note that George and Waters misunderstand and mistranslate the sentence which is omitted at the ellipsis; that sentence is discussed below, ch. 2, where Vespasiano's word *iscartabegli* is translated "volumes" or "manuscripts."

he was writing during the 1440s and 1450s.[141] He seems to have been particularly productive in the years roughly 1444 to 1449, when several substantial portions of the *Summa*, including the majority of parts 2 and 3, were completed, bound, and began to be copied.[142] Like Cosimo, Antoninus had a cell at San Marco for the rest of his life, including during his tenure as archbishop.[143] After his death, the autograph manuscripts of his *Summa* and *Chronicles* were kept in this cell into modern times, and displayed publicly on his feast day as relics.[144]

5. Antoninus the Counsellor

These three currents all flowed together to contribute to Antoninus's character and public ministry: the Dominican mission, the preaching and leadership of Giovanni Dominici, and the Observant reform. Their combined influence on Antoninus is readily visible in his most outstanding quality: his devotion to pastoral care.[145] I have already discussed the connection to the Dominican mission and to Giovanni Dominici; let me add here a brief word about Observant pastoral activity.[146] James Mixson wrote that, beyond their work of internal reform in the religious orders, "the Observants were also the leading architects of the era's most engaged and vigorous efforts at catechesis and moral formation."[147] They encouraged or shaped many of the most popular devotional practices of the late Middle Ages, from the processions of the Bianchi to the cult of the Holy Name to the praying of the Rosary.[148] Observants intensified the traditional mendicant commitment to pastoral care, particularly through preaching and hearing confessions, and added to this "an insistence on both spiritual and intellectual formation."[149] This Observant emphasis on the value of learning converged with the humanist movement; in fact, the whole Observant program of renewing religious life

141 See the description of Niccoli's collection of Latin books in Ullman and Stadter, *Public Library*, 85–9.

142 Dates of composition discussed below, ch. 2.

143 Vespasiano quotes Antoninus as saying in 1458, during an encounter to be narrated below, "I will go to my cell in S. Marco, of which I have the key beside me, and rest there in peace ..." George and Waters, *Vespasiano Memoirs*, 161–2; Vespasiano, "Arcivescovo Antonino," para. 11 (1:185).

144 Cornelison, *Art and the Relic Cult*, 14.

145 "Confession and preaching were the exercises he specially favoured, and in the one and the other he brought forth very great fruit." "Attese a dua esercizi molto necessari: l' uno fu il confessare, l' altro il predicare, e nell' uno e nell' altro fece grandissimo frutto." Vespasiano, "Arcivescovo Antonino," para. 1 (1:172).

146 On this topic, see the essays in Roest and Mixson, *Companion to Observant Reform*, especially Pietro Delcorno, "'Quomodo Discet Sine Docente?' Observant Efforts towards Education and Pastoral Care," in ibid., 145–84; Muessig, "Bernardino da Siena and Observant Preaching."

147 Mixson, "Observant Reform's Conceptual Frameworks," 82.

148 Mixson, "Introduction," 2; Van Engen, "The Church in the Fifteenth Century," 311.

149 Delcorno, "Observant Efforts towards Education and Pastoral Care," 183.

through a return to its sources is parallel to the cultural Renaissance focused on returning to the literature of classical Greece and Rome. Pietro Delcorno suggested that "with respect to the education of the laity, the Observant movement can thus be considered a powerful vector of modernity."[150]

For the instruction and edification of the laity, Observant friars produced both "a massive output of homiletic materials associated with preaching" and "many kinds of religious instruction literature, both in Latin and in the vernacular."[151] The latter we can describe here as *pastoralia*, "pastoral literature."[152] Antoninus contributed to both of these genres, preaching and *pastoralia*, through his own ministry and through his writing. He can readily be compared to St Bernardino of Siena (1380–1444), his Observant Franciscan counterpart, also a Tuscan and only slightly older than him.[153] Both were central players in the long-term success of the Observant movements in their orders.[154] Both were devoted to preaching, and both wrote lengthy treatises on doctrinal and moral topics. In fact, Antoninus drew extensively on Bernardino's writings, as will be discussed in chapters 3 and 4. The comparison, however, brings out some differences. Bernardino was not a prelate: he was never made a bishop, for example, but remained until the end of his life primarily an itinerant preacher. Antoninus, as archbishop, had to be a governor as well as a preacher; and indeed throughout his life he was noted as a gifted administrator – one of the reasons cited by Eugenius IV for making him archbishop. At the same time Antoninus did not have all of Bernardino's rhetorical gifts. Bernardino in his preaching could stoop lower and rise higher to conquer diverse audiences than Antoninus. When preaching to crowds of laypeople in the piazzas, parish churches, and cathedrals, the friars preached in the vernacular. Bernardino's Italian sermons are famous for their conversationality, folksiness, and even humour. Both Bernardino and Antoninus also preached and wrote Latin sermons which were directed at more learned audiences, primarily of clerics. In his Latin sermons, Bernardino wrote more elegantly and closer to classical standards than Antoninus. Antoninus's Latin is straightforward, relatively simple in its vocabulary, and at times rather inelegant. The difference in style is in parallel to a difference of character: Bernardino was more divisive, and more

---

150 Ibid., 184. See also ibid., 176–7.

151 Roest, "Observant Reform in Religious Orders," 455–6.

152 See Stansbury, ed., *A Companion to Pastoral Care in the Late Middle Ages (1200–1500)*; Boyle, *Pastoral Care, Clerical Education and Canon Law, 1200–1400*. For a fresh assessment of this literature and the boundaries of the genre *pastoralia*, see Samuel J. Klumpenhouwer's book on the *Summa de penitencia* of John of Kent, forthcoming from the Pontifical Institute of Mediaeval Studies.

153 On Bernardino, see Debby, *Renaissance Florence in the Rhetoric of Two Popular Preachers*; Polecritti, *Preaching Peace in Renaissance Italy*; Mormando, *The Preacher's Demons*; Origo, *The World of San Bernardino*.

154 Roest, "Observant Reform in Religious Orders," 449–50; Edelheit, "Introduction," 9.

prone to extremes in his teaching, while Antoninus was more moderate. There is an excellent example in relation to the subject of this book, economic teaching. Bernardino, preaching in Florence in the 1430s on the subject of usury, attacked the city's public debt (*monte*) so ferociously that when the Florentine Giannozzo Manetti encountered him in Vespasiano's bookshop he cried out, "You've consigned us all to damnation!" Bernardino replied, "I damn nobody; it's the sins and weaknesses of men that damn them."[155] At the same time, Bernardino went as far as any scholastic author in defending the legitimacy of certain claims to interest on loans, on the basis that money accumulated for business purposes has the character of capital. Antoninus's approach to the issue of usury versus legitimate interest is more moderate. He does not endorse all of the titles to interest put forward by Bernardino, but at the same time advises that confessors should be tolerant and not condemn penitents who sincerely believe that the interest they are taking is licit and does not cross over into usury.[156] In the chapters edited below he frequently advises against facile condemnation.

Antoninus was, in a word, a pastor before all else. He became possibly the supreme pastoral writer of the late Middle Ages: all of his literary output was either directly pastoral or aimed to support pastoral ministry and enable priests to carry it out well. He wrote for the instruction of both laity and clergy. His first catechetical work, his *Confessionale* mentioned above, was written for laypeople. For priests he wrote a pastoral handbook called *Medicina dell'anima* (or from its first words "Curam illius habe"), "to help the simple priests" in their ministry of taking care of souls, and later his great work, the *Summa*.[157] He also wrote works of spiritual direction for lay women, as his mentor Giovanni Dominici had done.[158] He was widely known for his devotion to and aptitude for resolving difficult moral issues, so-called cases of conscience. "So great was his reputation in cases of conscience that a vast number were submitted to him."[159] In the years 1439–42, sixty-nine such cases were submitted to him by Br. Dominic de Cathalonia.[160] Vespasiano reports:

> People came to consult him about contracts, as to whether they were lawful or not … when he had heard all, he decided at once which contracts were lawful.[161]

155 Vespasiano, *Vite*, 1:250, quoted in Armstrong, "Usury, Conscience, and Public Debt," 189.

156 This is discussed in some detail in ch. 4 below, in the section on Antoninus's chapter 3.8.3.

157 "Per aiutare li semplici sacerdoti." Quoted in Delcorno, "Observant Efforts towards Education and Pastoral Care," 182.

158 Ibid., 179, and see the references therein.

159 George and Waters, *Vespasiano Memoirs*, 157; Vespasiano, "Arcivescovo Antonino," para. 1 (1:171–2).

160 Marchetti, "Cronologia della vita e delle opera," 12. See Creytens, "Les cas de conscience soumis à S. Antoninus de Florence par Dominique de Catalogne, O.P."; Antoninus Florentinus, "Les 'consilia' de s. Antoninus de Florence O.P."

161 George and Waters, *Vespasiano Memoirs*, 159; Vespasiano, "Arcivescovo Antonino," para. 5 (1:178).

This question, "which contracts were lawful," is an example of a case for which Antoninus provided a written treatise in his *Summa*, disseminating solutions to common *dubia* (doubtful cases) which he had often received: it is dealt with in two of the six chapters edited below, namely 3.8.2 and 3.8.3. His skill in directing consciences, resolving doubts, and rendering just judgments in difficult cases earned him the nickname *Antoninus Consiliorum*, "Antoninus the Counsellor."[162]

6. Archbishop of Florence, 1446–1459

This is where things stood when the archbishop of Florence, Bartolomeo Zabarella, died in August 1445. Pope Eugenius IV reserved to himself the choice of the next archbishop, disallowing an election by the clergy of the cathedral chapter.[163] The Florentine leaders wrote to Eugenius to submit a list of five proposed candidates, asking that, at the very least, the city should be provided with one of her own sons as bishop.[164] Eugenius passed over their candidates and on 10 January 1446 issued a bull designating Antoninus.[165] The decisive reasons for Eugenius's choice are a matter of speculation. Eugenius's relationship with the city that had sheltered him was deteriorating, and beyond needing an archbishop he could work with, he also needed someone who could deal astutely with the complex relations between local clergy, commune, international religious orders, and papacy.[166] Morçay argued that by selecting Antoninus he gave the city a Florentine archbishop, while by reaching below the patrician class he chose a candidate who came from more neutral social territory – someone who was not a member of either the Medici partisans or their opponents.[167] Moreover, Peterson added, in Antoninus he had someone familiar with the local church and the politics of the city, but capable of not becoming embroiled in them.[168] In his bull of appointment Eugenius spoke most about Antoninus's skill in administrative affairs, expressing the hope that under him the church would be "usefully administered and prosperously

162 "Tanta enim erat in eo sacrarum litterarum cognitio, tanta consuetudo, tanta denique in consulendo experientia, ut non solum cives, verum et advenae plurimi, Principes ac Praelati, de rebus gravissimis ejus sententiam plurimi facerent. Ob quam rem etiam antea Frater Antoninus consiliorum appellari ceperat: sic enim ut plurimum diminutive, antequam Pontifex fieret, vocari consueverat." Castiglione, *Vita Beati Antonini*, c. 2 (317).

163 Peterson, "Archbishop Antoninus," 64–5.

164 Finucane, "Friar-Archbishop," 170.

165 Peterson, "Archbishop Antoninus," 63. See also Peterson, "An Episcopal Election in Quattrocento Florence."

166 See Peterson's skilful disentangling of these factors, "Archbishop Antoninus," ch. 1, esp. 63–84.

167 Ibid., 65, citing Morçay, *Saint Antonin*, 116; see also 101–23.

168 Peterson, "Archbishop Antoninus," 70.

augmented."[169] Vespasiano reports that he heard, via Nicholas V, that Eugenius was accustomed to say:

> … he had only made three prelates with an easy conscience: the Patriarch of Venice, the Bishop of Ferrara and Fra Antonino. Eugenius was full of praise of Antonino, having known him long. Pope Nicolas was the same.[170]

Antoninus resisted the appointment. The leaders of Florence's government expected that he would need to be convinced: though he was popular in the city, they knew that he preferred the quiet life, and they wrote a letter urging him to think of his city's need and the responsibility of the clergy to lead others to faith: "you ought rather to comply with the urging of the country, the ordering of the pope, and the calling of God."[171] Being urged by many citizens of Florence and many prelates,[172] and sternly commanded by the pope in an apostolic letter,[173] he reluctantly accepted the episcopal dignity. He entered Florence in the city's customary ritual procession in March 1446 and took up the duties of archbishop, which he performed for thirteen years, until his death on 2 May 1459.[174]

Antoninus's tenure as archbishop is by far the best documented portion of his life. His administration of the archdiocese has been the object of detailed study in recent years.[175] Chronicling his activity as archbishop as described in the sources would unduly lengthen this chapter. Instead, three themes deserve to be highlighted. The first is his continued attention to pastoral care and the support of the clergy in their ministry. Immediately after taking up the government of the Florentine church, he took an interest in the formation of both laity and clergy. He called a synod in April of 1446, declaring that hitherto there would be annual synods, and in August began an extensive visitation of parishes in his diocese.[176]

169 Quoted in Peterson, "Archbishop Antoninus," 66–7.

170 George and Waters, *Vespasiano Memoirs*, 158; Vespasiano, "Arcivescovo Antonino," para. 3 (1:174).

171 Quoted in Peterson, "Archbishop Antoninus," 77–9. The letter of the Florentine Republic to Antoninus after his appointment, 24 January 1446 (modern style), is printed in in "Autres documents," appendix 3-2 in Morçay, *Saint Antonin*, 439; see also Aliotti's letter to Antoninus, ibid., 440.

172 Vespasiano, "Arcivescovo Antonino," para. 3 (1:174–5).

173 Ibid., para. 2 (1:173). Morçay (*Saint Antonin*, 118 n1) rejects Vespasiano's report that the letter of Eugenius IV threatened excommunication if he did not obey. It would indeed have been an unheard-of procedure. Castiglione agrees with Vespasiano that Eugenius IV commanded Antoninus to accept in an apostolic letter, and makes no mention of a threat of excommunication.

174 Cornelison, *Art and the Relic Cult*, 12–13; Castiglione, *Vita Beati Antonini*, c. 1 para. 8 (316). On the entrance ritual and on the roles and duties of the archbishop of Florence, see Weinstein, *Savonarola*, 49–51.

175 The most thorough study is Peterson, "Archbishop Antoninus."

176 "His vicar continued the work into the 1450s." Finucane, "Friar-Archbishop," 171–2, citing Peterson, "Archbishop Antoninus," 30, 590–1.

He attempted to improve the education of the "secular" clergy (priests who are not members of religious orders), "considered both the weakest link and the most necessary element for a durable reform of society."[177] For the clergy also he continued writing the *Summa* and *Chronicles*, both largely composed during his tenure as archbishop.

> He worked at his *Summa*, a book which proved so useful and beneficial to the Christian faith. In spite of his heavy task of office he wrote the greater part of it while he was archbishop, by his prudent use of his time.[178]

For the education of the laity, Antoninus promoted the Florentine brotherhoods for the young, which had recently been reformed by Eugene IV.[179] He corresponded with several widows as their spiritual director and advocate in temporal affairs as part of his episcopal responsibility for widows and orphans; he composed several treatises on the spiritual life for these women, including one called *Opera a ben vivere* (*The Art of Living Well*) for Lucrezia Tornabuoni, the widow of a son of Cosimo de' Medici and mother of Lorenzo the Magnificent.[180] In addition to spiritual ministries, he promoted charitable endeavours. Vespasiano describes him providing bread for the poor of the city during a famine.[181] A new wave of the Black Death struck northern Italy in 1448–51, and Antoninus was one of the leading voices in Florence working for the provision of medical and spiritual care for the sick as well as charity for the poor in need. "He persuaded the *Signoria* to allocate 3,000 florins, and with some of the money he hired young people to seek out the sick and see to their needs."[182] He also requested that a *lazaretto* (plague

177 Delcorno, "Observant Efforts towards Education and Pastoral Care," 181. See also Trexler's discussion and edition of the diocesan constitution which Antoninus issued in 1455, "The Episcopal Constitutions of Antoninus of Florence."

178 George and Waters, *Vespasiano Memoirs*, 159; Vespasiano, "Arcivescovo Antonino," para. 6 (1:179).

179 Delcorno, "Observant Efforts towards Education and Pastoral Care," 176–77.

180 Antoninus, *Opera a ben vivere con altri suoi ammaestramenti*. A French translation of this edition was later published, which is the version consulted: *Une règle de vie au XVe siècle*, trans. Thiérard-Baudrillart (Paris, 1921). Two other such works are discussed in ch. 2.

For Antoninus's correspondence, see *Lettere di Sant'Antonino, Arcivescovo di Firenze, precedute dalla sua vita scritta da Vespasiano (da Bisticci) fiorentino*.

181 "At that time there was scarcity in Florence, and town and country alike suffered great want. He caused a vast quantity of bread to be baked and instructed the officials to give it, not only to the manifest poor, but also to those who were ashamed to let their distress be known … He did so many charitable works privately that all seemed well provided for in spiritual and temporal needs." George and Waters, *Vespasiano Memoirs*, 159; Vespasiano, "Arcivescovo Antonino," para. 5 (1:177–8).

182 Carmichael, *Plague and the Poor in Renaissance Florence*, 102. I thank my student Nick Levreault for this reference.

hospital) be provided as a refuge for the plague-stricken, for the sake of both administering food and medical care and avoiding contagion.[183]

A second theme in Antoninus's tenure as archbishop can be summed up in a word used repeatedly in the sources: "severity." Castiglione writes that, even as vicar general of the Observants, Antoninus governed "with great diligence and severity."[184] He uses the same term to describe him as archbishop: supervising all sorts of litigation and accusations, he displayed "severity … joined with mercy."[185] His clergy at one time asked the pope to order Antoninus to "go easier" on them.[186] Morçay, indeed, notes several cases of appeals from Antoninus's judgments being heard in Rome, the appellants alleging that Antoninus's judgment was too severe.[187] In his *Opera a ben vivere*, Antoninus tells a parable of a gardener who has let wild plants invade his garden, and now wishes to restore it to a good state: "he will first cut the wood, thorns, and weeds … second, he will tear up and extirpate all the roots and shoots which remain in the soil of the garden."[188] In this vein, Vespasiano tells many stories of Antoninus acting quickly and zealously to uproot sin or injustice.[189] The most extreme instance of this is Antoninus's condemnation of Giovanni da Montecatini in 1450, whom he handed over to the *podestà* (magistrate in charge of law and order) for execution. Baldovini, Antoninus's notary, records the case in most detail. This Giovanni da Montecatini was a doctor "well known for his evil opinion of the Catholic faith and teachings of the Church."[190] Finucane provides the following account, based on Baldovini's testimony:

> He was also thought to call up demons in his house in Florence's San Lorenzo parish. He and his followers resembled heretical *Fraticelli*, little sons of the devil – "figluoli del

---

183 Ibid., 102, 121.

184 Finucane, "Friar-Archbishop," 175, quoting: "… magna cum diligentia ac severitate Provinciam gubernavit." Castiglione, *Vita Beati Antonini*, c. 1 para. 4 (315).

185 "Erat tamen cum illa severitate summa bonitas misericordiaque conjuncta; …" Castiglione, *Vita Beati Antonini*, c. 2 para. 14 (318).

186 "Mitius nobiscum agat; … mitius, et benignius in rebus nostris se gerat." Peterson, "Archbishop Antoninus," 347–9, quoted in Finucane, "Friar-Archbishop," 175.

187 "Autres documents," appendix 3-2 in Morçay, *Saint Antonin*, 446, 469–70, 482, 487, 490–1.

188 "*Declina a malo et fac bonum, inquire pacem et persequire eam* [*Ps* 33:15]. … Je vous présenterai cette similitude: un homme qui posséderait un beau jardin qu'il aurait par négligence laissé envahir d'herbes sauvages, devrait pour le remettre en bon état faire quatre choses avant d'en tirer profit et récompense. Il coupera d'abord le bois, les épines et les mauvaises herbes, et j'entends par là, la première parole du Prophète: Écarte-toi du mal. En second lieu il arrachera et extirpera toutes les racines et les rejets qui resteraient dans la terre du jardin. Et c'est le second travail: Fais le bien …" Antoninus, *Règle de vie*, c. 1 (5–7).

189 See George and Waters, *Vespasiano Memoirs*, 159; Vespasiano, "Arcivescovo Antonino," para. 6 (1:179–80); Castiglione, *Vita Beati Antonini*, c. 3 para. 24 (320).

190 Finucane, "Friar-Archbishop," 176–7.

> diavolo." A group of high clergy, including theologians and Antoninus's vicar, interrogated Giovanni as he lay at home in his sickbed. He claimed that Nicholas V was not the true pope and that priests consecrated by Florence's archbishop weren't true priests and couldn't consecrate the body of Christ ... The attending clergy urged him to change his mind, but he was so stubborn (*tanta dura cervice*) that he neither confessed nor detested his errors. Out of compassion, Baldovini writes, Antoninus allowed him a certain term (unspecified) to think things over (not uncommon in such trials). Giovanni refused to budge. A platform was built outside the entrance to the cathedral, from which Antoninus and other prelates pronounced judgment. The heretic and invoker of demons was handed over [to] Florence's *podestà* Niccolò Vitelli, who committed him to the flames. His books of necromancy, chiromancy, and demonic invocations were also burned. Thus Giovanni died a "martyr to the devil" as the archbishop looked on. Gene Brucker claimed that he was "the only man to die in Florence for his beliefs in the 110 years between the execution of fra Michele da Calci (1389) and Savonarola (1498)."[191]

According to Castiglione, this execution was unpopular among the Florentines, yet Antoninus withstood the disapproval of the people.[192] "Nothing could move him from the ways of strict justice," says Vespasiano.[193] "He was of such severity that, having understood the truth of a thing, he stood firm and constant, and did not change for anything."[194]

This instance of Antoninus's severity is unlikely to endear him to contemporary readers. But it also shows his firmness in the face of opposition, and this brings us to our third theme: his independence from political interests. This is shown above all in his relations with the Medici regime. Though Cosimo de' Medici was the great patron of the Observant Dominicans of San Marco, Antoninus was not a creature of the Medici. Vespasiano writes:

> He made no distinction between rich and poor, and always gave equal justice. One day Cosimo de' Medici came to him asking him to favour a case he had in hand, and he replied that, if Cosimo had right on his side, he wanted no help from anyone.[195]

---

191 Ibid., 176–7, loosely translating Baldovini, *Vita di S. Antonino*, 430–1. In the final sentence Finucane cites Brucker, *Renaissance Florence*, 206–7.

192 "... quem haeretica pravitate infectum deprehenderat, non approbantibus id multis civibus, flammis concremandum esse adjudicavit." Castiglione, *Vita Beati Antonini*, c. 3 para. 24 (320).

193 George and Waters, *Vespasiano Memoirs*, 161; Vespasiano, "Arcivescovo Antonino," para. 10 (1:182).

194 "Ed era di tanta severità che intesa la verità d'una cosa, istava fermo e constante, e non se ne *mutava* per nulla." Vespasiano, "Arcivescovo Antonino," para. 1 (1:172). An excellent example of this trait of Antoninus is his conduct in the marriage case chronicled in Brucker, *Giovanni and Lusanna*.

195 George and Waters, *Vespasiano Memoirs*, 158; Vespasiano, "Arcivescovo Antonino," para. 4 (1:176–7). Likewise in the case of Giovanni and Lusanna (see previous note), Antoninus stood firm against political pressure and earned Cornelison's respect for "even-handed consideration of women." Cornelison, *Art and the Relic Cult*, 15.

Antoninus was even willing to stand up to the Medici and the *Signoria*. Perhaps the most celebrated episode in Antoninus's time as archbishop was his act of 26 July 1458. At a critical moment for the Medici regime, when by chance they temporarily had a majority of the priors and the ability to initiate legislation in the city's councils, they attempted to force measures through "which would give them effective control of the government."[196] In order to intimidate their opponents into voting as they wished, they pressed for open rather than secret ballots in the councils.

> It was at this juncture that, on July 26, just as they stood within reach of attaining their ends, Antoninus issued an edict which he ordered to be affixed to the doors of the cathedral and other churches in the city. In it, he declared it his pastoral duty to remind the councilmen and priors that open balloting comprised a violation of their oaths of office, and was therefore a mortal sin. Threatening excommunication without absolution, he forbade them to adopt the measure. Under such pressure from Antoninus, the strategy of the Medici partisans collapsed.[197]

Vespasiano describes the reaction:

> Certain of the leaders were much perturbed … [and sent] some prominent citizens to threaten him. Five of these waited on him and began to denounce him for what he had done, whereupon he replied that he had only played the part of a good pastor by saving their souls from damnation for perjury. This made them more furious than ever, though the archbishop spake gently and with humility. Then they threatened to deprive him of his see, and he at once began to laugh. "For God's sake, I beg you, do this at once. You will do me a great favour and lift a great burden from my shoulders. I will go to my cell in S. Marco, of which I have the key beside me, and rest there in peace. Such a deed would please me beyond anything." … Neither prayers nor threats could move the archbishop.[198]

In his preaching and writing, Antoninus commended the virtues not only of good Christians but of good citizens, and promoted the ideal of service to the common good of the republic; but he did not join the civic humanists in advocating Florentine imperialism and territorial expansion.[199]

---

196 Peterson, "Archbishop Antoninus," 87.

197 Ibid.

198 George and Waters, *Vespasiano Memoirs*, 161–2; Vespasiano, "Arcivescovo Antonino," para. 11 (1:184–5). The text of the archbishop's edict ("edipto"), in Italian, is provided by Baldovini, *Vita di S. Antonino*, 429–30.

199 Weinstein, *Savonarola*, 50–1. See Howard, *Beyond the Written Word*, 250; Lesnick, *Preaching in Medieval Florence*.

Antoninus has been called a model bishop down to modern times.[200] According to Vespasiano, not only was there a general desire for Antoninus to be made cardinal,[201] but in the papal conclave of 1447, in which Nicholas V was elected, several cardinals voted for Antoninus to be made pope: "had he been elected he would assuredly have reformed the Church."[202] In his final year, having reached age seventy, Antoninus had become (Vespasiano says) "old and greatly weakened by fasting and vigils."[203] He contracted a fever and died tranquilly at the episcopal residence at Montughi, just outside the Florentine city walls, on 2 May 1459 while Pope Pius II was visiting Florence.[204] In the last hours of his illness he was heard to murmer: *servire Deo regnare est*, "To serve God is to reign," and *laudate Dominum de caelis*, "Praise the Lord from the heavens."[205] He was given a splendid public funeral, conducted by Pius II himself.[206] Six bishops carried his remains to the cathedral, where the pope celebrated Mass.[207] The banker Tommaso Spinelli (discussed in chapter 4) paid for a large portion of the funeral expenses. After the funeral, Antoninus was carried to San Marco and lay in state while multitudes came to kiss his hands and feet.[208] The body was not buried until eight days after his death.[209] Nevertheless, Castiglione reports that the body remained fresh,

200 See, e.g., Barone, "Conclusioni"; Paoli, "Sant' Antonino 'vere pastor et bonus pastor.'"

201 Vespasiano, "Arcivescovo Antonino," para. 8 (1:181).

202 George and Waters, *Vespasiano Memoirs*, 162–3; Vespasiano, "Arcivescovo Antonino," para. 14 (1:188).

203 George and Waters, *Vespasiano Memoirs*, 162. "Era già vecchio in questo tempo, indebolito molto del corpo, per digiuni, astinenze e lunghe vigilie, in modo che il corpo suo era molto mortificato." Vespasiano, "Arcivescovo Antonino," para. 13 (1:187).

204 Finucane, "Friar-Archbishop," 178; Vespasiano, "Arcivescovo Antonino," para. 14 (1:188–9).

205 Morçay, *Saint Antonin*, 278; Cornelison, *Art and the Relic Cult*, 28.

206 "*The sanctity and death of Bishop Antonino of Florence:* It was at this time that Antonino, the archbishop of Florence, went to meet his maker. A member of the Dominican order and a man worthy of remembrance, he conquered avarice, trampled on pride, knew absolutely nothing of lust, consumed food and drink only sparingly and never gave in to anger or envy or any other passion. He was a brilliant theologian and wrote several books which were praised by scholars; he was a popular preacher even though he was violent in his denunciation of sin; he reformed the morals of clergy and laity; he worked hard to settle quarrels; he did his best to rid the city of feuds; he distributed the revenues of his church among the poor of Christ, but to his relatives and connections, unless they were very needy, he gave nothing. He used only glass and clay dishes and he desired his household (which was very small) to be content with little and to live by the precepts of philosophy. At his death he was accorded a splendid public funeral. In his house they found nothing but the mule he used to ride and some cheap furniture; the poor had taken everything else. All of Florence was sure that he had passed to a life of bliss – nor should we imagine their belief was unfounded." Pius II, *Commentaries*, 2.29.1 (1:318–21).

207 Finucane, "Friar-Archbishop," 178; Cornelison, *Art and the Relic Cult*, 17.

208 Castiglione, *Vita Beati Antonini*, c. 5 para. 34 (324).

209 "Nec nisi octava die post ejus obitum sepulcro condi posset." Ibid.

fragrant, and free of signs of rigor mortis.[210] He was buried, as he had wished, in the monastery of San Marco and attired in the friar's robe which he had worn even after his consecration as archbishop.[211]

7. St Antoninus and His Posthumous Influence

Antoninus was venerated as a saint immediately, and people began reporting miracles due to his intercession in subsequent decades.[212] A process for him to be officially declared a saint (canonized) was opened early in the next century. In 1513, Giovanni de' Medici was elected pope as Leo X. While visiting Florence in 1516, he was approached after the Mass of Ash Wednesday by his cousin the archbishop of Florence, Giulio de' Medici. With him there were

> the prior and *gonfaloniere di giustizia* [standard bearer of justice] of the Republic, Piero di Niccolò Ridolfi; and the master general of the Dominicans, Tommaso de Vio (Cajetan). In the names respectively of the Florentine Church, the *Signoria* and the people of Florence, and the Dominican order, the trio formally requested that Leo open a process for Antoninus's canonization.[213]

Leo granted their request and an ad hoc committee began taking testimonies at once. After this initial (first) process, a second and third were undertaken at a more leisurely pace after Leo left Florence, with Br. Roberto Ubaldini da Gagliano, OP, friar of San Marco, chronicler, and follower of Savonarola, as official procurator of the canonization process.[214] After three sets of testimony had been collected and

---

210 "Illudque sane multa admiratione dignum est, tanto tempore reservatum corpus exanime nullum tetrum odorem edidisse: quin potius mirabili semper fragrantia redolebat, videbaturque omnium judicio venustior laetiorque in mortuo facies quam fuerat in vivo. Insuper manus pedesque, nullo rigore contracti, nulloque maculati livore cernebantur: quod certe omnibus id cernentibus magnum sanctitatis signum esse ducebatur." Ibid.; Finucane, "Friar-Archbishop," 178. Vespasiano (two decades later than Castiglione) says the body lay in state for two days: Vespasiano, "Arcivescovo Antonino," para. 15 (1:190). Cornelison's measured discussion of possible embalming procedures (most likely none, or very limited), and the state of the body, is at *Art and the Relic Cult*, 18–19.

211 "Sic enim ipse testamento legaverat, ut juxta Fratres suos humi conderetur." Castiglione, *Vita Beati Antonini*, c. 5 para. 34 (324).

212 Finucane, "Friar-Archbishop," 178–80; Cornelison, *Art and the Relic Cult*, 22–3.

213 Finucane, "Friar-Archbishop," 184. The French king Francis I and his queen wrote to Leo X in support of Antoninus's canonization. "Autres documents," appendix 3-2 in Morçay, *Saint Antonin*, 499–500, cited by Cornelison, *Art and the Relic Cult*, 41 n99.

214 Finucane, "Friar-Archbishop," 185–6, 168; Cornelison, *Art and the Relic Cult*, 24. "The information they [Lorenzo Pucci and his clerical colleagues] gathered, as well as Castiglione's *Life of St. Antoninus*, the *Additiones*, and Verini's laud to Antoninus, were admitted as evidence in the canonization hearings." Cornelison, *Art and the Relic Cult*, 41 n103.

the matter discussed in several consistories, the next pope, Adrian VI, canonized Antoninus on Trinity Sunday, 31 May 1523, in a joint ceremony for Antoninus and Benno of Meissen (c. 1040–1106) in Old St Peter's, Rome.[215] The bull of canonization was delayed for reasons unknown, and it was Giulio de' Medici, one of the original trio requesting Antoninus's canonization process, who promulgated the bull a few months later as Pope Clement VII, on 26 November 1523, the day of his papal coronation.[216] Antoninus's feast, originally 2 May, was moved to 10 May in the Tridentine liturgical calendar. About 130 years after Antoninus's death, in 1589, his tomb in San Marco was opened to prepare for a translation of the body. He had been buried

> dressed as a simple friar, with only a pallium to show his archiepiscopal status. Much of the substance of the body remained – some friars claimed that (even after 130 years) he looked like the images familiar to them ... The body [was] redressed not as a friar but in sumptuous archiepiscopal gear, with fine footwear and vestments of silk and satin, silver and gold ornamentation, a pectoral cross, a beautiful miter, and on the right hand a ring of sky-blue sapphire. According to custom, the friar's simple garb was retained (and hidden) under the archiepiscopal finery.[217]

Antoninus was laid to rest again in San Marco, in a new altar-tomb at the centre of a chapel built and decorated by the patronage of the Salviati brothers, relatives of the Medici.[218] There, surrounded by sculptures and paintings in his honour, Antoninus's body remains today in its glass coffin and is seen daily by visitors to the church of San Marco.

The last matter to be discussed is the posthumous influence of St Antoninus. Only a few examples will be touched on very briefly here.[219] In the second half of the fifteenth century, Antoninus's shorter and longer works for the clergy were standard manuals in wide use.[220] The first commercial printing houses were opened in the 1440s, and printed books began appearing in ever increasing numbers after 1470.[221] During the next two centuries, Antoninus was one of the most frequently

---

215 A narrative of Antoninus's canonization is provided by Finucane, "Friar-Archbishop," 185–203; see also the articles referenced therein by Lorenzo Polizzotto, Klaus Pietschmann, and Stefano Orlandi. According to Cornelison, this was the first double canonization in Church history. Cornelison, *Art and the Relic Cult*, 24.

216 Cornelison, *Art and the Relic Cult*, 28.

217 Finucane, "Friar-Archbishop," 203.

218 Ibid., 205. This chapel is the main subject of Cornelison, *Art and the Relic Cult*.

219 Some additional examples from the fifteenth and sixteenth centuries are given by Sullivan, "Antonino Pierozzi."

220 See Wranovix, "Ulrich Pfeffel's Library."

221 Van Engen, "The Church in the Fifteenth Century," 307.

printed authors in Europe. Peter Howard reports that during the incunable period, counting editions of all of Antoninus's works, he was second only to the Bible.[222] Pope Sixtus IV is reported to have died († 1484) with the volumes of Antoninus's *Summa* beside his bed.[223] Cardinal Gabriel Paleotti († 1597) thought Antoninus's vernacular *Confessionales* were appropriate for the parish priest's library.[224] When St Robert Bellarmine was made a cardinal, he consulted Antoninus's *Summa* for advice about how to conduct himself appropriately.[225] An interesting use of Antoninus's *Summa* was made by the writer Tomaso Garzoni. In 1585 Garzoni published his *La piazza universale di tutte le professioni del mondo*, a comprehensive encyclopedia of the professions nearly a thousand pages long. Garzoni frequently cites part 3 of Antoninus's *Summa*, where the different professions and vocations are discussed, and at times even translates portions of it, transforming it "to a more popular key."[226] On the other hand, it is sometimes reported that Antoninus's *Summa* was among the books burned by Martin Luther, though this appears to be a confusion for Angelo Carletti's *Summa angelica*, which Luther burned in 1520 along with the papal bull announcing his excommunication and books of canon law.[227] Certainly Luther repudiated the whole framework for sacramental confession and moral theology practised by Antoninus and transmitted in his *Summa*.

In Catholic moral theology Antoninus remained an important figure into modern times, his works regularly consulted. In the eighteenth century Antoninus was called upon as an authority in two major controversies. Jansenist Catholics were waging a polemical war against the mainstream teaching of Catholic theology and doctrine. They attacked the discipline of moral theology specifically, calling it a system for minimizing moral obligations and widening the narrow way of the Gospel – the most famous Jansenist polemicist was Blaise Pascal, whose caricatures

222 Howard, *Beyond the Written Word*, 20–9.

223 Howard, *Aquinas and Antoninus*, 29.

224 Finucane, "Friar-Archbishop," 174, citing Black, *Church, Religion, and Society in Early Modern Italy*, 95, 258 n26.

225 "The thought of renouncing the purple is constantly in my mind, but how I am to do it I cannot see … To introduce novelties into my way of living by reducing the number of my suite or adopting a simple style in dress would give the impression that I was ambitious to initiate reforms which the most austere and upright cardinals have neither counselled nor adopted. St Antoninus, for instance, teaches in his treatise *De statu cardinalium* that a certain degree of splendour is necessary, if the dignity of this sacred order is to receive its due meed of respect from the world at large. I am trying as hard as ever I can to keep *my* splendour and dignity as modest as may be …" Letter of 16 June 1599, translated by James Brodrick, in *Robert Bellarmine*, 173–4. The treatise cited is Antoninus, *Summa*, 3.22 (21 in Ballerini) *de statu cardinalium et legatorum*.

226 McClure, *The Culture of Profession in Late Renaissance Italy*, 15. McClure analyses part 3 of Antoninus's *Summa* at 14–26 and Garzoni at 70ff.

227 Delcorno, "Observant Efforts towards Education and Pastoral Care," 183.

of Jesuit morality in particular still have left their imprint on popular culture. In the midst of this, Catholic moral theologians became divided into camps over their approach to resolving doubtful moral questions, with "laxism" and "rigorism" representing opposite extremes, and "probabilism," advocated primarily by the Jesuits, in the middle ground.[228] The seventeenth and eighteenth centuries were also years of controversy in Catholic economic and social teaching; the debate over usury specifically became embroiled in the contention between laxer and more rigorous schools of thought. For example, in their effort to check laxist tendencies in moral theology, popes Alexander VII and Innocent XI in the late seventeenth century condemned two propositions condoning titles to usury on loans.[229] These controversies prompted two priests, the brothers Pietro and Girolamo Ballerini, to prepare a new edition of Antoninus's *Summa* to bring his authority into both of these fields of battle. The Ballerinis were supporters of probabilism,[230] and on usury they were "among the last defenders of scholastic economics."[231] They prefaced part 1 of the *Summa* with essays on Antoninus's position as a probabilist,[232] and part 2 with "a sharp attack on modern usury."[233] The edition, published in Verona in 1740, coincided with the sale of a bond issue at 4 per cent by the city: "there broke out a lively public controversy over the morals of the subscribers to the bonds."[234] Pope Benedict XIV addressed himself to resolving the conflict, reasserting scholastic usury doctrine, with the encyclical *Vix pervenit* to the bishops of Italy, 1 November 1745.[235] Ballerini's edition remains today the most common one used by scholars, though, as I will show in subsequent chapters, its inaccuracies have led scholars astray and it ought to be replaced with a critical edition based on the original manuscripts. This is what I have endeavoured to provide for the chapters of the *Summa* edited in part two of this book.

Up to the turn of the twentieth century, Antoninus was primarily read and cited as a doctrinal writer. More recently there has been a strong current of study on his social, economic, and historical views, and his work has also been used as a primary source on the social history and culture of Renaissance Florence, as in the

228 Tutino, *Uncertainty in Post-Reformation Catholicism*, 352–4. Debate about "moral systems" persisted among moral theologians into the twentieth century, but the controversy would be settled somewhat by the intervention of St Alphonsus Liguori in the later decades of the eighteenth century. Ibid., and Slater, *A Short History of Moral Theology*, 48–50.

229 Noonan, *The Scholastic Analysis of Usury*, 355–6.

230 Tutino, *History of Probabilism*, 352.

231 de Roover, *San Bernardino of Siena and Sant'Antonino of Florence*, 6 n11.

232 Ballerini, vol. 1, praelectiones 1 and 2. For examples of Antoninus's moral system, see the chapter edited below: Antoninus, *Summa*, 2.1.1.6, sections 2.4, 2.7, and 3.1.3.3.4.

233 Noonan, *Scholastic Analysis of Usury*, 356. See Ballerini, vol. 2, praelectio 2.

234 Noonan, *Scholastic Analysis of Usury*, 356.

235 This encyclical's application was later extended to the universal Church by a decree of the Holy Office, 28 July 1835. Ibid., 357.

work of two leading scholars of Antoninus whom I have already cited, Peter Howard and David Peterson. Intellectual historians have explored Antoninus's ideas about psychology, free will, conscience, and legal philosophy, to note just a few.[236] Since 1900 there has been particularly strong interest in Antoninus's writing on economic topics.[237] This is the field to which this book primarily contributes. Before turning to that topic, however, the next chapter will introduce Antoninus's *Summa* and the most important manuscripts of it which survive, conclusively determining that they are the author's original autograph manuscripts, and examining what they show about Antoninus's writing process.

> Et io, che fui suo notaio et della sua corte et lungo tempo a presso di lui conversai, ricordare non mene posso sanza lagrime, vedendo me et la dolcie patria privati di tanto padre.[238]
>
> And I, who was his notary in his court and closely conversed with him, cannot remember him without tears, seeing myself and our sweet homeland deprived of such a father.

236 Amos Edelheit, "A Discussion of Conscience, Cognition and Will"; Spagnesi, "Sant'Antonino e il diritto."

237 E.g., Ilgner, *In S. Antonini Archiepiscopi Florentini sententias de Valore et de Pecunia Commentarius*; Ilgner, *Die volkswirtschaftlichen Anschauungen Antonins von Florenz*; Schumpeter, *History of Economic Analysis*, esp. 98; Jarrett, *St. Antonino and Mediaeval Economics*; Gaughan, *Social Theories of Saint Antoninus from His Summa Theologica*; Noonan, *Scholastic Analysis of Usury*; de Roover, *Great Economic Thinkers*; Spicciani, *Capitale e interesse tra mercatura e povertà nei teologi e canonisti dei secoli XIII–XV*; Langholm, *The Merchant in the Confessional*.

238 Baldovini, *Vita di S. Antonino*, quoted in Morçay, *Saint Antonin*, ix.

2 The *Summa*

Preamble. The Written Works of St Antoninus

The teaching of St Antoninus on trade, merchants, and workers is contained in six chapters of his *Summa*. Explaining Antoninus's *Summa* is the purpose of this chapter. Its argument is that the *Summa* is fundamentally a *Recollectorium*, that is, a "collecting-box" of material useful for pastoral care, especially for preaching, hearing confessions, and consulting about moral questions, within which Antoninus collected material from a wide range of theological, moral, and juridical literature, including also, in some form, his own written works: sermons, treatises, guides to confession, and histories.

First, by way of preamble, the *Summa* must be located in its place within Antoninus's whole body of writing. Any attempt to present even summary descriptions of each of Antoninus's written works would unduly extend this preamble. Let it suffice merely to indicate the broadest outlines of Antoninus's literary activity through his life, as known from his extant writings.[1]

As a member of the Friars Preachers, Antoninus's earliest literary activity was presumably the writing of sermons. Sermons are, indeed, among his oldest extant writings: a collection at the Biblioteca Nazionale Centrale (BNC) in Florence contains a cycle of sermons for the Lent of either 1427 or 1430. During the same era Antoninus also began producing the works he would be most known for, namely manuals of confession and moral theology. His first such work was written during his sojourn in Naples, and published April 1429: this is the Italian *Confessionale* directed to lay faithful, called from its incipit "Omnis mortalium cura," or

1 For basic information and bibliographical orientation on each of Antoninus's written works, see "Antoninus Florentinus archiep. (Antoni 1)"; Kaeppeli and Panella, *SOPMA*, 1:80–100, 4:27–31; Orlandi, *Bibliografia Antoniniana*; Michaud-Quantin, *Sommes de casuistique et manuels de confession au Moyen Âge (XII–XVI siècles)*.

popularly *Specchio di coscienza*. In the next decade Antoninus would produce two further practical manuals for use in confession:[2] first, another in Italian, this time directed to priests, called by its incipit "Curam illius habe," or popularly *Medicina dell'anima*; the second, in Latin, likewise directed to priests, called "Defecerunt" or just *Confessionale* and completed before July of 1440. This latter work is Antoninus's most popular by far, to judge by the number of manuscript copies, printed editions, and vernacular translations (Italian, Spanish, Croatian).[3] From the 1430s Antoninus also began writing *opuscula* (shorter works) addressing problems of moral theology. Although these *opuscula* are often described as *theologica* (theological), they tend to specialize in problems with a strong juridical component. In this genre are counted the *Tractatus de cambiis*, *Tractatus de censuris ecclesiasticis sive de excommunicationibus*, *Tractatus de restitutione*, and a famous one against female luxury, *De ornatu et habitu mulierum*.[4] From at least the 1440s other clerics began submitting queries, *dubia*, and cases of conscience to Antoninus "the Counsellor" for his resolution: from circa 1440, there are sixty-nine *Conclusiones et decisiones in foro conscientiae* replying to questions submitted by Br. Dominic de Catalonia, OP. Further collections of such responses and *consilia* are extant.[5] Antoninus likewise received requests for spiritual direction from lay men and women; his solicitude for such lay women, especially widows, produced a series of works of instruction about the spiritual life which were not made public and survived only in the one or two copies owned by the original recipients. These include the *Regola di vita cristiana (dello stato vedovile)*, directed to Ginevra de' Cavalcanti in 1441; the *Opera a ben vivere* of circa 1455, which survives in two autograph manuscripts, written for Dianora Tornabuoni and her sister Lucrezia, mother of Lorenzo the Magnificent;[6] and the recently discovered *Trattato della nave*.[7] An idiosyncratic work within his oeuvre is the *Trialogus inter Iesum et duos discipulos euntes in Emmaus*, an exegetical and apologetic work expounding the Messianic prophecies of the Old Testament as applying to Jesus Christ.[8]

The conclusion and crowning achievement of Antoninus's writing comes with the *Summa*, which was the focus of his writing activity during the last two decades of his life. Often treated as a separate work alongside the *Summa* is the *Chronica* (*Chronicles*), a history of the world in three volumes.[9] However, it will be seen

2 So described by Morçay in *Dictionnaire d'histoire et de géographie ecclésiastiques*, s.v. "Antonin (Saint)."

3 Howard, *Beyond the Written Word*, 22–4; Kaeppeli and Panella, *SOPMA*, no. 256.

4 See Izbicki, "The Origins of the *De ornatu mulierum* of Antoninus of Florence."

5 The crucial studies, with partial editions, are Creytens, "Les cas de conscience;" Creytens, "Les 'consilia' de s. Antoninus."

6 Morçay, "Antoninus (Saint)"; Thiérard-Baudrillart, *Règle de vie*.

7 Edited by Teresa di Graziana, OCD, 1967–80; see Kaeppeli and Panella, *SOPMA*, no. 261.01.

8 Orlandi, *Bibliografia Antoniniana*, xxiv–xxv.

9 The major studies are Walker, *"Chronicles" of Saint Antoninus*, and Morçay, *Chroniques*. This work goes under various titles, including *Chronicae*, *Chronicon*, and *Summa historialis*.

below that the *Chronica* should actually be considered a part and continuation of the *Summa*. It will also be seen that most or all of Antoninus's previous moral-theological writings were incorporated into the *Summa* in some form. It may truly be said, then, that the *Summa* represents the sum of Antoninus's literary estate. The present chapter will proceed by examining the *Summa* in three sections: first, introducing the author's conception of the *Summa* and its structure; second, establishing the most important textual witnesses by demonstrating that five volumes now held at San Marco and Santa Maria Novella in Florence are the author's own original autograph manuscripts; and, finally, probing what these textual witnesses reveal about the process of composition of the *Summa*, leading to the concluding argument of this chapter.

1. The Conception of the *Summa*

One of the goals of this book is to clarify the purpose of Antoninus's teaching on trade, merchants, and workers contained in the six chapters of his *Summa* edited and translated below. Here, we launch the inquiry by trying to identify Antoninus's conception of the *Summa* as a whole: how did Antoninus conceive its nature as a literary work, and what purpose or intention was he pursuing in composing it? A good place to begin is with the title of the work itself. The *Summa* of St Antoninus, like many works of medieval literature, does not go under a uniform title fixed by the author. It has been described as a *Summa* since it first saw the light of day, and this is the immutable element in the work's title in manuscripts and editions, though the author himself applied some alternative designations, as will be seen.[10] *Summa* is how the work is referred to on the flyleaves or first folios of the original manuscripts (to be discussed below):

> Originals of the first part of the *Summa* of brother Antonio of Florence of the Order of Preachers, archbishop of Florence.[11]

> Originals of the second part of the *Summa* of brother Antonio of Florence, archbishop of Florence.[12]

10 Today, and since at least the sixteenth century, it has been common to qualify the title *Summa* with various adjectives at the discretion of the editor or publisher. The most common are *Summa moralis*, *Summa theologica*, *Summa theologica moralis*, and *Summa doctrinalis*, but other variations exist. Fifteenth-century manuscript copies frequently use *Summa fratris Antonii* or *Summa sancti Antonini*, including the ones discussed below and Florence, BNC, Cod. n. (57) Landau Finaly 68.

11 "Originalia prime partis Summe fratris Antonii de Florentia ordinis predicatorum archiepiscopi Florentini." *N* fol. 1r, hand G. The hands A and G will be identified in section 2 below.

12 "Originalia secunde partis Summe fratris Antonii de Florentia archiepiscopi Florentini." M_1 flyleaf 2r, hand G.

> Third part of the *Summa* of dom Antonio, archbishop of Florence, drawn from the Order of Preachers.[13]

Likewise, Castiglione says that Antoninus called his "massive book and great volume" a *Summa*.[14] In light of these, the best-justified course of action for scholars today is to refer to the work simply as the *Summa* of St Antoninus of Florence (Antoninus Florentinus).

There are two yet older designations, however, which go back to the author himself in process of composition; they throw some light on the conception of the work, and lend support to the argument which runs through this chapter. These designations are *Recollectorium* and *Formica*.[15] The allusion to the *Formica*, "Ant," is employed in Antoninus's preamble to the *Summa*, in which he develops an extended comparison of himself to an ant, "foraging over the years and gathering together the fruits of a lifetime's experience and reading."[16] He takes Proverbs 30:6–8 as his theme for explaining the *Summa* and its conception, purpose, and method:

> Go to the ant, O sluggard, and consider her ways, and learn wisdom: Which, although she hath no guide, nor master, nor captain, Provideth her meat for herself in the summer, and gathereth her food in the harvest.[17]

The full passage from Antoninus's preamble will be translated and discussed shortly. For the moment, attending to the question of the title of the work:

> ... Therefore, no more or less of blame or praise ought to be ascribed to me than to the collectors of texts or copyists of books written by others. Hence I did not wish to apply my name nor a title to the work, unless in contempt, as one might want to name a most miserable ant, a despised animal, when telling a tale to someone.[18]

---

13 "<T>ertia pars Summe domini Antonii archiepiscopi Florentini assumpti ab ordine predicatorum." M_2 flyleaf 2v, hand G. The first half of the autograph manuscript of part 4 having been lost, it cannot be verified if a similar note was written on its first folios.

14 "... ingenti libro magnoque volumini, quam Summam appelavit." Castiglione, *Vita Beati Antonini*, c. 4 (322); quoted in Howard, *Beyond the Written Word*, 30 n49, and Orlandi, *Bibliografia Antoniniana*, x.

15 Noted by Orlandi, *Bibliografia Antoniniana*, x.

16 Howard, *Beyond the Written Word*, 32 n58; see more generally ch. 1 and 2 of the same.

17 *Vade ad formicam, o piger, et considera vias ejus, et disce sapientiam. Quae cum non habeat ducem, nec praeceptorem, nec principem, parat in aestate cibum sibi, et congregat in messe quod comedat.* Proverbs 30:6–8.

18 "Non igitur plus minusue uituperationis uel laudis mihi debet ascribi, quam collectoribus lectionum uel scriptoribus librorum ab aliis editorum. Vnde nec nomen apponere meum uolui, nec titulum operi; nisi in contemptum, tamquam uilissimam formicam, despectum animal, fabulando alicui nominare placuerit." Antoninus, *Summa*, 1 *prohemium* (*N* fol. 4r, hand G). My translation. Also translated in Howard, *Beyond the Written Word*, 40 n87.

If he refused to give it a title, how then did the author himself refer to the work? In the course of this passage, in addition to the key word *formica*, the work is also referred to as a *recollectio* and as a *collectorium*. Another witness to this is found in the original manuscripts of Antoninus's *Chronicles*. At the front of the third volume, in the *tabula titulorum et capitulorum* (table of contents), the following explanation is provided:

> This third volume of the historical part, which is the fifth with respect to the whole *Recollectorium*, contains material from various doctors and their books and more notable statements. From there the history is continued from Innocent III, who lived around the year of the Lord 1200, up to the present, namely the year 1458.[19]

This was written in 1458, after the four parts of the *Summa* had been largely or entirely finished. Two points are notable here. First, this provides further confirmation that the *Chronicles* were always considered by Antoninus as a continuation of the *Summa* itself: "the historical part, which is the fifth with respect to the whole." This is also how Castiglione characterized the relationship of the *Summa* and *Chronicles*; after saying that Antoninus called the work a *Summa*, he adds: "which he also wished to be divided into five parts ... And in the fifth he included a history from the beginning of the world up to his own times."[20] Second, Antoninus refers to the whole *Summa* by the word *Recollectorium*. Another manuscript, not autographic but donated to the convent of San Marco in 1465, witnesses to the same:

> The second volume of this historical part, that is the fifth volume of the whole work which is called the *Recollectorium* or *Formica*, contains the exploits of 900 years, namely from Constantine the Great and Pope Sylvestor, who lived in the year of the Lord 310, up to Emperor Frederick II and Pope Innocent III.[21]

---

19 "Tertium istud uolumen partis historialis, que est quinta respectu totius Recollectorii, continet materiam de quibusdam doctoribus et libris eorum et sententiis notabilioribus. Exinde continuatur historia ab Innocentio 3° qui fuit circa annum Domini millesimum ducentesimum, usque ad presens, scilicet annum millesimum quadringentesimum quinquagesimum octauum." Florence, Biblioteca Santa Maria Novella, I.B.55 fol. Ir; quoted from Orlandi, *Bibliografia Antoniniana*, xviii, 70. Based merely on Orlandi's descriptions of the autographs of the *Chronicles* (*Bibliografia Antoniniana*, 65–71), a reasonable hypothesis is that this note was written by Antoninus himself; for Giuliano Lapaccini died on 23 February 1458 modern style (Kaepelli and Panella, *SOPMA*, 3:56). A fuller explanation of this hypothesis is developed below.

20 "Summam appelavit. ... Quam etiam quinque partitam esse voluit. Et in prima parte de anima in genere ... In quinta vero historiam a principio orbis conditi usque ad tempora sua complexus est." Castiglione, *Vita Beati Antonini*, c. 4 (322).

21 "Secundum uolumen huius partis historialis, quod est quintum uolumen totius operis quod dicitur Recollectorium seu Formica, continet gesta noningentorum annnorum, uidelicet a

There is, then, evidence that the oldest designation of the work, and the one used by the author himself, is *Recollectorium* (Collecting-Box);[22] or more fancifully *Formica* (Ant).

This evidence is not rehearsed in order to argue for adopting *Recollectorium* or *Formica* as the designation for the work in scholarly discourse. *Summa* is, clearly, the standard title adopted during the author's own lifetime by his Dominican brothers and contemporaries – just as the work's author, despite being baptized Antonius, came to be called Antoninus. There is nothing improper about continuing to call it the *Summa* of Antoninus. But the author's own term, *Recollectorium*, does illuminate his conception of the work and his purpose in composing it. Thus, in his preamble, Antoninus writes:

> Indeed, when I was poised between the summer and autumn of my life, I deemed that it would be necessary to gather together some things for my sustenance from the harvest of doctrines; lest, if I should happen to reach the winter of old age, I falter from hunger. For old age is fogged by weak memory and sight; and, with the body's members exhausted and occupations sometimes multiplied, it has not the strength nor the time for paging through piles of books. But sensing that a certain sluggishness had entered into my bones, to shake it off I considered that the ant, contemptible creature and smallest of animals, is yet wiser than the wise, and therefore to be imitated: for *although she hath no guide nor master* in her work, nevertheless *she provideth for herself* for the winter time while she is able to run about. I confess that I had no guide in grammar except in my boyhood[23] … But drawn by the hunger and sweetness of truth, especially of moral wisdom, I have collected a few things which appealed to me from what it occurred to me to read. For neither does the ant gather all the food that she finds, nor the more precious, but rather what she knows is suited to her. Therefore the sublime theories enclosed in libraries I have left to the masters and those accomplished in learning. But what I have judged apt as material for preaching, for hearing confessions, and for consulting in the court of souls, I took up from many doctors in theology or experts in law; not intending to compose elegant verses, since I am unschooled and ignorant of every science, but to make a collection in the

---

Constantino magno et Siluestro papa qui fuerunt anno domino 310 usque ad Fredericum 2um imperatorem et Innocentium 3um papam." Florence, Biblioteca Laurenziana, cod. S. Marco n. 363 (vol. 2 of the *Chronicles*), fol. Ira; quoted in Orlandi, *Bibliografia Antoniniana*, xviii, 72–3. According to Orlandi, this manuscript appears to be written by the same hand as the manuscripts of the *Chronicles* volumes 1 and 3 held at the BNC, MS. II. I. 375 and 376. The latter manuscript's incipit likewise describes it as the "historical part": "Titulus iste est decimus octauus partis historialis …" Ibid., 72–3.

22 See *DMLBS*, s.v. "recollectio," "collectorium."

23 This sentence and the following two, in which Antoninus explains how, like the ant, he had no guide, master, or captain in his education, are translated and discussed above, ch. 1.

> tradition of the friars, for me and for my confrères who were with me, whose disposition does not soar to higher things, to whom a wealth of books is not always available, and from whom occupations take away the possibility of roaming through books … Therefore, no more or less of blame or praise ought to be ascribed to me than to the collectors of texts or copyists of books written by others.[24]

The author here has given a brief statement of the conception of the *Summa*. Antoninus's stated motive was the "hunger and sweetness of truth, especially of moral wisdom," which led him to prepare a collection drawn from "the harvest of doctrines," to provide for himself in his old age, for his brother friars, and for others with needs similar to his own. Its orientation is towards the pastoral duties of the friars, namely "preaching, hearing confessions, and consulting in the court of souls," and this is the principle which has guided the selection of material. It is a collection of material taken from "many doctors in theology and experts in law," providing a digest and reference work for those whose time or station does not permit them the possibility of "roaming through books." The nature of the *Summa* as a kind of miniature library, meant to provide a digest of many shelves' worth of books, brings to mind the extraordinarily rich library holdings available to St Antoninus, during the last fifteen years of his life, at San Marco.[25] The labour

24 "Equidem inter estatem et autumpnum etatis constitutus, arbitratus sum necessarium fore ex frumentis doctrinarum quedam recolligere ad mei substentationem: ne, si contingeret ad yemalem senectutem deuenire, fame deficerem. Senilis enim etas memoria et uisu debilitata caligatur, et exaustis corporis membris, occupationibus aliquando multiplicatis, non ualet nec ei tempus uacat ad reuoluendum multitudinem librorum. Intelligens autem in ossibus meis pigritiam insitam, ad eam excutiendam consideraui formicam inter animalia minimum et despicabile, sed sapientibus sapientiorem illam esse, et ideo imitandam: cum enim non habeat ducem nec preceptorem in opere suo, prouidet tamen sibi pro iemis tempore cum potest discurrere. Ducem fateor me non habuisse in grammaticalibus, nisi in pueritia, et debilem preceptorem. Nullum habui in alia facultate excepta parte dialectice, et satis interrupte, sed nec principem mihi studium imperantem ex prelatione. Auiditate tamen et suauitate tractus ueritatis, precipue moralis sapientie, ex his que mihi occurrerunt legenda, pauca recollegi mihi grata. Neque enim formica omnia inuenta cibaria colligit nec pretiosiora, sed que nouit sibi congrua. Illas igitur sublimes theorias in librariis comprehensas, magistris et scientia perfectis dimisi. Que autem iudicaui apta ad materias predicationum, et audientiam confessionum, et consultationem in foro animarum, accepi a doctoribus pluribus in theologia uel iure peritis; non intendens indoctus et omnis scientie ignarus poemata condere, sed recollectionem facere more fratrum, pro me et meis similibus qui mecum erant, quibus nec ingenium eminet ad altiora, nec librorum semper copia datur, et occupationes facultatem subtrahunt ad discurrendum per libros. … Non igitur plus minusue uituperationis uel laudis mihi debet ascribi, quam collectoribus lectionum, uel scriptoribus librorum ab aliis editorum." Antoninus, *Summa*, 1 *prohemium* (*N* fol. 3v–4r, hand G). Howard's translation of most of this passage has been consulted with profit: Howard, *Beyond the Written Word*, 37 n76; 32 n57; 35 n67; 39 n86; 41 n89; 32 n58; 40 n87.

25 "In qua re illud sane multa admiratione dignum est … potuisse tot librorum volumina, tam variis materiis conscripta, tot Doctorum ac sacrorum Canonum testimoniis et auctoritate firmata conscribere." Castiglione, *Vita Beati Antonini*, c. 4 (322); quoted in Howard, *Beyond the Written Word*, 47 n14.

which he spent digging through books in the library there, digesting, excerpting, and copying material suitable for "those like him" from the most important books of canonistic and theological scholarship, can be counted among Antoninus's acts of charity or almsgiving during his lifetime: for by doing so, he provided instruction and teaching out of his own wealth for those poorer than he in leisure and in books.[26]

It is a collection "in the tradition of the friars."[27] The nature of the texts employed in this tradition can be grasped from Michèle Mulchahey's study of Dominican education before 1350.[28] Mulchahey defines three *genera* (genres) of texts employed in the Dominican educational tradition: preaching aids, tools for biblical exegesis, and aids to the confessor (manuals of moral theology). Of these, the one to which Antoninus evidently does not see his *Summa* contributing is tools for biblical exegesis. But the other two *genera* go to the heart of the matter. The *Summa* is indeed a collection in the tradition of the friars: for the aid of the confessor it provides a manual of moral theology and casuistry, "the first of its kind embracing the study of moral theology on such a comprehensive plan."[29] In its individual chapters it provides many of the sorts of aids for preaching described by Mulchahey: model sermons; *florilegia* (excerpts) from Church Fathers, modern doctors, and to an extent even ancient pagan authors (Antoninus's sources will be discussed below, chapter 3); collections of exempla (moral examples); and instructions on the art of preaching. That the *Summa* was fundamentally conceived and designed "for preaching" is a major component of Howard's argument in *Beyond the Written Word*.[30] The argument need not be developed here; its accuracy will soon become evident, and it will be brought into play in later chapters.

---

26 This point is also made by Peterson in "Antoninus." Another quotation from Antoninus is illuminating: "So compilers of sentences from various books tend to irritate people to whom outstanding ability and plenty of leisure gives the chance of seeking out rich and honey-sweet doctrines in the original texts. But since these [compilers] aim to provide for their own and others' deficiency, it does not seem that they should be reproached since they do not do harm to those [authors], but, rather, further enlarge their glory by introducing to the dull-witted for their general erudition what they have never been able to see by chance in their dispersed state." Antoninus, *Summa*, 1 *prohemium* (*N* fol. 4r–4v); Howard's translation, *Beyond the Written Word*, 45 n9.

27 For the original *more fratrum* Ballerini prints *amore fratrum* (Ballerini, 1:4); scholars discussing Antoninus's preamble have often been misled by Ballerini's text here.

28 Mulchahey, *Dominican Education*, esp. part 3, "The Texts of Dominican Education."

29 Mandonnet, "Antonin (saint)."

30 Howard, *Beyond the Written Word*, esp. ch. 2, "For Preaching." Several chapters of Howard's book, along with subsequent publications, are devoted to exploring how Antoninus's "habit of mind" as a preacher, combined with the oral culture of Renaissance Florence, shaped the composition of the *Summa* and moulded Antoninus's "theologies." Howard, *Beyond the Written Word*, 259–62. See also Howard, *Aquinas and Antoninus*; Howard, "Antonino e la predicazione nella Firenze rinascimentale."

In the same preamble Antoninus describes the structural form of the *Summa.*

> But I have imposed some kind of order – even if not very serious since I am unschooled in method – so that the material may be more easily found. For I separated it into four principal parts, intending to go through the vices and virtues, dividing also each part into titles, and the titles into chapters, and the chapters into paragraphs.[31]

These make up the author's own division of the work. Antoninus then explains the contents of the four parts of the *Summa*:

> In the first part are treated certain general matters, namely the soul and its powers as well as their subjects: the passions as the sources [of sins], sins in general and their effects, the various laws by which vices are forbidden and virtues prescribed.[32]

Part 1 of the *Summa* is the most philosophical component. The material and method of treatment owe a great deal to St Thomas Aquinas.[33] This part falls into three main treatises: *On the soul and its powers*,[34] *On sin*,[35] and *On laws*.[36] This plan is not simply copied from Aquinas, but it does adapt the basic organization of the *prima secundae* (first part of the second part) of his *Summa theologiae*. The *prima secundae* deals, after man's last end, with the powers of the soul and the passions, followed by a *Treatise on habits* (where Aquinas deals with the nature of sin), and a *Treatise on law*. Antoninus follows this arrangement of the material, but precedes it with a treatment of the soul, dealt with by Aquinas in the *prima pars* in a *Treatise on man*. Antoninus's *Treatise on law*, however, shows a greater depth of interest and knowledge of the wealth of medieval jurisprudence, particularly evident in his inclusion of a treatment of *The rules of law* (from the decretal collections) as the final title of part 1.[37] This follows a precedent set by Antoninus's mentor Giovanni Dominici, who preached a Lenten cycle on the rules of law.[38]

---

31 "Aliqualem uero ordinem, etsi non multum seriosum ignarus ordinis, posui pro faciliori inuentione materiarum. Nam distinctum in quatuor partes principales feci, de uitiis et uirtutibus recitare intendendo, et quamlibet partem in titulos, et titulos in capitula, et capitula in paragraphos distinguendo." Antoninus, *Summa*, 1 *prohemium* (*N* fol. 4v).

32 "Et in prima parte quedam generalia, uidelicet de anima et potentiis eius, que subiecta eorum habentur: de passionibus tamquam principiis eorum, de peccatis in genere et effectibus eorum, de multiplicibus legibus quibus uitia prohibentur et uirtutes precipiuntur." Antoninus, *Summa*, 1 *prohemium* (*N* fol. 4v). The translation of this passage presents some difficulties. Cfr Howard, *Beyond the Written Word*, 63 n89.

33 Noted by Morçay, "Antoninus (Saint)."

34 Antoninus, *Summa*, 1.1–5: *De anima in comuni, De potentiis anime, etc.* Titles listed at *N* fol. 5r.

35 Ibid., 1.6–10: *De causis peccatorum et passionibus, De peccato, etc. N* fol. 6r.

36 Ibid., 1.11–20: *De lege in comuni, De lege eterna, De lege naturali, etc. N* fol. 6v.

37 Ibid., 1.20: *De regulis iuris, et habet unum capitulum cum omnibus regulis iuris que sunt in decretalibus et libro 6o cum glossis. N* fol. 6v.

38 See above, ch. 1.

Continuing through the parts of the *Summa*:

> In the second part: the vices in their species, namely the eight capital vices and their daughters and species; restitution, oaths and perjury, vows and their transgression, infidelity and its species, and superstitions; for each vice proposing corresponding sermons, and afterwards what pertains to cases of conscience and the exposition of the material. And as a theme a Psalm verse is taken because it is readily at hand and in wide use in the Church; and more profitable doctrine for all the material.[39]

The second and third parts of the *Summa* have tended to capture more attention from moral theologians and historians than the other two parts. Antoninus's treatment of greed (2.1 *de avaritia*) is especially renowned, for it is very compendious and was particularly useful to Antoninus's contemporaries in as much as it provides a digest of up-to-date magisterial opinions on subjects of urgent controversy.[40] It has been noted before that at the level of structure Antoninus in his second part has not followed Aquinas's plan of the *secunda secundae*, the moral part of *Summa theologiae*, despite this being a fundamental reference point for moral theology, especially among Dominicans. Aquinas proceeds through his moral material in order of the seven cardinal virtues: faith, hope, charity, prudence, justice, fortitude, and temperance. Antoninus does devote a major place to the seven virtues in part 4 of the *Summa*; but in this second part, he proceeds instead through the eight capital vices: greed (followed by a treatise on restitution), pride, vainglory, lust, gluttony, wrath, envy, and sloth, followed by the treatises on lies and perjury, vows, and infidelity. Antoninus nevertheless cites Aquinas as a preeminent authority, frequently following his doctrine and *sententie* (opinions) in dealing with his material, as is seen in the chapters edited below.

This departure from Aquinas's order of treatment in the *secunda secundae*, and from Aquinas's overall pedagogical plan in the *Summa theologiae*, has provoked some scholars to consider Antoninus's stated reliance on Aquinas as hypocritical, and to view Antoninus as in some sense betraying Aquinas, injuring his legacy, and undercutting what should have been a salutary influence exerted by Aquinas on the development of moral theology. Such criticisms, not so much of Antoninus in particular as of moralists generally from the fourteenth to the early twentieth

---

39 "In secunda parte: de uitiis in specie, uidelicet de octo capitalibus et eorum filiabus et speciebus; de restitutione, de iuramento et periuriis, de uotis et transgressionibus eorum, de infidelitate et speciebus eius et superstitionibus; ad singula uitia singulas predicationes ponendo, et postea que pertinent ad casus conscientie uel declarationem materie. Et pro themate sumitur uersus Psalmi, quia magis in promtu occurrit, et magis ecclesie in usu; et compendiosior doctrina ad omnem materiam." Antoninus, *Summa*, 1 *prohemium* (*N* fol. 4v). Cfr Howard, *Beyond the Written Word*, 63 n89.

40 Discussed at greater length below in ch. 4.

century, have been frequently issued by proponents of new approaches to moral theology.[41] This is the substance of Mark Jordan's brief critique of Antoninus in his book *Rewritten Theology*.[42] Peter Howard replied to Jordan in his *Aquinas and Antoninus*, which is very much worth reading.[43] What is wanting in this critique of Antoninus and other moralists is a recognition that these authors wrote for a different purpose, to fill a need not supplied by Aquinas's *Summa theologiae*. While the tendency to disparage late medieval scholastic authors is of very long pedigree, there has been a growing interest in the late Middle Ages among scholars who study the history of canon law and theology, and particularly in those "penitential" and pastoral works at the border of the two disciplines.[44] While authors of these sorts of

---

41 Critiques of this kind, as expressed in the first half of the twentieth century, are described and assessed by Ford and Kelly, *Contemporary Moral Theology*, vol. 1, *Questions in Fundamental Moral Theology*, esp. ch. 4–6. Some more recent examples of such critiques: Mahoney, *The Making of Moral Theology*, esp. ch. 6, "The Language of Law"; Cessario, *Introduction to Moral Theology*, esp. appendix, "The Flight from Virtue: The Outlook of the Casuist Systems"; Curran, *Catholic Moral Theology in the United States*, esp. ch. 1, "The Nineteenth Century," and ch. 2, "The Twentieth Century before Vatican II."

42 "I hold that rewriting Thomas erases a decisive feature of his texts, namely, their pedagogical structure … One of the deliberate structural accomplishments of Thomas's *Summa* is to reject an organization according to the seven capital sins … Yet not a few treatises on the seven capital sins were composed by excerpting Thomas – his deliberately scattered remarks gathered together, just as deliberately, into the treatise he refused to write. More grandly, the masterworks of fifteenth-century Dominican morality cite Thomas's *Summa* respectfully and actively resist its structural innovation. The *Theological Summa* of Antoninus of Florence refers to Thomas ostentatiously for many of its definitions and a few of its arguments, but it rewrites Thomas in two ways. First, Antoninus's entire *Summa* is concerned only with moral matters. Antoninus makes moral teaching a separate species of theology rather than an integral portion of it. Second, more importantly, Antoninus organizes his *Summa* not according to the structure of Thomas's *secunda pars* or either of its sub-parts, but according to a series of older schemata, including both the Ten Commandments and the seven capital sins." Jordan, *Rewritten Theology*, 6, 9–10.

This is not accurate: the Ten Commandments are not employed in Antoninus's *Summa* as an organizing principle, and the seven virtues are so employed in part 4. Jordan's description actually applies to Antoninus's *Confessionale "Defecerunt."* This point is made by Howard, *Aquinas and Antoninus*, 6. Indeed, Antoninus says, in the prologue of part 2, that transgressions of the Ten Commandments can be reduced to the seven capital vices. "Capita VII [i.e. draconis Apoc. 12] sunt VII uitia capitalia que dicuntur mortalia, que occidunt animam, cum filiabus suis, et ad ipsa reducuntur transgressiones X preceptorum signata per cornua X." Antoninus, *Summa*, 2 *prologus* (M_1 fol. IIr, hand G).

43 "An example of what seems to be an entrenched tendency to read Antoninus's *Summa* out of context, and therefore misread and misconstrue him, can be found in Mark Jordan's important and provocative book … " Howard, *Aquinas and Antoninus*, 6. The burden of *Aquinas and Antoninus*, originally an Etienne Gilson lecture at the Pontifical Institute of Mediaeval Studies, is to reveal Antoninus's intended audience and purpose in writing the *Summa*, inspired by a similar study of Aquinas by Boyle: *The Setting of the "Summa theologiae" of Saint Thomas.*

44 E.g., Pennington, "Canon Law in the Late Middle Ages."

works drew liberally on the classic thirteenth-century academic writers in canon law and theology, including Aquinas, they developed different, usually more practically focused ways of teaching about moral issues. As this book will show, Antoninus is an outstanding example of this practical pastoral approach.

The method of dealing with the vices in the second part follows a regular template: first a "corresponding sermon" for each vice, taking a Psalm verse as the theme – "because in moral matters particular sermons are more useful"[45] – followed by "what pertains to cases of conscience and the exposition of the material." Antoninus sums this up as proceeding *per modum predicationis*, "by the method of preaching," *deinde per modum doctrine*, "and then by the method of teaching."[46] Antoninus's treatment of his material in parts 2 and 3 will be discussed more fully below, in chapters 3 and 4.

Coming to the third part of the *Summa*:

> In the third part: the various states of life whether of layfolk or clerics, churches and the individual sacraments, ecclesiastical censures, and the states of those undergoing purgatory and of the blessed.[47]

The third part of the *Summa* is perhaps the most distinctively Antonine. The treatment of the moral life according to the different states of life or *status* in which people could be placed is not an innovation of Antoninus; however, the length, care, and detail of the treatment in the third part (to say nothing of its sagacity) do seem to have made Antoninus's *Summa* stand out. Castiglione's characterization of Antoninus's teaching makes one think immediately of the third part of the *Summa*: "He not only wrote about universal things, but he also adapted doctrine, coming down to the particulars, to our very way of living, to the basic practice of the specifics of human life."[48] The specifics to which Antoninus descends in this part are indicated by the title headings: *married people*, *the continent*, *temporal lords*, *soldiers and on the various kinds of war*, *doctors and scholars*, *advocates and procurators*, *merchants and workers* (edited below),[49] *secular and ecclesiastical judges*,

---

45 "Nunc autem, quia in materia morali sermones particulares sunt utiliores, ideo in hac secunda parte agetur de singulis uitiis in particulari, ..." Antoninus, *Summa*, 2 *prologus* (M_1 fol. IIr, hand G).

46 Antoninus, *Summa*, 2 *prologus* (M_1 fol. IIr, hand G).

47 "In tertia parte: de statibus uariis tam laicorum quam clericorum, de ecclesiis et sacramentis singulis, et de censuris ecclesiasticis, et statibus purgandorum et beatorum." Ibid., 1 *prohemium* (*N* fol. 4v). Cfr Howard, *Beyond the Written Word*, 63 n89.

48 "Non enim de universalibus tantum rebus scripsit: verum etiam ad particularia quaeque descendens, ad hunc nostrum vivendi usum et ad singularem quamdam humanae vitae operationem, doctrinam accommodavit." Castiglione, *Vita Beati Antonini*, c. 4 (322); translated by Howard, *Beyond the Written Word*, 52 n40.

49 Antoninus, *Summa*, 3.8.

the dying, hostellers and on jurisdictions and other pertinent things, churches and their patrons, clerics and the divine offices, the sacraments of the Church, the beneficed, religious, confessors, preachers, prelates (with titles on bishops, archbishops, patriarchs, cardinals, legates, and supreme pontiffs),[50] *universal councils*, a treatise of several titles *on excommunications and censures*,[51] and finally, *on God and the state of the blessed, on the various states of those having been taken*,[52] *on the punishment of purgatory*.

Continuing the comparison to Aquinas: the plan of Antoninus's third part has only a loose correspondence to the latter part of the *Summa theologiae*. The *secunda secundae* closes with a *Treatise on acts which pertain especially to certain men*, in which the various lay states are treated only at the most general level; the *tertia pars* and *supplementum* again deal with some of the same material in a roughly similar order (e.g., sacraments, ecclesiastical censures, those undergoing purgatory, and the blessed); but these are largely subordinated to other priorities – particularly in the *tertia pars*, whose overarching subject is the Incarnation of the Second Person of the Trinity.

> In the fourth part: virtue in general and in species, the cardinal and theological virtues in species, and their parts or things annexed to them; and if there is time, the seven gifts and grace will be dealt with.[53]

The fourth part appears to have been the least copied, and therefore, presumably, the least read; which is unfortunate, since it would appear to contain a great deal of Antoninus's practical teaching on ascetic theology and illustration of the moral life as a life of virtue supported by grace. After a title *on virtue in general*, the first half proceeds through the virtues of prudence, fortitude, temperance, justice, charity, hope, and faith.[54] Time enough was provided to the author to deal with divine grace and the seven gifts of the Holy Spirit.[55] These form the second half of this part, proceeding through the gifts of wisdom,[56] intellect, counsel, fortitude, fear,

50 Ibid., 3.19–22.

51 Ibid., 3.24–9.

52 *De diversis statibus comprehensorum*: ibid., 3.31. In context it appears that this title deals with the different human beings and angelic spirits who now reside in heaven.

53 "In quarta parte: de uirtute in genere et specie, de uirtutibus scilicet cardinalibus et theologicis in specie, et de earum partibus seu eis adnexis, et si tempus erit, agetur de septem donis et gratia. Restaret de articulis, si uita comitetur, que non minor ceteris erit. Qui inde aliquid utilitatis hauserit, pro eo oret ad Dominum nostrum." Ibid., 1 *prohemium* (*N* fol. 4v). Cfr Howard, *Beyond the Written Word*, 63 n89.

54 Antoninus, *Summa*, 4.1–8.

55 Two titles deal with these as a whole before their individual treatment: Ibid., 4.9–10.

56 The gift of wisdom is dealt with in the latter chapters of 4.10, *De donis Spiritus sancti*.

piety (incorporating a lengthy treatise on the Blessed Virgin Mary), and knowledge (*scientia*).[57]

Turning now from the structure of the *Summa* to the circumstances of its conception, Antoninus states that he conceived the project of the *Summa* "when I was poised between the summer and autumn of my life." This vague reference to his age is the most precise indication available of when Antoninus first put his hand to composing the *Summa*. Morçay supposes that "between the summer and autumn of my life" would be towards Antoninus's fiftieth year, circa 1440, and this has been accepted among scholars as a reasonable hypothesis.[58] However, I am inclined to read Antoninus's metaphor as equivalent to "midway in our life's journey,"[59] i.e., in about Antoninus's thirty-fifth year (circa 1424).[60] Since the earliest written works by Antoninus were composed at roughly this stage of his life, circa 1424–9, as discussed in chapter 1, it appears that Antoninus viewed all of his writing as part of the process of composing the *Summa*. How the *Summa* contains all of his earlier writing will be explored more in sections 3 and 4 of this chapter. What is clear from this statement is that Antoninus spent many years working on the *Summa*:

> I have worked on it enough over many years, although interrupted by many responsibilities, not of great value perhaps, yet time-consuming; whence, sometimes for months and years I left this work untouched, often taking time from it, now for sustaining the body, now for my duties as a prelate (in which I, though unworthy, have long been occupied), now for the exercise of religion, namely prayer and meditation.[61]

---

57 Ibid., 4.11–16.

58 So Lapidge et al., *CALMA*, Antoni 1.18; Kaeppeli and Panella, *SOPMA*, no. 239.

59 "Midway in our life's journey, I went astray / from the straight road and woke to find myself / alone in a dark wood. How shall I say ..." Dante Alighieri, *The Divine Comedy, Inferno*, trans. Ciardi, canto 1, ll. 1–3 (16).

60 The biblical lifespan is "threescore years and ten," i.e., seventy years. Ciardi, ibid., 21.

61 "Laboraui et ego satis per multos annos, et interrupte propter occupationes, etsi non magni ualoris, tamen tempus exigentes; unde aliquando per menses et annos opus dimisi, tempus sepe furando, aliquando necessarium corporis substentationi, aliquando exercitationi prelature, in qua diu indignus permansi, aliquando decentie religionis, scilicet orationis et meditationis." Antoninus, *Summa*, 1 *prohemium* (*N* fol. 4r); also translated in Howard, *Beyond the Written Word*, 30 n48.

Castiglione confirms, without any greater specificity, that the writing of the *Summa* took "a long time." Speaking of Antoninus's last illness and death: "Imposuerat etiam non multo antea extremam manum ingenti libro magnoque volumini, quam Summam apellavit. Quam longo tempore, magno labore, multoque artificio conscriptam (ut paullo post docebo) non ad meatus siderum naturaeque occultas vires demonstrandas, sed ad dandam edocendamque salutis scientiam ediderat ..." Castiglione, *Vita Beati Antonini*, c. 4 (322); quoted in Howard, *Beyond the Written Word*, 30 n49, and Orlandi, *Bibliografia Antoniniana*, x.

The author himself declares when the work was completed, in a colophon given in the penultimate paragraph of part 4:

> It should be noted that in treating of the the last three gifts (of the Holy Spirit) the order of enumeration set out by Isaias was not preserved: and for this reason, so that the lengthier material would be placed last. And therefore the gift of "fear" was dealt with earlier, then afterwards "piety" much more extensively by reason of the material annexed to it, namely about the Virgin Mary. And finally "knowledge" was dealt with. To which [i.e., to the title *de scientia*] is added a large work divided because of its length into two volumes,[62] not strictly of histories but also of many other things from sacred Scripture and the notable sayings of saints, and even some pagans, containing deeds from the beginning of the world up to the present time, namely the year of the Lord 1454 from the Incarnation;[63] if, that is, life shall accompany me to completing what has so far been brought up to the year of the Lord 600, namely up to the death of Gregory the Great and the reign of the Emperor Phocas. For since, as was said, it pertains to the gift of knowledge to conduct oneself well *in the midst of a crooked and perverse generation,*[64] and to know how to discriminate things to be believed from things not to be believed, things to be done from things not to be done, so that good things be approved and evil things disapproved, how very much, then, can the deeds of our forebears be of help towards this! … But let an end be made to this, the fourth part, which is about the virtues and the gifts of the Holy Spirit.[65]

---

62 At this place Ballerini writes "in tria uolumina" (4:1290), transmitting an updated text reflecting the final three-volume division of the *Chronicles.*

63 Ballerini writes "MCCCCV" (4:1291), which must be a typographical error.

64 Philippians 2:15. Antoninus's application of this text to the gift of knowledge follows earlier precedent. E.g., "Secundo ponit virtutem scientiae. Unde dicit *in scientia.* Et siquidem scientia referatur ad scientiam qua aliquis scit bene conversari in medio nationis pravae et perversae, sic refertur ad virtutem prudentiae." Thomas Aquinas, *Scriptum super II ad Corinthios,* reportatio vulgata, c. 6 lectio 2 (ad 2 Cor. 6:6), accessed via *Corpus Thomisticum.* Cfr, attributing this *sententia* to Augustine: Albertus Magnus, *Tratado sobre a prudência,* para. 489.

65 "Notandum quod in tractando de tribus ultimis donis non est seruatus ordo enumerationis positus ab Ysaia, et ratio fuit, ut prolixior materia posterius poneretur. Et ideo prius de timore, postea de pietate multo diffusior ratione materie adiuncte, scilicet de Virgine Maria. Et demum de scientia actum est. Cui additur magnum opus distinctum propter sui longitudinem in duo uolumina, non precise historiarum sed et multorum aliorum de scripturis sacris et dictis notabilibus sanctorum, sed et aliorum gentilium, continens gesta ab initio mundi usque ad presens tempus, scilicet anni Domini ab incarnatione 1454, si tamen uita fuerit chomes ad perficiendum quod iam perductum est usque ad annum Domini sexcentesimum, scilicet usque ad mortem Gregorii magni et imperium Foce. Cum enim, ut dictum est, ad donum scientie pertineat bene conuersari in medio nationis praue et peruerse, et scire discernere credenda a non credendis et agenda a non agendis, ut bona assumantur et mala renuantur, quamplurimum ad hoc possunt iuuare precedentium gesta … Sed finis sit huic 4[e] parti que est de uirtutibus et donis Spiritus Sancti." Antoninus, *Summa,* 4.16.1 para. penult. and ult. (M_4 fol. 277v, hand A). Also translated in Howard, *Beyond the Written Word,* 31 n54.

It is clear, then, that the author had completed part 4 of the *Summa* in 1454. In addition to this colophon, references within the *Summa* itself to dates and dateable events, combined with records of its binding and copying, permit the construction of a rough chronology for the composition of individual parts and titles of the *Summa*. These will be discussed below in the third section of this chapter, "The Composition of the *Summa*." First, however, the manuscripts and printed editions which transmit the text of the *Summa* will be introduced, and a crucial question will be answered: do we have access to the autograph manuscripts, i.e., the original manuscripts written by the author himself?

2. Textual Witnesses: Identifying the Autograph Manuscripts

The text of Antoninus's *Summa* is transmitted in numerous manuscripts and early modern printed editions. About fifty-four manuscripts of the *Summa* (each manuscript typically a single part) were described by Orlandi in 1961; some additions to this list have been made by subsequent research.[66] The *Summa* has been printed about twenty times in total since part 2 was first printed in Venice in 1474.[67] The most recent two editions were published between 1740 and 1756. At this time two teams of scholars, apparently independent of one another, made a concerted effort to republish and make available Antoninus's moral-theological teaching. These two projects produced the (to date) most recent and high-quality printed editions of Antoninus's *Summa*. The first team was that of the Dominican brothers Tommaso Mamachi and Dionisio Remedelli (assisted by Checherelli), based in Florence. Their goal was to publish Antoninus's *Opera omnia* (complete works) edited from the oldest surviving manuscripts, held at San Marco and Santa Maria Novella; these are the manuscripts which I will be analysing in detail in this section. They only succeeded in editing parts 1 and 2 out of the four parts of the *Summa*. Their edition of these parts is the most accurate and well-annotated edition produced up to this time; however, the volumes are now extremely rare.[68] The other team was that of the Ballerini brothers, Pietro and Girolamo; I introduced them and their interest in Antoninus above at the end of chapter 1. The Ballerinis published a complete edition of the *Summa*, in four volumes, adding to it some useful material, including Castiglione's *Vita*, copious doctrinal annotations and

66 Orlandi, *Bibliografia Antoniniana*, 25–64; Kaeppeli and Panella, *SOPMA*, 1:80, 4:28; Lapidge et al., *CALMA*, Antoni 1.18.

67 Orlandi, *Bibliografia Antoniniana*, 295–305; see also the other reference works just cited.

68 *Sancti Antonini archiepiscopi Florentini ordinis praedicatorum Opera omnia ad autographorum fidem nunc primum exacta, vita illius, variis dissertationibus, et adnotationibus aucta*, ed. Tommaso Maria Mamachi and Dionisio Remedelli, *Summa* parts 1 and 2 in 4 vols. (Florence, 1741–56). I consulted the volumes in the capitular library of Florence. They are also held at the BNC.

prefatory essays, and an analytical index to the whole work.[69] Ballerini's edition of the *Summa* was reprinted in 1959 and is today the standard one used by scholars. However, its text does not always reliably transmit Antoninus's teaching. Scholars have been accustomed, perforce, to make arguments about what Antoninus taught based on the text printed by Ballerini or in another early printed edition, and unfortunately this has sometimes led them astray, as these editions contain many passages which were never written by Antoninus or have been altered in their subsequent transmission (in addition to the example of *amore fratrum* for *more fratrum*, cited above in this chapter, there is a more significant example below in chapter 4, section 5). Nevertheless, Ballerini's edition is useful for research as the most widely available complete text of Antoninus's *Summa*, and in the absence of a new critical edition it should remain as the common reference point for scholars. For Antoninus's six chapters on trade, merchants, and workers, we now have the critical edition which I provide in part two of this book.

The bases of my edition are the most important textual witnesses, the original manuscripts prepared by the author himself, which he called *scartabelli* – an obscure word, perhaps translateable as "volumes" or "manuscripts."[70] These manuscripts, five in total (the third part being divided into two volumes), preserved by Antoninus's Dominican brothers, are today held at San Marco (parts 2 to 4) and Santa Maria Novella (part 1), along with the originals of the *Chronicles*.[71] These five manuscripts of the *Summa* are designated herein $N\ M_1\ M_2\ M_3\ M_4$. They have traditionally been considered autographs by scholars. The rest of this chapter is dedicated to demonstrating that these manuscripts are indeed autographs, and exploring what they can reveal about the process of composition of the *Summa*.

These five volumes have been described as autographs, *manu propria scripta* (written by the author's own hand), ever since their original production. That alone is sufficient to prompt a presumption in favour of their status as autographs. However, it will be worthwhile to make the presumption of autographic status as secure as possible, since it is the justification for the procedure adopted herein of editing chapters of the *Summa* solely from the autograph volume as if it were a *codex unicus* (sole surviving manuscript). The decisive proof of autographic status

69 *Sancti Antonini archiepiscopi Florentini ordinis praedicatorum Summa theologica in quattuor partes distributa* … , ed. Pietro Ballerini, 4 vols (Verona, 1740; facs. repr. with prologue by Innocenzo Colosio, Graz: Akademische Druck- U. Verlagsanstalt, 1959). The index is at the back of the first volume.

70 Evidently related to the Italian *scartabellare*, "to skim through."

71 The most detailed descriptions of these autographs are: for all volumes, Orlandi, *Bibliographia Antoninian*, 25–40; for part 1, G. Pomaro, "Censimento dei manoscritti della Biblioteca di S. Maria Novella, Parte II: Sec. XV–XVI," 306–7; Panella, "Catalogo dell'Archivio di S. Maria Novella in Firenze," I.B.54 (179).

rests upon a palaeographical examination of the hands in the manuscripts and comparison to extant documents known to have been written by Antoninus *manu propria*. By this means $N\,M_1\,M_2\,M_3\,M_4$ can be shown to be the originals prepared by St Antoninus himself, written in large part by his own hand. The next several sections will be rather technical.

First, a word about the palaeographical terminology employed. In classifying scribal hands, I use the nomenclature which was first proposed by Leiftinck and subsequently expanded by his disciples Gumbert and Derolez.[72] This nomenclature distinguishes, first, three families or *genera* of medieval scripts: early medieval, gothic, and humanistic. Only the latter two pertain to manuscripts of the *Summa*. As to gothic scripts, the Lieftinck-Gumbert-Derolez system classifies gothic scribal hands based on their treatment of a defined set of letter-forms: **a** in one or two compartments, **b h k l** with or without loops, **f** and straight **s** standing on the baseline or descending below it. The various combinations of these letter-forms in extant manuscripts yield six regular gothic script types: *textualis*, *semitextualis*, *cursiva antiquior*, *cursiva* (i.e., *recentior*), *hybrida*, *semihybrida*. These six types are employed here to classify gothic hands found in the manuscripts under discussion.

The only one of Derolez's script types which requires special attention here is his category *semihybrida*.[73] This category embraces scripts which "often mix Cursiva and Hybrida elements";[74] their characteristic letter-forms are single-compartment **a**, **f** and straight **s** descending below the baseline – these are *cursiva* letter-forms – and finally, ascenders on **b h k l** sometimes looped (like *cursiva*) and sometimes loopless (like *hybrida*). One variation on Derolez's nomenclature is employed here in connection with this script type. Derolez says:

> Many scribes were hesitant in their treatment of the ascenders in this kind of script and appear to have been indifferent in their tracing of looped or unlooped ascenders, either because they relapsed time and again into writing the customary Cursiva, or because the distinction held no significance for them. For other scribes, on the contrary, the writing of looped and loopless ascenders adheres to a strict rule. To all of these cases, whether conforming to a strict rule or not, we will apply the term Semihybrida as a classification of this intermediate type betwen Cursiva and Hybrida.[75]

In the discussion which follows, for hands which suggest scribes writing a *cursiva* script and merely "indifferent in their tracing of looped or unlooped ascenders,"

72 This nomenclature is explained in detail and employed in Derolez, *The Palaeography of Gothic Manuscript Books*.

73 Important remarks for present purposes: ibid., 163–5, 171.

74 Ibid., 23.

75 Ibid., 163.

the term *cursiva* is employed, with the inconsistent use of loops noted. In such cases the letter-forms are those of Derolez's *semihybrida*, but it is useful here for the sake of clarity to keep in the foreground the basically *cursiva* character of the script at hand. *Semihybrida* will be preferred for hands which appear to write a fundamentally *hybrida* script, yet with inconsistent ascenders.

1. The Hand A at M_1 *fol. 66v and* M_2 *fol. 69r*

When we turn to the examination of hands, a difficulty presents itself immediately upon examining these manuscripts: there is plainly more than one hand at work, but the number of distinct individuals to whom these hands belong is not obvious. It is well known that a competent medieval scribe had "a command of a variety of scripts appropriate to different functions and occasions."[76] Likewise, within the manuscripts, sometimes a change in the character of the writing is visible in the look of the page as a whole – a change in the angle of ascenders and descenders, for example, or in the degree of shading – but not necessarily evident in the letter-forms, such that it is possible that the same scribe is writing with a different pen, or the same pen after a good sharpening, or on a writing surface of different quality. In other words, a change in the character of the letters on the page need not compel the conclusion that a different individual is writing. On the other hand, a reasonable expectation that Antoninus sometimes employed secretaries to draft documents, to transcribe fair copies, and to take dictation leads one to expect that, even in the original manuscripts, some or all of the work would not be, strictly speaking, an author's autograph. Difficulties like these have led to some diversity of opinion among modern scholars in assigning autographic status to this or that manuscript of Antoninus's works. There are two main points of disagreement: first, whether the hand that wrote the *tabulae capitulorum* (tables of contents) for these volumes of the *Summa* is the hand of Antoninus himself;[77] second, whether a collection of Antoninus's sermons held at the BNC of Florence is an autograph.[78] The first point shall be discussed below. The second is not of prime concern for this book, though I may address it in a future article.

---

76 Clanchy, *From Memory to Written Record*, 99; quoted in Howard, *Beyond the Written Word*, 129.

77 This hand also wrote the notes describing these manuscripts as *originalia*, numerous notes for copyists within the volumes, and some sections and chapters of the text. Orlandi thought that this was Antoninus's own hand, against the general opinion of scholars. The question of the identity of this hand is dealt with in Panella, "Catalogo," following the lead of Pomaro, "Censimento," 306–7. Panella's argument is expounded below and accepted as successful.

78 Florence, BNC, Conv. soppr. A. 8. 1750, fol. 1r–61v: *Incipit quadragesimale quod intitulatur convertimini editum a venerabili patre fratre Antonino ser Nicolai de Florentia ordinis praedicatorum. Dominica LXXa* (fol. 1r). The debate about whether this manuscript is an autograph has yet to be resolved; opinions are rehearsed in Howard, *Beyond the Written Word*, 128–30.

For the immediate purpose of demonstrating that this edition is based on autograph witnesses, the difficulties just discussed are surmountable. It is sufficient to identify the hand which wrote the chapters edited below, namely *Summa* 2.1.16–17 and 3.8.1–4. The opening of *Summa* 2.1.16 is in manuscript M_1 located at fol. 66v (incipit: *De fraudulentia que commictitur*); the opening of 3.8.1 is in manuscript M_2 at fol. 69r (incipit: *Exibit homo ad opus*). The hand which wrote both of these folios wrote all, or very nearly all, of the chapters 2.1.16–17 and 3.8.1–4. This, then, is the primary hand whose identity is at stake for this edition. This hand shall be called "A." After identifying the hand of these two folios, the prominence of this hand throughout the five manuscripts as a whole will be discussed.

The general characteristics of hand A will now be described. See plates 1 and 2.

This hand A writes a *cursiva* at the *media* or *currens* level of execution. The letter-forms are typical of Italian *cursiva*, but with both looped and loopless ascenders. The **a** is always single-compartment, **b d h k l** have both looped and loopless forms, and **f** and straight **s** descend below the line. Minims have a slight leftward slant. The uncrossed 2-shaped Tironian **et** is consistent with Italian origin, as are the quite vertical angle of the **f** and straight **s**, the rather pointed descenders, and the absence of hairlines and horns. In these latter characteristics and in the general look of the page, the hand suggests *Cancelleresca* written in a casual fashion.[79] The hand does not write for display, but functionally and with some speed; yet not too rapidly for legibility. Nearly all the letter-forms are traced in a single stroke, the main exceptions being **e** and **r**. The scribe's haste, however, is not such as to result in letters collapsed or distorted beyond recognition: the only example of this is the lobe of **a** and **q**, which can become compressed to a mere diagonal line. As a rule, the letters' shapes are always discernible, and though the page is not beautiful, the writing is quite legible. Writing on pages without ruling, the scribe nevertheless keeps to fairly straight lines, with regular height and spacing. The lines are close, with only a minimum of vertical space, and extend across the page in a single column leaving regular margins. The ink is brown, varying from light to almost black, usually towards the middle of the spectrum. In general there is little shading, and no alternation of bold strokes and hairlines; the one exception being the body of **f** and straight **s**, whose ductus often produces a heavy top with descender tapering to a point. The presence of these heavy **f** and **s** forms contributes to the overall distinctive look of A's mise-en-page.

---

79 On *Cancelleresca*: Derolez, *Gothic Manuscript Books*, 156–7. Cfr Cherubini and Pratesi, *Palaeografia Latina*, tav. 105 (Italian "littera minuta cursiva") and 109 ("mercantesca diritta").

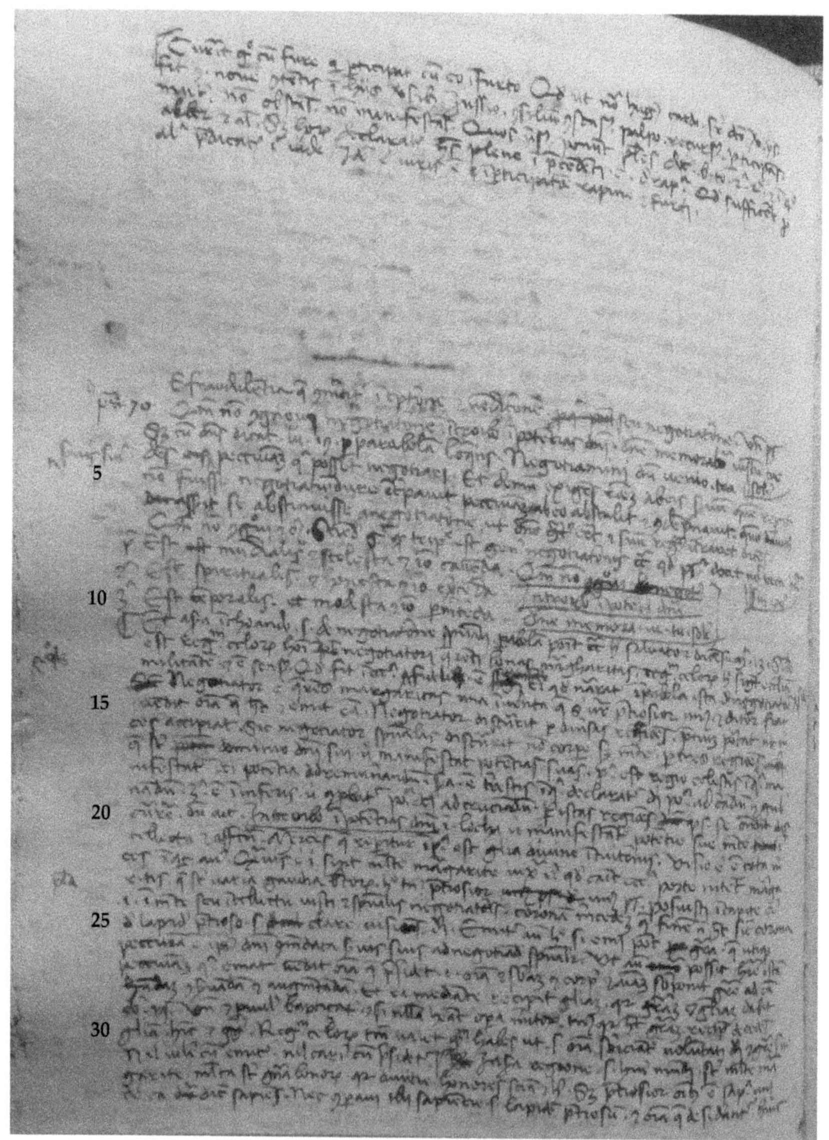

Plate 1: M_1 fol. 66v (Antoninus, *Summa*, 2.1.16), hand A

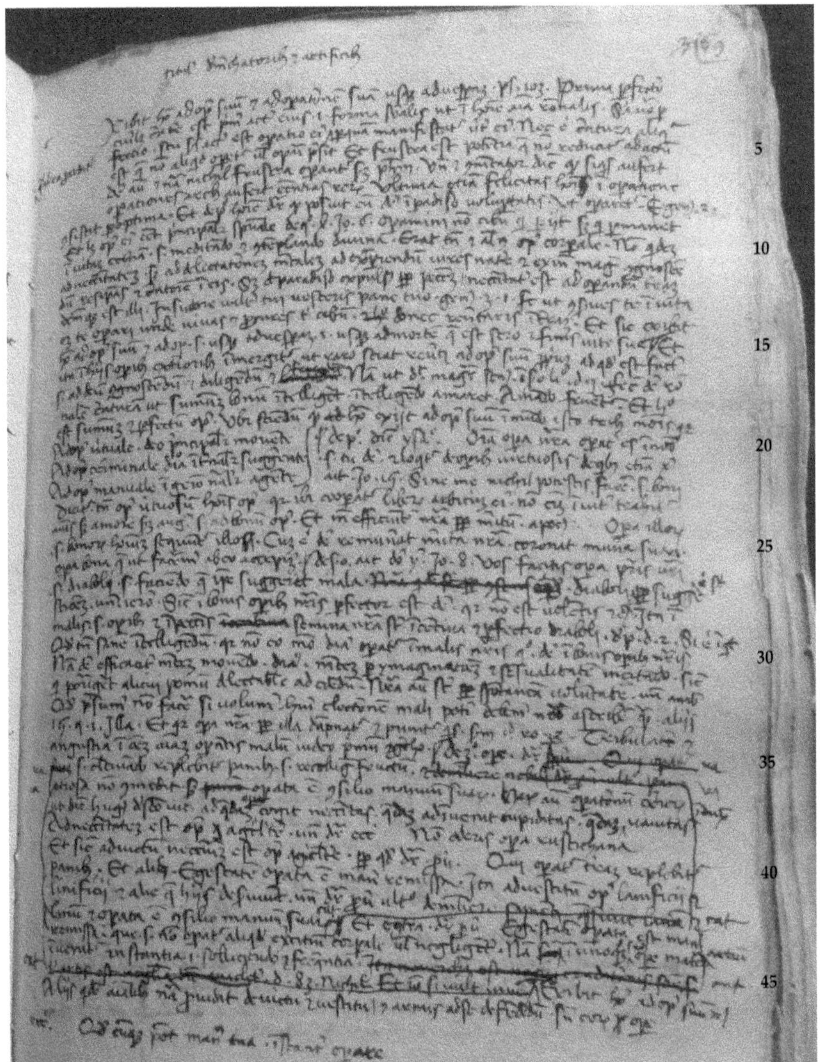

Plate 2: M_2 fol. 69r (Antoninus, *Summa*, 3.8.1), hand A

The hand A makes somewhat heavy use of abbreviations, though not excessive. The stock of abbreviations and their application conform to the standard practice of Italian scribes writing scholastic texts. Punctuation is minimal. At the sentence level, small units are indicated by periods (*punctus*), larger units by an initial majuscule letter; paragraphs and sections are introduced by paragraph marks, whose shape is a plain gibbet. Biblical quotations are sometimes underlined. New chapters begin with a space left for a decorated initial, which is always absent. The scribe also makes frequent deletions, corrections, and additions, employing all the typical means available to a medieval scribe. Small deletions are usually made by merely crossing out letters or words, larger deletions by marking a section with the label *uacat.* Additions are often inserted in any of the four margins, and their placement in the text is indicated with a tie-mark; different forms of tie-mark are employed, necessary because A at times makes four or even more marginal additions on a single page.

A detailed discussion of this hand's individual letter-forms, as well as samples of its majuscules, arabic numerals, and abbreviations, is provided in appendix 3.

2. *Comparison with Antoninus's Hand*

An extensive sample of the handwriting of St Antoninus of Florence is extant in an original document recording the separation of the convent of San Marco of Florence from the convent of San Domenico of Fiesole, formerly united under a single prior. A facsimile of the document has been published by Chiaroni; it provides the ideal sample for the identification of hand A.[80] The document was prepared in July of 1445. It records the consent of the Dominican brothers to the separation, each of whom affixed his signature to the document.[81] The comparison of Antoninus's hand in this document against the hand A was suggested by Panella.[82] Facsimiles

80 Chiaroni, *Gli autografi*, already cited above in ch. 1.

81 "Riproduco in tre tavole il prezioso documento originale in cui S. Antonino Pierozzi *scrive di sua mano* e narra come egli sia riuscito ad ottenere la separazione del Convento di S. Marco in Firenze dal Convento di S. Domenico di Fiesole uniti per 9 anni sotto un unico Priore … Il documento cartaceo in fol. che misura centim. 29 x 32, faceva parte della 'Miscellanea seconda' che apparteneva all'archivio del Convento di S. Marco. Nel 1876 passò al Museo di S. Marco e il Milanesi se ne valse per riprodurre la firma autografa del Beato Angelico ne 'La scrittura di artisti italiani'. Quando poi la Miscellanea suddetta fu assegnata nel 1883 alla Biblioteca Laurenziana il documento fu staccato per esser conservato nel Museo di S. Marco. Oggi si trova nella Biblioteca della Sopraintendenza alle Gallerie di Firenze." Chiaroni, *Gli autografi*, pref.

82 Panella, "Catalogo," I.B.54 (179).

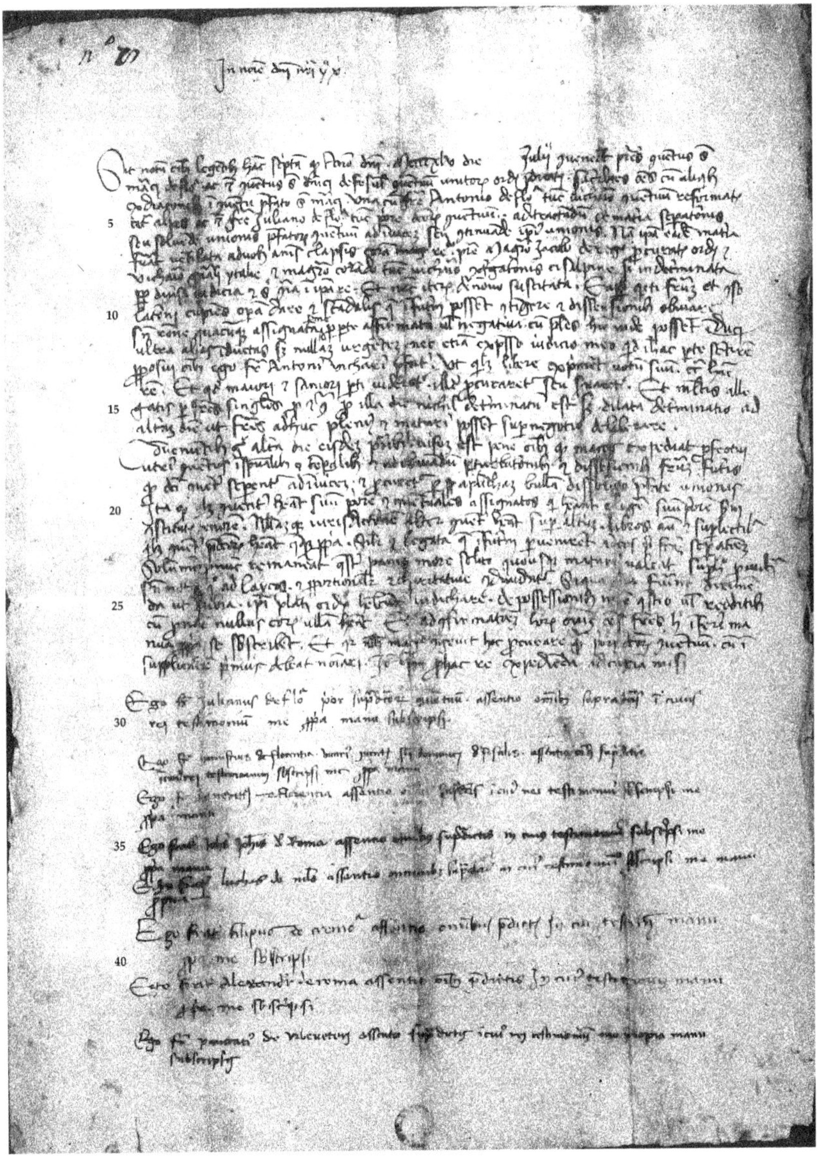

Plate 3: Antoninus, *Gli autografi*, tav. 1

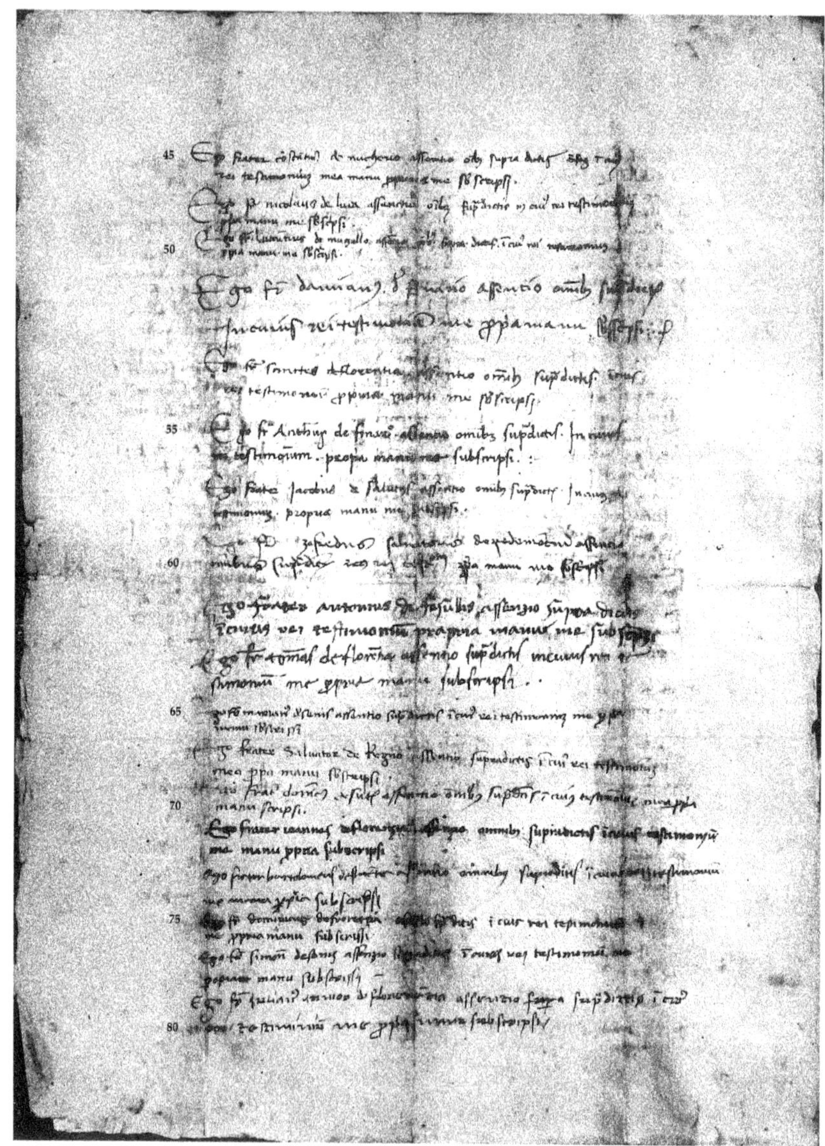

Plate 4: Antoninus, *Gli autografi*, tav. 2

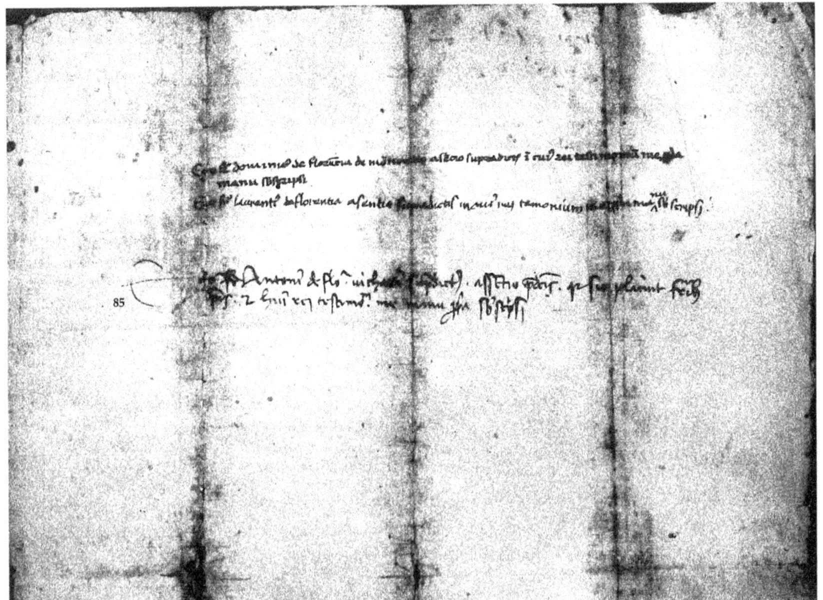

Plate 5: Antoninus, *Gli autografi*, tav. 3

Plate 6: Rolfi, Sebregondi, and Viti, *La Chiesa e la città*, tav. 2.3c (58)

of the document itself are provided here (plates 3–5), accompanied by a complete transcription.[83]

In nomine domini nostri Yesu Christi.[84]

Sit notum omnibus legentibus hanc scriptam quod Anno domini MCCCCXLV die … Iulii[85] conuenerunt patres conuentus sancti marci de florentia ac etiam conuentus sancti dominici de fesulis conuentuum unitorum ordinis predicatorum. sacerdotes omnes cum aliquibus ex diaconibus in conuentu prefato sancti marci, una cum fratre Antonio de florentia tunc uichario conuentuum reformatorum citra alpes ac etiam fratre Iuliano de florentia tunc priore dictorum conuentuum. ad tractandum de materia separationis seu soluende unionis prefatorum conuentuum ad inuicem seu continuande ipsius unionis. Nam ipsa eadem materia fuerat uentilata a duobus annis elapsis coram reuerendo patre Magistro Iacobo de regno procuratore ordinis et uichario generali ytalie et magistro corrado tunc uichario congregationis cisalpine sed indeterminata propter diuisa iudicia et sibi contraria in ipsa re. Et nunc iterum de nouo suscitata. Ea propter quieti fratrum et consolationi cupiens operam dare et scandalis que in futurum possent contingere et dissensionibus obuiare sine ratione quacumque assignata per me[86] et pro parte affirmatiua uel negatiua. cum plures hinc inde possent induci ultra alias inductas sed nullam urgentem. nec etiam expresso iudicio meo quod in hac parte sentirem proposui omnibus ego frater Antonius uicharius prefatus. Vt quilibet libere exprimeret uotum suum circa hanc rem. Et quod maiori et saniori parti uideretur. illud procuraretur seu seruaretur. Et multis allegatis per fratres singulos pro et contra pro illa die nichil determinatum est sed dilata determinatio ad alteram diem ut fratres adhuc plenius et maturius possent super negotio deliberare.

Conuenientibus igitur altera die eisdem patribus. uisum est pene omnibus quod magis expediat profectui utrius conuentus in spiritualibus et temporalibus et ad obuiandum perturbationibus et dissentionibus fratrum futuris quod dicti conuentus separentur ad inuicem. et procuretur per apostolicham bullam dissolutio prefate unionis. Ita quod quilibet conuentus habeat suum priorem et conuentuales assignatos qui habeant eligere suum priorem secundum constitutionis[87] tenorem. Nullamque iurisdictionem alter conuentus habeat super alterum. libros autem et superlectilia[88] quilibet conuentus predictorum habeat queque propria. Similiter et legata que in

83 Also transcribed in Chiaroni, *Gli autografi*, 11–12. Places where Chiaroni transcribes differently, apart from mere orthography, are noted herein.

84 *om. Chiaroni.*

85 July *Chiaroni.*

86 per me *s.l.*

87 constitutionibus *Chiaroni.*

88 supellectilia *Chiaroni.*

> futurum peruenirent ad eos post factam separationem. Solummodo pro nunc remaneat questus panis more solito quousque maturius ualeat super hoc prouideri, sine nota quoad laycos. et proportionaliter et charitatiue condiuidatur. Si qua alia fuerint dirimenda ut dubia. ipsi prelati ordinis habebunt iudichare. de possessionibus non est questio uel redditibus cum proinde nullus eorum ullam habeat. Et ad confirmationem horum omnium omnes fratres hic inferius manua[89] propria se subscribent. Et quia nulli magis congenet hoc procurare quam priori dictorum conuentuum. cum in supplicatione primus debeat nominari. Ideo ipsum pro hac re expedienda ad curiam misi.
>
> Ego fr. Iulianus de florentia prior supradictorum conuentuum, assentio omnibus supradictis in cuius rei testimonium me propria manu subscripsi.
>
> [...]
>
> Ego fr. Antonius de florentia. uicharius supradictus. assentio predictis. quia sic placuit fratribus ipsis. et[90] huius rei testimonium. me manu propria subscripsi.

The prior of the two convents, Giuliano Lapaccini ("of Florence"), signed the document first. The final signature is that of St Antoninus, at that time vicar of the cisalpine reformed Dominican convents:[91] "I, brother Antonio of Florence, aforenamed vicar, assent to the aforesaid, because so it pleased these brothers. And [in] witness of this thing I have signed my name with my own hand."[92] However, Antoninus did not merely affix his signature: he drafted the entire document himself. In the midst of its body, the document reads: "I, brother Antonio, aforenamed vicar, proposed to all that each of us should freely express his vote about this matter."[93] This document provides, then, in addition to an authentic signature, a sample of twenty-seven lines of handwriting, which by internal evidence is known to belong to St Antoninus himself. It is now possible to compare this against hand A and see the result. A sample of words and word-elements found in M_1 fol. 66vff. and M_2 fol. 69rff. are here presented in table 1 beside comparable elements in the separation document.

The visual comparison provided here speaks for itself on behalf of identifying hand A in M_1 and M_2 with the vicar Antonio of Florence – that is, St Antoninus –

89 manu *Chiaroni*.

90 et in *Chiaroni*.

91 "Vna cum fratre Antonio de florentia tunc uichario conuentuum reformatorum citra alpes ac etiam fratre Iuliano de florentia tunc priore dictorum conuentuum." Plate 3, ll. 4–5.

92 "Ego fr. Antonius de florentia. vicharius supradictus. assentio predictis. quia sic placuit fratribus ipsis. et (in) huius rei testimonium. me manu propria subscripsi." Plate 5, ll. 84–5.

93 "... proposui omnibus ego frater Antonius uicharius prefatus. Vt quilibet libere exprimeret uotum suum circa hanc rem." Plate 3, ll. 12–14.

Table 1: Comparison of St Antoninus's handwriting with hand A in M_1 and M_2

alias	alias	assentio	possent
congregationis	congregandi	continuande	continuando commutande
conuenerunt	emerunt	et	et
etiam	etiam	expediat	expedit
fr-	fraudulentia	fratrum	patrum
ipsius	ipsius	iudicia	iudiciali
manu	humanum	materia	materia
negotio	negotiatio	nichil	nichil
omnes	apud omnes ... nos	parte	parte

Table 1: (Continued)

who prepared the separation document. Antoninus writes an Italian *cursiva* with inconsistent loops at the *media* or *currens* level. His hand exhibits the same general characteristics and individual letter-forms as the samples from M_1 and M_2.[94] Virtually the only discrepancy is the use of round **s** in final position in the separation document. This appears in a number of places, indeed more regularly than not (pl. 3: l. 2 *patres conuentus*, l. 3 *sacerdotes omnes*, l. 5 *alpes, separationis*, l. 7 *elapsis*, l. 14 *multis*, l. 16 *fratres*, l. 26 *fratres*), against the practice of hand A. However, also seen is A's atypical tall **s** with tail in final position (pl. 3: l. 12 *alias*; pl. 5 l. 84 *predictis*).

Witnessing for the identification of hand A with Antoninus are, at the least, the following forms: the use of looped and loopless forms of **b d h k l** interchangeably (pl. 3: l. 2 *legentibus*, l. 2 *hanc*, l. 3 *aliquibus*, l. 4 *uichario*, l. 10 *obuiare*, l. 12 *ultra alias*, l. 12 *nullam*, l. 13 *hanc*, l. 15 *dilata determinatio ad*); flat **a** (pl. 3: l. 4 *reformatorum*, l. 5 *materia*, l. 6 *materia*, l. 8 *indeterminata*, l. 84 *assentio*); the joining of **ch** (pl. 3: l. 8 *uichario*[1,2]); the forms of **d** with or without loops, squashed like a majuscule, and clubbed (pl. 3: l. 2 *domini, die*, l. 3 *sacerdotes*, l. 4 *diaconibus*, l. 10 *dare, scandalis*, l. 12 *iudicio, quod*, l. 15 *ad*, l. 28 *expedienda ad*); **e** with a space between the strokes (pl. 3: l. 4 *reformatorum*, l. 6 *soluende*); **f** with a gap between the vertical strokes, and **f** as a large letter (pl. 3: l. 7 *fuerat*, l. 15 *fratres*, l. 16 *fratres*; pl. 5: l. 84 *frater*); the standard **g** (pl. 3: l. 2 *legentibus*, l. 8 *generali*, l. 10 *contingere*, l. 11 *negatiua*, l. 13 *ego*); insertion of **h** after **c** (pl. 3: l. 4 *uichario*, l. 8 *uichario*[1,2], l. 19 *apostolicham*, l. 25 *iudichare*); long **i** in final position, and occasionally dotted **i** (pl. 3: l. 2 *domini*, l. 2 *Iulii*, l. 3 *marci, dominici*, l. 11 *induci*, l. 28 *nominari*); frequent 3-shaped final **m** (pl. 3: l. 6 *inuicem*, l. 9 *fratrum*, l. 12 *urgentem*, l. 26 *confirmationem*); biting of **oe** (pl. 3: l. 3 *omnes*); the typical **p** and double **p** forms (pl. 3: l. 2 *scriptam*, l. 4 *prefato*, l. 5 *separationis*, l. 9 *propter*, l. 12 *parte*); flat **q** (pl. 3: l.3 *aliquibus*); the use of *textualis* **r** with a serif at the baseline, and 2-shaped **r** (pl. 3: l. 2 *conuenerunt patres*, l. 3 *ordinis*, l. 4 *reformatorum*, l. 5 *tractandum*, l. 7 *re(uerendo)*, l. 8 *procuratore*, l. 8 *re*, l. 11 *ratione*, l. 12 *urgentem*, l. 28 *re*); straight **s** in final position (pl. 3: l. 7 *annis* [cfr. *elapsis*], l. 19 *unionis*, l. 22 *eos*, l. 26 *nullus, omnes* [cfr. *fratres*]); the variant form of tailed straight **s** (pl. 3: l. 10 *scandalis*, l. 12 *alias* [cfr. *inductas*], l. 15 *-gatis* [cfr. *fratres singulos*]; pl. 5: l. 84 *predictis*, l. 85 *ipsis*); **s** with fat descender or separated vertical strokes (pl. 3: l. 8 *cisalpine*, l. 9 *suscitata*, l. 15 *singulos*, l. 28 *misi*); **t** curved or straight (pl. 3: l. 2 *sit notum, conuenerunt*); **x** in one stroke (pl. 3: l. 4 *ex*, l. 12 *expresso*, l. 13 *exprimeret*, l. 17 *expediat*, l. 28 *expedienda*).

Another published facsimile can be brought in to supplement Chiaroni's separation document.[95] Plate 6 reproduces a folio from a *registro di Entrate e Uscite* of the archdiocese of Florence under archbishop Antoninus, 1451–7.[96] On the last line of this folio, Antoninus approves the transaction concluded on 26 January 1453

94 Refer to appendix 3, where individual letter-forms are described in detail.

95 Suggested, like the previous comparison, by Panella, "Catalogo," I.B.54 (179).

96 Archivio Arcivescovile di Firenze, Mensa arcivescovile, I, Serie 10; reproduced in Rolfi, Sebregondi, and Viti, eds., *La Chiesa e la città a Firenze nel XV secolo*, fig. 2.3c (58).

Florentine style (1454 modern style): "Visa fuit per me f. An. ar. flo. dicta ratio et computus et approbata ut recte facta et ideo me manu propria ista s(ub)s(cripsi)." Again, archbishop Antoninus is seen writing the same sort of hand, employing the same letter-forms in the same fashion as in plates 1–5.

Having compared the hand A with two known samples of the handwriting of Antoninus of Florence, the resemblance is so strong that the natural conclusion is for their identity. At this point, the burden of proof is on the scholar who wishes to deny that hand A is Antoninus. Thus the conclusion: the text on M_1 fol. 66v and M_2 fol. 69r, and the rest of chapters 2.1.16–17 and 3.8.1–4 on the folios which follow, was written by Antoninus himself.[97]

3. *The Hand of Giuliano Lapaccini*

It was mentioned above that a major point of disagreement among scholars concerns the hand that wrote the *tabulae capitulorum* for each part of the *Summa* in these manuscripts. This hand, which Panella designated "G," also wrote the flyleaf notes describing these manuscripts as *originalia … concessa ad usum fratri Iuliano de Lapaccinis*, as well as numerous instructions for copyists throughout the volumes.[98] He also wrote some whole sections and chapters of the main text, including the preamble to the whole work, discussed and translated above.[99] Orlandi, against the general consensus of scholars, thought that this was "certainly the hand of St Antoninus," and printed facsimiles of folios written by both A and G as "autografi di S. Antonino."[100] The hand is visibly different from the hand A, however, and the difference was noticed by Orlandi.[101] This hand writes a neat and careful *hybrida* with a thin nib, on amply spaced lines; he has a particular preference for large lobes on majuscules and on minuscule **g**. This **g** is a particularly distinguishing letter: it is distinctive in having a closed loop completed by crossing the first downstroke, often with a large sinuous lobe. This hand G was first identified by Pomaro as that of brother Giuliano Lapaccini of San Marco.[102] By means of the same separation document already compared to hand A, the hand G can be identified as Lapaccini. In lieu of a laboured argument, a visual comparison is offered here. Plate 7 shows the note written on *N* fol. 1r by the hand G. In the table which follows, on the left are samples from Lapaccini's signature, on the right are samples from *N* fol. 1r.

---

97 The folios on which these chapters are written are described in further detail below, section 3.

98 The hand G writes *N* 3r–6v, 7r–7v, 16r–16v, etc.; M_1 second flyleaf recto and verso, IIr–VIIr, 100r, 381r–382v, 394r–395v, 407r–411v; M_2 flyleaf verso, Ir–VIIIr, etc.

99 Antoninus, *Summa*, 1 *prohemium* (*N* fol. 3r–5r, hand G).

100 Orlandi, *Bibliografia Antoniniana*, 26 and tav. I and II.

101 "… un'aggiunta di 1/2 fol. che lo stesso Autore, con mano leggermente differente, ma più accurata, ha fatto …" Ibid., tav. II.

102 Pomaro, "Censimento," 306–7, followed by Panella, who first compared it to the document reproduced herein as plates 3–5; Panella, "Catalogo," I.B.54 (179).

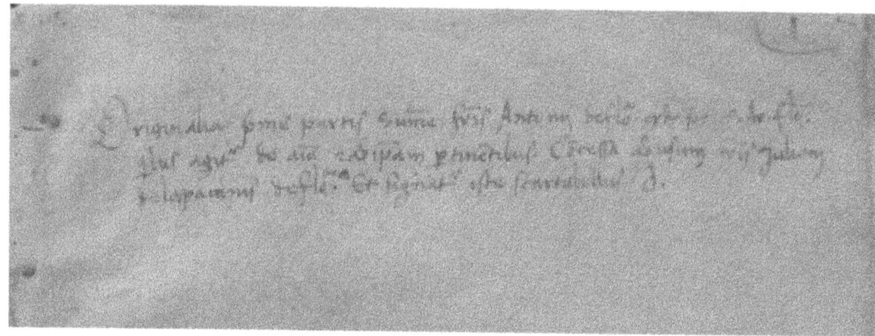

Plate 7: *N* fol. 1r, hand G

Table 2: Comparison of Giuliano Lapaccini's handwriting with hand G in *N*

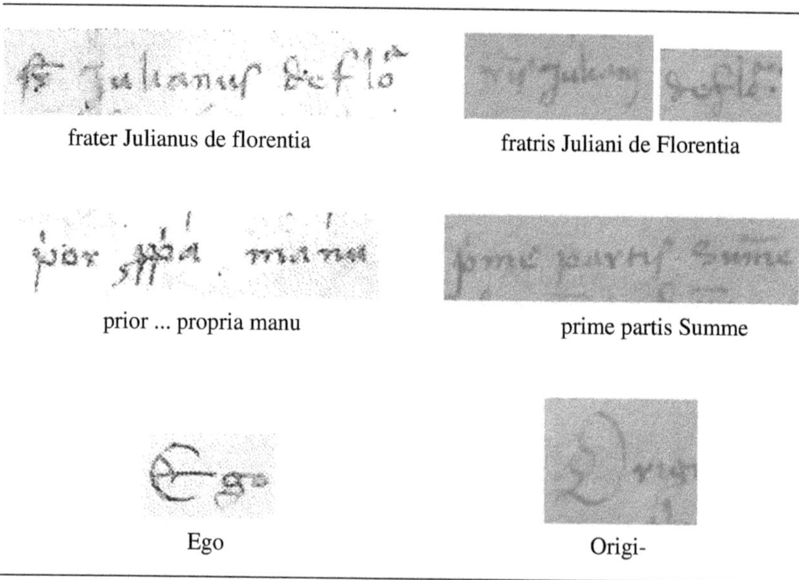

frater Julianus de florentia	fratris Juliani de Florentia
prior ... propria manu	prime partis Summe
Ego	Origi-

The comparison of hand G in manuscript *N* with the signature of Giuliano Lapaccini (Julianus Lapaccinis de Florentia) likewise yields a result of probable identity. That G is the hand of Lapaccini also fits in with a piece of circumstantial evidence. The hand G wrote a similar note in the front of each original volume of the *Summa*.[103]

103 With the qualification that this cannot be confirmed for part 4 of the *Summa*, since its first half has been lost; see the codicological descriptions in part two below.

These notes have a regular pattern: first, in describing each volume or part as *concessa ad usum fratri Iuliano de Lapaccinis*; second, in describing the work as a *Summa*. The first two original volumes of the *Chronicles* held at San Marco likewise bear similar notes:

> Originalia Cronice fratris Antonii de Florentia ... que poni debet in dono scientie in tractatu de dono scientie, et pertinet ad quartam partem Summe ... Concessa ad usum fratri Iuliano de Lapaccinis de Florentia ordinis predicatorum.[104]

> Secunda pars Cronice fratris Antonii de Florentia ordinis predicatorum et archiepiscopi Florentini ... Concessa ad usum fratri Iuliano de Lapaccinis de Florentia ...[105]

It can be assumed that both of these notes were also written by G, first, because of the repetition of the same pattern, and second, because Orlandi described them as written by the hand of Antoninus, which he believed G to be. There is a similar pattern here: in both of these notes the work is called a *Cronica*, and its individual volumes are called either *originalia* or *partes*; it is attributed to *frater Antonius de Florentia*; and it is described as *concessa ad usum fratri Iuliano de Lapaccinis*. In the first of these notes, the writer G again describes the other work as a *Summa*. The corresponding note in the third original volume of the *Chronicles*, however, is different:

> Tertium istud uolumen partis historialis, que est quinta respectu totius Recollectorii, continet materiam de quibusdam doctoribus et libris eorum et sententiis notabilioribus. Exinde continuatur historia ab Innocentio 3° qui fuit circa annum Domini millesimum ducentesimum usque ad presens, scilicet annum millesimum quadringentesimum quinquagesimum octauum.[106]

In this note, each element of the earlier pattern is absent: the volume is described as a *uolumen*, the work as a whole as the *pars historialis*, and the *Summa* as a *Recollectorium*; there is no attribution to its author; there is no *concessa ad usum* etc. Giuliano Lapaccini died on 23 February 1458 (1457 Florentine style).[107] Since this note states the time of its writing to be 1458, which in Florentine style began on 25 March, Lapaccini necessarily cannot have written it. It is more likely to be a note written by Antoninus himself, though only a direct examination and comparison of the hand could decide this. That the pattern of these notes was

104 Florence, Museo di San Marco, Inventario n. 507 (*Chronicles* vol. 1), fol. 1r; quoted from Orlandi, *Bibliografia Antoniniana*, 65.

105 Florence, Museo di San Marco, Inventario n. 508 (*Chronicles* vol. 2), fol. 1r; quoted from Orlandi, *Bibliografia Antoniniana*, 67.

106 Florence, Biblioteca Santa Maria Novella, I.B.55 fol. Ir; quoted from Orlandi, *Bibliografia Antoniniana*, XVIII, 70.

107 Kaepelli and Panella, *SOPMA*, 3:56.

maintained through the first seven volumes of the *Summa* and *Chronicles*, and abruptly changed with the last volume produced in 1458, the year following the death of Lapaccini, suggests that the identification of Lapaccini as the hand G which wrote these notes is likely correct.

4. Conclusion: Autograph Manuscripts

Antoninus himself wrote the text on M_1 fol. 66v and M_2 fol. 69r, and the rest of chapters 2.1.16–17 and 3.8.1–4 on the folios which follow: that is the conclusion reached thus far. What, however, is the overall role of Antoninus's hand A in the five manuscripts as a whole?

This hand A, the hand of the author Antoninus himself, is by a wide margin the most prominent hand in all five manuscripts N M_1 M_2 M_3 M_4. This is the hand which writes the majority of the base text in each volume. For example, in part 2 (M_1), of the 422 folios of text, about 337 were written by Antoninus: this makes about 80 per cent of the whole written *manu propria*. Other hands sometimes take over for particular chapters and, in a few places, whole titles, but their total contribution is less than a quarter of the whole *Summa*. Moreover, the vast majority of revisions, deletions, and supplements to the main text were written by the hand A; and the activity of the reviser certainly suggests the eye and mind of the author rather than a secretary or copyist.[108] The most important exception is the hand which wrote the *tabulae capitulorum*, hand G: this is Giuliano Lapaccini, whose role in the composition of the *Summa* will be discussed below in section 3. When the palaeographical comparison carried out here is added to the constant testimony that N M_1 M_2 M_3 M_4 were written *manu propria sua*, the argument for identifying A with the author St Antoninus becomes even more secure. These five volumes of the *Summa* are indeed, considered as a whole, autograph manuscripts.

3. The Composition of the *Summa*

Having demonstrated that these five manuscript volumes are indeed the original autographs of the *Summa*, I will now probe these manuscripts for what they reveal about the process of composition. This section cannot provide a comprehensive treatment of the entire *Summa*: the endeavour is too large to be carried out thoroughly at this time. Instead, what is offered is a sample of the sorts of evidence and suggestive hints which can be gleaned from a careful examination of the autograph manuscripts, helped along by forays already made by previous scholars. A few points have been singled out for particular attention: the role of Giuliano

108 Examples are given below in section 3; see also the critical apparatus and appendices to the chapters edited below.

Lapaccini; dates and datable references within the work which provide elements of a chronology of its writing; the writing of the chapters edited herein (*Summa* 2.1.16–17 and 3.8.1–4); the insertion into the *Summa* of Antoninus's previously written treatises and booklets; and the incorporation of Antoninus's sermons into the *Summa*.

1. Giuliano Lapaccini's Editorial Assistance

The hand G has already been identified as Giuliano Lapaccini. Lapaccini performed a crucial function: he appears to have acted as quasi-editor, assisting the author in preparing the work for publication. His activity can be seen throughout the manuscripts. In some places he copied the final version of a chapter or section: for example, the preamble to part 1 and the whole title on ecumenical councils in part 3. In both cases there are no annotations or corrections to Lapaccini's transcription. In other places, chapters were written out by Lapaccini and then annotated and revised by Antoninus, and the two hands can be seen together on the page. Lapaccini also seems to have been put in charge of assembling the originally detached notebooks, putting them in their final order, and tabulating their contents. There are notes in his hand throughout the volumes, instructing where a given section is meant to be placed in the sequence of chapters. A good example is in part 1, whose sequence of titles was rearranged at some point during composition. It appears that Antoninus wrote his *Treatise on laws* first, originally thinking it would constitute the first ten titles of the *Summa*. On review, he moved it to the second half of part 1, placing in the first half the other treatises on the soul, sin, etc.[109] Thus the first title of the *Treatise on laws* became, in the final version, *Summa* 1.11. On fol. 210r, where the *Treatise on laws* begins, at the top of the page there is a note by Antoninus: *In nomine Domini Nostri Iesu Christi*. Beside that, another note by the same hand, *primus quaternus*, indicates that this is the first quire of the *scartabellus*. Above this, however, a note has been added by Lapaccini, *undecimus titulus*, reflecting the final order of titles in part 1. Throughout the volumes there are many changes like this, with Lapaccini providing instructions for the copyist who would be tasked with preparing the first apograph (i.e., later non-autograph copy) manuscript.[110] At the end of the process, Lapaccini wrote the *tabulae capitulorum*. These not only indicate the intended order of the titles and chapters; they also indicate for the copyist on what folios each chapter will be found. This was very necessary if the work was to be copied intact and with its chapters in correct order: despite Lapaccini's work putting the quires in the

109 This was pointed out by Mamachi, 1.1:XIX; see also Orlandi, *Bibliografia Antoniniana*, 27. This matter is discussed at greater length below.

110 E.g., M_1 fol. 100r; M_2 fol. 70v, 77v, 94v, 115r, 116v; M_4 fol. 146r, 279r.

best arrangement possible, the titles and chapters of each part are not physically arranged in their final intended sequence. For the copyist, it was necessary to take the *tabula capitulorum* as the reference point: for each chapter proceeding to the folio indicated by Lapaccini as the starting point for that chapter, and then following his instructions within the chapter itself, pointing out places where supplements must be sought on later folios or changes of order made, as the case may be. In some cases, more than one set of folios is indicated for a single chapter in the *tabula*: these are chapters which Antoninus initially drafted, then returned to, adding supplementary sections written in later quires, to which the copyist had to proceed at the required point in the chapter. Some of the difficulties which copyists must have encountered in dealing with this process can be seen in the case of part 3: in an apograph manuscript in Florence's BNC (F_3), there are ten folios at the end of the volume containing sections of text which are to be inserted at various places within the chapters of part 3. For example, on fol. 360ra, a section of text begins, headed with this note: *Nota quod totum istud quod sequitur debet poni supra ad car. 221 columpna 3ª in principium ad tale signum.*[111] The transmission of the text in apograph manuscripts of the *Summa* would bear further investigation; it is not dealt with in this book.[112] Further light on Lapaccini's role could also be shed by examination of the third autograph volume of the *Chronicles*: since Lapaccini died before that volume was completed, Antoninus would have had to carry out the editorial process himself, or enlist a new assistant, and the task might have been carried out differently compared to what is seen in the volumes of the *Summa*. In any case, speaking of the four parts of the *Summa*, one thing is clear: the fact that the text was successfully copied from the autograph *scartabelli* and published in such a way as to accomplish, all things considered, a reasonably faithful rendition of the author's intent, must be credited to the editorial labours of Giuliano Lapaccini.

---

111 F_3 fol. 360ra. This fact about F_3 is briefly indicated by Orlandi, *Bibliografia Antoniniana*, 45.

112 Colosio supposes that the first apograph manuscript would have been a "public exemplar" from which, presumably, all later apographs are ultimately derived. "It appears to be the case that in some way a public exemplar was produced from the autograph, at the command of the Saint Author himself while he was still living, from which exemplar the other manuscripts and surviving printed editions would be made. For this explains the remarkable agreement they sometimes display together against the autograph, which the Author himself naturally revised up to the very end of his life." "Verisimile est, publicum quodam modo exemplar, ipso Sancto Scriptore duce, cum adhuc vitam ageret, ex autographo prolatum fuisse, a quo ceteri codices ac editiones reliquae prelo excusae futura essent: nam utrorumque hac re mira explanatur consensio quam interdum ostentant contra opus autographum, quippe quod Scriptor ipse usque ad ultimum vitae tempus emendaverit." Colosio, "Prologus in novam editionem," in Ballerini, 1:VIII.

2. *Dates and Datable References*

Dates and datable references within the work provide some elements of a chronology of the writing of the *Summa*. These references have been discussed before, but not always with recourse to the autograph manuscripts: a perilous procedure, since some were altered or added by later copyists and publishers, and others were vestiges copied in from earlier works.[113] For the sake of brevity, discussion of the context of these references will be kept to a minimum; they can be looked up in Ballerini's edition and the whole passage or chapter read there.

In part one on fol. 209r, Antoninus writes:

> Demum Nicholaus Papa 5ª qui nunc uiuit et regnat, anno Domini millesimo quadringentesimo quinquagesimo inchoante in festo Nativitatis Domini, fecit in missarum solempniis indulgentiam Iubilei publice insinuari scilicet plenariam remissionem ...[114]

This yields a date range for the writing of *Summa* 1.10.3: *post* the Jubilee of 1450, *ante* the death of Pope Nicholas V on 24 March 1455.[115]

In part 2, in the course of a very interesting discussion of the Great Schism:

> Greci etiam circa annum Domini nongentesimum scisma facientes, in heresim etiam inciderunt de Spiritu Sancto reprobatam ... Sed reducti ad unitatem ecclesie et ueritatem fidei sub Eugenio 4°, qui nunc Petri sedem tenet.[116]
>
> Scisma autem quod nunc regnat factum Basilee anno Domini MCCCCXL° vel circa sub Eugenio 4° videtur pertinere ...[117]

Two events are noted here as having occurred during the papacy of Eugenius IV, still incumbent at the time of writing. The bull of union with the Greeks, *Laetentur coeli*, was issued by the Council of Florence on 6 July 1439.[118] The schismatic Council of Basel attempted to depose Eugenius IV on 25 June 1439, and elected antipope Felix V on 5 November 1439.[119] Various countries, having once defected to Felix V, returned to the obedience of Eugenius IV between 1443 and 1446,[120]

113 See Ballerini's comment at 1:609–10 n14. Also suspected by Morçay, *Saint Antonin*, 415.
114 Antoninus, *Summa*, 1.10.3 (*N* fol. 209r, hand A). Noted in Morçay, *Saint Antonin*, 414.
115 Kelly, *The Oxford Dictionary of Popes*, 244.
116 Antoninus, *Summa*, 2.3.11.6 (M_1 fol. 165v in marg. infer., hand A). Noted in Morçay, *Saint Antonin*, 414; Orlandi, *Bibliografia Antoniniana*, X–XII.
117 Antoninus, *Summa*, 2.3.11.10 (M_1 fol. 169r, hand A).
118 Jedin, *Ecumenical Councils of the Catholic Church*, 133.
119 Ibid., 131.
120 Ibid., 135–6.

but the schism endured beyond the death of Eugenius IV on 23 February 1447.[121] Thus, for the writing of *Summa* 2.3.11, the date range is *post* 1440 (from which year Antoninus dates the schism of Basel), *ante* 23 February 1447. Shortly after this reference, there is an indication of the order of composition: *Hec pro paucis dicta sunt ratione scismatis. Sed de potestate pape et concilii infra dicetur in fine 3 partis si uitam concesserit Dominus.*[122] Thus these titles of part 3, on the supreme pontiff and on ecumenical councils,[123] were not yet written when Antoninus wrote *Summa* 2.3.11.

In part 3's title on advocates and procurators, in the course of explaining the dating clauses employed in various notarial and curial styles, Antoninus writes: … *uerbi gratia, nunc currit annus Domini MCCCCXLVIII*[us].[124] Shortly after, providing an example of a dating clause using the pontifical year, he again uses the year 1448: *In curia etiam ponuntur anni quibus papa resedit, puta anno Domini 1448 dicitur pontificatus sanctissimi domini Nicholai V anno secundo.*[125] Thus it can be surmised that *Summa* 3.6.3 was in composition during the year 1448.

In part 3, in the title on major excommunication: *Sed Eugenius quartus qui nunc est uoluit et declarauit non tenere seu ligare sententiam illam …*[126] This refers to a decree of Eugenius IV annulling a sentence of John XXII *contra mulieres facientes sibi tricas de capillis*. The decree of Eugenius IV was issued on 19 October 1437.[127] This reference, then, yields a date range between 19 October 1437 and 23 February 1447, the death of Eugenius IV. However, this particular reference requires further attention to its circumstances. It comes within the series of titles on excommunications and ecclesiastical censures, which were almost certainly transcribed into the *Summa* from Antoninus's earlier-published *Tractatus de censuris ecclesiasticis sive de excommunicationibus*. Creytens has shown that in Antoninus's replies (*Conclusiones et decisiones*) to cases of conscience submitted to him by Dominic of Catalonia, OP, he cited this *Tractatus* and directed the recipient to refer to it for further information.[128] The *Tractatus de censuris ecclesiasticis sive de excommunicationibus* thus predates the *Conclusiones et*

121 Kelly, *Oxford Dictionary of Popes*, 241. The schism was not finally resolved until antipope Felix V resigned on 7 April 1449, during the reign of Nicholas V.

122 Antoninus, *Summa*, 2.3.11.10ff. (M_1 fol. 169v, hand A).

123 I.e., ibid., 3.22–3 in Ballerini; 3.23–4 in the autograph (M_2 fol. IVv–Vr, hand G).

124 Antoninus, *Summa*, 3.6.3.5 (M_2 fol. 82v, hand A). Noted in Morçay, *Saint Antonin*, 414; Orlandi, *Bibliografia Antoniniana*, XII.

125 Antoninus, *Summa*, 3.6.3.5 (M_2 fol. 83r, hand A).

126 Ibid., 3.24.72.1 in Ballerini, 3.25.69 in the autograph (M_3 fol. 575v, hand G). This is the final paragraph of the chapter: in the autograph, this paragraph is written by Lapaccini on a folio inserted in between what were originally fol. 573 and 574, with a tie-mark indicating its proper place at the end of the chapter on what was originally fol. 574r (now fol. 576r). The preceding sections of this chapter, and the beginning of the next chapter, are written by a different scribal hand. These folios of the autograph manuscript will be discussed shortly below.

127 Creytens, "Les cas de conscience," 209; Orlandi, *Bibliografia Antoniniana*, XII; Morçay, *Saint Antonin*, 415.

128 Creytens, "Les cas de conscience," 209.

decisiones, which date from 1440. There is also a record of the binding of this *Tractatus* by Vespasiano da Bisticci in 1447, recorded by Giuliano Lapaccini.[129] The reference to Eugenius IV *qui nunc est* was most likely copied into the *Summa* as it was found in the earlier *Tractatus*, and thus does not reflect the time of composition of the *Summa*. The *Tractatus de censuris* will be discussed further below; the autographs appear to confirm that this treatise was transcribed into the *Summa* by scribes without major updating by Antoninus.

Again in part 3:

> Nam ab incarnatione Domini usque ad presens fluxerunt anni MCCCCXLVIIII, nondum completo ultimo anno; et quantum residui sit temporis usque ad finem mundi solus Deus nouit.[130]

This whole chapter is written in the autograph by Antoninus, with numerous revisions and additions made by his own hand at various points, including, at one place, on an inserted half-sheet.[131] An interesting point to note here is that there are three series of folio numbers at this point: in the modern numeration, this is fol. 653; in the old numeration referred to in the *tabula capitulorum*, and probably written by Lapaccini, this is fol. (*carta*) 650; in the older numeration, which appears to be written by Antoninus, this is fol. 514. The older numeration shows the final titles of part 3 (3.24–32/33) in a different order from their current order in the autograph and its *tabula capitulorum*. Interestingly, however, the order of titles indicated by the older numeration corresponds to their order as printed by Ballerini. In Ballerini's edition, the final three titles of part 3 are *De Deo et statu beatorum* (30), *De diversis statibus comprehensorum* (31), and *De poena purgatorii* (32); in the autograph, they are *De statu purgandorum in purgatorio* (31), *De statu comprehensorum* (32, corresponding to Ballerini's title 30), and *De diuersis statibus comprehensorum* (33). The order of titles followed in the manuscript F_3 appears to follow the current order of the autograph manuscript, though this requires confirmation.[132] A likely explanation is that

129 "Nei conti di S. Antonino col libraio-legatore Vespasiano da Bisticci, troviamo che in data 11 giugno 1447 Fr. Giuliano Lapaccini registra un pagamento per rilegatura *'d'alquanti quinterni negli quali è scripto il trattato delle Scomunicatione dell'Arcivescovo con due guardie e una choverta di pergamento'*; quindi il Trattato era già pubblicato avanti e separatamente dalla Somma." Orlandi, *Bibliografia Antoniniana*, xx–xxi.

130 Antoninus, *Summa*, 3.31.2.3 in Ballerini, 3.33.2 in autograph (M_3 fol. 653r, hand A). Noted in Orlandi, *Bibliografia Antoniniana*, xii.

131 M_3 fol. 653bis, hand A.

132 "Titulus XXXII. De unitate diuine essentie et Trinitate personarum et quinque modis essendi Dei in rebus, capitulum primum. Istud primum capitulum deficit supra ad car. 325, columpna prima, circa medium ad tale signum." F_3 fol. 362rb. Facsimiles of the full *tabula capitulorum* of this manuscript are not currently in my possession.

the first copies of part 3 were produced while the original order of titles stood; at some later point, Antoninus changed the order of titles, moving *De statu purgandorum* from final position to become the antepenultimate title: at least one later manuscript copy appears to reflect this change, but it may be that the older order became the received one.

All this is by the way. As to date, the reference found at this place in the autograph shows that the final titles of part 3 were being written in the year 1449.

Additional testimony about chronology can be brought in from payments to Vespasiano da Bisticci, stationer to the archbishop and the brothers of San Marco. Giuliano Lapaccini kept records of purchases of the paper on which to write the *Summa* and *Chronicles* as well as of the copying of some of their individual parts. Orlandi provides the following account.[133] On 13 February 1447, Lapaccini recorded, on behalf of the archbishop, an expense of 8 *solidi* to Bisticci for the binding of several "quinterns" of the *Summa di frate Antonino arcivescovo*.[134] On 4 October of the same year, he paid 16 *solidi* 6 *denarii* for the binding of two large books he describes as quarter-sheet *scartabelli*.[135] These octavo-size volumes, 9 inches by 6 inches, match the measurements of the autograph volumes (*scartabelli*) of the *Summa*. On 20 January 1452 Lapaccini paid Bisticci to bind "the third part of the *Summa* of the archbishop."[136] Copies were already being produced before the *Summa* had been completed: Br. Constantino Angeli da Nocera, OP, copied the following volumes, recorded 17 September 1450:

> *La* sechonda parte, cioè de vitii. Et prima chompiuta della somma di Messer Antonio Arcivescovo. di la quarta parte di detta cioè di virtute. Item la terza parte della detta somma non chompiuta. alla quale poco mancha. Item il principio (altra copia) della prima parte di detta somma.[137]

---

133 Orlandi, *Bibliografia Antoniniana*, xiii.

134 "Il 13 febbraio 1447 registrava, per conto dell'Arcivescovo, una spesa di soldi 8 pagati a Vespasiano *per legatura d'alquanti quinterni della Summa di frate Antonino arcivescovo*." Ibid.

135 "Il 4 ottobre dello stesso anno pagava all stesso libraio '*soldi 16 e den. 6 per leghatura di 2 libri grossi, cioè scartabelli a quarto di foglio dell'opere di frate Antonino*', che, probabilmente dovevano essere gli autografi dell P. I e II dallo stesso S. Antonino detti 'scartabelli'." Ibid. It should be noted that Orlandi's conjectures about which particular volume of the *Summa* was being bound in each of these transactions are difficult to confirm definitively from the evidence at hand.

136 "Mentre solamente il 20 gennaio 1452 (st. fior. 1451) pagava la rilegatura a Vespasiano de '*la terza parte* della somma dell'Arcivescovo', che è in due volumi, ancora nella sua rilegatura originale (P. I[a] et P. II[a] III[ae] partis)." Ibid.

137 Ibid.

On 3 November 1452, Lapaccini paid Bisticci for the paper to make a copy of the fourth part of the *Summa* for the convent of San Marco, although Antoninus had not yet completed writing the fourth part.[138] It has already been seen that the author completed the last chapter of part 4 in 1454, and considered the *Summa* finished at that point; he was then mid-way through the *Chronicles*.[139]

These references, though few, suggest two conclusions about the composition of the *Summa*. First, the writing of parts 2, 3, and 4 appears to have proceeded roughly in the order in which they now stand: for a reference at 2.3.11 places it *post* 1440, *ante* 23 February 1447; 3.6.3 circa 1448; 3.31.2 circa 1449; and 4.16.1 was finished in 1454. However, at least one chapter of part 1 (1.10.3) was not finished before the Jubilee year of 1450; this means that even while Antoninus was quite far into writing parts 2 and 3, he had not yet finished with part 1. Datable references within the *Summa*, then, combined with records of its binding and copying, are suggestive of a generally sequential progress through the parts, while keeping the files open, so to speak, for potential additions and revisions as they occurred to the author; until, presumably, circa 1454 when the whole *Summa* may have been considered complete and was committed "to the use of brother Giuliano Lappacini."

3. New Compositions at Summa *2.1.16–17 and 3.8.1–4*

Turning now to what the autograph manuscripts reveal about the composition of particular titles and chapters, the first matter to be dealt with is the writing of the chapters edited below (*Summa* 2.1.16–17 and 3.8.1–4). These appear to have been written by Antoninus in the course of composing the *Summa*, as original compositions rather than copies of older treatises; in the autograph manuscripts, each chapter shows signs of multiple stages of drafting.

The chapters edited below were written entirely by the hand of St Antoninus, with a few marginal notes added by Lapaccini. The chapters are these. *Summa* 2.1.16 (*De fraudulentia per modum predicationis*) is written on M_1 fol. 66v–70r, and is followed immediately by 2.1.17 (*De uariis fraudibus que commictuntur in negotiando*) on fol. 70v–73r. *Summa* 3.8.1 (*De merchatoribus et artificibus per modum sermonis*) is on M_2 fol. 69r–70v, followed by 3.8.3 (*De negotiatoribus et campsoribus*) on fol. 70v–73r (plus an addition in the upper margin of 73v) and 3.8.4 (*De diuersis generibus artificum*) on fol. 73v–79v. *Summa* 3.8.2 (*De diuersis*

138 "Il 3 novembre 1452 Fr. Giuliano Lapaccini pagava, per conto di S. Antonino, a Vespasiano da Bisticci la carta per fare una copia della '*quarta parte della somma sua la quale fa compiere per questo chonvento*', cioè di S. Marco, la quale P. IV, tuttavia, S. Antonino, come abbiamo detto, ancora non aveva finito di scrivere." Ibid.

139 Antoninus, *Summa*, 4.16.1 para. penult. and ult. (M_4 fol. 277v, hand A). Discussed above in section 1. Noted in Morçay, *Saint Antonin*, 414; Orlandi, *Bibliografia Antoniniana*, xii.

generibus contractuum) is on M_2 fol. 115v–116r, followed by an addition to to 3.10.5 (*De sepulturis*).

The autograph version of each of these chapters shows a process of composition involving at least two stages: a first draft followed by a revision and expansion. The two recensions for each chapter are documented in the appendices, to which the reader is referred. The paradigm is this. The first draft is written in the main text column by the hand A. Deletions are made by striking out individual words or indicating whole passages with *uacat*; additions are made above the line or in the margins, with tie-marks indicating where the added words are to be inserted in the text. The autograph version of 2.1.16 shows these sorts of revisions and expansions. Particularly frequent additions are canon-law references or material drawn from jurists' commentaries and theological and moral *Summae*. These suggest that after his initial draft, the author habitually returned to the books to refresh his memory and note further relevant material, which he then grafted into the draft, typically through marginal additions. See, for example, an addition made in the upper margin beginning with the word *quantum* and ending *satisfacere*, at 2.1.16, section 3.1.2.1; similarly the addition *et … constitueretur*, section 3.1.3.2; and the addition made in the lower margin, *in … fieri*, at the end of the same section. Chapter 2.1.17 is very similar. Many deleted words and phrases are visible throughout, struck through but still mostly legible, giving a glimpe of an idea or expression which Antoninus thought better of and recast. There are a few substantial additions to the first draft, in the form of paragraphs written in the upper or lower margins. The three largest of these, in the opening section (*thema*), sections 2.2–2.3, and section 3.2, add new scripture texts or canon-law citations to supplement what had been initially written, and so again they seem to show Antoninus returning to his books for further material.

Another good case study is 3.8.2, of which two versions are extant in the autograph manuscript M_2. On fol. 114v–115r, there is what appears to be an abandoned earlier version of 3.8.2 written mostly by a hand other than Antoninus. It very closely imitates a passage in John Duns Scotus's *Quaestiones in librum quartum Sententiarum* dealing with the different kinds of contracts;[140] I have included in the appendices a transcription of this first draft in parallel with the text of Scotus for comparison. The second version of 3.8.2, the one intended for publication by the author and edited below, shows a two-stage writing process just like 2.1.16. Antoninus wrote an initial draft, then reviewed it, making some revisions and expanding some material. Clarifying words are added in a few places; in one place a canon-law reference is added. Finally, at the end of the chapter a new paragraph is added in the upper margin, with a tie-mark indicating that it continues the text

140 John Duns Scotus, *In quartum*, 4, 15, 2, 2 in *Opera omnia*, vol. 18, 271–320.

which ends at the foot of the folio; this paragraph is copied in verbatim from the *Glossa ordinaria* to the *Decretum*, at C. 14 q. 3 c. 3 s.v. *precepta*.

The autograph of 3.8.1 bears the most interesting traces of the author's process of composition. This chapter shows the same sorts of expansions made upon reviewing the books, as in the very long addition beginning *Vnde et Crisostomus* and concluding *remanet nisi peccatum* (section 3.2.2), which was commenced in the lower margin of M_2 fol. 70r, continued in the upper margin of the same, and then, having run out of space, completed in the upper margin of the facing page, 69v. This chapter also shows a more primitive stage of outlining and drafting than is evident for the other two. On fol. 69r there is a paragraph which was drafted by the author and then struck out and marked for deletion with *uacat*. This paragraph contains the skeleton of some of the later sections of the chapter as it now stands, and assembles some of the texts to be cited at those places. As a method of developing this chapter's theme, *Exibit homo ad opus suum et ad operationem suam usque ad uesperam* (*Ps.* 103:23), applied morally to the subject of work (*opus*, *operatio*), Antoninus employs the typical preaching technique of division and subdivision. The first division divides work into *opus uirtuale*, *opus criminale*, and *opus manuale*. After dealing with the first two, the author, entering into the third point, initially posited a *sententia* of Hugh of St Victor to introduce a subdivision of manual labour into work which *cogit necessitas*, work which *inuenit cupiditas*, and work which *induxit uanitas*; the first recension on 69r shows him lining up scriptural quotations for each point and concluding with a moral exhortation to *instantia* (*id est sollicitudo et frequentia*), inspired by a quotation of Pope Anacletus taken from the *Decretum* at D. 83 c. 6. This first draft was then scrapped, and in the second recension Antoninus instead proceeds at this point (*opus manuale*) into a subdivision which lends itself to completion by the citation of Anacletus exhorting to *instantia*. The new subdivision sets out three necessary marks of *opus manuale*, namely *bona conscientia*, *apta conuenientia*, and *debita permanentia*. The *sententia* of Hugh of St Victor, and the further subdivision it prompts, is incorporated under the heading *apta conuenientia*, and at relevant places the scriptural texts collected in the first recension are brought in. Under the third heading, *debita permanentia*, the quotation of Anacletus is called upon to conclude the *thema* as a whole: *usque ad uesperam*.

In 3.8.3, small additions are made to the initial draft, mainly incorporating canon-law references (such as to D. 88 c. 11 in the preamble and *X* 3.34.7 in section 1.1); a few more extensive ones add part of a paragraph or, in two cases, a whole new paragraph. However, the most significant revision made by the author to 3.8.3 is its division from the next chapter, 3.8.4. The handwritten text of these two chapters runs seamlessly together: the last paragraph of 3.8.3, discussing small retail dealers (*pizicangnoli*), is in the upper margin of fol. 73v; the first paragraph of 3.8.4 begins immediately below it at the words *De merciariis*, "About outfitters." Indeed, it appears likely that when Antoninus initially drafted the text of 3.8.4, he did not conceive it as a new fourth chapter but merely as a continuation of 3.8.3's discussion of different sorts of traders; the division into two chapters was made later. The final chapter division is clear from the table of contents of the autograph manuscript M_2, where four chapters are enumerated in title 8, with 3.8.4 indicated as beginning on fol. 73 and its opening words given as *De merciariis*. However, the apograph manuscript F_3 only has three chapters in title 8, with the text belonging in my edition to 3.8.4 simply continuing chapter 3.8.3 without a break. In F_3 there is no chapter heading or decorated initial to signify a new chapter after the paragraph on *pizicangnoli* which concludes 3.8.3 in the final recension; the text simply continues directly into the paragraph *De merciariis* and on all the way through to the discussion of farmers at the end of 3.8.4. The manuscript F_3 thus appears to transmit an earlier recension of Antoninus's *Summa* than the autographs. This corroborates Colosio's supposition that at least some of the apograph manuscripts are derived from a "public exemplar" which did not incorporate all revisions Antoninus made to the autographs up to the end of his life.[141] Despite this discrepancy in the division of title 8 into chapters, F_3's text still seems, to my eye, very close to that of the autographs.

In 3.8.4 there are many additions which are of a piece with those made in the other chapters just discussed. Two revisions are worthy of note here. The first concerns the order of writing of the sections which compose this chapter. The sections I have numbered 1–8 (up to *De carpentariis*) appear to have been written in sequential order on fol. 73v–77v. The next section written, which commences on fol. 78r, was section 9 (*De aromatariis*). The whole of section 12 (*De agricolis*) was written next, on fol. 78v. After completing the section *De agricolis*, Antoninus then wrote several additional sections on fol. 79r–79v, and indicated where they are to be inserted within chapter 3.8.4: *pone hec ante precedentem* (one word is illegible here) *in fine faciei*. Following Antoninus's instructions, these become sections 8.1–8.2 and 10–11. Above the section *De agricolis* Antoninus wrote: *Iste §. in fine huius capituli ponatur.*

A final example of a particularly intricate process of drafting is present in the folios surrounding 3.8.4. The last folio of this chapter is fol. 79v. In the lower margin of that folio, there is an addition by Antoninus beginning with the words *Huiusmodi Psalmi*. Although at a glance this appears to be another paragraph of 3.8.4, in fact it is part of the final section of chapter 3.13.4: *de horis canonicis* (in the title *de clericis et diuinis officiis*). This chapter 3.13.4 begins in M_2 on fol. 303r and continues to fol. 306r, all written by a scribe, not Antoninus. In the lower margin of fol. 306r Giuliano Lapaccini has written a note: *Hic adde quare Psalmi Dauid cantantur in diuinis officiis. Quere supra ad cart. 80 et incipit: De Psalmis David, ad tale signum H.* On fol. 80v Giuliano wrote a corresponding note in the

141 Colosio, "Prologus in novam editionem," in Ballerini, 1:VIII. Quoted and translated above.

left margin: *Pone hunc §. infra, 315 cart.* [today fol. 306r] *ad tale signum H.* At this place on fol. 80v Antoninus began writing the new sections for 3.13.4 with the words ❡ *De Psalmis Dauith.* However, in writing this additional section on fol. 80v, Antoninus reached the foot of the folio and continued writing in the upper margin (indicating this with a tie-mark), and then again ran out of space, writing at the end of this marginal addition: *Reverte cartam, ad signum +*. On the reverse (fol. 80r), the + tie-mark is found in the lower margin, where the addition continues beginning with the words *secundum Tomam 2ª 2ᵉ*. Once again Antoninus reached the foot of the folio and placed a tie-mark; the corresponding tie-mark is found in the lower margin of fol. 79v, where this addition to 3.13.4 is continued, in the passage beginning with the words *Huiusmodi Psalmi*. Yet again Antoninus reached the foot of the folio and inserted a tie-mark, resuming the passage in the upper margin of fol. 80r at the words *dum eius dicta*. This is, at last, the final addition to 3.13.4, concluding at the words *ex se aptus ad omne peccatum*. In Ballerini's edition of the *Summa*, all of these additions appear in their intended order in 3.13.4 (vol. 3, columns 586e–588a). This is a remarkable example of the skill and care of the first copyist of Antoninus's *Summa*, who transcribed these in their correct order.

4. Confessionale "Defecerunt" *at* Summa *3.17 and Elsewhere*

It has just been seen how Antoninus proceeded in drafting several chapters as new compositions. However, it has often been noted that at some places in the *Summa* Antoninus incorporated his own previously written treatises and *opuscula*. In this and the next two sections, the autograph manuscripts are probed for what they reveal about this process.[142] In brief, it can be stated with certainty that Antoninus incorporated his previous works into the *Summa* at relevant places; however, the method of incorporation is not uniform, but takes various forms. Three examples

142 "Ce travail demande cependant beaucoup de prudence et de circonspection. La Somme n'est past une oeuvre qui reflète partout les opinions du Saint à la fin de sa vie. Elle contient plusieurs parties qui ont été composées à des époques antérieures et qui n'on pas été revues lors de leur insertion dans la grande compilation. Avant d'instituer ces comparaisons, il faudrait donc établir au préalable lesquels des traités, insérés dans la Somme, ont existé auparavant comme oeuvre séparée et originale, à quelles dates ils ont été composés et dans quelle mesure ils ont été mis a jour lors de leur incorporation à la Somme. Ce travail n'a pas encore été fait. Les érudits n'y ont donné que peu d'attention pour la simple raison qu'ils ont considéré les traités qui circulent à part comme des 'extraits' de la Somme, non pas comme des oeuvres indépendants. Les collections de cas de conscience pourront rendre ici quelque service par les nouvelles informations qu'elles apportent sur l'existence et la date de composition de quelques-uns de ces traités, considérés à tort comme des pièces détachées de la Somme. Pour d'autres, acceptés déjà comme oeuvres originales, elles fournissent de nouvelles lumières sur la date de composition." Creytens, "Les cas de conscience," 208.

are adduced here: the Latin confessional manual *"Defecerunt,"* the *Tractatus de censuris ecclesiasticis sive de excommunicationibus*, and a *sermo de indulgentiis*.

Morçay points out that much of the *Confessionale "Defecerunt"* was incorporated into the *Summa* at 3.17 (*de statu confessorum*).[143] The subject of this title corresponds to the first part of the *Confessionale*, namely *de potestate confessoris*. The relationship of these two texts shall now be examined.

The *Confessionale "Defecerunt"* exists in two known recensions, a briefer and a longer.[144] These are distinguished by their incipits. The briefer recension's incipit: *Defecerunt scrutantes scrutinio … Scrutantes aliorum peccata sunt confessores. Scrutinium autem est inquisitio facta in confessione.*[145] The longer recension's incipit: *Defecerunt scrutantes scrutinio … Scrutinium quidem est confessio, in quo et penitens scrutatur conscientiam suam et confessor cum eo.*[146] It would be a tenable hypothesis, *a priori*, that the longer recension is original, that its material was copied into the *Summa* at the relevant places, and that the briefer recension was produced by abbreviating the longer one. Having examined early printed editions of the *"Defecerunt"* and considered their text against the autograph manuscripts, I consider it more likely that the longer recension is the later one, and represents an expanded version produced by adding in material from the *Summa* at corresponding places in the original *Confessionale*.

The first part of the briefer recension of the *Confessionale "Defecerunt"* – i.e., chapters 1–8 *de instructione seu directione simplicium confessorum* – corresponds to *Summa* 3.17 *de statu confessorum*, chapters 1–19. The treatment in the *Confessionale*, about 42 printed octavo pages in large type, is relatively brief compared with that in *Summa*, about 33 printed columns on folio sheets in very small type.[147] In the autograph manuscript this whole section, from M_2 fol. 375v to 383v (9 folios), appears to be written by the hand of Antoninus.[148] A comparison of the text in the autographs of the *Summa* against the two recensions of the *Confessionale* suggests that Antoninus took the basic framework of the shorter recension and developed

143 Morçay, *Saint Antonin*, 405.

144 On these, see Lapidge et al., *CALMA*, Antoni 1.2; Kaeppeli and Panella, *SOPMA*, no. 256; Wilms, "Das *Confessionale Defecerunt* des hl. Antoninus"; Aranci, "I 'confessionali' di s. Antonino Pierozzi e la tradizione catechistica del '400."

145 Antoninus Florentinus, *Confessionale: Defecerunt scrutantes scrutinio. Add: Johannes Chrysostomus: Sermo de poenitentia* (Cologne, 1470); idem, *Libellus de audientia confessionum Domini Antonini de Florentia …* (Venice, 1472).

146 Antoninus Florentinus, *Summa confessionalis Do. Antonini Archiepiscopi Florentini. Adiecta est tabula, praecipuas huius operis materias, et scitu digniores summatim complectens …* (Lyon: apud Theobaldum Paganum, 1546).

147 Ballerini, 3:942–74.

148 It is certain that the majority of the text is by the hand A, and probable that the entirety is. It is possible, however, that some portions of the text are by an unidentified other hand, whose letter-forms are very similar.

the material into a more lengthy treatment. At times the *ex tempore* process of composition is visible in the manuscript. For example, at 379v, Antoninus (or possibly a scribe writing a similar hand) transcribed the text of a canon from the *Clementines*. Antoninus then glossed the text in the left and lower margins. It seems that two new gloss comments occurred to him after making his initial pass, and he then added them in the upper margin, indicating where they should be inserted within the overall apparatus of glosses with the letters **a b c d e**. In the printed edition of the *Summa*, this chapter has the text of the canon in italics followed by these glosses in their correct order.[149] The longer recension of the *"Defecerunt"* likewise prints the Clementine text followed by the glosses in their correct order.[150] If the longer recension were original, it would be hard to account for the writing process seen on fol. 379v: this hypothesis would have the author transcribe the Clementine canon and then his own glosses into the margins, missing glosses to two *lemmata*, which he then adds in the upper margin; the result being to produce a final *Summa* text identical to the original in *"Defecerunt."* On the other hand, the briefer recension does not print the Clementine text and is much shorter at the corresponding place.[151] If the briefer recension is original, then the process of composition suggested by the autographs becomes lucid: the whole of *Summa* 3.17 represents an expansion and development of material treated with deliberate brevity in his earlier *summula* on confession. The process of drafting a lengthier and more substantial treatment for the *Summa* left the footprints just described in the autographs. It appears likely that an editor later replaced the original chapters of *"Defecerunt"* by substituting the longer treatment from the *Summa*, to produce a more compendious and up-to-date confessional manual, yet still short enough to function as a handbook.[152]

The second part of the *"Defecerunt"* is an *Interrogatorium* providing question-prompts for confessors. It proceeds through three lists: the Ten Commandments, the capital vices, and the various states of life. Obviously, the treatment of the capital vices and the various states of life correspond to the main material of the *Summa* parts 2 and 3. However, there is no clear evidence in the autograph of part 2 to indicate dependence on the *"Defecerunt."* Although the scheme of the capital vices is the same, their order of treatment is different, as is the approach to the material – for example, its development *per modum predicationis*, alien to the short *summula* form of the *"Defecerunt."* In length there is no comparison.

149 Ballerini, 3:954.

150 Antoninus, *Summa confessionalis* (Lyon, 1546), 32–6.

151 Antoninus, *Confessionale: Defecerunt* (Cologne, 1470), c. 4ff.; idem., *Libellus de audientia confessionum* (Venice, 1472), 11–17.

152 The longer recension of *"Defecerunt"* is about 400 octavo pages in moderate-sized type. The shorter recension averages about 250 octavo pages in large type.

As for part 3 of the *Summa*, there is what appears to be an earlier draft of the opening of this part on M_2 fol. 17r. This folio and the several following show a base text written in a very neat and upright *cursiva* script, with red highlighting and rubrication marks – which are never present on the typical page written by Antoninus's hand. The base text has been heavily revised and annotated by more than one hand; the principal revisions, however, are by Antoninus. The base text begins:

> *Post tractatum de singulis uitiis sequitur tertia pars de quibusdam statibus hominum. Et primo agetur de coniugatis seu de matrimonio. Secundo de dominis et bellis et represaliis. Quinto de medicis. Sexto de magistris et doctoribus. Septimo de clericis secularibus. Octauo* (corrected to *Nono*) *de religiosis. Nono* (corrected to *Decimo*) *de confessoribus.* (inserted in the right margin by hand A:) *Undecimo de predicatoribus. Duodecimo de prelatis. Cui addetur breuis tractatus de uirtutibus.*

Immediately after this, there is the former beginning of a chapter, which has been deleted by Antoninus: *Et quantum ad primum uidendum est primo de impedimentis eius.* … A tie mark then directs the reader to the upper margin, where Antoninus has written a new incipit for the chapter: *Relinquet homo patrem et matrem et adherebit uxori sue* … This is the beginning of what is now *Summa* 3.1.2 (*de impedimento matrimonii quod dicitur error persone*). At some later time, Antoninus drafted a preamble to part 3, which begins *Astitit Regina*, and a new opening chapter of title 1 *de statu coniugatorum*, which begins *Beatus es*. These are found at later places in the autograph, commencing on M_2 fol. 38r and 49v.

This folio appears to represent an early stage in the planning and drafting of the *Summa*; its dependence on Antoninus's previous works is not evident. The order of items in the list just quoted is not the same as in either recension of *"Defecerunt"* or in the final version of the *Summa*. Nor does *"Defecerunt"* have a treatise on the virtues following the *interrogatorium* based on *status*. The *Summa* does have a treatise on the virtues in its fourth part, but in the final version it follows the treatise on ecclesiastical censures and the several other titles which conclude part 3. Another as yet unexplained fact is that on the final folios of what is now *Summa* part 2, there appears to be another draft of the opening of part 3. On M_1 fol. 393r, an unidentified hand writes a chapter incipit: *Relinquet homo patrem et matrem et adherebit uxori*. In the left margin the word *uacat* stands next to this paragraph. In the upper margin, Antoninus has written: *Tertia pars principalis operis*.

5. De censuris ecclesiasticis sive de excommunicationibus *at* Summa *3.24–9*

The clearest example of a preexisting treatise which was transcribed directly into the *Summa* is Antoninus's *Tractatus de censuris ecclesiasticis sive de excommunicationibus*. This corresponds to *Summa* 3.24–9 in Ballerini's edition, 3.25–30 in the autographs. In the autographs, this whole sequence of titles was copied by scribes other than Antoninus. It begins on fol. 538r in a fresh quire. A cursory look shows it was copied by a secretary, not Antoninus. It displays a different mise-en-page, with ample space left for initials; the page is rubricated and marked with red highlights. It bears a few marginal notes which may be, but are not certainly, by A; some of them have the appearance more of a user of the book than of its author, for example on fol. 542r: *Nota.* On fol. 543r and further, large red initials are found rather than blank spaces. Antoninus has made some additions on fol. 548v, and there is also a supplement in the hand of Lapaccini; but it goes on from there with few such revisions. A new quire and a new hand begin on fol. 554 and this proceeds until fol. 569v. Here is the end of this quire and a catchword; on fol. 570 the text is taken up again from approximately the same place, but in a more cursive hand with a different mise-en-page, notably lacking red. On fol. 575r the text breaks off again and the hand of Lapaccini writes: *uolue cartam et uide in principio alterius faciei.* On the verso there are two additions by Lapaccini, and then the text resumes on fol. 576r. Although a new quire begins at fol. 587 and again at fol. 603, it appears to be the same hand all the way to fol. 612r. A few notes by Lapaccini are found, but the only significant revisions are from fol. 591r to fol. 592v, in the hand of Antoninus. At the foot of fol. 612v, which is blank, is another catchword, and on fol. 613 the final section of this treatise begins. The text is copied here in an elegant *cursiva* hand and decorated with red initials. The treatise ends on fol. 625r.

At least three different hands copied this treatise, and the transitions from one hand to the next always come at the beginning of a new quire; sometimes there is blank space at the end of the last quire. This suggests that Antoninus divided his treatise into three sections and assigned each section to a different secretary, all of whom probably copied simultaneously. This was a common method for copying long works, in both universities and Dominican houses; it was famously used by St Thomas Aquinas.[153] After his secretaries had copied the original treatise, Antoninus reviewed the work with the help of Lapaccini, revising, expanding, and supplementing, to produce the final version which stands in the *Summa.*

6. Sermo de indulgentiis *at* Summa *1.10.3 and the Writing of Part 1*

Many chapters of the *Summa* take the form of sermons, and in some cases there are extant manuscripts which witness the text of an earlier or later sermon by Antoninus on the same topic. These are, of course, of interest to scholars who wish to study the development of Antoninus's ideas and rhetoric, because they can compare his treatment of the same subject matter in two different contexts of time,

153 Derolez, *Gothic Manuscript Books*, 29–31; Jean Destrez, *La pecia dans les manuscrits universitaires du XIIIe et du XIVe siècle*; Dondaine, *Secrétaires de Saint Thomas.*

place, and circumstance.[154] In the case of the chapter *de indulgentiis* (1.10.3), in addition to the *Summa* version there are also extant manuscripts and early printed editions of a *Sermo de indulgentiis*.[155] At this point a comparison of these versions has not been carried out. However, the autograph version in *N* does prompt some conjectures about the development of this sermon, and, from there, about the composition of part 1 of the *Summa* as a whole.

The *de indulgentiis* is one of several sermons copied into part 1 of the *Summa* by a secretary, in this case by Giuliano Lapaccini. This is a chapter of what is described in the autograph as the *Libellus de peccato*, embracing titles 7 to 10 of part 1.[156] The first folios of this *Libellus* are written by Antoninus.[157] The next thirteen folios are written by a different, unidentified, scribe. Giuliano Lapaccini takes over at the bottom of 200r, writing the last three paragraphs of a chapter which ends on the verso. The next chapter, *De purgatorio*, was copied very neatly by Giuliano Lapaccini, with no significant annotations added. It bears a rubric indicating that it is a sermon for All Souls Day: *pro die animarum*.[158] The *De indulgentiis* begins on 204r, headed by two rubrics. The first: *pro feria 5 post dominicam de passione, super illud: Dimissa sunt ei peccata etc.*[159] The second: *Pro dominica 19 post festum Trinitatis, super illud: Confide fili remictuntur tibi peccata etc.*[160] The first two folios of this chapter are written by Lapaccini, again with very few annotations. This section ends halfway down fol. 205v. On 206r a new section is introduced, written by Antoninus himself: *Demum uidendum est de indulgentia plenaria*.[161] This is the final part of the chapter, embracing several sections, all dealing with plenary indulgences. On the last face (fol. 209v), Antoninus's hand leaves off after writing the first five lines, and Lapaccini takes over, finishing the paragraph which Antoninus had left in progress and then copying the final paragraph, which begins *Notandum*

154 This is a major avenue of Peter Howard's research. See, for example, his *Beyond the Written Word*, ch. 7 ("Sermons and *Summa*"); Howard, *Creating Magnificence in Renaissance Florence*.

155 Orlandi, *Bibliografia Antoniniana*, 95; Lapidge et al., *CALMA*, Antoni 1.1.5; Kaeppeli and Panella, *SOPMA*, no. 242. It is called in these reference works a *Tractatus de indulgentiis*, but in form it is a sermon, and several of the manuscripts listed in Orlandi describe it as such. The incipits of these other manuscript witnesses are identical to the *Summa* chapter.

156 "Incipit libellus J intitulatur de peccato. Titulus septimus." *N* fol. 179r *in marg. super.*, hand G.

157 A summary of what follows is provided here. Hand A: *N* fol. 179r–187v; unidentified hand: *N* fol. 188r–200r; hand G: *N* fol. 200r–205v; hand A: 206r–209v; hand G: 209v.

158 *N* fol. 201r *in marg. super.*, hand G.

159 Note that the sermon for this day in Antoninus's Lenten cycle of 1427 or 1430 does not correspond to the *sermo de indulgentiis*. Orlandi, *Bibliografia Antoniniana*, 126–7.

160 *N* fol. 204r *in marg. super.*, hand G. Another manuscript collection of Antoninus's sermons contains a sermon for this Sunday; it does not correspond to the *sermo de indulgentiis*. Orlandi, *Bibliografia Antoniniana*, 149.

161 *N* fol. 206r, hand A.

de Iubilee.[162] Lapaccini reached the bottom of the folio with two lines of the chapter still left to copy, and inserted them in the upper margin. The explicit here is identical to the chapter printed in Ballerini: *determinationem uniuersalis ecclesie.*[163] Within the section of this chapter written by Antoninus himself, there is a datable reference, discussed above, which puts the composition of this chapter between 1450 (modern style) and 1454 (Florentine style), i.e., after significant portions of parts 2 and 3 were written.[164]

Taking a larger view of part 1 as a whole: the first half of part 1 (*N* fol. 8r–209v) is written by a rather bewildering variety of hands. Antoninus's hand is still visible frequently and for large stretches, probably amounting to more folios than any other single hand; but very much mingled with multiple different hands which are similar enough that it is not easy to distinguish them. By contrast, the majority of the *Tractatus de legibus* (*N* fol. 210r–323v) is written by Antoninus: of about 113 folios, roughly 25 were written by hands other than A.

In advance of collating extant witnesses of the *de indulgentiis*, the following hypothesis may be offered cautiously. Antoninus wrote what are now part 1's titles 11–20 (*de legibus*) earlier than he wrote titles 1–10 (*de anima, de peccato*). If Antoninus started composing the *Summa* as a whole at part 1, then the *de legibus* would be the oldest portion of the *Summa*: it may be conjectured that part 1, titles 11–20 were written at some time between about 1440 and 1450. Titles 1–10 were written after titles 11–20, and it is certain from the remark in *Summa* 1.10.3 that these titles were not completed before 1450. This is congruent with the state of the autograph manuscript: it may be expected that Antoninus had more scribes at his disposal after his elevation to the archiepiscopacy in 1446; and, indeed, the autograph manuscripts show that the assistance of scribes was more frequently employed in drafting titles 1–10 than titles 11–20. In the case of the chapter *de indulgentiis*, it appears likely that Antoninus had his collaborator Giuliano Lapaccini transcribe a preexisting *sermo de indulgentiis*. To this base, he added a new treatment of the plenary indulgence, drafting this original section with his own hand, including the note about the Jubilee indulgence of Nicholas V, who was reigning at the time. Antoninus either dictated the final paragraph of the chapter to Lapaccini or had it copied from a previously written discussion of the Jubilee. It may be that the older *sermo de indulgentiis* ended with a treatment of the Jubilee, and in preparing the *Summa* version Antoninus opted to draft a new discussion of plenary indulgences to insert immediately before that point.

162 *N* fol. 209v, hand G.

163 *N* fol. 209v, hand G; Ballerini, 1:612.

164 *N* fol. 209r, hand A. Reproduced in Ballerini, 1:609–10.

4. Conclusion: The *Summa* as *Recollectorium*

The *Summa* is indeed a *Collecting-Box*. Its author called it such, i.e., *Recollectorium*, while he was at work on it, and it was so called in at least one other contemporary manuscript witness. What the author collected in the box goes beyond what he himself outlined in his preamble to the work. It is, as he said, a collection "in the tradition of the friars" of material apt "for preaching, for hearing confessions, and for consulting in the court of souls," taken up from "doctors in theology or experts in law."[165] It is, therefore, a kind of miniature library of *pastoralia*. It is also, however, the definitive and complete collection of all of Antoninus's own writings and, it may be said, of his theological, moral, and ascetic teaching. This is seen in the incorporation into the *Summa* of Antoninus's earlier written treatises and *summula*. Some of Antoninus's preached doctrine was also incorporated, as seen in the *sermo de indulgentiis* copied into the *Summa*. It is seen, finally, in the author's conception of his three-volume *Chronicles*, the last written undertaking of his life, as the fifth part of the *Summa*: as an adjunct to and application of the gift of knowledge with which part 4 closes, "to illustrate from the past how men should live in this world."[166] In sum, Antoninus conceived his *Summa* as encompassing in some form everything he wrote since he first felt the need to begin writing, around mid-life. All of it was meant to provide a library of moral teaching and prepared material for the poor preacher, confessor, or pastor who has not the leisure and wealth for roaming through books.

> Pro ipsis conficiendis plures uigilias et labores contemplationesque simul et orationes ipse sanctus operatus est.[167]

> For the writing of these that holy man toiled through many sleepness nights, many labours, much contemplation, and many prayers.

165 Antoninus, *Summa*, 1 *prohemium* (*N* fol. 3v–4r, hand G).

166 Walker's phrasing in "Antoninus, St."

167 Alessandro Capocchi, OP, at *N* fol. IIv–IIIr.

3 The Scholastic Tradition on Justice in Buying and Selling

Preamble. Antoninus's Authorities in the *Summa* as a Whole

Before approaching the main subject of this chapter, it is opportune to take a glance at the authors and works whom Antoninus cites as authorities for his doctrine in the *Summa* as a whole. To return to the preamble of the *Summa*: there, immediately following the section translated above in chapter 2, the author himself provides a list of his principal authorities.[1] A translation of this passage is provided now, with the individual authors and works identified in the footnotes.

> But the following testimonies are incorporated in proof of the aforesaid matters, beyond the authorities of the divine Scriptures and the sacred canons, which are frequently adduced, and the individual doctrines of the ancient doctors of the Church, Augustine,[2] Jerome,[3] Gregory,[4] Ambrose,[5] Chrysostom,[6] Basil,[7] Isidore,[8]

1 Antoninus also discusses the authors and books most useful for preaching and teaching doctrine in *Summa*, 3.18 *de statu predicatorum et inquisitorum*, c. 3, c. 5, and esp. c. 6 *de modis dilatandi materiam et libris authenticis ecclesie et de apocrifis*. In the autograph, this is chapter 3.19.5, and it begins on M_2 fol. 190v, proceeding to 192v. On these chapters, see the thorough discussion in Howard, *Beyond the Written Word*, ch. 4 "The Preacher's Art." Antoninus also discusses many of these authors in his *Chronicles*, tit. 23–4 about the Dominican and Franciscan orders, on which see Howard, *Beyond the Written Word*, 54–7; Walker, *"Chronicles" of Saint Antoninus*, 93–100.

2 St Augustine (Augustinus Aurelius), 354–430, bishop of Hippo Regius. For names of late antique and medieval authors, the English form is taken from *The Oxford Dictionary of the Christian Church*; Vauchez, *Encyclopedia of the Middle Ages*; or *The Oxford Dictionary of the Middle Ages*; the Latin form is taken from *Bibliotheca Scriptorum Latinorum Medii Recentiorisque Aevi*.

3 St Jerome (Hieronymus Stridonius), c. 345–420, biblical scholar.

4 St Gregory the Great (Gregorius I, Gregorius Magnus), c. 540–604, pope from 590.

5 St Ambrose (Ambrosius Mediolanensis), c. 339–397, bishop of Milan.

6 St John Chrysostom (Iohannes Chrysostomus), c. 347–407, bishop of Constantinople.

7 St Basil the Great (Basilius Caesariensis), c. 330–79 (or possibly slightly earlier), bishop of Caesarea.

8 St Isidore (Isidorus Hispalensis), c. 560–636, bishop of Seville and metropolitan of Baetica.

Bernard,[9] Anselm,[10] etc., [and] sometimes of the pagans, Plato,[11] Aristotle,[12] Tully,[13] and Seneca.[14]

The determinations and statements are added of many moderns in theology or of experts in law, whose names are these.

In theology: St Thomas, whom I set before all others in the things which he commented on,[15] Albert the Great,[16] Peter of la Palud,[17] Peter of Tarentaise who was Pope Innocent V,[18] Durandus,[19] Cardinal Hugh,[20] William Peraldus in his *Summa of Vices and Virtues*,[21] Master Giovanni Cardinal Dominici of Florence,[22] Raniero in the *Pisan Summa*,[23] Vincent in the *Mirror of History*.[24] All the aforesaid

---

9 St Bernard (Bernardus Claraevallensis), 1090–1153, abbot of Clairvaux.

10 St Anselm (Anselmus Cantuariensis), 1033–1109, archbishop of Canterbury.

11 Plato (Lat. Plato, Gk Plătōn), c. 427–347 BC, Greek philosopher of Athens, founder of the Academy. For ancient Greek and Latin authors, see *The Oxford Companion to Classical Literature*, *The Oxford Encyclopedia of Ancient Greece and Rome*, and *The Oxford Classical Dictionary*.

12 Aristotle (Aristoteles), 384–322 BC, Greek philosopher, pupil of Plato.

13 Marcus Tullius Cicero (Cicero M. Tullius), 106–43 BC, Roman orator and statesman. Known by the name Tully (Tullius) down to the early nineteenth century (*Oxford Companion to Classical Literature*, s.v. "Tully").

14 Lucius Annaeus Seneca the Younger (Seneca philosophus), c. 4 BC–AD 65, Roman philosopher, moralist, and tragic poet.

15 St Thomas Aquinas (Thomas de Aquino), OP, 1224/5–1274, philosopher and theologian, "Doctor Communis" or "Doctor Angelicus."

16 St Albert the Great (Albertus Magnus), OP, c. 1200–1280, theologian, philosopher, and scientist.

17 Peter of la Palud (Petrus de Palude), OP, 1275/80–1342, theologian and canonist, Latin patriarch of Jerusalem from 1329.

18 Peter of Tarentaise (Innocentius V), OP, c. 1224–22 June 1276, theologian, pope from 11 January 1276.

19 Durandus of Saint-Pourçain (Durandus de Sancto Porciano), OP, c. 1275–1334, philosopher, "Doctor Modernus" or "Doctor Resolutissimus."

20 Hugh of St Cher (Hugo de Sancto Caro), OP, c. 1190–1263/4, theologian and cardinal. On Hugh of St-Cher's manual for confessors, see Mulchahey, *Dominican Education*, 539–40.

21 William Peraldus (Guillelmus Peraldus), OP, c. 1200–1271. On Peraldus's *Summa de vitiis et virtutibus*, see ibid., 540–1.

22 Bl. John Dominici (Iohannes Dominici de Florentia), OP, 1355/56–1419, prior of Santa Maria Novella in Florence 1385–7, vicar general of the reformed convents in Italy 1393–9, founder of San Domenico of Fiesole in 1406, cardinal bishop of Ragusa. On Dominici, see above, ch. 1.

23 Two works are confounded here. The true author of the *Summa pisana* (*Summa de casibus conscientiae*) is Bartolomeo of San Concordio (Bartholomaeus de Sancto Concordio), OP, 1260/62–1347, jurist and theologian. Raniero of Pisa (Rainerus Iordanis de Pisis), OP, † 1348, theologian, wrote a work (*Pantheologia*) sometimes described as a *Summa casuum conscientiae*. On these two authors and their works, see Langholm, *Merchant in the Confessional*, 123–30.

24 Vincent of Beauvais (Vincentius Bellovacensis), OP, c. 1190/94–c. 1264. His *Speculum maius*, a vast popular encyclopedia and florilegium, is divided into three parts: *Speculum naturale*, *Speculum doctrinale*, *Speculum historiale*. To these was added an inauthentic *Speculum morale* towards the end of the thirteenth century. Antoninus's approach to writing his *Chronicles* drew much inspiration from Vincent of Beauvais (Walker, *"Chronicles" of Saint Antoninus*, 55–7); it is not far-fetched to suppose this to be true of the *Summa* as well, since it is a kind of moral-theological encyclopedia.

are of the Order of Preachers. Cardinal Bonaventure,[25] Richard of Middleton,[26] Alexander of Hales,[27] John Scot,[28] Nicholas of Lyre,[29] of the Order of Friars Minor. Augustine of Rome in his *Quodlibetal questions*,[30] Augustine of Ancona on the power of the Church,[31] Gregory of Rimini,[32] of the Order of Hermits [of St Augustine].

In law: in glossing the *Decretum*, Hugo,[33] Bartholomew of Brescia,[34] Bernard;[35] in glossing the *Decretals*, Raymond of the Order of Preachers in his oldest *Summa* of them all,[36] Innocent IV,[37] Hostiensis in his *Apparatus* and *Summa*,[38] William in his

---

25 St Bonaventure (Bonaventura de Balneoregio), OFM, 1217/21–1274, theologian, master general of the Franciscans, cardinal bishop of Albano, "Doctor Seraphicus."

26 Richard of Middleton (Richardus de Mediavilla), OFM, c. 1249–1308, philosopher and theologian.

27 Alexander of Hales (Alexander Halensis), OFM, c. 1186–1245, theologian, "Doctor Irrefragabilis."

28 Bl. John Duns Scotus (Iohannes Duns Scotus), OFM, c. 1265/66–1308, philosopher and theologian, "Doctor Subtilis" or "Doctor Marianus."

29 Nicholas of Lyre (Nicolaus de Lyra), OFM, 1270/75–1349, biblical exegete.

30 More correctly Giles of Rome (Aegidius Romanus), OESA, c. 1243/47–1316, philosopher, author of a large number of *Quaestiones*, archbishop of Bourges, "Doctor Fundatissimus."

31 Augustine of Ancona (Augustinus de Ancona), OESA, c. 1270/75–1328, theologian, author of a *Summa de potestate ecclesiastica*.

32 Gregory of Rimini (Gregorius Ariminensis), OESA, 1300/1305–1358, philosopher, "Doctor Authenticus."

33 Huguccio (Hugutio Ferrariensis), fl. 1180–1210, canonist, author of an extremely influential *Summa decretorum*, bishop of Ferrara. On jurists, see Pennington et al., *Bio-Bibliographical Guide to Medieval and Early Modern Jurists*; Brundage, *Medieval Canon Law*, esp. appendix 2, "Major Canonists of the Classical Period: Biographical Notes"; Clarence Smith, *Medieval Law Teachers and Writers*; Hartmann and Pennington, eds., *The History of Medieval Canon Law in the Classical Period, 1140–1234*.

34 Bartholomew of Brescia (Bartholomaeus Brixiensis), fl. 1234–1258, canonist, updated the *Glossa ordinaria* on the *Decretum* originally compiled by Johannes Teutonicus.

35 Bernard of Pavia (Bernardus Papiensis), † 1213, canonist, the most important twelfth-century decretist after Huguccio (Pennington et al., *Bio-Bibliography*, s.v. "Bernardus Papiensis"), author of glosses on the *Decretum* which were the basis of the *Glossa ordinaria* until Johannes Teutonicus. Bishop of Pavia.

36 St Raymond of Peñafort (Raymundus de Pennaforti), OP, c. 1180–1275, canonist, compiler of the *Liber Extra* promulgated by Gregory IX in 1234, master general of the Dominican Order 1238–40, author of several *Summae* on penance, canon law, and moral theology. On Peñafort's *Summae*, see Mulchahey, *Dominican Education*, 533–9; Langholm, *Merchant in the Confessional*, 32–40.

37 Sinibaldo de' Fieschi (Innocentius IV), before 1200–1254, canonist, author of an influential *Apparatus* on the *Liber Extra*, pope from 1243.

38 Henry of Susa (Henricus de Segusio), c. 1200–1271, canonist, author of a *Summa* and a *Lectura* (*Apparatus*) on the *Liber Extra*, chaplain to Innocent IV, cardinal bishop of Ostia, hence the nickname "Hostiensis."

Speculum,[39] the Archdeacon in his *Rosary*,[40] Giovanni d'Andrea in his *Novella* and the gloss on the *Sext* and the *Clementines*,[41] Giovanni da Legnano,[42] Giovanni Calderini,[43] Giovanni da Imola the most recent doctor of all,[44] Pietro d'Ancarano,[45] Lorenzo Ridolfi in his *Treatise on Usury*,[46] Francesco Zabarella,[47] Nicholas the abbot of Sicily,[48] Antonio da Budrio,[49] Peter of the Order of Friars Minor in his *Directory of Law*,[50]

---

39 William Durand (Guillelmus Duranti senior, dictus Speculator), 1236–1296, canonist, auditor general of the Rota, bishop of Mende, author of the *Speculum iudiciale*, "the most widely used procedural treatise of the middle ages" (Pennington et al., *Bio-Bibliography*, s.v. "Guillelmus Durandus"), hence the nickname "the Speculator."

40 Guido de Baysio (Guido de Baysio), c. 1246/56–1313, canonist, author of *apparatus*, *quaestiones*, and *tractatus*, but most famously an enormous commentary on the *Decretum*, the last produced in the Middle Ages, called *Rosarium Decretorum*. Archdeacon of Bologna, hence the nickname "Archidiaconus."

41 Giovanni d'Andrea (Iohannes Andreae), c. 1270–1348, lay canonist, author of extensive commentaries on the *Corpus iuris canonici*, including two commentaries on the *Liber Extra*, the later one (*Novella*) being the more famous, the *Glossae ordinariae* on the *Sext* and the *Clementines*, as well as *tractatus*, *consilia*, and *quaestiones* on the rules of law (*Quaestiones mercuriales*). He is nicknamed *iuris canonici fons et tuba*.

42 Giovanni da Legnano (Iohannes de Lignano), c. 1320–1383, doctor of both laws, author of a *Concordantia canonum*, *Summa de confessione*, *tractatus*, *consilia*, etc.

43 Giovanni Calderini (Iohannes Calderinus), † 1365, canonist, author of *repetitiones*, *tractatus*, *consilia*, etc. His son also became a canonist, Gaspare Calderini senior (Gaspar Calderinus senior), 1345–1399; the *Repetitiones et distinctiones in Decretales* of father and son are transmitted together in manuscripts.

44 Giovanni da Imola (Iohannes de Imola), c. 1372–1436, doctor of both laws, author of commentaries and *repetitiones* on canon law, *consilia*, etc. In fact, of the jurists listed, Niccolò de Tudeschi is the most recent.

45 Pietro d'Ancarano (Petrus de Ancharano), c. 1333–1415, doctor of both laws, author of commentaries, lectures, *repetitiones*, *consilia*, etc.

46 Lorenzo Ridolfi (Laurentius de Rodulphis), 1362/63–1443, lay canonist and prominent Florentine statesman; his best-known work is his *Tractatus de usuris*, "the most influential study of usury and interest in the later middle ages" (Pennington et al., *Bio-Bibliography*, s.v. "Laurentius de Ridolfis"). On Ridolfi and for an edition of his *Questio de monte* from the *Tractatus*, see Armstrong, *Usury and Public Debt in Early Renaissance Florence*.

47 Francesco Zabarella (Franciscus Zabarella), 1360–1417, doctor of both laws, author of commentaries, *repetitiones*, and *consilia* on canon law as well as an instructional work on studying law, cardinal of antipope John XXIII.

48 Niccolò de Tudeschi (Nicolaus de Tudeschis), OSB, 1386–1445, canonist also learned in theology, author of a *lectura* on the *Liber Extra* and other *lecturae*, *repetitiones*, *consilia*, etc., abbot of St Maria de Maniaco in Messina until 1435, thereafter archbishop of Palermo, hence the nicknames "Abbas Siculus" and "Panormitanus."

49 Antonio da Budrio (Antonius de Butrio), c. 1360–1408, doctor of both laws, author of commentaries, treatises, *consilia*, etc. on canon law.

50 Peter Quesnel (Petrus de Quesnell), OFM, † 1299, author of a *Directorium iuris in foro conscientiae et iudiciali*. On this work, see Langholm, *Merchant in the Confessional*, 66–8.

Lapo da Castiglionchio,[51] Frederic of Siena in his consultations,[52] Bartolo,[53] Baldo.[54]

Examples are put forward from histories: Gregory in the *Dialogue*,[55] Vincent in the *Speculum*,[56] Martin in the *Chronicles*,[57] Valerius Maximus,[58] Paul Orosius,[59] *The Lives of the Fathers*,[60] *The Lives of the Brothers*,[61] *The Seven Gifts*.[62]

Many others of the wise are cited, but because not so frequently, I have not taken care to name them.[63]

---

51 Lapo da Castiglionchio (Lapus Castelliunculus senior), doctorate c. 1353, † 1381, canonist, author of *consilia, repetitiones, tractatus*, and *allegationes iuris*.

52 Federico Petrucci (Fridericus Petruccius de Senis), doctorate c. 1321, † c. 1348, canonist, author of *consilia*.

53 Bartolo da Sassoferrato (Bartholus de Saxoferrato), 1313/14–1357, civilian, author of extensive commentaries on the *Corpus iuris civilis* and treatises on civil law.

54 Baldo degli Ubaldi (Baldus de Ubaldis), 1319/27–1400, canonist, author of commentaries and treatises on canon law as well as a vast number of *consilia*.

55 St Gregory the Great (Gregorius I, Gregorius Magnus), *Dialogorum libri IV*. On Gregory the Great, see above, note 4.

56 Vincent of Beauvais (Vincentius Bellovacensis), OP, *Speculum historiale*, on which see above, note 24.

57 Martin of Troppau (Martinus Oppaviensis), OP, c. 1230–1279, *Chronica summorum pontificum et imperatorum* (*Chronicon pontificum et imperatorum*). Martin was a Dominican of the province of Poland, chaplain and penitentiary to Clement IV, and in 1278 was consecrated archbishop of Gnesen, but died on his way there. The *Chronica* were meant to provide a chronological parallel of popes and emperors for use in connection with the *Decretum* of Gratian (Walker, *"Chronicles" of Saint Antoninus*, 58–60). On Antoninus's use of this and the preceding two histories in his *Chronicles*, see ibid., 53–102; Morçay, *Chroniques*, I–XII.

58 Valerius Maximus (Valerius Maximus), fl. c. 27–31, *Factorum et dictorum memorabilium libri IX*.

59 Orosius (Orosius Paulus), fl. e. fifth century, † after 418, *Historiarum adversus paganos libri septem*, written c. 417.

60 Probably *Vitae patrum*, an anonymous work whose tradition goes back to the sixth century or earlier, on which see Hwang, "*Vitas* (*vitae*) *patrum*."

61 Probably Gerard de Frachet (Gerhardus de Fracheto), OP, 1205–1271, *Vitae fratrum Ordinis Praedicatorum*, on which see Walker, *"Chronicles" of Saint Antoninus*, 61.

62 Perhaps Stephen of Bourbon (Stephanus de Borbone), OP, 1185/90–1260/61, *Tractatus de diversis materiis praedicabilibus ordinatis et distinctis in VII partibus secundum VII dona Spiritus Sancti*. Stephen of Bourbon's work is a collection of exempla, containing nearly three thousand narratives, as well as biblical and patristic citations, organized according to the seven gifts of the Holy Spirit (Berlioz, "Stephen of Bourbon").

63 "Que autem inducuntur testimonia ad probationem dictorum, ultra auctoritates diuinarum Scripturarum et sacrorum canonum que frequenter apponuntur, et sententias proprias antiquorum doctorum ecclesie [ecclesia *N*] Augustini, Ieronymi, Gregorii, Ambrosii, Crisostomi, Basilii, Ysidori, Bernardi, Anselmi etc., aliquando gentilium Platonis, Aristotelis, Tullii et Senece. Addiciuntur determinationes et dicta multorum modernorum in theologia uel iure peritissimorum, quorum hec sunt nomina. In theologia: Sanctus Tomas, quem omnibus prepono in suis dictis, Albertus magnus, Petrus de Palude, Petrus de Tarantasio, qui fuit Innocentius V, Durandus, Hugo cardinalis, Vilielmus Peraltus in Summa uitiorum et uirtutem, Dominus Ioannes

Several observations about this list are in order; first, about the authors included as authorities. The list of ancient doctors is traditional and presents nothing exceptional; in the High and late Middle Ages, the patristic period was considered to have closed with St Bernard († 1153) as the last Latin father. The inclusion of the pagans Plato, Aristotle, Cicero, and Seneca is likewise typical, particularly in a *Summa* on moral doctrine. The list of sources for histories shows a combination of ancient sources with thirteenth-century Dominican authors; the blend is somewhat different from the main sources employed in composing the *Chronicles.*[64] Setting aside the ancients and the historians, the lists of theologians and jurists make for an interesting comparison. As to number, out of the total forty-one individual authors named, nineteen are theologians and twenty-two are jurists. Theologians are exclusively represented by members of the mendicant orders: Dominicans (11), Franciscans (5), and Hermits of Saint Augustine (3).[65] All of the theological authors cited date from the century circa 1250 to 1350, with the sole exception of Giovanni Dominici, OP († 1419), Antoninus's mentor. The earliest theologian is Alexander of Hales, OFM († 1245); the latest, apart from Dominici, is Gregory of Rimini, OESA († 1358). There is a striking similarity here to the results of Langholm's survey of pre-Reformation penitential manuals:

> Omitting authors antedating Gratian and Peter Lombard … a complete list of primary authorities quoted in this study runs to upward of forty names … [The predominance of early authors] is most striking in the case of the theologians, who don't count a single name of any significance after c. 1350.[66]

Dominici cardinalis de Florentia, Raynerius in Summa pisanus, Vincentius in Speculo ystoriali. Ordinis predicatorum omnes isti prenominati. Bonauentura cardinalis, Riccardus de Mediauilla, Alexander de Ales, Ioannes Scotus, Nicolaus de Lira, ordinis minorum. Augustinus de Roma in Quodlibetis, Augustinus de Ancona de potestate ecclesie, Gregorius de Arimino, ordinis eremitarum. In iure: in glossa Decreti, Hugo, Bartolomeus Brixiensis, Bernardus; in glossa Decretalium, Raymundus ordinis predicatorum in Summa sua antiquissima omnium, Innocentius IV, Hostiensis in Apparatu et Summa, Gulielmus in Speculo, Archidiaconus in Rosario, Ioannes Andreas in Nouella et glossa Sexti et Clementinarum, Ioannes de Lignano, Ioannes Calderini, Ioannes de Imola omnium nouissimus doctor, Petrus de Ancarano, Laurentius de Ridulfis in Tractatu de usuris, Franciscus Zamberellus [Çambẽs *N*], Nicolaus abbas de Sicilia, Antonius de Butrio, Petrus ordinis minorum in Directorio iuris, Lapus de Castiliunco, Fredericus de Senis in consiliis, Bartolus, Baldus. De ystoriis exempla ponuntur: Gregorius in Dyalogo, Vincentius in Speculo, Martinus in Cronicis, Valerius maximus, Paulus Orosius, De uita patrum, De uita fratrum, De septem donis. Allegantur et multi alii sapientes, sed quia non ita frequenter non curaui nominare." Antoninus, *Summa,* 1 *prohemium* (*N* fol. 4v–5r, hand G).

64 Walker, *"Chronicles" of Saint Antoninus,* 53–102.

65 The Hermits of Saint Augustine were conceived as a quasi-mendicant order: "From 1256, [Alexander IV] decided on the creation of a new order, likened to the mendicant orders …" Baloup, "Hermits of Saint Augustine, Order of."

66 Langholm, *Merchant in the Confessional,* 258–9.

This shows that a canon of theological authorities for moral theology and penitential doctrine was rapidly established after 1350, and remained a stable tradition thereafter, with the canon not admitting any new post-1350 writers for a long time. Antoninus here does not show himself to depart from this theological tradition in the authors he puts forward as his authorities; however, this matter is somewhat more complex than it first appears, as will be seen shortly.

On the other hand, the list of jurists shows a marked contrast to Langholm's findings. Langholm saw the same "predominance of quite early authors" in citations of jurists:

> The case of the canonists is not very different. Most of the sources used date from the thirteenth century or earlier ... The most prominent exception to this overall reliance on early canonistic authorities is the late Italian summists' frequent use of Panormitanus, who died in 1445.[67]

This is not the case for Antoninus's list of juristic authorities. The jurists cited – all canonists or doctors of both laws, except for the great civilian Bartolo († 1357) – form a continuous series, beginning with the famed decretist Huguccio († 1210), continuing with decretists and decretalists of the thirteenth century (e.g., Bartholomew of Brescia [† 1258], Hostiensis [† 1271]), through fourteenth-century authors of commentaries, treatises, and *consilia* (e.g., Guido de Baysio [† 1313], Giovanni d'Andrea [† 1348], Baldo degli Ubaldi [† 1400]), and reaching Antoninus's contemporaries Giovanni da Imola († 1436) and Niccolò de Tudeschi (Panormitanus), OSB († 1445). Although Antoninus's coverage of the canonical tradition is unusually extensive, the prominence of canon lawyers as authorities in the *Summa* is in harmony with the overall character of moral-theological writing in the late Middle Ages, particularly in manuals and *summae* for confessors. Once again Langholm's observations are germane:

> I once characterized the major names in medieval economic thought as theologians writing with a sidelong glance at canon law. This description will have to be considerably modified and clarified if it is to be applied to authors of penitential handbooks and if the period to be examined is extended from the Middle Ages through the entire pre-Reformation era. Many of the authors reviewed looked rather more directly to canon law and not a few looked beyond canon law to its basis in Roman law. The legal element in penitential doctrine is further enhanced by the fact that much of the theological source material on which it built was formally legalistic.[68]

---

67 Ibid., 259.
68 Ibid., 258.

The legal mould in which moral theology developed within the scholastic tradition has often been noted;[69] it will be apparent in the course of this chapter and is reinforced by the prominence of canon-law texts and lawyers among Antoninus's sources.[70] For the moment it is sufficient to notice that Antoninus stands out from the main stream of the moral-theological and penitential tradition for the breadth and chronological coverage of his engagement with canonical jurisprudence.[71]

Antoninus places the divine Scriptures at the head of his list of authorities. The chapters edited herein show that this should not be taken to mean the Vulgate Bible simply as a freestanding book. Through the Breviary and the *Glossa ordinaria*, Antoninus knows and at times draws upon other translations of the Scriptures than Jerome's Vulgate; for example, alternate translations of the Septuagint transmitted in the Roman Psalter, which provided the Psalm texts for the office. The lectionary is another significant road of access to the Scriptures, particularly within the model sermons which make up so many chapters in Antoninus's *Summa*. In a similar vein, Antoninus's access to the "sacred canons" and the patristic authors is very frequently gained through intermediaries: above all Gratian's *Decretum*, secondarily Peter Lombard's *Sentences*. This is likewise evident in the chapters edited herein. Aristotle, similarly, is frequently cited via St Thomas Aquinas or other scholastic theologians. The case is similar for jurists, who are sometimes cited via the *summae* or *tractatus* of other authors: for example, in chapter 2.1.16, Giovanni da Legnano and Giovanni Calderini are cited, almost certainly not directly but via Lorenzo Ridolfi's *Tractatus de usuris*.[72]

Another point to be made about this list is that, as mentioned by Antoninus in his final caveat, it is not exhaustive. Many other authors are cited by Antoninus at various places within the *Summa*; for example, to the list could be added the "Master of Sentences" (*Magister sententiarum*) Peter Lombard,[73] Gerard Odonis, OFM,[74] John of Naples, OP,[75] and Henry of Rimini, OP.[76] Henry of Rimini's *Liber*

69 For example, in connection with Raymond of Peñafort's *Summae* in Mulchahey, *Dominican Education*, 533–9. See also Mahoney, *Making of Moral Theology*, ch. 6, "The Language of Law."

70 Essays examining the influence of canon law on the medieval theologian St Thomas Aquinas will soon be available in *Thomas Aquinas and Medieval Canon Law: Historical and Systematic Perspectives*, ed. Justin Anderson and Atria Larson.

71 On law in Antoninus's *Summa*, see Spagnesi, "Sant'Antonino e il diritto."

72 Antoninus, *Summa*, 2.1.16 (below), section 3.1.3.2 (M_1 fol. 69v, hand A). See the final footnote in the present chapter.

73 Peter Lombard (Petrus Lombardus), 1095/1100–1160, teacher at the cathedral school in Paris, author of the *Sententiae* in four books, bishop of Paris from 1159.

74 Gerard Odonis (in Occitan Guiral Ot, Lat. Gerhardus Odonis), OFM, c. 1290–1349.

75 John of Naples (Iohannes de Regina), OP, fl. 1298–1347, † c. 1350.

76 Henry of Rimini (Henricus de Arimino), OP, fl. c. 1300, † c. 1314, prior of the Dominican convent of Ss. Giovanni e Paolo at Venice.

de quattuor virtutibus cardinalibus ad cives Venetos was taken by Antoninus as the basis for his treatise on the virtues in part 4:

> After dealing with the virtues in general, we must consider each of them in particular. And in the first place the cardinal [virtues], then the others. And that treatment of the cardinal [virtues] is nearly all taken from the book which Henry of Rimini of the Order of Preachers composed. Much has been added [to Henry's treatment], however, as the whole matter demands in relation to these four connected virtues. And even certain things with regard to the four themselves, when extracted from the book, have occasionally been abbreviated.[77]

Indeed, Antoninus's treatment of the cardinal virtues in part 4 repeats extensive portions of Henry of Rimini verbatim.[78] Antoninus adapts the text to better suit his purposes, "by expunging details that tie the text to its original locale of Venice, and by adding further material from other, more recent, authorities,"[79] such as Giovanni d'Andrea and Peter of la Palud; he also modifies the structure of the material and reorders the treatment of the virtues.[80]

More enigmatic are the authors from whom Antoninus draws extensively without ever explicitly citing their names. The most famous known instance is Antoninus's use of the sermons of St Bernardino of Siena, OFM,[81] in *Summa* 2.1 on the capital vice of greed. Antoninus's quotations and adaptations from St Bernardino in chapter 2.1.16, edited herein, are indicated in the *apparatus fontium* to the edition and in the footnotes to the English translation. St Antoninus's dependence on St Bernardino here was not widely known among scholars until the publication of Raymond de Roover's *San Bernardino of Siena and Sant'Antonino of Florence: The Two Great Economic Thinkers of the Middle Ages*.[82] Schumpeter and Ilgner both supposed the doctrine of threefold value (*virtuositas, raritas, complacibilitas*) found in 2.1.16 to be original to St Antoninus.[83] This threefold value doctrine was, in

77 Antoninus, *Summa*, 4.2.1 (Ballerini, 4:27); translated in Howard, *Creating Magnificence*, 92–3, 95.

78 This was discovered by Peter F. Howard. Antoninus's chapter on magnificence (a species of the virtue of fortitude), copied verbatim from Henry of Rimini, is analysed extensively in Howard, *Creating Magnificence*, ch. 5 and ch. 6.

79 Ibid., 95.

80 Ibid., 95–8.

81 St Bernardino of Siena (Bernardinus Senensis), OFM, 1380–1444, very famous in Italy as a preacher, a partisan of the Observant reform. His complete works have been published in a critical edition of exceptional quality: *Opera omnia*, 9 vols (Quaracchi: Collegio San Bonaventura, 1950–65).

82 This dependence is pointed out in de Roover, *Great Economic Thinkers*, 18–19.

83 Schumpeter, *History of Economic Analysis*, 98; Ilgner, *Die volkswirtschaftlichen Anschauungen Antonins von Florenz*. On this point, see Spicciani, *Capitale e interesse*, 167–8.

turn, taken by Bernardino from Peter John Olivi.[84] Bernardino also drew from Peter John Olivi his concept of money as capital.[85] This passage in Bernardino appears to have been copied, paraphrased, into Antoninus's *Summa* by a later copyist or editor, and thus was transmitted in early printed editions under Antoninus's name; hence several distinctive lines of analysis developed by Olivi came to be attributed to Antoninus, for example by John T. Noonan.[86] On this passage falsely attributed to Antoninus, see below, chapter 4, section 5. Peter John Olivi's place in the scholastic tradition will be discussed briefly in the postscript to the present chapter. For elucidation of this subject the reader is directed to the work of Amleto Spicciani and Bertram Schefold and the references therein.[87]

Having sketched Antoninus's principal authorities for the *Summa* as a whole, I shall now turn to the main subject of this chapter: the intellectual sources of the core moral doctrines which Antoninus employed in his teaching on trade, merchants, and workers edited herein, namely the scholastic tradition on justice in buying and selling.

1. Introductory Remarks

The scholastic economic tradition is the body of economic thought developed by scholars and doctors – philosophers, theologians, and jurists – in the universities of Europe from roughly AD 1150 to 1450.[88] The present chapter is concerned specifically with scholastic thought on the obligations of justice which apply to the act of buying and selling, particularly in relation to price. Its focus is on prescriptive norms which apply in the economic sphere: the moral analysis of the duties

84 Peter John Olivi (Petrus Iohannis Olivi), OFM, 1247/48–1296/98, Franciscan theologian, partisan of the Spirituals, died under suspicion of heresy. His *Tractatus de contractibus, de usuris, de restitutionibus* is edited by Piron in *Traité des contrats*. An English translation of Piron's edition is now available: *A Treatise on Contracts*, trans. Thornton and Cusato.

85 Bernardinus Senensis, *De evangelio aeterno*, sermon 42, 2, 2 (*Opera omnia*, 4:358–9), repeating Petrus Iohannis Olivi, *Quodlibet* 1, q. 17, co. (printed in Piron, *Traité de contrats*, 398).

86 Noonan, *Scholastic Analysis of Usury*, 128. The relevant passage of Antoninus's *Summa* is 2.1.7.15 (Ballerini 2:98d–99b; 2.1.6.15 in Mamachi 2:136–8).

87 Spicciani, *Capitale e interesse*, esp. appendix 1, "Le fonti del pensiero economico di sant'Antonino da Firenze"; Schefold, "Thomas von Aquin, Petrus Johannes Olivi und Antoninus von Florenz. Mittelalterliche Kapitalkritik und die Weberthese."

88 The most concise and systematic overview of scholastic economic thought as a whole is Langholm, "The Medieval Schoolmen (1200–1400)." An ambitious argument for the analytical completeness and enduring utility of scholastic economic thought is made in Mueller, *Redeeming Economics*. For further bibliographical orientation, see Langholm, *Merchant in the Confessional*; Diana Wood, *Medieval Economic Thought*; James Davis, "Economic History," esp. the section "Economic Thought." For introduction to scholasticism more generally: Brady and Gurr, "Scholasticism," and Leinsle, *Introduction to Scholastic Theology*.

and pitfalls of buying and selling in the market. As such, it is not an examination of the whole tradition of economic analysis developed by the scholastics. It likewise leaves aside the scholastic analysis of usury, an enormous subject in its own right.[89] The present chapter is intended to elucidate the sources and intellectual background of Antoninus's teaching in the chapters of his *Summa* edited below: namely the scholastic teaching on buying and selling, particularly on the "just price."[90]

The method applied in this chapter and the choice of sources to be examined can be introduced through a scheme employed by Odd Langholm in his monograph *Economics in the Medieval Schools*. The scheme can be called "Langholm's triangle" (represented in figure 1). This triangle shows, on its outside, the principal source texts which provided *loci communes* (common reference points) for scholastic economic analysis; on its inside, it shows the different literary genres in which this economic analysis was developed and disseminated.

There are six sets of books which provide the fundamental reference points for scholastic economic thought: the texts surrounding the triangle. The scholastics themselves wrote about economics in the genres within the triangle. This scheme usefully illuminates the nature of the scholastic method, which proceeds through expounding, teaching, and reflecting upon a given collection of texts, as exemplified in the curricula of the medieval universities and academic disciplines. For present purposes, however, a slight adjustment of the paradigm is called for. With our focus on the specific topic of justice in buying and selling, particularly "just price" doctrine, it is more convenient to adopt a paradigm which illustrates the ancient sources of key doctrines and principles, and the medieval texts in which the scholastics identified and applied those principles.[91]

Adopting this paradigm, the outside of the triangle can be reduced to three sets of ancient sources providing crucial principles for scholastic "just price" doctrine (see figure 2). Within the triangle are the medieval texts which assembled these principles and doctrines and transmitted them to later scholastics like St Antoninus and others in the moral-theological tradition.

---

89 In addition to the references in the previous note, the large literature on usury can be approached through Armstrong, *The Idea of a Moral Economy*; Armstrong, *Usury and Public Debt*; Spicciani, *Capitale e interesse*; Noonan, *Scholastic Analysis of Usury*.

90 The classic study is Baldwin, "The Medieval Theories of the Just Price." Particularly valuable contributions to this literature: Gordley, "*Ius commune*," ch. 2 in *The Jurists*; Kaye, *Economy and Nature in the Fourteenth Century*; Zimmermann, "*Emptio venditio* I," ch. 8 in *The Law of Obligations*; de Roover, "The Concept of the Just Price."

91 This is an application of the concepts of *fons materialis* (material source, i.e., original source of a doctrine) and *fons formalis* (formal source, intermediary text which transmits a doctrine) used by scholars of canon law.

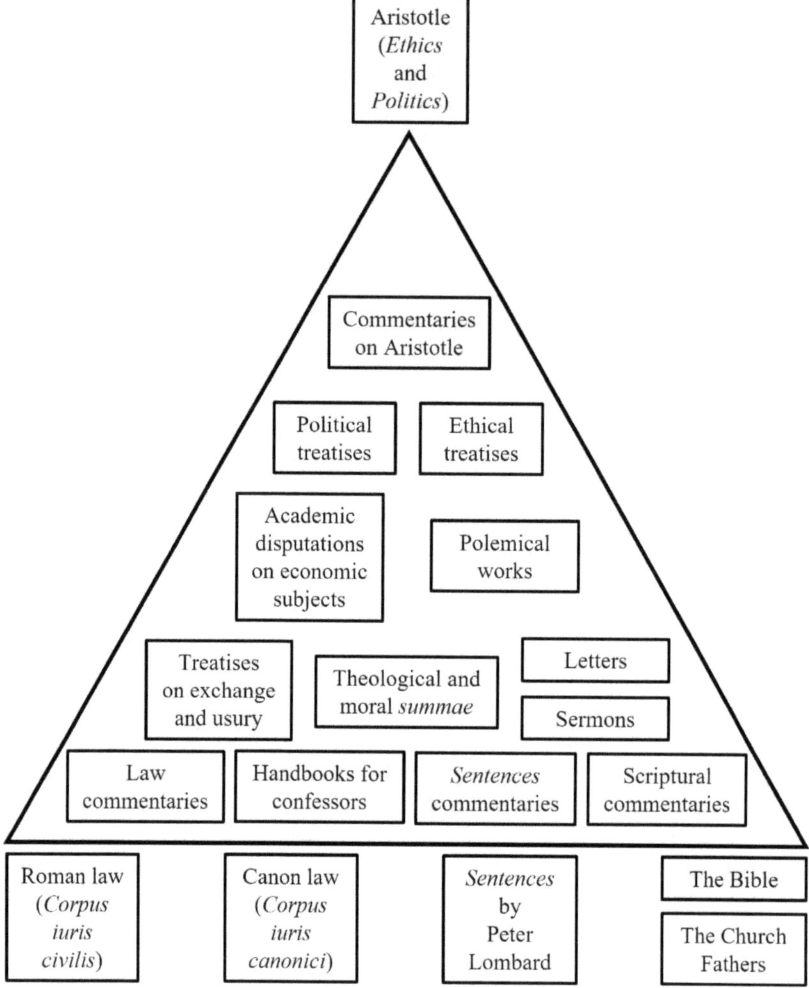

Figure 1: Source texts and genres of scholastic economic analysis

(based on Langholm, *Economics in the Medieval Schools,* 26)

These three sets of ancient sources are:

1. The Bible, the Church Fathers, and the sacred canons. The principal medieval texts which brought doctrines from these sources into the scholastic tradition are Peter Lombard's *Sentences* and Gratian's *Decretum.*
2. Roman law, especially the *Digest* and the *Code*. The medieval intermediaries to the scholastic tradition are the canon-law collections, especially the *Liber*

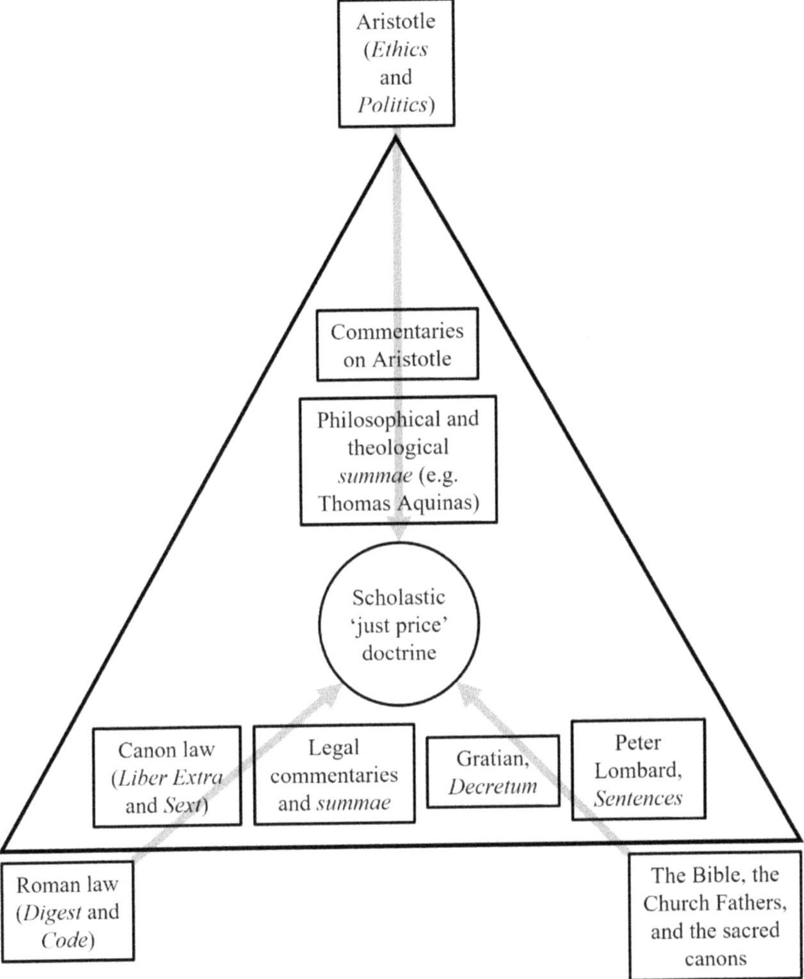

Figure 2: Ancient sources of "just price" doctrine and their medieval intermediaries

Extra (to a lesser extent the *Liber Sext*), and the jurists' commentaries and *summae* on canon law.

3. Aristotle, especially the *Nicomachean Ethics* and *Politics*. The medieval intermediaries are the commentaries and *summae* of scholastic philosophers and theologians. The *Summa theologiae* of St Thomas Aquinas is the most important work in this genre, but there are many others.

These three sets of ancient sources, as interpreted and drawn out by the scholastics in their lectures and teaching, provided all of the crucial principles forming the framework for the scholastic tradition on justice in buying and selling, and in particular their doctrine of the "just price." The exposition of this material in the present chapter shall proceed in the order just listed, which follows the order in which the medieval intermediary texts were produced: first Peter Lombard and Gratian (twelfth century), then the *Liber Extra* (1234), then Thomas Aquinas's *Summa theologiae* (*secunda secundae* composed 1271–2). It will be seen that each stage builds upon the last; and with Aquinas a synthesis is achieved, drawing together the principles developed by his forebears out of all three sets of ancient sources.

2. The Bible, Church Fathers, and Sacred Canons via Peter Lombard and Gratian

The medievals told a story – probably never meant to be taken literally – about the founders of the sciences of biblical studies, canon law, and theology:

> There had once been three brothers, born of an adulterous union. Their mother, on her deathbed, confessed her sin, but professed an inability to feel compunction, in view of the great good that had come of it, since each of her sons had become a luminary of the Church. The three brothers born of this unrepented sin were Peter Comestor, Gratian, and Peter Lombard.[92]

These three were contemporaries, teaching and writing in the early to mid-twelfth century. Each one founded a science, in the sense of inaugurating a tradition of rational, disciplined teaching and study of a defined body of material. For present purposes, Peter Comestor and his *Scholastic History* can be set aside. Peter Lombard produced the basic textbook of the science of theology, *The Sentences*. Gratian produced the basic textbook of canon law, *The Harmony of Discordant Canons* or *Decretum*. These two books are of similar character: they are textbooks for classroom teaching and they are structured as casebooks.[93] The intention of the authors, it may be fairly surmised from their work, was not merely to deliver a body of content or doctrine but also, in their capacity as teachers, to train the minds of their students to think in a certain way. The two rely on a similar corpus of authorities, namely the Scriptures and the patristic writers, especially the four Latin doctors of the Church, Augustine, Jerome, Ambrose, and Gregory. Gratian also brings in the canons of Church councils and papal decretal letters. In each book, the author collects authorities or precedents in order to elucidate the chief

92 Petrus Lombardus. *The Sentences*, trans. Silano, 1:VII.

93 On these texts as casebooks, see Silano, "The *Sentences* as Medieval Casebook," ibid., 1:XIX–XXX; Gratianus, *The Concord of Discordant Canons and the Ordinary Gloss*, trans. Silano, Introduction.

principles, arguments, and doctrines to be employed in his discipline. Neither Lombard nor Gratian is inclined to use these authorities to settle definitively any particular question. Instead, they bring out the contradictions in the authorities, and invite the student to become a participant in debating the ensuing questions. In other words, they teach a problem-based approach to the sources.[94] They are not laying down a body of dogma to be memorized, but rather introducing the student to the precedents which set out the ground for the discussion, and teaching the principles by which the discussion should be conducted. The frame of mind in view may be described as *fides quaerens intellectum*, "faith seeking understanding," and, by analogy, as *ius quaerens intellectum*, "law seeking understanding."[95]

Each one is truly a founding text; neither was the last word in its discipline. They were followed up on in the thirteenth century by theological commentaries and *summae* and by further canon-law compilations and glosses. *The Sentences* remained the basic textbook in theology until the sixteenth century, and left a permanent mark thereafter; the *Decretum* was taught in the law faculties through the rest of the Middle Ages, and, as the first part of the *Corpus iuris canonici*, remained an essential component of the canon law of the Roman Catholic Church until the publication in 1917 of the "new code" produced at the order of St Pius X, the *Codex iuris canonici*. Every later medieval theologian engaged with Peter Lombard, and many published their own commentaries on his *Sentences*. Every medieval canonist engaged with, and often lectured on, Gratian. The examination of the scholastic tradition, then, begins with these two. In reading them it is possible to anticipate somewhat, and to look ahead to consequences drawn and uses made of their texts in subsequent generations. By the end of this chapter it will be seen that quite a few essential principles and arguments which are cited and applied by later scholastic authors are already present in these founding texts.[96]

Peter Lombard's Sentences

The contribution, however, is unequal. Discussions of economic questions in Peter Lombard's *Sentences* are few and far between. What Lombard did was provide three *loci* for later theologians' comments on economic matters. The first is in book 3, distinction 33, on the virtue of justice.[97] Later authors connect this

---

94 The characterization of these texts here is indebted to Giulio Silano's teaching in Toronto.

95 The formula "faith seeking understanding," *fides quaerens intellectum*, comes from Anselm of Canterbury, the "Father of Scholasticism." See Leinsle, *Scholastic Theology*, 79, and the whole of ch. 2 "The Self-Concept of Early Scholastic Theologies." The phrase "law seeking understanding" was turned by James Gordley, "*Ius quaerens intellectum*."

96 For another summary of this material, see Baldwin, "Medieval Theories of the Just Price," 12–16.

97 Lombard, *Sentences*, 3, 33, 1–3 (3:135–6). English quotations of the *Sentences* are from the translation by Silano.

material with Aristotle's discussion of justice in the *Nichomachean Ethics*; but in the text of the *Sentences* itself there is nothing here on economics. The second *locus* is 3, 37, on the commandment against theft. Lombard comments: "Here usury is also forbidden, since it is contained under theft with violence."[98] Jerome and Augustine are cited defining usury as any excess beyond the principal in a loan, whether of money or of other countable goods, and establishing the prohibition of usury as a species of robbery. This combination of texts is foundational for scholastic moral teaching on usury. A similar combination is found in the *Decretum*, which shall be discussed briefly below.

The third *locus* in the *Sentences* is 4, 14–16, on the sacrament of penance. It is not necessary here to expound Lombard's whole teaching on penance, although it does have applications and consequences for moralists and penitential authors. The *dictum* (statement) for this study is at d. 16 c. 3, where Lombard discusses the third necessary element in penance: after compunction and confession, the final thing required is "satisfaction." Gregory VII is cited:

> If a soldier or trader, or one given to some office which cannot be exercised without sin, should come to penance bound by graver faults, either while he detains unjustly another's goods, or while he bears hate in his heart, let him acknowledge that he cannot perform true penance unless he abandon trade or leave his office, and expel hatred from his heart, and make restitution of the goods which he has taken unjustly.[99]

There are two points here. First, there is an apparent blanket condemnation of trade, as well as of soldiery. It shall be seen, however, that the scholastics found texts like this to be very much in need of interpretation. The second point is more crucial. Gregory lays down restitution of unjustly acquired goods as a condition for penance. This has momentous consequences for confessors dealing with merchants, traders, and bankers: profits gained through usury, and by extension through fraud or injustice, must be restored as a condition of sacramental absolution.

This is the extent of the treatment of economic issues in *The Sentences*. Peter Lombard's textbook provided a few important doctrines, and several *loci* which are occasions for later interpretation and argument over the prohibition of usury and the moral quality or turpitude of trade.

Gratian's Decretum

An impressive number of fruitful principles and key points for debate were set in place in Gratian's *Decretum*, the foundational text of canon-law jurisprudence.

98 Ibid., 3, 37, 5 (3:155).

99 Gregory VII, Council of Rome V, in ibid., 4, 16, 3 (4:91).

Principles developed by Gratian would continue to be applied to justice in buying and selling throughout the scholastic period. Once again, there are several *loci communes* to be examined.

In the second part of the *Decretum*, Gratian sets out thirty-six hypothetical situations, called causes, which give rise to legal issues to be pursued through a series of questions. The framework for the following three centuries of discussion on usury is found in cause 14:

> The canons of a certain church have begun an action regarding some estates; they produce witnesses from among their brethren; they had lent money to traders, in order to receive gains from their merchandise.[100]

Question 3: "Whether it is usury to exact that gain?" The authorities ranged on this point are Augustine, Jerome, Ambrose, and the council of Agde. From the latter we have:

> It is usury, where more is required than is given; for example, if you have given ten shillings, and you have sought more, or if you have given one measure of wheat, and you have exacted something above that.[101]

This becomes the standard scholastic definition of usury: any exaction beyond the principal in a loan of a fungible good. This is the definition employed, adjoined with certain later scholastic distinctions, in the 1917 *Codex iuris canonici*.[102]

Question 4: "Whether it is lawful for clerics or laypeople to seek usuries from anyone?" In the first part of the *Decretum*, clergy were forbidden to lend money at interest.[103] Here, by the authority of Leo the Great, Ambrose, and Augustine, that prohibition is extended to all without distinction. Thus Ambrose: "Whoever has taken usury commits theft, and does not live life."[104] Thus, as in Lombard, usury is

100 Gratian, in C. 14 dict. ante q. 1 (*Canonici*). English quotations of the *Decretum* are from the translation by Silano, *Concord of Discordant Canons*. Latin quotations of the *Decretum* are from *Corpus iuris canonici*, ed. Friedberg, vol. 1, *Decretum magistri Gratiani*. I include the Latin incipit (opening words) of each canon in parentheses, since these are used by Antoninus and other scholastic authors to cite legal texts. See Brundage, *Medieval Canon Law*, appendix 1.

101 Council of Agde, in C. 14 q. 3 c. 4 (*Usura est*).

102 "Si res fungibilis ita alicui detur ut eius fiat et postea tantundem in eodem genere restituatur, nihil lucri, ratione ipsius contractus, percipi potest; sed in praestatione rei fungibilis non est per se illicitum de lucro legali pacisci, nisi constet ipsum esse immoderatum, aut etiam de lucro maiore, si iustus ac proportionatus titulus suffragetur." *Codex iuris canonici*, c. 1543. Quoted from *Codex iuris canonici Pii X Pontificis Maximi iussu digestus, Benedicti Papae XV auctoritate promulgatus.*

103 D. 46–7.

104 Ambrose, *On the Good of Death*, 12, in C. 14 q. 4 c. 10 (*Si quis usuram*).

classified as a species of the sin of theft. Another important principle is established in these questions. In theft, the intention is what makes the sin, and not only the outward acts. "God questions the heart, not the hand," says Ambrose;[105] and Jerome: "It is not the thing taken by theft which is marked, but the mind of the thief."[106] This will be come to be applied to "mental usury": if the lender intends to reap a profit from a loan, he is guilty of the sin, even if the form of the loan does not strictly betray usury.

Question 5: "Whether alms may be given from usury?" By the authority of Augustine, Jerome, and Ambrose, it is proven that one must return to the original owner what one has reaped as usurious profits. Only if this is impossible may those things be given as alms to the Church or to the poor. Thus Ecclesiasticus says: "The offering is tainted which is sacrificed from iniquitous gain."[107] The taking of usury, then, is not cleansed by giving the profits in alms.

Finally, question 6: "Whether usurers are able to do penance without restoring what they have taken?" Augustine attests: "If penance is truly done, the sin is not remitted, unless the stolen good is returned, when it can be returned."[108] If the goods have been consecrated, then their value is to be repaid. As was seen in Peter Lombard, restitution, where possible, is strictly required as a condition for the absolution of one who has taken usurious profits.

Thus far, Gratian has marshalled patristic authorities and laid down five principles which will structure the usury discussion for centuries:

1. Usury is any exaction beyond the principal in a loan, whether of money or other fungibles.
2. It is a kind of theft.
3. Not only the outward acts but also the intention are relevant to the sin of usury.
4. Usurious profits are to be returned, not given as alms, unless restitution is impossible.
5. Restitution is a condition for absolving a usurer's sins in the confessional.

Each of these principles will be applied by analogy to fraudulent practices in the market more generally, including frauds and deceptions committed in buying and selling. The defrauding of the neighbour of his wealth is, like usury, a species of theft. The guilt of "mental usury" applies also to unjust frauds in trade: if the

105 Ambrose, *Homilies*, 50, 9, in C. 14 q. 5 c. 6 (*Si quid invenisti*).

106 Jerome, *Letter to Titus*, 2, in C. 14 q. 6 c. 4 (*Fur autem*).

107 Sirach 34:21, in C. 14 q. 5 c. 2 (*Immolans*). Douay-Rheims: "The offering of him that sacrificeth of a thing wrongfully gotten, is stained."

108 Augustine, *Letter to Macedonius*, 54, in C. 14 q. 6 c. 1 (*Si res aliena*).

perpetrator intends to deceive, he is guilty of the sin, even if he does not succeed. Profits gained through fraud are to be returned to the original owner as a condition for absolution; only if this is impossible may such profits be given in alms as a form of satisfaction. All these principles are constantly applied by St Antoninus in the chapters edited below as he examines market practices.

The next *locus* is in the first part of the *Decretum*, distinction 88. Gratian juxtaposes a combination of patristic texts here, beginning with those which express a low view of commerce. The point of departure for the Church Fathers was the New Testament, certain texts of which could be called upon as indictments of the merchants' profession and of worldly wealth in general: the account of the rich young man whom Christ commanded to sell his possessions and give the money to the poor;[109] the Apostle Paul's statement *the desire of money is the root of all evils*;[110] and the Lord's casting of buyers and sellers out of the Temple.[111] However, as mentioned above, these texts were found to cry out for interpretation. The texts gathered here in D. 88 offer contrasting opinions about the liceity of commerce and the merchant's profession. The authorities establish clearly enough that clerics may not engage in trade.[112] As to the laity, the question remains whether trade is illicit *per se*, or only contingently. Two texts from Augustine seem to contradict one another on the point. The first says trade is "at times lawful, at times unlawful."[113] The second, citing Psalm 70, *Because I have not known trade*, says, "let Christians

109 "And behold one came and said to him: Good master, what good shall I do that I may have life everlasting? … Jesus saith to him: If thou wilt be perfect, go sell what thou hast, and give to the poor, and thou shalt have treasure in heaven: and come follow me. And when the young man had heard this word, he went away sad: for he had great possessions. Then Jesus said to his disciples: Amen, I say to you, that a rich man shall hardly enter into the kingdom of heaven. And again I say to you: It is easier for a camel to pass through the eye of a needle, than for a rich man to enter into the kingdom of heaven. And when they had heard this, the disciples wondered very much, saying: Who then can be saved? And Jesus beholding, said to them: With men this is impossible: but with God all things are possible." Matthew 19:16–26.

110 *Radix enim omnium malorum est cupiditas*. 1 Timothy 6:10.

111 "And Jesus went into the temple of God, and cast out all them that sold and bought in the temple, and overthrew the tables of the money changers, and the chairs of them that sold doves: And he saith to them: It is written, My house shall be called the house of prayer; but you have made it a den of thieves." Matthew 21:12–13. "And the pasch of the Jews was at hand, and Jesus went up to Jerusalem. And he found in the temple them that sold oxen and sheep and doves, and the changers of money sitting. And when he had made, as it were, a scourge of little cords, he drove them all out of the temple, the sheep also and the oxen, and the money of the changers he poured out, and the tables he overthrew. And to them that sold doves he said: Take these things hence, and make not the house of my Father a house of traffic. And his disciples remembered, that it was written: The zeal of thy house hath eaten me up." John 2:13–17. Cfr Mark 11:15–19; Luke 19:45–8.

112 D. 88 c. 1–9.

113 Augustine, *Questions of the Old and New Testament*, 127, in D. 88 c. 10 (*Fornicari*).

correct themselves and not trade."[114] Here Gratian has set up an excellent occasion to make distinctions and draw out the principles underlying the critique. The threads of contrasting *sententiae* (opinions) will be teased out and brought into coherence by Thomas Aquinas, as will be seen below.[115] For the moment, one canon (D. 88 c. 11) deserves special commentary. It was known to the scholastics as *Eiiciens* from its opening word, and was erroneously attributed to John Chrysostom; in fact, it comes from a pseudonymous Greek work called the *Opus imperfectum in Matthaeum*.[116] The canon *Eiiciens* condemns usurers and then sets out to show why usury is distinguished from renting out a property:

> Above all merchants, a usurer is the most accursed. Indeed, he sells a thing given by God, and not one purchased, as does a merchant; furthermore, after the interest, he also seeks the return of his thing, taking another's and his own property. At this point, someone says: One who rents out a field, in order to receive agrarian dues, or a house, in order to receive rents, is he not similar to one who lends money at usury? Far be it. First, because money is not intended for any use other than purchasing. Second, because one who has a field, ploughs it and takes a fruit from it; one who has a house, takes from it the use of inhabiting it. And so, one who rents a field or a house is seen to give its use and to receive money, so that he is seen to exchange in some way gain for gain; if money is set aside, you receive no use from it. Third, the field or house is aged by use. But money, when it is lent, neither diminishes, nor ages.[117]

Eiiciens anticipates or suggests a number of natural-law arguments which will later be used to explain the usury prohibition: the usurer sells what is God's (i.e., time); money's use is consumption; money does not bear fruit of itself; the usurer takes the fruit of another man's labour; money does not deteriorate with use. Ambrose also, at D. 47 c. 8, condemns usury as unnatural because money by itself is not fruitful: "Through the iniquitous practice of usury, gold is born from gold."[118] These texts

---

114 Augustine, *Enarrationes in Psalmos*, *Ps* 70, 1, 17–20, in D. 88 c. 12 (*Quoniam non*). On this Psalm and its different Latin texts, see below, ch. 4, at the discussion of Antoninus, *Summa*, 2.1.16.

115 In addition to the present chapter, I explore Thomas Aquinas's use of Gratian's D. 88 in my chapter of the forthcoming volume on *Thomas Aquinas and Medieval Canon Law*, ed. Anderson and Larson.

116 This text is introduced by Noonan, *Scholastic Analysis of Usury*, 38–9.

117 Pseudo-Chrysostom, *Opus imperfectum in Matthaeum*, 38, in D. 88 c. 11 (*Eiciens*). This canon is marked as a *palea* in the *Decretum*, along with the two subsequent canons, c. 12–13. I discuss the importance of the fact that they were not lectured on or glossed in the law schools in my chapter of *Thomas Aquinas and Medieval Canon Law*.

118 Ambrose (pseudo?), *Sermons*, 81, in D. 47 c. 8 (*Sicut hii* [*ii* vulg.]).

are seminal for the scholastic analysis of usury; further pursuit of this subject, however, would be tangential to the present chapter.

The canon *Eiiciens* also makes two judgments about the moral legitimacy of trade: the profession is dishonest, and it is unproductive:

> In casting sellers and buyers from the Temple, the Lord signified that a man who engages in trade can rarely or never please God. And so no Christian must be a merchant, or, if he should wish to be one, let him be cast out of God's Church, as the Prophet says: *Because I have not known trade, I will enter into the powers of the Lord* (*Ps.* 70.16). One who buys and sells cannot be free of lying and perjury. But all men seem to be merchants. And so I will show who is not a trader, so that you will understand anyone to be a trader who does not fit my description. Whoever purchases a thing, not in order to sell it whole and unchanged, but in order to have matter to work into something else, he is not a trader. But he who buys a thing in order to gain something by alienating it whole and unchanged, he is a trader who is cast out of God's Temple.[119]

The line that a trader "can rarely or never please God" will be a staple for later comments on the spiritual dangers of trade; as will the similar line from another place in the *Decretum*, attributed to Leo the Great, "it is difficult for sin not to intervene in the commerce between buyer and seller."[120] There is also in D. 88 a critique of trade based on the frequent use of lies by merchants – "burdening their merchandise more with perjuries than prices," as is said by Cassiodorus.[121] This will be carried into confessors' manuals, instructing pastors that lying is a characteristic vice of merchants for which they must be scrutinized. So also the critique of trade as unproductive. The definition given in *Eiiciens* of illicit speculative trade, as against trade which adds something to the product, will be standard for centuries. It is reiterated in another *locus*:

> Whoever, at the time of harvest of wheat or grapes, buys wheat or wine, not by any need, but out of cupidity, so that, for example, he buys a measure for two pennies and keeps it until it is sold for four, or six, or more pennies, we say that he is engaging in a shameful gain.[122]

This canon expresses a common theme in medieval preaching and confessors' manuals: the condemnation of regrating, that is, the practice of speculators who

119 Pseudo-Chrysostom, *Opus imperfectum in Matthaeum*, 38, in D. 88 c. 11 (*Eiciens*).

120 Leo I, *Epistolae*, 167, 11, in *De pen.* D. 5 c. 2 (*Qualitas*).

121 Cassiodorus, *In psalmos*, *Ps* 70, in D. 88 c. 13 (*Quid est aliud*).

122 Attributed to Julius I, but Friedberg assigns it to a Carolingian capitulary of 806, in C. 14 q. 4 c. 9 (*Quicumque*).

buy up large quantities of commodities and induce dearth. This practice would be distinguished by later scholastics from the legitimate purchase and storage of commodities for sale at a later date.

Two additional important principles are raised in these sections. The more essential of the two is the germ of scholastic thought on private property. Ambrose, attacking the avaricious and miserly man, says:

> Is God not unjust in not sharing out equally to all of us those things which support life? In allowing you to be affluent and rich, while others lack and are in need? And yet, having received God's gifts, you treat them as if they had come from your own breast; do you really believe that you are doing no evil by keeping for yourself alone the aids to life of so many? For who is as unjust, greedy, and avaricious as the one who takes the food of many, and not for his own use, but for his plenty and pleasures? Nor, indeed, is it a lesser crime to refuse to give to the needy what you can from your abundance than to take something away from one who has it. The bread which you keep for yourself belongs to the hungry; the clothes which you lock up belong to the naked; the money which you bury in the earth is the redemption and freedom of the poor.[123]

Ambrose here has planted the seed of a dual principle governing property: private ownership but common destination or right of use. The scholastics defend private property as a general right under the *ius gentium* ("law of nations," a set of rational customary norms), though not strictly of *ius naturale* ("natural law," a set of unchanging universal moral norms); but those who have more than enough have a duty to use their wealth to help the poor. This is a consistent standard applied by later canonists, as also what follows from "the bread belongs to the hungry, the clothes to the naked," namely: in need all is common. Thus the conclusion that for one in grave and mortal need, the taking of another's property for sustenance is not theft.

Finally, there are two comments on worldly ambition which are noteworthy. Rather than establishing specific canonical principles, they set out a general picture of the vice of avarice and of its consequences on the moral and spiritual life. Gregory the Great accuses those who devote themselves to temporal gain of neglecting the service of God:

> All the lovers of this world are strong in earthly things, but weak in the heavenly ones. Thus, for temporal glory they desire to labour even to death, and for the everlasting hope they do not even bear with a little effort. For the sake of earthly gains, they bear any injuries, but for the sake of the heavenly reward they refuse to suffer the insults even

123 Ambrose (pseudo?), *Sermons*, 81, in D. 47 c. 8 (*Sicut hii* [*ii* vulg.]).

> of the least offensive word. They are sufficiently strong to stand before an earthly judge even for the whole day, but in praying before God, they become exhausted even within a single hour. Often, they suffer nakedness, dejection, hunger for the sake of acquiring riches and honours, and they punish themselves by abstaining from those things for whose acquisition they work so feverishly, but they omit to seek with effort the things which are above, all the more as they hold them to be paid back with great delay.[124]

The outlook just described by Gregory the Great coincides very closely with what Max Weber called "worldly asceticism" in *The Protestant Ethic and the Spirit of Capitalism*.[125] The attitude which Gregory condemns here is the attitude recommended as virtuous conduct by Benjamin Franklin in the quotations with which Weber opens his second chapter.[126] In the pursuit of profit or success the avaricious man denies himself the enjoyment even of the worldly goods which his wealth can acquire. This shows the essentially disinterested character of the "spirit of capitalism," as defined by Weber: the true capitalist builds up a business, not for the sake of his own happiness, but in obedience to a transcendental ethic. In D. 88, Augustine makes the same point about the anti-hedonism of the capitalist, punning on the Latin: "It is deservedly called trade (*negotium*) because it denies leisure (*negat otium*), to do which is evil, nor does it seek true rest, which is God."[127] These observations should be compared to those made by Langholm in the concluding chapter of *The Merchant in the Confessional*,[128] where he points out that Weber's concept of the "spirit of capitalism" corresponds closely to what medieval writers like Gregory the Great described as the vice of avarice. This topic will be discussed more fully in the preamble of the next chapter.

Thus has Gratian introduced reflection on economic issues into his *Decretum*. If we are seeking early formulations of the key doctrines of scholastic economic ethics, we have found the prohibition of usury clearly stated and a framework proposed for its practical application, but we have not yet found a clear statement of the doctrine of "just prices." Aside from the condemnation of speculation and regrating, there are only two incidental and as yet undeveloped references to exchange at a just price.[129] The development of detailed and practical canonical

124 Gregory the Great, *Morals on the Book of Job*, 19, 27, in D. 47 c. 3 (*Omnes*).

125 Weber, *The Protestant Ethic and the Spirit of Capitalism*, trans. Parsons.

126 Ibid., ch. 2 "The Spirit of Capitalism."

127 Augustine, *Enarrationes in Psalmos*, *Ps* 70, 1, 17–20, in D. 88 c. 12 (*Quoniam non*).

128 Langholm, *The Merchant in the Confessional*, ch. 16 "The Fortunes of Avarice."

129 Justinian, *Nov*. 7, in C. 10 q. 2 c. 2 (*Hoc ius porrectum*); Council of Tarragona, 3, in C. 14 q. 4 c. 5 (*Si quis[2] clericus*). The layers of decretist commentary on these canons track successive stages in the development of just price doctrine; the combination of civil-law principles described in the next section does not fully appear until the Archdeacon comments on C. 10 q. 2 c. 2. So, at least, it appears from the attributions of the glosses.

and moral principles applicable to justice in contracts would be the work of the next century, spurred on, perhaps, by several factors not yet compelling in the early twelfth century. These include the growth of commerce and concomitant rise of a professional merchant and business class,[130] as well as the increased drive for religious education for priests and laity alike, particularly with a view to valid and fruitful sacramental confession.[131] Both of these factors are relevant to the purpose of Antoninus's teaching in the *Summa*.

That is one angle from which to view the question. Another is to observe sources available to and employed by the scholastics. As described in the introductory remarks, there were three foundational corpora (bodies of texts) on which the scholastics drew. But Gratian and Peter Lombard draw mainly from the first corpus, illustrated at the lower right point of our triangle. This is why the usury prohibition makes up the mainstay of their economic thought: the source of this prohibition was the Bible, the sacred canons, and the writings of the Church Fathers. As John T. Noonan pointed out: "Usury analysis would not have begun if the Church had not prohibited usury, and no other intellectual or economic force exerted so strong a pressure on the formation of the early theory."[132] The importance of usury theory in canon law and theology rested on the dogmatic authority of Scripture and the Church Fathers. The theory of the "just price" and the general principles of just dealing in exchange, on the other hand, took their origins more from the other corpora, at the other two points of our triangle: Roman-law jurisprudence, which Gratian made only a limited use of,[133] and Aristotle's *Ethics* and *Politics*, which had not yet been translated into Latin and subjected to study.

Of these two fountainheads of theology and canon law, Lombard's *Sentences* and Gratian's *Decretum*, Gratian is distinguished for the abundance of material he provides dealing with economic ethics. The reason for this presumably hinges on the different purposes aimed at in the two disciplines. Lombard's book begins with the Trinity and ends with the Four Last Things: as he says at the end, "the writer began from the face of the One sitting upon the throne and, proceeding by way of the middle things, has now come to the feet."[134] In Lombard's milieu, it may be that commerce did not make for a very consequential or interesting part of those "middle things." Gratian, however, is concerned with the regulation of life in the

130 Langholm, "The Medieval Schoolmen," 441–2.

131 On this point, see the illuminating chapter by Joseph Goering, "The Internal Forum and the Literature of Penance and Confession," ch. 12 in Hartmann and Pennington, *Medieval Canon Law in the Classical Period*.

132 Noonan, *Scholastic Analysis of Usury*, 11.

133 Gratian's acquaintance with Roman law is a subject of controversy among historians of canon law. The literature can be approached through Pennington, "The 'Big Bang.'"

134 Lombard, *Sentences*, 4, 50, epilogue (4:276).

Church, and the ancient authorities raise a number of practical questions about that life. May Christians take usury? May clergy participate in business? May a Christian legitimately occupy himself as a trader? These questions are both legal and ethical. Gratian – and this also applies to the scholastic authors to be examined below – is primarily interested in economic activities insofar as they present legal and ethical dilemmas: occasions for distinguishing licit from illicit, moral from immoral behaviour. In time, a great deal of descriptive economics is drawn out of this, but it is drawn out primarily with the motive of more clearly discerning how to apply ethical principles and direct the Christian flock towards virtue. Hence it has long been recognized that it is the prescriptive motive which gave the impetus to the scholastics' descriptive economics.[135]

3. Roman Law via the *Liber Extra* and the Decretalists

Odd Langholm was quoted above as saying of the authors of penitential handbooks, "not a few looked beyond canon law to its basis in Roman law."[136] The following section of this chapter shows this process in reverse: it illustrates how principles from Roman law came to be the basis of canonical thought on justice in buying and selling, particularly the concept of the "just price." The basic framework of the "just price" was developed by civilians (jurists who studied Roman civil law) and canonists (jurists who studied the Catholic Church's canon law) in the twelfth and thirteenth centuries. It then became part of the common stock of analytical tools and moral principles both for theologians and canonists, as well as for the moral theologians who straddle the two disciplines. The canon law of just prices had its classic formulation over the century from circa 1160–1270. It was defined both in papal decretal letters and in jurists' commentaries upon them. When cases dealing with contracts of purchase and sale were brought before popes of the twelfth and thirteenth centuries like Alexander III (1159–81) and Innocent III (1198–1216), they drew on Roman-law precedents to resolve the cases justly. In a famous decretal, Lucius III (1181–5) stated that Roman law was permitted

135 "With the growing complexity of the later medieval economy, the opportunities for new and more subtle types of illicit gain multiplied apace. If priests were to judge wisely in the internal forum [of confession] they needed to understand some of the intricacies of the new profit-economy. It is generally acknowledged that the groundwork for the modern discipline of economics was laid by medieval canonists and theologians in their discussions of usury, simony, tithes, and just price. This scholastic analysis was undertaken not for its own sake, however, and not for its relevance to the church courts, but because it was necessary for preparing confessors and judges in the internal forum." Goering, "Internal Forum and the Literature of Penance," 403.

This point is explored at greater length in Langholm, "The Medieval Schoolmen," and Langholm, *Economics in the Medieval Schools*, Introduction.

136 Langholm, *Merchant in the Confessional*, 258.

to speak where canon law was silent.[137] In their rescripts, the popes took solutions directly from Roman law and applied them in ecclesiastical courts.

These papal decretals were collected by various jurists into the *Quinque compilationes antiquae* (c. 1191–1226) for use and analysis in the university faculties of law.[138] When a definitive collection of canon law was compiled by Raymond of Peñafort and promulgated by Gregory IX on 5 September 1234 as the *Decretales Gregorii IX* or *Liber Extra*, these decretal letters were established as the basic legal texts to be used by canonists for the next several centuries in discussions of the nature of prices. The key *loci* on the just price are nine canons of the *Liber Extra*.[139] Simultaneously, the canonists went to Roman-law jurisprudence as a source for legal principles and maxims to analyse purchase and exchange contracts. The foundational commentaries were made by Innocent IV in his *Commentaria*, Bernard of Parma and the other jurists whose comments were compiled into the *Glossa Ordinaria* (standard commentary), and Hostiensis in his *Summa* and *Commentaria*. These were produced between 1234 and 1271.[140] These canonists built a framework of the just price as both subjective and objective. They did not invent this framework from scratch: they drew as a matter of course on the jurisprudence of civilians, their confrères in the faculty of law, whose object of study was the recently rediscovered materials of Roman law. When Irnerius, the father of civil-law jurisprudence, rediscovered the *Digest* of Justinian, he found a well-developed and deeply thoughtful way of doing justice, born of centuries of experience ordering a society with a unique genius for law. Roman law became, for the scholastics, a rich source for principles governing purchases and sales and other contracts. Three key principles were brought together, each associated with a civilian maxim: free bargaining (*licet contrahentibus*); protection of buyers and sellers from gross injury (*laesio enormis*); and the true value or just price as the current market price (*res tantum*).

*Free Bargaining (*licet contrahentibus sese invicem decipere*)*

Free bargaining was a foundational principle governing the Roman law of purchases and sales. Each party was permitted to seek, and, if the other consented, to get, the most advantageous price. This was pointedly expressed in a maxim attributed to the Roman jurist Pomponius: "As regards the price in purchase and sale, it

137 "Quia vero, sicut leges non dedignantur sacros canones imitari, ita et sacrorum statuta canonum principum constitutionibus adiuvantur, ..." Lucius III, in *X* 5.32.1. Latin quotations of the *Liber Extra* are from *Corpus iuris canonici*, ed. Friedberg, vol. 2, *Decretalium collectiones*.

138 On the compilations see Brundage, *Medieval Canon Law*, 194–7.

139 *X* 2.20.42; *X* 3.13.11; *X* 3.17.1; *X* 3.17.3; *X* 3.17.5; *X* 3.17.6; *X* 5.19.6; *X* 5.19.10; *X* 5.19.19.

140 Brundage, *Medieval Canon Law*, 57–8, 201, 214, 225–6.

is naturally permitted for contracting parties to get the better of one another."[141] Similarly Paul: "In buying and selling natural law permits the one party to buy for less and the other to sell for more than the thing is worth; thus each party is allowed to outwit the other."[142] Being thus founded on a general rule of free bargaining, classical Roman law had no requirement of a just price in purchases and sales.[143]

The weight of canonical authorities before the twelfth century tended to resist a blanket approval of free bargaining. Against the Roman-law maxim, the Apostle Paul could be cited as a counter-text forbidding dishonest or fraudulent dealing: "that no man overreach, nor circumvent his brother in business."[144] The Church Fathers' many aspersions against merchants and their practices have already been seen via Gratian. Carolingian legislation also attempted to regulate exchange on the basis of fair or just prices. The canon *Placuit* is one such law that was incorporated into the *Liber Extra*.[145] This canon requires priests to admonish their flocks not to sell their goods to travellers at higher prices than they could in the local market; if they should do so, then let such travellers refer it to the priest, who shall bid them to sell "with humanity."[146] *Placuit* thus forbade departing from local market prices to take advantage of travellers.

With the rediscovery of the Digest circa 1100, the Roman-law principle of free bargaining became part of the stock of tools applicable to questions of law and justice. It was brought into play in canon law to resolve certain difficulties raised in cases dealing with contracts of purchase and sale. The papal rescripts in the *Liber Extra* never explicitly refer to Pomponius's maxim *licet contrahentibus*; but it is implicit in the popes' application of the Roman-law doctrine of *laesio*

141 "In pretio emptionis et venditionis naturaliter licere contrahentibus se circumvenire." Ulpian quoting Pomponius, in *Dig.* 4.4.16.4. English translation from *The Roman Law of Sale: Introduction and Select Texts*, ed, and trans. de Zulueta. Latin quotations of Roman law are from *Corpus iuris civilis*, ed. Theodor Mommsen et al.

In the Watson translation: "the contracting parties are in the course of nature allowed to overreach each other." *The Digest of Justinian*, trans. Watson et al.

142 "Quemadmodum in emendo et vendendo naturaliter concessum est quod pluris sit minoris emere, quod minoris sit pluris vendere et ita invicem se circumscribere, ita in locationibus quoque et conductionibus iuris est." Paul, in *Dig.* 19.2.22.3. English from *Roman Law of Sale*, 136.

143 The limitation on free bargaining discussed below (*laesio enormis*) is supposed to have been a later development in Roman law. See Berger, *Encyclopedic Dictionary of Roman Law*, s.v. *pretium iustum*.

144 *Ut ne quis supergrediatur neque circumveniat in negotio fratrem suum.* 1 Thessalonians 4:6. Sometimes quoted in the sources with the phrasing *nemo in negotio* etc.

145 *X* 3.17.1. For discussion of the canon's Carolingian origins, see Baldwin, "Medieval Theories of the Just Price," 33.

146 "Placuit ut presbyteri plebes suas admoneant, ut … non carius vendant transeuntibus, quam in mercato vendere possunt, alioquin ad presbyterum transeuntes hoc referant, ut illius iussu cum humanitate sibi vendant." *X* 3.17.1.

enormis, discussed below, that bargaining over price, within a reasonable range, is legitimate. The decretalists, however, in commenting on these canons, consistently invoke *licet contrahentibus*. Although the decretalists sometimes cite the Roman principle of free bargaining and let it stand on its own,[147] they usually specify that it is bounded by certain limitations. The *Glossa ordinaria* consistently interprets *licet contrahentibus* with reference to *laesio enormis*, namely, that it is lawful for contracting parties to mutually deceive one another up to half of the just price.[148] Innocent IV and Hostiensis likewise recognize a limit of half the just price on the freedom to bargain.[149] Both Innocent IV and Hostiensis specify that freedom of bargaining excludes fraud, once again with reference to Roman law: Roman law identified several kinds of fraud in contracts of purchase and sale, on grounds of which the defrauded party could take legal action.[150] These frauds were called *fraus* and *dolus malus* and against them separate remedies were granted.[151] Free bargaining thus did not permit parties to outright lie or cheat to gain an advantage, but did allow for reasonable salesmanship in haggling over prices.[152]

---

147 "Si decepti essent, cum liceat contrahentibus se invicem decipere, non esset peccatum." Innocent IV, *Commentaria, X* 5.19.6 s.v. *promittunt*. "Licet contrahentibus se decipere." Ibid., s.v. *ex forma*². Quotations of Innocent IV are from *Commentaria super libros quinque Decretalium* (Frankfurt, 1570).

"Licitum est contrahentibus decipere se in pretio." Hostiensis, *Commentaria, X* 5.19.6 s.v. *usurarum*. Quotations of Hostiensis are from *In Decretalium libros commentaria*.

148 "Licitum est contrahentibus adinvicem se decipere; verum est usque ad dimidiam, sed non ultra." *Glossa ordinaria, X* 2.20.42 s.v. *deceptionis*. "Si autem sum deceptus minus dimidia iusti pretii, non possum agere ad aliquid: quia licitum est contrahentibus sese invicem decipere usque ad dimidiam iusti pretii." Ibid., *X* 3.17.3 s.v. *deceptione*. "Licet contrahentibus sese adinvicem decipere usque ad dimidium iusti pretii." Alanus, in *Glossa ordinaria, X* 5.19.6 s.v. *comparant*. Quotations of the *Glossa ordinaria* are from *Corpus iuris canonici cum glossis*, 4 vols (Rome, 1582).

149 Innocent IV, *Commentaria*, X 5.19.6 s.v. *promittunt* (quoted below, note 155). Hostiensis, *Commentaria*, X 3.17.3 s.v. *proponendam* (quoted below, note 150). "Usque ad dimidiam iusti pretii licet contrahentibus se ad invicem decipere." Ibid., *X* 5.19.6 s.v. *quinque libras*. Hostiensis also says that restitution will not be granted for a small injury in price; within limits, parties may get the best bargain possible: "Alias pro modico non daretur restitutio." Ibid., *X* 3.13.11 s.v. *enorme*.

150 Innocent IV, *Commentaria, X* 5.19.6 s.v. *promittunt* (quoted below, note 155). "Si deceptio non excedat dimidiam, licitum est naturaliter, scilicet sine fraude et sine dolo, adinvicem se decipere posse." Hostiensis, *Commentaria, X* 3.17.3 s.v. *proponendam*.

151 On the categories of fraud in Roman and later civil law, see Baldwin, "Medieval Theories of the Just Price," 55; Zimmermann, "*Metus* and *Dolus*," ch. 21 in *Law of Obligations*; and the relevant chapters in du Plessis, *Borkowski's Textbook of Roman Law*.

152 On this point, another Roman-law text (one of the *loci* for *laesio enormis*) described with approval the legitimate higgling and haggling over price that goes on in free bargaining. "Quod videlicet si contractus emptionis atque venditionis cogitasses substantiam et quod emptor viliori comparandi, venditor cariori distrahendi votum gerentes ad hunc contractum accedant vixque post multas contentiones, paulatim venditore de eo quod petierat detrahente, emptore autem huic quod obtulerat addente, ad certum consentiant pretium ..." Diocletian and Maximian, 1 December 293, in *Cod*. 4.44.8.

In some of their approaches to *licet contrahentibus*, the canonists come to grips with the apparent dissonance of the Roman-law maxim with the canonical authorities and the New Testament.[153] Hostiensis in one place reformulates the maxim in a form that is less susceptible to a mischievous reading, by putting the verb *decipere* in the passive voice: "contracting parties may naturally be mistaken about the price."[154] As a description of free bargaining, the picture drawn is not of two parties each trying to get the better of one another, but of two parties each attempting to approximate the true value of the good offered for sale. It shall become evident below how well this accords with the overall scholastic concept of the "just price" and of market exchange in general. Innocent IV likewise in one place offers an exposition of 1st Thessalonians 4:6. He explains that the "circumvention" which Paul forbids is just the set of categories of fraud established in Roman law. This includes fraud giving rise to a contract (*dolus dans causam*), fraud arising in a contract (*dolus incidens*), and injury beyond half the just price (*laesio enormis*). However, Innocent IV makes a seminal distinction about this permission of deception within half the just price when he adds the qualifying remark that this is according to the law of the forum, but perhaps not according to divine law: *iure fori sed forsan non iure poli*.[155] This distinction, *iure fori non iure poli*, shall be discussed more fully below. It becomes a key element in the approach of moral theologians to "just prices."

Juristic interpretation of the canon *Placuit* lends further support to the view that, although the law permits free bargaining within limits, this is not to be understood as a licence to take advantage of others, but as a recognition that there is legitimate uncertainty about prices. The *Gloss* simply repeats that one is not to sell more dear to travellers than in the local market.[156] Innocent IV, commenting on the requirement that priests admonish their parishioners not to gouge travellers in prices, adds that if they are notorious for this sin then they may be excommunicated.[157] Hostiensis equates the "humanity" with which locals ought to sell with

---

153 On this theme, see Kuttner, "Harmony from Dissonance."

154 "Naturaliter possunt in precio decipi contrahentes." Hostiensis, *Commentaria*, *X* 2.20.42 s.v. *quantitatem*. English adapted from Baldwin, "Medieval Theories of the Just Price," 56.

155 "Nec obicit quod dicit apostolus: Nemo in negotio circumveniat fratrem suum, ut exponatur in negotio, id est, in negotiatione; sed dic, nemo circumveniat ita, quod circumventio det causam contractui, quia ipso iure non tenet, sicut quando incidit potest agi ut rescindatur. Vel nemo circumveniat in negotio supple, venditionis, ultra dimidiam iusti pretii: intra non dimidiam possent se decipere iure fori. Sed forsan non iure poli accipiunt." Innocent IV, *Commentaria*, *X* 5.19.6 s.v. *promittunt*.

This phrase is the theme of a recent article by James Brundage, "*Ius fori* and *Ius poli*."

156 "Nota, quod transeuntibus nihil carius vendendum est, quam in mercato." *Glossa ordinaria*, *X* 3.17.1 s.v. *placuit*.

157 "Et si necesse fuerit compellant; secundum Alanum, sed nos contra: nisi esset notorium, quia tunc posset excommunicare, nisi emendaretur, vel interdiceret nocentes." Innocent IV, *Commentaria*, *X* 3.17.1 s.v. *admoneant*.

"equity" and "piety," invoking the Golden Rule: "do unto others as you would have them do unto you."[158] There is, then, a moral requirement upon Christians not to gouge travellers, even if, apart from the more extreme or notorious cases, this is not compelled by human law. In light of this, along with the canonistic interpretations of *licet contrahentibus*, the permission given by canon law to free bargaining is not meant to imply that a Christian can, with a clean conscience, knowingly charge someone more than the just price; rather, the haggling over prices is a mutual search precisely for this value. This matter of the conscience is brought out more explicitly by the theologians, as discussed below.[159] Among the canonists the legal doctrine is clear: within the limits of half the just price, *licet contrahentibus sese invicem decipere*: freedom of bargaining is the rule.

*Protection from Gross Injury (*laesio enormis*)*

In discussing *licet contrahentibus*, I have already alluded to a competing Roman-law doctrine, the restriction on free bargaining known as "gross injury" (*laesio enormis*). The *locus communis* for this doctrine is a law from Justinian's *Code*:

> If your father sold the land at a price below its value, it is equitable that either you should repay the price to the buyers and recover the land with the assistance of the authority of the court, or should, if the buyer prefers, receive the amount of deficiency of a fair price. The price is considered too low if less than half of the true price has been paid.[160]

The suit for *laesio enormis* in Roman law only protected a seller of land. If he received less than half the "fair" or "true price" (*verum pretium, iustum pretium*) he

---

158 "Id est aequitate, et pietate praedicta. Iuxta illud, "quod tibi vis fieri, mihi fac. Quod non tibi noli ..." Hostiensis, *Commentaria, X* 3.17.1 s.v. *humanitate*.

159 See also Baldwin, "Medieval Theories of the Just Price," 68ff. However, *pace* Baldwin, I interpret the canonists as being in essential agreement with the theologians on the obligation in conscience to observe a "just price" in purchases and sales. For my full argument, see the chapter in *Thomas Aquinas and Medieval Canon Law.*

160 "Rem maioris pretii si tu vel pater tuus minoris pretii, distraxit, humanum est, ut vel pretium te restituente emptoribus fundum venditum recipias auctoritate intercedente iudicis, vel, si emptor elegerit, quod deest iusto pretio recipies. Minus autem pretium esse videtur, si nec dimidia pars veri pretii soluta sit." Diocletian and Maximian, 28 October 285, in *Cod.* 4.44.2. English from *Roman Law of Sale*, trans. de Zulueta.

The other precedent-setting text for *laesio enormis*: "Hoc enim solum, quod paulo minori pretio fundum venumdatum significas, ad rescindendam emptionem invalidum est ... nisi minus dimidia iusti pretii, quod fuerat tempore venditionis, datum est, electione iam emptori praestita servanda." Diocletian and Maximian, 1 December 293, in *Cod.* 4.44.8.

On these two passages in the Code, see Jusztinger, "The Principle of *Laesio Enormis* in Sale and Purchase Contracts in Roman Law"; Westbrook, "The Origin of *Laesio Enormis*."

could sue to have the sale rescinded under judicial authority, refunding the price to the buyer, or to receive what was lacking from the just price. It was up to the buyer which alternative to choose. The principle of *laesio enormis* is key to the canonistic framework of just prices.

The popes imported *laesio enormis* whole cloth into the canon law through their resolutions of cases. Three decretal letters, issued under popes Alexander III and Innocent III, were fundamental. Alexander III's decretal *Cum dilecti* concerned a piece of forest sold by some members of the cathedral chapter of Beauvais to the monks of Chaalis.[161] The monks paid 10 pounds for it; the canons claimed the property was then worth 40 marks.[162] The dean of Rheims, appointed to decide the case, pronounced that the sale did not hold because the monks paid less than half the just price, and he returned possession to the canons. Alexander III, however, nullified the sentence as contrary to law, because, "when a thing is bought for less than half the just price, it is in the judgment of the buyer whether he supply the just price or rescind the sale."[163] He thus returned possession to the monks but left open the possibility of a new suit being opened concerning the property. This sentence is noteworthy because, even though it appeared likely on several grounds that the property should ultimately be returned to the cathedral chapter, Alexander III scrupulously applied Roman law's procedural requirements for *laesio enormis*, resulting in a judgment in favour of the monks of Chaalis.

A decretal of Innocent III, *Ad nostram noveritis*, of 29 March 1206, dealt with the problem of gross injury and was an important text drawn on by later legal commentators in their discussions of *laesio enormis*.[164] In this sentence, the property was to be returned, not only because the price paid was much less than its worth, but also because it had been sold under compulsion of poverty. The one who had purchased the property was allowed to keep the profits he had gained from it in the intervening years, which amounted to substantially more than the price paid.

Baldwin called Innocent III's decretal *Cum causa*, 27 November 1207, the *cause célèbre* of *laesio enormis*.[165] It introduced the conditions of *laesio enormis*, as

---

161 Alexander III, in *X* 3.17.3. For discussion, see Baldwin, "Medieval Theories of the Just Price," 43.

162 Establishing the equivalent value of these different measures is not easy. Estimating based on the general range of values of the mark, the land might have been worth between 24 and 32 pounds. For an orientation to moneys of account, see Spufford, *Money and Its Use in Medieval Europe*, 411–14.

163 "Quia vero in arbitrio emptoris est, si velit supplere iustum pretium, aut venditionem rescindere, cum res minus dimidia iusti pretii comparatur." Alexander III, in *X* 3.17.3.

164 Innocent III, in *X* 3.13.11. The decretal is edited in full in *Die Register Innocenz' III*, ed. Hageneder, Sommerlechner, et al., vol. 9, no. 56 (9:102–3). For discussion, see Baldwin, "Medieval Theories of the Just Price," 43–4.

165 Baldwin, "Medieval Theories of the Just Price," 44.

understood in Roman law, into the body of canon law without modification.[166] Innocent III settled a case concerning a monastery which in a sale of its lands had received substantially less than the current price. The resolution established several clearly defined principles:

1. A seller of property can claim gross injury if he received less than half the just price.
2. If gross injury is proved, then it is up to the buyer whether to return the property and receive a refund or to pay what is lacking from the just price.[167]
3. The just price is what the property was commonly worth at the time of sale.
4. This price is to be established in court through the testimony of local witnesses.[168]

The decretalists accepted and built on this basic doctrine originating in Roman law and assimilated by the popes into canon law.[169] The civilians had already led the way by extending *laesio enormis* to also protect buyers, and applying it not only to purchases of land but to any good which could fetch a price.[170] In applying *laesio enormis* to buyers, the choice was assigned to the seller whether to pay back the excess or rescind the sale, on the general principle that in a case of gross injury the choice of alternatives belongs to the party who benefited from the injury, i.e., the "deceiving" party.[171]

There was some debate about the precise value beyond which *laesio enormis* enters. For the seller this was normally anything below precisely half the just price;

---

166 Innocent III's decretal is split into two chapters in the *Liber Extra*: *X* 2.20.42; *X* 3.17.6. Edited in full in *Die Register Innocenz' III*, vol. 10, no. 162 (10:271).

167 "Cum constitisset nobis, monasterium in venditione ultra dimidiam iusti pretii fuisse deceptum, sententiando decrevimus ut praefati cives aut recepto pretio possessiones restituerent memoratas, aut supplerent quantum constaret legitimae venditionis tempore iusto pretio defuisse." Innocent III, in *X* 3.17.6.

168 "Cum igitur abbas et fratres eiusdem loci probare intendant, quanti pretii venditionis tempore possessiones praedictae fuere, mandamus quatenus recipiatis testes, quos alterutra partium super hoc duxerit producendos." Innocent III, in *X* 2.20.42.

169 See *Glossa ordinaria*, *X* 2.20.42, passim; ibid., *X* 3.13.11 s.v. *enorme*; ibid., *X* 3.17.3 s.v. *cum dilecti*; ibid. s.v. *deceptione*; ibid., *X* 3.17.6 s.v. *cum causa*; ibid. s.v. *dimidiam*; Innocent IV, *Commentaria*, *X* 2.20.42, passim; ibid., *X* 3.13.11 s.v. *monasterium*; ibid., *X* 3.17.3 s.v. *arbitrio*; ibid., *X* 3.17.6 s.v. *recepto*; ibid., s.v. *restituerent*; Hostiensis, *Commentaria*, *X* 3.17.3, s.v. *induxit*; ibid., s.v. *in arbitrio emptoris*; ibid., s.v. *proponendam*; ibid., *X* 3.17.6 s.v. *vertebatur*; ibid., s.v. *restituerent*.

170 Armstrong, *Usury and Public Debt*, 303.

171 "Quid ergo, si plus dimidia, ex quo casus conversus est? In arbitrio venditoris debet esse, utrum rem recuperet, vel quod minus habuerit, restituat conversa ratione, et sic in utroque casu datur electio decipienti." Hostiensis, *Commentaria*, *X* 3.17.3 s.v. *minus dimidia*. Thus also the *Glossa ordinaria*, *X* 3.17.6 s.v. *dimidiam*; Hostiensis, *Commentaria*, *X* 5.19.6 s.v. *quinque libras*.

but there were alternative opinions noted, including slightly above half.[172] When the doctrine was applied to buyers, a dilemma emerged about the value equivalent to less than half the just price. Should this be calculated by the same ratio of two to one, or by deviation of half the value? The *Glossa ordinaria* notes that some keep to the same ratio, saying the buyer must have paid twice the price and more: as in a buyer who pays 21 for a thing worth 10. But the glossator refutes this opinion, "because no law says it," and because the buyer then is deceived in more than the whole price.[173] Hostiensis says that if this were applied equally to the seller then he could only claim *laesio enormis* if he received no price at all.[174] The glossator explains the correct opinion, with which "dominus Jacobus" and Azo agree: if a buyer pays 16 for a good worth 10, he may claim *laesio enormis*, because he is deceived beyond half the just price; but if he were deceived only in 5, he would have no legal recourse.[175] Hostiensis, using the same example, says that the buyer could claim *laesio enormis* if he paid 15 plus a single penny.[176]

With canon law having received the Roman principle *licet contrahentibus*, the concomitant reception of *laesio enormis* granted some protection to buyers and sellers from gross injury within a normal framework of free bargaining. The question remains how, within a framework of free bargaining, can the the just price, on which *laesio enormis* depends, be calculated? When *laesio enormis* applied only to land, as in its origin, there were certain arithmetical methods available: for

172 Affirming anything below precisely half: *Glossa ordinaria, X* 3.17.6 s.v. *dimidiam*; Hostiensis, *Commentaria, X* 3.17.6 s.v. *dimidiam*. Noting the alternative opinion: Innocent IV, *Commentaria, X* 3.17.6 s.v. *restituerent*.

173 "Alii dicunt quod necessarium est ut duplum iusti pretii et ultra dederit emptor: ut ecce, res valet decem, et ego emi pro viginti unum, quod nulla lex dicit: et nihil est quod dicunt: quia hic decipitur emptor in plus quam sit totum iustum pretium." *Glossa ordinaria, X* 3.17.6 s.v. *dimidiam*.

174 "Quod secundum hoc sequeretur, quod nec venditor deceptus esset, nisi quoniam emptio nulla esset, nam quantum addis emptori exemplificando, tantum debes detrahere venditori, sed si detrahis X lib. quas superaddis venditori, iam detrahis totum pretium, ergo de nullo pretio convenit inter contrahentes, ergo nulla fuit emptio, quae nec sine precio contrahitur." Hostiensis, *Commentaria X* 3.17.6 s.v. *dimidiam*.

175 "Et sic etiam in emptore decepto pone quod res valeat decem, et emptor solvit sexdecim, potest agere ad pretium recipiendum quod plus dedit, vel in totum recedere a contractu: quia sic patet, quod est deceptus ultra dimidiam iusti pretii; solvit enim sex ultra dimidiam [*sic*] iusti pretii, quod fuit decem. Si enim deciperetur in quinque tantum, non ageretur: quia quinque sunt dimidia decem. Et ita non est deceptus emptor in aliquo ultra dimidiam iusti pretii. Sed quia sex dedit, ultra dimidiam deceptus est, ideo aget. Azo intelligit ista verba ita ... Et dominus Iacobus dicit eodem modo cum Azone." *Glossa ordinaria, X* 3.17.6 s.v. *dimidiam*. A likely identification of Dominus Iacobus is Jacobus de Arena; however, Jacobus Butrigarius is cited (as Iac. Bu.) soon after in the *Glossa ordinaria* to the same canon, s.v. *restituerent*. For identifications, see Bryson, *Dictionary of Sigla and Abbreviations to and in Law Books before 1607*, s.v. *dom. Iacobus*; ibid. s.v. *Iac. Bu.*

176 "Pone, quod ipse emit XV libris et uno denario, patet, quod est deceptus in V libris, quae faciunt dimidiam iusti precii, et in uno denario ultra, et sic est deceptus ultra dimidiam: unde et ipse agere potest contra te venditorem." Hostiensis, *Commentaria*, X 3.17.6 s.v. *dimidiam*.

example, the value of the property's income over a certain number of years.[177] In *Ad nostram noveritis* the value of the property was reckoned based on its annual revenue.[178] But once *laesio enormis* was extended to apply to any kind of goods for sale, another method was needed.

The Current Market Price (res tantum valet quantum vendi potest, sed communiter)

Once again from Roman law came the standard formula for reckoning the value of a good: the current market price. A celebrated text from the Digest concerned transfer of ownership of a farm which had been pledged, and whether a *cautio* (security) should be given: "the farm should be valued at what it is worth without this *cautio*, that is, at the sum for which it might be sold without a *cautio*."[179] The principle, then, is that the value of a thing, at least for legal purposes, is the price for which it can normally be sold. Further texts of the Digest specified this: "The prices of things are to be taken generally and not according to personal affections nor their special utility to particular individuals."[180] The standard example was of a man who owns his own son as a slave. He is not thereby richer because his son is of particular value to him; the value of the slave (for instance if someone kills him and is obliged to pay compensation) is what he would normally sell for, not the value which the father might put on his son.[181] This produced the maxim *res tantum valet quantum vendi potest*, always completed by some form of *sed communiter*.[182] The value of a thing is its current market price.[183]

---

177 "Sed qualiter hoc probatur? Dico quod ex qualitate rei et quantitate reddituum probatur pretium rei. Quandoque res aestimatur quantum potest colligi in quinquaginta annis. Quandoque etiam consideratur quantum in XX annis possit colligi." *Glossa ordinaria*, *X* 2.20.42 s.v. *ad alium*. Likewise Hostiensis, *Commentaria*, *X* 2.20.42 s.v. *articulum*.

178 Innocent III, in *X* 3.13.11.

179 "Aestimandum fundum, quanti valet sine hac cautione, hoc est quanti vendere potest sine cautione." Ulpian, in *Dig.* 36.1.1.16. English from *Digest*, trans. Watson et al.

180 "Pretia rerum non ex affectione nec utilitate singulorum, sed communiter fungi." Paul, in *Dig.* 9.2.33. English from *Digest*, trans. Watson et al. See also *Dig.* 36.2.63.

181 "Si servum meum occidisti, non affectiones aestimandas esse puto, veluti si filium tuum naturalem quis occiderit quem tu magno emptum velles, sed quanti omnibus valeret." Paul, *Dig.* 9.2.33.

182 "Immo videtur quod tantum valeat: res enim tantum valet, quantum vendi potest. Pretia enim rerum non ex affectu singulorum, sed communiter aestimantur." *Glossa ordinaria*, *X* 5.19.6 s.v. *non valent*. "Communi aestimatione." Innocent IV, *Commentaria*, *X* 5.19.6 s.v. *non valent*. "Sed verius est, quod dicatur quantum vendi posset tempore ipsius contractus, communi aestimatione considerata non speciali affectu." Hostiensis, *Commentaria*, *X* 2.20.42 s.v. *articulum*. Glossing *quam in mercato vendere possunt*: "communi pretio." Ibid., *X* 3.17.1 s.v. *possunt*. "Immo videtur, quod tantum valet, quantum vendi potest. Quod et verum est communi pretio considerato non affectu ementis, quia pretia rerum non ex affectu singulorum, immo communiter aestimantur. Intelligas ergo, quod hic dicit non valet, subaudi communi pretio aestimato." Ibid., *X* 5.19.6 s.v. *non valent*.

183 Noonan (a judge as well as a historian) pointed out that "the law today has achieved little more precision." "Review: The Medieval Theories of the Just Price by John W. Baldwin."

In ancient Roman law this principle was not applied as a check against free bargaining. The texts just cited were concerned with calculating the value of various kinds of property for legal purposes, not for enforcing just prices generally.[184] In purchases and sales, *licet contrahentibus* was the rule, with the postclassical protection of *laesio enormis* reserved specifically for sales of land. In classical canon law, however, the principle that prices are established by common estimation and not by individual affection did work as a check against certain excesses in free bargaining. It was employed as part of the moral condemnation of price discrimination, as was foreshadowed in the canon *Placuit*, and as will be seen in the discussion of St Thomas Aquinas below.[185] In canon-law jurisprudence, it was brought into application in connection with *laesio enormis*. In commenting on *Cum causa*, where the standard of value being employed was not made explicit, Hostiensis mentions the annual income test as a possibility, but concludes that the better standard is to consider what the property would commonly sell for.[186]

The canonists judged that this value could be determined by summoning local witnesses and asking them what the goods, or a similar piece of property, would normally sell for.[187] This is what Innocent III mandated in *Cum causa*: the testimony of local witnesses on both sides would settle the true price.[188] The original witnesses had testified that the property was worth more than twice the price paid. The buyer therefore was faced with the alternative of rescinding the sale or supplying what was lacking from the price. If he chose to supply the just price, it would become necessary to know this value precisely. Hence witnesses were to be called in a second time, on both sides, to attest to the just price. The same witnesses could be called in again, because formerly they had only been answering whether the true value exceeded twice the price, whereas now they are answering what was its exact value.[189]

---

184 However, Roman law did deal sternly with monopoly: see de Roover, "Monopoly Theory prior to Adam Smith," 274.

185 On scholastic condemnation of price discrimination and market manipulation more generally, see Langholm, "Monopoly and Market Irregularities in Medieval Economic Thought"; Langholm, *The Legacy of Scholasticism in Economic Thought*; and de Roover, "The Concept of the Just Price," 426ff.

186 "Sed qualiter probabitur verum precium rei? … Sed verius est, quod dicatur quantum vendi posset tempore ipsius contractus, communi aestimatione considerata non speciali affectu." Hostiensis, *Commentaria*, *X* 2.20.42 s.v. *articulum*.

187 "Sed non constitit inquantum ultra, ideo mandantur recipi testes super hac quantitate." Ibid., *X* 3.17.6 s.v. *iusti pretii*. Hostiensis grants that the true value could by known also by the agreement of the adversarial party: "Per consessionem partis adversae, vel per testes conductos, ut innuitur." Ibid., *X* 3.17.6 s.v. *constitisset*.

188 Innocent III, in *X* 2.20.42. Hostiensis, *Commentaria*, *X* 2.20.42 s.v. *alterutra*.

189 "Cum igitur abbas et fratres eiusdem loci probare intendant, quanti pretii venditionis tempore possessiones praedictae fuere, mandamus, quatenus recipiatis testes, quos alterutra partium super hoc duxerit producendos … Si vero pars monasterii ad hunc articulum eosdem

The need to establish the true value of a thing arose in several other papal decretals incorporated into the *Liber Extra.* Innocent III, in *Ad nostram noveris* of 4 March 1203, settled a case in which a pretended contract of sale was used to disguise a usurious loan. An excessively small price was considered as evidence that the sale was fraudulent. Here the phrase *iustum pretium* is used as synonymous with the current market price.[190] In other decretals on the subject of usury, the true worth of a thing was understood to be the price the goods would normally sell for, i.e., the usual market price. A decretal of Alexander III, *In civitate*, answered a question about a certain type of contract where someone buys goods not worth more than 5 pounds at the time of the purchase, promising to pay over 6 pounds at a later time.[191] Two points are worth noting. The legal value was presumed to be the current market price.[192] This value was known to vary with time: the pope explained that the seller incurs sin unless there is doubt whether the commodities will be worth more or less at the time of payment; in this case the seller is clear

---

testes produxerit, quos ad alium probandum produxit, vos nihilominus eos recipere procuretis, quoniam aliud est probasse deceptionis excessum, et aliud probare quantitatem valoris." Innocent III, in *X* 2.20.42. "Sed non determinaverunt testes quanta fuerit illa laesio: Et haec probatio sufficiebat si emptores voluissent emptionem rescindere: sed quia dicebant se velle iustum pretium supplere, fuit dubitatum, nunquid monasterium posset de novo probare quantitatem excessus, cum dicta testium fuissent publicata super deceptione? Et respondetur quod sic: quia ista est nova materia, licet habeat partem inclusam de antiqua, non oportebit iterum probare monasterium fuisse deceptum, sed de novo nunc determinabitur, quantitas deceptionis. Nota quod diversus modus agendi est probare, quod quis sit deceptus ultra dimidiam iusti pretii, et probare quantum deceptus est ultra dimidium, unde testes recepti in uno articulo publicatis attestionibus eorum, possunt recipi in <alio>, nec dicuntur recipi super eodem capitulo." *Glossa ordinaria, X* 2.20.42 s.v. *cum causa.* See also ibid., *X* 2.20.42 s.v. *ad alium.* "Scilicet, quantitatem valoris, forte enim valet 400 quod est quadruplum pretii." Innocent IV, *Commentaria, X* 2.20.42 s.v. *articulum.* "Scilicet, deceptionis excessum, qui plene probatus fuit, si res vendita esset pro 100 probavit valorem 200, quibus 200 Abbas non vult, nec debet esse contentus cum valeat 400." Ibid., *X* 2.20.42 s.v. *ad alium.* "Scilicet quantitatem valoris, ut sequitur secundum dominum nostrum, et nota quod argumentum habes hoc imo expressum, quod potest probari, quod res vendita valebat ultra medietatem iusti precii, licet non probetur, quantum ultra. Puta cum esset vendita precio X librarum testes dicebant, quod scilicet valebat plus quam viginti, sed non determinabant quantum, illud ergo quantum potest modo probari ad hoc. Quid enim si emptor offerat undecim, vel duodecim? Potest venditor dicere non sufficit, quia res valebat triginta, vel quadraginta tempore contractus, qui inspicitur." Hostiensis, *Commentaria, X* 2.20.42 s.v. *articulum.* See also ibid., *X* 2.20.42 s.v. *quos ad alium.*

190 "XL uncias Tarenorum, quae vix dimidiam iusti pretii contingebant." Innocent III, in *X* 3.17.5. *Die Register Innocenz' III*, vol. 6, no. 15 (6:28). See Baldwin, "Medieval Theories of the Just Price," 51.

191 Alexander III, in *X* 5.19.6. See Baldwin, "Medieval Theories of the Just Price," 53–4, 56.

192 "Alias merces comparant, quae tunc ultra quinque libras non valent." Alexander III, in *X* 5.19.6.

of sin.[193] A decretal of Urban III, *Consuluit*, also condemned one selling a good for more than it was worth because payment was delayed.[194] Hostiensis added the comment that this assumes there was no doubt about the future value of the goods; if there were, then, as in *In civitate*, the contract would be clear of sin.[195]

A final text from canon law, *Naviganti*, is attributed to Pope Gregory IX; it was drafted for the *Liber Extra* by Raymond of Peñafort and placed into the title *De usuris*.[196] In addition to condemning sea loans (*foenus nauticum*), *Naviganti* summarized the principle of *In civitate* that it is permissible to sell goods for a higher price because of delayed payment if there is genuine doubt about their future value; however, this was not meant to justify speculation, since it only applied if the seller "was not otherwise intending to sell."[197] The principle is extended to permit buying goods for less than their value if delivery is deferred.[198] The rubric once again uses *iustum pretium* as synonymous with the current market price.[199]

The recognition that the value of goods can change over time has its own precedents in Roman law: "Sometimes place or time brings a variation in value; oil will not be equally valued at Rome and in Spain nor given the same assessment in periods of lasting scarcity as when there are crops."[200] No item has a permanently stable price. Instead, to determine the just price in any particular situation, one must rely on the current market price in a given time and place. Hence, in treating of *laesio enormis*, the canonists explain that the determination of price must always

193 "Venditores peccatum incurrunt, nisi dubium sit, merces illas plus minusve solutionis tempore valituras." Alexander III, in *X* 5.19.6. The rubric repeats this with emphasis: "Vendens rem plus, quam valeat, quia solutionem differt, peccat, nisi dubium sit, an tempore solutionis erit valor rei variatus, et venditor non erat venditurus tempore, quo vendidit." Ibid.

194 Urban III, in *X* 5.19.10.

195 "Nec aliquod dubium occurrit, utrum plus, vel minus sint solutionis tempore valituræ, alioquin contra: supra eodem *In civitate*." Hostiensis, *Commentaria*, *X* 5.19.10 s.v. *pretio*.

196 Gregory IX, in *X* 5.19.19.

197 "Ratione huius dubii etiam excusatur, qui pannos, granum, vinum, oleum vel alias merces vendit, ut amplius, quam tunc valeant, in certo termino recipiat pro eisdem; si tamen ea tempore contractus non fuerat venditurus." Gregory IX, in *X* 5.19.19. The quotation is from the rubric to this canon: "Propter dubium excusatur is, qui ex eo, quod differt solutionem pretii, vendit rem plus, quam valeat, si non erat eam alias venditurus." Ibid. On the various forms of speculation condemned by the scholastics, see de Roover, "The Concept of the Just Price," 428ff.

198 "Ille quoque, qui dat X solidos, ut alio tempore totidem sibi grani, vini vel olei mensurae reddantur, quae licet tunc plus valeant, utrum plus vel minus solutionis tempore fuerint valiturae, verisimiliter dubitatur, non debet ex hoc usurarius reputari." Gregory IX, in *X* 5.19.19.

199 "Non est usurarius emptor rei minus iusto pretio, si tunc verisimiliter dubitetur, an tempore solutionis plus vel minus sit res valitura." Ibid.

200 "Nonnullam tamen pretio varietatem loca temporaque adferunt: nec enim tantidem Romae et in Hispania oleum aestimabitur nec continuis sterilitatibus tantidem, quanti secundis fructibus." Paul, in *Dig.* 35.2.63.2. English from *Digest*, trans. Watson et al.

be based on the time of the sale itself.[201] The *Glossa ordinaria* asks: what if a thing that sold for 10 was worth 10 at the time, but now, because of the care of the new owner or some other reason, is worth 30? In that situation, the seller cannot claim *laesio enormis*, because it is the value at the time of sale that matters.[202]

The civilians and canonists of the classical period of medieval jurisprudence thus produced a framework for purchase and exchange in which the value of things is both subjective and objective. It is subjective in relation to the thing itself considered in general, and in relation to time and to place: because the value of a thing cannot be permanently fixed at a particular sum. This is recognized in the formula *res tantum valet quantum vendi potest*, "a thing is worth as much as it can be sold for." However, protection of buyers and sellers in the context of *laesio enormis* requires some standard of value beyond the simple consent of the parties. Thus *res tantum* is completed by *sed communiter*, "yet commonly." The just price has an objective quality with regard to the individual transaction: because in any given exchange there is a knowable outside standard, namely the normal going market price. This does not obliterate free bargaining; the principle *licet contrahentibus* still applies. Each party may bargain and use salesmanship in order to persuade the other to agree to an advantageous price. What the objective standard does is set some bounds for this. On the one hand, *laesio enormis* sets a boundary on the advantage one can gain beyond the usual market price; on the other hand it sets a boundary on the loss a person can suffer without recourse.

A fully expounded doctrine of the nature of value was not necessary for the operation of canon law. It sufficed to cite the common legal principle *res tantum valet quantum vendi potest, sed communiter*. It was the scholastic philosophers and theologians who made explicit the theory of value implicit in the legal framework, as will be seen in the next section.

4. Aristotle via Thomas Aquinas: Aquinas's Synthesis

The third foundational corpus for scholastic economic analysis is the philosophical writings of Aristotle. Indeed, it has been pointed out more than once by historians

---

201 "Tempus enim contractus inspiciendum est." *Glossa ordinaria*, *X* 2.20.42 s.v. *tempore*. "Tempus venditionis spectandum est." Ibid., *X* 3.17.3 s.v. *tunc valentem*. "Tempore venditionis, quod spectandum est." Innocent IV, *Commentaria*, *X* 3.17.3 s.v. *tunc*. "Tempus enim contractus inspiciendum est." Hostiensis, *Commentaria*, *X* 2.20.42 s.v. *venditionis tempore*. "Scilicet tempore contractus. Hoc enim inspiciendum est." Ibid., *X* 3.17.3 s.v. *tunc valentem*. Likewise, ibid., *X* 3.17.6 s.v. *venditionis tempore*. "Scilicet tempore contractus, qui spectandus est, quando quaeritur de aestimatione rei emptae." Ibid., *X* 5.19.6 s.v. *quae tunc*.

202 "Sed pone quod tempore venditionis valeret decem, tempore litis contestatae valeret triginta, sive studio monachorum, vel alio modo; nunquid modo revocabitur venditio? Non: quia tempus venditionis spectandum est." *Glossa ordinaria*, *X* 3.17.3 s.v. *tunc valentem*.

of economic thought that Aristotelian economics is a creation, not of Aristotle or the ancient Greeks or Romans, but of the thirteenth-century scholastics.[203] A great deal of scholastic economic analysis was worked out in commentaries on Aristotle's *Nicomachean Ethics* and *Politics*. This Aristotelian-inspired scholastic economics has been very ably and thoroughly studied, and the reader is directed in particular to the publications of Odd Langholm, whose life's work this is.[204] For present purposes, it will suffice to elucidate what St Thomas Aquinas did to advance the analysis of value and just prices by extrapolating from a small number of key *loci* in Aristotle.[205] In so doing, it will be shown that the principles and arguments drawn from all three corpora were brought together and to a great extent harmonized and synthesized by Aquinas into a coherent body of teaching on justice in buying and selling.

St Thomas Aquinas dealt with economic subjects and employed intellectual tools for economic analysis at a number of places in his writings.[206] However, all the relevant threads can be found intertwined in the *Summa theologiae, secunda secundae*, question 77, "of cheating which is committed in buying and selling."[207] In the four articles which are part of this question, two directly concern the subject: a. 1, "whether it is lawful to sell a thing for more than its worth?" and a. 4,

---

203 "Even among the Greeks, says Schumpeter, economic analysis is confined almost entirely to Aristotle ... After Aristotle, there is what Schumpter calls the 'Great Gap,' which encompasses the period between the death of Aristotle and the work of Thomas Aquinas in the thirteenth century. Insofar as anyone deserves the title of founder of economics, according to Schumpeter, it was the 'Scholastic doctors' of the Middle Ages." Mueller, *Redeeming Economics*, 13, citing Schumpeter, *History of Economic Analysis*, 9, 57, 60, 93. "Starting with Albert the Great and Thomas Aquinas, historians are able to trace the transmission of economic theories from teacher to student, and from one 'school' to another, right down the present. But no earlier tradition of a purely Aristotelian economics has been found, even though the Greek Academy continued to operate until A.D. 529." Mueller, *Redeeming Economics*, 28.

204 In addition to the publications already cited, there is Langholm's series (1979–84): *Price and Value in the Aristotelian Tradition*; *Wealth and Money in the Aristotelian Tradition*; *The Aristotelian Analysis of Usury*.

205 It should be noted that Aquinas is greatly indebted to his forebears, in both philosophy and theology, who led the way in their teaching and annotation of Aristotle. Above all others stands St Albert the Great, OP, the first to comment on the entire Aristotelian corpus. See Resnick, ed., *A Companion to Albert the Great*, 9–10.

206 Even a bare abbreviated list of these would be lengthy. See the references collected in Langholm, "The Medieval Schoolmen," and the two chapters on Aquinas in *Economics in the Medieval Schools*.

207 Unless otherwise noted, English quotations are from *The Summa Theologica*, trans. Fathers of the English Dominican Province. Another English translation of this question is in *Summa theologiae: Latin Text and English Translation, Introductions, Notes, Appendices and Glossaries*, vol. 38, *Injustice*, trans. LeFébure; quotations therefrom are indicated where they are used. Latin quotations are from the *editio Leonina*: *Opera omnia*, vols. 4–10.

"whether it is lawful in trading to sell a thing at a higher price than was paid for it?" A few points are also worthy of note in the other two articles.

Following his normal procedure in the *Summa theologiae*, Aquinas approaches the question "whether it is lawful to sell a thing for more than its worth" by first setting out arguments against the thesis he will adopt.[208] Each of these three objections argues that it is lawful to sell a thing for more than its worth. The first argues from the civil law, citing the jurists' maxim *licet contrahentibus sese invicem decipere*: "according to these laws it is just for buyer and seller to deceive one another" (*secundum eas licitum est emptori et venditori ut se invicem decipiant*).[209] The second argues from common custom, citing a saying of St Augustine, as well as Proverbs 20:14, *It is nought, it is nought, saith every buyer: and when he is gone away, then he will boast.*[210] The third argues from the demands of honesty: sometimes "the utility accruing to the receiver … is worth more than the thing given," and in that case honesty demands that the receiver provide a corresponding recompense to the deliverer.[211]

Aquinas's *sed contra* corresponds to the objection raised by Hostiensis against a supposed blanket permission of "deception" in buying and selling:

> *All things therefore whatsoever you would that men should do to you, do you also to them.*[212] But no man wishes to buy a thing for more than its worth. Therefore no man should sell a thing to another man for more than its worth.[213]

In his reply, Aquinas first sets aside the question of actual deceit (*fraus*) in order to sell a thing for more than its just price: this is altogether sinful.[214] As was just seen in the discussion of law, *fraus* was dealt with under a separate remedy; the question here concerns selling a thing for more than its worth "apart from fraud."[215] In the first half of the reply, Aquinas makes use of Aristotle, drawing upon two notions elucidated in Aristotle's *Politics* and *Nicomachean Ethics*. The first is that buying and selling "seem to be established for the common advantage of both parties" (Aquinas), they arise "at first from what is natural, from the circumstance

208 Aquinas, *Summa theologiae*, q. 77 a. 1.

209 Ibid., arg. 1. Cfr *Cod.* 4.44.8; *Cod.* 4.44.15.

210 *Malum est, malum est, dicit omnis emptor; et cum recesserit, tunc gloriabitur.* Proverbs 20:14.

211 Aquinas, *Summa theologiae*, q. 77 a. 1 arg. 3.

212 *Omnia ergo quaecumque vultis ut faciant vobis homines, et vos facite illis.* Matthew 7:12.

213 Aquinas, *Summa theologiae*, q. 77 a. 1 *sed contra*. Cfr Hostiensis, *Commentaria*, X 3.17.1 s.v. *humanitate*, quoted above in section 3.

214 "Respondeo dicendum quod fraudem adhibere ad hoc quod aliquid plus iusto pretio vendatur, omnino peccatum est …" Aquinas, *Summa theologiae*, q. 77 a. 1 co.

215 Ibid.

that some have too little, others too much" (Aristotle);[216] "and consequently all contracts between them should observe equality of thing and thing" (Aquinas).[217] The second notion is that "the quality of a thing that comes into human use is measured by the price given for it, for which purpose money was invented" (Aquinas),[218] as Aristotle points out in the *Nicomachean Ethics*:

> But these must be equated. This is why all things that are exchanged must be somehow comparable. It is for this end that money has been introduced, and it becomes in a sense an intermediate; for it measures all things, and therefore the excess and the defect – how many shoes are equal to a house or to a given amount of food ... All goods must therefore be measured by some one thing, as we said before. Now this unit is in truth demand, which holds all things together (for if men did not need one another's goods at all, or did not need them equally, there would be either no exchange or not the same exchange); but money has become by convention a sort of representative of demand.[219]

Therefore, Aquinas concludes, "if either the price exceed the quantity of the thing's worth, or, conversely, the thing exceed the price, there is no longer the equality of justice: and consequently," it is unjust and unlawful to sell a thing for more than its worth or to buy for less.

It was mentioned above that for the canonists a fully expounded doctrine of the nature of value was not necessary. The passage in Aquinas just quoted, however, combined with several other passages in the same question (2a 2ae q. 77), does provide the framework for such a doctrine. Skipping ahead to a. 2, in Aquinas's reply to objection 3, he approaches the nature of economic value with a key distinction first drawn by St Augustine:

> As Augustine says, the price of things salable does not depend on their degree of nature, since at times a horse fetches a higher price than a slave; but it depends on their usefulness to man.[220]

The point of this distinction, expressed with Aquinas's usual brevity, is that the place held by a thing in nature (e.g., sentient versus that which has no sensation) is not what determines economic value, but rather its "convenience" or "how

216 Aristotle, *Politics*, 1, 9 (1256b40–1258a20; McKeon, 1137–40). English quotations of Aristotle are from *The Basic Works of Aristotle*, ed. McKeon.
217 Aquinas, *Summa theologiae*, q. 77 a. 1 co.
218 Ibid.
219 Aristotle, *Nicomachean Ethics*, 5, 5 (1133a15–35; McKeon, 1011).
220 Aquinas, *Summa theologiae*, q. 77 a. 2 ad 3.

it meets [one's] need" (Augustine).[221] "Who would not rather have bread in his house than mice, gold than fleas?"[222] Hence, returning to Aristotle, the unit by which economic value is measured "is in truth demand ... but money has become by convention a sort of representative of demand."[223] Conjointly, Aquinas notes another factor which alters the economic value of goods:

> The measures of salable commodities must needs be different in different places, on account of the difference of supply: because where there is greater abundance, the measures are wont to be larger.[224]

The phrasing of this observation suggests that it was inspired by Aristotle, who says, in a place quoted by Aquinas in a. 1, that "wine and corn measures are not everywhere equal, but larger in wholesale and smaller in retail markets."[225] Nevertheless, that the prices of goods are altered by abundance or deficiency of supply was already well known apart from Aristotle; many illustrations could be cited.[226] Aquinas also, a little further on, describes the scenario of a merchant selling wheat at a place where it fetches a high price, who knows that many other merchants will soon arrive carrying wheat, which will then "make it of less value."[227] "The seller, since he sells his goods at the price actually offered him, does not seem to act contrary to justice."[228] In other words, the merchant in this case is permitted to sell his goods at the current market price, and commits no sin in so doing, even if the goods will shortly be worth less because of the arrival of greater supplies. This leads naturally back to the second half of Aquinas's reply in a. 1, where he defines what Odd Langholm calls the "double rule of just pricing."[229]

> Secondly we may speak of buying and selling, considered as accidentally tending to the advantage of one party, and to the disadvantage of the other: for instance, when a man has great need of a certain thing, while an other man will suffer if he be without it. In such a case the just price will depend not only on the thing sold, but on the loss which the sale brings on the seller. And thus it will be lawful to sell a thing for more

---

221 Augustine, *The City of God*, 11, 16.

222 Ibid.

223 Aristotle, *Nicomachean Ethics*, 5, 5 (1133a15–35; McKeon, 1011).

224 Aquinas, *Summa theologiae*, q. 77 a. 2 ad 2.

225 Aristotle, *Nicomachean Ethics*, 5, 7 (1135a; McKeon, 1014–15).

226 E.g.: "Nonnullam tamen pretio varietatem loca temporaque adferunt: nec enim tantidem Romae et in Hispania oleum aestimabitur nec continuis sterilitatibus tantidem, quanti secundis fructibus." Paul, in *Dig.* 35.2.63.2.

227 Aquinas, *Summae theologiae*, q. 77 a. 3 ad 4.

228 Ibid.

229 Langholm, *Merchant in the Confessional*, 253ff.

> than it is worth in itself, though the price paid be not more than it is worth to the owner. Yet if the one man derive a great advantage by becoming possessed of the other man's property, and the seller be not at a loss through being without that thing, the latter ought not to raise the price, because the advantage accruing to the buyer, is not due to the seller, but to a circumstance affecting the buyer. Now no man should sell what is not his, though he may charge for the loss he suffers.[230]

Aquinas concludes the reply by another remark pregnant with implications for the moralists and for judging in the court of souls:

> On the other hand if a man find that he derives great advantage from something he has bought, he may, of his own accord, pay the seller something over and above: and this pertains to his honesty.[231]

This principle comes to be associated with its own maxim, drawn from the rules of law in the final title (*de regulis iuris*) of the *Liber Sext*: *scienti et consentienti non fit iniuria neque dolus*, "no injury or fraud is done to one who knows and consents."[232] Since a seller has the freedom to simply give away the good which he is selling, if he so choose, and it would be licit for the buyer to receive it, similarly a buyer may willingly pay more for the good which he purchases than its normal value in the market; and, assuming he "knows and consents" to this, it is licit for the seller to receive it.

In his reply to the first objection, which was based on the civil-law maxim *licet contrahentibus*, Aquinas develops a fully explicit explanation of what was expressed cautiously and laconically by Innocent IV with the formula *iure fori, forsan non iure poli.*

---

230 Aquinas, *Summa theologiae*, q. 77 a. 1 co.

Langholm's exposition of this rule: "The full significance of the double rule emerges. It follows, that the market principle will trump both the labour and cost principle and the nonexploitation principle. If a thing is of little value to the seller, he can still, according to the Thomistic rule, charge the current, competitive market price from a needy buyer if the buyer can afford it, for no one is expected, as a matter of justice, to sell below the market price. If, on the other hand, the seller puts a high value on a good that the buyer needs, he can keep himself indemnified, that is, cover his cost, but only up to the level of the market price if the buyer has access to a competitive market, because the buyer then has a cheaper alternative there. Thus interpreted, Thomas Aquinas's double rule of just pricing contains, in a nutshell, the essential elements of penitential price doctrine." Langholm, *Merchant in the Confessional*, 255.

231 Aquinas, *Summa theologiae*, q. 77 a. 1 co.

232 *VI* 5.[13.]27 (*Scienti*). My translation, adapted from Gauthier, *Roman Law and Its Contribution to the Development of Canon Law*, 110. Gauthier translates all of the rules of law (*regulae iuris*) from the *Sext* in appendix 2 therein. On the principle encapsulated in this rule, cfr Antoninus, *Summa*, 2.1.16, section 3.1.2.1; ibid., *Summa*, 1.20.1.94.

> As stated above,[233] human law is given to the people among whom there are many lacking virtue, and it is not given to the virtuous alone. Hence human law was unable to forbid all that is contrary to virtue; and it suffices for it to prohibit whatever is destructive of human intercourse, while it treats other matters as though they were lawful, not by approving of them, but by not punishing them. Accordingly, if without employing deceit the seller disposes of his goods for more than their worth, or the buyer obtain them for less than their worth, the law looks upon this as licit, and provides no punishment for so doing, unless the excess be too great, because then even human law demands restitution to be made, for instance if a man be deceived in regard to more than half the amount of the just price of a thing.[234]

Aquinas's answer to the objection addresses the civil- and canon-law doctrine of *laesio enormis*, which demands restitution for "deception" beyond half the amount of the just price; but if the deception amounts to less than half the just price, then it "looks upon this as licit." Aquinas's explanation is that this is a matter of human law – i.e., "the law of the forum" (*ius fori*) in Innocent IV's phrase – which, as Aquinas has previously shown, permits, in the sense of "not punishing," many matters which are contrary to virtue, aiming only at prohibiting "whatever is destructive of human intercourse."[235] This suffices for human, i.e., civil, law.

> On the other hand the Divine law leaves nothing unpunished that is contrary to virtue. Hence, according to the Divine law, it is reckoned unlawful if the equality of justice be not observed in buying and selling.[236]

Once again, Aquinas makes explicit what was expressed cautiously by Innocent IV in his phrase *forsan non iure poli accipiunt*, "but it may be that they do not receive this according to the celestial law," i.e., Aquinas's divine law, *lex divina*. Although in the order of enacted human law, "deception" within half the just price is not prohibited and goes unpunished, in the moral order ("according to Divine law") it is unlawful "if the equality of justice be not observed in buying and selling." Glancing ahead to later centuries, this is the exact intepretation which will be applied by later canonists to Innocent's IV's formula:

> … And Innocent's dictum should proceed so that in the contentious forum this [deception] be tolerated, but not in the penitential forum, because we ought not

233 "Human laws should be proportionate to the common good. Now the common good comprises many things. Wherefore law should take account of many things, as to persons, as to matters, and as to times." Aquinas, *Summa theologiae*, 1a 2ae q. 96 a. 1–3. See also ibid., q. 90 a. 2.

234 Ibid., 2a 2ae q. 77 a. 1 ad 1.

235 Ibid.

236 Ibid.

to suffer that a neighbour be deceived, whom we ought to love as ourselves. Hence Innocent says that this has place in the law of the forum, not the celestial law, that is, the law of heaven or of God, i.e. in the penitential forum.[237]

The moral conclusion, then, is that buyers and sellers are obliged to observe "real equality" in the price of goods which they exchange: "in buying [the recompense] should be equal to the thing bought."[238] Following Augustine, Aquinas says that although "the desire to buy cheaply and sell dearly" appears to some to be "shared by everybody," "this common desire is not a natural but a vicious one," and "anybody can acquire the virtue of justice to resist and overcome it," by observing a just price in buying and selling even when one might have the opportunity or temptation to depart from it.[239] Hence:

> He who has received more than he ought must make compensation to him that has suffered loss, if the loss be considerable. I add this condition, because the just price of things is not fixed with mathematical precision, but depends on a kind of estimate, so that a slight addition or subtraction would not seem to destroy the equality of justice.[240]

This final point, that the just price is not precise, but a kind of estimate, is another seminal one which is developed by later scholastics. Probably the most influential extension is made by John Duns Scotus, who says that the just price has a "latitude."[241]

We have covered the first article of q. 77. The final article of this question, a. 4, addresses "whether in trading it is lawful to sell at a higher price than what was paid for it?" In this article, Aquinas approaches the complex conjunction of patristic and pseudo-patristic texts assembled by Gratian at D. 88 c. 9–13.[242] Just as, in a. 1–3 of this question, Aquinas drew out and made explicit a theory of economic

---

237 "Aut intervenit deceptio ex re ipsa, et ex proposito, non tamen intervenit dolus partis, et procedat dictum Inno. ut in foro contentioso toleretur, sed non in poenitentiali, quia non debebat pati proximum decipi, quem debet diligere sicut seipsum. Unde Inno. dixit quod illud habet locum iure fori, sed non iure poli. id est iure coeli, seu Dei. id est in foro poenitentiali." Panormitanus, *Commentaria, X* 2.20.42 no. 4. See also ibid., *X* 5.19.6 no. 6. Quotations of Panormitanus (Nicolaus de Tudeschis) from *Commentaria in quinque Decretalium libros.*

238 Aquinas, *Summa theologiae*, 2a 2ae q. 77 a. 1 ad 3.

239 Ibid., 2a 2ae q. 77 a. 1 ad 2 (LeFébure, *Injustice*, 216–17).

240 Ibid., 2a 2ae q. 77 a. 1 co.

241 John Duns Scotus, *In quartum*, 4, 15, 2, 15 in *Opera omnia*, 18:283b.

242 On Aquinas's use of these texts, see my chapter in Anderson and Larson, *Thomas Aquinas and Medieval Canon Law.*

value which was implicitly contained in the combined corpora of Aristotle and Romano-canonical jurisprudence, in a. 4 he draws out and makes explicit a doctrine of the liceity of trade which is implicitly contained in the combined corpora of Aristotle and the Church Fathers.

The initial objections in a. 4 make the argument that commerce is sinful by its very nature. The argument can be expressed in the form of a syllogism:

- Major premise: to make profits by selling for more than the purchase price is a sin.
- Minor premise: commerce is to make profits by selling for more than the purchase price.
- Conclusion: therefore, commerce is a sin.

To establish the minor premise, Aquinas cites Aristotle,[243] as well as some of Gratian's canons in D. 88, namely pseudo-Chrysostom and Cassiodorus;[244] the latter two also serve to establish the major premise,[245] to which is added a citation of Jerome,[246] as well as a logical argument from Aquinas's conclusion in the first article.[247]

243 "When the use of coin had once been discovered, out of the barter of necessary articles arose the other art of wealth getting, namely, retail trade; which was at first probably a simple matter, but became more complicated as soon as men learned by experience whence and by what exchanges the greatest profit might be made. Originating in the use of coin, the art of getting wealth is generally thought to be chiefly concerned with it, and to be the art which produces riches and wealth; having to consider how they may be accumulated." Aristotle, *Politics*, 1, 9 (1256b40; McKeon, 1137–8).

"There are two sorts of wealth-getting, as I have said; one is a part of household management, the other is retail trade: the former necessary and honorable, while that which consists in exchange is justly censured; for it is unnatural, and a mode by which men gain from one another." Aristotle, *Politics*, 1, 10 (1258a38; McKeon, 1141).

244 "But he who buys a thing in order to gain something by alienating it whole and unchanged, he is a trader who is cast out of God's Temple." Pseudo-Chrysostom, *Opus imperfectum in Matthaeum*, 38, in D. 88 c. 11 (*Eiciens*).

"What else is trade, except to wish to sell more dearly those things which can be purchased more cheaply? ... The Lord cast out such people from the Temple." Cassiodorus, *In psalmos*, *Ps* 70, in D. 88 c. 13 (*Quid est aliud*).

245 "But nobody is thrown out of the temple unless he has committed some sin. Such commerce is, therefore, a sin." Aquinas, *Summa theologiae*, q. 77 a. 4 obj. 1 (LeFébure, *Injustice*, 227).

246 "Negotiatorem clericum, ex inope divitem et ex ignobili gloriosum, quasi quasdam pestes fuge." Jerome, *Epistola ad Nepotianum de vita clericorum*, 5, in D. 88 c. 9 (*Negotiatorem*).

"The only reason why clerics are forbidden to practise commerce is apparently that it constitutes sin." Aquinas, *Summa theologiae*, q. 77 a. 4 obj. 3 (LeFébure, *Injustice*, 227).

247 Aquinas, *Summa theologiae*, q. 77 a. 4 obj. 2.

On the contrary, Augustine says in commenting on Psalm 70:15,[248]

> The businessman consumed by the profit motive blasphemes when he incurs a loss and lies and perjures himself to obtain the highest prices. But such vices belong to men who engage in commerce, they are not intrinsic to commerce as such, which can be conducted without them.[249]

This is a fuller exposition of the *sententia* attributed to Augustine at D. 88 c. 10 (*Fornicari*):

> To fornicate is always unlawful for everyone, but to engage in trade is at times lawful, at times unlawful. Before someone becomes an ecclesiastic, it is lawful for him to be in trade; once he has become one, it is no longer lawful.[250]

The reason why clerics are bound to abstain from commerce is not because it is sinful *per se*, but because "clerics are bound to abstain not merely from things that are bad but from things that look bad," "because of the likelihood of their falling victim to the vices of business men," and because "commercial activity engrosses a person too much in secular cares."[251]

In Aquinas's reply he provides the exposition of a basic doctrine of the liceity of trade which was only implicit in the complex of texts collected by Gratian. Aquinas's exposition hangs upon Aristotle's distinction between "household management" and "the so-called art of getting wealth" in the *Politics*:

> For natural riches and the natural art of wealth-getting are a different thing; in their true form they are part of the management of a household; whereas retail trade is the art of producing wealth, not in every way, but by exchange ... And there is no bound to the riches which spring from this art of wealth-getting ... But the art of wealth-getting which consists in household management, on the other hand, has a limit; the unlimited acquisition of wealth is not its business ... The source of the confusion is the near connection between the two kinds of wealth-getting; in either, the instrument is the same, although the use is different, and so they pass into one another; for each is a use of the same property, but with a difference: accumulation is the end in the one case, but there is a further end in the other. Hence some persons are led

248 "Because I have not known learning, I will enter into the powers of the Lord"; but in an alternate translation, "Because I have not known trade," etc. Psalm 70:15, *Quoniam non cognovi litteraturam* [*negotiationes*], *introibo in potentias Domini.*

249 Augustine, *Enarrationes in Psalmos, Ps* 70, 1, 17–20, in D. 88 c. 12 (*Quoniam non*); quoted here from Aquinas, *Summa theologiae*, 2a 2ae q. 77 a. 4 *sed contra* (LeFébure, *Injustice*, 227).

250 Augustine, *Questions of the Old and New Testament*, 127, in D. 88 c. 10 (*Fornicari*).

251 Aquinas, *Summa theologiae*, q. 77 a. 4 ad 3, citing Sirach 26:28 and 2 Timothy 2:4.

> to believe that getting wealth is the object of household management, and the whole idea of their lives is that they ought either to increase their money without limit, or at any rate not to lose it. The origin of this disposition in men is that they are intent upon living only, and not upon living well; and, as their desires are unlimited they also desire that the means of gratifying them should be without limit.[252]

Now Aquinas points out that, although the "art of getting wealth" – commerce, "the sort of exchange that belongs to business men in the strict sense" – is rightly open to criticism since it feeds the acquisitive urge which knows no limit but tends to increase to infinity, nevertheless, "profit, which is the point of commerce … does not carry the notion of anything vicious or contrary to virtue either."[253] What is necessary for commerce to be practised licitly is that it be "subordinated to an activity that is necessary, or even right. And this is the way in which commerce can become justifiable."[254] In other words, commerce is licit and can even be praiseworthy if used as a means or instrument for the achievement of good ends, as Aquinas says in another place:

> Now it is evident that man's happiness cannot consist in natural wealth. For wealth of this kind is sought for the sake of something else, viz. as a support of human nature: consequently it cannot be man's last end, rather is it ordained to man as to its end.[255]

It is the conversion of profit making into an end rather than a means which constitutes the characteristic fault of those who practise the art of getting wealth. "Even profit-making can become justifiable … provided this is not the ultimate aim and

252 Aristotle, *Politics*, 1, 9 (1256b40ff; McKeon, 1137–8).

253 Aquinas, *Summa theologiae*, 2a 2ae q. 77 a. 4 co. (LeFébure, *Injustice*, 227–9).

254 Ibid. LeFébure comments on this passage (*Injustice*, 228–9): "The author proceeds with such finesse that it would be easy to miss the fact that he has, especially in the second paragraph of the body of this article, broken discreetly but definitely with Aristotle on the question of commercial activity for profit. The immediate occasion for making the break was, no doubt, the immense development of commerce about his own time, but it is perhaps paradoxical that the real reason why he was able to initiate this break seems to be that he was writing as a theologian and not merely as a political economist. For it was the fact that he was in possession of an assured vision of the contemplative goal of individuals in society, and of the subordination of the earthly to the heavenly society, which enabled him to apply the basic Aristotelian distinction between means and ends even to the subject-matter of commerce and profit-making in a way which Aristotle had not explained it – although for that very reason he also imposed stringent limitations on profit-making. The essential characterization of material resources and money as utilities and means is summarized in e.g. 2a 2ae q. 118 a. 1 and q. 117 a. 3, whilst the positioning of riches in relation to man's final end is summarized in e.g. 1a 2ae q. 1 a. 1; q. 2 a. 8; q. 3 a. 8; q. 4 a. 7; 2a 2ae q. 50 a. 3 ad 1. And for a synthetic statement of man's position in the universe and of the liberties and limitations implied by his pull towards fulfilment and happiness, see *Summa contra Gentiles* 3 c. 37."

255 Aquinas, *Summa theologiae*, 1a 2ae q. 2 a. 1 co.

is meant to fulfil some necessary and worthy purpose."[256] This is how Aquinas answers the objection proffered from pseudo-Chrysostom: the sort of business condemned is that which pursues profit for its own sake. Once again, as was seen above with Gratian, the scholastic economic outlook shows a neat correspondence with Weber's description of "economic traditionalism," and it condemns the "spirit of capitalism" as avarice and as a confusion of means for ends.

This doctrine of the liceity of trade, seen at least implicitly in Gratian's combination of patristic texts and drawn out explicitly by Aquinas, is the starting point for the more complete analysis of commerce which is found in Antoninus's chapters 2.1.16–17 and 3.8.1–4 below. Once it is recognized that commerce is a means which can be put to a good use or a bad one – in Augustine's phrase, that the vices of commercial traders are the "vices of the man, not of the craft"[257] – the way is opened for an analysis of all the attributes which are required for virtuous trade. Hence it becomes useful to scrutinize trade according to the seven circumstances of a human act, all of which must be correct in order for the act to be good.[258]

To conclude, by the late thirteenth century, the crucial principles governing justice in buying and selling were drawn out of the three corpora: the Scriptures, the Church Fathers, and the sacred canons; Roman law; and Aristotle. With Aquinas a synthesis of all these is reached. Scholastics of the fourteenth and fifteenth centuries did, of course, develop further analyses and refinements of the doctrines concerning commerce, value, and justice in buying and selling elucidated so far. Doctors and authors in all branches of scholastic learning contributed: philosophers (e.g., John Buridan, Nicholas Oresme), theologians (e.g., Gerard of Siena), specialists in moral theology and confession (e.g., Raymond of Peñafort, John of Freiburg, Bartolomeo of San Concordio), canonists (e.g., Giovanni da Legnano, Gaspare Calderini, Lorenzo Ridolfi), and preachers (e.g., Bernardino of Siena). It is not necessary to lengthen this chapter to an extreme by expounding all of this material: it could not be done with much more brevity than that with which Antoninus himself deals with it in the chapters of his *Summa* edited below. For the purpose of understanding the intellectual background of Antoninus's teaching on justice in buying and selling, Aquinas supplies a worthy foundation. As Langholm noted, "one is tempted to say, as is so often the case in scholastic thought, that 'it's all in Aquinas.'"[259]

256 Ibid., 2a 2ae q. 77 a. 4 ad 1 (LeFébure, *Injustice*, 229). On wealth and commerce as means, see also Aquinas, *Summa theologiae*, 2a 2ae q. 118 a. 1; ibid., q. 117 a. 3; ibid., 1a 2ae q. 2 a . 8; ibid., 1a 2ae q. 3 a. 8; ibid., 1a 2ae q. 4 a . 7; ibid., 2a 2ae q. 50 a. 3 ad 1.

257 Augustine, *Enarrationes in Psalmos*, *Ps* 70, 1, 17–20, in D. 88 c. 12 (*Quoniam non*); quoted from Aquinas, *Summa theologiae*, 2a 2ae q. 77 a. 4 sed contra.

258 "Tully, in his Rhetoric, gives seven circumstances, which are contained in this verse: 'Quis, quid, ubi, quibus auxiliis, cur, quomodo, quando' – who, what, where, by what aids, why, how, and when." Aquinas, *Summa theologiae*, 1a 2ae q. 7 a. 3 co.

259 "… In the present case, considering the contribution of Carletti, it would perhaps be more correct to say that it's all in the *Summa Angelica*." Langholm, *Merchant in the Confessional*, 255.

5. Postscript: Peter John Olivi via Bernardino of Siena

The Franciscan Peter John Olivi is an anomaly in the tradition of scholastic economics, as an early theologian whose recognition was greatly delayed, and whose acute economic ideas were nearly lost to posterity. The teaching of Olivi, written in the late thirteenth century, was introduced into preaching and penitential literature in the mid-fifteenth century via the Latin sermons of Bernardino of Siena.[260] Bernardino possessed a manuscript of Olivi's *Tractatus de contractibus*;[261] the concepts which he found therein impressed him enough that he incorporated them, in some cases nearly verbatim, into his own *Tractatus de contractibus* in the sermon series *De Evangelio aeterno*.[262] St Antoninus, encountering these ideas in Bernardino's sermons, was taken with them and copied them in his turn into the sermon on fraud committed in buying and selling (*Summa* 2.1.16), in his discussion of the appraisal and valuation of things (section 3.1). From Bernardino and Antoninus they were picked up by other Franciscan and Dominican authors in the next century, shorn of any attribution to Olivi. Although Olivi's *Treatise on Contracts* "has come to be recognized as a classic of the economic thought of the scholastics,"[263] the legacy of Olivi's ideas in subsequent centuries has not yet been traced in detail by scholars. Olivi's ideas which Antoninus incorporated into his own sermon 2.1.16 are summarized in the next chapter in section 2. The reader is also directed to Olivi's original text, whose first part, on purchases on sales, is brief yet conceptually dense.[264]

> In hoc cum beato Toma concordant Iohannes de Lignano et Iohannes Calderinus et plures alii canoniste, dicentes illam decretalem [*X* 3.17.3] habere locum "iure fori, non iure poli," et hoc ad uitanda multa litigia que de leui possent cotidie fieri.[265]

> In this Giovanni da Legnano and Giovanni Calderini and many other canonists agree with blessed Thomas, saying that this decretal has force "by the law of the forum and not the law of heaven" – and its purpose is to avoid the excessive lawsuits which could otherwise lightly be brought daily.

260 Ibid., 259.

261 Bernardino's own marginal annotations are printed in Piron, *Traité des contrats*.

262 For references, see notes 81 to 87 above.

263 Piron, quoted from Thornton and Cusato, *Treatise on Contracts*, xix.

264 Peter John Olivi, *Traité des contrats*, 1 q. 1 (94–109) and 1 q. 5 n. 52–61 (126–35).

265 Antoninus, *Summa*, 2.1.16 (below), section 3.1.3.2 (M_1 fol. 69v, hand A). Cfr Iohannes and Gaspar Calderinus, *Repetitiones et distinctiones in decretales*, *X* 5.19.19 (Vatican City, Biblioteca Apostolica Vaticana, Vat. lat. 2652, fol. 281v–282r); Iohannes de Lignano, *Commentaria in Decretales*, *X* 5.19.19 (Florence, Biblioteca Medicea-Laurenziana, Edili 54, fol. 99v); Lorenzo Ridolfi, *Tractatus de usuris*, 2 op. 6 (Armstrong, *Usury and Public Debt*, 161).

4 St Antoninus's Teaching on Trade, Merchants, and Workers

Preamble. The Business Culture of Renaissance Florence

"To know a medieval Italian was to know his city." – Augustine Thompson, OP[1]

Antoninus's teaching on trade, merchants, and workers was written in the milieu of mid-fifteenth-century Florence. Born and raised there, son of a prominent member of the guild of notaries and of the communal government, founder of the Dominican house of San Marco, friend of bankers and members of the civic elite like Tommaso Spinelli and Cosimo de' Medici, and finally archbishop of the city, Antoninus was a Florentine through and through. While Antoninus's teaching cannot be described simply as a product of his environment – particularly since much of it comes from thirteenth-century authors like Thomas Aquinas and Peter John Olivi, as just discussed in chapter 3 – nevertheless, it is worth knowing something about his social context in the world of Renaissance Florence, and the audience to whom his teaching was addressed. Florence was indeed the most appropriate place in Europe, and perhaps the globe, for a moralist in the 1400s to write a treatise on the ethics of business and trade. The stakes of Antoninus's teaching, if taken seriously by his fellow citizens, were high; and the stakes of his teaching for historians of capitalism remain high.

Medieval and Renaissance Florence has, relative to other cities, attracted an extraordinary amount of interest and scholarship. One feature which makes Florence particularly attractive to historians is the amount of documentation which survives from the late medieval and Renaissance periods, more than for any other European city.[2] Beyond that, interest in Florence primarily has to do with the

1 Thompson, *Francis of Assisi*, 3.

2 I credit this remark to Lawrin Armstrong in his course on Communal Florence, who in turn quoted Christiane Klapisch-Zuber: "Florence remains – by the enormous wealth of its archival

city's association with three historical developments which decisively shaped the trajectory of Western modernity. Each of these developments has its own lineage of scholars who seek out its origins in Florence and Italy more broadly between 1200 and 1500. The first is republicanism. In Florence this took both the concrete form of a government based on popular participation and the theoretical form of an ideology glorifying liberty and rule for the common good.[3] The second is the Renaissance, that is, both the humanist movement to recover, study, and emulate the literature of classical Greece and Rome, and the glorious works of painting, sculpture, and architecture which Florentine artists produced, first in imitation of Greek and Roman models, later arguably surpassing them.[4] Antoninus has a place in the history of both of these developments. As archbishop, Antoninus defended the integrity of the Florentine republic's legislative voting from manipulation by the party of Cosimo de' Medici, and furthermore, San Marco went on to become the home base of Girolamo Savonarola during his republican revolution against the Medici in the generation after Antoninus's death. In relation to the Renaissance, Antoninus took part in a lineage of Dominicans who engaged critically with humanism. He was a protégé of Giovanni Dominici, who had exchanged fire with Coluccio Salutati, chancellor of Florence, over the value and proper use of humanistic studies.[5] Antoninus influenced Marsilio Ficino's thought through directing him to study Thomas Aquinas's *Summa contra gentiles*.[6] This lineage of Dominicans grappling with humanism was continued by, for instance, Giovanni Caroli, whom Antoninus mentored and who made Antoninus the main speaker in a fictional dialogue about the spiritual faults of the Dominican order in the late fifteenth century.[7] Antoninus also touched on republicanism and Renaissance humanism in his writings, both the *Summa* and the *Chronica*.[8] However,

resources – one of the best [historical] laboratories." See Herlihy and Klapisch-Zuber, *Tuscans and Their Families*, and the Florentine Renaissance Resources hosted by Brown University: https://library.brown.edu/create/cds/projects/.

3 As an example of a historian who viewed this as the most important trait of the medieval Italian town, see Frederic C. Lane's presidential address to the American Historical Association in 1965, published as "At the Roots of Republicanism." On historiography, see Molho, "The Italian Renaissance, Made in the USA."

4 Giorgio Vasari, "Preface to Part Three," in *The Lives of the Artists*, 277–83.

5 Giovanni Dominici (Iohannes Dominici de Florentia), *Lucula noctis*; Coluccio Salutati, "Letter to Giovanni Dominici."

6 See Morçay, *Saint Antonin*, 310–19.

7 Edelheit, "Introduction," *Humanism, Theology, and Spiritual Crisis*, 9, 13, 34–6.

8 Remarks on these aspects of Antoninus's thought can be found in essays by Lorenz Böninger, Isabella Gagliardi, David S. Peterson, Fausto Arici, Leonardo Cappelletti, and Timothy Verdon collected in Cinelli and Paoli, *Antonino Pierozzi*. See also, revising the view of Antoninus as a stern opponent of humanism, E. Sanesi, *La Rinascita* 3 (1940): 105–16 (cited in Ullman and Stadter, *Public Library*, 4 n1).

these topics are not central to this book. It is the third pioneering development in medieval and Renaissance Florence which requires some space here.

To define this third development as "capitalism" would cause many medievalists and economic historians to bristle. It would immediately raise the highly controverted question of how we define capitalism and why we define it that way.[9] Bypassing this question for now, what can be said concretely is that Florence in the late Middle Ages and Renaissance gives us the earliest known example of the pattern of modern economic development.[10] At the broadest level, Florence went through a secular (centuries-long) period of per capita economic growth, becoming the wealthiest commercial centre in Europe during the period from roughly 1200 to 1500, with the presumed highest output, life expectancy, and literacy rates.[11] Moreover, the Florentines developed methods of doing business and economic policies which are still integral to Western economies; indeed, the path which Florence's merchant entrepreneurs and ruling elite forged remains, in its main lines, the one which countries around the world follow in trying to attain high levels of productivity and prosperity.[12] Florence was thus the forerunner of modern "development," characterized by rapid economic and demographic growth.[13]

Whether all of this equals "capitalism," or in what sense Renaissance Florence may be called "capitalistic," will be addressed below. Here, it is worth sketching out in brief the story of Florence's ascent as a commercial centre, and the kind of social classes to which this gave rise.[14]

Florence's growth from a diminished Roman town into a major urban commercial centre began in the context of a much broader process, the medieval "Commercial Revolution."[15] After trade and the use of money had sunk to very low levels

9 Robert Fredona and Sophus A. Reinert dive into the "semantic battle" over the term "capitalism" in the opening pages of their lead article, "Italy and the Origins of Capitalism," in the special coedited issue of the *Business History Review*, esp. 5–9 and 30–2.

10 Ibid., 34–6.

11 Ibid., 32–4; see especially 33, figure 7.

12 "With the still dubious examples of a select number of petro-states, the *only* truly successful stories of economic development understood as rapid and sustained increase in output and human welfare outside the Western tradition remain China, Korea, Japan, Singapore, and Taiwan, all of which essentially followed or are following a playbook – based on a conscious emphasis on high-value-added industries and 'Western' modes of business – codified and theorized already in Renaissance Italy and quite purposefully and explicitly emulated by the Low Countries, Britain, Germany, the United States, and practically everyone since." Ibid., 34.

13 Ibid., 31–2.

14 For the discussion which follows, the most important monograph is Goldthwaite, *The Economy of Renaissance Florence*. See also Brucker, *Renaissance Florence*; Najemy, *A History of Florence 1200–1575*; Martines, *The Social World of the Florentine Humanists 1390–1460*.

15 The term is used here to describe the medieval period of European economic growth, as in Lopez, *The Commercial Revolution of the Middle Ages, 950–1350*.

during the Carolingian era, mercantile activity and long-distance trade began to be revived in the ninth and tenth centuries. The Mediterranean was reopened for Christian trade with the Levant and the Byzantine Empire, and merchants began importing luxury goods and spices from Africa and Asia via Mediterranean ports.[16] The need to find or produce merchandise which could be traded abroad stimulated a great increase and diversification of economic activity in western Europe. The basic picture drawn by Henri Pirenne in the early twentieth century of trade-led growth of the European economy – in other words, of a relatively backward economic region developing through trade with a more advanced and wealthy one – has been justified by subsequent research, and still forms the basic groundwork of economic historians' understanding of the conditions for the Commercial Revolution.[17] Italian port cities like Genoa, Pisa, and Venice were the leaders in building regular trade links around the Mediterranean, but many other towns also grew into trade cities and built up their own particular fields of business. Cities swelled through immigration from the countryside, which became possible as agricultural productivity increased.[18] Urbanization was most extensive in northern Italy and southern France at first, but during the High Middle Ages the Low Countries also became a highly urbanized region, plugged into Mediterranean trade through the fairs of Champagne; London and the North Sea and Baltic cities joined in as well, eventually forming the commercial league of the Hanse. By the time of Giotto and Dante a little after 1300, Florence's population was, according to historians' best estimates, between 90,000 and 130,000, making it one of the five largest cities in Europe.[19] The population of Florence was decimated by the arrival of the Black Death in 1348; in many cities across Europe, within just two years, upwards of a

---

16 Pirenne, *Economic and Social History of Medieval Europe*, esp. ch. 1, "The Revival of Commerce." See also Braudel, *Civilization and Capitalism, 15th–18th Century*, vol. 2, *The Wheels of Commerce*, esp. ch. 3–4; de Roover, "The Organization of Trade."

17 "As early as the eighth and ninth centuries Italian merchants ventured out to cross the boundaries separating three major areas: the new Carolingian Empire, in economically backward Europe; the Byzantine heir of the old Roman Empire, extending from southern Italy to Constantinople; and the Arab world, rapidly expanding along the southern and eastern Mediterranean … The major dynamic driving this enterprise arose out of the imbalance in the relative development of two vast economic areas, Europe and the Near East … The initiatives for this trade came from the undeveloped West, not from the Near East; thus, during the later Middle Ages, from the twelfth to the fifteenth century, the European economy expanded, while the economies in the Levant stagnated and declined." Goldthwaite, *Economy of Renaissance Florence*, 3–6; on this theme see ibid., "Introduction: The Commercial Revolution."

18 The citizens of Florence began to construct a new set of city walls at the end of the thirteenth century, which "enclosed an area almost fifteen times the area enclosed two centuries earlier." Ibid., 5. However, the city's growth was arrested temporarily by the plagues and famines of the next fifty years, so that the built-up area of the city did not fill the newest circuit of walls until the sixteenth century; see the map, ibid., 24.

19 Ibid., 22; "Florence," in *The Grove Encyclopedia of Medieval Art and Architecture*.

third to three-fifths of the inhabitants had died from the epidemic.[20] Nevertheless, the trend towards urbanization continued into modern times.

Florence was initially, prior to about 1200, not a leading city of the Commercial Revolution; its Tuscan neighbours Pisa and Siena were larger and wealthier.[21] During the twelfth and thirteenth centuries, Florentine merchants were going abroad, carrying products to sell and seeking grain to import. These international import-export merchants were the main protagonists in the story of Florence's rise to the greatest commercial city of the late Middle Ages. They found a new avenue for business in the lucrative wool trade: purchasing unfinished wool cloth manufactured elsewhere, such as Flanders, transporting it to Florence for finishing, and exporting it for sale in other regions, "laying the foundation for their great international commercial and financial network."[22] Their business activities took them so far and wide that circa 1300 Boniface VIII said Florentines were the fifth element of the universe.[23] As they gained experience and skill handling the different local and international currencies across Europe, they found in this a new business opportunity. Using their accumulated capital, they began to offer banking services, including moneychanging, providing bills of exchange for merchants travelling on trading ventures, extending commercial credit, and finally lending money on a large scale to monarchs and popes (these functions are described in more detail below in the discussion of Antoninus's chapter 3.8.3). Thus Florence's merchant entrepreneurs became the greatest bankers of the fourteenth and fifteenth centuries, building "medieval Europe's largest and most integrated trade and banking network."[24] The symbol of Florence's monetary clout was the *florin*, the city's gold coin, stamped with the lily and a portrait of John the Baptist.[25] The first medieval gold coin to be minted in large numbers, it was used internationally as a trade currency, whose metallic purity was rigorously protected since it was first struck in 1252.[26] Later, the manufacturing of wool cloth was brought into Florence itself, run by merchant entrepreneurs who employed a vast number of workers carrying out the many steps in the manufacturing process, including washing, fulling, stretching, carding, and napping.[27] Florence became the Europe-wide leader in the production of woollen cloth.[28] The wool industry in the fourteenth century

20 Vargas, *Taming a Brood of Vipers*, 13.
21 Caferro, "Florence"; Cohn, "Florence (Firenze)."
22 Goldthwaite, *Economy of Renaissance Florence*, 26.
23 Brucker, *Florence: The Golden Age*, 8.
24 Goldthwaite, *Economy of Renaissance Florence*, 32.
25 Weinstein, *Savonarola*, 43.
26 Brucker, *Florence: The Golden Age*, 247.
27 Florence Edler (de Roover) describes the steps of manufacturing woollen cloth in *Glossary of Mediaeval Terms of Business*, 328–9.
28 Caferro, "Florence."

was estimated by Giovanni Villani to employ about a third of the city's population, some 30,000 people.[29] Florentine business and economic activity came to revolve around the wool trade and international banking for the rest of the Middle Ages.[30] In the century after about 1340, a silk industry was also built in Florence.[31] While these industries had a primarily outward focus, producing for export,[32] there was also a diverse variety of artisanal trades producing goods for the local market, which prospered throughout the Middle Ages.[33] The professional classes also flourished, with the city's notaries, lawyers, teachers of grammar and rhetoric, and civic officials becoming the leading representatives of humanistic studies.[34] Through the textile and banking industries, enormous wealth flowed into Florence, above all into the hands of the leading merchant families, who channelled it sometimes back into the business, sometimes into purchasing rural land or building ostentatious *palazzi* for themselves, sometimes into charitable endeavours, and sometimes into patronizing artistic projects and the construction of magnificent civic and ecclesiastical buildings.[35] The Renaissance in art was, to put it bluntly, financed by the city's businesspeople; but it was Florence's artisans, hired by the merchant classes, who transformed the wealth generated by the textile and banking industries "into the patrimony of urban architecture, artwork, and a tradition of craftsmanship unequaled in any other city."[36] The most visible example today of the partnership of Florentine citizens of all classes in the beautifying of their city is the Cathedral of Santa Maria del Fiore, the "Duomo," constructed over many generations, the spiritual heart of the city which still dominates its skyline.

During the era of its early growth, roughly the eleventh to the fourteenth centuries, Florence also participated in the broader phenomenon by which Italian and French cities threw off the dominion of episcopal or feudal lords and established

29 Cited in Papi, "Florence."

30 "Textile production represented by far the city's most important industrial activity, though taking the measure of its impact on the economy is not easy." Goldthwaite, *Economy of Renaissance Florence*, 336.

31 Ibid., 602.

32 "The strength of the sector [production of textiles] lay in its orientation to international markets for its products." Ibid., 265.

33 "The people in this chapter ["Artisans, Shopkeepers, Workers"] worked in many activities, but they can be lumped together in one composite sector of the economy that produced goods and services primarily, if not exclusively, for the local market, not for export … The sector grew as a result of the increased demand for consumer goods that arose from the wealth that flowed into the city in the form of profits from textile exports and merchant banking abroad." Ibid., 341.

34 See Kristeller, *Renaissance Thought*, esp. ch. 1 "The Humanist Movement." A recent book about the humanist movement which has not received enough attention is Field, *The Intellectual Struggle for Florence*.

35 "Florence," in *Grove Encyclopedia of Medieval Art and Architecture*.

36 Goldthwaite, *Economy of Renaissance Florence*, 607.

self-governing communes. This is not the place for a discussion of the incredibly intricate history of Florence's popular republic.[37] However, a couple of points are worth noting about the role of merchants and of guilds in the city's politics. The international merchants and their wealthy family dynasties were the leaders in creating the communal government and for most of its history were able to hold its reins tightly. Florentine citizens participated in the city government through guild membership. It is emblematic of the leading role of international merchants that they were the first to organize themselves into a guild, the *Arte di Calimala*, established in the second half of the twelfth century.[38] They also established a mercantile court in 1308, the *Mercanzia*, to adjudicate disputes among merchants.[39] "In the early thirteenth century other guilds appeared – the *Cambio* (moneychangers) in 1202, followed in the next decade by the *Lana* (wool manufacturers), the *Por Santa Maria* (retail cloth merchants), and the *Giudici e Notai* (judges and notaries)."[40] All the various categories of merchants, artisans, shopkeepers, and workers in Renaissance Florence came to be grouped into seven major guilds and fourteen minor guilds.[41] Nevertheless, the actual importance of the guilds in defining the economic life of the city is much debated.[42] According to Goldthwaite, guild membership was primarily a means of political participation, and many people joined guilds regardless of whether they actually practised that guild's trade; hence "it makes little sense to categorize workers [in Florence] according to guilds."[43] Nor does Antoninus use the framework of guild membership to categorize workers in the chapters edited below. Possibly as a result of this peculiarity of the Florentine guild system, citizens of Florence may have enjoyed more freedom than usual in choosing their own profession or trade.[44] A charming example is given by the sixteenth-century art historian Giorgio Vasari: he relates that Cimabue discovered the young Giotto, whose father Bondone "was a tiller of the soil and a humble person," sketching on a rock while tending his father's sheep, "sketching one of them in a lifelike way … led on by his natural inclination towards the art of drawing …

37 A concise overview of this aspect of the city's history can be found in Brucker, *Florence: The Golden Age*, 243–59.
38 Goldthwaite, *Economy of Renaissance Florence*, 109.
39 Ibid., 109–14; Papi, "Florence."
40 Goldthwaite, *Economy of Renaissance Florence*, 109–10.
41 See the chart of Florentine guilds, ibid., 344–5.
42 On the historiography of guilds, see ibid., 342ff.
43 Ibid., 347.
44 "The ranks of any particular group of craftsmen were not protected by a guild oligarchy in an effort to secure access for sons as a hereditary right … A young Florentine, less bound by the guild ties, and hence family traditions, so characteristic of guild society elsewhere, had the possibility, at least in theory, of selecting the trade he wanted to practice (or entering the one his father wanted to direct him to) … The father of Brunelleschi was a notary, as was the father of Leonardo da Vinci." Ibid., 349–50.

Cimabue therefore asked Bondone, and he lovingly gave his consent and allowed Cimabue to take Giotto to Florence."[45] While the strict veracity of the story may be doubted, it does suggest that the Florentine valued the possibility of choosing a trade suited to his own talents. This is expressed by Antoninus as well: in chapter 3.8.1 below, he teaches that one should choose a trade suitable for one's interests, capacities, and temperament, in which, Antoninus says quoting Aristotle, "pleasure perfects the work."[46]

In Antoninus's time, the city's guild-based republican government was in the process of being subverted by the Medici. Beginning as merchants in the fourteenth century, in the wake of the collapse of the Peruzzi and Bardi banks in 1345, the Medici family went on to build the largest and wealthiest banking firm in Europe, deriving vast profits from becoming the pope's bankers.[47] As discussed above in chapter 1, in the fifteenth century the leader of the family, Cosimo "il Vecchio," surreptitiously took control of the city of Florence through influence, intimidation, and manipulation of elections, becoming the unofficial "first citizen" and *Pater Patriae*, while maintaining the appearance that republican institutions were still functioning.[48] Cosimo became a great patron of Renaissance art and culture, and had a close, though certainly complex, relationship with Antoninus. Cosimo funded the construction of the new building for the Dominican house of San Marco, and as benefactor he is personally portrayed in some of Fra Angelico's paintings therein.[49] Cosimo kept a cell for himself at San Marco, where he would make spiritual retreats. Nevertheless, Cosimo's patronage did not prevent Antoninus from opposing him at times, as in the celebrated episode when as archbishop he condemned the Medici regime's attempt to use open balloting.

At this point let us turn to a discussion of the business culture of Renaissance Florence and relate it to St Antoninus's teaching in his *Summa*. In Antoninus's Florence circa 1450, the four most important businesses were large-scale banking based on international currency exchange, wool production for international markets, silk production for international and local markets, and artisanal crafts in both mundane and luxury products for the local market, including art and architecture. At the top rung of the business classes were the the import-export merchants, the *calimala*, who operated Florence's international commercial and

45 Giorgio Vasari, "The Life of Giotto, Florentine Painter, Sculptor, and Architect," in *The Lives of the Artists*, 15–16. I owe the reference to this story to Goldthwaite, *Economy of Renaissance Florence*, 350.

46 Antoninus *Summa*, 3.8.1 (below), section 3.2; cfr Aristotle, *Nicomachean Ethics*, 10, 4 (1174b30ff.; 1175a20ff), in McKeon, 1099–1100.

47 Caferro, "Premodern European Capitalism, Christianity, and Florence," 65–6.

48 Goldthwaite, *Economy of Renaissance Florence*, 484–5; "Florence," in *Grove Encyclopedia of Medieval Art and Architecture*.

49 St Cosmas in the San Marco altarpiece is usually considered a portrait of Cosimo "il Vecchio."

banking network.[50] The manufacturers of wool cloth (*lanaioli*) and silk (*setaioli*) employed many different categories of textile worker, who by and large worked at piece rates, carrying out individual stages of the lengthy production process. Thus, most of the workers in the textile sector were industrial employees operating on the putting-out system.[51] These workers were among the most disenfranchised of the city's productive classes, and, as mentioned in chapter 1, at one point in Florence's history they banded together to temporarily overthrow the merchant oligarchy during the Ciompi Revolt, 1378–82, when the wool carders briefly gained direct representation in government, though the mercantile elite regained and strengthened their dominance afterwards.[52] Beyond the textile sector, there was an exceptionally large number of artisans, shopkeepers, and professionals in Florence, for whom establishing and haggling over prices was a daily routine, whether dealing in their own goods or retailing the goods of others.

Antoninus has all of these specific businesses in view in the chapters edited below. While the subject of Antoninus's teaching in chapter 2.1.16 – the obligation to pay a just price for what one purchases, and to purchase without fraud – has a nearly universal applicability, since practically everyone must purchase food, clothing, and other necessities of life, the more precise audience for Antoninus's teaching is those people and social classes who are obliged by their trade to make daily decisions about buying and selling. The textile and artisan sectors, being oriented fundamentally towards the production, purchase, and sale of merchandise, are the focus of much of Antoninus's discussion in the remaining chapters, especially 2.1.17 and 3.8.4. The subject of banking receives its own special treatment in chapter 3.8.3. A lively picture of those social classes emerges from Antoninus's enumeration of the variety of individual trades and the fraudulent and illicit practices in which they are often implicated when buying and selling. These social classes – from the merchant entrepreneurs down to shopkeepers, artisans, and humble peasants – are the audience whom Antoninus's teaching is meant to reach, and whose conduct it is meant to guide.

Did these social classes in Florence represent a capitalistic business culture? We return now to the question of capitalism and its hypothetical origins in medieval and Renaissance Italy. As mentioned above, a great many scholars who study the history of capitalism have been very interested in the business culture of Florence from the thirteenth to the fifteenth century, as illustrated recently by a special issue

50 Goldthwaite, *Economy of Renaissance Florence*, 343–5.

51 The putting-out system in the textile industry is described in ibid., 317–36. Antoninus's comments on labour relations in the Florentine textile industry can be found at *Summa*, 2.1.17 and 3.8.4; in addition to the present book, for a brief summary see de Roover, *Great Economic Thinkers*, ch. 7 "The Problem of the Just Wage."

52 Trivellato, "Renaissance Florence and the Origins of Capitalism," 241.

of the *Business History Review* devoted to "Italy and the Origins of Capitalism." But one of the most striking characteristics of the historiography on the origins of capitalism is how disparate scholars' approaches are.[53] Even among recent publications it is possible to find extremes of opposition. In his introduction to the first volume of *The Cambridge History of Capitalism*, published in 2014, Larry Neal defines four elements as central to capitalism: private property, enforceable contracts, responsive markets, and supportive governments.[54] This "incredibly capacious" definition allows for capitalism to be found as far back as Babylonia in the first millennium BC, the subject of the volume's opening chapter.[55] At the other extreme, in a book published just the next year, Sven Beckert argued that the plantation slavery of the seventeenth and eighteenth centuries was pivotal to the development of global capitalism.[56] Closer to the main stream of economic history scholarship are two schools which are likewise opposed to one another about the origins of capitalism. On the one hand is the school of thought associated with Max Weber and Werner Sombart, which seeks to identify a quintessence or "spirit" of capitalism; on the other hand is what could be called the business history school, which focuses instead on the tools and methods of modern enterprises, including accounting techniques, forms of corporation and contract, and state fiscal policies. Finally, the Marxist approach to history attempts to define capitalism as a set of relations to the means of production giving rise to a distinct class system and ideological superstructure; while Marx located the genesis of capitalism in the early modern period, some Marxist historians have argued that the crucial transformation of class relationships took place in the late Middle Ages.[57] For purposes of this book, I leave aside this approach to the history of capitalism; however, brief introductions to the Weber-Sombart school and the business history school are warranted.

For Weber and Sombart, the quintessence or spirit of capitalism is in fundamental opposition to the "traditionalist" ethos of most premodern and non-Western societies, including the Catholic culture of the Middle Ages. The traditionalist, as defined by Weber, pursues economic activity – whether as an agricultural labourer or an international banker – for the purpose of satisfying human wants. When one has done enough work or made enough profit to satisfy the customary wants of

53 This point was also made by Caferro, "Premodern European Capitalism," 39.

54 Larry Neal, "Introduction," in Neal and Williamson, eds., *The Cambridge History of Capitalism*, vol. 1, *The Rise of Capitalism*, 2–4.

55 Fredona and Reinert, "Italy and the Origins of Capitalism," 30.

56 Beckert, *Empire of Cotton*. See the review by Thierry Drapeau.

57 Much of this debate has revolved around the "Brenner thesis." The literature can be approached through Ghosh, "Rural Economies and Transitions to Capitalism"; Wood, *The Origin of Capitalism*; Hoppenbrouwers and van Zanden, eds., *Peasants into Farmers?*; Aston and Philpin, eds., *The Brenner Debate*.

oneself and one's family, in principle there is no motive to work any more or build up the business further; as in the example of the labourer whose wage is increased to motivate him to work harder, but whose response is simply to work a shorter day, since he can now take home his accustomed wage in fewer hours.[58] "This is an example of what is here meant by traditionalism. A man does not 'by nature' wish to earn more and more money, but simply to live as he is accustomed to live and to earn as much as is necessary for that purpose."[59] Money, here, is earned in order to be spent. Weber's capitalist, however, pursues profits not in order to spend them – whether on actual necessities or on hedonistic pleasures – but in order to reinvest them in the business and increase its profits without limit.[60] "The *summum bonum* of this ethic, the earning of more and more money … is thought of so purely as an end in itself, that from the point of view of the happiness of, or utility to, the single individual, it appears entirely transcendental."[61] Werner Sombart, in similar vein, contrasted the *Bedarfsdeckungsprinzip* (pursuit of one's needs), characterizing premodern business culture, and the *Erwerbsprinzip* (pursuit of gain), characterizing the "ethos of full capitalism."[62] After defining these two spirits, Weber argued that the capitalistic spirit was born in Protestant Europe, specifically out of Luther's idea of serving God in a "calling" combined with the "worldly asceticism" of Calvinism, and that the traditionalist spirit, associated by Weber with Catholic culture, represented "the most important opponent with which the spirit of capitalism … has had to struggle."[63] It is worth noting here that although some scholars think Weber's analysis should not be taken seriously any longer,[64] at least this much must be said in favour of it: something closely approximating Weber's "traditionalist" spirit is found expressed in a great many ancient and medieval texts which touch on economics and trade.[65] In chapter 3 above I mentioned some quotations from Gregory the Great and Augustine of Hippo collected in Gratian's *Decretum* as examples. As we saw in the discussion of Thomas Aquinas's teaching, scholastic writers described money and work as means, not ends. Medieval and

58 Weber, *Protestant Ethic*, 23–5. My first history professor, Karl Koth, illustrated the same attitude with a South American example (possibly proverbial) of a fisherman who would end his work day as soon as he had caught enough fish to pay his expenses, and was told by a visiting American businessman that if he instead worked a full day every day he could invest in a bigger boat, expand his business, earn more money, and one day retire to enjoy time with his wife and family. The fisherman reportedly saw no point in this, since he could already enjoy time with his wife and family now, simply by completing his work day as quickly as possible.

59 Ibid., 24.

60 Ibid., 13–23.

61 Ibid., 18.

62 Sombart, *Der moderne Kapitalismus*, quoted in Caferro, "Premodern European Capitalism," 45. See also Sombart, *The Quintessence of Capitalism.*

63 Weber, *Protestant Ethic*, 23; see also 122–5.

64 See, e.g., Jon Balserak's review of Patterson's *Representing Avarice in Late Renaissance France*, 1078.

65 On this theme, see Schefold, "Mittelalterliche Kapitalkritik und die Weberthese."

even Renaissance writers usually described the desire to make money without limit as the vice of avarice.[66] Thus Aquinas and Antoninus wrote:

> It is natural to man to desire external things as means to an end: wherefore this desire is devoid of sin, in so far as it is held in check by the rule taken from the nature of the end. But avarice exceeds this rule, and therefore is a sin.[67]

> Therefore a right intention is required in every exercise of a craft, so that the remote and ultimate end be God, according to what the Apostle says, *All whatsoever you do in word or in work, do to the glory of God;*[68] and the proximate end be some rational thing, for instance the support of one's need or that of neighbours.[69]

In light of the apparent dominance of economically traditionalist attitudes up to the Protestant Reformation, Weber and Sombart dated the birth of capitalism to the sixteenth century at the earliest.[70] For scholars in the school of Weber and Sombart, then, "economic history does not know the Renaissance," as Nussbaum observed.[71] From this point of view, the Renaissance is irrelevant to the birth of capitalism.

A century of scholarship in the field of business history, however, has shown that Renaissance Italy is "of critical significance in the development of modern economic forms."[72] Techniques and institutions which are essential to modern business were developed by Italian merchants and bankers, and propagated from Italy to the Low Countries, England, Spain, and thereafter to their colonies.[73] Innovations include marine insurance, the limited partnership, the bill of exchange, double-entry book-keeping, and government finance in the form of public debts and later annuities and bonds.[74] There was also the elaboration of mercantile, property, and contract law both in court practice and in city statutes.[75] The classic works of business history have been studies of the account books and business records of individual

66 This observation is also made by Langholm, *Merchant in the Confessional*, 264.

67 Aquinas, *Summa theologiae*, 2a 2ae q. 118 a. 1 ad 1.

68 Colossians 3:17; 1 Corinthians 10:31.

69 Antoninus, *Summa*, 3.8.1, section 3.1.1. See his whole discussion of "Right intention" there.

70 Trivellato, "Renaissance Florence and the Origins of Capitalism," 232.

71 Nussbaum, "The Economic History of Renaissance Europe," 527; I owe this reference to Caferro, "Premodern European Capitalism," 47.

72 Nussbaum, "Economic History," 528. See also Trivellato, "Renaissance Florence and the Origins of Capitalism," 235–7.

73 For an overview, see de Roover, "The Organization of Trade," esp. part 3, "Italian Hegemony in the 14th and 15th Centuries," 70–105.

74 Trivellato, "Renaissance Florence and the Origins of Capitalism," 235. See Munro, "The Medieval Origins of the Financial Revolution"; Gleeson-White, *Double Entry*.

75 Goldthwaite, *Economy of Renaissance Florence*, 110.

firms or merchants, including Raymond de Roover's studies of the Alberti and Medici banks,[76] Federigo Melis's and Iris Origo's work on Francesco Datini,[77] and Edwin Hunt's study of the Peruzzi and Bardi banks.[78] Scholars of business history sometimes discern in the business practice of merchants the hallmarks of modern capitalism. As early as 1914, Henri Pirenne argued that "all the essential features of capitalism – individual enterprise, advances on credit, commercial profit, speculation, etc. – are to be found from the twelfth century on, in the city republics of Italy – Venice, Genoa, or Florence."[79] Similarly, Armando Sapori found the medieval Italian merchant to be a heroic figure forging the path to modernity; Lujo Brentano traced the mentality of capitalism to them, and thought that the the Medici exemplified the impulse for infinite wealth.[80] Raymond de Roover stated boldly in the opening pages of his *Rise and Decline of the Medici Bank*: "Modern capitalism based on private ownership has its roots in Italy during the Middle Ages and the Renaissance."[81] Jacques Heers recently argued that capitalism was born in the Middle Ages among the moneychangers, usurers, and grand financiers.[82] In this vein, Richard Goldthwaite, in the most comprehensive monograph on the economy of Renaissance Florence, has suggested that some essential aspects of a capitalistic culture were present there, albeit with qualifications:

> By the standard definition of the term, the economy of Florence qualifies as a capitalist economy. The entrepreneur conducted his affairs relatively free from some of the strongest cultural restraints of medieval Europe ... This was an economy notable not just for the presence of capitalists in it; it was an economy organized around some of the basic principles of the capitalist system.[83]
>
> In other respects, however, these men were somewhat lacking in their "spirit of capitalism," as this phenomenon is often known. They seem not to have been driven

76 de Roover, "The Story of the Alberti Company of Florence, 1302–1348, As Revealed in Its Account Books"; de Roover, *The Rise and Decline of the Medici Bank, 1397–1494.*

77 Melis, *Aspetti della vita economica medievale (Studi nell'Archivio Datini di Prato)*, and Melis, *Documenti per la storia economica dei secoli XIII–XVI*; Origo, *The Merchant of Prato.*

78 Hunt, *The Medieval Super-Companies.* See also Hunt and Murray, *A History of Business in Medieval Europe, 1200–1550.*

79 Pirenne, "The Stages in the Social History of Capitalism," 495–6; quoted in Trivellato, "Renaissance Florence and the Origins of Capitalism," 233.

80 Sapori, *The Italian Merchant in the Middle Ages*; Brentano, *Der wirtschaftende Mensch in der Geschichte.* On these works, see Fredona and Reinert, "Italy and the Origins of Capitalism," 14; Trivellato, "Renaissance Florence and the Origins of Capitalism," 234.

81 De Roover, *Rise and Decline of the Medici Bank*, 2; quoted in Fredona and Reinert, "Italy and the Origins of Capitalism," 24.

82 Heers, *La Naissance du capitalisme au Moyen Âge.*

83 Goldthwaite, *Economy of Renaissance Florence*, 583, 588. See the more extensive remarks at 583–8.

> by a strong competitive instinct … In running their government they followed an economic policy of laissez faire, and privately they ran their business as highly individual enterprises. Yet their behavior at home and abroad often reveals an underlying spirit of corporatism … This stage in the history of capitalism, as exemplified by the Florentine experience, was still too early for us to talk about a natural link to the kind of individualism exemplified by *homo oeconomicus*, so important to later economic thinkers, not to mention today's economic historians.[84]

There is an echo here of the classic antithesis of modernity as individualistic, as against the "corporatism" of the Middle Ages. This raises the question of a possible link between the birth of a capitalistic culture and the humanist movement, especially the civic humanists of Florence, with the humanists, as the narrative goes, advocating individualism, freedom, and mobility, in opposition to the corporatist and static social order supposedly advocated by the medieval Church.[85] This link between humanism and a new capitalistic ethos has been made by Amintore Fanfani and H.M. Robertson, and more recently by Odd Langholm and Jonathan Patterson.[86] They see a new capitalistic ethos rising with the humanist movement, a lay-led movement pursuing secular values, individualism, and the goods of this world rather than those directed towards the next. While many scholars of Florentine history would add nuance and qualifications to a view I have stated very simply, I think most would agree that there has been a longstanding tendency to find a tension between the business culture of Renaissance Florence and the traditional teaching of the Church. This has made it common to see, in the way scholars talk about Renaissance business culture, merchants and bankers associated with civic humanists on the one side, and the Church's scholastic doctors, bishops, and mendicant preachers arrayed against their worldly values on the other side; in a word, to see an apparent friction between lay and clerical cultures.[87]

A radical revision of this view was advanced by Lester Little, who proposed that the mendicant friars created, for the first time, a Christian spirituality fully compatible with life in the new towns and with lay intellectual and material culture.[88] Giacomo

84 Ibid., 588–90.

85 The terminology of individualism and corporatism go back to Burckhardt, *The Civilization of the Renaissance in Italy*. Caferro, "Premodern European Capitalism," 43, writes that Alfred von Martin fleshed out Buckhardt's ideas in his *Sociology of the Renaissance* (London, 1944), describing Renaissance Florence as the prototype of the modern world.

86 Fanfani, *Catholicism, Protestantism and Capitalism*; Robertson, *Aspects of the Rise of Individualism*; Langholm, *Merchant in the Confessional*, esp. 260–71; Patterson, *Representing Avarice in Late Renaissance France*, esp. 14–17. See also Nuccio, *La storia del pensiero economico italiano come storia della genesi dello spirito capitalistico*.

87 For example in Goldthwaite, *Economy of Renaissance Florence*, 584–6.

88 Little, *Religious Poverty and the Profit Economy in Medieval Europe*.

Todeschini has taken this train of thought much further, suggesting that the medieval Christian church, and specifically Franciscan writers like Peter John Olivi and preachers like Bernardino of Siena, created a Christian conception of the economy and of the virtuous role of the merchant therein; indeed, suggesting that we are still embedded in it, with modern economics continuing to use the providential language of Christianity only in secularized form.[89] I wish to make a parallel argument here. My proposal is that an open mind may find more harmony than dissonance in comparing the moral outlooks of merchants and humanists on trade to those of scholastic doctors, bishops, and mendicant preachers.

Let us consider the merchants first. There is plenty of evidence that Italian merchants and bankers took seriously the Church's moral teaching in relation to trade, including its condemnation of usury. Take the case of Enrico Scrovegni, a banker who tried to make amends for his sins of usury by building the Arena Chapel in Padua and having it decorated by Giotto, producing one of the finest examples of western Christian art.[90] Moreover, lay Florentine citizens took an active interest in the disputes of theologians and canonists over the possibly usurious character of their city's public debt, the *monte*.[91] There was particular concern about whether trading in the secondary market in *monte* credits would implicate one in usury or illicit profit. Lawrin Armstrong has found a significant number of testaments in which Florentine citizens expess reservations about the morality of participating in the debt market or even accepting the interest payments which the commune paid out to lenders.[92] These testaments include orders for at least partial restitution of interest payments or forgiveness of the city's debts.[93] One rich wool merchant, Angelo Corbinelli, was particularly articulate in his testament: he declared that "he never bought credits in any of the *monti* of the commune of Florence."[94] In this he was following the advice and example of the lay canonist Lorenzo Ridolfi, a leading citizen of Florence from a patrician family, who had written in his *Tractatus de usuris* of 1404 that although he considered the market licit, "Nevertheless in doubtful cases the safer way should always be chosen, and therefore I recommend that those who can do so should abstain [from the market] … as indeed I myself

89 Todeschini, *Come l'acqua e il sangue*; see the helpful review by Robert Fredona. Todeschini has developed this theme in many publications, including *Ricchezza francescana*, translated into English by Michael Cusato (*Franciscan Wealth*); *I mercanti e il tempio*, translated into French by Ida Giordano (*Les marchands et le temple*).

90 Armstrong, *The Idea of a Moral Economy*, 3–4. See Derbes and Sandona, *The Usurer's Heart.*

91 See Lawrin Armstrong's account of the Florentine *monte* and the controversies over it in *Usury and Public Debt.*

92 Armstrong, "Usury, Conscience, and Public Debt," 173–200. On debates about the *monte* and citizens' interest in the controversy, see esp. 188–90, and the references therein.

93 Ibid., 195–200.

94 Ibid., 187.

have always done."[95] With regard to the forced loans (*prestanze*) which Angelo Corbinelli and his family had made to the city, and for which he had received annual interest payments, his testament reads:

> And because the testator himself often witnessed many masters, bachelors and other theologians dispute whether it was licit to accept payments on the aforesaid sums, and because he both saw and heard it said that highly judicious masters and theologians hold contrary opinions on this question, he was unable to be certain in his conscience.[96]

The testament goes on to direct his heirs to obey any future judgment by the Church, a general council, or a theological commission about the public debt. Had the Church ever condemned interest payments on the *monte* as usurious, Corbinelli's testamentary instructions would have involved a considerable sacrifice of the family's wealth. When merchants represented their views of moral uprightness in works of art they commissioned, they aligned with those of the Church's teachers on the obligations of truthfulness, justice, and charity to the poor. Brian Pollick has recently analysed some important examples in his doctoral thesis on the "merchant's moral eye," including the Palazzo Datini, built and decorated by the famed "merchant of Prato" Francesco Datini.[97] Some merchants wrote manuals on trade and business administration; although they show a different set of priorities from works by theologians and canonists, nevertheless these manuals tend to stress the same sort of moral duties and warn about the same moral pitfalls as one finds in clerical writers.[98] An early example is Domenico Lenzi's *Lo specchio umana*, a unique manuscript which Lenzi personally had copied and illuminated by a professional scribe according to his instructions circa 1340.[99] In Pollick's words, Lenzi represents himself therein as "an honest and knowledgeable grain merchant, a compassionate Christian, and a stern Christian moralist."[100] The illumination spanning fol. 57v and 58r shows Siena expelling its poor in time of famine and Florence taking them in and caring for them.[101] Paolo da Certaldo condemns usury in his *Libri di buoni costumi*.[102] The two greatest Renaissance manuals for

95 Ibid., 188.

96 Ibid., 187.

97 Pollick, "The Merchant's Moral Eye," 204–72.

98 A brief summary of some representative manuals is in Langholm, *Merchant in the Confessional*, 265–7. A vast number of sources produced by merchants are described and summarized in Dahl, *Trade, Trust, and Networks*.

99 Pollick, "Merchant's Moral Eye," 138; on this work, see 138–203.

100 I quote from a talk given by Brian Pollick at the University of Victoria Centre for Studies in Religion and Society, 26 May 2022. See also his "Merchant's Moral Eye," 140.

101 See the reproductions at ibid., 410–11.

102 Paolo da Certaldo, "Book of Good Practices."

merchants were written by Benedetto Cotrugli in 1458 and Luca Pacioli in 1494. Luca Pacioli, celebrated today as the "father of modern accounting" for his precise description of the double-entry method (although the practice goes back at least a century and a half before him in parts of Italy), ironically was not a lay writer at all – he was a Franciscan friar.[103] Once again with Pacioli we have a counter-example to the hypothetical friction between the clergy and lay business culture. The merchant writer Benedetto Cotrugli can serve as a final example, all the more interesting because Cotrugli's work shows the signs of some humanistic sensibilities and learning.[104] Much of his *Libro dell'arte di mercatura* (*The Book of the Art of Trade*),[105] completed in 1458, deals with the ins and outs of commercial activity – the location of the firm, the choice of merchandise, the different forms of exchange, resource allocation, partnership, insurance, correspondence, record keeping, and accounting.[106] Book 2, however, is "On the Religion Incumbent on the Merchant." It expresses serious Christian piety. "Man's greatest prize is religion alone."[107] Chapters 1 to 3 instruct merchants to attend Mass, to pray, and to give alms. To my mind the most interesting part is chapter 4, "On Matters of Conscience; What Is, and What Is Not Permissible." In this chapter Cotrugli hands on the traditional scholastic teaching on usury, illicit contracts, the just price, fraud, and restitution. He cites canon law repeatedly, and in his discussion of the just price and fraud he restates the teaching of Thomas Aquinas and Raymond of Peñafort, two of Antoninus's principal sources. Cotrugli even cites St Antoninus's discussion of sales on credit (contained in chapter 3.8.4 below): after analysing the practice and explaining when it is licit, when illicit, he concludes, "All this is endorsed by the venerable Brother Antoninus, master of theology and Bishop of Florence, in his *Antonina*."[108] Far from contesting the teaching of scholastic doctors and mendicant friars, Cotrugli emphasizes the importance of merchants learning it well: "To no man more than themselves is it necessary to know canons, because they [merchants] have to untangle many knotty problems in their profession."[109] If I may say so, in his merchant manual Cotrugli appears to be striving to

103 Caferro, "Premodern European Capitalism," 51, 54–5.

104 Ibid., 59–60.

105 The most recent critical edition is Benedetto Cotrugli, *Libro de l'arte de La Mercatura*, ed. Ribaudo (2016). An English translation is now available: Benedetto Cotrugli, *The Book of the Art of Trade, with Scholarly Essays from Niall Ferguson, Giovanni Favero, Mario Infelise, Tiziano Zanato and Vera Ribaudo.*

106 Summarized in Langholm, *Merchant in the Confessional*, 266.

107 Cotrugli, *Book of the Art of Trade*, 2, pr. (85).

108 Ibid., 2, 4 (100).

109 Ibid., 2, pr. (86). "Ma non sanno che a nulla generacione di homini è più necessario il sapere di canoni quanto ad loro, perché avendo multi scropulosi ligamenti, è di bisogno habino de li sc[i]ogliere" (Cotrugli, *Libro de l'arte de La Mercatura*, ed. Ribaudo, 98).

live up to Christ's words: *He therefore that shall break one of these least commandments, and shall so teach men, shall be called the least in the kingdom of heaven. But he that shall do and teach, he shall be called great in the kingdom of heaven.*[110]

Now let us briefly consider the Renaissance humanists. First, one must recognize that insofar as humanists wanted to revive classical culture, so much the more were they likely to be hostile to commerce and to deplore the activity and moral character of merchants. The foremost Greek and Roman philosophers, including Aristotle and Cicero, were indeed quite negative about trade.[111] Early humanists of the *trecento* were likewise.[112] Dante, whether he counts as a humanist or not, wrote a scorching condemnation of usury in his *Divine Comedy*.[113] Later "civic humanists" have often been cited as emphasizing the positive aspects of wealth for the individual and for the state, employing the classical concepts of liberality and magnificence.[114] But here there is no material departure from the scholastics. Thomas Aquinas counted both liberality and magnificence as virtues, species of justice and fortitude.[115] Antoninus himself both preached and wrote on the "virtue of magnificence" as one of the "virtues concerning money and its use."[116] Peter Howard has recently published a book evaluating Antoninus's teaching and preaching on magnificence and his influence upon the culture of Renaissance Florence.[117] Antoninus categorized magnificence, following Aquinas, as a part of the cardinal virtue of fortitude or courage: "its practice was seen in spending a great deal of money and the resolute accomplishment of imposing projects such as churches and chapels, hospitals for the poor, hospices for pilgrims, and even *palazzi* appropriate to the status of eminent citizens – all built or rebuilt for the honour of God and the good of the republic."[118] Nor can Antoninus's recommendation of

110 Matthew 5:19. This happens to be the Gospel for the day I am writing these words, 8 June 2022.

111 This is emphasized in Baldwin, "Medieval Theories of the Just Price," 12–13. For a fuller account, see Lowry and Gordon, eds., *Ancient and Medieval Economic Ideas and Concepts of Social Justice*.

112 See Baron, "Franciscan Poverty and Civic Wealth as Factors in the Rise of Humanistic Thought."

113 Dante Alighieri, *The Divine Comedy*, trans. Ciardi, *Inferno*, canto 17. See also in canto 11: "'Go back a little further,' I said, 'to where / you spoke of usury as an offense / against God's goodness. How is that made clear?' … 'Philosophy makes plain by many reasons,' / he answered me, 'to those who heed her teachings, / how all of Nature, – her laws, her fruits, her seasons, – / springs from the Ultimate Intellect and Its art / … near the beginning of Genesis, you will see / that in the will of Providence, man was meant / to labor and to prosper. But usurers, / by seeking their increase in other ways, / scorn Nature in herself and her followers.'"

114 See, for example, Goldthwaite, *Economy of Renaissance Florence*, 307, 584–6; Langholm, *Merchant in the Confessional*, 268. Both cite, among others, Leon Battista Alberti, e.g., *Della famiglia*, 2, in *Opere volgari*, vol. 1, 141–2.

115 Aquinas, *Summa theologiae*, 2a 2ae q. 117 and q. 134.

116 Antoninus, *Summa*, 4.3.6 (Ballerini, 4:85–6).

117 Howard, *Creating Magnificence*.

118 Ibid., 108; see also ibid., 119–21, for an English translation of Antoninus on magnificence.

magnificence as a virtue for the rich be attributed to the influence of the new civic humanism of Florence, since Antoninus's chapter in the *Summa* is an adaptation of the teaching of the Dominican Henry of Rimini, written circa 1300 in Venice, a manuscript of which was owned by Santa Maria Novella in Florence.[119] It is true that there were contemporary preachers who spoke in a more sceptical way about the "magnificence" of the Florentines. St Bernardino, in particular, when he preached in Florence for the Lent of 1425, "criticized the Florentines' propensity for almsgiving and for building chapels and hospitals as a substitute for true repentance."[120] This, however, only shows the diversity of views that could exist even among the Church's most outstanding spokesmen – disagreeing not necessarily about the usefulness of wealth in general, but perhaps about the spiritual and pastoral priority of the moment. Considering, however, that Antoninus, Henry of Rimini, and Thomas Aquinas can all be cited as recommending the classical virtue of magnificence, civic-humanist discourse about magnificence cannot, *per se*, be counted as a marker of cultural change. Likewise, in his treatise on the family, Leon Battista Alberti shows a social consciousness (Goldthwaite's phrase) about the purposes of wealth and business very much in harmony with Antoninus's teaching on these matters.[121] As Antoninus denounces the vice of avarice, the "inordinate love or appetite for money,"[122] so Alberti and Giovanni Rucellai both denounce avarice.[123]

But what about Poggio Bracciolini's dialogue *De avaritia* (*On Avarice*)?[124] This work has a reputation as the great humanist salvo calling into question "the ancient stigma of avarice surrounding the love of money."[125] Yet the interpretation of it is not straightforward. It is a Ciceronian dialogue consisting of a debate between three speakers on the subject of avarice. The second speaker, Antonio Loschi, who speaks in praise of avarice and calls it a virtue not a vice, has usually been considered the mouthpiece of Poggio himself, delivering the true message of the dialogue and acting as spokesman for the humanists' more worldly values.[126] If correct, then

119 Ibid., 92–9.

120 Ibid., 110.

121 Alberti, *Della famiglia*, 3, translated in Goldthwaite, *Economy of Renaissance Florence*, 307.

122 "Et sic diffinitur auaritia, quod est inordinatus amor uel appetitus peccunie." Antoninus, *Summa*, 2.1.1 ([*De avaritia*] *per modum predicationis*) (M_1 fol. 96v, hand A).

123 See Alberti, *Della famiglia*, 2 (146), and 3 (164); Giovanni Rucellai, *Zibaldone*, 15; both cited in Langholm, *Merchant in the Confessional*, 269.

124 Poggio Bracciolini, *On Avarice*, trans. Kohl and Welles, in *The Earthly Republic*, 241–89. The original Latin is printed in *Opera Omnia*, 1:1–31. See also Poggio Bracciolini, *De avaritia (Dialogus contra avaritiam)*.

125 Patterson, *Representing Avarice*, 15.

126 Garin, *L'umanesimo italiano*, 54–5, followed by many. Similarly see Langholm, *Merchant in the Confessional*, 270–1.

Poggio would seem to be a representative of a kind of proto-capitalism;[127] he even "anticipates Hume's famous dictum about avarice as the spur of industry."[128] However, I think it is more likely that John Oppel was correct in his reinterpretation of the *De avaritia* as an intensely conservative attack on avarice.[129] Oppel sited the *De avaritia* in the context of Poggio's longstanding conflict with the mendicant friars, particularly the Observant Franciscans, and his personal animosity towards St Bernardino of Siena.[130] Read alongside Poggio's statements about Bernardino in his correspondence, the polemical target of the dialogue appears to be the hypocrisy of the Observant mendicants, who proclaim their adherence to the rule of poverty but build extravagant new monasteries for themselves all over Tuscany with the patronage of the wealthiest bankers. Within the dialogue itself, what prompts the discussion of avarice is the speakers hearing Fra Bernardino preaching in Rome in 1427.[131] Antonio praises Bernardino generously, but Bartolomeo, the first speaker, complains that because the friars desire popularity and applause, they do not attack the vices to which Tuscans are most prone: "your Bernardino, whom you have praised so much, never treated avarice."[132] What is worse, preachers, "if they do indeed reprove avarice, they do so in the most jejune, arid, and insipid fashion and never with dignity of expression or conviction, so that it would have been better for them to have remained silent. They do not engender a hatred, but rather a desire, for sinning."[133] Poggio almost certainly has in mind here Bernardino's sermons on merchants and trade; as mentioned above, Bernardino and other Franciscan writers proposed a positive view of the Christian merchant. When Antonio speaks in defence of avarice, his arguments about the naturalness of trade and the profit motive and the social benefits of avarice paraphrase Bernardino's Latin sermon on merchants.[134] Oppel describes Antonio as effectively a parody of Bernardino.[135] The third speaker in the dialogue, the Greek theologian Andrea of Constantinople, is portrayed with the greatest *gravitas* and is given the last word.[136] He makes a forceful and learned statement against avarice, copiously citing classical and Christian authors, and at one point making a verbal echo of the canon

127 This was argued by Bec, *Les marchands écrivains*, 379–82.

128 Langholm, *Merchant in the Confessional*, 270.

129 Oppel, "Poggio, San Bernardino of Siena, and the Dialogue on Avarice." George Holmes takes a middle view, calling the dialogue a game in which "neither side is seriously in favour of avarice." *The Florentine Enlightenment 1400–50*, 147.

130 Oppel, "Poggio, San Bernardino," 566–7.

131 Bracciolini, *On Avarice*, 243.

132 Ibid., 247.

133 Ibid., 245–6.

134 Oppel, "Poggio, San Bernardino," 573–5. The sermon is Bernardinus Senensis, *De evangelio aeterno*, 33 (*Opera omnia*, 4:140–62).

135 Oppel, "Poggio, San Bernardino," 579.

136 Ibid., 577, 581–5.

Eiciens attributed to Chrysostom,[137] source of the statement that "a merchant can rarely or never please God."[138]

This reading of Poggio's *De avaritia* as an attack on avarice strikes me as highly probable.[139] Seen in this light, Poggio appears as a sterner and more conservative moralist in relation to commerce than the scholastics and mendicants. The apparent incongruity of this is, I think, an artifact of the Burckhardtian construct of lay humanist culture. There is a ready parallel to Poggio as the stern anticlerical moralist in Blaise Pascal, so famous for his attacks on the moral laxity of the Jesuits. Indeed, the scholastics and mendicants have been attacked for their liberality at least as often as they have been attacked for their rigidity. And it is true that the medieval scholastics were willing to err in favour of leniency towards merchants; some concrete examples are noted in my discussion of Antoninus's chapter 3.8.4 below. Scholastic writers asserted the basic necessity and utility of buying and selling and of the construction of businesses for pursuing certain trades.[140] They taught that merchants can and often do provide benefits not only for the individuals involved but also for the wider community, and that their commerce is licit so long as it is exercised in conformity with the requirements of moral law.

It must be acknowledged that merchants evidently found it difficult to follow all of these moral requirements, as spelled out in the teaching of Antoninus or even in manuals for merchants.[141] They did not always act honestly, shun usury, or limit themselves to pursuing the "moderate gain" which scholastic writers like Antoninus advised as the proper limit of trade. Francesco Datini's wife wrote to him once begging him to come home from his commercial travels and retire, since he had made more than enough money already.[142] The merchant writer Benedetto Cotrugli, speaking of the need for merchants to restore ill-gotten gains, wrote, "You will find only a small number of merchants, among many, who make full restitution, because they have entrusted their happiness to riches."[143] But that does

137 "Avaros omnes decreto meo eiciendos sentio e civitatibus." The echo is discernible in Poggio's original Latin; it is included in the extracts printed in Garin, ed., *Prosatori latini del Quattrocento*, 300.

138 "Homo mercator vix aut numquam potest Deo placere." Pseudo-Chrysostom, *Opus imperfectum in Matthaeum*, 38, in D. 88 c. 11 (*Eiciens*).

139 Arthur Field also rejects the hypothesis of Poggio as a proto-capitalist in *The Intellectual Struggle for Florence*, 308–15. "Poggio condemned 'avarice' consistently in his letters, and he did so in a way that fit in with the condemnations delivered in this dialogue. Indeed in his letters he refers to the dialogue as a piece 'against' avarice." Ibid., 314.

140 For supporting citations, see Langholm, "The Medieval Schoolmen," 444–59.

141 Obviously I am not the first to make this point. See, for example, Caferro, "Premodern European Capitalism," 57, 59, 64–6, and the references therein.

142 Personal communication from Brian Pollick, 27 May 2022. See Crabb, *The Merchant of Prato's Wife*.

143 Cotrugli, *Book of the Art of Trade*, 2, 4 (109).

not mean they disbelieved in the teaching. On the contrary, several outstanding works of scholarship in recent years have stressed how deeply embedded medieval merchants, buyers, and sellers were in a "moral economy."[144] There is a perfect illustration in the life of Tommaso Spinelli, reconstructed by William Caferro from the surviving Spinelli family archive. Spinelli was banker to Pope Eugenius IV, and was a close friend of Antoninus; on Antoninus's death in 1459, Spinelli helped pay for his funeral, and in his will stipulated that his letters from Antoninus be buried with him (causing them to be lost to us).[145] Spinelli seems to have been a genuinely pious Christian, and was generous in giving both to charity and to the Church, most famously supporting the building of Sante Croce.[146] But like Datini before him, Spinelli was known for focusing on his business to the exclusion of everything else, including his family, and for being extremely stingy about raising his employees' wages.[147] In Rome during the Jubilee of 1450, one of Spinelli's employees boasted of the huge profits he was making by speculating in gold. Spinelli told him to stop immediately: "Gabriello, I don't have such great need nor such great desire to earn as you may think. It is enough that I preserve myself and don't go backwards. I don't want too much … don't buy any more gold."[148] There is a strong parallel here with Antoninus's teaching on profit as a means, not as an end in itself:

> Hence it can be ordered towards an honest and necessary end, and thus trade will be made licit. Say if a trader orders the profit he seeks, moderate profit mind you, towards the end of sustaining himself and his family, that is in accordance with what is appropriate to their state, or suppose he intends to help the poor from his profit, or suppose he pursues trade for public utility, to ensure that the country does not run short of the necessities of life, and if he makes a profit not as an end in itself, but as a wage for his labour, observing all the due circumstances which will be discussed: one acting thus cannot be condemned. But if he places the ultimate end in profit, intending only to increase his wealth into immensity and to store it up for himself, he remains in a state of damnation.[149]

Similarly in several more places in the chapters edited below, Antoninus stresses that traders and businesspeople should seek "moderate profit" (*moderatum lucrum*).[150]

---

144 This point is emphasized in Armstrong, *The Idea of a Moral Economy*, 25–8. See James Davis, *Medieval Market Morality*; Romano, *Markets and Marketplaces in Medieval Italy, c. 1100 to c. 1440.*

145 Caferro, "Premodern European Capitalism," 67–70.

146 Caferro, "Tommaso Spinelli."

147 Ibid., 309–10.

148 Quoted in ibid., 314–15.

149 Antoninus, *Summa*, 2.1.16, section 2.1. See his whole discussion here of "End: greed," i.e., avarice.

150 Ibid., 3.8.1, section 3.2.2; 3.8.3, section 4.1; ibid., 3.8.4, esp. section 3.2, as well as sections 1 and 10.1. This is echoed in Cotrugli, *Book of the Art of Trade*, 2, 4 (106).

However, despite Spinelli's insistence on this principle, when eight days later he actually saw how large his employee's profits were, he could not resist their allure and resumed the gold trade.[151]

Yes, there was a tension in Renaissance Florence between Christian ideals and the pursuit of profit. The tension existed within the merchants and businesspeople themselves. However much a merchant might believe in the duties of honesty, justice, charity, and self-restraint in business, one could still be tempted by large profits, by opportunities for fraud, by usury, or by the compulsion to never stop working. Antoninus the pastor knew this. I will return to this point in the conclusion of this chapter. We turn now to Antoninus's teaching.

The next section will explain St Antoninus's teaching on trade, merchants, and workers as contained in the six chapters edited and translated below: 2.1.16 (*On fraud*), 2.1.17 (*On the various frauds which are committed in trading*), 3.8.1 (*On merchants and workers*), 3.8.2 (*On the various kinds of contracts*), 3.8.3 (*On traders and bankers*), and 3.8.4 (*On the various kinds of workers*).[152] For each chapter, a brief summary is provided, followed by a more lengthy exposition of its doctrine, method, and sources. This exposition is meant to summarize the main points, elucidate the key principles and logical steps of Antoninus's arguments, provide any necessary context, and indicate authorities to whom he is indebted, insofar as this is clear. It should be understood that all of this represents the editor's interpretation, and is no substitute for a careful reading of the text itself.

In explaining Antoninus's doctrine here, it is more convenient to depart from the original order of the chapters, and discuss first 3.8.1, then 2.1.16 and 2.1.17, and finally 3.8.2–4. This proceeds from more general topics to more specific ones. In 3.8.1, Antoninus gives a theological view of human work at the broadest level. In 2.1.16 he provides a detailed treatment of the moral principles which apply to buying and selling, with particular attention to the duty of observing justice in exchange by buying and selling at a just price. In 2.1.17 he discusses ways people can violate justice through various kinds of fraud. In the remaining chapters, which come from title 3.8 *On merchants and workers*, Antoninus applies all of these principles to specific cases: various types of contracts (3.8.2); exchange banking, insurance, and different types of commercial trade (3.8.3); and finally the various kinds of workers of all sorts (3.8.4).

---

151 Caferro, "Tommaso Spinelli," 318.

152 Other studies which examine St Antoninus's economic teaching: Cremona, *Carità e "interesse" in s. Antonino da Firenze (15o secolo)*; Gordon, *Economic Analysis before Adam Smith*; Bazzichi, "Antonino da Firenze"; Howard, "'Where the Poor of Christ Are Cherished'"; Ilgner, *Die volkswirtschaftlichen Anschauungen Antonins von Florenz*; Jarrett, *St. Antonino and Mediaeval Economics*; Noonan, *Scholastic Analysis of Usury*; de Roover, *Great Economic Thinkers*; Schumpeter, *History of Economic Analysis*; Spicciani, *Capitale e interesse*.

Chapters 3.8.1, 2.1.16, and 2.1.17 have the form of sermons, proceeding, in Antoninus's words, *per modum predicationis*, "by the method of preaching." The other three chapters, 3.8.2–4, are not sermons, proceeding instead *per modum doctrine*, "by the method of teaching."[153]

1. Theology of Work: *Summa* 3.8.1

This is a chapter of the *Summa*'s part 3. Most of part 3 is devoted to the different states of life: their special duties and characteristic vices. Title 8 is *On the state of merchants and workers*. In this first chapter of title 8, *On merchants and workers, arranged for a sermon*, Antoninus unfolds a theology of work arranged in a way suitable for preaching. The first component is the theology of merit as applied to good and evil acts or "works." The second is a theology of manual work: that the different sorts of manual work were instituted by God; the conditions for their goodness; their origins; and that restraint and good conscience are necessary in their exercise. Antoninus's approach to a theology of work here depends on three doctrines central to scholastic moral theology. In modern terms, these are the sources of morality, obedience to the duties of one's state in life, and the application of circumspection or discernment to every action.

Chapter 3.8.1 is organized according to the general scheme of the *sermo modernus* or scholastic sermon form, which had been standard since the thirteenth century. The hallmark of the *sermo modernus* is the use of a scriptural verse as a *thema*, and the unfolding of the sermon through division and development of this *thema*.[154] Chapter 3.8.1 proceeds in this way. It has the following structure:[155]

I. *Thema*: *Exibit homo ad opus suum, et ad operationem suam usque ad vesperam* (*Ps* 103.23).

II. Introduction of the subject.
Division of work into three types. Note the parallelism:

(1) Ad opus	virtuale,	Deo	principaliter	movente.
(2) Ad opus	criminale,	diabolo	internaliter	suggerente.
(3) Ad opus	manuale,	ingenio	naturaliter	agente.

153 Antoninus, *Summa*, 2 *prologus* (M_1 fol. IIr, hand G).

154 On the *sermo modernus*, see Mulchahey, *Dominican Education*, ch. 6 "Preaching Aids: Sermon Collections, Florilegia, *Exempla*, and *Artes*," esp. 400–10. For medieval descriptions of the method, see Thomas Waleys Anglicus, *De modo componendi sermones*; Wenzel, *Medieval Artes Praedicandi*. Antoninus's own instructions on preaching are found in *Summa*, 3.18.

155 The presentation of the structure of these chapters is adapted from the method employed by Alexander Andrée in the introduction to *Christopherus Laurentii de Holmis*, 9–39.

Confirmation of each of these types with biblical quotations and development:
1. To virtuous work.
2. To criminal work.
3. To manual work.

III. Development of the *thema*.
Restatement of the *thema*. Division of the *thema* into three principal parts, which are subsequently developed in the rest of the sermon. Again, note the parallelism:

3.1. Bonam conscientiam, ibi *Exibit homo ad opus suum.*
The first principal part is further divided according to the three ways in which *every one must prove his own work* (*Gal* 6.4).
- 3.1.1. Si est rectum in intentione,
- 3.1.2. Si est licitum ex improhibitione,
- 3.1.3. Si est congruum in discretione.

3.2. Aptam convenientiam, ibi *Ad operationem suam.*
The second principal part is likewise divided according to a three-fold distinction of exterior human works.
- 3.2.1. Ad quedam cogit necessitas;
- 3.2.2. Quedam invenit cupiditas;
  An exemplum is included of a merchant redeemed from vice.
- 3.2.3. Quedam induxit vanitas.

3.3. Debitam permanentiam, ibi *Usque ad vesperam.*
The third principal part functions as the conclusion of the whole sermon.

The subject of this chapter is work (*opus, opera, operatio*), presented in the form of a sermon. The sermon proceeds from the most general and universal level to the more particular, ultimately descending to the sort of work proper to "merchants and workers," the subject of the title as a whole. Antoninus takes as his *thema* a Psalm verse which speaks of man's work and labour (*opus, operatio*). Before introducing and dividing this *thema*, however, Antoninus sets out a very brief summary of the position of "work" in an Aristotelian-Thomistic philosophy of being. Each creature has its own work proper to it, intrinsically related to the fulfilment of its fundamental nature. Man, therefore, as a creature, has his own sort of work which fulfils his nature: this is revealed in Sacred Scripture to be twofold, a spiritual work and a corporal work. The spiritual work, which is man's "own proper work for which he was made," "the highest and perfect work," is "knowing and loving and enjoying God."[156] There is also, however, a corporal work proper to man, which was present even in the "paradise of pleasure" before the Fall; but after the Fall and

156 Antoninus, *Summa*, 3.8.1, opening section (*thema*).

the expulsion of man from paradise because of sin, "he was compelled to work the earth," as a necessity in order to live and to procure food, *till thou return to the earth* (Gen 3.19), that is, "until death."[157]

Antoninus then, as an introductory section of the sermon, divides human work into three kinds: virtuous work, criminal work, and manual work. Each of these has its own source of inspiration or principle of action: namely God, the devil, and one's own natural disposition. Antoninus confirms the definition of each type of work with biblical quotations and patristic commentary (the latter quoted via Lombard's *Sentences* and Gratian's *Decretum*) and briefly develops it in a short paragraph. As to virtuous and criminal work, Antoninus outlines how God and the devil are implicated in man's good and evil works, and how by them man can merit reward or punishment.

Arriving at manual work, Antoninus enters into the main subject of the sermon. He defines the manual work which distinguishes man from other animals as that by which, "through the exterior works of different occupations, he may provide himself with means of sustenance and garment and defence from harmful things. And practically all the exterior works of man are ordered towards these."[158] At this point Antoninus returns to the *thema*, restating it and applying it specifically to manual work; he then divides it into three principal parts: good conscience, apt suitability, and necessary perseverance. The development of these three principal parts will produce the remainder of the sermon.

As to good conscience, Antoninus points out that every work must be carried out "not only following the rule of that craft, but also following the rule of a good conscience."[159] Antoninus here reduces the requirements of "good conscience" to three: right intention, non-prohibition, and appropriate discretion. These three requirements readily correspond to the standard moral-theological "sources of morality," which are end (i.e., intention), object (i.e., non-prohibited), and circumstances (which are judged by discretion).[160] Antoninus's discussion of the first two requirements employs recognizably common scholastic doctrine: some sorts of work ("objects" in moral-theological terminology) are illicit or prohibited in themselves, as is the case with prostitution and usury, and no good intention can make them licit; all other sorts of work, however, take their morality, first, from the intention ("end") for which they are done. A distinction can be made here between the remote end and the proximate end. The remote or ultimate end of

157 Ibid.

158 Ibid., section 3.

159 Ibid., section 3.1.

160 "What have we to attend to in order to know whether an action is according to right reason or not? There are three such elements … They are the object, the end, and the circumstances of the action." Slater, *A Manual of Moral Theology for English-Speaking Countries*, 1, 4, 2 (1:21–6).

every human act must be God, as is taught in the Scriptures.[161] The proximate end must be "some rational thing";[162] for instance, when in agriculture, wool working, smithing, etc., the profits are employed to provide what is necessary for the corporal sustenance of oneself or one's neighbour. Antoninus then illustrates how such a proximate end can be the first link in a chain of ends terminating in God as the remote end:

> And rightly spoke Christ and the Apostle, *For the labourer is worthy of his wage.*[163] The end of his wage ought to be that, from it, he may take care and provide for himself and others in accordance with his state; the end of sustaining himself and his own ought to be that they may live virtuously; the end of virtuous living is the attainment of glory: for as Augustine says on John, "For to this end ought every one to live well, that it may be given him to live for ever."[164]

As for "appropriate discretion," this pertains to observing the due circumstances of a work whose object and intention are good. Antoninus's discussion of this point is brief and merely introduces the principle. A much fuller exposition of it is provided in 2.1.16, where Antoninus explains each of the seven circumstances of a human act as applied to trade and commerce.

The second principal part of the sermon is about the "apt suitability" of work. Antoninus introduces this subject as a question, not so much of what causes a work to be moral, but of what causes it to be fit and suitable to a particular person. For each person should go forth to "his" labour, as the *thema* states, that is, "to that craft which he judges to be more suitable and pleasing to him."[165] Antoninus cites both Aristotle and the Scriptures in support of this. This portion of the sermon seems to anticipate pastoral teaching about discernment of a state in life more commonly associated with St Ignatius of Loyola and St Francis de Sales. Antoninus applies the theory, received from natural philosophy, of the four common human temperaments: melancholic, phlegmatic, sanguine, and choleric. Each of

161 Antoninus cites here Colossians 3:17 and 1 Corinthians 10:31. Although Antoninus does not spell this out himself, the Aristotelian-Thomistic philosophy which he began with also supports this conclusion. If the fulfilment of man's nature is "knowing and loving and enjoying God," and man's actions are good or bad according to whether they contribute to the fulfilment of his nature, then it logically follows that man's actions are good or bad according to whether they contribute to his knowing and loving and enjoying God. Hence, at least the remote end of every human act must be God.

162 Antoninus, *Summa*, 3.8.1, section 3.1.1.

163 Luke 10:7; 1 Timothy 5:18.

164 Antoninus, *Summa*, 3.8.1, section 3.1.1. At the end Antoninus quotes Augustine, *In Evangelium Ioannis*, 45, 2; see *Tractates on the Gospel of John*, trans. Gibb.

165 Antoninus, *Summa*, 3.8.1, section 3.2.

these inclines a person to the practice of different virtues, to the study of different sciences, and to the exercise of different corporal works or mechanical crafts.[166] A person should, as far as possible, choose that mechanical craft or trade which is "more suitable and pleasing to him,"[167] for "pleasure … perfects work."[168] This urbane piece of pastoral direction stands out as particularly suited to Antoninus's Florentine audience: as noted above, people in Renaissance Florence enjoyed a relative freedom to enter and pursue a trade of their own choosing.

Antoninus continues his discussion of "exterior human works" by introducing a threefold distinction drawn from a *sententia* of Hugh of St Victor: some works are compelled by necessity, some were invented by cupidity (greed), and some were introduced by vanity. Under these three headings the sermon is carried through to its conclusion. The latter two sorts of work are inventions of man, and from the beginning were deformed by his vices and inordinate passions; the works compelled by necessity, however, were instituted by God. Antoninus briefly confirms how each of the typical works compelled by necessity has its own progenitor or forbear in Sacred Scripture: agriculture, husbandry, viticulture, shepherding, wool and linen working and the making of clothes, the building of dwelling-places and cities (first done by Cain!), tent making, and smithing. "And thus step by step all the necessary crafts were invented."[169]

"The exterior work invented by cupidity is trade."[170] Antoninus here mentions in passing Aristotle's statement that trade, understood as the art of wealth getting, has a certain distastefulness, though, according to Antoninus following Aquinas, it may be made licit by serving a good end. This *sententia* was already cited above in discussing Aquinas (chapter 3); it will return in the discussion of 2.1.16 below. Antoninus then introduces the scriptural progenitors of trade: the Ishmaelites, whom he identifies as the ancestors of the Saracens (Arabs or Muslims) of his own day.[171] In his eyes, the Saracens are a people specially associated with trade: first, because it was the original profession of Mohammed; and second, because they now trade in Christians by capturing them and perverting them "to their perfidy."[172] They have a further association with trade, because a multitude of

166 Antoninus cites Albert the Great in support of this; on further investigation, however, he appears to be handing on a doctrine expounded by his mentor Giovanni Dominici in a work, *Dialogus*, which is no longer extant. Dominici also wrote a handbook on the care and upbringing of children – a subject to which knowledge and experience of the different temperaments is very pertinent.

167 Antoninus, *Summa*, 3.8.1, section 3.2.

168 Ibid., quoting Aristotle, possibly via Aquinas.

169 Ibid., section 3.2.1.

170 Ibid., section 3.2.2.

171 See *DMLBS*, s.v. *Saracenus*.

172 Antoninus, *Summa*, 3.8.1, section 3.2.2.

papal decretals have prohibited traders, on pain of papal excommunication, from delivering certain merchandise to Egypt or others of their lands. Antoninus passes on to warning about the dangers to salvation inherent in trade, drawing largely on familiar patristic texts collected in Gratian's *Decretum* at D. 88 (discussed above, chapter 3). He provides an exemplum for the inspiration and imitation of the faithful, drawn from the *vita* of the hermit St Paphnutius, of a merchant who carried out his trade in a way pleasing to God and in the end received heavenly glory rivalling that of Paphnutius himself.

As to arts introduced by vanity, typical examples are the art of silk making, lace, embroidery and other ways of ornamenting fabric, and cosmetics. It is notable that these are among the arts or industries for which Antoninus's own city of Florence was, and continues to be, justly famous. Antoninus passes brief judgment on these arts, noting that they are often misused, abused, and thus debased, though they can be used fittingly by those for whom they are appropriate if they employ them in a restrained manner.

The third principal part, "necessary perseverance," provides the conclusion of the whole sermon. Its inspiration is a saying attributed to Pope Anacletus: "Diligence is the mother of the works of each craft."[173] This is the meaning of the *thema*'s saying that man shall go forth to his labour *until the evening*, "that is, the end of life."[174] Here Antoninus's exemplum is of conduct to be avoided: he cites the "son of inconstancy," a parable which originated in a thirteenth-century pseudo-Boethian work, *De disciplina scholarium*, and in Antoninus's time had become proverbial.[175] Finally, the reward for persevering in labour is held out to the faithful: *Call the labourers and give them their wage*,[176] "namely of glory."[177]

The principal sources employed by Antoninus in developing this sermon are theological. The books of the Bible provide, by a wide margin, the majority of Antoninus's quotations and citations. In the second place come Church Fathers quoted via Gratian's *Decretum* and, to a lesser extent, Peter Lombard's *Sentences*. A few points in the sermon are supported by references to canon law, including the *Liber Extra* and papal *decretales extravagantes*. Similarly, a small number of notions drawn from philosophy are employed, cited from Aristotle, Averroës, and Albert the Great. Although citations of Thomas Aquinas are few, nevertheless several common scholastic doctrines are employed in this sermon whose formulation Antoninus probably received from Aquinas. Finally some other works are cited only once, such as those of Seneca, pseudo-Boethius, and the anonymous *Vitae*

173 Anacletus, *Epistola cunctis fidelibus* (Pseudoisidore, 1, 8) in D. 83 c. 6 (*Nichil*).

174 Antoninus, *Summa*, 3.8.1, section 3.3.

175 Boethius (pseudo), *De disciplina scholarium*, 104–8. See also Sanford, "*De disciplina scholarium*."

176 Matthew 20:8.

177 Antoninus, *Summa*, 3.8.1, section 3.3.

patrum. Hugh of St Victor likewise is cited only once, though he provides the key *sententia* which structures the development of the second part of the *thema.*

2. Justice in Buying and Selling: *Summa* 2.1.16

This chapter comes from the second part of the *Summa* in the lengthy treatise on the seven capital vices, from the title on *avaritia* "greed." Under the rubric of "greed," the scholastic moralists were accustomed to deal with all kinds of "economic" sins.[178] Antoninus is no exception; the first fifteen chapters of the title *de avaritia*, after several general sermons and two chapters on simony, deal with usury and its various kinds; disguised usury and cooperation in usury; the public debts (*montes*) of the Italian cities and the controversy over trading in debt credits; robbery; unjust taxes, tolls, imposts, and forced loans (*prestanze*); and theft with its various means, including unjust prescription.

This chapter, 2.1.16, *On fraud* in the form of a sermon, is one of the two longest of the six edited herein. It has three sections. In the first, Antoninus shows what sort of trade is entirely virtuous and is recommended in Sacred Scripture, namely spiritual trade, which is symbolized by the merchant seeking good pearls. In the second section, Antoninus deals with "criminal trade," which is vicious and to be avoided. Here he presents a comprehensive exposition of the doctrine of the "sources of morality" as applied to trade; i.e., the ways in which trade can become wicked because of a disorder in end, object, or due circumstances. He examines this according to the traditional seven circumstances of a human act: why, who, when, where, by what aids, how, what. In the third section, on "temporal trade," Antoninus considers the moderation or restraint required in exercising licit trade, as regards the price given or received. This section could be considered an eighth circumstance: assuming all the first seven due circumstances are observed, the final circumstance to be considered is the price, which has its own requirements in order for the whole contract to be virtuous. In sum: merchandise must be exchanged at a just price, i.e., a price which equalizes the value of what is given and what is received. Antoninus expounds the doctrine of the just price in detail. First, he considers what causes prices, i.e., the nature and origin of economic value. Second, he considers the latitude which pertains to the just price, employing the doctrines of *laesio enormis*, free bargaining, and Aquinas's double rule (see above, chapter 3). Finally, he considers what is the consequence of an excess in price (too high or too low), and here there are three kinds of excess. The first two are unjust, namely excess against law and excess against conscience. The third, however, is neither unjust nor sinful, namely inadvertent minor excess.

178 On this see Langholm, *Merchant in the Confessional*, 261–3.

Chapter 2.1.16, in the form of a sermon, has the following structure:

I. *Thema*: *Quoniam non cognovi negotiationem, introibo in potentias Domini; Domine, memorabor iustitie tue solius* (*Ps* 70:15–16).

II. Division of the *thema* into three principal parts. Note the parallelism.
Triplex est genus negotiationis:

(1) Prima est	mundialis et scelesta	et ideo	cavenda:	*Quoniam non cognovi negotiationem.*
(2) Secunda est	spiritualis et honesta	et ideo	exercenda:	*Introibo in potentias Domini.*
(3) Tertia est	temporalis et modesta	et ideo	permittenda:	*Domine memorabor iustitie tue solius.*

III. Development of the *thema*.
The majority of the sermon proceeds by development of the *thema*, beginning from the second principal part, with each part subdivided in turn.

1. De negotiatione spirituali.
This part is divided into three regions where spiritual trade is carried out.

1.1. Prima est	regio celestis,	in qua	manifestatur	Dei potentia ad remunerandum,
1.2. Secunda est	terrestris,	in qua	declaratur	Dei potentia ad creandum et gubernandum,
1.3. Tertia est	in inferis,	ubi	comprobatur	potentia Dei ad cruciandum.

2. De negotiatione mundiali.
This part is divided according to the seven circumstances of a human act, by which the act of trade can become iniquitous and to be avoided.
Septempliciter autem negotiatio est iniqua et cavenda:

2.1. Ratione	finis	cupidi.
2.2. Ratione	persone	clerici.
2.3. Ratione	temporis	feriati.
2.4. Ratione	loci	sacrati.

It is noted at this point that profits gained through trade involving the above four undue circumstances should be paid out upon the poor, with directions about how this should be preached and counselled in the confessional.

2.5. Ratione	consortii	iniusti.
2.6. Ratione	medii	iniqui.
2.7. Ratione	materie	mali.

3. De negotiatione temporali modesta.
   The third principal part is divided according to the three ways by which trade may be carried out against the justice of God. Only the first member of the division is developed in this sermon; the remaining two are left for the next sermon in 2.1.17.
   (3.1) Ex iniqua appretiatione.
   (3.2) Ex varia sophisticatione vel fraudatione.
   (3.3) Ex illicita permutatione.

   Development of the first member.
   - 3.1. Ex iniqua appretiatione.
     The development of the first member proceeds through further divisions.
     Pro pleniori declaratione materie tria videnda sunt:
     - 3.1.1. Unde accipiendus sit debitus valor rei.
       Ipse valor rerum ... tripliciter pensatur:
       - 3.1.1.1. Ex eius virtuositate.
       - 3.1.1.2. Ex eius raritate.
       - 3.1.1.3. Ex eius complacibilitate.
         The next member is introduced here.
     - 3.1.2. Que sit latitudo competens valoris rei.
       Tripliciter hoc [latitudo] innotescere potest:
       - 3.1.2.1. Ex iure.
       - 3.1.2.2. Ex consuetudine.
       - 3.1.2.3. Ex discretione.
     - 3.1.3. Quid dicendum quando fit excessus valoris rei.
       Tripliciter potest fieri excessus in pretio rerum ... vel defectus:
       - 3.1.3.1. Excessus ultra dimidiam iusti pretii.
       - 3.1.3.2. Excessus notabilis infra dimidiam iusti pretii.
       - 3.1.3.3. Excessus minor.
         Si fiat diminutio vel excessus iusti pretii in contractibus in modicho, non est neccesse restitutionem fieri, ad quod probandum inducunt triplicem rationem:
         - 3.1.3.3.1. Ratione pacis et salvationis.
         - 3.1.3.3.2. Ratione mutue concordationis.
         - 3.1.3.3.3. Ratione humane extimationis.
         - 3.1.3.3.4. Si quis autem obstaret et diceret ...

III. Conclusion.
   The conclusion explains that the second and third members, (3.2) ex varia sophisticatione vel fraudatione and (3.3) ex illicita permutatione, are left to the next sermon in 2.1.17.

The subject of this chapter is buying and selling, i.e., "trade" (*negotiatio*). The *thema* is a Psalm verse: *Because I have not known trade* (negotiationem), *I will enter into the powers of the Lord: O Lord, I will be mindful of thy justice alone.*[179] This is a quotation of the Psalm numbered 70 in medieval Bibles, verses 15–16 (71:15–16 in modern Bibles), but drawing on a different biblical translation from the Vulgate. The Vulgate text reads, *Because I have not known learning* (litteraturam), *I will enter into the powers of the Lord.* However, the Vaticanus manuscript of the Greek Septuagint here reads *pragmateia* (mercantile affairs) in place of *grammateia* (learning).[180] This reading, *pragmateia*, became the basis of the Latin translation, *negotiationem*, contained in the Roman Psalter.[181] It was cited by many Church Fathers, including Pope Gelasius, Augustine, and Cassiodorus, whose comments on this text were quoted by Gratian in the *Decretum*, D. 88 c. 2, c. 12, and c. 13.[182] The reading *negotiationem* (or *-es*) is also recorded in the *Glossa ordinaria* to the Bible, alongside the Vulgate's reading *litteraturam.*[183] This alternate translation of Psalm 70:15 was regularly quoted by scholastic writers discussing trade; Bernardino of Siena took this same text as the *thema* of a sermon on the subject *Quo pretio aestimari debeant res venales, et de culpa vendentium res maculatas.*[184] Nevertheless, Bernardino's division and development of the *thema* are quite different from those of Antoninus in 2.1.16.

Antoninus sets up the division of the sermon by pointing out an apparent contradiction between the *thema* and the Lord's parable of the talents in Luke 19, where the servants are told, *Trade till I come.*[185] In scholastic fashion, Antoninus resolves the dilemma by means of distinction and definition: "trade is of three kinds."[186] This provides the division of the *thema.* The rest of the sermon will proceed by development of each of the three principal parts of the *thema.* Trade is divided into spiritual trade, which is honest; worldly trade, which is dishonest; and temporal trade, which is modest.

Spiritual trade is recommended by the Lord in a parable in Matthew 13: *The kingdom of heaven is like to a merchant seeking good pearls, who when he had found one pearl of great price, went his way, and sold all that he had, and bought it.*[187] Antoninus interprets this as signifying the Church militant (i.e., the Church in

---

179 Psalm 70:15–16 in the Roman Psalter, my translation.
180 Haydock, *Haydock's Catholic Bible Commentary*, *Ps* 70.15 s.v. *Learning.*
181 See Lefébure, *Injustice*, 226–7.
182 The latter two texts were discussed above in ch. 3, section 2.
183 *Bibliorum sacrorum glossa ordinaria*, *Ps* 70.15 (3:950).
184 Bernardinus Senensis, *De evangelio aeterno*, 35 (*Opera omnia*, 4:189–90).
185 Luke 19:11–27.
186 Antoninus, *Summa*, 2.1.16, opening section (*thema*).
187 Matthew 13:45–6.

this world) and each of the faithful in it;[188] he divides the subject according to the three regions in which the merchant proverbially travels to carry out his spiritual trade: in heaven, on earth, and in hell. To each region, Antoninus applies the parable, explaining what is the pearl of great price to be found therein, and what is the money with which it is bought. Antoninus makes a clever pun here, playing on two Latin words: *merx, mercis*, "merchandise, wares," and *merces, mercedis*, "wage, reward." The pun cannot be reproduced perfectly in my English translation; Antoninus uses the homography between the two words to connect the merchandise sought by the spiritual trader – a pearl of great price – with the rewards received in heaven. In heaven, the pearl of great price is the "glory of the direct perception of the divine,"[189] and the money to buy it is grace: "Nothing is cheaper when bought, nothing is dearer when possessed."[190] On earth, the pearl of great price is wisdom, and the money is the "labour of curbing and moderating one's passions."[191] In hell, the pearl of great price is indulgence, "that is, the remission of the penalty of eternal fire or of the temporal purgatory which everyone has earned for their sins,"[192] and the money is penance. This part of the sermon, on spiritual trade, is much briefer than the next two parts. It is less doctrinal and more oriented towards edification and exhortation. Scriptural quotations constitute by far the most frequent source, with a few quotations embedded from Church Fathers (mostly via Gratian or Aquinas) or other sources, including a hymn from the breviary and a verse from the poet Vergil.

In turning to dishonest worldly trade, the sermon shifts towards a more doctrinal orientation. Antoninus expounds here the seven circumstances which can make trade iniquitous, unjust, and to be avoided. These circumstances correspond to the classical seven circumstances of a human act:[193]

1. *Cur* ("why"), "because of end: greed."
2. *Quis* ("who"), "because of person: cleric."
3. *Quando* ("when"), "because of time: holiday."

188 This is a typical use of the allegorical and moral senses of Scripture. See Mulchahey, *Dominican Education*, 410, and the references therein.

189 Antoninus, *Summa*, 2.1.16, section 1.1.

190 Gregory I, *XL homiliarum in Evangelia*, 1, 5 (PL 76:1093–4), on Matthew 4:18–22; quoted in Antoninus, *Summa*, 2.1.16, section 1.1. Cfr Aquinas, *Summa theologiae*, 2a 2ae q. 100 a. 1.

191 Antoninus, *Summa*, 2.1.16, section 1.2.

192 Ibid., section 1.3.

193 Aquinas's explanation: "Tully, in his Rhetoric, gives seven circumstances, which are contained in this verse: 'Quis, quid, ubi, quibus auxiliis, cur, quomodo, quando – who, what, where, by what aids, why, how, and when.' … But Aristotle in Ethic. iii, 1 adds yet another, to wit, 'about what,' which Tully includes in the circumstance 'what.'" Aquinas, *Summa theologiae*, 1a 2ae q. 7 a. 3 co. Cfr Hostiensis, *Summa aurea*, 5.38 §. 50 (Venice, 1574, col. 1811).

4. *Ubi* ("where"), "because of place: sacred."
5. *Quibus auxiliis* ("by what aids"), "because of combination: unjust."
6. *Quomodo* ("how"), "because of means: iniquitous."
7. *Quid* ("what"), "because of matter: evil."[194]

This is another place where Antoninus's exposition has much in common with a sermon of Bernardino of Siena.[195] Nevertheless, he has adapted the material for his own purposes, applying some of the circumstances differently: for example, where Bernardino has *circumstantia communis damni*, Antoninus has *ratione materie mali*, and Antoninus's interpretation of *consortium*, "combination," is quite different. Analysis of trade according to the circumstances which can render it illicit has a long scholastic pedigree: Raymond of Peñafort led the way in his *Summa de paenitentia*, employing, however, only the first four of Antoninus's circumstances.[196] Hostiensis employed a similar scheme in his *Summa aurea* in the title on penance, at the place where he discussed restitution of wrongly acquired goods.[197] The major sources for Antoninus's discussion as a whole are Thomas Aquinas in the *Summa theologiae, secunda secundae*, q. 77; Raymond of Peñafort, *Summa de paenitentia*, 2.8; Hostiensis, *Summa aurea*, 5.38 on penance; and Bernardino of Siena, *De evangelio aeterno*, sermon 33.

It is not necessary here to expound Antoninus's treatment of each circumstance in more than summary form. Only a few points will be highlighted. The explanation of the circumstance of end, "greed," is based on Aquinas, *secunda secundae*, q. 77 a. 4, which was already discussed above in chapter 3. The circumstance of person, "cleric," weaves together the substance of three texts: Aquinas's

---

A twentieth-century explanation: "Moral circumstances are those moral conditions which are added to and modify the already existing moral substance of the act ... From the earliest times it has been customary to list seven circumstances contained in the following verse ..." Prümmer, *Handbook of Moral Theology*, 21–2.

194 Antoninus, *Summa*, 2.1.16, section 2.

195 Bernardinus Senensis, *De evangelio aeterno*, 33, 2, 1–7. "Fit autem ex septemplici circumstantia illicita mercantia: primo, ex circumstantia personae; secundo, ex circumstantia causae; tertio, ex circumstantia temporis; quarto, ex circumstantia loci; quinto, ex circumstantia consortii; sexto, ex circumstantia communis damni; septimo, ex circumstantia modi. Sexta circumstantia est Scoti, reliquae vero Alexandri de Hales" (*Opera omnia*, 4:145).

196 Raymundus de Pennaforti, *Summa de paenitentia*, 2.8 (557–8): "Circa hoc nota quod negotia: alia inhonesta sui natura, alia non. ... Alia plura sunt quae non sunt inhonesta sui natura, sed ex causa, vel ex tempore, vel ex persona, vel ex loco, ut emptio-venditio, locatio-conductio et similes contractus; similiter et quasi contractus, ut tutela, cura, negotiorum gestorum iudicium et similia. Et breviter: in hoc concluditur exercitium omnium artium mechanicarum, ut artis textoriae, sutoriae et similium quae necessaria sunt usui humano."

197 Hostiensis, *Summa aurea*, 5.38 §. 61 (col. 1858–9). Hostiensis writes, for the circumstance of "end," *fraudulenta intentione*, synonymous with *iniusto exercitio*.

reply to the third objection in q. 77 a. 4; Raymond of Peñafort's explanation of the circumstance of person; and the corresponding circumstance in Bernardino of Siena's sermon on this subject.[198] The circumstance of time, "holiday," however, owes little to these three sources; it does suggest some debt to Raymond of Peñafort's title *de feriis*,[199] which provides precedent both for intepreting the Third Commandment as forbidding "servile works" and for classifying trade among these.[200] Antoninus adds a pastoral note that moderate trading in the markets on feast days can be licit if the proper church offices have been heard;[201] he attributes this *sententia* to Peter of la Palud.[202] On place, "sacred," namely trade in a church, Antoninus's discussion does not draw conspicuously on any of the usual sources. It is a straightforward declaration of why this is forbidden, with the Gospel of John the only source cited.[203] Antoninus does raise the question, "what about those selling candles there?"[204] and provides the requirements for this activity to be licit.

At this point, Antoninus adds a pastoral note about what is required of the profits gained in trade carried out in one of the four aforesaid circumstances. Addressing the clerical reader, his instruction is to preach and counsel penitents that such profits should be paid out on the poor. "Nevertheless this does not seem to be necessary for salvation."[205] He briefly indicates the grounds for his opinion and then explains that this need not be mentioned, because

> it is not proper to open up every truth in preaching, because of the danger of people who are prone to loosening their consciences abusing the truths they are told.[206]

---

198 Aquinas, *Summa theologiae* 2a 2ae q. 77 a. 4 ad 3; Raymundus de Pennaforti, *Summa de paenitentia* 2.8.1 (Ochoa-Diez, 1B:559); Bernardinus Senensis, *De evangelio aeterno* sermo 33, 2, 1 (*Opera omnia*, 4:145–6). The authorities Antoninus cites are those cited by the former three authors, except for the citation of Pope Leo ("difficile est …") in *De pen.* D. 5 c. 2, and Psalm 100:6 (*ambulans in via immaculata*), both of which appear to be Antoninus's additions. Cfr also Hostiensis, *Summa aurea* 5.38 §.61 (*Restitutione male acquisitorum quibus, et qualiter, et inquantum sit facienda*) (col. 1858–9).

199 Raymundus de Pennaforti, *Summa de paenitentia*, 1.12 §. 4 (*In diebus festivis*) (Ochoa-Diez, 1B:398–9).

200 Exodus 20:10. Cfr Antoninus, *Summa*, 2.1.16, section 2.3.

201 Antoninus, *Summa*, 2.1.16, section 2.3.

202 I have not found this *locus* in Peter of la Palud. The relevant volume is *Quartus sententiarum liber* (Paris, 1514).

203 John 2:16. *Et his qui columbas vendebant, dixit : Auferte ista hinc, et nolite facere domum patris mei, domum negotiationis.* "And to them that sold doves he said: Take these things hence, and make not the house of my Father a house of traffic."

204 Antoninus, *Summa*, 2.1.16, section 2.4.

205 Ibid.

206 Ibid.

The remaining types of illicit trade, which occupy the rest of the sermon, constitute violations of justice; therefore, any profits gained by means of them are not to be paid out as alms but rather must be returned to the owner who suffered loss.[207]

The next circumstance, combination, "unjust," appears most indebted to Hostiensis;[208] towards the end of the section, there are also elements drawn from Bernardino of Siena.[209] In this circumstance, Antoninus condemns monopolies and cartels, drawing on both canon and civil law, and also warns those who join in partnerships with monopolists or unscrupulous businessmen that they become implicated in their sins. He also says that, where a legally established price exists (by ecclesiastical or, "what is better," by municipal law),[210] then merchants may not increase their prices beyond it without sin.

Coming to the circumstance of means, "wicked," Antoninus says: "Trade is illicit on account of means, that is when one trades by means of perjuries and lies and duplicities."[211] Antoninus proceeds largely by weaving together and glossing Raymond of Peñafort and Hostiensis on the same subject, with some reference to Aquinas.[212] The substance of the discussion is devoted to which such sins are mortal and which are venial. "Now about lies, Raymond says that if they do this in order to deceive, they also sin mortally, and are bound to make restitution of the thing concerning which they committed deception."[213] A difficulty of interpretation raised by the gloss on Peñafort's *Summa* is dealt with. There follows a discussion on lying in order to keep oneself indemnified (a venial sin), which is quite close in wording to Bernardino of Siena.[214] Another difficulty of interpretation is dealt with, this time raised by a *sententia* of Hostiensis, with Antoninus taking Aquinas's side *contra* the jurist. Antoninus's final word on the subject of wicked means: "about duplicities which are committed in trade, and frauds," it must be said that they are "mortal when a notable deception of neighbour is intended, otherwise they are venial."[215]

207 On this point, see Noonan, *Scholastic Analysis of Usury*, 30–1, who cites this place in Antoninus's *Summa* for "a clear and traditional distinction between unjust profit and *turpe lucrum*," as well as Aquinas, *Summa theologiae*, 2a 2ae q. 62 a. 2, and Raymundus de Pennaforti, *Summa de paenitentia*, 2.7.5.

208 Hostiensis, *Summa aurea*, 5.38 §. 61 (col. 1859).

209 Bernardinus Senensis, *De evangelio aeterno*, 33, 2, 7 (in the section *de circumventionibus malitiosis*) (*Opera omnia*, 4:153–4).

210 Antoninus, *Summa*, 2.1.16, section 2.5.

211 Ibid., section 2.6.

212 Raymundus de Pennaforti, *Summa de paenitentia*, 2.8 §. 5 (*De poena eorum qui cum iuramentis et mendaciis emunt vel vendunt*) (Ochoa-Diez, 1B:563–4); Hostiensis, *Summa aurea*, 5.38 §. 61 (col. 1859); Aquinas, *Summa theologiae*, 2a 2ae q. 77 a. 2 co.

213 Antoninus, *Summa*, 2.1.16, section 2.6.

214 Bernardinus Senensis, *De evangelio aeterno*, 33, 2, 7 §. 1 (*de mendaciis multis*) (*Opera omnia*, 4:152).

215 Antoninus, *Summa*, 2.1.16, section 2.6.

The final circumstance is matter, "evil," which applies to trades which "in themselves have an evil nature, such as usury, simony, and so forth."[216] Apart from the opening paragraph (adapted from Peñafort), Antoninus does not make conspicuous use of any of his four standard sources.[217] First, Antoninus briefly explains that all must abstain from trading in things which cannot be used without mortal sin, or which are commonly used for evil. This subject is dealt with at other places in the *Summa*, including the brief discussion in 3.8.1 of arts which serve vanity, and in other chapters of part 2.[218] Next, Antoninus mentions certain doubtful matters, namely trading in the various public debt instruments of Italian communes, "which some say are licit, some illicit and usurious."[219] These are discussed by Antoninus at great length in 2.1.11 (*De materia montis de Florentia et inprestitarum Venetiis et locis Ianuensium*), where "arguments are set out that support both sides."[220] A major source for that discussion is Lorenzo Ridolfi, whose advice is echoed by Antoninus: "therefore this is not to be facilely condemned; and so what is safer should be counselled."[221]

Finally, Antoninus comes to modest temporal trade, that is, trade which is exercised in accordance with the justice of God. After introducing the subject in general, Antoninus again divides it:

> Now just as God's justice, that is justice according to God, is served in trading when the price is just, not excessive, and the whole good is handed over in the expected condition, not counterfeited, and/or in a barter the exchange is equitable; so also by contrast, traders – taking the word in a wide sense for buyers and sellers – transgress against God's justice in three ways:
>
> 1. By wrongful appraisal;
> 2. By various tricks and frauds; or
> 3. By illicit exchange.[222]

---

216 Ibid., section 2.7; quoting Raymundus de Pennaforti, *Summa de paenitentia*, 2.8.6 (*An liceat facere vel vendere gladios, venena et ornamenta*) (Ochoa-Diez, 1B:564–6).

217 The argument is similar at the general level to Peñafort's at the place just cited.

218 E.g., Antoninus, *Summa*, 2.1.17 (*De variis fraudibus que commictuntur in negotiando*); 2.1.23 (*De turpi lucro et ibi de ludo alearum*); 2.4.5 (*De presumptione nouitatum et ibi agitur de ornatu mulierum inordinato*).

219 Ibid., 2.1.16, section 2.7.

220 Ibid.

221 Ibid. Cfr ibid., 2.1.11, §. 24–5.

Ridolfi advised abstention from trading in *monte* credits as the safer course. "Contrast Peter of Ancharano, who argues that the principle of 'in dubio via tutior est eligenda' has no application here" (Kirshner, "From Usury to Public Finance," 200; quoted in Armstrong, *Usury and Public Debt*, 373). See Lorenzo Ridolfi, *Tractatus de usuris*, 2 q. 7 and 3 co. (Armstrong, *Usury and Public Debt*, 180, 249).

222 Antoninus, *Summa*, 2.1.16, section 3.

The latter two types of transgression are left out of this sermon, and taken up again in the next one, *Summa* 2.1.17. The rest of the sermon in 2.1.16 is about the "just price." It is the most doctrinally sophisticated and pastorally complex component of the sermon. Four sources predominate in this section: Thomas Aquinas, *secunda secundae*, q. 77 a. 1; John Duns Scotus, *Quaestiones in librum quartum Sententiarum* (*Collationes Oxonienses*), d. 15, q. 2; Bernardino of Siena, *De evangelio aeterno*, sermon 35, a. 1; and, via Bernardino, Peter John Olivi, *Tractatus de contractibus*, part 1 q. 1. The central moral principle is established in the introductory paragraph: "a good cannot licitly be sold for more than it is worth, neither can it be bought for less, with their value reckoned with respect to our use and a probable judgment of human estimation measuring the value of the thing within the limits of the applicable latitude."[223] The elucidation of each component of this thesis is then divided into three subjects: the origin of value in exchange (i.e., economic value), the latitude of this value, and the consequences which follow when a thing is exchanged at an excessive or defective value (i.e., price).

The origin of economic value is introduced by employing the twofold doctrine of value drawn from Augustine and employed by both Aquinas and Scotus:[224] everything has two kinds of value, natural value and use-value. Use-value, that is, value taken according to things' utility for human purposes, is the sort of value which is relevant to buying and selling. The explanation of use-value which follows is an essentially complete transcription of Bernardino of Siena transmitting Peter John Olivi, with a few small changes of wording.[225] This use-value in a thing for sale is assessed, according to Antoninus following Bernardino and Olivi, from three factors. The first factor, *virtuositas*, touches a thing's real powers, properties, and efficacy for human use. The second, *raritas*, touches scarcity and difficulty of acquisition. This factor, Antoninus notes, varies with time; he does not mention place, though he certainly understood that scarcity applies to place as well. *Complacibilitas* touches desirability and attractiveness: "no small part of the value of things for sale is weighed based on how pleasing they are to the will."[226] This threefold scheme of value was reckoned as an impressive and subtle piece of analysis by the economic historians Raymond de Roover and Joseph Schumpeter.[227] In addition to specifying scarcity on the supply side, on the demand side it specifies an objective factor pertaining to the merchandise and a subjective factor pertaining to the human buyer. While the sum of *virtuositas* and *complacibilitas* may produce

223 Ibid., section 3.1, repeating verbatim Bernardinus Senensis, *De evangelio aeterno*, 35, 1, 2 (*Opera omnia*, 4:191–2).

224 Discussed above, ch. 3, in the section on Aquinas.

225 Bernardinus Senensis, *De evangelio aeterno*, 35, 1, 1 (*Opera omnia*, 4:190–1); Peter John Olivi, *Tractatus de contractibus*, 1 q. 1 (Piron, *Traité des contrats*, 94–109).

226 Antoninus, *Summa*, 2.1.16, section 3.1.1.3.

227 De Roover, *Great Economic Thinkers*, 18–20; Schumpeter, *History of Economic Analysis*, 98.

a quantified "demand" factor, specifying the sources of value according to Olivi's scheme adds a certain psychological and epistemological precision.

The next matter to be considered is the latitude of this value. "The value of things for sale can rarely or never be determined by us except as a matter of conjecture and probable opinion. Even then it cannot be determined down to an exact point on an unchanging standard or measure which can be applied at all levels, but rather there is an appropriate range of values applicable for any given time, place, and set of persons."[228] This latitude, i.e., the boundaries of a just price, may be known in three ways: from law, from custom, and from discretion. This section follows generally, though not exactly, Bernardino of Siena.[229] As to law: "if the price at which a thing is sold exceeds half of the just price, or the price at which it is bought fails by half of the just price … then according to the laws the contract is null, and to be voided by a judge, or the party who perpetrated the wrongful price is to be compelled to make up the difference."[230] This is the civil- and canon-law doctrine of *laesio enormis*. After introducing the doctrine, Antoninus jumps ahead to the subject of notable excess or defect which does not reach the legal limit of half the just price; this anticipates his more thorough discussion in the final section of the sermon, and is better explained at that point. As to custom: quoting Scotus via Bernardino, Antoninus says, "customarily it is left up to the exchanging parties if, taking account of the need on either side, they consider themselves to give equivalent value and hence to receive equivalent value from the transaction";[231] therefore, Antoninus concludes after further exposition, "it is probable enough that when the contracting parties are mutually content, they wish to mutually remit to each other whatever small amount, provided it is not gross, may depart from perfect justice."[232] Finally, as to discretion: Antoninus here explains Aquinas's "double rule" of just pricing, discussed above in chapter 3.

The final part of the sermon addresses the consequences which follow when a thing is exchanged at an excessive or defective price. Such an excess or defect can be of three kinds: beyond half the just price, notable but less than half, or minor. The discussion proceeds argumentatively. At each point, one or more objections are introduced, which Antoninus then answers in order to support the true *sententia*. The first objection, a jurists' argument, is raised against the doctrine of *laesio*

---

228 Antoninus, *Summa*, 2.1.16, section 3.1.1.3, repeating nearly verbatim Bernardinus Senensis, *De evangelio aeterno*, 35, 1, 1 (*Opera omnia*, 4:191).

229 Bernardinus Senensis, *De evangelio aeterno*, 35, 1, 2 (*Opera omnia*, 4:191–2). Cfr ibid., *De christiana religione*, 37, 2, 1 (*Opera omnia*, 1:470–2).

230 Antoninus, *Summa*, 2.1.16, section 3.1.2.1; see the additional references provided at this place in the edition and translation.

231 Ibid., section 3.1.2.2; Bernardinus Senensis, *De evangelio aeterno*, 35, 1, 2 (*Opera omnia*, 4:193); John Duns Scotus, *In quartum*, d. 15 q. 2 n. 15 (18:283b–284a).

232 Antoninus, *Summa*, 2.1.16, section 3.1.2.2.

enormis, by which a party cheated beyond half the just price may rescind the contract or sue for a restoration of his loss. Antoninus here is indebted to Bernardino of Siena, though he does not follow him exactly.[233] The objection relies upon two Roman-law principles, *unusquisque in re sua est moderator et iudex* ("each person is the moderator and judge of his own property"), and *res tantum valet quantum vendi potest* ("a thing is worth as much as it can be sold for," on which see above, chapter 3). Antoninus cites the canonists Hostiensis and Antonio da Budrio in reply to the objection.[234]

The second argument concerns whether a notable excess not reaching half the just price is licit and may be retained: "some say that it is licit, and one [who benefits from such a deception] is not bound to restitution, because the laws permit this … but blessed Thomas, 2a 2ae q. 77, and Scotus, in book 4 d. 15, reprove this opinion as erroneous and dangerous to the salvation of souls."[235] The reply, drawing on Bernardino,[236] follows the lines of Aquinas's discussion of human law versus divine law.[237] Antoninus concludes by agreeing with Aquinas and with the canonistic maxim that such excess is permitted *iure fori, non iure poli*.[238]

The final argument is more lengthy than the others, and is the last section of the sermon.

> The third kind of excess is when in such contracts a small injury is committed, so that the thing is sold for a little more, or bought for a little less, than the just price. And then … some say without distinction that no sin is committed nor is one bound to restitution, because the price of things does not consist of an unchanging quantity but has an appropriate range of higher and lower values.[239]

Against this, Antoninus cautiously advances two theses.[240] The first thesis:

> if someone sells for more or buys for less than the just price against conscience, that is, believing that it exceeds the highest degree of the price's latitude, even by a small amount, then he cannot be excused from at least venial sin, for every deception and fraud is a sin.[241]

233 Bernardinus Senensis, *De evangelio aeterno*, 35, 1, 3 (*Opera omnia*, 4:194).
234 See the references at Antoninus, *Summa*, 2.1.16, section 3.1.3.1.
235 Antoninus, *Summa*, 2.1.16, section 3.1.3.2.
236 Bernardinus Senensis, *De evangelio aeterno*, 35, 1, 2 (*Opera omnia*, 4:192).
237 Aquinas, *Summa theologiae*, 2a 2ae q. 77 a. 1 ad 1.
238 Antoninus cites the maxim from Giovanni da Legnano and Giovanni Calderini, probably via Lorenzo Ridolfi. The maxim appears to have originated with Innocent IV; see above, ch. 3.
239 Antoninus, *Summa*, 2.1.16, section 3.1.3.3.
240 "Nevertheless, it seems more true that we must say …" Ibid.
241 Ibid.

The second thesis is that in such cases, although the guilty party is bound to satisfaction, this should be done by paying out the unjust gains upon the poor: restitution to the original owner is not necessary. Antoninus attributes this thesis, and the three arguments by which he supports it in the next section, to Gerard of Siena, OESA,[242] and John of Naples, OP;[243] but this attribution is doubtful.[244] The thesis is not found in Gerard of Siena's treatises on usury, prescription, and restitution. John of Naples did write a *Quodlibet* on the just price, wherein Antoninus may have found the thesis just stated.[245] However, neither John of Naples nor Gerard of Siena is the true source for Antoninus's three supporting arguments: the immediate source is Bernardino of Siena, whom Antoninus transcribes essentially verbatim, and who in turn selected and transcribed the arguments from Peter John Olivi's *Treatise on contracts*.[246] The arguments in favour of the thesis are its conduciveness to temporal peace and the salvation of souls, the mutual agreement of the parties, and the uncertainty of human estimation. Finally, the objection is raised that whatever is illicit and sinful in contracts, being contrary to divine law,

242 Gerard of Siena (Gerhardus Senensis), OESA, c. 1295–1336, a theologian who may have had legal training, author of a highly esteemed commentary on the *Sentences* as well as *quaestiones* on legal problems. His treatises on usury, restitution, and prescription have recently been edited and translated by Lawrin Armstrong in *The Idea of a Moral Economy*.

243 In fact, Antoninus writes "Io. de Rip.," which is difficult to construe; John of Naples is Langholm's solution (discussed in the next note) and is the best conjecture so far.

244 Odd Langholm addresses this attribution in *Merchant in the Confessional*, 152 n53. This section of Antoninus's *Summa* was, apparently, copied in substance and perhaps even verbatim in the *Interrogatorium* of Bartolomeo Caimi and the *Somma* of Pacifico of Cerano. Langholm may have been unaware that this passage quite likely derives from Antoninus's *Summa*. He investigated these names as they are printed in Caimi and Pacifico's texts, and identified the first author as Gerard Odonis making use of Olivi: Gerhardus Odonis, *De contractibus*, 4 (Siena BCom U.V.8, fol. 81v). As for the second author: "One of the authorities cited by Caimi and Pacifico at this point is at first sight troublesome. They refer to *Decretum*, II.14.5.14 and to Gerald Odonis and 'Jo. de ripole' … As to the last-mentioned reference, recourse to the manuscript tradition solved the puzzle. In Bologna BArch A.241, which, among other things, contains Caimi's *Interrogatorium*, the reference in question is to 'Jo de neapolis' (f. 129ra). Checking the *quodlibet* collections of the fourteenth-century Dominican John of Naples, I found that Caimi's true reference is to *Quodl.* IV.18: Naples BNaz VII.B.28, ff.64va–65ra, where the author discusses the question of the just price, drawing copiously on Thomas Aquinas. This correction supports the hypothesis that Pacifico of Cerano drew on Bartolomeo Caimi and not vice-versa, and that Pacifico used a corrupt text (perhaps that of the first edition) of Caimi's *Interrogatorium*" (Langholm, *Merchant in the Confessional*, 152 n53). My own investigation, explained in the text, casts doubt on the conclusion for John of Naples as a genuine source, though this is the most probable reading of Antoninus's citation.

245 Iohannes de Regina, *Quodlibeta*, 4, 18 (Naples, Biblioteca Nazionale, VII.B.28, fol. 64va–65ra).

246 Bernardinus Senensis, *De christiana religione*, 37, 2, 1 (*Opera omnia*, 1:470–2); Peter John Olivi, *Tractatus de contractibus*, 1 q. 5 n. 52–61 (Piron, *Traité des contrats*, 126–35).

cannot be of any force, and consequently cannot transfer ownership to the one sinning. The objection is answered initially by a somewhat obscure and subtle distinction between the "inner intention" and the "outer act"; but finally by a *reductio ad absurdum*:

> otherwise all such illicit excess of price will be a mortal fault for those who acquire it … every seller or buyer would also be bound to restore every such excess, and thus everyone who did not restore it would be damned, which is indeed an extremely evil and harsh thought.[247]

These theses, however, "must be preached with great discretion, since the people are prone to loosening their consciences."[248] "And therefore the safer things are the ones we must say."[249]

The treatment of fraud is continued in chapter 2.1.17, which enumerates and discusses specific varieties of fraud committed in buying and selling and in exchanges of goods.

3. Fraudulent Practices, Especially Those Known in Florence: *Summa* 2.1.17

Chapter 2.1.17 picks up where 2.1.16 left off, completing its third principal part by dealing with the two remaining ways by which trade may be carried out against the justice of God: "by various tricks and frauds" or "by illicit exchange."[250]

This chapter 2.1.17, *On the various frauds which are committed in trading*, is structured as a sermon with four main sections. The first three sections address the "three evils which the guileful man or deceiver commits in trading or selling," namely craftiness, malice, and fraudulence. The first section defines craftiness as a vice against prudence. The second, on malice, briefly states the three ways in which guile or fraud may be present in a contract. The third, on fraudulence, is the longest part of the sermon. It enumerates six types of fraud, and under each type Antoninus highlights frauds which are particularly practised in Florence in his day. The fourth and final section discusses "exchanges of goods or barter," completing the topics related to buying and selling which Antoninus had laid out at the beginning of chapter 2.1.16.

---

247 Antoninus, *Summa*, 2.1.16, section 3.1.3.3.4, repeating Bernardino and Olivi.
248 Ibid., repeating Bernardino.
249 Ibid. These are Antoninus's own words.
250 Antoninus, *Summa*, 2.1.16, section 3.

Chapter 2.1.17, in the form of a sermon, has the following structure:

I. Thema: *Tota die iniustitiam cogitauit lingua tua; sicut nouacula acuta fecisti dolum* (*Ps* 51.4).

II. Division of the thema into three principal parts. Note the parallelism.
Notat tria mala que facit dolosus seu deceptor in negotiando seu uendendo:

(1) Primum est	astutia	in modos ad decipiendum	exquirendo, ibi:	*Tota die iniustitiam cogitauit lingua tua.*
(2) Secundum est	malitia	in decipiendos	liniendo, ibi:	*Sicut nouacula acuta.*
(3) Tertium est	fraudulentia	in excogitatos	exequendo, ibi:	*Fecisti dolum.*

III. Development of the thema.
The majority of the sermon proceeds by development of the thema through the three principal parts: *astutia* (craftiness), *malitia* (malice), and *fraudulentia* (fraudulence).

1. Craftiness.

2. Malice.
The following subjects are dealt with after an an introduction connecting *malitia* to *dolus*.
2.1. Guilde and fraud.
2.2. Guile giving rise to a contract.
2.3. Guile incidental in a contract.

3. Fraudulence.
The third principal part is divided into six different type of fraud. Again note the parallelism.
Fit ergo fraudulentia: (1) in rei quiditate, (2) in sui quantitate, (3) in eius qualitate, (4) in soluendi tarditate, (5) in pretii ad res mutabilitate, (6) in bono opere cum intentionis prauitate.
3.1. Fraud in a thing's essence.
3.2. Fraud in a thing's quantity.
Various frauds involving quantity are treated here. Only the first three are introduced in advance: In quantitate fit fraus in pondere numero et mensura.
3.2.1. In weight.
3.2.2. In measure.
3.2.3. In number.
3.2.4. The customary practice when giving material to be spun.
3.2.5. Tavern keepers.

3.2.6. Wool merchants and shoemakers.
3.2.7. *Lanini* putting out material to be spun.
3.3. Fraud in a thing's quality.
The following subjects are dealt with, without an introductory division.
3.3.1. When a thing's defect ought to be revealed.
3.3.2. Selling defective cloth or clothing.
3.3.3. Cloth menders.
3.4. Fraud in late payment.
The following subjects are dealt with, without an introductory division.
3.4.1. Bankers.
3.4.2. Civic officials.
3.5. Fraud in payment of the price in kind.
3.6. Fraud in a good work with crooked intention.
Triplex fraus commictitur in bono opere, quod est opus Dei:
3.6.1. From the heart.
3.6.2. From the mouth.
3.6.3. From the work.

4. Exchanges of goods or barter.
This fourth principal part wraps up the material begun in 2.1.16, and functions as the conclusion of the two sermons.

The subject of this chapter is fraud (*fraus*, *fraudulentia*, *dolus*). The *thema* is a verse of Psalm 51: *All the day long thy tongue hath devised injustice: as a sharp razor, thou hast wrought guile.*[251] The Latin word which I have translated "guile" here is *dolus*; in the Douay-Rheims translation of the Vulgate, *dolus* is translated "deceit." In the initial statement of the *thema*, Antoninus lays out three scriptural condemnations of *dolus*, *circumventio*, and *fraus*. He then divides the *thema* into three principal parts:

> Now the Psalmist notes three evils which the guileful man or deceiver commits in trading or selling.
> The first is craftiness in seeking out methods for deceiving, at *All the day long thy tongue hath devised injustice.*
> The second is malice in coaxing people to be deceived, at *As a sharp razor.*
> The third is fraudulence in executing methods contrived, at *Thou hast wrought guile.*

251 Psalm 51:4. Bernardino of Siena also used this Psalm as a *thema* in two of the sermons in his series on contracts; however, Antoninus makes a more extensive use of the *thema* to structure this sermon than Bernardino does. Bernardinus Senensis, *De evangelio aeterno*, 33 (*Opera omnia*, 4:141); ibid., 44, 1, 3 (4:392).
Antoninus may have been inspired by another of Bernardino's sermons in his use of the "mark of the Beast" to signify fraud and guile: cfr ibid., 33, 2, 7 (4:151–5).

This provides the overall division of the majority of the sermon into three parts, dealing in turn with craftiness, malice, and fraudulence. The first topic, craftiness, is dealt with briefly. Antoninus closely follows Thomas Aquinas's discussion of craftiness (*astutia*), defining craftiness as a vice against the virtue of prudence, which consists in thinking out fictitious and counterfeit means to achieve an end, "as in the intention to deceive a neighbour in temporal things."[252] Antoninus then cites several condemnations of craftiness in Scripture.

A note here is warranted on my translation of several Latin terms in this chapter. In the standard translations of Thomas Aquinas's *Summa theologiae*,[253] *astutia* is translated as "craftiness," and I have followed this precedent. The word *dolus* in a legal context is often translated "fraud," but Antoninus distinguishes *fraus* from *dolus* at several points in this chapter, and so I have likewise distinguished the two by translating *fraus* as "fraud" and *dolus* as "guile," again in agreement with translators of Aquinas.

In the next part of chapter 2.1.17, Antoninus turns to the topic of malice, which he associates with *dolus*, "guile," consisting in "the execution of the aforementioned false ways which are thought out through craftiness ... with the purpose of deceiving."[254] Here again he follows Thomas Aquinas closely and provides several scriptural condemnations of guile. He then, in three subsections, introduces the legal rules related to *dolus* employed by canonists and civilians. According to Zimmermann, the distinction between *dolus causam dans* (fraud giving rise to the contract, i.e., when fraud induced the fact that a contract had been concluded) and *dolus incidens* (fraud incidental to the contract, i.e., when the innocent party would still have entered into the contract, but on better terms) was "the most important and, in the long run, influential contribution of the medieval lawyers to the doctrine of dolus."[255] Langholm argues (drawing on the opinion of many legal historians) that moral theologians found the civil- and canon-law doctrines on *dolus* difficult to make sense of and apply in penitential handbooks. Nevertheless, in my opinion, Antoninus has made an effective pastoral use of the legal doctrines here and in *Summa* 2.1.16.[256] His exposition of the legal rules closely follows Bernard of Parma in the *Glossa ordinaria* on *X* 3.17.3 (*Cum dilecti*). Antoninus then adds his own striking image of the "unjust avaricious man" who uses his tongue like a barber's razor, and sharpens it with the oil of flattery "in order to trim hair,

252 Antoninus, *Summa*, 2.1.17, section 1. See Aquinas, *Summa theologiae* 2a 2ae q. 55 a. 3–5.

253 *Summa Theologica*, trans. Fathers of the English Dominican Province; see also Alfred J. Freddoso's *New English Translation of St. Thomas Aquinas's Summa Theologiae (Summa Theologica)*, currently in progress and available at: https://www3.nd.edu/~afreddos/summa-translation/TOC.htm.

254 Antoninus, *Summa*, 2.1.17, section 2.

255 Zimmermann, "*Metus* and *Dolus*," ch. 21 in *Law of Obligations*, 670.

256 Scholastic legal analysis of fraud (*dolus*) is summarized in Langholm, *Merchant in the Confessional*, 71–8.

that is, to carry off temporal goods," committing guile "through laudatory words full of falsehoods, coaxing with kindly and reverent words, making himself out to be the friend of the buyer and so forth."[257]

Antoninus then comes to the third and longest section of the sermon, on "fraudulence which consists in acts."[258] To begin, he sets out three key points: 1) this sort of fraudulence is sometimes a mortal sin, 2) and creates a requirement for restitution, 3) if it involves a "notable" deception. He enumerates six ways fraudulence happens, and then proceeds by discussing them in turn.

Antoninus follows a fairly consistent method in explaining these six kinds of fraud. First, he defines the nature of the fraud. He then provides specific examples, and usually they appear to be practices known to him locally; in one place he says outright that he discussed a fraud of silk merchants "because this is very much practised in Florence."[259] Sometimes he takes up possible counter-examples, where a practice which might otherwise be fraudulent is in fact tolerable. Finally he applies the principles of moral theology to the case at hand, stating, for example, if a practice is illicit and sinful, if it creates an obligation of restitution, and so forth. Some of the frauds which he mentions are discussed at greater length in chapters 3.8.3 and 3.8.4, namely the various frauds committed by butchers, apothecaries, tavern keepers, wool merchants, *lanini*, shoemakers, second-hand dealers, mediators and brokers, cloth menders, and silk merchants. There is no need to summarize all six of the subsections here, but I will highlight a few points.

In the first three subsections, on fraud in a thing's essence, quantity, and quality,[260] Antoninus closely follows the exposition of Bernardino of Siena in *De evangelio aeterno*, sermon 35,[261] while the moral-theological doctrine is that of Aquinas.[262] At several places the question of custom arises, and whether a local custom excuses a practice which would normally be sinful fraud. In one case we have a custom in the textile industry of Florence: when spinners of wool or linen are paid for what they have spun, the spun material is counted as if thirteen ounces make one pound. Antoninus says that this "seems like a distasteful custom," but nevertheless since it is well known and understood when the spinners take on the work, it seems that it is not fraud: for, invoking one of the rules of law in the *Liber Sext*, "to one who knows and consents no injury nor guile is done."[263] This

257 Antoninus, *Summa*, 2.1.17, section 2.3.

258 Ibid., section 3.

259 Ibid., section 3.5.

260 Ibid., sections 3.1–3.3.1.

261 Bernardinus Senensis, *De evangelio aeterno*, 35, 3, 1–3 (*Opera omnia*, 4:199–202).

262 Aquinas, *Summa theologiae*, 2a 2ae q. 77 a. 2–3.

263 Antoninus, *Summa*, 2.1.17, section 3.2.4, citing *VI* 5.[13.]27 (*Scienti*). Gauthier translates this and the other rules of law from the *Sext* in his *Roman Law and … Canon Law*, appendix 2. For Antoninus's fuller discussion of this rule, see *Summa*, 1.20.1.94 (*N* fol. 323r, Ballerini 1:899, Mamachi 1:1422): *scienti et consentienti*.

rule of law, which Antoninus cites by the shorthand *scienti et consentienti* (from its opening words), will be invoked repeatedly in the subsequent sections as well as in chapters 3.8.3 and 3.8.4. In another case, we have the custom of tavern keepers dispensing a "tun" of wine or another measure, but only filling the tun up to the neck. That this is customary does not excuse them; "for the buyers are deceived, since they intend to have the full measure and it is diminished against their will," and this custom must be described as "corrupt."[264] However, Antoninus notes, the tavern keepers can be excused if they

> do this in order to protect themselves from loss or to receive some reasonable profit, when otherwise they would not make a profit if they gave full measures, because it would be necessary to increase the price, and then they would not find any buyers, or only a few.[265]

Sometimes a person can be excused from sin and from any debt of justice, when they use some "fraudulent" practice not in order to get an unjust price, but in order to protect themselves from loss or practise their trade on a level field with their competitors. This principle is applied throughout chapter 2.1.17, and sometimes in 3.8.3 and 3.8.4 as well; it is characteristic of Antoninus's pastoral attention to the concrete dilemmas faced by well-meaning Christian people engaged in business.[266]

At section 3.3.2, on selling defective cloth or clothing, Antoninus's focus shifts decidedly towards practical specifics. He begins describing fraudulent practices of wool merchants and clothes dealers, and continues on through bankers and civic officials to silk merchants.[267] One cannot help but think Antoninus is describing current practices known to him in the Florence of his day. The most interesting and original section of this whole chapter is section 3.5, on fraud in payment of the price in kind, which opens thus:

> Fifth, fraud is committed through paying in kind rather than money, and through this the due price promised is diminished: because sometimes the people hired for some sort of work, not needing such goods, when they sell them, receive a price lower than that which they agreed to. And against these James says, in chapter 5: *Behold the wages of your wage-labourers, which by fraud has been kept back by you, crieth against you* etc.[268]

264 Antoninus, *Summa*, 2.1.17, section 3.2.5.

265 Ibid., section 3.2.5.

266 For another example, see ibid., section 3.1, lines 108–19.

267 Ibid., sections 3.3.2–3.5.

268 James 5:4.

Indeed, in the Catholic tradition, defrauding labourers of their wages is considered a sin which cries out to God for vengeance. This section on payment in kind is one of three places where Antoninus discusses and censures the abuses and frauds commonly present in the "truck" system in Florence.[269] If someone is hired, and promised his pay in money, then the hirer should not pay him in kind (foodstuffs or cloth or other things). "Such devices are commonly invented to deceive and oppress the poor."[270] Nevertheless, if the terms of the employment agreement were that payment would be partly in money and partly in kind, then in principle the hirer commits no fraud, since "To one who knows and consents no injury or guile is done."[271] Antoninus goes on to analyse the details of several specific cases involving payment in kind, and allows that, although this method is "distasteful enough,"[272] some of these practices which involve a diminution of the nominal wage do not involve true fraud, since all parties involved are familiar with them and can take into account the real value of the contract.

However, Antoninus says, in all cases the person hired – a weaver in this case – must receive "a proper profit for his labour," i.e., "an appropriate wage." In a rather momentous passage in the history of moral theology and Catholic social teaching, Antoninus writes:

> Note, however, that if because of this the weaver does not receive a proper profit for his labour according to common estimation, but a diminished one – and his due profit is reckoned to be what they agreed to in money, e.g., 10 florins – but because he is poor he has to accept less, even a lot less, just to sustain himself and his family: then without a doubt the silk merchant would be bound to pay a supplement up to 10 or thereabouts, if he pays him cloth which he only sells for 6; because just as *the labourer is worthy of his wage* as a matter of justice, so he is also worthy of an appropriate wage. Otherwise the contract would go against the equality of justice; just as in a contract of purchase and sale it is injustice and a sin when a thing is bought for less than the just price due to the seller's need.[273]

In this passage we see the doctrine of the "just price" applied directly to wages. It would be fair, in my opinion, to describe this as a statement of the "just wage" doctrine of Catholic social teaching. In substance it is somewhat different from the famous formulation of Pope Leo XIII in *Rerum novarum*, that natural justice

---

269 In addition to this section, see also *Summa*, 3.8.3, section 3, and *Summa*, 3.8.4, section 3.9 and 5.1.

270 Antoninus, *Summa*, 2.1.17, section 3.5, lines 323–4.

271 *VI* 5.[13.]27 (*Scienti*).

272 Antoninus, *Summa*, 2.1.17, section 3.5, line 312.

273 Ibid., lines 313–22.

demands that a worker ought to receive a wage sufficient to support himself and his family.[274] What it does is apply the scholastic rule of justice in prices to the case of wages, treating the worker as a "seller" of his work and the hirer as the "buyer." Just as a buyer may not take advantage of the necessity of a seller, coerced by poverty or what have you, to purchase his good for less than the just price, so a hirer may not take advantage of a labourer's poverty or fear of unemployment.[275] The hirer, like the buyer, is in all cases obliged to pay a price which observes the equality of justice. In the case of buying and selling, this is normally considered to be the common, current, local market price; so in hiring of labour, the proper profit or wage is what "is considered an appropriate wage" "according to common estimation."[276]

Antoninus concludes with a pastoral note, speaking directly to the clergy:

> Because such devices are commonly invented to deceive and oppress the poor, silk merchants and retail merchants should be induced to abstain from them, and to make satisfaction to those injured from frauds of this kind, or to bestow alms on the poor if they did not notably burden the weavers, by the argument of C. 14 q. 5 c. 14 and c. 15. And the same must be said about those hiring labourers in other crafts and occupations. But silk merchants and weavers were discussed because this is very much practised in Florence.[277]

In the final subsection of this part of the sermon, Antoninus shifts from looking at outward acts to intentions.[278] He discusses the sixth fraud, which is committed "when a person does works which are good in their nature, but in doing them seeks something other than the glory of God … for example, he seeks recompense in this world."[279] The whole subsection is based on a passage in Gregory the Great's *Morals on the Book of Job*, where Gregory says that one is "guilty of deceit in the work of God, whosoever loving himself to excess, by that which he may have done well, is only making the best of his way to transitory good things in compensation."[280] The examples of good works which Antoninus mentions are almsgiving,

---

274 "There underlies a dictate of natural justice more imperious and ancient than any bargain between man and man, namely, that wages ought not to be insufficient to support a frugal and well-behaved wage-earner." Leo XIII, *Rerum novarum: On Capital and Labor* (15 May 1891), para. 45. For background on Leo XIII's teaching, mentioning Antoninus's doctrine, see Healy, *The Just Wage 1750–1890*.

275 The fear of unemployment is highlighted by Antoninus at *Summa*, 3.8.4, section 5.1.

276 Antoninus, *Summa*, 2.1.17, section 3.5, line 319.

277 Ibid.

278 Ibid., section 3.6–3.6.3.

279 Ibid., 2.1.17, section 3.6.

280 Gregory I, *Morals on the Book of Job*, 9, 53 (trans. Parker, 1:534–5).

fasting, praying, and so forth; fraud is committed in them when done to gain friendship and favour, or human applause and praise, or a reward from God in this world such as through obtaining ecclesiastical dignity or gaining others' trust in one's goodness. This section has a less legal and more ascetical flavour than the earlier sections of the sermon; appropriately, the quotations are from the Scripture and two Church Fathers, Gregory the Great and St Augustine.

The final part of this sermon addresses exchanges of goods or barter (*de permutationibus ... que vulgariter dicuntur baracti*), the final topic introduced originally in chapter 2.1.16.[281] Antoninus follows the same approach as already outlined: he defines the transaction, provides some examples, and then applies the relevant moral principles to it. The examples he gives all have to do with the Florentine textile industry, involving exchanges of silk or wool for silk cloth or wool cloth, etc. The last example of local practice which Antoninus highlights is this: say a trader and a wool merchant exchange wool valuing 90 florins for wool cloth also valuing about 90 florins, but each one claims that his good is worth 100 florins, and they both know that the other is likely doing the same; since the unjust prices are equalized, and each party is trying to protect himself from losing in the transaction, properly speaking fraud is not present. "Nevertheless," Antoninus says, "devices like this are devised out of cupidity, and therefore should be shunned."[282]

The source most frequently cited throughout this sermon is the Bible: by my count, thirty-one separate scripture texts are cited, a few more than once. Canon law is the next most frequently cited source, with seventeen separate citations of canon law, several of them repeatedly invoked as supplying standard principles. There is also a general reference to civil law.[283] Thomas Aquinas is also a major source, specifically q. 55 and q. 77 of the *Summa theologiae*, 2a 2ae, which Antoninus draws on copiously in sections 1, 2, and 3; indeed, Aquinas supplies most of the core doctrinal principles which Antoninus applies to specific practices and frauds. Bernardino of Siena is another reference point for Antoninus: in parts of section 3 Antoninus follows him closely, including copying in most of one paragraph; however, there are also significant differences of approach between Antoninus's sermon here and Bernardino's sermons on the subject of fraud.[284] The final two sources cited are Gregory the Great and Augustine of Hippo.

4. Types of Contracts: *Summa* 3.8.2

In the next chapter, 3.8.2, *On the various kinds of contracts*, Antoninus provides a list of the different kinds of contracts in which property rights are transferred,

281 Antoninus, *Summa*, 2.1.17, section 4.
282 Ibid.
283 Ibid., section 2.1.
284 Cfr Bernardinus Senensis, *De evangelio aeterno*, 33 (*Opera omnia*, 4:141); ibid., 44, 1, 3 (4:392).

and a summary of the conditions for their liceity. The names of the contracts are standard among the late medieval moralists, who inherited them from Roman law via medieval civilian and canonical jurisprudence. Antoninus's method of classifying them will be discussed below. About their liceity, Antoninus says, in sum: these contracts are all licit *per se* if the due circumstances are observed; they become illicit if one or more of the circumstances is disordered. This is an application of the doctrine of the "sources of morality."

Chapter 3.8.2 is not arranged as a sermon. Its structure is as follows:

1. Transfer of ownership. In the first paragraph, transfer of things is divided: (1) sometimes ownership of the thing is transferred, (2) sometimes only the use of the thing, with ownership being retained. Transfer of ownership is then subdivided as carried out in six ways.
   - 1.1. Gift. It is noted here that this first mode is liberal, the following five illiberal.
   - 1.2. Exchange of goods.
   - 1.3–4. Purchase and sale.
   - 1.5–6. Giving and receiving a loan.
   - 1.7. Liceity of these six conveyances.

2. Transfer of use. Six methods, as it were corresponding to the aforesaid six.
   - 2.1. Loan for use.
   - 2.2. Accommodation.
   - 2.3–4. Hire and lease.
   - 2.5–6. Pledge and mortgage.

3. Evasion of law. Evasion of the law is defined in the first paragraph. Now evasion of law is committed in four ways.
   - 3.1. From thing to thing.
   - 3.2. From person to person.
   - 3.3. From contract to contract.
   - 3.4. From contract to contract in a different fashion.

This chapter, unlike three just discussed, does not proceed *per modum predicationis* but rather *per modum doctrine*, "by the method of teaching."[285] It is very brief. First, Antoninus enumerates six recognized types of contract by which ownership is transferred, and then six types of contract by which the use of a thing is transferred without transferring ownership. The contracts by which ownership is transferred are gift (*donatio*), exchange of goods (*permutatio*, with the innominate

285 Antoninus, *Summa*, 2 *prologus* (M_1 fol. IIr, hand G).

contracts also in this category),[286] purchase and sale (*emptio-venditio*), and giving and receiving a loan (*mutui datio-acceptio*). "And these six contracts are licit when they are carried out in the proper manner."[287] Antoninus then briefly lays out basic conditions for the liceity of each of these types of contract, e.g., that they be free of fraud, that there be no departure from a just price, that they involve no usury. The contracts by which use is transferred are loan for use (*commodatum*), accommodation (*accomodatio*), hire and lease (*conductio-locatio*), and pledge and mortgage (*pignus-ypotheca*). In this list, Antoninus states the conditions for liceity as he enumerates the individual contracts; the conditions correspond to those of the contracts which transfer ownership.

This chapter draws much material from John Duns Scotus's *Quaestiones in librum quartum Sententiarum* (*Collationes Oxonienses*), d. 15, q. 2, a. 2: on transfer of property to another. This is part of Scotus's longer discussion of restitution, in which he provides his most comprehensive statement of a political and economic philosophy.[288] There, Scotus divides property transfers into acts which are *mere liberalis*, "purely free," i.e., in a gift, when the person expects no recompense, and acts which are *secundum quid liberalem*, "free in a qualified sense," i.e., when the person expects something in return, as in the other contracts. Antoninus makes the same division between "liberal conveyance," i.e., gift, and "illiberal conveyance," i.e., the other five contracts. Antoninus's list of six contracts which transfer ownership is identical to Scotus's in terminology and order. Like Scotus, Antoninus then defines corresponding contracts in which use only is transferred, without transferring ownership. However, the placement of *pignus* as a contract corresponding to *mutuum* is not found in Scotus; Antoninus admits that it has only "some similarity, though small."[289] It is curious that Antoninus never names Scotus as a source in this chapter, though he does cite Scotus by name in chapter 2.1.16. A final note: in the autograph manuscript, there is what appears to be a first draft of chapter 3.8.2 on fol. 114v–115r, written mostly by a hand other than Antoninus. This first draft follows Scotus's article 2 far more closely than the final version of 3.8.2, sometimes copying essentially verbatim, sometimes loosely paraphrasing or adapting. I have included in appendix 1 a transcription of this first draft in parallel with the text of Scotus for comparison.

---

286 Antoninus, *Summa*, 3.8.2, section 1.7.

287 Ibid.

288 Johannes Duns Scotus, *Political and Economic Philosophy: Latin Text and English Translation*, ed. Wolter. When I cite Scotus in the chapters edited below, I normally provide page numbers in the *Opera Omnia*, vol. 18. Here I will cite Wolter.

Bernardino of Siena has his own discussion of contracts based the same article in Scotus; Bernardino follows Scotus more closely. Bernardinus Senensis, *De evangelio aeterno*, 32, 3 (*Opera omnia*, 4:134–9).

289 Antoninus, *Summa*, 3.8.2, section 2.5–6.

The final part of this chapter is a corollary on "evasion of the law," which is committed by one who "respects the words of the law but circumvents its intention."[290] This subject is pertinent to the liceity or morality of contracts, since a formally legal contract may be the vehicle for subversion of the law's intent, as in the oft-cited case of hidden usury. The rest of the chapter, defining the four types of evasion of law, is an adaptation of the *Glossa ordinaria* to C. 14 q. 3 c. 3 at the word *precepta*. Antoninus quotes each sentence of the gloss, with few or no changes of wording, as the leading sentence of a paragraph, then expands upon each point with his own explanation of relevant cases.

In this chapter, John Duns Scotus and the *Glossa ordinaria* to the *Decretum* are the major sources from which Antoninus directly draws material. The other sources cited in this chapter are entirely legal: from canon law, Gratian's *Decretum* and its gloss, the *Liber Extra*, and the *Liber Sext*; from civil law, the *Digest*. All of the citations of the *Digest* appear to be copied from the *Glossa ordinaria* to C. 14 q. 3 c. 3.

The list of named contracts employed here comes from Roman law. It has often been noted that the Roman law of contract was based on distinct types of discrete transactions ("contracts"), each with its own set of rules.[291] Each "contract" had its own name, e.g., *stipulatio, emptio, pignus*. These Roman contracts became part of the general jurisprudential apparatus in medieval Europe. Antoninus, like other late medieval moralists, makes use of them when he addresses the obligations of justice in business transactions. Various ways of dividing these contracts into categories were attempted across the periods of Roman and medieval civilian jurisprudence. One such distinction, of great practical significance in law and employed both in Justinian's time and in the High Middle Ages, was between contracts *stricti iuris* and *bonae fidei*.[292] The most influential classification, however, was the one employed by the Roman jurist Gaius and adopted by Justinian, which divides contracts according to the means by which the obligation is contracted: consensual contracts, verbal contracts, contracts *re*, and contracts *litteris*.[293] This division of contracts, however, does not correspond to the division Antoninus employs in 3.8.2, following Scotus: the contracts listed by Antoninus, i.e., contracts in which property rights are transferred, include some contracts *re* and some consensual contracts, but not all of the latter (e.g., *societas, mandatum* are omitted). It appears that Scotus and Antoninus are experimenting to find a classification scheme which

290 *Glossa ordinaria*, C. 14 q. 3 c. 3 s.v. *precepta*; quoted in Antoninus, *Summa*, 3.8.2, section 3. On the concept of *fraus legi facta*, see *Dig.* 1.3.30 and Berger, *Dictionary of Roman Law*, s.v.

291 See, for example, du Plessis, *Borkowski's Textbook on Roman Law*, 259–60.

292 On early Roman classification schemes, see ibid., esp. ch. 9, 256ff.

293 Ibid., 258ff. See Gaius, *Institutes*, 3.90–162, in *The Institutes of Gaius*, ed. and trans. de Zulueta, 1:178–207; Justinian, *Institutes*, 3.14–26, in *The Institutes of Justinian*, ed. and trans. Thomas, 200–49.

best answers to the requirements of their moral and pastoral priorities; as mentioned, they divide these contracts into liberal and illiberal, and into those which transfer ownership and those which only transfer use. This sort of experimentation in contract doctrine was continued by jurists and moral theologians of the late fifteenth and sixteenth centuries;[294] compare, for example, the novel division imposed by Jean Bodin in his *Iuris universi distributio* (1578).[295]

5. Exchange Banking and Other Commercial Transactions: *Summa* 3.8.3

Chapter 3.8.3, *On traders and bankers*, is not arranged as a sermon. Its structure is simple. It covers four different kinds of trade: exchange banking, i.e., moneychanging and its many permutations; assurances (including insurance, security or surety on loans, safe-conducts, and "pledges" or bets); exchange of goods or barter; and purchase and sale. Moneychanging, exchange of goods, and purchase-sale are introduced in the opening preamble, while the inclusion of assurance may have been prompted by the topic arising at the end of the section on exchange. The structure of the chapter, including subheadings, is as follows:

Pr. Who is properly called a trader? A trader properly so called is one who buys a thing in order to make a profit by selling it whole and unchanged. This preamble introduces three kinds of trade:
- (1) of money for money, i.e., banking or exchange (moneychanging),
- (2) of merchandise for merchandise, i.e., exchange of goods or barter,
- (3) of merchandise for money, i.e., purchase and sale.

1. Exchange, i.e., moneychanging. Now exchange is carried out in many different ways.
   - 1.1. Petty exchange.
   - 1.2. Exchange by bill.
   - 1.3. Dry exchange.
   - 1.4. Mixed exchange which seems to savour of usury. This section contains two paragraphs, the first introducing the nature of the transaction, the second arguing that in it mental usury is committed.
   - 1.5. Usury in exchanges.
   - 1.6. Mental usury.
   - 1.7. Particularly illicit exchange carried out in the Roman curia.

294 A monumental and exceptionally rich study on the subject is Decock, *Theologians and Contract Law*.

295 Jean Bodin, *A Division of All Law: "The Iuris Universi Distributio" of Jean Bodin*, ed. Lee, trans. Brown.

2. Assurance. Although this topic was not introduced in Antoninus's preamble on the three kinds of trade (above), nevertheless it seems to represent its own heading in the chapter. The first paragraph states that assurances can be applied to merchandise, to money, and to persons.
   2.1. Assurance on merchandise (i.e., insurance).
   2.2. Assurance on money (i.e., security or surety on loans).
   2.3. Assurance on persons (i.e., safe-conducts and wagers).

3. Exchange of goods or barter. This section contains two paragraphs. The first addresses the general requirements of justice to be observed in exchanging goods. The second paragraph condemns exchanges in which two people cooperate to defraud a third.

4. Purchase and sale. The first paragraph summarizes when it is licit to trade by buying things in order to sell them for a greater price.
   4.1. Retail cloth merchants and second-hand dealers.
   4.2. Food merchants.
   4.3. Butchers and small retail dealers.

This chapter is both doctrinal and casuistic. In it, Antoninus identifies specific commercial transactions which existed in practice in his time, and addresses their liceity and the possible frauds committed within them. The discussion has a pastoral orientation but engages in more learned analysis than 3.8.1, which is oriented directly to preaching, or 3.8.4, which is almost purely casuistic and practical. Canon law and its jurisprudence provide the majority of sources cited or drawn on by Antoninus. The *Decretum* and the *Liber Extra* are both cited regularly, and the *Rules of Law* in the *Liber Sext* are cited three times. Antoninus makes significant use of Lorenzo Ridolfi's *Tractatus de usuris*, and also cites the opinions of other canonists, including the Archdeacon (Guido de Baysio), Peter Quesnel, OFM, Hostiensis (Henricus de Segusio), Goffredo da Trani, Astesanus of Asti, OFM, Bernard of Parma (or possibly Bernard of Pavia), Innocent IV, and Giovanni Calderini.

The most interesting part of this chapter for intellectual and economic history is section 1, discussing exchange banking. Noonan, in his review of scholastic analysis of banking from 1150–1450 AD,[296] describes Antoninus's chapter 3.8.3 as "the fullest discussion yet attempted of exchange."[297] Antoninus's most important

---

296 Noonan, *Scholastic Analysis of Usury*, ch. 8 "Banking," 171–92.

297 Ibid., 188. Antoninus also discusses exchange at *Summa*, 2.1.7.47–50 (M_1 fol. Vr, 30rff. and Ballerini 2:122b–125; 2.1.6.47–50 in Mamachi 2:165–70): *de cambiis* (or *canbiis*). "The wording is not exactly the same, but there is nevertheless a great deal of duplication in the two versions." De Roover, *Great Economic Thinkers*, 36 n193.

source in this section is Lorenzo Ridolfi's *Tractatus de usuris*, on which he relies heavily.[298] The operations Antoninus describes all involve exchanging two different currencies; to help the reader understand them, a brief outline of exchange banking and its context is called for.[299]

There were a large number of currencies in use locally in the different regions of Europe in the late Middle Ages. In Italy, the larger commercial cities minted their own currencies in coins of both gold and silver, so that even within that one region a variety of different coins circulated and several different systems of denomination were current. For example, in Florence, the gold florin was the largest coin, while a variety of silver coins were accounted in terms of Florentine pounds, shillings, and pence (£ s. d. *a fiorino*). International merchants had to be able to deal in many different currencies in the course of trade: a Florentine merchant might go to London and purchase wool, transport it to Florence and sell it to a *lanaiuolo* there to be turned into finished cloth, then purchase the cloth for export to another region. As discussed in the preamble above, Florentine merchants built up an extensive trade network, and expanded their activities into banking. Florentine banking firms operated branches in many major cities across Europe.

The simplest service the bankers provided was the on-the-spot exchange of one coinage for another: "as of silver or gold coinage for copper and vice versa."[300] This was literal moneychanging, *cambium*, from which the name *campsores* came to designate their trade: originally "moneychangers," but in Italy in the late Middle Ages "bankers." This simple moneychanging transaction was called petty or manual exchange.[301] Antoninus gives the example of someone exchanging gold florins for pounds, shillings, and pence (in local Florentine currencies); the exchange rate which Antoninus gives here, of about 96 shillings for someone to buy one large gold florin (*fiorino d'oro largo*), agrees with Peter Spufford's figure of 96s. per florin in the year 1450.[302] This simple exchange transaction, according to Antoninus, is entirely licit, provided all frauds are excluded and provided the banker charges the reasonable customary fee. This is the most basic transaction on which all exchange banking is founded, and in principle it is licit; from here, Antoninus is prepared to view any sort of exchange as licit, provided that it serves a useful purpose and the banker's profits do not involve usury.

---

298 Laurentius de Rodulphis, *Tractatus de usuris*, 3, 1–4 (TUI 7:37r–38v).

299 In the following brief account of exchange banking, I draw principally on the following works: Mueller, *The Venetian Money Market*; Spufford, *Money and Its Use*; Noonan, *Scholastic Analysis of Usury*; Goldthwaite, *Economy of Renaissance Florence*.

300 Antoninus, *Summa*, 3.8.3, section 1.1.

301 Noonan, *Scholastic Analysis of Usury*, 175.

302 See his table of exchange rates in Spufford, *Money and Its Use*, 291. See also Spufford, *Handbook of Medieval Exchange*, 27, giving a rate of 96s. for the years 1448–52.

There is a sharp distinction to be made, for Antoninus and the other medieval scholastics, between usury, i.e., profit sought on a loan, and legitimate remuneration for a service. When one provides a service involving labour and expenses, *the labourer is worthy of his wage* (1 Tim 5.19), and so it is licit for a banker who provides such a service to seek a moderate profit from it. However, it is not licit to demand or even to desire a profit on a loan of money or a loan of another consumption good – this sort of loan is called a *mutuum*. Profits on such a loan were normally usury, at least when sought in advance, and prohibited to Christians. However, exchange operations could be used to evade the Church's prohibition on usury, as will be seen.

This brings us to the next kind of exchange operation: exchange by bill. Antoninus's example will suffice: "Someone gives to a banker or merchant in Florence 100 florins, to be returned to him or to a third party on his behalf in Rome where he needs them, and this is done so that he may have them more safely and conveniently; for which the banker prepares a bill of exchange, writing to another banker in Rome that at the request of the person carrying the bill he should give to the person the 100 florins which he received in Florence."[303] The great immediate advantage of the bill of exchange was how it facilitated long-distance trade. A merchant could transfer assets from one city to another without the inconvenience or risk of transporting physical coins. The bill of exchange, being a simple piece of paper drawn up in-house, was also cheaper than a notarized legal instrument. The breadth of Florentine merchant-bankers' networks, with branches in many of Europe's largest cities, put them in a position to provide this service and to profit from it. The banker made a profit either through charging a fee for the bill or through a favourable rate of exchange between the currency paid by the purchaser and the currency delivered in the other city. Antoninus considers this type of exchange legitimate and the banker's profit straightforwardly licit: the banker deserves to make a profit for serving the customer's utility and for labour, expenses, and risk.

In the exchange by bill just described, the customer paid up front and then received the money in the other city at a later date. However, the transaction could be done in reverse: a person could ask for a sum of money from the banker here and now, to be repaid later in another city in the currency which circulates there. In this case, the banker is the one who "buys" the exchange in a foreign city. In this form, the banker is in effect extending credit to the opposite party, who has the use of the money for a period of time until the date of maturity on the bill, when the sum must be repaid. Noonan describes this as "the common form" used by merchants and bankers both for commercial credit to finance the wool trade and to extend credit to governments.[304] One very important characteristic of this

303 Antoninus, *Summa*, 3.8.3, section 1.2.

304 Noonan, *Scholastic Analysis of Usury*, 189; see also 176–7.

credit, however, was that it did not take the form of a straight *mutuum* loan, and therefore on the face of it did not implicate the lender in usury. The bankers' profits did not normally come from charging interest at a rate fixed in advance. The banker could charge a transaction fee, but normally the banker's profit came from a favourable exchange rate. The value of one currency in terms of another differed from place to place, and went through seasonal fluctuations; the banker depended on knowing these rates and being able to predict them, but also on luck – bankers could lose if the rates went against them.

The credit function of this type of exchange by bill could also be extended through rechange. In rechange, the bill of exchange is presented in the other city without really repaying it there; the branch there draws up a new bill of exchange to be paid to the home branch where the loan was originally taken, say in Florence, and thus the borrower has the use of the money for another term (a month in the common case of rechange between Florence and Venice), and at the end repays it to the home branch, with a favourable exchange rate yielding a profit for the banker. Renewing a loan through rechange was known as "stare in su cambi" or "stare su interessi."[305]

The third and fourth transactions which Antoninus describes in 3.8.3 are variations on this type of exchange. In both of these exchanges, Antoninus's overriding concern is whether they involve disguised usury. First, Antoninus describes a form of exchange which is in reality a purely fictitious currency exchange used to disguise a loan. It was called "dry exchange" or exchange *ad libras grossorum*, i.e., into Venetian pounds of groats (£ *di grossi*), or *ad Venetias*, because in the fifteenth century it was most often used between Florence and Venice, on a term of one month.[306] Antoninus describes it this way (1 pound of groats equals 10 ducats):

> Someone receives 10 pounds of groats in Florence, i.e., 100 ducats, from a banker or merchant, which he is obliged to repay in Florence a month from then, and at the value which 100 ducats were worth in Venice ten days after the contract was concluded, i.e., when the said money was received. And if he wants to hold the said quantity of 100 ducats from month to month, the contract is renewed in the way just described.[307]

In this case, the movement of currencies is purely fictitious. There is simply a loan effected through a contract of exchange, with the interest due being calculated

305 Mueller, *Venetian Money Market*, 290; see also the examples at 323–6. This type of exchange is also described by Noonan, *Scholastic Analysis of Usury*, 177–8.

306 See Mueller, *Venetian Money Market*, 288–92; de Roover, *Great Economic Thinkers*, 36 n192; Noonan, *Scholastic Analysis of Usury*, 177–8.

307 Antoninus, *Summa*, 3.8.3, section 1.3.

based on the exchange rate between Florence and Venice ten days after the money is lent. Although a profit was not guaranteed for the banker, the bankers knew the seasonal patterns of exchange rates well enough that they would usually take a profit – as Antoninus says, "commonly, more often than not, [the money is] worth more at the time of repayment than when received ... hence at year-end it is always turned into a profit, and a large one."[308] Dry exchange is an example of how some bankers and borrowers tried to work around the prohibition on usury; it was discussed by Lorenzo Ridolfi,[309] and though, in Noonan's words, "there is a note of hesitancy in his final condemnation,"[310] Antoninus concludes that Ridolfi considers the contract usurious, with which he agrees.[311]

Next Antoninus discusses a fourth kind of exchange, the most interesting, also called exchange by bill: "it seems a kind of mixture of the second and third kinds, and drawn more to the nature of the third. Hence it also seems to savour of usury."[312] Antoninus describes it as "used very frequently."[313] The transaction Antoninus describes here appears to take the form of exchange by bill involving an extension of credit, as just described above. The explanation in Antoninus's first paragraph is compressed, making it difficult to follow how the accounting works; the analogy which is provided in the second paragraph goes some way towards clarifying it. In light of it, it seems we can say that it works like this. A banker provides a certain sum of money to a customer, for example 100 florins in Florence; the 100 florins paid out are accounted as having "purchased" the equivalent value of foreign coinage, such as Venetian pounds of groats, at the then-current local rate of exchange; the foreign coinage is to be delivered at a later date in the other city, where, presumably, its value in terms of florins would be greater – Antoninus takes it as a general rule that a coin is normally worth more in its home city where it circulates.[314] Thus the dealer will make a profit from the increased value he receives versus what he paid out. As a hypothetical exchange rate, let us say that with the 100 florins paid out to the customer, the banker has "purchased" 10 pounds of groats (i.e., 100 Venetian ducats) to be delivered in Venice in one month's time. In one month, the customer has 10 pounds of groats paid to the banker's agent in Venice; where, at this time, they are worth more in terms of florins – let us say they are now worth 102 florins – and hence the banker makes a profit when he sells

308 Ibid., section 1.3.

309 Laurentius de Rodulphis, *Tractatus de usuris*, 3, q. 1 (TUI 7:37v–38r).

310 Noonan, *Scholastic Analysis of Usury*, 187.

311 Antoninus, *Summa*, 3.8.3, section 1.4.

312 Ibid., section 1.4.

313 Ibid., section 1.5.

314 Antoninus, *Summa*, 3.8.3, section 1.4 and 1.2; see also where Antoninus affirms this general rule in *Summa*, 2.1.7.47–50 (M_1 fol. Vr, 30rff. and Ballerini 2:122b–125; 2.1.6.47–50 in Mamachi 2:165–70): *de cambiis* (or *canbiis*).

the ducats in Venice to repurchase florins. In my hypothetical example, he ends up with 102 florins one month later in return for the 100 he originally paid out, yielding an annual interest rate of 24 per cent, which would have been unusually high.[315] The customer, on the other hand, has the use of the 100 florins for the specified period of time, effectively as a loan.

After describing the transaction, Antoninus asks if it is licit, and initially sets out an argument that it is. "For it seems comparable to someone," i.e., the banker, "arranging to buy a great quantity of *bolognini* in Florence," when they are worth 24 d. (pence), then transporting them to Bologna where they are worth 26 d., and thus in selling them again in Bologna, "he receives for one *bolognino* two more pence than it cost him."[316] "But one can reply that it is not comparable," Antoninus responds, for in the aforesaid transaction:

> although it is called an "exchange" nevertheless in reality it seems to be a loan. For Peter, needing money in Florence in order to provide for himself, receives that 100 as a loan from Martin in a so-called "exchange through Venice or Barcelona" or what have you, to be repaid there, when he does not ever have any business to carry out there or money to bring back to himself from there. From this loan to be repaid there, Martin hopes to make a profit; hence it seems to savour of usury ...[317]

Antoninus concludes by citing with approval Peter Quesnel, who follows Hostiensis and Goffredo da Trani in concluding that in this sort of exchange, since it is in effect a loan with hope of profit, a banker "can hardly be excused from mental usury."[318] Noonan makes some perceptive remarks about the apparent disconnect between the outlook of leading theologians like Antoninus and the common practice of merchants and bankers.[319] It seems reasonable to suppose that, notwithstanding the opinions of Antoninus, Hostiensis, and so forth, the merchants and bankers probably did not believe that they were engaging in usury when they extended credit to one another in order to finance trade journeys abroad. Returning to this transaction at the end of the next section, Antoninus has a note of uncertainty: "with due respect for a better judgment, this kind of exchange seems to savour of usury, although it is nevertheless used very frequently. And I have heard many very learned and God-fearing men hold this opinion."[320]

In the next two sections Antoninus discusses usury in exchanges and mental usury, all seemingly with reference to the credit transaction just discussed in

315 See Mueller, *Venetian Money Market*, 323–6.
316 Antoninus, *Summa*, 3.8.3, section 1.4.
317 Ibid., section 1.4.
318 Ibid., section 1.4.
319 Noonan, *Scholastic Analysis of Usury*, 190–2.
320 Antoninus, *Summa*, 3.8.3, section 1.5.

section 1.4. He addresses the arguments made in the *Summa Astensis* (drawing on Alexander Lombard) to defend the liceity of exchange banking: that this is useful for the commonwealth, and that the Roman curia tolerates it. Antoninus's position is that exchange banking is in itself licit, as he has said before, but usury can be committed in it, and neither of the two arguments excuses usury. However, the banker in the example above seems to be "a mental usurer."[321] In relation to mental usury and its consequences, Antoninus follows closely the opinion of Bernard of Parma, compiler of the *Glossa ordinaria* on the *Liber Extra*, who says:

> In relation to the form of contract they are not called usurers; but, because of the intention which they had, they must be judged as acting wickedly in the tribunal of the soul, and they are to be induced, but not compelled, to restore what they have received in this way. And they are not to be punished as usurers, but in truth in the eyes of God they appear to be usurers, because they are bound to restore what they have received in this way. And here you have it manifest, that the intention makes a man a usurer – and understand, with effect.[322]

Finally, in the last section on exchange, Antoninus comes to a transaction carried out in the Roman curia by bankers or merchants "which seems even more illicit and usurious."[323] In this kind of exchange, ecclesiastics who received dignities or benefices in Rome borrowed money from bankers there to pay the apostolic treasury the required portion of their benefice's first year's revenue. The bankers disguised the loan as an exchange, to be paid in the region of the benefice in the local currency, but at a very unfavourable rate for the borrower.[324] On the transaction itself I have little comment to add: Antoninus condemns it as straightforward usury, disguised in a currency exchange. However, in the course of the discussion Antoninus raises a counter-example which merits some attention.

The bankers could defend themselves from the charge of usury through this example:

> For the doctors concede that when a person wants and intends to engage in trade through making use of money which he has, hoping that a profit will genuinely be

321 Ibid., section 1.6.

322 Bernardus Parmensis in *Glossa ordinaria*, *X* 5.19.10 (*Consuluit*) s.v. *male agere* (2:1739). My translation.

323 Antoninus, *Summa*, 3.8.3, section 1.7.

324 In de Roover's words: "The fifth kind of exchange was the most pernicious in Sant'Antonino's opinion because its principal victims were ecclesiastics residing at the Curia who raised money by drawing at an unfavorable rate of exchange on the prospective income of their benefices abroad." *Great Economic Thinkers*, 37. Noonan translates the first part of section 1.7 in *Scholastic Analysis of Usury*, 189–90.

> produced for himself from it, and someone, knowing this and needing money, asks that he lend him that money with which he was prepared to engage in trade and to make a profit, and because of this he will pay him the profit which can reasonably be estimated in the state of uncertainty, the trader is able to lend and receive that profit licitly; nor is this usury, but it is sought as interest, that is, the avoidance of his loss, since he is not moved by the intention of making a profit from a loan, which is usury, but of serving his neighbour, yet while avoiding his own loss.[325]

There are several points to unpack here. First, Antoninus makes a distinction between "usury" and "interest." In scholastic terminology, interest (*interesse*) means compensation for a loss which a creditor has incurred through lending: the noun is formed from the Latin phrase *quod interest*, "that which is the difference,"[326] i.e., the difference between the creditor's present position and the position he would have been in otherwise.[327] It was widely accepted that interest could be claimed if the debtor delayed repaying the loan, causing a loss to the lender. There was an ongoing controversy among the canonists and theologians about whether interest could ever be claimed from the beginning of a loan; the controversy centred on two possible titles to interest, *damnum emergens* (loss occurring) or *lucrum cessans* (profit ceasing).[328] Hostiensis (circa 1271) broke away from previous consensus by giving qualified approval to interest from the beginning of a loan on grounds of *lucrum cessans* in cases like the one just described by Antoninus, where the lender was a merchant or businessman who lent money with which he would otherwise engage in trade, in order to help someone seeking a loan from him.[329] Hostiensis's opinion did not prevail over all opposition; the controversy continued for more than two centuries. Hostiensis's opinion was taken up and espoused by, among others, Peter John Olivi (circa 1293), Astesanus (1317), Lorenzo Ridolfi (1404), and Bernardino of Siena (circa 1440).[330] It was opposed by Thomas Aquinas in the *Quaestiones disputatae de malo* (circa 1270–2),[331] by the canonist Giovanni d'Andrea (circa 1348) in his *Novella in Decretales*, citing

---

325 Antoninus, *Summa*, 3.8.3, section 1.7.

326 Noonan, *Scholastic Analysis of Usury*, 105–6.

327 On titles to interest, see ibid., ch. 5, "Titles to Payment beyond the Principal."

328 See ibid., 118–28.

329 Hostiensis, *Commentaria* ad *X* 5.19.16 (*Salubriter*) n. 4–5 (4:58v–59r); see Noonan's translation of this passage, *Scholastic Analysis of Usury*, 118.

330 Petrus Iohannis Olivi, *Quodlibet* 1, q. 17, co. (Piron, *Traité des contrats*, 398); Astesanus, *Summa Astensis*, 3.11 *De usuris* a. 4 (ed. Lamberti, 1:330); Laurentius de Rodulphis, *Tractatus de usuris*, 2, 24 (no. 6 in TUI 7:22v); Bernardinus Senensis, *De evangelio aeterno*, 42, 2, 2 (4:358–9).

331 The date of the *De malo* is from Torrell, *Saint Thomas Aquinas*, vol. 1, *The Person and His Work*, 336. Thomas Aquinas seems to approve *damnum emergens* as a title to interest from the beginning of a loan in *Summa theologiae* 2a 2ae q. 78 a. 2 ob. 1 and ad 1; but condemns it except for in the case of delayed repayment in *De malo* q. 13 a. 4 ad 14.

Innocent IV (circa 1245),[332] and by many theologians who rejected the title of *lucrum cessans* from the start of a loan.[333]

Antoninus discusses the topic here in 3.8.3 as well as in the second part of the *Summa*, at 2.1.7. Noonan stated that "the fullest acceptance of *lucrum cessans* and *damnum emergens*, as well as the most detailed analysis of what they mean, is given by the two saints from capitalistic Tuscany, Bernardin[o] and Antoninus."[334] However, Noonan did not correctly ascertain Antoninus's opinion because he did not have access to the autograph manuscripts; more on this in a moment. Bernardino discusses the topic in sermons 41 and 42 of the *De evangelio aeterno*, in which he presents three arguments defending *lucrum cessans*, saying that the merchant lending money in this circumstance "gives not money in its simple character, but he also gives his capital."[335] Noonan comments that this is the first use of the term *capitale* by a prominent scholastic with the precise sense of "money accumulated for business purposes" – however, Bernardino here is actually repeating what Peter John Olivi (circa 1296) wrote in *Quodlibet* 1, 17.[336] Noonan states that Antoninus likewise says, in 2.1.7, that a businessman's money "has the nature of capital, so he has from the beginning of a loan a right to *lucrum cessans* up to the probable amount of profit lost, allowing for its uncertainty and deducting for expenses."[337] However, this account of Antoninus's opinion on *lucrum cessans* must be modified by recourse to the autograph manuscripts. Noonan was reading Antoninus's *Summa* in the edition printed in Venice, 1581–2. The passage which Noonan cites, in which money is described as having the nature of capital, is printed in Ballerini's edition of Antoninus's *Summa* at columns 98d–99b.[338] However, this passage is not extant in the autograph manuscript of part 2 of the *Summa* where Antoninus discusses *lucrum cessans* as a title to interest.[339] Here, Antoninus begins by citing the different opinions of Innocent IV, Hostiensis, Giovanni d'Andrea, Giovanni Calderini, and Giovanni da Legnano; the rest of the passage runs thus:

> Also what Hostiensis says about profit, it seems must be understood as excluding doubtful profit, namely when he could also have not profited or taken a loss. And

---

332 Iohannes Andreae, *Novella* ad *X* 5.19.19 (*Naviganti*) n. 5 (Venice, 1581, 4:77v).

333 See additional references in Noonan, *Scholastic Analysis of Usury*, 119–21 and 126.

334 Ibid., 126.

335 English trans. Noonan, *Scholastic Analysis of Usury*, 126. "Non tradit sibi solam simplicis pecuniae rationem, sed etiam tradit sibi capitale suum." Bernardinus Senensis, *De evangelio aeterno*, 42, 2, 2 (4:358).

336 Petrus Iohannis Olivi, *Quodlibet* 1, q. 17, co. (Piron, *Traité des contrats*, 398).

337 Noonan, *Scholastic Analysis of Usury*, 128.

338 Antoninus, *Summa*, 2.1.7.15 (Ballerini 2:98d–99b; 2.1.6.15 in Mamachi 2:136–8).

339 Antoninus, *Summa*, 2.1.7.15 (M_1 fol. 25r). Mamachi notes the absence of this passage in the codex, and prints it in italics in his edition (see col. 126, note m).

before the fact, this should be prohibited, but after the fact in the court of conscience, where one must be believed in favour of oneself just as against oneself, when one has asserted that he did this without fraud, it seems it can be overlooked.[340]

A marginal note has been added beside these words, barely legible today and probably not written by Antoninus, which refers to Bernardino, sermon 41 or 42, a. 2, c. 1–2.[341] The passage which Ballerini prints here in his edition of Antoninus's *Summa* continues discussing *lucrum cessans* through another four paragraphs, which, in fact, largely repeat Bernardino of Siena's discussion of money as capital in sermon 42.[342] Noonan read these paragraphs in the Venice edition of Antoninus's *Summa,* but it turns out that they were not written by Antoninus. The first person to discover the dicrepancy was, as far as I am aware, Amleto Spicciani.[343] These paragraphs appear to have been added to Antoninus's *Summa* later, copied in from Bernardino's sermons. Indeed, every instance of the word *capitale* or *capitalitas* in Ballerini's edition is part of this passage which is absent from the autograph manuscripts, and appears to have been added to the text of the *Summa* by a later copyist or editor drawing from Bernardino's sermons. Based on the autograph manuscripts, which lack this passage cited by Noonan, it seems that Antoninus's opinion on *lucrum cessans* is more qualified than Bernardino's. He never directly describes it as licit, as Bernardino does.[344] Indeed, he says that "before the fact, this

340 "Respondet Inno. in c. fi. e. ti. dicens quod licet quidam contrarium dicant, ipse putat hunc contractum usurarium, nec scit sic contrahentem excusare. Hosti. uero in c. Salubriter dicit quod talis est mihi obligatus ad interesse illius lucri quod facturus eram uerisimiliter ex peccunia, dummodo nil fiat in fraudem usurarium. Io. An. approbat dictum Inno. Et quod dicitur de interesse habet locum post moram debitoris, contrarium dicendo pararetur uia aperta ad fenus. Et hoc etiam placet Io. Cald. Sed Io. de Lig. dicit quod quamuis communiter teneatur cum Inno., ne uia fraudibus aperiatur; ipse tamen credit ueram oppinionem Hosti., dummodo nil fiat in fraudem. Tutum tamen est ab hoc abstinere, Lau. de Ridol. Quod etiam dicit Hosti. de lucro uidetur intelligendum deducto etiam dubio lucri, cum scilicet potuisset etiam non lucrari uel perdere. Et ante factum prohibendum est, post factum uero in foro conscientie ubi credendum est pro se sicut contra se, cum asserit sine fraude egisse uidetur posse pertransire." Antoninus, *Summa* 2.1.7.15 (M_1 fol. 25r).

341 My transcription of this note: "Hic deficit ratio quare talis contractus sit licitus que habetur in 41 (corrected from 42?) sermone Bernardini ar. 2. c. 2. Inter istum §. et §. sequentem ponitur §. qui habetur in eodem sermone 41 ar. 2 c. 1."

342 Bernardinus Senensis, *De evangelio aeterno*, 42, 2, 2 (4:358–9).

343 In his 1990 book *Capitale e interesse*, 188–95. Spicciani transcribes the marginal note slightly differently: "Hic deficit ratio quare talis contractus sit licitus, quod habetur in 42 Sermone Bernardini articulo 2, capitulo 2, inter istum § et § sequentem positum. Et quod habetur in aliam partem 42 articulo 2, capitulo 1." Spicciani, *Capitale e interesse*, 188.

344 "Et de hoc quod licitus sit contractus triplex ratio dari potest: primo enim licet hoc ratione aequitatis; secundo, ratione indemnitatis; tertio, ratione utilitatis." Bernardinus Senensis *De evangelio aeterno* 42, 2, 2 (4:358).

should be prohibited." The furthest he goes in approving it is to say that "after the fact in the court of conscience ... it seems it can be overlooked." This is an example showing how advantageous it is to verify what Antoninus authentically wrote by recourse to the autograph manuscripts.

After concluding the discussion of this final kind of exchange, by noting that the bankers who carry it out often also act as mediators in simony, Antoninus moves on to the next topic of this chapter, assurances. He did not introduce this topic in his opening preamble; perhaps it was prompted by the mention of how the bankers at the Roman curia demand security for the credit they extend to prelates there.[345] This section is straightforward and I have little to add by way of comment. Antoninus discusses assurance on merchandise, i.e., insurance; money, i.e., security or surety for a loan (which is sometimes used to evade the usury prohibition); and persons. He mentions two kinds of "assurance" on persons. The first is when a lord provides a safe-conduct. The second is when merchants or others bet on whether a certain person will die within a specified time; they also sometimes make bets about other events, including "wagers" (*inuadiationes*) among scholars and doctors about how some question will be decided. "And all these," i.e., such bets, "appear to be vain and shameful kinds of gain."[346]

In the third main section of the chapter, Antoninus discusses exchange of goods (*permutatio*), i.e., barter between merchants, which "are very frequently made use of today because of the shortage of coins."[347] In highlighting the frauds which are sometimes committed therein, Antoninus makes some sharp comments about commercial practices and the deceptive character of merchants in his day. This topic is treated more fully in 2.1.17 (discussed above) and 3.8.4 (below); no further comment is needed here.

The fourth and final section of this chapter addresses purchase and sale. Once again this topic is dealt with more fully by Antoninus elsewhere, in 2.1.16 and 2.1.17. The principles Antoninus applies here are the same: trading in goods of whatever sort is licit, provided that it is done without fraud, observing the proper circumstances, and at just prices. After the opening paragraph, Antoninus begins enumerating different sorts of traders and merchants who buy and sell various

---

Cfr Ballerini's text of Antoninus, *Summa*, 2.1.7.15 (98d–e): "Quod enim licitus sit talis contractus, simpliciter intuitu pietatis factus, non in fraudem usurae, tripliciter potest probari. Primo ratione aequitatis et pietatis. ... Secundo hoc licet ratione indemnitatis. ... Tertio licet hoc ratione utilitatis." This passage is absent from M_1.

345 Antoninus, *Summa*, 3.8.3, section 2. Antoninus also discusses assurance at Antoninus, *Summa* 2.1.7.45–46 (M_1 fol. Vr, 29v–30r and Ballerini 2:121–2; 2.1.6.45–6 in Mamachi 2:164–5): *de securitatibus*.

346 Antoninus, *Summa*, 3.8.3, section 2.3.

347 Ibid., section 3.

types of goods commercially, and highlights the frauds and vices they often perpetrate.[348] This leads directly into chapter 3.8.4, *On the various kinds of workers.*

6. The Different Sorts of Workers and Their Vices: *Summa* 3.8.4

Chapter 3.8.4, *On the various kinds of workers,* is not arranged as a sermon. It proceeds by enumerating twelve different categories of workers and discusses the characteristic vices and moral duties of each. Within the twelve general categories, Antoninus discusses specific occupations or tasks. In the autograph manuscript, this structure is indicated by a two-level hierarchy of paragraph marks: a large gibbet indicates a new heading, while a small gibbet indicates a subheading. This two-level hierarchy of headings is not preserved in the manuscript F_3 or in Ballerini's edition, but I have reproduced it in my edition. The structure of the chapter is as follows:

1. Outfitters, goldsmiths, and gem dealers. It is noted in the first paragraph that all these workers sometimes act as merchants selling goods made by others, sometimes as artisans.
   The rest of this section primarily discusses goldsmiths and the sale of precious metals.
   1.1. Goldsmiths.
   1.2. Let them not sell alchemically produced gold and silver for the real thing.
   1.3. On mixing copper into gold or silver.

2. Agents and brokers. General principles are set out in the first paragraph.
   2.1. If one is a mediator in contracts.
   2.2. If one is a mediator in the purchase of credits in the *monte.*
   2.3. The same applies to all who are mediators.

3. Wool merchants. This section on wool merchants is the longest in the chapter. The first paragraph merely states that the wool craft is necessary for human life.
   Now this craft has many members who serve it.
   3.1. Purchase on credit.
   3.2. On moderate profit.
   3.3. The wool merchant in a case of usury.
   3.4. Depositing money with wool merchants.
   3.5. If a wool merchant receives money at his discretion.

348 Ibid., section 4.1–3.

- 3.6. Employees in the workshop.
- 3.7. Consuls.
- 3.8. Officials.
- 3.9. Employees in the wool craft. This section contains three paragraphs, discussing workers in the successive stages of wool manufacturing: wool-carders, *lanini*, spinners, weavers, washers, fullers, dyers, and cloth stretchers.
- 3.10. The craft of menders.
- 3.11. Retail cloth dealers.

4. Tailors, makers of boots and shoes, and so forth. The first paragraph discusses tailors and boot- and shoemakers.
   - 4.1. The craft of fabric decorators. These may include textile printers as well as embroiderers.
   - 4.2. Those who lend precious garments and jewelled items.
   - 4.3. Cobblers and slipper makers.
   - 4.4. Furriers.

5. Silk makers or silk merchants. The first paragraph comments on the use of silk cloth. This is licit, but it often serves vanity, especially today when luxurious fabrics are worn by people whose status they do not befit.
   - 5.1. Weavers and dyers. The first sentence notes that they can be expected to recompense the silk merchant for defects they cause; the rest of this paragraph condemns various ways silk merchants defraud weavers or dyers. The rest of section 5 deals with other frauds committed by silk merchants.
   - 5.2. Those who defraud taxes or tolls.
   - 5.3. Buying silk from those who have stolen it.
   - 5.4. Selling on credit or making exchanges.

6. Architects and builders. The first paragraph explains that this work is necessary but can be used to build excessive palaces and buildings.
   - 6.1. Let them beware of frauds.
   - 6.2. Masons and bricklayers.
   - 6.3. Stonecutters.

7. Smiths. The first paragraph divides craftsmen (*fabri*) into smiths (*fabri ferrarii*) and carpenters (*carpentarii*), and begins enumerating the different types of smiths.
   - 7.1. Farriers, that is, smiths who make shoes for oxen.
   - 7.2. Armourers, that is, smiths who make arms.
   - 7.3. Craftsmen devoted to other sorts of work.

8. Carpenters. The first paragraph comments on moon phase harvesting of lumber and introduces several kinds of carpenter.
   8.1. Those who make galleys, ships, and boats.
   8.2. Mariners. It is peculiar that mariners are discussed here in the section on carpenters, but presumably it is because of the connection to ships. The autograph manuscript uses a small gibbet at the start of this paragraph, indicating that it is a subheading and not a new section of its own.

9. Apothecaries. The first paragraph states the necessity of this craft and begins listing ways apothecaries can do wrong; this continues through several short paragraphs.
   9.1. Employees in this craft.
   9.2. Barber-surgeons. Discussed here because they perform medicinal bloodletting.
   9.3. Working on the sabbath. This subsection ends with an unfinished sentence: "Above all they must beware lest in their shops …"

10. Artisans whose work relates to writings and pictures. The first paragraph discusses paper and parchment makers.
    10.1. Booksellers.
    10.2. How scribes do wrong.
    10.3. Painters. This section ends with a sentence about illuminators.

11. The occupation of musicians in singing and playing. The first paragraph discusses liturgical music specifically and the musicians who practise it.
    11.1. Laypeople playing instruments recreationally.
    11.2. The craft of performing.

12. Farmers. The first paragraph observes that farming is certainly licit and necessary, and notes that it is common for buyers to take advantage of farmers in several ways.
    12.1. If they work the lands of others.
    12.2. If they hold animals in agistment.
    12.3. They do wrong in not paying tithes.
    12.4. How they commonly do wrong. This paragraph lists, rather laconically, many different sins which farmers are prone to. It concludes, however, with a stern admonition addressed to parish clergy, holding them responsible for checking the vices of their flock.

This chapter, like the preceding two, is not crafted as a sermon. It is also the least doctrinal and most "casuistic" of all the chapters edited herein. It proceeds serially through a list of different kinds of workers, categorizing them into crafts (*artes*), in each case commenting on the general necessity or utility of the craft (sometimes supported by a scripture text),[349] and then discussing the typical vices or frauds committed by workers in this craft. The most frequently cited sources in this chapter are the Scriptures and the canon law, especially Gratian's *Decretum*. Thomas Aquinas is also cited in several places. Compared to the other chapters already discussed, this one makes a lighter use of source references. Instead, what comes to the fore is Antoninus's direct knowledge and experience. The length and detail of his treatment of wool merchants, for example, shows his first-hand contact with this chief industry of Florence. A linguistic indication that Antoninus is drawing on his acquaintance with local practice is the frequent use of Italian terms: sometimes directly, such as the Italian words *zappas* (section 7.3) and *cozones* – "tales tamen uulgariter dicuntur cozones" (7.1) – but often fully Latinized, such as the Italian phrase *a discrezione*: "ad discretionem secundum uulgare" (3.5). Of all the chapters edited herein, this one best exemplifies Francesco da Castiglione's description of the qualities of Antoninus's teaching: "He not only wrote about universal things, but he also adapted doctrine, coming down to the particulars, to our very way of living, to the basic practice of the specifics of human life."[350] Indeed, Antoninus's comments on the various sorts of workers and their practices are often interesting and revealing. I hope they will be of use to historians and students of social and cultural history.

In discussing the different crafts, Antoninus applies the governing principles about the liceity of work and the requirements of justice which he has set out in the previous chapters, especially 3.8.1, 3.8.2, and 2.1.16, to the particular activities and circumstances of each case. There is no need to go through this chapter paragraph by paragraph here, since it has just been summarized in diagrammatic form above. Instead, this section will outline the standard overall principles applied most frequently in this chapter, and highlight a few notable cases and comments made by Antoninus.

The most fundamental principle underlying Antoninus's approach to the crafts in this chapter is that all of them are licit in themselves, since they serve some genuine necessity or utility. Each craft has a legitimate use, and its practitioners can, in principle, be morally safe in making a living from it. Indeed, Antoninus frequently states that a given craft is worthy of a suitable reward or has the right

349 The following crafts are provided with a scriptural precedent or a patron saint in this chapter: furriers, architects and builders, sculptors, smiths, carpenters, singers and musicians, and farmers.

350 "Non enim de universalibus tantum rebus scripsit: verum etiam ad particularia quaeque descendens, ad hunc nostrum vivendi usum et ad singularem quamdam humanae vitae operationem, doctrinam accommodavit." Castiglione, *Vita Beati Antonini*, c. 4 (322); English from Howard, *Beyond the Written Word*, 52 n40.

to charge a just price for its products and thereby earn a wage: "since one is not obliged to soldier at his own expense,"[351] "because all labour desires its reward,"[352] and "the labourer is worthy of his wage."[353] It is only the motives of the worker, or the methods used, or the circumstances in which the craft is done, which make it illicit. The same seven circumstances which were analysed in relation to buying and selling, in chapter 2.1.16, are applicable to all the crafts: "observing the due places and times along with other circumstances,"[354] i.e., why, who, when, where, by what aids, how, what. In addition, what I called the "eighth circumstance"[355] also applies: the requirement of justice in exchange, i.e., a just price must be charged or a just wage paid. Business profits which meet these terms are licit.

In relation to motive, Antoninus reaffirms what he has said above in chapter 3.8.1: one's desire to make a profit or receive a wage "in order to provide for his needs and for the governance of his family according to the character of his state" is licit.[356] The principal bad motives which infect the otherwise licit crafts are greed and vanity. For example, even if the purchase of credits in the *monte* may be licit in itself, a motive of greed, rather than reasonable human utility, renders such profit "shameful."[357] Some of the merchants and artisans who made Florence's wealth and fame are tainted by their service to vanity: notably the silk merchants, but also tailors, cobblers and slipper makers, furriers, barbers, and at times even carpenters.[358]

Certain principles are particularly applicable to employers who hire workers. They must not defraud the workers through paying them in bad money.[359] They must not delay paying the workers' wages: *If any man hath done any work for thee, immediately pay him his wage, and let not the wages of thy hired servant remain with thee at all.*[360] A practice which was current in several industries in Florence, which Antoninus comments on at length in several places, is the practice of payment in kind or "truck."[361] On this practice: employers must not cause a loss of income for their workers by paying them in goods when the original agreement was for money; frequently such workers have no use for the goods, such as foodstuffs or cloth, and in selling them they end up receiving less than the agreed-upon wage.[362]

351 Antoninus, *Summa*, 3.8.4, section 1, quoting C. 13 q. 1 c. 1 Gr. p. §. 4 (1:719).
352 Ibid., section 2.3.
353 Ibid., section 7.1, quoting Luke 10:7 or 1 Timothy 5:18.
354 Ibid., section 11.1.
355 See above in the discussion of chapter 2.1.16.
356 Antoninus, *Summa*, 3.8.4, section 2.2.
357 Ibid.
358 Ibid., section 5, 4.1, 4.3, 4.4, 9.2, 8.
359 Ibid., section 6.1.
360 Tobias (Tobit) 4:15, quoted in Antoninus, *Summa*, 3.8.4, section 3.9. See also section 5.1, 6.1.
361 See de Roover, *Great Economic Thinkers*, 26.
362 Antoninus, *Summa*, 3.8.4, section 3.9, 5.1, 5.4.

However, if payment in kind was agreed to by the worker at the time of hire, then it is licit: for, according to a maxim of canon law, "to one who knows and consents no injury or fraud is done."[363] Nevertheless, the terms of the contract should provide the worker with an acceptable wage "according to the common judgment of the craft," not taking advantage of a worker's fear of unemployment – to do so and pay an unjust wage would be an injustice on the part of the employer.[364]

Employees, conversely, are obliged to do their work faithfully and attentively, not wasting time or working incompetently.[365] Indeed, Antoninus holds that workers can be obliged to compensate their employers for defects which they cause, if such defects reduce the value of the merchandise.[366] In such cases the employers can hold them to account by charging a financial penalty or by subtracting from their wages. Employees must also act faithfully with goods entrusted to them in their work: for example, tailors must not keep superfluous cloth provided for a garment without the owner's knowledge,[367] nor may throwsters and weavers keep some of the silk which they are supposed to throw or weave;[368] if they do, "they are thieves and robbers and are bound to make satisfaction,"[369] applying the same rules which Antoninus discusses in his chapters on theft.[370] However, if an employer has defrauded his employee by illegitimately subtracting from his wages, then – provided the employee knows this with certainty – the employee has the right to recover his lost wages through keeping some of the goods which come into his hands.[371] Known in traditional moral theology as "occult compensation," this is a controversial doctrine which potentially admits of much abuse; hence Antoninus attempts to place strict limits on it.[372]

---

363 Ibid., section 5.1, quoting *VI* 5.[13.]27 (*Scienti*).
364 Ibid., section 5.1.
365 Ibid., section 3.9, 4, 6.1, 7.1, 10.1, 12.1.
366 Ibid., section 3.9, 5.1, 7.1.
367 Ibid., section 4.
368 Ibid., section 5.3.
369 Ibid., section 4.
370 Antoninus, *Summa*, 2.1.12–15 (M_1 fol. Vr and Ballerini; 2.1.11–15 in Mamachi 2:259–331).
371 Antoninus, *Summa*, 3.8.4, section 5.3.
372 On occult compensation, see, for example, McHugh and Callan, *Moral Theology*, part 2, q. 2, a. 4, §. 1927–38 (2:167–73). On the lawfulness of occult compensation, they write: "Ordinarily, or *per se*, it is not lawful; for it contains such evils as disregard of due process of law, scandal, infamy, public disturbance, the menace that the common good will be harmed by frequent abuse, the danger that the debtor will suffer loss through a second payment of the same debt, etc. ... Exceptionally, or *per accidens*, it is lawful; for under certain conditions it offends neither public nor private welfare and it is necessary for the vindication of a right. Just as the natural law gives authority to occupy the goods of another in case of extreme need, so does it justify occult compensation in the special cases just mentioned."

The first case they indicate in which occult compensation may be used is employees: "Employees (i.e., servants, workingmen, artisans, officials, etc.) have a strict right when they are injured

In relation to sellers, the requirements are essentially those analysed in detail in chapters 2.1.16 and 2.1.17. Sellers must not use false weights or measures.[373] They must be faithful with goods or money entrusted to them; for example, a bookseller who sells a book on behalf of the owner for a greater price than the owner intended may not keep the additional amount – this is theft.[374] They must not buy goods which they plausibly believe are stolen;[375] and if one does not take care to avoid buying stolen goods "because he gets a good deal on them," then "when he becomes aware of it later, he may neither keep the thing itself nor seek a refund from the thing's owner of the price which he paid."[376] They must not profit from the buyer's ignorance by concealing hidden defects which reduce the value of the good; although it is not necessary that they reveal defects unless they are likely to cause harm to the buyer, they must reduce the price proportionally.[377] They must not lie and especially they must not commit perjury, confirming a lie with an oath.[378]

The principal requirements which apply specifically to buyers are to pay a just price and not to take advantage of another's necessity or compulsion. This is mentioned particularly sharply in relation to farmers: "such is the subtlety and craftiness of men today that the farmers themselves are rather deceived by buyers."[379] Antoninus highlights the practice of "buying in the blade" or purchasing commodity futures, in which farmers frequently take a loss, selling for a lower price because of their immediate need for cash.[380]

In some crafts, shoddy work may bring people to harm, such as in architecture.[381] Practitioners are obliged not to involve themselves in the craft unless they have sufficient skill and expertise: Antoninus mentions this specifically in connection with barber-surgeons and farriers who practise veterinary medicine.[382]

---

by the employer's non-observance of the contract (e.g., the stipulated salary is not paid; unjust subtractions are made from the salary, as by fines for the inadvertent and infrequent breaking of tools, etc., about which there was no agreement in the contract; labors not contracted for are exacted), or when an unjust contract is imposed on them (e.g., they are induced by force or threats to accept less than a living wage; advantage is taken of their grave necessity to wring from them agreement to such a wage)." See also their *notanda confessariis* (§. 1938), very much of the same spirit as St Antoninus.

373 Antoninus, *Summa*, 3.8.4, section 3.11, 6.2, 7.3, 9, 12.

374 Ibid., section 10.1.

375 Ibid., section 1.1, 5.3.

376 Ibid., section 1.1.

377 Ibid., section 1.2, 1.3, 2.1, 3.10, 5, 10.1, 12.2.

378 Ibid., section 2, 9.1, 12.4.

379 Ibid., section 12.

380 Ibid.

381 Ibid., section 6.1.

382 Ibid., section 7.1, 9.2.

Conversely, in certain crafts, especially the fine arts like sculpture, painting, and working in gold, the skill of the artisan makes a great difference to the quality of the product, and therefore to the price. For some comments on this, as well as on Antoninus's stylistic preferences, see Creighton Gilbert's insightful article in the *Art Bulletin*.[383]

The danger of cooperation in sin, or consent to another's sin, is present in several crafts, particularly armourers, shipbuilders, mariners, booksellers, and performers;[384] merchants who borrow money are also to beware of giving another person the occasion of usury.[385] Antoninus cites Romans 1:32,[386] the canon *Notum sit*,[387] and refers twice to the canon *Qui consentit*: "He who consents to sinners and defends another in his sin shall be cursed before God and men, and he will be corrected with a most severe reproof." The *Glossa ordinaria* glosses the words *he who consents*: "by cooperation and approval."[388]

All of these admonitions look to the conscience and eternal soul. Antoninus expects employers, employees, buyers, and sellers to act with honour and moral integrity: they should follow the requirements of the moral law even if they could, in practice, get away with perpetrating some fraud or taking an illegitimate profit.[389] The court (*forum*) in which these cases are tried is not principally the external court of secular or canon law but the internal court of confession and penance (*forum internum*, *forum penitentie*, etc.).[390]

A specific application of this last point, of the highest importance, is the requirement of restitution. Whenever justice is violated in favour of one party, that party is obliged to make satisfaction to the injured party by returning to them whatever they have lost.[391] This obligation of restitution is mentioned frequently throughout the chapter with the verb *tenere* in the passive voice, which I have translated in

383 Gilbert, "The Archbishop on the Painters of Florence, 1450."

384 Antoninus, *Summa*, 3.8.4, section 7.2, 8.1, 8.2, 10.1, 11.2.

385 Ibid., section 3.5.

386 Romans 1:32: "Who, having known the justice of God, did not understand that they who do such things, are worthy of death; and not only they that do them, but they also that consent to them that do them."

387 C. 2 q. 1 c. 10 (*Notum sit*): "Do not in any way allow anyone, by any sort of temerity, to hold in contempt canonical institutes, because an equal penalty binds the one who commits a deed and the one who consents to it." See Antoninus, *Summa*, 3.8.4, section 3.5.

388 C. 11 q. 3 c. 100 (*Qui consentit*); *Glossa ordinaria*, ibid., s.v. *consentit*. See Antoninus, *Summa*, 3.8.4, section 2.2.

389 On this point, see especially Antoninus, *Summa*, 3.8.4, section 2.3.

390 See above, ch. 3.

391 "Justice not only commands that one pay or give back what is due in voluntary transactions, but also that one repair injury which one has caused in involuntary transactions ... Restitution is the act by which one places another in renewed possession or ownership or chance of ownership of that which is owed to him because it is his by reason of a strict right *in re* or *ad*

various ways as the syntax requires: "a person deceiving another *is bound* to make satisfaction to the injured party," "otherwise *they owe* their employers," "they *are obliged* to the injured party for all losses," etc.[392] The stakes, of course, are the highest, since unrepented mortal sin will condemn the soul eternally, and repentance in the confessional requires a firm intention of making amends by restoring what one has unjustly taken.[393]

While the example of restitution shows Antoninus applying a rigid rule, a certain equity is also evident in his willingness to admit accommodations to people's practical needs. The two examples I would like to note here are Antoninus's approach to the observance of feast days and his application of the prohibition on usury.

On feast days: in this chapter Antoninus comments with some frequency on the violation of the due circumstance of time, through work being done on feast days. The Church's legislation required ceasing from labour – normally understood to mean servile, manual, or remunerative labour – from the evening of the vigil, i.e., the day before, to the evening of the feast day itself. However, Antoninus makes three qualifications in the interest of peoples' practical needs. First, he says that if people work on a feast day because they are unable to provide for themselves sufficiently otherwise or because they would suffer great detriment if they did not, this can be excused.[394] Second, some crafts need to be available to serve people even on feast days, such as apothecaries and others who provide medicinal things: "cities that are well administered are accustomed to provide that some of these should keep their shops open, say, one per quarter and so forth."[395] Third and most interesting is Antoninus's discussion of apothecaries and barber-surgeons

rem; in other words, it restores the equality that existed before an injury was done to the goods of another. Thus, restitution is not due for violation of virtues other than justice, because these virtues are not concerned with strict obligations and rights." McHugh and Callan, *Moral Theology*, §. 1751–3 (2:66–7). See also Noonan, *Scholastic Analysis of Usury*, 30–1.

392 Antoninus, *Summa*, 3.8.4, section 1.1, 3.9, 7.1.

393 A summary of this doctrine: "The obligation of restitution. The obligation is both of natural and divine law. Reason itself dictates that everyone should receive his due, and revelation expressly commands restitution, as when it declares that he who has injured his neighbor's field or vineyard must restore according to the damage done (Exod., xxii. 5). The obligation is both of means and of precept, for without restitution the offender does not obtain pardon from God (Ezech., xxxiii. 13 sqq.; Tob., ii. 20 sqq.). Hence, one who has seriously injured his neighbor cannot be saved unless he actually makes restitution, if he is able, or intends to make restitution when possible, if here and now he is not able to do so ... As to absolution, the penitent lacks true contrition if he is under a serious obligation to make restitution and is wilfully opposed to the performance of this duty at all or at the proper time. Such a one may not be absolved." McHugh and Callan, *Moral Theology*, §. 1759–60 (2:70–1).

394 Antoninus, *Summa*, 3.8.4, section 3.9, 4, 4.4, 6.2, 9.2, 9.3, 12.4.

395 Ibid., section 9.

working on the sabbath.[396] He points out that although the Church's legislation would permit people to resume working on the evening of the feast day, commonly people do not in fact start working again before the middle of the night; "and thus it seems that this compensation may be admitted in the evening of the vigil alongside the evening of the festival." In other words, Antoninus supposes that it would be legitimate to allow people to work until the middle of the night on the vigil, provided that they will also abstain from work until the middle of the next night; the safest and most equitable way to bring this about would be for local officials to embody this in a law recognizing the existing custom, and establishing a definite start and end time for feasts with a penalty for violation. This way, people in the business could observe the Church's law without losing the "concourse of persons" to their competitors who kept their shops open until the middle of the night on the vigil; "and in observing it, no prejudice would come to any of them."

On the usury prohibition: Antoninus, as we have seen already, stands by the Church's traditional prohibition on usury, and takes up the standard scholastic framework in which usury is fundamentally when "more is taken than given" in a loan. Since usury is a violation of justice, all usurious profits must be returned to the borrower who paid them, as an essential component of the usurer's repentance. Moreover, Antoninus cites several decretals which enact a penalty of excommunication for those who compel borrowers to pay usury, protect usurers by preventing borrowers from suing to recover the usuries they have paid, or block the Church from hearing usury cases in ecclesiastical courts.[397] All this represents a firm application of the usury doctrine. However, in certain cases where the presence of usury is doubtful, or an argument can be made in defence of the lender, Antoninus is disposed to adopt a charitable interpretation. Two examples stand out. The first is in relation to credits in the *monte comune*; Antoninus's approach has already been mentioned above, and it is the same here.[398] The second is in relation to the practice, very common in the wool and silk industries, of selling on credit.[399] "Now this is commonly observed," Antoninus says, "that someone selling wool or cloth sells it for more when selling on credit than when selling for money counted out to him right then (or "for cash"[400] in the vernacular), at a rate of 10 per cent."[401] Following the rulings of the decretals *Consuluit* and *In civitate*,[402] this practice would be usury if the merchant sells for more

396 Ibid., section 9.3.
397 Ibid., section 3.8.
398 Ibid., section 2.2.
399 Ibid., section 3.1–3.3, 5.4.
400 "Contanti, a; for cash." Edler, *Terms of Business*, 86.
401 Antoninus, *Summa*, 3.8.4, section 3.1.
402 *X* 5.19.10 (*Consuluit*); *X* 5.19.6 (*In civitate*).

than the just price merely because of a time delay. However, "it is necessary to observe what is judged to be the just price."[403] Antoninus takes up this question in the next section. His overall argument in section 3.2, "On Moderate Profit," is that the customary higher price in credit sales, of 10 per cent or thereabouts, is within the bounds of the just price. For the just price is not fixed at one precise unchanging point, "but has a latitude within a range of values."[404] Antoninus lays out three further practical considerations. The cash price, e.g., of 45 for a unit of finished wool, can be regarded as a discounted price, which merchants are induced to accept because of their need for cash on hand to pay their employees; "for if a wool merchant wanted to sell his cloth on credit at the price at which he sells for cash, at the end of the year he would find himself in his capital and he would have put his labour out for others in vain, as they say, or he would obtain an extremely minute and unsuitable profit, and this not only one time or in one year but practically always." Selling on credit is a kind of favour to the buyer, since it departs from the common principle of sale "that the price should be received when the goods are delivered," and it occasions much inconvenience and trouble for the sellers while they await payment, including the cost of employing people to try to collect these debts; "and often enough the purchasers do not pay on time … and sometimes the purchasers default and do not pay at all." The higher price of 50 in credit sales, viewed in this light, is a kind of compensation for the inconveniences and risks which the seller suffers in extending this favour to the buyer. Finally, Antoninus addresses the crucial point of intention: a key criterion of usury.[405] If a merchant could make a suitable profit by selling wool for 45 florins cash, but would rather sell on credit because this will yield greater profits (*ubi superlucrabitur*), he could "hardly be excused from usury."[406] But Antoninus observes that the merchants themselves say that they

> would sell their cloth much more willingly at a price of 45 or 46 for cash if they could sell all of it or the greater part in this way, than for 50 on credit, because then with the money in hand they would be quick to reinvest it regularly throughout the year in making cloth, and the difference in price they receive by selling however much cloth for cash rather than on credit would be made up for by the increased amount of cloth manufactured, because they would make 100 cloths where they make 50 for lack of the money which they are stuck waiting for on a term of credit.[407]

403 Antoninus, *Summa*, 3.8.4, section 3.1.

404 Ibid., section 3.2. Cfr Iohannes Duns Scotus, *In quartum*, d. 15 q. 2 n. 15 (18:283b); Bernardinus Senensis, *De evangelio aeterno*, 35, 1, 2 (4:191–2).

405 See Noonan, *Scholastic Analysis of Usury*, 32–6.

406 Antoninus, *Summa*, 3.8.4, section 3.3.

407 Ibid., section 3.2.

"All these put together, even if no one of them in and of itself, seem to render tolerable this mode of selling on credit."[408]

In my opinion, this discussion of credit sales shows Antoninus at his best and most characteristic. Rather than a formalistic or teleological analysis of contracts,[409] it represents an effective application of the casuistic method to a "case of conscience" in the realm of business ethics: analysing the details of the situation and the practical economic considerations which ordinary people have to juggle in their trade. He concludes that the customary method in the wool industry of selling on credit seems tolerable, and the same norms apply to sales on credit in other industries such as silk.[410] He adds, however, a pastoral note, warning that the subject is extremely involved and not fully clear, and "people who carry out this sort of trade sometimes deceive even themselves, concealing their intention."[411]

The final underlying principle which is worthy of note is made explicit at the end of this chapter. The clergy have the duty of teaching their flock and leading them off of the "wide way of the vices"[412] through preaching, the confessional ministry, and private warnings. Although throughout this chapter Antoninus speaks of the duties incumbent upon people who practise these crafts, in the final paragraph he returns to the duties of pastors. Speaking about farmers, Antoninus concludes: "this is what helps them to be led to perdition through the wide way of the vices: the ignorance and negligence of their pastors with bad conscience," "not caring for the sheep committed to them but for their wool …"[413] With these appropriate final words of 3.8.4 in mind, we shall now turn to the purpose of Antoninus's teaching in these chapters.

7. Purpose: Preaching, Hearing Confessions, and Consulting in the Court of Souls

The last matter to be dealt with in this introduction to Antoninus's teaching on trade, merchants, and workers is its intended purpose. The author himself made it clear in the preamble to the first part what overall purpose he had in view for his *Summa*:

> But drawn by the hunger and sweetness of truth, especially of moral wisdom, I have collected a few things which appealed to me from what it occurred to me to read.

408 Ibid. Although this sentence comes in the middle of the paragraph in my edition, it concludes an addition by Antoninus written in the lower and upper margins of this folio (M_2 fol. 74v), and thus was probably written last. It seems to represent his concluding thought on the matter.

409 On Aristotle's teleological argument against usury, and Thomas Aquinas's formalistic one, see Noonan, *Scholastic Analysis of Usury*, 52.

410 Antoninus, *Summa*, 3.8.4, section 5.4.

411 Ibid., section 3.3.

412 Ibid., section 12.4; cfr Matthew 7:13.

413 Ibid., section 12.4.

> For neither does the ant gather all the food that she finds, nor the more precious, but rather what she knows is suited to her. Therefore the sublime theories enclosed in libraries I have left to the masters and those accomplished in learning. But what I have judged apt as material for preaching, for hearing confessions, and for consulting in the court of souls, I took up from many doctors in theology or experts in law; not intending to compose elegant verses, since I am unschooled and ignorant of every science, but to make a collection in the tradition of the friars, for me and for my confrères who were with me, whose disposition does not soar to higher things ...[414]

Antoninus's stated purpose for compiling the *Summa* as a whole, then, is to provide material apt "for preaching, for hearing confessions, and for consulting in the court of souls," that is, for resolving difficult moral dilemmas. We can now proceed to examine how this purpose applies to the teaching contained in these six chapters, 2.1.16–17 and 3.8.1–4.

It is helpful at this point to bring in another distinction sometimes employed in more modern moral theology. This distinction is quoted from two Dominican moral theologians of the first half of the twentieth century, the Revs McHugh and Callan, OP, in *Moral Theology: A Complete Course*. They describe three methods which are used in moral theology:

> (a) The *positive* method is a simple statement of moral principles and doctrines, with little attention to argument, except such as is found in the positive sources (e.g., Scripture, tradition, the decisions of the Church).
> (b) The *Scholastic* method is a scientific statement of moral teaching through accurate definition of terms, systematic coordination of parts, strict argumentation and defense, attention to controversies, and recourse to philosophy and other natural knowledge.
> (c) The *casuistic* method, or case-system, is the application of moral principles to the solution of concrete problems of lawfulness or unlawfulness.
>
> The *Scholastic* method is the one best suited for the study of Moral Theology, because it is more scientific, and fits one better to understand, retain, and apply what one learns. But it is not exclusive of the other methods, since

---

414 "Auiditate tamen et suauitate tractus ueritatis, precipue moralis sapientie, ex his que mihi occurrerunt legenda, pauca recollegi mihi grata. Neque enim formica omnia inuenta cibaria colligit nec pretiosiora, sed que nouit sibi congrua. Illas igitur sublimes theorias in librariis comprehensas, magistris et scientia perfectis dimisi. Que autem iudicaui apta ad materias predicationum, et audientiam confessionum, et consultationem in foro animarum, accepi a doctoribus pluribus in theologia uel iure peritis; non intendens indoctus et omnis scientie ignarus poemata condere, sed recollectionem facere more fratrum, pro me et meis similibus qui mecum erant, quibus nec ingenium eminet ad altiora, ..." Antoninus, *Summa*, 1 *prohemium* (*N* fol. 3v–4r, hand G). For the full passage see above, ch. 2.

> it perfects the *positive* method, and is the groundwork for the *case* method. Each method has a special suitability for certain ends. Thus: (a) the positive method is well adapted to preaching, and hence was much in favor with the Fathers of the Church, as can be seen from their moral homilies and treatises; (b) the Scholastic method is the best for study, teaching, apologetic, and was followed by the great classical works of theology in the Middle Ages and later; (c) the case method is very helpful to the seminarian and the priest in the exercise of the ministry of the confessional.[415]

This provides some markers to look for as evidence of Antoninus's intention in his teaching. Does he tend to favour the scholastic method in these chapters, or the positive, or the casuistic? Antoninus does to some extent make use of all three. Predominantly, however, Antoninus employs a combination of the positive and the casuistic methods.

Taking the latter first: the clearest examples of the casuistic method are the whole of 3.8.4, *On the Various Kinds of Workers*, and the latter sections of 2.1.16 dealing with questions about the just price. Moreover, the discussions of contracts in 3.8.2 and exchange banking in 3.8.3 correspond to a very "casuistic" episode in Antoninus's life recounted by Vespasiano da Bisticci:

> People came to consult him about contracts, as to whether they were lawful or not ... when he had heard all, he decided at once which contracts were lawful.[416]

This is a clear example of material oriented towards "consulting in the court of souls" and resolving "concrete problems of lawfulness or unlawfulness." The case is similar for Antoninus's discussions in 2.1.16 about the obligation of restitution of goods acquired unjustly. This matter is of great practical importance for hearing confessions, since the confessor must decide whether to grant the penitent absolution or not; if the penitent intends to retain goods which in justice belong to another, then he lacks the purpose of amendment which is a necessary element for a valid confession. It is crucial for the confessor, then, to know how to correctly

415 McHugh and Callan, *Moral Theology*, introduction, nn. 13–14. Cfr Prümmer, *Handbook of Moral Theology*, introduction (1): "Three methods are used in this science: 1. The *scholastic or speculative* method, which considers carefully the various moral truths, proving and defending them against their adversaries but without ignoring completely their practical applications; 2. the *casuistic* method, which is chiefly concerned with passing judgement on individual moral cases; 3. the *ascetical* method, which has for its chief subject the practice of the virtues as the means of achieving Christian perfection. The best method is one which makes use of all three without sacrificing either clarity or brevity."

416 *Vespasiano Memoirs*, trans. George and Waters, 159; Vespasiano, "Arcivescovo Antonino," para. 5 (1:178).

distinguish between cases in which a penitent is strictly obliged to restitution and cases in which he is not, even if it is encouraged as part of penance and satisfaction. Hence, it is consistent with the purpose of providing material helpful for hearing confessions that Antoninus takes care to distinguish between these situations in 2.1.16.

The method most used by Antoninus in the other chapters is the positive one, which McHugh and Callan say was in favour with the fathers of the Church in their moral homilies and treatises. This is the dominant method in 3.8.1, 2.1.16, and 2.1.17. It is fitting that McHugh and Callan distinguish the positive method as "well adapted to preaching," because Antoninus arranges the material of these chapters "for preaching," *per modum predicationis*. Although the casual reader might overlook it, it is undeniable that these chapters are designed for use in sermons: Antoninus arranges both of them according to the standard scholastic schema of the *sermo modernus*. As noted above, this is evident in his use of a *thema* and his practice of dividing the *thema* in parallel rhyming sentences: all hallmarks of the scholastic sermon form.[417] His favoured authorities also fit McHugh and Callan's description of the positive method: he quotes the Scriptures far more often than any other source, and also makes extensive use of "tradition," i.e., patristic texts, and "decisions of the Church" as contained in the *Decretum* and the other canon-law compilations. His attentive reading of the sermons of St Bernardino of Siena, a renowned preacher, and his occasional borrowing of large extracts from these sermons, likewise show his focus on preaching.

The purpose of these chapters can be illuminated also by contrast with works exemplifying the "scholastic or speculative" method as applied to moral questions. This method, according to McHugh and Callan, is specially suitable for study, teaching, and apologetic; in the context of the late Middle Ages, one would expect the ideal milieu for such texts to be the university, in the faculties of arts, theology, or law. A brief comparison of some examples of such texts is sufficient to illustrate the marked contrast with Antoninus's method. Here is a very brief list of scholastic texts of diverse genres, products of all three university faculties, occupied with some of the same questions which Antoninus treats in these chapters.

a. Thomas Aquinas, OP, *Summa theologiae, secunda secundae*, especially q. 77. Genre: theological *summa*, introductory textbook. Setting: University of Paris, Faculty of Theology; various Dominican *studia*.

417 "The difference between the two techniques, as Waleys describes it, was this: the *modus antiquus* consisted in a complete verse-by-verse commentary on the Gospel reading of the day, while a modern sermon was based on the careful elaboration of a single selected *thema*, an individual line from Scripture, analogous to the *lemma* of biblical exegesis ... [The *thema*] should contain latent within it the whole sermon [the preacher] imagined, to be drawn out through a complex yet organic development." Mulchahey, *Dominican Education*, 402.

b. Peter John Olivi, OFM, *Tractatus de contractibus*, especially q. 1. Theologico-legal *tractatus*, quodlibetal question. University of Paris, Faculty of Theology; Franciscan *studia* in Provence.
c. John of Naples, OP, *Quodlibet* 4, especially q. 18. Quodlibetal question. University of Paris, Faculty of Theology; thereafter Dominican *studium* in Naples.
d. John Duns Scotus, OFM, *Quartus sententiarum (Oxoniensis)*, especially d. 15 q. 2. *Sentences* commentary. University of Oxford, Faculty of Theology; thereafter University of Paris and Cambridge and Franciscan *studia*.
e. John Buridan, *Quaestiones super decem libros Ethicorum Aristotelis*, especially book 5, c. 16. Philosophical commentary. University of Paris, Faculty of Arts.
f. Hostiensis, *Summa aurea*, especially 3.17. Legal *summa*. University of Bologna, Faculty of Law.
g. Panormitanus, *Commentaria in decretales*, especially on *X* 3.17. Legal commentary. University of Bologna, Faculty of Law; thereafter universities of Parma, Siena.

These texts, though they originate in different university faculties and represent distinct genres, all have certain features of the "scholastic or speculative method" in common. They are concerned with the systematic analysis of problems, with constructing a rational account of their solution, and with the defence of such solutions against possible objections. They tend to proceed argumentatively, frequently employing locutions such as *obiicitur* ("it is objected"), *aliqui dicunt* ("some say"), *sed contra* ("but on the other hand"), and *respondeo* ("I answer"). There is freedom, indeed sometimes exercised to excess, in coordinating apparently contradictory texts or premises, and in exploring the implications of one possible answer or another. Among the authorities cited, the Scriptures occupy a relatively minor place, or at least are no more prominent than philosophical and legal authorities, including non-Christian authors. It is not necessary to labour this point by mustering quotations from these texts or examining passages in detail, as was done in the previous chapter with Aquinas's *Summa* and a corpus of thirteenth-century legal commentaries. The interested or sceptical reader is free to consult some of these texts and compare their method with Antoninus's in, for example, 2.1.16 and 3.8.4.

In saying that Antoninus does not habitually use the scholastic or speculative method, there are some exceptions which can be cited. In 3.8.3 Antoninus engages with the arguments of learned doctors, principally jurists, about the liceity of exchange transactions; similarly in his chapter on the *monte* of Florence and other Italian cities (not edited here). The reason for the speculative procedure is the same in both cases: these transactions were subjects of controversy and enduring dispute among the doctors, and so Antoninus was obliged to rehearse the arguments and draw what seemed to him the best-justified conclusion – in both cases, following the lead of Lorenzo Ridolfi. The most interesting use of the speculative method is in 2.1.16's final sections, numbered in this edition 3.1.3.1–3, on "excess in valuation." Here, as noted above, Antoninus proceeds argumentatively.[418] His cited authorities are modern doctors in theology and law; apparently contradictory texts are brought together and harmony is produced through distinctions. The reason for the change of method is fairly clear: there was a degree of controversy among doctors and moralists about the moral and legal obligations which truly apply in each of the situations discussed. If one is concerned with delivering the right answer, or at least the best-grounded, and the matter is not a settled one where the authorities are in agreement, then it is necessary to rely on reason as expressed and tested through argument; honesty also demands acknowledging that one's own position is in opposition to others of high repute. Hence Antoninus's procedure is to raise the key objections, enumerate some of the chief interlocutors, state his own opinion, and provide some of the arguments in its favour or authors whom he is following. The most controversial and uncertain case would seem to be the one dealt with in 3.1.3.3, minor excess against the just price; and, at that place, he ceases to attempt to answer the objections in his own words, but transcribes several passages taken from a truly scholastic or speculative work, that of Peter John Olivi (via Bernardino). All of this serves to reinforce the contrast with Antoninus's predominant approach in 2.1.16, *per modum predicationis*, which fits the description of the "positive" method.

As to the intended audience for these chapters: initially, the foregoing discussion should suffice to clarify that the intended audience was not university students or teachers, and the work's intended use was not primarily in the classroom, as is the case for most or all of the contrasting exemplars of university texts. The intended audience would appear to be, primarily, Dominican preachers and confessors as well as other mendicants, and the clergy more generally, whether secular or religious, who carry the burden of pastoral care. Antoninus's characterization of those for whom he wrote confirms this: "for me and for my confrères who were with me, whose disposition does not soar to higher things." Another pair of facts support the conclusion.

First, the description of chapters 3.8.1, 2.1.16, and 2.1.17 as "arranged for preaching" should be qualified: they are not fully prepared sermon texts (i.e., model sermons), ready to be preached, but rather "sermon material" which would have to be adapted by

418 Some of his typically scholastic locutions: "nec obstat si dicatur," "respondeo," "secundum Hostiensem," "secundum Antonium de Butrio," "aliqui dicunt," "hanc oppinionem … reprobant beatus Tomas … et Schotus," "ad rationem … respondet beatus Tomas," "concordant Iohannes de Lignano et Iohannes Caldrinus," "quamvis quidam dicant … verius tamen videtur dicendum," "ad quod probandum inducunt triplicem rationem." Antoninus, *Summa*, 2.1.16, section 3.1.3.1–3.1.3.3.1.

the cleric to produce an actual preachable sermon. This would be straightforward, to be sure, since Antoninus has provided both a collection of scriptural *themata* suited to the material and examples of their division and development. It is clear, nevertheless, that the chapters are not complete sermons because of the absence of a standard element of the scholastic *sermo modernus*: the *captatio benevolentiae* and invocation of divine aid at the outset of the sermon. An illustrative contrast is ready to hand, from a surviving manuscript of Antoninus's sermon notes, which provides evidence (usually only in outline) about his actual preaching practice. For instance, in his sermon for Septuagesima Sunday (1427 or 1430), Antoninus concludes the opening paragraph with the expected invocation of divine aid: ... *propter gratiam acquirendam: quam ut impetremus, Virginem salutabimus*.[419] Most of Antoninus's sermons in this collection begin with a similar invocation of divine aid through the Virgin Mary.[420] However, neither 3.8.1 nor 2.1.16 and 2.1.17 contain such an invocation. Other common elements prescribed in scholastic sermon manuals are also absent.

Another argument against viewing Antoninus's chapters "arranged for preaching" as true model sermons is that Antoninus includes within these chapters occasional pastoral notes.[421] In 2.1.16 he makes several asides advising how best to preach on a given subject or what is required in the confessional; for example, in sections 2.3 and 2.4. Note also his words at the close of the final section: these theses "must be preached with great discretion, since the people are prone to loosening their consciences,"[422] "and therefore the safer things are the ones we must say."[423] Such asides address the clerical reader directly, and were meant to be grasped by the cleric and applied to his preaching and ministry; they show that the chapters were not meant to be simply read out verbatim by the preacher. Moreover, Antoninus warns the preacher that he must have a certain circumspection in what he openly discusses with or teaches to a lay audience, more than once noting the tendency of "the people" towards "loosening their consciences" and "abusing the truths they are told."[424] Such warnings preclude Antoninus's *Summa* being intended for general consumption by laity and clergy alike.

The intended audience for these chapters, then, was twofold. The proximate audience was the clergy, particularly the mendicant and secular clergy who had

419 Florence, BNC, Conv. soppr. A. 8. 1750, fol. 1r; quoted from Howard, *Creating Magnificence*, appendix 1, 115–16.

420 Their incipits and explicits are printed in Orlandi, *Bibliografia Antoniniana*, 106–40.

421 This is a direct parallel with the practice of the twentieth-century Jesuit moral theologian Henry Davis, SJ, in his *Moral and Pastoral Theology*.

422 Antoninus, *Summa*, 2.1.16, section 3.1.3.3.4, repeating Bernardinus Senensis, *De christiana religione*, 37, 2, 1 (*Opera omnia*, 1:470–2).

423 Antoninus, *Summa*, 2.1.16, section 3.1.3.3.4. These are Antoninus's own words.

424 Ibid., section 2.4.

pastoral care as a foremost duty. For these sorts of clergy, it provided a compendium of doctrine and practical advice to aid them in their ministry, especially the ministries of preaching, hearing confessions, and resolving doubtful moral questions. The remote audience was the Christian people generally, and especially those social classes and professions who habitually engaged in buying and selling as part of their business. Though Antoninus's teaching was surely intended to be applicable and useful in more or less any commercial town, the social classes with whom he would have been most familiar and experienced are those merchant entrepreneurs, bankers, artisans, shopkeepers, and workers who made up the main fabric of Florentine society, discussed above in the preamble.

As we saw in chapter 3, scholastic doctors in the university faculties of canon law and theology constructed a Christian ethical code for economic actors. Antoninus evidently considered it important that this ethical code not remain in the lecture chambers and debate halls of the universities, but that it reach the laypeople plying their trades in the markets, fairs, and ports of medieval cities. What he has done in writing chapters 2.1.16–17 and 3.8.1–4 in his *Summa* is act as intermediary for the propagating of scholastic economic ethics. He has taken the substance and reworked it into a form which will enable it to be put to use by the clergy in their duties as confessors, counsellors, and preachers. Indeed, discussing the importance of this ministry, Antoninus writes: "No fewer souls in modern times are drawn to God through confession when done diligently than through preaching, as experience teaches."[425]

This, I conclude, is the primary purpose of Antoninus's teaching on trade, merchants, and workers. Its purpose is to transmit the common doctrine of the best doctors on the liceity of commerce, the obligations of justice in business, and the particular obligation of observing equality of exchange in buying and selling; and to transmit this in a form that answers to the needs of the mendicants and the parochial clergy who carry the burden of pastoral care for their flock. Antoninus provides instruction on the application of this doctrine to the hearing of confessions and counselling of penitents with moral doubts; he argues for the best resolution of difficult and controversial questions; and, where possible, he arranges the material for preaching, so that it will be readily adapted to produce a preachable sermon.

Antoninus surely knew that businesspeople find it difficult in practice to resist all the temptations of fraud, usury, and excessive profits. This informs the rhetorical aspects of his writing. He constantly supports the bare teaching of what to do

425 "Non minus trahuntur anime ad Deum per confessionem quando diligenter fit quam per predicationem moderno tempori, ut experientia docet. Debet igitur non tardare quando vocatur ad huiusmodi." Antoninus, *Summa*, 3.17.5 (M_2 fol. 382v in the upper margin, hand A; 3.17.17 in Ballerini, 1:966).

or what not to do with passages from the Scriptures: texts suited to inspire the full range of interior responses, from fear of God's punishments, to reverence for God's commands and designs, to hope in God's promises. He uses images, like the image of a scammer's tongue as a razor, to make his points. As mentioned earlier, he warns clerics not to lay open the full extent of the grey area in which merchants might get away with pushing the ethical bounds, as this could be a source of temptation. This all underscores the pastoral orientation of Antoninus's teaching. His *Summa* may be counted as one of the more comprehensive and sophisticated contributions to medieval *pastoralia.*

That Antoninus did have the capacity to reach actual businesspeople in his own time is shown by two examples which I already discussed in the preamble of this chapter. Benedetto Cotrugli, the merchant writer, drew on Antoninus's chapters edited herein in his *Libro dell'arte di mercatura,* written only four years after Antoninus had finished writing the *Summa.* Tommaso Spinelli tried, only partially successfully, to follow the ethical code contained in Antoninus's teaching. Antoninus's goal was ultimately to teach, persuade, and fortify merchants and workers like these men, the men and women in Renaissance Florence, and all Christians in business, to keep God's commandments and to act morally in the market.

Hoc peccatum est grave quia est contra Deum, contra proximum, contra se ipsum.[426] Peccat avarus contra Deum in quantum propter bonum temporale divitiarum contempnit bonum ecternum … Item avarus peccat in proximum, cum scilicet plus debito accipit et conservat peccunias et bona alia temporalia in dampnum et nocumentum proximorum. Cum enim bona temporalia non possint simul presideri[427] a multis, non potest unus homo in bonis temporalibus superhabundare nisi alteri deficiat, et sic avaritia est directe contra proximum … Tertio peccat avarus in se ipsum quia per hoc deordinatur affectus eius. Licet non deordinetur corpus sicut per vitia carnalia, substinet etiam corpus multa incommoda contra rationem … Est autem avaritia mortale tripliciter, et tunc gravat et deicit ad infernum: primo ratione equitatis quam offendit, secundo ratione charitatis quam excludit, tertio ratione finis quem pervertit.[428]

This is a grave sin because it is against God, against neighbour, and against self. The avaricious one sins against God in as much as for the temporal good of riches he despises the eternal good. The avaricious one also sins against neighbour, namely

426 In the left margin (*M_1* fol. 97v, hand A): "secundum Thomam, 2a 2ae q. 118 a. 1; ad Ephe. 5."
427 Ballerini prints *possideri* (2:11c).
428 Antoninus, *Summa,* 2.1.1 ([*De avaritia*] *per modum predicationis*) (*M_1* fol. 97v, hand A).

when he takes more than he is due and hoards money and other temporal goods to the injury and harm of his neighbours. For since temporal goods cannot be owned by many at the same time, one man cannot have superabundance of temporal goods unless another lacks them, and thus avarice is directly against neighbour. Third, the avaricious one sins against himself because through this his affection is disordered. Although the body is not disordered as it is through carnal vices, nevertheless the body sustains many inconveniences contrary to reason. Avarice, then, is a mortal sin in three ways, and moreover oppresses and throws into hell: first because of the equity which it offends, second because of the charity which it excludes, third because of the end which it perverts.

PART TWO

Latin Text and English Translation

Introduction to the Edition

Textual Witnesses

Autograph Manuscripts

N Florence, Biblioteca Santa Maria Novella, I.B.54 (Antoninus, *Summa*, part 1)
M_1 Florence, Museo di San Marco, Inventario n. 504 (Antoninus, *Summa*, part 2)
M_2 Florence, Museo di San Marco, Inventario n. 505 (Antoninus, *Summa*, part 3 vol. 1)
M_3 Florence, Museo di San Marco, Inventario n. 506 (Antoninus, *Summa*, part 3 vol. 2)
M_4 Florence, Museo di San Marco, Inventario n. 503 (Antoninus, *Summa*, part 4)

Apograph Manuscripts

F_1 Florence, BNC, Conv. soppr. A. 4. 2555 striscia 78 (Antoninus, *Summa*, part 1)
F_2 Florence, BNC, Conv. soppr. A. 4. 2555 striscia 79 (Antoninus, *Summa*, part 2)
F_3 Florence, BNC, Conv. soppr. A. 4. 2555 striscia 80 (Antoninus, *Summa*, part 3)

Notes on the Manuscripts

The autographic status of the manuscripts which I have designated *N* M_1 M_2 M_3 M_4 was demonstrated above in chapter 2. Full codicological descriptions of them are provided in the next section. First, a note on other manuscripts of the *Summa*. About fifty-four manuscripts of the *Summa* (each manuscript typically a single part) were described by Orlandi in 1961; some additions to this list have been made by subsequent research.[1] Only one set of apograph volumes have been consulted in preparing this edition, designated herein F_1 F_2 F_3. They form a set and

1 Orlandi, *Bibliografia antoniniana*, 25–64; Kaeppeli and Panella, *SOPMA*, 1:80, 4:28; Lapidge et al., *CALMA*, Antoni 1.18.

can be described together. These volumes belonged to the Badia Fiorentina (the Benedictine abbey of Beata Maria Virginis): each volume is marked as owned by *Abbatiae Florentiae*.[2] The colophon of part 1: *Explicit prima pars fratris Antoni* (sic) *archiepiscopi Florentini scripta per me Lottum [de Bancosis] indignum presbiterum. Explevique eam hac die XIII mensis Maii, anno vero M°CCCC°LXXIII. Ex quo gratias refero Christo. Amen*.[3] These are large and exceptionally beautiful volumes, *libri pulchrissimi*, bound in leather with metal clasps. The writing surface is parchment, very white and strong. The text is written in two columns. Black ink is used to write the text, with red and blue highlights, paragraph marks, initial letters, and pen work throughout; purple and orange are sometimes used as well. The first folio of each volume bears a historiated initial enclosing an image of St Antoninus: F_1 (striscia 78) shows Antoninus in his Dominican habit standing below Jesus crucified, with a gold background; F_2 (striscia 79) shows Antoninus in profile wearing the bishop's mitre, holding a maroon book which bears a more than passing resemblance to the autograph volumes of the *Summa* (blue background); F_3 (striscia 80) has the largest and most attractive historiated initial, with a portrait of St Antoninus seen from the front, on a blue background, with his face in half-profile, wearing episcopal garb over his Dominican habit, holding a crozier in his right hand and a green book in his left, with marks of the stigmata showing on his hands. The script and hand vary, with the script typically either gothic *textualis* or humanistic. Each volume contains marginal notes at certain chapters, but a large portion of the folios remain free of marginal annotations. Full description of these manuscripts can be found in Orlandi, *Bibliografia antoniniana*.

Codicological Descriptions

General codicological descriptions of the five autograph volumes are now provided. For the demonstration that they are indeed Antoninus's own autographs, see above in chapter 2, where the hand of Giuliano Lapaccini is also identified. Under the manuscripts M_1 and M_2 are also included detailed descriptions of the quires which contain the chapters edited below.

The volumes are alike in size, appearance, and overall codicological character. They measure about 225 x 150 mm (9 inches by 6). They are bound in wooden boards covered with red velvet. The main distinction in outward appearance is in the binding: *N* is decorated more ornately than the rest; M_1 and M_2 the most simply, in plain red velvet; the velvet covers of M_3 and M_4 have a pattern themed on the lily of Florence, with a decorative thread border, and are in slightly poorer

2 F_1 fol. Ir.
Iste liber est abbatie Florentine. F_2 fol. 1r. An identical note is on F_3 fol. 1r.
3 F_1 fol. 219v; quoted in Orlandi, *Bibliografia antoniniana*, 44.

condition. Each volume consists of between about 290 and 430 folios, assembled from booklets which Antoninus called *quaterni* (quaternions, quires), although the number of folios in each is irregular, usually between 10 and 20.[4] The quires' leaves are paper, but frequently their inner and outer bifolia are parchment. The text is written in a single column throughout, generally without ruling, by a multitude of different hands but with a single hand, that of St Antoninus, predominating. The scripts' size and care of execution vary, as does the size of the text column. In a few places red highlighting and rubrication are used, but these are the exception. Divisions in the text are indicated by paragraph marks, sometimes written in the body, sometimes in the margin. There is space for an ornamental initial at the opening of most chapters, but the letters themselves are normally absent. The manuscripts abound with annotations, corrections, and deletions, sometimes filling the margins to the edge of the page. Each volume has modern folio numbers and sometimes also the remains of older numeration or even two older series; some but not all quires are numbered and provide catchwords. The occasional appearance of antique numeration, quire numbers, and catchwords reveals that the quires have been reordered one or more times before they received their current arrangement. Descriptions of the individual codices follow.[5]

N: *Florence, Biblioteca Santa Maria Novella, I.B.54*

Paper and parchment, 335 folios, 225 x 150 mm, *s.* XV^{mid}, Florence, Italy
Antoninus Florentinus, *Summa*, 1
2nd fol. inc. *Nullum habui in alia facultate*
Collation: iii + 1^{42} (attached initially: $1a^{7}$; attached finally: $1b^{1}$) + 2^{21} + 3^{22} + 4^{19} + 5^{14} + 6^{28} + 7^{32} + 8^{13} + 9^{14} + 10^{23} + 11^{23} + 12^{22} + 13^{21} + 14^{10} + 15^{3} + 16^{16} + 17^{7} + ii

This is a codex of 335 folios measuring approximately 225 mm x 150 mm, with a writing space that varies widely in size and nature through the different quires of the codex.[6] It is bound in a fifteenth- or sixteenth-century binding of wooden boards covered in red velvet. There are several layers of velvet wrapping the boards; the outermost layer forms a bag descending from the base of the codex, fringed with red and yellow strings which continue into a tail a little over a foot long. The

4 "¶ In isto quaterno est materia de rapina quintuplici et de talliis et prestantiis et de gabellis. Et de participatione in furtis et rapina. Item de furto et de fraudulentia VII modis." M_I fol. 57r, hand A.

"¶ In isto quaterno agitur de fraudulentia ¶ de falsificatione ¶ de iniustitia in iudiciis ¶ de acceptione personarum ¶ de sacrilegio." M_I fol. 71r, hand A.

5 Further description and commentary on these manuscripts can be found in Orlandi, *Bibliografia Antoniniana*, 25–40.

6 On this manuscript, see also Panella, "Catalogo," I.B.54 (179); Pomaro, "Censimento," 306–7.

Photo 4. F_3 fol. 1 (Antoninus, *Summa*, part 3): apograph manuscript (i.e., later non-autograph copy)

Photo 5. *N* (Antoninus, *Summa*, part 1): autograph manuscript

front cover is adorned with a metal decoration in the centre: a circle surrounded by a diamond, with intricate lace and leaf-shapes sprouting within and without. The back cover has one decorative metal guard on the bottom right corner, of similar pattern. Attached to the back cover, in its centre, is a large (three-inch) hexagonal portrait of St Antoninus in bishops' vestments, with a halo. The portrait is enclosed under a thick piece of crystal in a heavy metal frame. The placement of this portrait on the back cover indicates that, for reading, the volume would have been laid on its front cover and opened from the back. The binding of *N* is similar to the binding acquired by Br. Roberto Ubaldini for the Antoninus's bull

Photo 6. M_1 (Antoninus, *Summa*, part 2), M_2 (part 3, vol. 1), M_3 (part 3, vol. 2), M_4 (part 4): autograph manuscripts

of canonization in 1523.[7] On the spine are two raised bands, which, inside the volume, can be seen to be of white leather and attached to the cover with nails. Apart from these, there are no markings on the outer binding or spine. No pastedowns are present. There are three parchment flyleaves, marked in pencil by a modern hand as I, II, III. The first flyleaf is blank, except for a label in a modern hand, in blue pen: *Arch. S. M[e] N[e] / I. B. 54.*

The second and third flyleaves are a bifolium, with a note written on the inside (IIv–IIIr), by a large italic humanist hand in dark brown ink:

> Yhesus.
>
> Hec est prima pars Summe doctrinalis sancti Antonini archiepiscopi Florentini manu eius sanctissima scripta: que fuit bone memorie fratris Antonii Thome de Stiatentsibus eximi magistri in sacra theologia et filii conuentus sancte Marie Nouelle

7 "Fra Roberto Ubaldini spent forty-eight ducats on a copy of the Bull for San Marco, which he had encased in a book-like red velvet cover reinforced with silver filigree at the corners ... [The cover] was further adorned on the front and back with a niello medallion framed by an inscription and a decorative acanthus-leaf border." Cornelison, *Art and the Relic Cult*, 28.

qui obiit anno Domini 1480.[8] Et de ista Summe parte legitur in libro de miraculis operatis a sancto Antonino post mortem ipsius sic.

Magister Antonius de Stiattensibus theologus ordinis predicatorum excellentissimus sepe sepius dolore illiaco grauiter laborabat. Et imposita loco doloris prima parte Summe doctrinalis sancti Antonini manu sanctissima scripta, pro reliquiis ab eodem ex deuotione seruata, sanabatur semper. Testificatur hoc testis 40 primi fol. 134 frater Petrus Benedicti Angeli annorum 72 qui sciuit ab ipso magistro Antonio sanato a quo habuit cum magna commendatione originalem partem illam sancti uiri scriptam.

Deinde talis liber peruenit ad manus fratris Victori Mathei magistri et predicatoris deuotissimi. Qui librum dedit michi fratri Alexandro Petri de Capocchiis. Et ego anno dicto 1580 feci eum ornare ut seruetur in sacrario (pro) deuotione ad sanctum nostrum pissimum Antoninum.

Anno domini 1550 obiit frater Raphael Francisci de Monte Morello et michi fratri Alexandro Petri dedit cum magna deuotione tertiam partem Summe historialis sanctissimi Antonini manu eius scriptam. Quam partem dedi fratri Dionisio Iuntino sacriste ut eam ornaret et in sacrario poneret pro reliquiis anno Domini 1580 die 14 aprilis. Ad laudem et honorem Domini nostri Yhesu Christi et beate Virginis et sancti Antonini. Amen. Fr. Alexander manu propria.

Isti libri diligenter et reuerenter seruandi sunt non solum propter sanctitatem admirabilem uiri sed quia multa misteria in ipsis leguntur et pariter (quia) pro ipsis conficiendis plures uigilias et labores contemplationesque simul et orationes ipse sanctus operatus est.[9]

At the back of the volume are two flyleaves, labelled in pencil by a modern hand I', II'. The first is paper; the recto is blank, the verso has a faint remnant of the letters *dne q* in a textualis hand, and in blue ink a modern hand has written *Arch. S. M. M*[e] (sic) / *I. B. 54.* The second flyleaf is parchment, cut from a manuscript with a French text written in two columns by a gothic *textualis* hand with brown ink and red highlighting.[10] The flyleaf is a bifolium turned clockwise 90 degrees (thus four columns are visible) and cut down to fit in the codex.

The first seven folios of the codex were attached, by glue, to the front of the first true quire, which begins on fol. 8 and continues to 41 (fol. 8 and 41 are a bifolium); another leaf (fol. 42) was glued in at the end. The folios of *N* are marked with two number series, the older one at the top right of each folio, the modern at the foot. Both series appear (and agree) on fol. 1–2; on fol. 3–6 there is only

8 It appears that originally "1580" was written, then the "5" was scratched out and replaced with "4."

9 *N* fol. IIv–IIIr, hand of Alessandro Capocchi. On this Alessandro Capocchi, OP († 8 October 1581), see the references provided in Orlandi, *Bibliografia Antoniniana,* 25 n1, where this note is also transcribed.

10 Panella describes it as "frammenti omiletici in lingua d'oil." Panella, "Catalogo," I.B.54 (179).

the modern series; on fol. 7 the older series resumes, and from that point the two series are always in disagreement, though usually not distant. On fol. 1r there are two notes, one at the top, one at the bottom; in the middle of the page are some pen trials by an ornate *hybrida* hand. The upper note was written by Giuliano Lapaccini:

> Originalia prime partis Summe fratris Antonii de Florentia ordinis predicatorum archiepiscopi Florentini. (In) quibus agitur de anima et ad ipsam pertinentibus. Concessa ad usum fratris Iuliani de Lapaccinis de Florentia. Et signatur iste scartabellus D.

The lower note is by Dionysius Remedelli, collaborator in Mamachi's edition. It reads:

> Contulit diligentissime trium annorum spatio hoc sancti Antonini Autographon, et ad illius fidem edidit Florentiae notisque et obseruationibus illustrauit Primam Partem Summae Moralis eiusdem sancti Antonini, Frater Dionysius Remedelli Ragusinus, una cum F. Thoma Maria Mamachi Chio Ordinis Praedicatorum. Typis Petri Caietani Viuiani anno Christi 1741. A. 1742 F. Dionysius Remedelli manu propria.

Fol. 1v–2v are blank. On fol. 3r the *Summa* proper begins:

> Incipit prima pars Summe fratris Antonii de Florentia ordinis predicatorum et archiepiscopi Florentini. In qua agitur de anima et de pertinentibus ad ipsam. Incipit prohemium totius operis:
>
> Quam magnificata sunt opera tua domine.

From here, 3r to 7v, the text is written by Giuliano Lapaccini. The *prohemium* continues to 5r, where the *tabula capitulorum* commences: *Huius autem prime partis tituli sunt isti. Primus titulus de anima in comuni.* The *tabula capitulorum* terminates on 6v. On fol. 7 there are two unrelated sections of text, one on each face, each written by Giuliano Lapaccini and constituting parts of later chapters of this volume; the old number series marked this fol. 38, and the chapters are indicated as found on fol. 38 in the *tabula capitulorum*. The section on 7r incipit: *Una anima et unus intellectus*. This is a section of chapter 1.3.1 *de intellectu possibili et agente*. On 7v incipit: *Deinde uidendum est quomodo ipse intellectus*. This is the beginning of 1.3.2 *de multiplici oculo uarie exercendo*. This fol. 7, bearing the antique number 38, should fall in the modern sequence of folios between 41 and 42; it appears that it was written by Giuliano Lapaccini to replace a lost folio there written by the hand of St Antoninus. At the top of 42r is a note:

> Chartam 38 quae hic deest habes initio huius I. Partis post indicem capitulorum. Scribebam Fr. Dionysius Remedelli O.P. die 9 Nouembris anni 1740.

At the foot of fol. 42r is another note by the same hand:

> Quae hoc fol. 39 continentur et medio folio 38 quod prestat, ante iudicem, ut supra monui, non sunt exarata manu sancti Antonini. Ceterum haec eadem suprosunt (?) adhuc scripta manu sancti Praesulis et exstant in hoc ipso Volumine folio 61 ex altera parte.
> + Vide +

The true beginning of part 1's chapters is fol. 8r, written probably by the hand of St Antoninus. Text incipit (8r): *Venite audite et narrabo omnes qui timetis Deum.* The text of this manuscript is part 1 of the *Summa* of St Antoninus in its final stage of composition. The quires of the codex were originally discrete booklets which were assembled and bound together at a late stage of composition. In principle for each quire the outer and inner bifolia are parchment, the rest are paper; but some quires are paper all the way through, and for some the outer and inner bifolia are paper reinforced with parchment at the fold. See the overview of all five volumes, above, for general description of the mise-en-page. On the last written page, 325v, the final paragraph explicit: *Nam omnis uenialiter peccauerunt.* These are the final words of an addition which begins on fol. 324r, written by Giuliano Lapaccini, which is meant to be inserted in an earlier chapter. At the head of 324r is a note: *De conceptione Virginis Marie. Et debet poni supra ad cartam 186 in fine etc.* This ought to follow 191v in the modern foliation, on whose foot Giuliano Lapaccini wrote: *Hic deest unum capitulum uidelicet de conceptu Virginis per modum predicationis. Et incipit: Nondum erant etc. Quere infra ad cartam 317.* When the chapters are placed in their intended order, the true final chapter is 1.20.1 (*de regulis iuris*), in 101 sections, whose explicit (323v): *finalis efficiens et occasionalis tunc cessat constitutio.*

M_1: *Florence, Museo di San Marco, Inventario n. 504*

Paper and parchment, 431 folios, 225 x 150 mm, *s.* XV^{mid}, Florence, Italy
Antoninus Florentinus, *Summa*, 2
2nd fol. inc. *Luxuria per cecitatem Samsonis*
Collation: iii + 1^{8} + 2^{9} + 3^{13} + 4^{16} + 5^{8} + 6^{10} + 7^{14} + 8^{12} + 9^{6} + 10^{14} + 11^{14} + 12^{10} + 13^{12} + 14^{14} + 15^{16} + 16^{18} + 17^{18} + 18^{16} + 19^{14} + 20^{9} + 21^{18} + 22^{24} + 23^{26} + 24^{33} + 25^{12} + 26^{10} + 27^{16} + 28^{6} + 29^{22} + 30^{13} + iiii

This is a codex of 431 folios measuring approximately 225 mm x 150 mm, with a writing space that varies widely in size and nature through the different quires of the codex. It is bound in a fifteenth- or sixteenth-century binding of wooden boards covered in red velvet, with three raised bands. Inside the covers there are no pastedowns; three leather straps are visible. There are no markings on the outer binding or spine. Inside the front cover are two paper stickers: the first reads *N° 4.*, the second R. MUSEO DI S. MARCO | *Inventario 1918* | *N°. 504*. There are three parchment flyleaves. The first is blank, with four glued parchment tabs attaching it to the spine; these tabs are cut from an older manuscript, written in brown, blue, and red ink. The second and third flyleaves are a bifolium made out of a public instrument, the text of which is on the inside. The recto of the first of these leaves (i.e., flyleaf 2r) bears two notes. The first, in the hand of Giuliano Lapaccini:

> Originalia secunde partis Summe fratris Antonii de Florentia archiepiscopi Florentini. Quibus tractatur de uitiis in particulari. Et signatur hic scartabellus E. Concessus ad usum fratri Iuliano de Florentia qui dicitur de Lapaccinis.

The second, in a later hand:

> Pastor piissime Deus, gratia Spiritus Sancti corda nostra clementer illustrans quatinus beati Antonii gloriosi pontificis tui edita uitae (?) sancta cristiane religionis prosequi ualeamus; eiusque piis intercessionibus omnibus meritis terrenis despectis et amatis celestibus, ueniamus ad patriam claritatis eterne per Christum Iesum nostrum. Amen.

Immediately below, another note has been erased of about the same size and shape: most of the words are unreadable, but it is possible to discern *illustrans* on the first line, which suggests this may have been a first attempt of the previous note. On the verso (flyleaf 2v) Giuliano Lapaccini has written a short note followed by a description of the volume: *In principio huius secunde partis debet poni unus sermo qui est in fine de auaritia ante titulum de restitutione, et incipit: Filii hominum usquequo graui corde. Et habet ista pars duodecim titulos.* He then provides a list of the titles in this volume:

> Primus est de auaritia. 1.
> 2. De restitutione. 102.
> 3. De superbia. 127.
> 4. De inani gloria. 171.
> 5. De luxuria. 204.
> 6. De gula. 244.
> 7. De ira. 270.
> 8. De inuidia. 288.
> 9. De accidia. 310.
> 10. De iuramento et periurio. 345.
> 11. De voto et transgressione uoti. 360.
> 12. De infidelitate et superstitionibus. ~~366~~. 375.
> Quilibet titulus habet plura capitula de speciebus et filiabus illius uitii. Et quodlibet uitium habet unum sermonem predicabilem, et etiam quilibet titulus in genere.

The parchment of the public instrument folds out and the text can still be read on the recto of the second leaf (flyleaf 3r). A dating clause indicates the last day of December in 1445.[11] It was prepared for Giovanni Vaultier, rector of a benefice in the diocese of Constance:[12] *dominus Iohannes Vaultier Rector ... Constantiensis diocesis in utroque iure Bacalarius necnon litterarum Apostolicarum Abbreviator.*

The first folio (I, numbered 1*) is blank. The text of the prologue begins in a single column on IIr (numbered 2*). A note above the prologue on IIr reads: *Incipit prologus in secundam partem Summe fratris Antonii de Florentia ordinis predicatorum et archiepiscopi Florentini. In qua agitur de uitiis in particulari.* Prologue incipit: *Tu contribulasti capita draconum.* The prologue continues to the bottom of IVv, where the *tabula capitulorum* begins: *Incipiunt capitula. Et habet ista 2ª pars 12 titulos, et quilibet titulus habet multa capitula, et capitula paragraphos plures, etc.* The titles and chapters of the work are listed on Vr–VIIr. The prologue and *capitula* were all written by Giulano Lapaccini. After a blank leaf (VIII) the text begins.

The text of this manuscript is part 2 of the *Summa* of St Antoninus in its final stage of composition. Text incipit (1r): *De auaritia in genere per modum predicationis.* This, however, is properly the beginning of the second chapter (2.1.2). As indicated in Giuliano's flyleaf note quoted above, the intended first chapter is to be found further into the codex; its incipit (96r): *Ps. Filii hominum usquequo graui corde.* The quires of the codex were originally discrete booklets that were assembled and bound together at a late stage of composition. The folios are almost all paper, but in a few quires the outer or inner bifolia are parchment, and for some others the outer and inner bifolia are paper reinforced with parchment at the fold. See the overview of all five volumes, above, for general description of the mise-en-page. On the last written page, 423v, the final paragraph (explicit: *ex circumstantiis eius*) is marked for deletion (*uacat quia hoc supra in titulo de superbia*), with a marginal note attached: *hic pone capitulum de superstitione quod est supra.* Immediately above this is the text explicit (423v): *Et hoc ad uitandum maius scandalum persecutionis.* These are the final words of title 12 (*de infidelitate*) ch. 5 (*de apostasia multiplici*). When the chapters are placed in their intended order, this is not the last chapter of the second part but is followed by five more, the final chapter being 2.12.10 (*de fato*), whose explicit (406r): *que omnia falsa sunt.*

---

11 "A natiuitate eiusdem Domini millesimo quadringentesimo quadragesimo quinto, indictione octaua, die Decembris ultima." M_1 flyleaf 3r.

12 Orlandi, *Bibliografia Antoniniana*, 29.

M_1 *quires 7–8 (fol. 57–70, 71–82)*

Paper, 26 folios, 225 x 150 mm
Antoninus Florentinus, *Summa*, 2, chapters of title 1 *de auaritia*
Quire 7 inc. *Nolite sperare*
Quire 8 inc. *cum perpendit*

These are two quires of 14 folios and 12 folios measuring 225 mm x 150 mm, with a writing space generally in the range 160–180 mm height x 110–130 mm width, accompanied by numerous marginal annotations. The quires are paper throughout, with the outer and inner bifolia reinforced with parchment at the fold. The text of 2.1.12 (*de rapina per modum predicationis*) begins in a single column on 57r (inc. *Nolite sperare in iniquitate*) and the chapters continue in one column until part of the way through 2.1.21 (*de sacrilegio*) on 82v. One chapter included in the list of *capitula* at the beginning of the volume, 2.1.15 (*de multis speciebus seu modis furti*), was apparently written later and is found on fol. 381–2, 394–5, 409–11.

The main text is written in a single hand, that of St Antoninus; letter size and care of execution vary throughout. Ink is dark brown. Marginal annotations mostly appear to be the same hand, but a few have a different appearance, sometimes being written with another sort of ink or instrument; some are in pencil. Tie marks are frequently used and corrections are numerous. Divisions in the text are indicated by paragraph marks, sometimes written in the body, sometimes in the margin especially where marking larger textual units. Fol. 64r is blank. There is space for an ornamental initial at the opening of certain chapters, on fol. 59v, 62v, 64v, 66v, 73r, 74v, 79r, and 80v. There is no ruling of any sort, and consequently the size of writing and number of lines per page vary widely; nevertheless the lines of text are fairly straight and neat. The height and width of the text column vary according to the author's whim – on 68r, 72r, 76r–77v, 80v, and 81v the text fills nearly the whole height of the folio – and margins are sparse or full according to the number of annotations which the author saw fit to make. The quires are numbered with arabic numerals 5 and 6 dotted on either side, but now are properly quires 7 and 8 of the codex. There is a note above each quire number, written later but probably by the hand of the author. The note on 57r reads: ¶ *In isto quaterno est materia de rapina quintuplici et de talliis et prestantiis et de gabellis. Et de participatione in furtis et rapina. Item de furto et de fraudulentia VII modis.* The note on 71r reads: ¶ *In isto quaterno agitur de fraudulentia* ¶ *de falsificatione* ¶ *de iniustitia in iudiciis* ¶ *de acceptione personarum* ¶ *de sacrilegio.*

M_2*: Florence, Museo di San Marco, Inventario n. 505*

Paper and parchment, 406 folios, 225 x 150 mm, *s.* XV^{mid}, Florence, Italy
Antoninus Florentinus, *Summa*, 3, vol. 1 of 2

2nd fol. inc. *Quintus titulus de doctoribus et scolaribus*
Collation: ii + 1^{8} + 2^{20} + 3^{16} + 4^{20} + 5^{18} + 6^{6} + 7^{20} + 8^{16} + 9^{14} + 10^{23} (nested: $10a^{6}$) + 11^{23} + 12^{20} + 13^{20} + 14^{20} + 15^{15} + 16^{22} + 17^{18} + 18^{18} + 19^{24} (nested: $19a^{2}$) + 20^{16} + 21^{16} + 22^{16} + 23^{9} + i

This is a codex of 406 folios measuring approximately 225 mm x 150 mm, with a writing space that varies widely in size and nature through the different quires of the codex. It is bound in a fifteenth- or sixteenth-century binding of wooden boards covered in red velvet, with three raised bands. Inside the covers there are no pastedowns; three leather straps are visible. There are no markings on the outer binding or spine. Inside the front cover are two paper stickers; the first reads *Nº 5.*, the second R. MUSEO DI S. MARCO | *Inventario 1918* | *Nº. 505*. There are two flyleaves. The first flyleaf is parchment, blank, with four glued parchment tabs attaching it to the spine; these tabs are cut from an older manuscript, written in brown, blue, and red ink. The second flyleaf is paper and has been damaged, with about a quarter of it torn away at the far edge. The verso bears a note by Giuliano Lapaccini reading:

> (T)ertia pars Summe domini Antonii archiepiscopi Florentini assumpti ab ordine predicatorum. In qua agitur de statibus. Conuentus Sancti Marci de Florentia eiusdem (ordinis.) (C)oncessa ad usum fratri Iuliano de Lapaccinis de Florentia eiusdem ordinis predicatorum.[13]

The *tabula capitulorum*, written by Lapaccini, begins on the recto of fol. I (numbered 1*):

> Incipiunt rubrice titulorum et capitulorum omnium istius tertie partis. Primo ponitur quasi per modum sermonis materia istius tertie partis, id est de status multiplici acceptione. Et incipit: Astitit regina etc. 38.

The *tabula capitulorum* continues to VIIIr; it lists the chapters of the whole third part of the *Summa*, including those contained in the second physical volume (M_3). The prologue to the third part is not at the front of the volume, but begins on fol. 38r, in the hand of St Antoninus: *Astitit regina a dextris tuis* ... Above this is a headnote: *In nomine Yesu Christi*.

The text is the first half of part 3 of the *Summa* of St Antoninus in its final stage of composition. Text incipit (1r): ... *propter pecuniam contra iura*. This, however, is not the true beginning of the third part. The first sixteen folios (1r–16v) of this

13 Text in parentheses supplied from Orlandi, *Bibliografia Antoniniana*, 31; Orlandi may have viewed the manuscript before this folio was damaged.

volume do not appear to be part of the text proper. There is one discrete unit at 1r–7v, which appears to be a section taken from an older treatise or draft by St Antoninus with his own revisions and marginal annotations added. A headnote on 1r reads: *in quibus casibus sit restituendum*. On 8r a new mise-en-page begins. The text here appears to be a supplement meant to be inserted at a place in the preceding section; a note in the lower margin reads: *Istud §. totum qui incipit utrum usurario pone supra in §. qui incipit quantum ad quintum in isto e. c.° ante ¶ Hosti. in Summa*. This supplement continues to 9v. On 10r another new unit begins, with a changed mise-en-page and space for an initial letter: *Nunc de uoto uidendum est sic*. This new unit continues to 12v. On 13r the mise-en-page returns to that of 1r–7v, again appearing to represent a section of an older treatise or draft in the process of being worked over by St Antoninus. Two section headings are seen on 13r: *De transgressione uoti*, at the top of the text body, and at the middle, *De obligatione uoti*. The page 13r appears to have had a large block of text erased and overwritten by Antoninus himself, with parts of the original nevertheless retained. From 13v to 15v the text body is the original, with Antoninus's revisions and supplements in the margins. On 16r another new section begins: *Sciendum igitur quod matrimonium in lege ciuili*, in the hand of Antoninus. This continues to the very bottom of 16v.

The true text of the third part begins on 17r, incipit: *Relinquet homo patrem et matrem*. This incipit, however, replaced the original, which is still visible: *Post tractatum de singulis uitiis sequitur tertia pars de quibusdam statibus hominum*. This original incipit was written by a scribe, not St Antoninus, and scribes wrote the majority of the body text from this point up to 37v. Marginal revisions and annotations, often very substantial, have been added by St Antoninus in his own hand. The revised incipit on 17r was written by Antoninus. These folios are discussed above, in chapter 2, section 3.

The chapter which begins on 17r is, in the final intended sequence, chapter 2 of the first title. The chapters of this volume are indeed very much out of order: to find a desired location, the reader is obliged to consult the *tabula capitulorum* carefully to learn on what folios the required chapter is located. The quires of the codex were originally discrete booklets that were assembled and bound together at a late stage of composition. In principle for each quire the outer and inner bifolia are parchment, the rest are paper; but some quires are paper all the way through, and for some the outer and inner bifolia are paper reinforced with parchment at the fold. See the overview of all five volumes, above, for general description of the mise-en-page. The first chapter of the first title (*de statu coniugatorum*) begins on fol. 49v, incipit: *Beatus es et bene tibi erit*. On the last written page, 391v, the text explicit: *quod inde raro accidit*. This, however, does not appear to be one of the chapters of the third part: it is an unconnected fragment of text (incipit: *Queritur utrum utar corruptis ponderibus uel mensuris*), covering two-thirds of 391v, which is preceded by several blank folios (384v–391r). Working backwards, the next section of text has the appearance of another discrete fragment, beginning (384r): *Utrum aliquo modo liceat uendere tempus dic secundum Gerardum Obdonem*. The last section that appears truly to belong to the third part is a unit at fol. 382r–383v. The text begins on 382r (389 in the old numeration): *Dicto de potestate confessoris nunc uidendum est de scientia eius*. This is 3.17.4 (*de scientia quam debet habere confessor*). This section continues to 3.17.5, and the text ends on 383v with the explicit: *sequitur in ipsis et in populis*. At the foot of 383v there is a catchword: *de penitentia iniugenda*. These words lead into the following chapter, 3.17.6, which is taken up on fol. 400r in M_3 with the incipit: *De penitentia seu satisfactione iniungenda*.

M_2 *quires 5, 6, 8 (fol. 57–74, 75–80, 101–16)*

Paper and parchment, 40 folios, 225 x 150 mm
Antoninus Florentinus, *Summa*, 3, chapters of titles 1, 3, 8, 9, 10, 14, 15, 21
Quire 5 inc. *Casus autem in quibus*
Quire 6 inc. *Item cum quis*
Quire 8 inc. *Quia sententia appellationis*

These are three quires of 18, 6, and 16 folios measuring 225 mm x 150 mm, with a writing space generally in the range 160–80 mm height x 110–30 mm width, accompanied by numerous marginal annotations. The quires are paper throughout, except for quire 5's outer bifolium (fol. 57 and 74), which is parchment. The text is in a single column throughout. The quires contain a disorderly collection of chapters and additions to chapters from different sections of part 3 of the *Summa*: sections come from title 1 *de statu coniugatorum*, title 3 *de dominis temporalibus*, title 8 *de statu mercatorum et artificum*, title 9 *de statu iudicum secularium et ecclesiasticorum*, title 10 *de statu morientium*, title 14 *de septem sacramentis ecclesie et statu ministrantium et conferentium ea*, title 15 *de statu beneficiatorum*, and title 21 (20 in Ballerini's edition) *de statu episcoporum, archiepiscoporum, et patriarcharum*.

The main text was written by four or five different hands. The bulk of the work was written by the hand of St Antoninus; letter size and care of execution vary throughout. The hands are as follows: Antoninus from 57r; possible change of hand (*hybrida*) fol. 61v (compare body 63r with additions in lower margin); Antoninus resumes 63v; change of hand 66r (humanistic cursive); Antoninus resumes 68r and continues until 80v, the end of this quire. In the third quire we are discussing here, the hand is Antoninus at the outset on 101r; there is a change of hand 104r (humanistic); 105v is blank; Antoninus resumes 106r; change of hand 107r (*hybrida fere semitextualis*); Antoninus resumes 115r. Ink is dark brown. Marginal annotations mostly appear to be the hand of St Antoninus, but some other hands are present as well. Tie marks are frequently used and corrections are numerous. Divisions in the text are indicated by paragraph marks, sometimes written in the body, sometimes in the margin, especially where marking larger textual units. There is space for an ornamental initial at the opening of certain chapters, on fol. 58v, 59v, 62v, 63v, 64v, 66r, 69r, 80r, and 101r. There is no ruling of any sort, and consequently the size of writing and number of lines per page vary widely; nevertheless the lines of text are fairly straight and neat. The height and width of the text column vary according to the usage of the scribe or the whim of the author, and margins are sparse or full according to the number of annotations which the author saw fit to make. Two of the three quires are numbered with arabic numerals: in the lower margin of 57r is the number 18 and in the upper margin the letter "s"; this is now properly quire 5. Fol. 101r bears 22 in the lower and "y" in the upper margin, but is now quire 8. Fol. 75 (the beginning of quire 6) is unnumbered.

Up to three series of folio numbers remain in the upper right corners of the recto sides. The oldest series, like the text, is written in brown ink, probably by St Antoninus himself. This series runs through quire 5, marking these folios 305–22. The series is absent in quire 6. In quire 8, this series marks the folios 383–98. A second series, which may be by the same hand, appears on some folios of quire 5 and quire 8; this hand has either written over the original series or has struck them out and replaced them. On some folios of quire 5 this second series provides the same numeration as the current series. On quire 8, however, this series marks the folios 111–26. The most recent series, by a modern hand, was written in pencil, usually just below the older numbers, and is present on all folios of these quires; on quire 6, this is the only numeration.

There is a note in the upper margin of 57r, written later but probably by the hand of the author, which reads: *¶ Omnia que sequuntur in isto quaterno usque ad titulum de merchatoribus, qui incipit exibit homo, pertinent ad titulum primum de coniugatis et sunt additiones.* Chapters 1, 3, and 4 of title 8 *de statu mercatorum et artificum* are written continuously on fol. 69r–79v. An addition to title 14 c. 16 begins on 80r. Quire 7, fol. 81–100, contains text from titles 3, 4, 6, and 7 (out of order). In quire 8, on 101r, an addition to title 9 c. 14 begins. On 107r, title 3 c. 3 begins; c. 2 begins on 110r. Chapter 2 of title 8 *de statu mercatorum et artificum* (3.8.2 edited herein) is written on fol. 115v–116r. On 116v, the final page of this quire, there is an addition to title 10 c. 5. On 117r, the beginning of quire 9, a continuation of title 1 c. 23 begins.

M_3: *Florence, Museo di San Marco, Inventario n. 506*

Paper and parchment, 292 folios, 225 x 150 mm, *s.* XV^{mid}, Florence, Italy
Antoninus Florentinus, *Summa*, 3 vol. 2 of 2
2nd fol. inc. *Quia non reputat*
Collation: i + 1^{20} + 2^{20} + 3^{17} + 4^{19} + 5^{14} + 6^{18} + 7^{10} + 8^{8} + 9^{8} + 10^{4} + 11^{16} + 12^{16} + 13^{17} + 14^{16} + 15^{10} + 16^{13} + 17^{6} + 18^{24} + 19^{27} + 20^{10} + i

This is a codex of 292 folios measuring approximately 225 mm x 150 mm, with a writing space that varies widely in size and nature through the different quires of the codex. It is bound in a fifteenth- or sixteenth-century binding of wooden boards covered in red velvet decorated with the Florentine lily and a lace border. There are no markings on the spine. Inside the front cover there is a paper pastedown and one paper sticker, which reads R. MUSEO DI S. MARCO | *Inventario 1918* | *N°. 506*. Below the sticker the pastedown is stamped: *N° 6*. There is one flyleaf, paper, blank. After the flyleaf, looking at the first folio, the two leather straps of the binding are visible. At the back of the volume there is a final quire (20) of ten blank paper folios, followed by a final flyleaf, which is pasted to the cover. There is no table of contents or any introductory note; the text and folio numeration continue directly from the end of M_2. The text is the second half of part 3 of the *Summa* of St Antoninus in its final stage of composition. Text incipit (400r): *De penitentia seu satisfactione iniungena.* This is chapter 3.17.6. In the header there is a note, very faint now, which appears to read: *dimictatur spatium unius carte cum principio istius quaterni.*

The quires of the codex were originally discrete booklets which were assembled and bound together at a late stage of composition. In principle for each quire the outer and inner bifolia are parchment, the rest are paper; but some quires are paper all the way through, and for some the outer and inner bifolia are paper reinforced with parchment at the fold. See the overview of all five volumes, above, for general description of the mise-en-page. The text from fol. 400r to 444r was written entirely, or almost entirely, by St Antoninus. The first place where a different hand is clearly at work is the body of 444v, which also has marginal annotations by both Antoninus and another hand. From that point on, text written by Antoninus's hand alternates with blocks written by other scribes; annotations by the author are frequent, as well as by other hands. Beginning at 518r there is an extensive section written by Giuliano Lapaccini, introduced: *Incipit titulus de conciliis universalibus*. This ends on 537r. The *titulus de excommunicatione* (begins 538r) is written by other hands and with a different mise-en-page; this is discussed more fully in chapter 2, section 3. The title *de statu purgandorum in purgatorio* begins on 626r in the hand of St Antoninus; his hand writes the mainstay of the text up to the end on 681v. On the last written page, 681v, the text explicit: *quando nemo operari potest, scilicet meritorie. Io. 9.* These are the final words of 3.33.10. For St Antoninus's intended final chapter, 3.33.11, the reader is referred (in the table of contents in M_2) to chapter 3.2.1, which is in M_2, fol. 40r–46v.

M_4 : *Florence, Museo di San Marco, Inventario n. 503*

Paper and parchment, 291 folios, 225 x 150 mm, *s.* XV^{mid}, Florence, Italy
Antoninus Florentinus, *Summa*, 4
2nd fol. inc. *Timor mundanus est*
Collation: i + 1^{25} + 2^{44} (nested: $2a^{15}$) + 3^{12} + 4^{6} + 5^{4} + 6^{25} + 7^{28} + 8^{24} + 9^{32} + 10^{32} + 11^{32} (attached: $11a^{3}$) + 12^{10} + 13^{12} + iii

This is a codex of 291 folios measuring approximately 225 mm x 150 mm, with a writing space that varies widely in size and nature through the different quires of the codex. It is bound in a fifteenth- or sixteenth-century binding of wooden boards covered in red velvet decorated with the Florentine lily and a lace border. There are no markings on the spine. Inside the front cover there is a paper pastedown and one paper sticker, which reads R. MUSEO DI S. MARCO | *Inventario 1918* | *N°. 503*. Below the sticker the pastedown is stamped: *N° 3*. There is one flyleaf, paper, blank. This flyleaf has a watermark in the shape of a cross standing atop three circular stones piled in the shape of a pyramid.[14] It is not possible to see straps or the structure of the binding. At the back of the volume are three blank paper folios, followed by a final flyleaf, which is pasted to the back cover. On the verso of the penultimate flyleaf a note is written, in a probably early modern hand: *Iste liber est conuentus sancti Marci de Florentia quem scripsit dominus Antonius archiepiscopus Florentini ordinis predicatorum manu propria.*

This volume is incomplete: it contains only the second half of part 4 of the *Summa*. The whole first half of part 4 has become separated from the rest, and its location is now unknown. The quires of the codex were originally discrete booklets that were assembled and bound together at a late stage of composition. In principle for each quire the outer and inner bifolia are parchment, the rest are paper; but some quires are paper all the way through, and for some the outer and inner bifolia are paper reinforced with parchment at the fold. See the overview of all five volumes, above, for general description of the mise-en-page. In M_4 as it exists today, there is no table of contents or any introductory note. The recto of the first folio (1r) has suffered wear and is difficult to read. In the header there is a note, probably by a later hand, which reads: *prologus*. The text is not the first chapter of part 4, but rather is chapter 4.14.1. The first several lines set out the order of chapters in title 14 (*de dono timoris*) before the text proper begins. Text incipit (1r): *Timor Domini est donum Spirtus Sancti*. The first two words are almost entirely worn away; these are the opening words of this chapter in Ballerini's edition,[15] and the visible letters in M_4 confirm the reading. The chapters of title 14 follow on the next folios and continue until 69v. The folios show an old number series which was, presumably, the one used when the first and second half were still together. Folios now numbered 1–69 were then 432–504. The text in M_4 was largely written by the hand of St Antoninus, with additions by Giuliano Lapaccini; there are a few sections written by other hands.

---

14 A search for this watermark in Briquet, *Les filigranes, dictionnaire historique des marques du papier jusqu'en 1660*, was unsuccessful. Unhappily, I only noticed this watermark at the end of the hours permitted for studying the manuscripts at San Marco, and was unable to carry out a comprehensive search through M_4 and the other codices for additional watermarks.

15 Ballerini, 4:727.

The final folios, 283–8, contain plans of two sermons, written by the hand of Giuliano Lapaccini. It is not evident if these sermons are meant to be included in the text of part 4 or are separate items. The text explicit (388r): *et conclude totum etc.* The true final chapter of part 4, 4.16.1 (*de dono scientiae*), begins on 269r (505): *Notum fac mihi.* This continues to 277v (513), where the text explicit: *Sed finis sit huic 4*[e] *parti que est de uirtutibus et donis Spiritus Sancti.* On this folio (277v), Antoninus wrote the colophon:

> Et demum de scientia actum est. Cui additur magnum opus distinctum propter sui longitudinem in duo uolumina ... continens gesta ab initio mundi usque ad presens tempus, scilicet anni Domini ab incarnatione 1454 ...

Editorial Principles

This edition aims, for each chapter of the *Summa*, at reproducing the final recension of the text as the author intended it to stand. Since we possess the author's original autograph volumes of each part (except the first half of part 4, not relevant to this edition), the text of each chapter has been transcribed and edited from the autograph volume as if it were a *codex unicus*. There are, however, two qualifications to be made. First, the initial transcription was made with reference to the text printed in the editions of Ballerini and, for 2.1.16 and 2.1.17, of Mamachi. Ballerini's text was found to conform generally to the autograph at the chapter and paragraph levels, but it contains many changes at the sentence level, principally replacement or corruption of individual words and introduction of explanatory clauses or additional references into the text; moreover, Ballerini prints some passages which do not exist at all in the autograph manuscripts. Mamachi's text, on the other hand, which is limited to parts 1 and 2 of the *Summa*, is nearly faultless in its adherence to the autograph, with only the occasional misreading or typographical error introduced. (Note: I have not included a full collation of the text of the autograph against Ballerini and Mamachi; however, I have indicated a selection of the most substantial differences in the *apparatus criticus*.) The second qualification is that wherever the autograph is visually obscure or illegible, in addition to consulting Mamachi and Ballerini, I have consulted the apograph manuscript volumes which I designate F_1 F_2 F_3, held in Florence, written circa 1473. These manuscripts provided enough help to resolve the difficulties, though I have not always adopted their readings. The text of these manuscripts, from the samples I have taken, is mostly very close to that of the autographs; in addition, the disposition of the titles and chapters of part 3 mimics the organization of the autographs (with the exception of the chapter divisions in part 3, title 8), whereas the printed editions and (according to Orlandi) non-Florentine apographs have adopted a different scheme. This is intriguing evidence about the *Summa*'s textual tradition after it left the hands of the author; it would merit further investigation, but for the present has been left unexplored.

The orthography of the autograph manuscripts is generally followed, apart from obvious misspellings. There are many nonstandard usages in the autograph which have been retained: collapsed diphthong **e** for **ae** and **oe**, **ci** for **ti**, doubled letters such as **cc** for **c**, use of **n** for **m**, insertion of initial **h** before a vowel, substitution of **y** for **i**, and epenthetical **p** as in *condempnavit*. There are two exceptions where orthography has been standardized: the letter **j** (long-**i**) is always printed as **i**; minuscule **u** and **v** in the autograph are always printed as **u**, while majuscule **U** and **V** are always printed as **V**. For numbers, I have reproduced the autograph's usage of arabic or roman numerals, but have written out numbers in a few places where it is necessary for the comprehension of the text. The use of capital letters has been normalized. The autograph's punctuation has been taken as a guideline but not consistently followed; I have adapted the punctuation to be more comprehensible to the modern reader. Paragraph breaks generally follow the autograph, but are occasionally introduced for clarity. Abbreviations have been expanded, except for ambiguous citations of biblical and legal texts.

There are two *apparatus* on each page of the edition. The first is the *apparatus fontium*. Entries in the *apparatus fontium* provide the exact reference in modern format for sources cited within the text, as well as sources which are not explicitly mentioned but correspond closely to or are probable reference points for the text. Sources not explicitly cited within the text are preceded by *cfr*, *vide*, or, in the case of extensive near-verbatim transcription, by *textus ex*. Many texts of the Church Fathers are cited by Antoninus from Peter Lombard's *Sentences* or Gratian's *Decretum*; in such cases the original author is indicated, followed by the reference to the *Sentences* or *Decretum*. References to the Bible are included in the *apparatus fontium*; biblical quotations within the text are italicized when they are verbatim or nearly so. Latin abbreviations for books of the Holy Bible follow those employed in *The Holy Bible: Translated from the Latin Vulgate… [Douay-Rheims Version]*, Dumbarton Oaks Medieval Library. Citations to texts of the canon and civil laws follow the standard format in use among historical scholars: see above, Abbreviations, and for further explanation consult James A. Brundage, "The Romano-Canonical Citation System," appendix 1 in *Medieval Canon Law*, 190–205.[16] Abbreviated Latin forms for the names of medieval authors are expanded in the bibliography below. Abbreviated Latin titles for works of ancient and medieval

16 My treatment of legal citations is based on the norms laid out in Kuttner, "Notes on the Presentation of Text and Apparatus in Editing Works of the Decretists and Decretalists." To locate the legal texts cited by Antoninus, I have used the following indices: Ochoa and Diez, *Index canonum et legum totius Corporis iuris canonici et civilis*; Germovnik, *Indices ad Corpus Iuris Canonici*; Peters, "*Ius decretalium*."

literature are from the *Novum glossarium mediae latinitatis*, the *Thesaurus linguae latinae*, or have been created by employing the same principles. In addition to citing sources according to their internal divisions (e.g., part, question, article, chapter; sermon, article, chapter; etc.), wherever possible, the page, column, or folio number in the edition consulted has been provided within parentheses. The edition used can be found under the author's name in the bibliography below. However, page numbers are omitted for frequently used texts that have standard and accessible editions. To wit:

Biblia sacra: Latin text is from Weber's edition, *Biblia Sacra iuxta Vulgatam versionem*; English is from *Holy Bible: Douay-Rheims*. The *Glossa ordinaria* is quoted from *Bibliorum sacrorum glossa ordinaria* (Venice, 1603).

Corpus iuris canonici: Latin text is from Friedberg's edition; English translations of the *Decretum* are from Silano's translation (not yet published). The *Glossa ordinaria* is from the Roman edition, *Corpus iuris canonici cum glossis* (1582).

Corpus iuris civilis: Latin text is from the edition by Mommsen et al.; English translations of the *Digest* are from Watson's translation; English translations of the Code are from *Annotated Justinian Code* by Blume.

Petrus Lombardus, *Sententiae*: Latin text is from the 3rd ed. (Grottaferrata: Editiones Collegii S. Bonaventurae ad Claras Aquas, 1971–81); English translations are from Silano, *The Sentences*.

Thomas de Aquino: Latin text is quoted from the Leonine edition accessed online through *Corpus Thomisticum* or, for the *Summa theologiae* in Latin and English, through the website of the Dominican House of Studies.

One novelty in my edition is that I have included in the *apparatus fontium* excerpts from the sources which Antoninus cites.[17] This is meant to unburden the reader who wishes to understand the meaning of Antoninus's references, see how he makes use of sources, or discern if he is quoting from memory: rather than having to look up the text independently, the reader can find the relevant passage included in the *apparatus*. Whenever I have access to an English translation of the source, I have also included the passage in English in the footnotes to my translation.

The *apparatus criticus* indicates peculiarities of the autograph manuscripts: principally, these are deletions, corrections, and supralineal and marginal additions. It also indicates editorial interventions, which are few, wherever it has been necessary to emend the autograph's text on account of grammar or sense.[18]

17 This procedure was suggested by the example of Alexander Andrée's edition in *Christopherus Laurentii de Holmis*.

18 The principal abbreviations which I employ in the *apparatus criticus* are expanded below. For a fuller explanation of standard abbreviations used in critical editions, see Maurer, "Commonest Abbreviations, Signs, etc., Used in the Apparatus to a Classical Text."

I have added headings in the left margin which show the divisions and subdivisions of each chapter. These headings are not present in the autographs, with the exception of the heading "Exemplum" at one point in 3.8.1; however, the divisions which they represent are indicated within the text, and follow conventions of scholastic writing and preaching. Each chapter is preceded by a *summarium* which shows the overall structure of that chapter; as with the marginal headings, I have devised these for the utility of the reader.

Each chapter is introduced, at the head of its first page, by a rubric of one or two lines. These are supplied from the *tabula capitulorum* of the relevant volume, and the folio from which they are taken is indicated in the right margin. Folio numbers continue in the right margin, with the transition from one folio to the next indicated by | within the text.

The appendices provide some of the information contained in the edition in the form of summary tables. Appendix 1 provides summary tables of substantial additions made to the first recension of each chapter. The autograph of part 3 contains remnants of early drafts of chapters 3.8.1 and 3.8.2, on M_2 fol. 69r and fol. 114v–115r; transcriptions of these early drafts are also provided in appendix 1. For a discussion of what these folios reveal about the composition of 3.8.1, see above, chapter 2, section 3, as well as for a discussion of the first draft of 3.8.2. Appendix 2 provides a summary table of sources and parallel passages for 2.1.16. Appendix 3 is a supplement to chapter 2, providing a more thorough palaeographical description of the hand A's letter-forms, and visual tables showing its majuscules, arabic numerals, and abbreviations.

Note on the Translation

While the reader may require little explanation of the English translation, I should like to provide some account of what I tried to achieve with it. In doing so, the modicum of a "translation theory" to which I subscribe will become apparent. I have had three ideals in mind while translating Antoninus's Latin: fidelity to the author's thought, reflection of the author's style, and clarity of communication with the reader.

The first ideal is certainly the most difficult to achieve. It has entailed resisting the tendency to translate by reflex, and instead I have endeavoured in translating every sentence to attend not just to the words themselves but also to the context, trying to determine precisely what thought the author meant to convey. The greatest challenges in this text have been two: Antoninus's sometimes awkward or confusing syntax – I will comment more on this below – and his use of some obscure Latin vocabulary (often derived from then current Italian). Examples of obscure vocabulary are especially abundant in 3.8.4, where I have frequently provided footnotes citing the dictionaries which helped me determine the meaning.[19] Antoninus also uses some peculiar idioms to express certain ideas. I will only mention three examples here. Antoninus frequently uses the Latin verb *dare* (to give) to mean "to pay," as in paying wages, paying money to purchase a good, etc. This usage is frequent throughout the chapters, and I have accordingly translated *dare* as "to pay" in such contexts. In 3.8.3, and in a few other places, Antoninus uses the preposition *de* (of, from, about) governing a noun of money to mean "for." Thus *de* must be understood in the following sentence as meaning "for" and not "of" or "from" as one would typically expect: *hic tantum dat de bononenis quantum ualent Florentie, scilicet 24 denarios, et Bononie uel alibi tantum permutando cum alia moneta quantum ibi ualet, scilicet 26 denarios, accipit.*[20] Finally, Antoninus very commonly uses the verb *tenere* in the passive voice to mean "to owe, to be in debt or obliged for, to be bound (to repay something)." Thus the reader will frequently see phrases like "he is bound to make satisfaction," "they owe them the money," "he is in debt for X amount," which translate phrases built on *tenetur* or *tenentur*.

As for the second ideal, I believe that a successful translation should give the reader a sense of the style of the translated work. This entails finding some way to reproduce the form which the work has in its original language. Translating the sense alone, without any attempt to appoximate the original work's style or form, enables the reader to understand what the author said, but without any sense of how he or she said it. I mean no slight to such translations, which are often extremely helpful – for instance, when I wish to look up a passage of the *Aeneid* in English, I prefer to consult H. Rushton Fairclough's prose translation over Stanley Lombardo's verse translation. Nevertheless I have tried to produce not just a translation of the sense but also an English which represents Antoninus's Latin style to the extent that this is feasible in our language without causing great difficulty for the reader. Thus I have reproduced Antoninus's sentence structure as regularly as possible. For the most part this sentence structure is simple, relative to other Latin authors, and somewhat repetitive. Antoninus did not strive after elegance through the complex, highly involuted sentences of a Cicero or Ciceronian humanist. Although he writes long sentences, they become long through the accumulation of additional clauses and thoughts, rather than in fulfilment of an elaborate design. Another obvious element of Antoninus's style is its repetitiveness. Antoninus did not generally employ "elegant variation" to express the same thought in different words. He was content

19 The dictionaries which I have consulted in preparing the translation are listed in the bibliography below under the following surnames or titles: Berger; Bryson; Deferrari; Du Cange; Edler; *Grande Dizionario della lingua italiana*; Latham; Lewis; *Oxford English Dictionary Online*; *Oxford-Paravia Italian Dictionary*; University of Chicago, "Logeion"; Whitaker.

20 Antoninus, *Summa*, 3.8.3, section 1.4.

to use the same words or syntax many times. This reflects the practical character of the *Summa*, and is in keeping with the style of "scholastic" Latin generally, whose purpose was precise and clear communication rather than persuasive or beautiful. None of this is to say that Antoninus did not have any aesthetic sense, or did not strive after elegance, only that it is not very evident in his sentence structure. It seems to me, for instance, that there is a certain sense of elegance or fitness underlying his approach to the use of scriptural texts, though I would be hard pressed to define it. Antoninus's sense of elegance is best seen in the structural design of his three sermon-chapters (2.1.16, 2.1.17, 3.8.1), which has never been reflected in any previous edition of these texts. This is the most important formal aspect of Antoninus's writing that I have reproduced: in my summaries of the chapters and in my marginal headings, I have employed Antoninus's division of the chapters into sections, subsections, and (sometimes) sub-subsections; for the most part he states these divisions outright in the text, though sometimes they are merely indicated by a hierarchy of paragraph marks.

Finally, the third ideal, clarity of communication, has forced me in many places to stray from strictly reproducing Antoninus's sentence structure in my English translation. This has been the case especially in revising the translation. A few examples of difficulties and how I have dealt with them in the interest of clarity can be provided from chapter 3.8.4, sections 3.2 to 3.7, where all of the following cases can be found. Sometimes I have changed singular verbs to plural (or vice versa) in order to be consistent with nearby sentences or in order to highlight that Antoninus is making a general statement. Sometimes I have broken up one long sentence into two – English readers find very long sentences fatiguing, and do not easily follow the constant adversative or concessive structure which Antoninus uses ("although ... nevertheless ... since ... yet ... etc."). I have found that these long sentences can be turned into more effective English by introducing full stops. Sometimes I have added clarifying words where Antoninus's Latin is very compressed: he frequently writes long sentences with many verbs in which he never repeats the subject nouns; directly translated into English, they would produce ambiguous statements lacking signposts about who is being referred to: "they ... they ... they ... etc." I have thus inserted subject nouns where they were most needed. Sometimes, however, I myself am not certain exactly what Antoninus meant with a particular sentence; in such cases I have preferred to formulate an ambiguous or obscure sentence in English, reflecting the obscurity of the Latin, rather than rephrase the sentence into one that is clear in English but represents only my own guess at what the author means. An example of this is in section 3.7 of chapter 3.8.4: I do not understand the lending practice which Antoninus is describing there, and so, although I have restructured the paragraph slightly to bring the main verb to the fore, I have not been able to formulate a clear way of expressing Antoninus's thought therein. I have to leave it vague.

I have also tried to be reasonably consistent in my translation of Latin words. Complete consistency could never be feasible, since there is no one-to-one correspondence between Latin and English words, but I have adopted a standard way of translating most of the key terms. For example I normally translate *ars, artis* as "craft," *artifex* as "worker," *negotium* as "trade," etc. Where Antoninus quotes from the Bible, in my translation I quote the English of the Douay-Rheims translation, since this is a translation of the Latin Vulgate and thus closer to what Antoninus was reading than would be, for instance, the Authorized Version or the Revised Standard Version, which translate from Hebrew and Greek manuscripts. However, I have updated the forms of personal names with the forms used in the Revised Standard Version, since these are more familiar to contemporary readers than the archaic forms used in Douay-Rheims. For example, I have replaced the Douay-Rheims's form "Noe" with "Noah," "Henoch" with "Enoch," "Agar" with "Hagar," and so forth.

Finally, in the footnotes, I have included excerpts from the sources which Antoninus cites whenever I have access to an English translation of those sources. If I do not have access to an English translation, I have provided a citation in modern format without quoting from the source.

Apparatus Abbreviations

a.c.	ante correctionem	before correction
add.	addidit	added
cap.	capitulum	chapter
cfr	confer	compare to
cod.	codex -icis	the autograph manuscript(s)
del.	delevit	deleted
dext.	dexter -tra -trum	right-hand
e.g.	exempli gratia	for example
fol.	folium -ii	folio(s)
infer.	infer -fera -ferum	lower
marg.	margo -inis	margin
om.	omisit	omitted
p.c.	post correctionem	after correction
praeb.	praebet	provides
sin.	sinister -tra -trum	left-hand
s.l.	super lineam	above the line
super.	superus -a -um	upper
tr.	transposuit	transposed
ut vid.	ut videtur	as it seems
< >	addenda	letters or words not in the manuscript which are to be added
[ ]	delenda	letters or words in the manuscript which are to be deleted

EDITION AND TRANSLATION

Antoninus Florentinus, *Summa*, 2.1.16
De fraudulentia per modum predicationis

Summarium ab editore confectum

Thema. *Quoniam non cognoui negotiationem, introibo in potentias Domini; Domine, memorabor iustitie tue solius* (*Ps* 70.15–16).

- **1. De negotiatione spirituali.**
  - **1.1. In regione celesti.**
  - **1.2. In regione terrestri.**
  - **1.3. In regione infera.**
- **2. De negotiatione mundiali.**
  - **2.1. Ratione finis cupidi.**
  - **2.2. Ratione persone clerici.**
  - **2.3. Ratione temporis feriati.**
  - **2.4. Ratione loci sacrati.**
    Quid consulendum sit de lucris in hiis quattuor casibus.
  - **2.5. Ratione consortii iniusti.**
  - **2.6. Ratione medii iniqui.**
  - **2.7. Ratione materie mali.**
- **3. De negotiatione temporali modesta.**
  - **3.1. Ex iniqua appretiatione.**
    - **3.1.1. Debitus ualor rei.**
      - **3.1.1.1. Ex virtuositate.**
      - **3.1.1.2. Ex raritate.**
      - **3.1.1.3. Ex complacibilitate.**
    - **3.1.2. Latitudo ualoris rei.**
      - **3.1.2.1. Ex iure.**
      - **3.1.2.2. Ex consuetudine.**
      - **3.1.2.3. Ex discretione.**
    - **3.1.3. Excessus ualoris rei.**
      - **3.1.3.1. Excessus ultra dimidiam iusti pretii.**
      - **3.1.3.2. Excessus notabilis infra dimidiam iusti pretii.**
      - **3.1.3.3. Excessus minor.**
        - **3.1.3.3.1. Ratione pacis et saluationis.**
        - **3.1.3.3.2. Ratione mutue concordationis.**
        - **3.1.3.3.3. Ratione humane extimationis.**
        - **3.1.3.3.4. Contra quoddam obiectionum.**

St Antoninus, *Summa*, 2.1.16
On fraud, arranged for preaching

Summary prepared by the editor

Thema. *Because I have not known trade, I will enter into the powers of the Lord: O Lord, I will be mindful of thy justice alone* (*Ps* 70.15–16).

- **1. Spiritual trade.**
  - **1.1. In the heavenly realm.**
  - **1.2. In the terrestrial realm.**
  - **1.3. In the infernal realm.**
- **2. Worldly trade.**
  - **2.1. End: greed.**
  - **2.2. Person: cleric.**
  - **2.3. Time: holiday.**
  - **2.4. Place: sacred.**
    What should be counselled about such profits in these four cases.
  - **2.5. Combination: unjust.**
  - **2.6. Means: wicked.**
  - **2.7. Matter: evil.**
- **3. Modest temporal trade.**
  - **3.1. Wrongful appraisal.**
    - **3.1.1. Valuation of things.**
      - **3.1.1.1. From efficacy.**
      - **3.1.1.2. From scarcity.**
      - **3.1.1.3. From desirability.**
    - **3.1.2. Latitude in valuation.**
      - **3.1.2.1. From law.**
      - **3.1.2.2. From custom.**
      - **3.1.2.3. From discretion.**
    - **3.1.3. Excess in valuation.**
      - **3.1.3.1. Excess beyond half the just price.**
      - **3.1.3.2. Excess notable but less than half.**
      - **3.1.3.3. Minor excess.**
        - **3.1.3.3.1. Argument from peace and salvation.**
        - **3.1.3.3.2. Argument from mutual agreement.**
        - **3.1.3.3.3. Argument from human estimation.**
        - **3.1.3.3.4. Against an objection.**

PRIMUS TITULUS: DE AVARITIA. M_1 fol. Vr

16^m capitulum: de fraudulentia per modum predicationis.
De fraudulentia que commictitur in emptione et uenditione seu negotiatione. fol. 66v

Thema. Vnde Ps. 70, *Quoniam non cognoui negotiationem, introibo in potentias Domini; Domine, memorabor iustitie tue solius.* Sed cum Dominus dicat Lu. 19 per parabolam loquens, *Negotiamini, dum uenio*, tradens *seruis suis* peccuniam qua possent negotiari, et demum exigens rationem ab eis, seruum quem reperit non fuisse negotiatum dure increpauit peccuniam ab eo abstulit et condempnauit: quomodo Dauith asserit se abstinuisse a negotiatione ut Domino gratus esset et suum regnum intraret dicens, *Quoniam non cognoui* etc.? Sciendum igitur quod triplex est genus negotiationis, circa quod Psalmista docet nos recte habere sui exemplo.

Prima est mundialis et scelesta et ideo cauenda: *Quoniam non cognoui negotiationem.*

Secunda est spiritualis et honesta et ideo exercenda: *Introibo in potentias Domini.*

Tertia est temporalis et modesta et ideo permittenda: *Domine memorabor iustitie tue solius.*

1. De negotiatione spirituali. Et a secunda inchoando, scilicet de negotiatione spirituali, parabolam ponit circa hoc Saluator dicens Matth. 13, *Simile est regnum celorum homini negotiatori querenti bonas marghabitas.* Regnum celorum hic significat ecclesiam militantem, et est sensus: quod fit in ecclesia a quolibet fideli est simile ei quod narratur in parabola ista de negotiatore. Negotiator enim querens margaritas, *una inuenta* que sibi uidetur pretiosior unde et ditior fiat, *uendit*

---

4 Quoniam…**5** solius] *Ps* 70.15–16 in *Septuaginta Vaticana* et *Psalt. Rom.* Cfr VULG.: Os meum annuntiabit justitiam tuam, tota die salutare tuum. Quoniam non cognovi litteraturam, introibo in potentias Domini; Domine, memorabor justitiae tuae solius.

6 Negotiamini…uenio] *Lc* 19.11–27: Haec illis audientibus adjiciens, dixit parabolam, eo quod esset prope Jerusalem : et quia existimarent quod confestim regnum Dei manifestaretur. Dixit ergo : Homo quidam nobilis abiit in regionem longinquam accipere sibi regnum, et reverti. Vocatis autem decem servis suis, dedit eis decem mnas, et ait ad illos : Negotiamini dum venio …

19 Simile … **24** eam] *Mt* 13.45–6: Iterum simile est regnum caelorum homini negotiatori, quaerenti bonas margaritas. Inventa autem una pretiosa margarita, abiit, et vendidit omnia quae habuit, et emit eam.

---

3 emptione] eptione *cod.* | uenditione] + pro qua ponit *a.c.* **4** 70] *om. cod. sed in marg. sin. suppl. Iulianus de Lapaccinis ut vid.* **6** seruis suis] *in marg. sin. add.* : eis *a.c.* **12** est] *bis a.c.* **13** negotiationem] li(tteraturam?) *a.c.* **21** a quolibet] *in marg. sin. add.* | simile] *in marg. dext. add.* : sign- *a.c.* **22** Negotiator] Sicut *a.c.*

TITLE ONE: ON GREED.

Chapter 16: On fraud, arranged for preaching. On fraud which is committed in buying and selling or trade.

Thema. From Psalm 70: *Because I have not known trade, I will enter into the powers of the Lord: O Lord, I will be mindful of thy justice alone.*[1] But since the Lord said in Luke 19 when speaking through a parable, *Trade till I come*, handing over *to his servants* money with which to trade, and then later when exacting an account from them he harshly upbraided the servant who he learned had not traded, took the money from him, and condemned him;[2] how then can David declare that he has abstained from trade in order to please the Lord, and to enter into his kingdom, saying, *Because I have not known trade* and so on? It must be understood therefore that trade is of three kinds, in which the Psalmist teaches us to conduct ourselves rightly with himself as our exemplar.

The first is worldly and criminal and therefore to be avoided: *Because I have not known trade.*

The second is spiritual and honest and therefore to be exercised: *I will enter into the powers of the Lord.*

The third is temporal and modest and therefore to be permitted: *O Lord, I will be mindful of thy justice alone.*

1. Spiritual trade. And beginning with the second, namely spiritual trade, the Saviour sets out a parable on it saying in Matthew 13, *The kingdom of heaven is like to a trader seeking good pearls.*[3] The kingdom of heaven here signifies the Church militant, and the meaning is: what is done in the Church by any of the faithful is comparable to that which is narrated about the trader in the parable. For the trader seeking pearls, *when he has found one* which seems to him more precious, by which he will be enriched, *he sells all that he has, and buys it.* A trader travels around different realms; he carries a price in order to acquire rewarding

1 *Ps* 70.15–16. Antoninus's translation of this Psalm verse is drawn from the Roman Psalter, which has *trade* (*negotiationem*) where the Vulgate translation has *learning* (*litteraturam*). See my discussion of this alternate translation of *Ps* 70.15–16 above in ch. 4, section 2. The Vulgate reads: "My mouth shall shew forth thy justice; thy salvation all the day long. Because I have not known learning, I will enter into the powers of the Lord: O Lord, I will be mindful of thy justice alone."

2 *Lc* 19.11–27: "As they were hearing these things, he added and spoke a parable, because he was nigh to Jerusalem, and because they thought that the kingdom of God should immediately be manifested. He said therefore: A certain nobleman went into a far country, to receive for himself a kingdom, and to return. And calling his ten servants, he gave them ten pounds, and said to them: Trade till I come …"

3 *Mt* 13.45–6: "Again the kingdom of heaven is like to a merchant seeking good pearls. Who when he had found one pearl of great price, went his way, and sold all that he had, and bought it."

omnia que habet, et emit eam. Negotiator discurrit per diuersas regiones; pretium portat ut merces accipiat. Sic negotiator spiritualis discurrit non corpore sed mente, per tres regiones que sunt dominio Domini sui, ubi manifestat potentias suas.

Prima est regio celestis, in qua manifestatur Dei potentia ad remunerandum.

Secunda est terrestris, in qua declaratur Dei potentia ad creandum et gubernandum.

Tertia est in inferis, ubi comprobatur potentia Dei ad cruciandum.

1.1. In regione celesti.

Per istas regiones Psalmista se ostendit discurrere dum ait: *Introibo in potentias Domini*, id est locha ubi manifestantur potentie sue, mente intellectu et affectu. Merces que reperitur in prima est gloria diuine intuitionis. "Visio," enim "est tota merces," inquit Augustinus. Quamuis enim ibi sint multe margarite, iuxta illud quod canit Ecclesia, "Porte nitent margaritis," que sunt uaria gaudia beatorum; hec tamen pretiosior, unde Ps., *Posuisti in capite eius*, id est in mente seu intellectu iusti et spiritualis negotiatoris, *coronam*, mercedem que finem non habet, sicut corona *de lapide pretioso*, scilicet clare uisionis Dei. Emitur autem hec, si emi potest, gracia; que utique peccunia est ipsius Domini commendata seruis suis ad negotiandum spiritualiter. Vt autem possit habere istam peccuniam qua emat, uendit omnia que presidet, id est omnia, et substantiam et corpus et animam, subponit gracie ad eam habendam conseruandam et augmentandam; et ea mediante recipit gloriam, quia *graciam et gloriam dabit Dominus*, Ps. Vnde et paruulus baptizatus, etsi nulla habeat opera meritorum, tamen quia habet graciam, recipit decedens gloriam. Hinc et

---

35 Visio … merces] Aug. *Trin.* 1, 8–9: Contemplatio quippe merces est fidei. … In eius [filii] visione merces tota promittitur dilectionis et desiderii nostri. Cfr Thom. Aq. *Sum. th.* 1a 2ae q. 4 a. 1 ob. 1.

36 Porte … **37** margaritis] *Breviari Romani* hymn. *Urbs Ierusalem beata dicta pacis visio* (§. 3) ex officio dedicationis ecclesiae: Portæ nitent margarítis / ádytis paténtibus … Cfr *Apc* 21.9–21.

38 Posuisti … **40** pretioso] *Ps* 20.4: Quoniam praevenisti eum in benedictionibus dulcedinis; posuisti in capite ejus coronam de lapide pretioso.

45 graciam … **46** Dominus] *Ps* 83.12: Quia misericordiam et veritatem diligit Deus, gratiam et gloriam dabit Dominus.

---

26 que] ubi *a.c.* | dominio] potentia *a.c.* **32** Psalmista] Dominus *a.c.* **37** gaudia] + plura *in marg. sin. add. sine indicatione quo ponendum* **37–8** unde Ps.] *bis scr.* + dicit *a.c.* **41** gracia] pe(ccunia?) *a.c.* **42** autem] + emere *a.c.* **46** baptizatus] baptiçatus *cod.*

merchandise.[4] Even so the spiritual trader travels around, not in body but in mind, through the three realms which are in the kingdom of his Lord, where He manifests his powers.

The first is the heavenly realm, in which is manifested the power of God for rewarding.

The second is the terrestrial realm, in which is declared the power of God for creating and governing.

The third is in the infernal realm, in which is proven the power of God for tormenting.

1.1. In the heavenly realm. The Psalmist shows himself travelling around those regions when he says: *I will enter into the powers of the Lord*; that is, the places where his powers are manifested, in mind, intellect, and affect. The reward which is found in the first is the glory of the direct perception of the divine. For, "vision is the whole reward," says Augustine.[5] For although there are in that realm many pearls, according to that text which the Church sings, "Thy gates shine bright with pearls,"[6] which are the various joys of the blessed; nevertheless this one is more precious, whence the Psalm says: *thou hast set on his head*, that is, in the mind or intellect of the just and spiritual trader, *a crown*, a reward which has no end, just like a crown *of precious stones*, namely of the clear vision of God.[7] And this is purchased, if it can be purchased, by grace; which is the money which that Lord commended to his servants to carry out spiritual trade. But in order to have that money with which to buy, he sells all that belongs to him, that is he submits everything, his wealth and his body and his soul, to grace, in order to possess it, keep it, and increase it; and with grace mediating he receives glory, because *The Lord will give grace and glory*, Psalm 83.[8] Hence even a little baptized child, although he has no works of merit, nevertheless because he has grace, when he dies he receives glory. Hence also Gregory says: "The kingdom of heaven is worth as

4 Antoninus makes a pun here which cannot be reproduced perfectly in English. He plays on the similarity between two Latin words: 1) *merx, mercis*, "merchandise, wares," and 2) *merces, mercedis*, "wage, reward." The accusative plural of the former is *merces*, a homograph with the nominative singular of the latter. Thus here he writes *merces* (merchandise) and in the second and third sentences of the next paragraph he writes *merces* (reward). Through this pun he connects the merchandise sought by the spiritual trader with the rewards received in heaven.

5 Aug. *Trin.* 1, 8–9: "For contemplation is the recompense of faith … The whole reward of our love and longing is held forth as in the sight of Him [the Son]." Cfr Thom. Aq. *Sum. th.* 1a 2ae q. 4 a. 1 ob. 1.

6 Hymn *Urbs Ierusalem beata dicta pacis visio*, §. 3, in the Tridentine Missal (1570), Office for the Dedication of a Church, Vespers ("Blessèd city, heavenly Salem," trans. Neale, 36–8): "Bright thy gates of pearl are shining; They are open evermore; And by virtue of his merits Thither faithful souls do soar …" Cfr *Apc* 21.9–21.

7 *Ps* 20.4: "For thou hast prevented him with blessings of sweetness: thou hast set on his head a crown of precious stones."

8 *Ps* 83.12: "For God loveth mercy and truth: the Lord will give grace and glory."

Gregorius: "Regnum celorum tantum ualet quantum habes," ut scilicet omnia subiciantur uoluntati Dei et gracie sue. "Nil uilius cum emitur, nil carius cum possidetur."

1.2. In regione terrestri.

In secunda regione, scilicet huius mundi, sunt multe margarite. Multa sunt genera bonorum, quia diuitie honores scientia et huiusmodi; sed pretiosior omnibus est sapientia. Vnde de ea dicit sapiens: *Nec comparaui illi*, sapientie scilicet, *lapidem pretiosum*, et *omnia que desiderantur huic* | *non ualent comparari*, fol. 67r Sapientie 7. Sapientiam autem uocho uirtutem infusam tantum, et sic accipitur communiter in sacra Scriptura. Ipsa comprehendit in se omnes uirtutes morales, quibus in uita nil est utilius, ut dicit ibi sapiens. Peccunia qua emitur est labor cohibendi et moderandi suas passiones. Nam ut dicit Philosophus, "uirtus est scientia circa difficilia." Et Virgilius, "Sursum attollere gradum," scilicet ad uirtutem, "hoc opus, hic labor est." Et Prouerb. <2> dicitur, *Si quesieris sapientiam quasi effodiens tesaurum, inuenies*. In effossione thesauri est

---

48 Regnum … **49** possidetur] Greg. M. *In evang.* 1, 5 on *Mt* 4.18–22 (1093–4): Sed fortasse alliquis tacitis sibi cogitationibus dicat: ad vocem dominicam uterque iste piscator quid aut quantum dimisit, qui pene nihil habuit? … Multa, fratres, relinquitis, si desideriis terrenis renuntiatis. Exteriora etenim nostra Domino quamlibet parva sufficiunt. Cor namque, et non substantiam pensat; nec perpendit quantum in eius sacrificio, sed ex quanto proferatur. Nam si exteriorem substantia perpendamus, ecce sancti negotiatores nostri perpetuam angelorum vitam datis retibus et navi mercati sunt. Aestimationem quippe pretii non habet, sed tamen regnum Dei tantum valet quantum habes. … Valuit Petro et Andreae dimissis retibus et navi (Matth. iv, 20), valuit viduae duobus minutis (Luc. xxi, 2), valuit alteri calice aquae frigidae (Matth. x, 42). Regnum itaque Dei, ut diximus, tantum valet, quantum habes. Pensate igitur, fratres, quid vilius cum emitur, quid charius cum possidetur?
Cfr Thom. Aq. *Sum. th.* 2a 2ae q. 100 a. 1.

52 Nec … **53** pretiosum] *Sap* 7.9: Propter hoc optavi, et datus est mihi sensus; et invocavi, et venit in me spiritus sapientiae; et praeposui illam regnis et sedibus, et divitias nihil esse duxi in comparatione illius. Nec comparavi illi lapidem pretiosum, quoniam omne aurum in comparatione illius arena est exigua, et tamquam lutum aestimabitur argentum in conspectu illius.

53 et … comparari] *Prv* 3.15: Beatus homo qui invenit sapientiam, et qui affluit prudentia. Melior est acquisitio ejus negotiatione argenti, et auri primi et purissimi fructus ejus. Pretiosior est cunctis opibus, et omnia quae desiderantur huic non valent comparari.

58 uirtus … difficilia] Arist. *Ethica Nic.* 2, 3 (1105a10); vide Ant. Flor. *Chron.* 1.4.3 pr. (*Chronicorum opus* [Lyon, 1586], 122bd): Quicumque enim removetur a corporalibus et hoc ipso gaudet, castus qui autem tristatur incontinens, idem, Difficilius est passionem delectationis repellere quam irae, quemadmodum Heraclitus, Circa difficillimum autem semper et ars sit et virtus, In his quae sunt secundum virtutem requiritur qualiter habens operetur. Primum quidem si sciens, deinde si volens, Praeter hoc autem tertium si firme et immutabiliter operetur. Haec autem ad habendum alias artes non connumerantur praeter ipsum scire. Ad habendum igitur virtutes scire quidem partum aut nihil prodest, ad alia vero non parum, sed omne. Lib. 2 Eth. c.3.
Cfr Arist. *Ethica Nic.* 3, 3 (1112b9); Thom. Aq. *Sum. th.* 1a 2ae q. 68 a. 7 ad 3.

58 Sursum … **59** est] Verg. *Aen.* 6, 128–9 (*Opera*, 231): Sed reuocare gradum superasque euadere ad auras, / hoc opus, hic labor est.

59 Si … **60** inuenies] *Prv* 2.4–5: Si quaesieris eam [sapientiam] quasi pecuniam, et sicut thesauros effoderis illam : tunc intelliges timorem Domini, et scientiam Dei invenies.

---

52 dicit] dicitur *a.c.* **54** Sapientie 7] *in marg. super. add.* | 7] 8 *cod.* | uirtutem] + secundum quod eam uocant stoyci *a.c.* **57** Philosophus] Sa- *a.c.* **59** Prouerb.] Sapientie *cod.* | 2] *spatium duarum litterarum praeb. cod.*

much as you have," namely it is worth making all things subject to the will of God and his grace. "Nothing is cheaper when bought, nothing is dearer when possessed."[9]

1.2. In the terrestrial realm.

In the second realm, namely of this world, there are many pearls. There are many different goods, for there is wealth, honour, knowledge, and so on; but more precious than all is wisdom. Hence the wise man says about her: *Neither did I compare unto her*, namely wisdom, *any precious stone*, and *all the things that are desired are not to be compared with her*, Wisdom 7.[10] Now I call "wisdom" only the infused virtue, and it is commonly taken thus in sacred Scripture. It comprehends in itself all the moral virtues; and in this life, nothing is more useful than they are, as the wise man says there. The money with which wisdom is bought is the labour of curbing and moderating one's passions. For as the Philosopher says, "virtue is knowledge in relation to difficult matters."[11] And Vergil says, "To climb up the steps," namely to virtue, "this is is the task, this the toil."[12] And it is said in Proverbs 2, *If thou shalt seek wisdom as if digging for a treasure, thou shalt find.*[13] In the digging of treasure there is labour in throwing aside the earth, akin to disdaining earthly desires; there is also the

9 Greg. M. *In evang.* 1, 5 on *Mt* 4.18–22. Cfr Thom. Aq. *Sum. th.* 2a 2ae q. 100 a. 1.
This text of Gregory the Great was widely diffused and variously attributed. E.g. St Robert Bellarmine attributed it to St Augustine in one place; Bellarmine, *The Eternal Happiness of the Saints*, 190–2.

10 *Sap* 7.7–9: "Wherefore I wished, and understanding was given me: and I called upon God, and the spirit of wisdom came upon me: And I preferred her before kingdoms and thrones, and esteemed riches nothing in comparison of her. Neither did I compare unto her any precious stone: for all gold in comparison of her, is as a little sand, and silver in respect to her shall be counted as clay."
Prv 3.15: "Blessed is the man that findeth wisdom and is rich in prudence: The purchasing thereof is better than the merchandise of silver, and her fruit than the chiefest and purest gold: She is more precious than all riches: and all the things that are desired, are not to be compared with her."

11 I find this passage difficult to interpret. Antoninus also gives this phrase in similar form in his *Chronica*, part 1 tit. 4 c. 3 pr. (*Chronicorum opus* [Lyon, 1586], 122bd), where he cites Arist. *Ethica Nic.* 2, 3 (1105a10; McKeon, 955): "It is harder to fight with pleasure than with anger, to use Heraclitus' phrase, but both art and virtue are always concerned with what is harder; for even the good is better when it is harder."
Cfr Arist. *Ethica Nic.* 3, 3 (1112b9; McKeon, 969–70); Thom. Aq. *Sum. th.* 1a 2ae q. 68 a. 7 ad 3.

12 Verg. *Aen.* 6, 128–9 (LCL 63:540–1): "But to recall one's steps and pass out to the upper air, this is the task, this the toil!"

13 *Prv* 2.4–5: "If thou shalt seek her [wisdom] as money, and shalt dig for her as for a treasure: Then shalt thou understand the fear of the Lord, and shalt find the knowledge of God."

labor in abiciendo terram, id est terrena affectu despiciendo; est et desiderium tesauri magnum; est et profundatio que innuit humiliationem.

1.3. In regione infera.

In tertia regione, scilicet inferni, merces que descendendo meditatione ad eam in uita presenti potest emi est uenia, id est remissio pene ecterne inferni uel temporalis purgatorii, cuius quisque est debitor pro peccatis suis. *Non enim est homo* super terram, *qui non peccet*, ait Salomon, 3 Regum 8. Nulla pretiosior margarita ex illa regione inde potest trahi, et utilior ista, scilicet uenia. Multa inde meditando possunt trahi, ut cognitio diuine iustitie, compassio ad illos, et huiusmodi, sed hec utilior. Peccunia autem qua emitur ista merces et margarita pretiosa est penitentia. Vt enim dicit Leo Papa: "Venia non datur, nisi correcto," *De re. iur.* in *6º*. Et plenius declarat Augustinus, *De p.* D. 1, inquiens: "Neminem putes de errore ad ueritatem, de quocumque magno uel paruo uitio ad uirtutem sine penitentia posse transire." Per penitentiam enim principaliter cordis et contritionem ueram tollitur culpa, et de pena debita plus et minus secundum quantitatem doloris. De ista igitur negotiatione spiritualiter intelligitur quod Dominus precepit dicens, *Negotiamini.* Et ad hanc exercendam dicit Psalmista se intraturum *in potentias Domini*, id est in regiones sue potentie, suo exemplo nos ad idem prouocans.

2. De negotiatione mundiali.

Reuertendo ad primum genus negotiationis, scilicet quam faciunt mundani, quia plena est multis uitiis, ideo cauenda in quantum uitiosa. Quod ipse Psalmista nos docet suo exemplo dicens, *Non cognoui negotiationem.* Et hic textus est secundum aliam Biblie translationem, loco cuius nostra translatio habet: *Non cognoui litteraturam*, hoc est exercitium iniquorum. De quibus dicitur Baruch 3, *Filii Agar exquisierunt prudentiam que de terra est, negotiatores Teman* etc. Et ideo

---

65 Non … **66** peccet] *3 Rg* 8.46: Quod si peccaverint tibi (non est enim homo qui non peccet) et iratus tradideris eos inimicis suis, et captivi ducti fuerint in terram inimicorum longe vel prope.

70 Venia … **71** correcto] Non Leo sed Gelas. in *VI* 5.[13.]5 (*Peccati*): Peccati venia non datur, nisi correcto. Cfr *De pen.* D. 5 c. 2 (*Qualitas*). Vide etiam Ant. Flor. *Summa* 1.20.1.69 (apud *N* fol. 320r, Ballerini 1:887–8, Mamachi 1:1405–6): *peccati venia.*

72 Neminem … **73** transire] Aug. in *De pen.* D. 1 c. 43 (*Neminem*): Neminem putes ab errore ad ueritatem, et a peccato quocumque seu paruo seu magno ad correctionem sine penitencia posse transire.

81 Non … **83** litteraturam] Cfr Aug. in D. 88 c. 12 (*Quoniam non*); *Glossa ord.* ad *Ps* 70.15–16.

83 Filii … **84** Teman] *Bar* 3.23: Filii quoque Agar, qui exquirunt prudentiam quae de terra est, negotiatores Merrhae et Theman, et fabulatores, et exquisitores prudentiae et intelligentiae : viam autem sapientiae nescierunt, neque commemorati sunt semitas ejus.

---

63 meditatione] mente *a.c.* **64** remissio] + ille *a.c.* **66** 8] 7 *cod.* **73** uirtutem] *ut vid.* | sine … transire] *tr. p.c.* **83** 3] *p.c.* : 2 *a.c.*

great desire for the treasure; and there is the downward descent which signifies being humbled.

1.3. In the infernal realm. In the third realm, namely of hell, the reward which can be bought during the present life, by descending there in meditation, is indulgence, that is, the remission of the penalty of eternal fire or of the temporal purgatory which everyone has earned for their sins. *For there is no man* on the earth *who sinnith not*, Solomon says in 3rd Kings 8.[14] No pearl more precious or of greater profit can be drawn out of this realm than that one, namely indulgence. Many a thing can be drawn out of there by meditating on it, such as the thought of divine justice, compassion for the denizens, and so forth, but this is more profitable. Now the money with which you purchase that reward and precious pearl is penance. For as Pope Leo says: "Indulgence is not given unless the fault has been corrected," *On the rules of law* in the *Sext.*[15] And Augustine explains this more fully, *De pen.* D. 1, saying, "Do not think that anyone can pass from error to truth, or from any vice whether large or small to virtue, without penance."[16] For through penance – in the first place, of the heart – and true contrition, the fault is taken away; and of due punishment more or less according to the quantity of sorrow. Therefore what the Lord commanded when he said, *Trade*, is understood to signify that spiritual trade. And to practise it the Psalmist says that he will enter *into the powers of the Lord*, that is into the realms of His power, prompting us by his example to do the same.

2. Worldly trade. Returning to the first kind of trade, namely that which the worldly carry out: since it is full of many vices, it is to be avoided in as much as it is vicious. The Psalmist himself teaches us this by his example when he says: *I have not known trade*. And this is the text according to the other translation of the Bible, in place of which our translation has: *I have not known learning*, which is the occupation of the iniquitous.[17] About these it is said in Baruch 3: *The children of Hagar have sought after the wisdom that is of the earth, the traders of Teman* etc.[18] And therefore the Lord Jesus prohibits this when he says in John 2, *Make not the house of my Father a house of*

---

14 *3 Rg* 8.46: "But if they sin against thee (for there is no man who sinneth not) and thou being angry deliver them up to their enemies, so that they be led away captives into the land of their enemies far or near."

15 Not Leo but Gelas. in *VI* 5[.13].5 (*Peccati*). The *Glossa ord.* (s.v. *peccati venia*) says that this rule is deduced from a canon of Pope Gelasius, C. 24 q. 2 c. 2 (*Legatur*). In attributing this canon to Leo, Antoninus may have been thinking of *De pen.* D. 5 c. 2 (*Qualitas*). Augustine states the same opinion at *De cons.* D. 4 c. 96. For Antoninus's further comments on this rule of law, see also *Summa* 1.20.1.69 (apud *N* fol. 320r, Ballerini 1:887–8, Mamachi 1:1405–6): *peccati venia.*

16 Aug. in *De pen.* D. 1 c. 43 (*Neminem*): "Do not hold that anyone can pass without penance from error to truth, or from any sin, whether large or small, to correction."

17 Cfr Aug. in D. 88 c. 12 (*Quoniam non*); *Glossa ord.* ad *Ps* 70.15–16. Discussed above in ch. 4.

18 *Bar* 3.23: "The children of Agar also, that search after the wisdom that is of the earth, the merchants of Merrha, and of Theman, and the tellers of fables, and searchers of prudence and understanding: but the way of wisdom they have not known, neither have they remembered her paths."

hanc Dominus Yesus prohibet dicens Io. 2, *Nolite facere domum patris mei domum negotiationis*. Domus patris est non solum ecclesia materialis sed multo magis spiritualis, id est collectio fidelium, que tunc fit domus negotiationis cum fideles intendunt negotiationibus iniquis et iniustis. Vnde et Crisostomus de huiusmodi dicit quod "merchator numquam potest Deo placere." Septempliciter autem negotiatio est iniqua et cauenda.

1°. Ratione finis cupidi.
2°. Ratione persone clerici.
3°. Ratione temporis feriati.
4°. Ratione loci sacrati.
5°. Ratione consortii iniusti.
6°. Ratione medii iniqui.
7°. Ratione materie mali.

2.1. Ratione finis cupidi.

Quantum ad primum clarum est quod cuius finis est malus et ipsum opus necessario est malum. Si ergo finis negotiandi sit principaliter *cupiditas*, que *est radix omnium malorum*, negotiatio erit iniqua. Sed pro huiusmodi declaratione sciendum secundum beatum Tomam, 2^{a} 2^{e} q. 77 articulo 4, quod ad negotiatores pertinet commutationibus rerum insistere, inportat enim negotiatio in facto quamdam commutationem. Est autem duplex commutatio rerum, secundum Philosophum in primo *Polit.* Vna quidem quasi naturalis et neccessaria per quam uidelicet fit commutatio rei ad rem uel rerum et denariorum propter neccessitatem uite: et talis commutatio non proprie pertinet ad negotiatores sed magis ad ychonomichos et politicos, id est hiis qui habent prouidere domibus et familie sue aut ciuitati de rebus neccessariis uite. Hec igitur commutatio secundum Philosophum de se est laudabilis, quia habet finem

---

85 Nolite … **86** negotiationis] *Io* 2.16: Et his qui columbas vendebant, dixit : Auferte ista hinc, et nolite facere domum patris mei, domum negotiationis.

89 quod … placere] Chrys. (pseudo) *Opus imperf.* in D. 88 c. 11 (*Eiciens*): Eiciens Dominus uendentes et ementes de templo, significauit, quia homo mercator uix aut numquam potest Deo placere. Et ideo nullus Christianus debet esse mercator, aut, si uoluerit esse, proiciatur de ecclesia Dei.

98 cuius … **99** malum] Vide Boeth. *Diff. top.* 2 (PL 64:1189); Thom. Aq. *Sum. th.* 1a 2ae q. 18 a. 4.

99 cupiditas … **100** malorum] *1 Tim* 6.10: Radix enim omnium malorum est cupiditas : quam quidam appetentes erraverunt a fide, et inseruerunt se doloribus malis.

101 ad … **126** laboris] Textus ex Thom. Aq. *Sum. th.* 2a 2ae q. 77 a. 4, quibusdam mutatis.

103 Est … rerum] Arist. *Polit.* 1, 3 (1253b13); ibid. 1, 9 (1256b40).

108 Hec … **109** laudabilis] Arist. *Polit.* 1, 10 (1258a38).

---

89 Septempliciter] *p.c.* : *dub. a.c.* **94** 4° … **95** iniusti] *tr. per litteras* a (ratione temporis feriati) c (ratione consortii iniusti) b (ratione loci sacrati) *cod.* **108** Hec] Alia enim com- *a.c.*

trade.[19] The house of the Father is not only the material church but much more the spiritual one, that is, the congregation of the faithful, which is made into a house of trade when the faithful engage in iniquitous and unjust types of trade. Hence also Chrysostom says about such trade that "a merchant can never please God."[20] Now trade is iniquitous and to be avoided because of seven circumstances.

1. Because of end: greed.
2. Because of person: cleric.
3. Because of time: holiday.
4. Because of place: sacred.
5. Because of combination: unjust.
6. Because of means: iniquitous.
7. Because of matter: evil.

2.1. End: greed. As to the first, it is clear that if the motivation of an action is evil, the action itself is also necessarily evil.[21] If therefore the end of trading is principally *cupidity*, which *is the root of all evils*, the trade will be wicked.[22] But for the explanation of these things, it must be understood, according to blessed Thomas, 2a 2ae q. 77 a. 4, that it is in the nature of traders to engage in exchanges of goods, for the act of trading involves some kind of exchange.[23] Now there are two sorts of exchange of goods, according to the Philosopher in the first book of the *Politics*.[24] The first sort indeed is, as it were, natural and necessary, and consists in the exchange of one good for another or of goods and money for the necessities of life; this sort of exchange does not, strictly speaking, pertain to traders but more to heads of households and statesmen, that is those who are responsible for providing the necessities of life for their households and their family or for the state. Therefore this kind of exchange, according to the

19 *Io* 2.16: "And to them that sold doves he said: Take these things hence, and make not the house of my Father a house of traffic."

20 CHRYS. (pseudo) *Opus imperf.* in D. 88 c. 11 (*Eiciens*): "In casting sellers and buyers from the Temple, the Lord signified that a man who engages in trade can rarely or never please God. And so no Christian must be a merchant, or, if he should wish to be one, let him be cast out of God's Church."

On this canon and the next, AUG. in D. 88 c. 12 (*Quoniam non*): "Both the texts quoted exercised a great influence on moral thinking about commerce in the Middle Ages, although in fact they are both of doubtful authenticity. The text attributed to Chrysostom is in fact an apocryphal Latin work of the 6th century, which goes under the title of *Opus imperfectum in Matthaeum* (and as such is to be found in PG 56, 840) … Both the texts were included in his *Decretum* by Gratian, who thereby added his immense authority to their influence." LeFébure, *Injustice*, 226–7.

21 See BOETH. *Diff. top.* 2 (PL 64:1189); THOM. AQ. *Sum. th.* 1a 2ae q. 18 a. 4.

22 *1 Tim* 6.10: "For the desire of money is the root of all evils; which some coveting have erred from the faith, and have entangled themselves in many sorrows."

23 THOM. AQ. *Sum. th.* 2a 2ae q. 77 a. 4. The rest of this paragraph is a close paraphrase of the majority of Aquinas's article 4. Antoninus intersperses his own comments and expansions throughout. My English translation here is indebted to LeFébure, *Injustice*, 224–31.

24 ARIST. *Polit.* 1, 3 (1253b13); ibid., 1, 9 (1256b40). I discuss these passages above in ch. 3.

honestum, quia scilicet deseruit neccessitati uite humane. Possent tamen in ea commicti diuersa peccata, sed illa sunt uitia hominum, non artis in se. Alia commutatio est denariorum ad denarios, ut in cambiendo, uel denariorum ad merces, ut in emptione et uenditione, uel rerum ad res, ut in permutatione que dicuntur baratti, non propter res neccessarias uite sed ordinata ad hunc finem, scilicet lucrum ex ipsa commutatione consequendum: et hec proprie dicitur negotiatio. Et quia quantum est de se deseruit cupiditati lucri que terminum nescit sed infinitum tendit, ideo secundum se considerata habet quamdam turpitudinem, in quantum in sui ratione non importat aliquem finem honestum uel neccesarium. Nichil tamen importat in sui ratione uitiosum uel rationi contrarium. Vnde ordinari potest ad finem aliquem honestum et neccessarium, et sic efficietur negotiatio licita. Puta si negotiator, lucrum quod querit, moderatum tamen, ordinat ad hunc finem, scilicet ad substentationem sui et familie, secundum scilicet statum suum decentem, aut etiam ut inde pauperibus subueniat, | fol. 67v uel etiam cum negotiationem intendit propter publicam utilitatem, ne scilicet res neccessarie ad uitam patrie desint; et lucrum inde expedit non quasi finem, sed quasi stipendium laboris, seruatis aliis debitis circumstantiis de quibus dicetur: sic non potest condempnari. Sed si finem ponat ultimum in lucro, intendens solum diuitias augere in immensum et sibi reseruare, in statu permanet dampnationis. Et de huiusmodi negotiatoribus dicit beatus Tomas esse intelligendum quod ait Crisostomus super Mattheum, “Quicumque rem comparat ut integram immutamque uendendo lucretur, ille est qui de templo eicitur,” ut habetur D. 88 c. *Eiciens*. Quod uerum est quando ultimum finem constituit in lucro, tunc enim est extra ecclesiam quoad meritum. *Nolite* hoc modo *facere domum meum domum negotiationis* etc. Hic tamen summimus large negotiationem, et in sequentibus huiusmodi sectionibus.

2.2. Ratione persone clerici.

Secundo negotiatio est mala ratione persone, cum scilicet aliquibus personis specialiter aliquo iure prohibetur, quod fit cunctis clericis et multo magis religiosis, *Extra*, *Ne clerici uel mona.*, per totum, ubi non solum negotiatio sed plura negotia ibi ponuntur eis interdicta. Dicit etiam Augustinus: “Negotiari

---

111 uitia … artis] Vide Aug. in D. 88 c. 12 (*Quoniam non*).
130 intelligendum … **133** lucro] Thom. Aq. *Sum. th.* 2a 2ae q. 77 a. 4 obj. 1; ibid. ad 1.
131 Quicumque … **132** eicitur] Chrys. (pseudo) *Opus imperf.* in D. 88 c. 11 (*Eiciens*).
138 cunctis … **140** interdicta] *X* 3.50 *Ne clerici vel monachi saecularibus negotiis se immisceant.*
140 Negotiari … **142** licet] Aug. in D. 88 c. 10 (*Fornicari*): Fornicari omnibus semper non licet: negotiari vero aliquando licet; aliquando non licet. Antequam enim ecclesiasticus quis sit; licet ei negotiari: facto iam, non licet.

---

117 secundum se] de se *a.c.* **122** ordinat] intendit ordinari *a.c.* **122** substentationem] -ne *cod.* **132** Eiciens] Quoniam *cod.* **134** meritum] *in marg. dext. add. ut vid.* | meum] *dub.* | Nolite … **136** sectionibus] *in marg. sin. add.* **139** Extra … **140** etiam] *in marg. super. add.*

Philosopher,[25] in itself is praiseworthy, because it has an honest end, namely supplying the needs of human life. Nevertheless various sins may be committed in it, but these are the vices of men, not of the craft as such.[26] The other sort of exchange is of money for money, as in moneychanging, or of money for merchandise, as in buying and selling, or of goods for other goods, as in exchange of goods, which is called barter, not on account of the necessities of life, but ordered towards the end of gaining profit from the exchange; this is properly called trade. And in as much as in itself it serves the desire for profit which knows no limit but extends to infinity, it follows that considered in itself it has a certain shamefulness, in so far as it does not intrinsically entail any honest or necessary end. Nevertheless it does not intrinsically entail anything vicious or contrary to reason. Hence it can be ordered towards an honest and necessary end, and thus trade will be made licit. Say if a trader orders the profit he seeks, moderate profit mind you, towards the end of sustaining himself and his family, that is in accordance with what is appropriate to their state, or suppose he intends to help the poor from his profit, or suppose he pursues trade for public utility, to ensure that the country does not run short of the necessities of life, and if he makes a profit not as an end in itself, but as a wage for his labour, observing all the due circumstances which will be discussed: one acting thus cannot be condemned. But if he places the ultimate end in profit, intending only to increase his wealth into immensity and to store it up for himself, he remains in a state of damnation. And blessed Thomas says that we must understand Chrystostom to be speaking about these sorts of traders when he says, on Matthew, "Anybody who buys something in order to make a profit by selling it whole and unchanged, this is the one who is thrown out of the temple,"[27] as we read in D. 88 c. 11.[28] Which is true when he places the ultimate end in profit, for then he is outside the Church through lacking merit. *Make not*, in this way, *my house a house of trade* etc. Here, however, we take "trade" in its wide sense, as we do in the following sections of this discussion.

2.2. Person: cleric. Second, trade is evil on account of person, namely when it is specially prohibited by law to certain persons, which is the case for all clerics and much more for religious, as in *Extra*, the whole title *That clerics and monks not involve themselves in secular affairs*, where not only trade but many other types of business are set out as forbidden to them.[29] Augustine also says: "To engage in trade is at times licit, at times not licit: before you become a cleric, it is licit; after you have been made a cleric, it is no longer licit," D. 88 c. 10.[30] The reason for

25 Arist. *Polit.* 1, 10 (1258a38).

26 See Aug. in D. 88 c. 12 (*Quoniam non*).

27 Thom. Aq. *Sum. th.* 2a 2ae q. 77 a. 4 obj. 1; ibid. ad 1.

28 Chrys. (pseudo) *Opus imperf.* in D. 88 c. 11 (*Eiciens*).

29 *X* 3.50 *Ne clerici vel monachi saecularibus negotiis se immisceant.*

30 Aug. in D. 88 c. 10 (*Fornicari*): "To fornicate is always unlawful for everyone, but to engage in trade is at times lawful, at times unlawful. Before someone becomes an ecclesiastic, it is lawful for him to be in trade; once he has become one, it is no longer lawful."

aliquando licet, aliquando non licet: antequam sis clerichus, licet; postquam effectus es clerichus, non licet," D. 88 *Fornichari*. Ratio huius est, secundum beatum Tomam, 2^{a} 2^{e} q. 77 articulo 4, quia clerici abstinere debent non solum a malis, sed etiam ab hiis que habent speciem mali, quod in negotiatione contingit, et hoc tripliciter. Primo, quia negotiatio est ordinata ad lucrum, cuius clerici debent esse contemptores. Vnde Ieronymus: "clerichum negotiatorem ex inopi diuitem tamquam quamdam pestem deuita," D. 88. Secundo, propter frequentia negotiatorum uitia, quia *difficulter exuitur negotiator a peccatis labiorum*, ut dicitur Ecclesiastici 26. Et Leo Papa: "Difficile est inter uendentis ementisque commercium non interuenire peccatum," *De pen.* D. 5 *Qualitas*. Sed clerichus debet se multum cauere a peccatis iuxta illud: *Ambulans in uia immaculata, seruabat mihi* etc. Tertio, quia negotiatio nimis implicat mentem curis secularibus et per consequens a spiritualibus retrahit, unde Apostolus, 2 ad Thim., *Nemo militans Deo implicat se negotiis secularibus*, et ad idem D. 88 *Consequens*. Habent autem frequenter uacare diuinis. Licet tamen clericis

---

143 clerici ... **157** uendendo] Textus ex THOM. AQ. *Sum. th.* 2a 2ae q. 77 a. 4 ad 3, quibusdam mutatis et additionibus.

146 clerichum ... **147** deuita] HIER. in D. 88 c. 9 (*Negotiatorem*). Cfr THOM. AQ. *Sum. th.* 2a 2ae q. 77 a. 4 ob. 3.

148 difficulter ... **149** labiorum] *Sir* 26.28: Duae species difficiles et periculosae mihi apparuerunt : difficile exuitur negotians a negligentia, et non justificabitur caupo a peccatis labiorum. Cfr *Sir* 27.2: Sicut in medio compaginis lapidum palus figitur, sic et inter medium venditionis et emptionis angustiabitur peccatum.

149 Difficile ... **150** peccatum] LEO in *De pen.* D. 5 c. 2 (*Qualitas*): Qualitas lucri negotiantem aut accusat, aut arguit, quia et est honestus questus, et turpis. Verumtamen penitenti utilius est dispendia pati, quam periculis negotiationis astringi, quia difficile est inter ementis uendentisque commercium non interuenire peccatum.

151 Ambulans ... **152** mihi] *Ps* 100.6: Oculi mei ad fideles terrae, ut sedeant mecum; ambulans in via immaculata, hic mihi ministrabat.

154 Nemo ... secularibus] *2 Tim* 2.4: Nemo militans Deo implicat se negotiis saecularibus : ut ei placeat, cui se probavit.

154 D. ... **155** Consequens] D. 88 c. 2 (*Consequens*): Consequens est, ut illa quoque, que de Piceni partibus nuper ad nos missa relatio nuntiauit, non pretereunda putaremus, id est, plurimos clericorum negotiationibus inhonestis et turpibus lucris inminere, nullo pudore censentes euangelicam lectionem, qua ipse Dominus negotiatores ex templo uerberatos asseritur expulisse, nec Apostoli uerba recolentes, quibus ait: "Nemo militans Deo implicat se negociis secularibus;" psalmistam quoque Dauid surda dissimulantes aure, cantantem: "Quoniam non cognoui negotiationes, introibo in potentias Domini." Proinde huiusmodi aut ab indignis posthac questibus nouerint abstinendum, et ab omni cuiuslibet negotiationis ingenio cupiditateque cessandum, aut, in quocumque gradu sint positi, mox a clericalibus offitiis cogantur abstinere, quoniam domus Dei domus orationis et esse debet et dici, ne per offitia negotiationis potius sit latronum spelunca.

---

146 Vnde ... **147** 88] *in marg. sin. add.* **149** 26] 27 *cod.* **151** Sed ... peccatis] *in marg. dext. add.* | iuxta] *ut vid.* | iuxta ... **152** etc] *in marg. dext. add. Iul. de Lapacc.* **152** seruabat] s. *cod.* **154** 2] 1 *cod.* **155** Habent ... diuinis] *in marg. sin. add.*

this is, according to blessed Thomas, 2a 2ae q. 77 a. 4,[31] that clerics are bound to abstain not merely from things that are evil but from things that have the appearance of evil, which is the case in trade, and in three ways. First, because trade is ordered towards profit, which clerics should scorn. Hence Jerome: "Avoid like the plague any cleric who, engaging in trade, has gone from poverty to riches," D. 88.[32] Second, because of the frequent vices of traders, since *a trader can hardly keep from sins of the lips*,[33] as is said in Ecclesiasticus 26. And Pope Leo: "It is difficult for sin not to intervene in the commerce between buyer and seller," *De pen.* D. 5 c. 2.[34] But a cleric ought very much to guard himself from committing sins according to that text: *The man that walked in the perfect way, he served me* etc.[35] Third, because trade involves the mind too much in secular cares and thereby withdraws it from spiritual ones, hence the Apostle says in his second letter to Timothy, *No man, being a soldier to God, gets entangled in secular business*,[36] and on the same D. 88 c. 2.[37] For they must frequently take time for divine things. Nevertheless it is licit for clerics to use the first kind of exchange, which is ordered towards providing the necessities of life through buying and selling. And if, having bought foodstuffs or books or clothing and so forth for their own use and later no longer needing them

31 Thom. Aq. *Sum. th.* 2a 2ae q. 77 a. 4 ad 3. Most of this paragraph is a paraphrase of Aquinas.

32 Hier. in D. 88 c. 9 (*Negotiatorem*). Cfr Thom. Aq. *Sum. th.* 2a 2ae q. 77 a. 4 obj. 3.

33 *Sir* 26.28: "Two sorts of callings have appeared to me hard and dangerous: a merchant is hardly free from negligence: and a huckster shall not be justified from the sins of the lips." Cfr *Sir* 27.2: "As a stake sticketh fast in the midst of the joining of stones, so also in the midst of selling and buying, sin shall stick fast."

34 Leo in *De pen.* D. 5 c. 2 (*Qualitas*): "The quality of his gain either accuses, or condemns a trader, because there is an honourable and a shameful profit. And yet, for a penitent, it is more useful even to suffer expenses than to be bound by the dangers of trade, because it is difficult for sin not to intervene in the commerce between buyer and seller."

35 *Ps* 100.6: "My eyes were upon the faithful of the earth, to sit with me: the man that walked in the perfect way, he served me."

36 *2 Tim* 2.4: "No man, being a soldier to God, entangleth himself with secular businesses; that he may please him to whom he hath engaged himself."

37 D. 88 c. 2 (*Consequens*): "It also follows that we believe not to be passed over what a report sent to us from the regions of Picenum has brought to our attention, namely that several clerics attend to dishonest trade and filthy lucre. With no shame, they see the Gospel reading by which the Lord himself is said to have expelled the traders from the Gospel, striking them with whips, nor do they recall the words of the Apostle, by which he says: *No man, being a soldier to God, entangles himself with secular businesses* (2 Tim. 2.4); feigning a deaf ear, they also fail to hear the psalmist David, who sings: *Because I have not known trade, I will enter into the powers of the Lord* (Ps. 70.16). And so these people know either that they must henceforth abstain from these unworthy gains, and to cease from any pursuit of trade or cupidity, or, in whatever grade they may be placed, they must be compelled immediately to abstain from clerical offices, because the house of God is to be and to be called a house of prayer, lest it become rather a den of thieves by the offices of trade (cf. Lc. 19.46)."

uti prima commutationis specie que ordinatur ad neccessitatem uite emendo uel uendendo. Et si emendo ad sui usum uictualia uel libros uel uestes et huiusmodi, postea non indigendo hiis uel alia querendo, empta charius uendant clerici, quia tunc plus ualent quam prius: non peccant, clerici uel layci. Similiter licet eis rudem materiam emere et inde artificilia facere honesta, tamen que congruant statui suo, sicut emere ferrum inde facere ligones et uendere, et alia huiusmodi honesta exercitia, non tamen ex hoc dimittendo ecclesie officia, arg. D. 91 *Clerichus*. *Nolite* ergo, qui clerici uel religiosi estis, negotiationibus uacando, *facere domum patris mei domum negotiationis*.

2.3. Ratione temporis feriati.

Tertio negotiatio est mala ratione temporis feriati, id est diebus festiuis. Quilibet enim debet talibus diebus [debet] abstinere ab operibus seruilibus iuxta Domini preceptum, Exo. 20, *Omne opus* seruile *non facietis in eo*. Sed computatur inter opera seruilia negotiari, nisi emendo que sunt neccessaria uictui cotidiano; et de hoc habetur diffuse infra, titulo <nono> c. <7.> Per huiusmodi enim negotiationem non solum uiolantur festa, sed frequenter ommictuntur diuina officia, quibus uacandum est diebus festiuis. *De cons.* D. 3 <c. *Ieiunia*> dicitur, "In illa sancta die," scilicet festiua, "nil aliud agendum nisi Deo uacandum." Dicit tamen Petrus de Palude in 4°, in nundinis negotiando, auditis diuinis, non quidem causa auaritie, id est congregandi ad superfluitatem, sed aliquo fine honesto, scilicet ad prouidendum ex lucro necessitati sue et familie uel dandum

---

157 Et … **159** layci] Cfr Thom. Aq. *Sum. th.* 2a 2ae q. 77 a. 4 ad 2; Raym. Penn. *Sum. paen.* 2.7.9 (1B:547).

163 arg … Clerichus] D. 91 c. 3 (*Clericus*[1]): Clericus uictum et uestimentum, sibi artificiolo uel agricultura, absque offitii sui dumtaxat detrimento, preparet. §. 1. Clericus enim, qui absque corpusculi sui inequalitate uigiliis deest, stipendio priuatus excommunicetur.
D. 91 c. 4 (*Clericus*[2]): Clericus quilibet uerbo Dei eruditus artificio uictum querat. Item: §. 1. Omnes clerici, qui ad operandum ualidi sunt, et artificiola, et litteras discant. Qui uero non pro emendo aliquid in nundinis uel in foro deambulant, ab offitio suo degradentur. Inter temptaciones autem ab offitio declinantes uel negligentius agentes ab ipso offitio remoueantur.

167 Omne … eo] *Ex* 20.10: Septimo autem die sabbatum Domini Dei tui est : non facies omne opus in eo, tu, et filius tuus et filia tua, servus tuus et ancilla tua, jumentum tuum, et advena qui est intra portas tuas.

167 Computatur … **168** negotiari] Vide Raym. Penn. *Sum. paen.* 1.12.4 (1B:398–9).

169 de … 7] Ant. Flor. *Summa* 2.9.7 (apud M_1 fol. 324v–327v, Ballerini 2:975–87, Mamachi 2:1305–21): *de negligentia circa obseruationem festorum, et ibi quomodo festa debeant celebrari.*

172 In…uacandum] *De cons.* D.3 c.16 (*Ieiunia*): Die autem dominica nichil aliud agendum est, nisi Deo uacandum. Nulla operatio in illa die sancta agatur, nisi tantum ymnis, et psalmis, et canticis spiritualibus dies illa transigatur.

173 in[2] … **177** tollerant] Locum Petr. Pal. non inveni.

---

160 rudem] *ut vid.* : crudam *F_2 fol. 47ra p.c.* : eamdem *F_2 fol. 47ra a.c. una cum Mamachi et Ballerini* **167** 20] 21 *a.c.* **169** nono … 7] *spatia quattuor litterarum praeb. cod.* **171** c. Ieiunia] *supplevi cum F_2 fol. 47rb* : *spatium duarum litterarum praeb. cod.* **174** fine] *in marg. sin. add. Iul. de Lapacc. ut vid.*

or wanting other things, clerics sell the things they bought for a higher price, because they are worth more then than before: they commit no sin, clerics or laymen.[38] Similarly it is licit for them to buy raw material and from it to make honest crafts, assuming they are congruent to their state, like buying iron to make hoes from it and sell them, and other honest occupations of this sort, and nevertheless in doing so not neglecting the offices of the Church; by the argument of D. 91 c. 3–4.[39] *Make not*, therefore, you who are clerics or religious, by devoting time to trade, *the house of my Father a house of trade.*

2.3. Time: holiday. Third, trade is evil on account of holiday time, that is on feast days. For everyone is obliged on those days to abstain from servile works according to the Lord's commandment in Exodus 20, *Thou shalt do no* servile *work on it.*[40] But trade is counted among servile works,[41] except for buying such things as are necessary for daily sustenance; and about this there is a lengthy discussion below in title 9, chapter 7.[42] Through this sort of trade not only are the feasts violated, but frequently the divine offices are omitted, to which one must attend on feast days. In *De cons.* D. 3 c. 16 it is said, "On that holy day," namely feast day, "nothing else is to be done than to attend to God."[43] Nevertheless Peter of la Palud in book 4 says, people who trade in the markets, having heard the divine offices, not indeed for the sake of greed, that is of accumulating beyond what is necessary, but for some honest end, namely to provide from the profit for their need or their family, or to give to the poor or to provide things necessary for the good of the community: such people may be excused,

38 Cfr Thom. Aq. *Sum. th.* 2a 2ae q. 77 a. 4 ad 2; Raym. Penn. *Sum. paen.* 2.7.9 (1B:547).

39 D. 91 c. 3 (*Clericus*[1]): "A cleric may gain his food and clothing by some little work or the work of the fields, but yet without detriment to his office. *Also.* § 1. A cleric who, without unequalness of body, is absent from the vigils, deprived of his stipend, is to be excommunicated."

D. 91 c. 4 (*Clericus*[2]). "A cleric, however learned in the word of God, is to seek his sustenance by some little work. *Also.* § 1. All clerics who are able to work are to know both some little work and their letters. As for those who walk in the fairs or the market without having anything to buy, they are to be degraded from their office. Those brokers who avoid their office, or carry it out more negligently, are to be removed from their office."

40 *Ex* 20.10: "But on the seventh day is the sabbath of the Lord thy God: thou shalt do no work on it, thou nor thy son, nor thy daughter, nor thy manservant, nor thy maidservant, nor thy beast, nor the stranger that is within thy gates."

41 Vide Raym. Penn. *Sum. paen.* 1.12.4 (1B:398–9).

42 Ant. Flor. *Summa* 2.9.7 (apud M_I fol. 324v–327v, Ballerini 2:975–87, Mamachi 2:1305–21): *de negligentia circa obseruationem festorum, et ibi quomodo festa debeant celebrari.*

43 *De cons.* D. 3 c. 16 (*Ieiunia*): "As for Sunday, nothing else is to be done than to attend to God. No work is to be done on that holy day; that whole day is to be passed only in hymns, psalms, and spiritual canticles."

pauperibus uel prouidendum bono communitatis de rebus necessariis: possent tales excusari, ex quo prelati ecclesiarum sciunt et tollerant. Secus, si sint prohibite per aliquam exchommunicationem et huiusmodi. Conuenientius tamen prouideretur per penas peccuniarias, que magis timentur si exigantur.

2.4. Ratione loci sacrati.

Quarto est mala ratione loci, cum scilicet exercetur negotiatio in ecclesia: fit enim ex hoc magna irreuerentia locho sacro, et per consequens Deo, cuius est domus. Vnde et Dominus uendentes et ementes in templo eiecit dicens: *Nolite facere domum patris mei domum negotiationis*. Sed dignius et sacratius est in tempori gratie templum ecclesie quam templum Salomonis; ibi enim offerebantur animalia et sanguis hirchorum et uitulorum, hic autem offertur corpus et sanguis Christi uerum. Et cum plura peccata perpetrentur in emptione et uenditione, grauiora etiam fiunt ratione loci sacri, sicut et alia ibi perpetrata. Impeditur etiam deuotio orantium propter tumultum, qui solet contingere in huiusmodi. Sed quid de uendentibus ibi candelas in ecclesia? Dicendum uidetur quod clerici uel religiosi qui hoc faciunt principaliter ad satisfaciendum deuotioni fidelium, qui solent eas accendere in honorem Dei, excusari possunt. Si autem ad cupiditatem et lucrum principaliter, non uidentur posse excusari a uitio eis prohibito negotiationis, et precipue in tali loco, sicut nec sacerdotes ueteris testamenti in hiis que uendebant in templo.

Quid consulendum sit de lucris in hiis quattuor casibus.

Et in hiis quattuor casibus predictis, quamuis consulendum sit quod lucra facta in huiusmodi pauperibus erogentur, non tamen uidetur hoc esse de neccessitate salutis. Et ratio est quia datio et acceptio peccunie in huiusmodi de se non est prohibita, sed actus negotiandi, non simpliciter, sed in tali loco, tempori, persona, uel fine. Licet aliqui contrarium dicant, non tamen inueni aliquod ius uel doctorem solempnem hoc expresse dicentem, scilicet quod de necessitate sit pauperibus dandum illud lucrum. Quod autem predicetur hoc pauperibus dandum, cautum est absque alia declaratione, esse scilicet de neccessitate uel consilii honestate. Nec enim oportet omnem ueritatem aperire in predicatione propter periculum abutentium | sententiis ueritatis, qui proni (fol. 68r) sunt ad conscientiam dilatandam: quinymmo et in interrogationibus super

---

195 quamuis … **197** salutis] Cfr Raym. Penn. *Sum. paen.* 2.7.11 (1B:548–50); ibid. 2.5.44 *De forma restitutionis* (1B:524–5).

203 Nec … **206** eludere] D. 43 c. 2 (*In mandatis*): Quod si ingesserit se, et prouocabit nos dicere, que eum minus recte agentem non oporteat audire, prudenter eum debemus eludere. Vide etiam *Glossa ord.* ad idem s.v. *prudenter*: transferendo nos callide ad alienam materiam: cum nec ipsi debeant alieni regni scrutari arcana …

---

177 sint] *ut vid.* **183** et] + ho- *a.c.* **192** cupiditatem] + sic *a.c.* **195** quod] *scilicet negotiatio iniqua ratione finis vel persone vel temporis vel loci* **196** de] *s.l.* **201** pauperibus] pauper- *haud leg.* **205** super] *ut vid.*

because the prelates of the churches know and tolerate this.[44] It is otherwise if they are prohibited under an excommunication or what have you. Nevertheless this is more conveniently dealt with by pecuniary penalties, which, if they are enforced, are feared more.

2.4. Place: sacred. Fourth, trade is evil on account of place, namely when trade is carried out in a church: for by this a great irreverence is committed against the sacred place, and consequently against God, whose house it is. And hence the Lord cast out the sellers and buyers in the temple saying: *Make not the house of my Father a house of trade*. But the temple of the church in the time of grace is more worthy and sacred than the temple of Solomon: for there animals were offered, and the blood of he-goats, and of calves; but here is offered the true body and blood of Christ. And since many sins are perpetrated in buying and selling, their gravity is increased by the circumstance of sacred place, the same as for other sins perpetrated there. The devotion of those praying is also impeded by the tumult which generally attends this sort of business. But what about those selling candles there in the church? It seems we must say that clerics or religious who do this principally to satisfy the devotion of the faithful, who are accustomed to light them in honour of God, may be excused. But if it is principally for cupidity and profit, it does not seem that they may be excused from the vice of trade prohibited to them, and particularly in such place, just as the priests of the Old Testament were not excused in those things which they would sell in the temple.

What should be counselled about such profits in these four cases. And in these four aforesaid cases,[45] although one must counsel that the profits made in such transactions should be bestowed on the poor, nevertheless this does not seem to be necessary for salvation.[46] And the reason is that the giving and receiving of money in these matters is not in itself prohibited, but rather the act of trading, not simply, but specifically in such place, at such time, by such person, or for such end. Granted that some say the contrary, nevertheless I have not found any law or solemn doctor expressly saying this, namely that such profit must by necessity be given to the poor. But it is circumspect to preach that it should be given to the poor, without affirming specifically whether this is strictly required or recommended as upright behaviour. For it is not proper to open up every truth in preaching, because of the danger of people who are prone to loosening their consciences abusing the truths they are told; moreover even in questions about this it is fitting sometimes "to prudently sidestep," by

44 I have not found the *locus* in Petr. Pal. in his *Quartus sententiarum liber* (Paris, 1514).

45 Namely, trade engaged in for greed, by a cleric, on a holiday, or in a church or sacred place.

46 Antoninus's doctrine seems to roughly follow the lines laid down by Raym. Penn. *Sum. paen.* 2.7.11 (1B:548–50); similarly ibid., 2.5.44 *De forma restitutionis* (1B:524–5).

hoc decet aliquando "prudenter eludere," ar. D. 43 *In mandatis*. Semper etiam tutior uia consulenda, sed non imperanda, ar. 26 q. 7 *Alligant*.

2.5. Ratione consortii iniusti.

Quinto negotiatio redditur illicita ratione mali consortii: puta si inter se mercatores conueniant et pactum faciant, quod omnes uendant tali pretio tales merces, uel unus solus uendat et non alii certam rerum speciem. Tales si pactum faciant, quod uendant certo pretio competenti et non plus, sed in minus sint liberi, iustum est. Ymmo consulit Hostiensis quod ad hoc quod mercatores sua officia exerceant bona fide, de licentia sui episcopi sciant quantum possunt lucrari in mensura bladi et uini et huiusmodi, uel quantum possunt pro libra ultra id quod emerunt uendere in recompensatione laboris industrie et expensarum, et secundum pretium taxatum ab eo uendant sine mendaciis, et tuti erunt a peccato negotiationis, *Extra, De emptione et uenditione*, c. 1. Bonum et equum consilium est, sed quia consilium est non obligat, cum consuetudo ubique quasi sit in contrarium. Vbi tamen siue per episcopum, siue, quod melius fieret, prouideretur per rectores ciuitatis, scilicet quod taxato pretio ab eis uenderentur uictualia et alia que sunt ad usum neccessaria, non possent mercatores seu uendentes pretium augere absque peccato. Sed si pactum faciunt mercatores insimul, quod certo pretio uendant merces suas et

---

206 Semper … **207** imperanda] C. 26 q. 7 c. 12 (*Alligant*): Deinde, etsi erramus modicam penitenciam inponentes, nonne melius est propter misericordiam rationem dare, quam propter crudelitatem? Ubi enim paterfamilias largus est, dispensator non debet esse tenax. Si Deus benignus, ut quid sacerdos eius austerus uult apparere?

Vide etiam *Glossa ord.* ad idem s.v. *melius est*: Misericordia est praeferenda rigori.

212 consulit … **217** mendaciis] Hostien. *Sum.* 5.38 *De poenitentiis et remissionibus* §. 61 *Quid de negotiatoribus* (5:1859): Verum sacerdos debet tales in viam rectam dirigere, et inducere quantum potest, ut recto fine laborent, et rectam intentionem habeant, et sine omni fraude officia sua exerceant bona fide: et consulerem talibus quod de licentia episcopi sui scirent, quantum possent lucrari in mensura bladi et vini, et similibus, vel quantum pro libra possent ultra quam emerent vendere, in recompensatione laboris et expensarum, et sic venderent sine mendacio: ipsos crederem esse in tuto, quo ad peccatum negotiationis. arg. supra de contrah. empt. c. j. supra de voto. c. j. et c. magnae. §. fi. 10. q. j. regenda. et sic possent intelligi 88. dist. fornicari. Hi autem qui hoc non faciunt, sine periculo vix evadunt. et sic potest intelligi quod dicit Leo, Difficile esse inter ementis vendentisque commercium non intervenire peccatum. de poe. di. 5. qualitas. et c. seq.

217 Extra … **218** 1] *X* 3.17.1 (*Placuit*): Cogit episcopus, ne carius vendatur transeuntibus, quam in mercato venderetur.

---

206 hoc] + oportet aliquando *a.c.* **209** et … faciant] *in marg. dext. add.* **210** merces] + et non minus *a.c.* **212** Ymmo] + fieri debet taxatio pretii *a.c.* **221** alia] + co- *a.c.*

the argument of D. 43 c. 2.[47] Also the safer way is always to be counselled, but not commanded, according to the argument of C. 26 q. 7 c. 12.[48]

2.5. Combination: unjust. Fifth, trade is rendered illicit on account of evil combination: say, if merchants agree among themselves and make a pact that all shall sell such and such merchandise at such and such price, or only one shall sell, and not the others, a certain type of thing. If such merchants make a pact to sell at a certain suitable price and not more, but they are free to sell for less, it is just. Hostiensis actually counsels[49] that in order for merchants to exercise their business in good faith, they should know from the permission of their bishop how much profit they may take on a measure of grain and wine and so forth, or how much per pound beyond what they paid in buying they may sell for in compensation for labour, industry, and expenses, and according to the price assessed by him they may sell without resort to lies, and they will be safe "from the sin of trade, *Extra*, *On buying and selling*, c. 1."[50] It is a good and fair counsel, but because it is a counsel they are not required to obey it, when custom practically everywhere runs counter to it. Nevertheless where provision is made by the bishop, or what is better, by the governors of the state, namely that foodstuffs and other things which are necessary for use be sold at a price assessed by them, then merchants or sellers may not increase the price without sin. But if the merchants make a pact collectively to sell their merchandise at a certain price and no less, by this not intending to protect themselves from loss when they place a just price on their merchandise based on its value at the time, but rather to seek immoderate profits from an excessive price, they do a most wicked thing. And these

---

47 D. 43 c. 2 (*In mandatis*): "If he should push himself forward and induce us to speak those things which it is not lawful for him to hear, because of the less than righteous nature of his actions, then we must prudently avoid him."

See also *Glossa ord.* ad idem s.v. *prudenter*: "By prudently changing the topic, as they must not pierce the mysteries of a kingdom which is not their own ..."

48 C. 26 q. 7 c. 12 (*Alligant*): "Finally, even if we err in imposing a slight penance, is it not better to render an account for mercy than for cruelty? For where the father of the household is generous, the administrator must not be stingy. If God is full of benignity, how can his priest be austere? Do you wish to appear holy? Be austere as to your own life, but full of benignity as to the life of another."

See also *Glossa ord.* ad idem s.v. *melius est*: "Mercy is to be preferred over rigour." My translation.

49 Hostien.*Sum.* 5.38 *De poenitentiis et remissionibus* §. 61 *Quid de negotiatoribus* (5:1859). Cfr Panorm. *Comm. X* 3.17.1, n.9 (1583 ed., 3:96r).

50 *X* 3.17.1 (*Placuit*): "The bishop compels that people not sell more dear to travellers than they may sell in the market." My translation.

non minus, per hoc non tam intendentes se conseruare indempnes cum iustum pretium ponunt mercibus secundum ualorem illius temporis, quam lucra immoderata [lucra] querere ex nimietate pretii, pessime faciunt. Et dicuntur hii monopolite a monos, quod est unum, et pola, quod est uenditor, uel polis, quod est ciuitas, quasi unus solus uendens in ciuitate. Et tale pactum monopolitarum est illicitum, et a iure prohibitum secundum Hostiensem, *Codex*, *De monopoliis*, l. una. Et cauetur in dicta lege quod exercens tale officium, propriis bonis spoliatus exilio perpetuo dampnetur. Si quis etiam societatem facit cum eo quem nouit esse male conscientie et per phas et nephas negotiari, licet ipse ab illicitis commertiis caueat et socium admoneat ab illicitis abstinere, non excusatur nisi prohibeat in quantum potest, et societatem cum eo soluat si potest, uel protestetur, si non potest, de illicitis lucris participare non uelle nec ipsum in illis se intromittere, ar. D. 83 *Error*, et c. *Facientis*. Et super hoc debet inquirere, ne laboret crassa ignorantia que non excusat.

2.6. Ratione medii iniqui.

Sexto est illicita ratione medii, id est cum mediantibus periuriis et mendaciis et dupplicitatibus negotiatur. Vnde Cassiodorus: "Illi negotiatores abhominabiles sunt" coram Deo, "qui iustitiam Dei minime considerantes, per immoderatum peccunie ambitum merces suas plus periuriis quam pretiis honerant," D. 88 <*Quid est*> in palea. Et de periuriis quidem non est dubium, quod qui utuntur eis, etiam unicho periurio scienter, scilicet falsum iurando, quod

---

229 Codex … **230** una] *Cod.* 4.59.1[2] (*Iubemus ne quis*): Iubemus, ne quis cuiuscumque vestis aut piscis vel pectinum forte aut echini vel cuiuslibet alterius ad uictum vel ad quemcumque usum … monopolium audeat exercere, neve quis illicitis habitis conventionibus coniuraret aut pacisceretur, ut species diversorum corporum negotiationis non minoris, quam inter se statuerint, venumdentur. … Si quis autem monopolium ausus fuerit exercere, bonis propriis spoliatus perpetuitate damnetur exilii.

230 tale … **231** dampnetur] Non Hostien. sed potius Bern. Sen. *Evang. aet.* 33, 2, 7 §. 5 *de circumventionibus malitiosis* (4:153–4).

236 D. … Error] D. 83 c. 3 (*Error*): Error, cui non resistitur, approbatur, et ueritas, cum minime defensatur, obprimitur. Negligere quippe, cum possis perturbare peruersos, nichil est aliud quam fouere. Nec caret scrupulo societatis occultae, qui manifesto facinori desinit obuiare.

236 c. Facientis] D. 86 c. 3 (*Facientis*): Facientis proculdubio culpam habet, qui quod potest corrigere negligit emendare. Scriptum quippe est: "Non solum qui faciunt, sed etiam qui consentiunt," participes iudicantur. … Et nichil prodest alicui non puniri proprio, qui puniendus est alieno peccato.

239 Illi … **241** honerant] Cass. in D. 88 c. 13 (*Quid est aliud*): Negotiatores ergo illi abhominabiles existimantur, qui iustitiam Dei minime considerantes per inmoderatum pecuniae ambitum polluuntur, merces suas plus periuriis onerando quam preciis. Tales eiecit Dominus de templo, dicens: "Nolite facere domum patris mei domum negotiationis."

---

226 lucra] *bis* **230** l.] *bis a.c.* | cauetur] *in marg. dext. add.* | quod] *s.l.* **236** 83] 82 *cod.* | Facientis] + Contractus in negotiando facere cum hiis qui sciuntur exchommunicati non licet quia hoc fieri non potest nisi participando *a.c.* **242** Quid est] *spatium duarum litterarum praeb. cod.* | dubium] dubiis *a.c.*

are called monopolies, from *monos*, which is "one," and *pola*, which is "seller," or *polis*, which is "city," as if there is only one seller in the city.[51] And such a monopolistic pact is illicit, and prohibited by law, according to Hostiensis, *Code*, *On monopolies*, l. 1.[52] And it is warned in said law that one exercising such monopoly "shall be stripped of his property and condemned to perpetual exile."[53] Also if someone makes a partnership with a person who he knows is of bad conscience and uses any means good or bad in trade, even though he himself holds back from illicit commerce and admonishes his partner to abstain from it, he is not excused unless he prevents him insofar as he can, and dissolves the partnership with him if possible, or if not, if he protests that he will not participate in illicit profits nor allow himself into them, by the argument of D. 83 c. 3 and D. 86 c. 3.[54] And about this one should inquire, lest he labour under crass ignorance, which does not excuse.[55]

2.6. Means: wicked. Sixth, trade is illicit on account of means, that is when one trades by means of perjuries and lies and duplicities. Hence Cassiodorus: "Those traders are abominable" in God's sight, "who, not considering God's justice, by their immoderate ambition for money burden their merchandise more with perjuries than

51 "Monopoly, n … Etymology: < classical Latin *monopōlium* exclusive right to sell a commodity < ancient Greek *μονοπώλιον* right of monopoly (compare the synonymous and cognate *μονοπωλία*), in Hellenistic Greek also trade mart enjoying a monopoly < *μονο-* mono- comb. form + *πωλεῖν* to sell (see -pole comb. form) + *-ιον* , suffix forming nouns (compare -y suffix[4])." *Oxford English Dictionary Online*, s.v. "monopoly," accessed 23 September 2017.

52 Not Hostien. but rather Bern. Sen. *Evang. aet.* 33, 2, 7, §. 5 *de circumventionibus malitiosis* (4:153–4). I have not found this in Hostien. *Sum.* 3.17 or 5.38; the word *monopolit-* is not listed in the index of the 1574 ed.

53 *Cod.* 4.59.1[2] (*Iubemus ne quis*): "We order that no one shall have a monopoly … of any kind of cloth, fish, shell-fish, sea-urchin, or of any other article used for food or for any other purpose … nor shall anyone swear or agree in any unlawful meeting not to sell the various articles of commerce for less than the price agreed on … And if anyone shall dare to carry out a monopoly, his goods shall be confiscated and he shall be sent into perpetual exile."

54 D. 83 c. 3 (*Error*): "He who does not resist errors consents to them. The error, which is not resisted, is approved, and the truth is oppressed when it is not defended. Certainly, to be negligent, when you are able to trouble the perverted, this is nothing else than to give support. Nor does he lack the scruple of secret fellowship who fails to oppose a manifest crime."

D. 86 c. 3 (*Facientis*): "He who neglects to emend what he can shares the guilt of the doer … Indeed, it is written: *Not only they that do them, but they also that consent to them that do them* are adjudged to be sharers (Rom. 1.32) … And it profits one nothing to avoid being punished for his own sin who becomes punishable for another's."

55 Prümmer explains the kinds of ignorance this way: "According to the degree of carelessness vincible ignorance is either simply vincible, crass, or studied. Ignorance is *simply vincible* when there is some slight lack of care; it is *crass* or *supine* when the carelessness is grave and hardly any attempt is made to remove the ignorance. Such ignorance is either gravely or slightly culpable depending on the gravity of the matter of which one is ignorant … Ignorance is *studied (affected)* when it is deliberately fostered by the agent as a means of being excused from sin or of not avoiding some sin." *Handbook of Moral Theology*, 10.

peccant mortaliter, secundum Raymundum et beatum Tomam, 2^{a} 2^{e} <q. 98 a. 3>, quia expresse contra preceptum Dei faciunt, notabilem irreuerentiam committendo. De mendaciis autem dicit Raymundus quod si hoc faciunt ut decipiant, etiam mortaliter peccant, et tenentur ad restitutionem eius in quo deceperunt. Et glossa dicit ibi quod non distinguit, utrum in modicho uel in magno decipiat. Credo Raymundum loqui de mendacio, ex quo quis intendit nocere seu decipere in multo si posset, sicut in modicho, cum dicit esse mortale: nam si in modicho tantum intendat decipere, non est ratio quare debeat esse mortale. Et quod dicit glossa, uidetur referendum ad factum non ad intentionem, quod ex modo loquendi patet, hoc est cum et si intendat decipere in multo, actu tamen non decipit nisi in modico, quia non potest. Vel etiam potest referri ad factum restitutionis, quia ita in modicho decipiens tenetur ad illud modicum, sic ad multum qui in multo decipit. Sed si quis mendacio utitur in uendendo et emendo ut conseruet se indempnem, puta ut uendat iusto pretio rem suam dicit constitisse sibi plus quam constitit et huiusmodi, peccat talis uenialiter secundum Raymundum. Sed Hostiensis dicit, si hoc

---

244 secundum Raymundum] Raym. Penn. *Sum. paen.* 1.9.4–5 *Species iuramenti* (1B:367–8): Qualiter autem hoc fiat ostendit Augustinus ponens hos tres modos periurii … Secundus, cum scit vel putat falsum esse, et tamen pro vero iurat. … Duo ultima mortalia [sunt].

244 beatum … **245** 3] Thom. Aq. *Sum. th.* 2a 2ae q. 98 a. 3: Utrum [periurium] semper sit peccatum mortale. … Sed contra, omne peccatum quod contrariatur praecepto divino est peccatum mortale. Sed periurium contrariatur praecepto divino, dicitur enim Levit. XIX, non periurabis in nomine meo. Ergo est peccatum mortale. … Periurium autem de sui ratione importat contemptum Dei, ex hoc enim habet rationem culpae, ut dictum est, quia ad irreverentiam Dei pertinet.

246 si … **248** deceperunt] Raym. Penn. *Sum. paen.* 2.8.5 (1B:563): Ad hoc dico quod, quoties scienter et causa decipiendi proximum peierat vel mentitur, peccat mortaliter, et tenetur ad restitutionem in quantum deceperit proximum, illi eidem decepto faciendam, si scit vel potest, vel heredi eius; vel si nescit personam, vel non potest, procedat ut dixi supra De usuris, § Sed pone, in fine [Lib. II tit. 7 n. 16: UBI 1 B 555] et supra De raptoribus, § Forma restituendi [Lib. II tit. 5 n. 44: UBI 1 B 524].

247 non … **248** decipiat] Guil. Red. *Glossa* in Raym. Penn. *Sum. paen.* 2.8.5 s.v. *in quantum* (1603 ed., 247): Non distinguit utrum in modico, vel in magno.

259 peccat … Raymundum] Raym. Penn. *Sum. paen.* 2.8.5 (1B:563–4): Si autem ignoranter dicit falsum credens dicere verum, vel etiam scienter, sed intendit et scit per mendacium illud sibi prodesse, ut sic se servet indemnem, et proximo non obesse, quia non decipit eum in re unam pro alia vendendo, nec in valore rei, quia non vendit ei ultra debitum valorem, tale mendacium potest dici forte veniale.

259 si … **260** peccare] Hostien. *Sum.* 5.38 *De poenitentiis et remissionibus* §. 61 *Quid de negotiatoribus* (5:1859): Veruntamen ex quo assidue et de consuetudine mentitur, quicquid dicat Ray. et ex aequitate et benignitate, tamen de veritate mortale videtur; sicut et ebrietas, si assidua sit, est mortalis. 25. dist. §. alias. et ut patet in his quae no. supra e. §. quae interrogationes. sub §. dixisti unquam mendacium.

259 Sed … **262** Alias] Cfr Bern. Sen. *Evang. aet.* 33, 2, 7 §. 1 *de mendaciis multis* (4:152).

---

244 q. … **245** 3] *spatium quinque litterarum praeb. cod.* **247** et … **248** deceperunt] *in marg. sin. add.* **249** Credo] Sed dicendum *a.c.* | loqui] intelligere *a.c.* **250** nocere] + in multo *a.c.* **256** Sed] Et *a.c.*

prices," D. 88 c. 13.[56] And about perjuries indeed there is no doubt that any people who make use of them, even one deliberate perjury, namely by swearing falsely, sin mortally, according to Raymond[57] and blessed Thomas, 2a 2ae q. 98 a. 3,[58] because they act expressly against the commandment of God, committing a notable irreverence. Now about lies, Raymond says that if they do this in order to deceive, they also sin mortally, and are bound to make restitution of the thing concerning which they committed deception.[59] And the gloss says there that Raymond does not distinguish whether one deceives in a small or a large amount.[60] I believe he is speaking about a lie by which one intends to do harm or to deceive for a lot if he can, or a little if not, when he says that it is mortal: for if he only intends to deceive in a small amount, then there is no reason why this should be mortal. And it appears that what the gloss says ought to be taken with reference to fact, not intention, which is evident from this manner of speaking, that is, when and if he intends to deceive for a lot, nevertheless in the actual deed he only deceives for a little, because he does not succeed. Or also it may be in reference to the fact of restitution, for just as one deceiving for a little is bound to restitution of that little amount, so one who deceives for a large amount is bound to restore that large amount. But if someone uses a lie in selling and buying in order to protect himself from loss[61] – for instance, in order to sell his thing at a just price, he says that it cost him more than it did, or something like this – such a one sins venially according to Raymond.[62] But Hostiensis says, if one does this "persistently and as a regular practice," he seems to sin mortally.[63] He argues by analogy with drunkenness,

56 Cass. in D. 88 c. 13 (*Quid est aliud*). "And so those traders are esteemed to be abominable who, with no consideration of God's justice, are polluted by their immoderate desire for money, burdening their merchandise more with perjuries than prices. The Lord cast out such people from the Temple, saying: *Do not make the house of my Father a house of trade* (Jn. 2.16)."

57 Raym. Penn. *Sum. paen.* 1.9.4–5 *Species iuramenti* (1B:367–8).

58 Thom. Aq. *Sum. th.* 2a 2ae q. 98 a. 3: "On the contrary, Every sin that is contrary to a divine precept is a mortal sin. Now perjury is contrary to a divine precept, for it is written (Lev. 19:12): 'Thou shalt not swear falsely by My name.' Therefore it is a mortal sin … Now perjury, of its very nature implies contempt of God, since, as stated above (Article [2]), the reason why it is sinful is because it is an act of irreverence towards God."

59 Raym. Penn. *Sum. paen.* 2.8.5 (1B:563). Cfr Hostien. *Sum.* 5.38 *De poenitentiis et remissionibus* §. 61 *Quid de negotiatoribus* (5:1844).

60 Guil. Red. *Glossa* in Raym. Penn. *Sum. paen.* 2.8.5 s.v. *in quantum* (1603 ed., 247).

61 For the next several sentences, cfr Bern. Sen. *Evang. aet.* 33, 2, 7 §. 1 *de mendaciis multis* (4:152).

62 Raym. Penn. *Sum. paen.* 2.8.5 (1B:563–4).

63 Hostien. *Sum.* 5.38 *De poenitentiis et remissionibus* §. 61 *Quid de negotiatoribus* (5:1859).

facit "assidue et ex consuetudine," mortaliter uidetur peccare. Arguit a simili de ebrietate, quam dicit Augustinus esse mortale "si sit assidua," ut patet D. 25 §. *Alias*. Hoc tamen non credo uerum, quia ueniale de se quantumcumque continuetur et multiplicetur, numquam fit mortale secundum beatum Tomam 1^a 2^e q. <88 a. 4>, et de hoc supra in prima parte titulo 6°. Sed bene disponit ad mortale. Nec est simile de ebrietate, unde et dictum illud Augustini exponit beatus Tomas, 2^a 2^e q. <150 a. 2>. Est igitur illud mendacium ueniale, nisi addatur contemptus. Et idem dicendum de duplicitatibus que ibi fiunt et fraudibus, scilicet quod sit mortale, ubi intenditur notabilis deceptio proximi, alias ueniale. De hoc plenius infra.

2.7. Ratione materie mali.

Septimo ratione materie mali: quedam enim negotia sunt, que sunt de se mala in sui natura, ut usura symonia et huiusmodi. Vnde Ambrosius:

---

261 ebrietate … assidua] AUG. in THOM. AQ. *Sum. th.* 2a 2ae q. 150 a. 2 ob. 1: Augustinus enim, in sermone de Purgatorio, dicit ebrietatem esse peccatum mortale, si sit assidua.

262 D. … Alias] D.25 c.3 Gr. p. §. 3 (*Alias*): Multa enim ex deliberatione procedunt, que nisi sepius iterata et in consuetudinem fuerint deducta, quamuis grauent post mortem, non tamen eternaliter perdunt: quia etsi quadam ratione crimina appellentur, tamen mortifera, et capitalia non sunt. … et si longo tempore teneatur, iracundia, et ebrietas, si assidua sit, in eorum numero computatur.

262 ueniale … **263** mortale] THOM. AQ. *Sum. th.* 1a 2ae q. 88 a. 4: Ea quae differunt in infinitum, non transmutantur in invicem. Sed peccatum mortale et veniale differunt in infinitum, ut ex praedictis patet. Ergo veniale non potest fieri mortale. … Quod si sic intelligatur quod ex multis peccatis venialibus integraliter constituatur unum peccatum mortale, falsum est. Non enim omnia peccata venialia de mundo, possunt habere tantum de reatu, quantum unum peccatum mortale. … Augustinus loquitur in illo sensu, quod multa peccata venialia dispositive causant mortale.

Cfr ibid. a. 5 ad 1; *Glossa ord.* ad D. 25 c. 3 Gr. p. §. 3 (*Alias*) s.v. *criminale* et s.v. *ebrietas*.

264 de … **265** 6°] ANT. FLOR. *Summa* 1.6 (apud *N* fol. 6r et Ballerini et Mamachi): *de causis peccatorum et passionibus*.

265 Nec … **267** contemptus] THOM. AQ. *Sum. th.* 2a 2ae q. 150 a. 2 ad 1: Ad primum ergo dicendum quod assiduitas facit ebrietatem esse peccatum mortale, non propter solam iterationem actus, sed quia non potest esse quod homo assidue inebrietur quin sciens et volens ebrietatem incurrat, dum multoties experitur fortitudinem vini, et suam habilitatem ad ebrietatem.

269 De … plenius] Infra in hoc capitulo, §. 3.1.3 *Excessus valoris rei*. Cfr ANT. FLOR. *Summa* 2.1.17 (infra).

---

260 assidue et] *in marg. sin. add.* | consuetudine] + peccare *a.c.* **262** quia] + de se *a.c.* **264** 88 … 4] *spatium quinque litterarum praeb. cod.* **266** 150 … 2] *spatium quinque litterarum praeb. cod.* **271** natura] + et per consequens *a.c.*

which Augustine says is mortal "if it is persistent,"[64] as is evident from D. 25 c. 3 §. 3.[65] Nevertheless I do not believe this is true, because a venial sin, in itself, no matter how much it is continued and multiplied, never becomes mortal, according to blessed Thomas, 1a 2ae q. 88 a. 4.[66] This is treated above in part 1, title 6.[67] But it certainly disposes one to mortal sin. Nor is it analogous to drunkenness, and thus blessed Thomas expounds that statement of Augustine, 2a 2ae q. 150 a. 2.[68] That lie, therefore, is venial, unless contempt is added. And the same must be said about duplicities which are committed in trade, and frauds, namely that they are mortal when a notable deception of a neighbour is intended, otherwise they are venial. This is discussed more fully below.[69]

2.7. Matter: evil. Seventh, <trade is wicked> on account of evil matter: for there are some kinds of trade which in themselves have an evil nature, such as usury, simony, and so forth. Hence Ambrose: "Many are found who, by their trade in this gift,

---

64 Aug. in Thom. Aq. *Sum. th.* 2a 2ae q. 150 a. 2 ob. 1: "It would seem that drunkenness is not a mortal sin. For Augustine says in a sermon on Purgatory [*Serm. civ in the Appendix to St. Augustine's works] that "'drunkenness if indulged in assiduously, is a mortal sin.'"

65 D. 25 c. 3 Gr. p. §. 3 (*Alias*): "For there are many actions proceeding from deliberation which, unless they are frequently repeated and become customary and even though they are a burden after death, nevertheless they do not cause eternal loss; although these deeds are somewhat reasonably called crimes, nevertheless they are not deadly and capital ... If they should be practised for a long time, anger and frequent drunkenness are also counted among these [capital sins]."

66 Thom. Aq. *Sum. th.* 1a 2ae q. 88 a. 4: "Things that differ infinitely are not changed into one another. Now venial and mortal sin differ infinitely, as is evident from what has been said above (Q. 72, a. 5, ad 1; Q. 87, a.5, ad 1). Therefore a venial sin cannot become mortal ... If this be taken as meaning that many venial sins added together make one mortal sin, it is false, because all the venial sins in the world cannot incur a debt of punishment equal to that of one mortal sin ... Augustine is referring to the fact of many venial sins making one mortal sin dispositively."

Cfr ibid. a. 5 ad 1; *Glossa ord.* ad D. 25 c. 3 Gr. p. §. 3 (*Alias*) s.v. *criminale* and *ebrietas*, where the same argument is made.

67 Ant. Flor. *Summa* 1.6 (apud *N* fol. 6r et Ballerini et Mamachi): *de causis peccatorum et passionibus.*

68 Thom. Aq. *Sum. th.* 2a 2ae q. 150 a. 2 ad 1: "Assiduity makes drunkenness a mortal sin, not on account of the mere repetition of the act, but because it is impossible for a man to become drunk assiduously, without exposing himself to drunkenness knowingly and willingly, since he has many times experienced the strength of wine and his own liability to drunkenness."

69 See below in this chapter, section 3.1.3 "Excess in valuation." Cfr Ant. Flor. *Summa* 2.1.17 (below).

"Reperiuntur quamplurimi negotiatione muneris merchari uelle gratiam Spiritus Sancti," 1 q. 1 *Reperiuntur*. Et horum negotiatio, id est exercitatio, omnibus prohibetur clericis et laycis secundum Raymundum.

Quedam alia sunt, que non sunt in sui natura mala, tamen eis utuntur homines, ut in pluribus, ad malum: ut facere taxillos cartas seu naybos, fuchos, et ornamenta superflua uestium, et huiusmodi. Et ab horum negotiatione, id est emptione et uenditione et factione, debet quilibet abstinere, et per maxime ab hiis que sine peccato mortali fieri non possunt, seu quorum usus communiter est ad mortale peccatum. Et sic intelligendum est quod dicit Innocentius in c. *Fratres nostros*, *De pen.* D. 5, "Verum falsa penitentia est, cum penitens ab officio," id est actu "negotiali non recedit, quod sine peccatis agi non potest," et quod ait Gregorius in omelia, scilicet negotia "que ad peccatum implicant, neccesse est ut ad hec post conuersionem animus non recurrat," *De pen.* D. 5 *Negotium*. Loquuntur enim de mortalibus peccatis. Nam si de quibuscumque etiam uenialibus intelligantur, nullus posset etiam negotia licita exercere. De huiusmodi tamen artibus, quarum artificia sunt frequenter ad peccata, dicetur infra in sequenti capitulo.

---

272 Reperiuntur … **273** Sancti] AMBR. in C. 1 q. 1 c. 7 (*Reperiuntur*) (Rome, 1582 ed., 1:653–4): Reperiuntur quamplurimi negotio [† al. negotiatione] muneris perituri, mercari velle gratiam spiritus sancti.

274 secundum Raymundum] RAYM. PENN. *Sum. paen.* 2.8.1 (1B:558): Circa hoc nota quod negotia: alia inhonesta sui natura, alia non. Inhonesta sui natura sunt omnia quae sine peccato exerceri non possunt, ut contractus usurarum, simoniae et similes. Ista omnibus sunt prohibita indistincte, tam clericis, quam laicis cuiuscumque sexus sint vel condicionis vel aetatis, dummodo sint doli capaces. 14 q. 4 Nec hoc quoque [C. 14 q. 4 c. 8(7); 1 q. 1 Reperiuntur, in fine [C. 1 q. 1 c. 7]; dist. 88 Fornicari [D.88 c.10]; Extra de delictis puerorum, Pueris [X 5.23.1]; Extra de iureiurando, Etsi Christus, ultra medium, versu Quaedam enim prohibentur quia per se mala sunt [X 2.24.26]. Cfr RAYM. PENN. *Sum. paen.* 2.8.6 (1B:564–6).

281 Verum … **283** potest] INNO. II in *De pen.* D. 5 c. 8 (*Fratres*): Falsa est etiam penitencia, cum penitens ab offitio uel curiali uel negotiali non recedit, quod sine peccatis nullatenus agi preualet.

284 negotia … **285** recurrat] GREG. M. in *De pen.* D. 5 c. 7 (*Negotium*): Que ergo ad peccatum inplicant, ad hec necesse est ut post conuersionem animus non recurrat.

287 De … **288** peccata] ANT. FLOR. *Summa* 2.1.17 (infra).

---

271 Vnde … **272** Reperiuntur] *in marg. infer. add.* **273** negotiatio] + omnibus *a.c.* **275** que] + sunt *a.c.* | mala] + sed possunt honestis uti bene et male. Sicut *a.c.* **276** facere] + uenena ad mortem *a.c.* **279** possunt] *ut vid.* **282** id … actu] *in marg. sin. add.* **286** de] *s.l.*

are seeking to traffic in the grace of the Holy Spirit," C. 1 q. 1 c. 7.[70] And trade in these things, that is practising them, is prohibited to all clerics and laymen alike according to Raymond.[71]

There are some other matters which do not have an evil nature, but nevertheless men use them at least for the most part for evil: as in the making of dice, playing cards or games,[72] cosmetics and superfluous ornamentation of clothing, and so forth. And everyone should abstain from trading in these things, that is buying and selling and making them, and most of all from those which cannot be done without mortal sin, or whose use commonly tends to mortal sin. And this is how we must interpret what Innocent says in *De pen.* D. 5 c. 8, "A penance is indeed false when the penitent does not withdraw from the office," that is the act, "of trading, which cannot be carried out without sin,"[73] and what Gregory says in a homily, namely, as for those trades "which involve one in sin, it is necessary that one's mind not return to these after conversion," *De pen.* D. 5 c. 7.[74] For they are speaking about mortal sins. For if these statements were understood as also applying to venial sins of whatever sort, then no one could practise even the licit kinds of trade. However, crafts of this kind, whose products frequently lead to sin, will be discussed below in the following chapter.[75]

---

70 AMBR. in C. 1 q. 1 c. 7 (*Reperiuntur*). The text of this canon in Friedberg differs from the Roman edition of 1582 (1:653–4). Silano translates the Roman text: "Many are found who, by seeking to traffic in the grace of the Holy Spirit, will perish by their trade in this gift."

71 RAYM. PENN. *Sum. paen.* 2.8.1 *Quaenam negotia inhonesta dicantur* (1B:558); cfr RAYM. PENN. *Sum. paen.* 2.8.6 (1B:564–6).

72 Cfr Du Cange s.v. *naibis, naibes*: "Ital. Naibi, Ludi puerilis genus."

73 INNO. II in *De pen.* D. 5 c. 8 (*Fratres*): "A penance is also false when the penitent does not withdraw from a court or trade function which can in no way be fulfilled without sin."

74 GREG. M. in *De pen.* D. 5 c. 7 (*Negotium*): "But as for those things which involve one in sin, it is necessary that one's mind not turn to these after conversion."

75 ANT. FLOR. *Summa* 2.1.17 (below).

Quedam alia sunt dubia, ut emere prestantias solutas communitati ab aliis, seu denarios montis et imprestita Venetorum et loca Ianuensium, que quidam dicunt licita, quidam illicita et usuraria. Et ab huiusmodi etiam abstinendum, quia: "In dubiis tutior uia est eligenda," *Extra*, *De spons.*, *Iuuenis*. Et de hac materia diffuse habes supra eodem tit. c. <11>. Ibi ponuntur rationes ad utramque partem: et ideo non de facili condempnandum, et sic consulendum quod tutius est, ut dictum est. |

3. De negotiatione temporali modesta.

Quantum ad tertium principale, scilicet de negotiatione temporali modesta, fol. 68v sciendum quod tunc negotiatio est modesta et licita quando <quis> eam exercet secundum iustitiam Dei, id est secundum iustitiam quam exigit Deus ab hominibus, non secundum iustitiam hominum. Et hoc est quod ait Ps., *Memorabor iustitie tue solius*, scilicet in negotiando et alia opera faciendo. Iustitia hominum cauet sibi solum a magnis excessibus deceptionis, puta ultra dimidiam iusti pretii, irritans tales contractus, ut *Extra*, *De empt. et uen.*, *Cum dilecti*. Sed iustitia Dei non permictit aliquam etiam paruam deceptionem scienter factam. Qui autem sequuntur iustitiam hominum, non memorantur iustitie Dei, de qua dicit Psalmista: *Memorabor iustitie tue solius*. Illi sunt negotiatores qui de templo ecclesie militantis quoad meritum eiciuntur, et de templo ecclesie triumphantis quoad consortium. Vnde Cassiodorus super dicto uersiculo Psalmi: "Illi abhominabiles sunt," scilicet "qui iustitiam

---

293 In … eligenda] *X* 4.1.3 (*Iuvenis*): Quia igitur in his, quae dubia sunt, quod certius existimamus tenere debemus, tum propter honestatem ecclesiae, quia ipsa coniux ipsius fuisse dicitur, tum propter praedictam dubitationem, mandamus tibi, quatenus consobrinam ipsius puellae, quam postmodum duxit, dividas ab eodem.

Vide *Glossa ord.* ad idem, casus: Respondet Papa, in his quae dubia sunt, quod certius est, servari debet … Notandum ergo quod in dubiis semper tenendum est illud, quod securius est et certius.

Vide etiam Ant. Flor. *Summa* 1.20.1.16 (apud *N* fol. 311r, Ballerini 1:856–7, Mamachi 1:1363–4). Cfr Laur. Rod. *Tr. usur.* 2 q.7 (Armstrong, 180); ibid. 3 conclusio (Armstrong, 249).

293 de … **294** diffuse] Ant. Flor. *Summa* 2.1.11 (apud M_1 fol. Vr, 31v–36v, Ballerini 2:159–91; 2.1.10 apud Mamachi 2:213–59): *de materia montis de Florentia et inprestitarum Venetiis et locis Ianuensium.*

303 ultra … contractus] *X* 3.17.3 (*Cum dilecti*): Tenet venditio, licet venditor sit deceptus ultra dimidiam iusti pretii; potest tamen venditor agere, ut restituatur res vel iustum pretium suppleatur, et, si alterum praecise petit, succumbit.

309 Illi … **311** polluunt] Cass. in D. 88 c. 13 (*Quid est aliud*): vide supra.

---

290 ut] *ut vid.* **294** 11] *spatium quattuor litterarum praeb. cod.* **295** sic] *ut vid. cod.* : si F_2 *fol. 47vb* | et^{2} … consulendum] *ut vid. propter detrimentum cod.* | de … **296** est^{2}] *in marg. infer. add.* **298** modesta] iusta *a.c.* | quis] *supplevi cum* F_2 *fol. 47vb* **300** iustitiam] *bis* **305** sequuntur] sequentes *cod.* | hominum] + ob *a.c.* **308** et] preca- *a.c.* **309** scilicet] *s.l.* : negotiatores *a.c.*

Certain other matters are doubtful, such as buying *prestanze*[76] paid out to the community by others, or credits in the *monte*,[77] and *imprestiti* of Venice,[78] and *luogi* of Genoa,[79] which some say are licit, some illicit and usurious. And one should also abstain from things of this sort, because: "In doubtful things the safer path ought to be chosen," *Extra, On engagements*, c. 3.[80] A copious treatment of this matter is found above in the same title, c. 11.[81] There, arguments are set out that support both sides, and therefore this is not to be facilely condemned; and so what is safer should be counselled, as already said.

3. Modest temporal trade. As for the third principal part, namely modest temporal trade, it must be understood that trade is modest and licit when <one> practises it in accordance with God's justice, that is, following the justice which God demands from men, not following men's justice. And this is what the Psalmist says: *I will be mindful of thy justice alone*, namely in trading and in doing other works. The justice of men restrains itself only from great excesses of deception, say beyond half of the just price, voiding such contracts, as in *Extra, On buying and selling*, c. 3.[82] But the justice of God does not permit any deception to be done knowingly, however small. Now those who follow the justice of men are not mindful of God's justice, about which the Psalmist says, *I will be mindful of thy justice alone*. These are the traders who are cast out from the temple of the Church militant in that they lack merit, and from the temple of the Church triumphant

---

76 "Compulsory loan to the commune." Armstrong, "Glossary," in *Usury and Public Debt*, s.v. *prestantias*, 393.

77 "Consolidated public debt of Florence, the *monte comune* … The public debt of Venice was also called the *mons*." Ibid. s.v. *mons*, 391.

78 "Compulsory loan to the commune of Venice analogous to the Florentine *prestanza*." Ibid. s.v. *imprestitis*, 388.

79 "Luogo; a share in the public debt (in Genoa)." Edler, *Terms of Business*, 165. This is the government security of Genoa, parallel to those of Florence and Venice. See also Kirshner, "From Usury to Public Finance," 28.

80 *X* 4.1.3 (*Iuvenis*). See the *Glossa ord.* ad idem, casus.

See also Ant. Flor. *Summa* 1.20.1.16 (apud *N* fol. 311r, Ballerini 1:856–7, Mamachi 1:1363–4). Cfr Laur. Rod. *Tr. usur.* 2 q. 7 (Armstrong, 180); Laur. Rod. *Tr. usur.* 3 conc (Armstrong, 249).

81 Ant. Flor. *Summa* 2.1.11 (apud M_I fol. Vr, 31v–36v, Ballerini 2:159–91; 2.1.10 apud Mamachi 2:213–59): *de materia montis de Florentia et inprestitarum Venetiis et locis Ianuensium.*

82 *X* 3.17.3 (*Cum dilecti*). "Originally a remedy for sellers of land, the Roman law title of *laesio enormis* (C. 4.44.2) was extended by medieval civilians to buyers as well as sellers and made applicable to all sales transactions. The title permits a party to a sale to appeal a price that varies by more than half the current market or legally regulated price. In such cases, the sale may be rescinded and the original price refunded or the fair value paid. *Laesio enormis* was recognized as a canonical title by Alexander III (1159–81) in *X* 3.17.3. It was endorsed by Innocent III in *X* 3.17.6." Armstrong, *Usury and Public Debt*, 303.

"The gloss to both canons [*X* 3.17.3 and 6] notes that parties to a purchase-sale may circumvent one another without invalidating the contract: 'But if I am deceived for less than half the just price, I have no action, for it is licit for contracting parties to deceive one another by up to half the just price.' [gl. ord. ad *X* 3.17.3, v. *Deceptione*]." Ibid., 368.

Dei minime considerantes, per nimium peccunie ambitum merces suas polluunt," D. 88. Sicut autem seruatur iustitia Dei, id est iustitia secundum Deum, cum in negotiando datur iustum pretium non excessiuum, et res integra debita non sophisticata, et aut permutatio equa; ita econtra negotiantes, largo sumpto uocabulo pro ementibus et uendentibus, tripliciter faciunt contra iustitiam Dei:

1°. Ex iniqua appretiatione.
2°. Ex uaria sophisticatione uel fraudatione.
3°. Ex illicita permutatione.

3.1. Ex iniqua appretiatione.

Quantum ad primum, sciendum secundum beatum Tomam, 2ª 2ᵉ q. 77 articulo primo, quod "emptio et uenditio uidentur introducta pro communi utilitate utriusque, dum scilicet unus indiget re alterius, et econuerso, sicut patet per Philosophum in 1° *Politice*. Quod autem pro communi utilitate introductum est, non debet magis esse unius, quam alterius, et ideo debet inter eos secundum equalitatem contractus institui. Quantitas autem rerum, que in usum hominum ueniunt, mensuratur secundum pretium datum, ad quod est inuentum numisma, ut dicitur 1° *Ethicorum*. Et ideo si pretium excedat quantitatem ualoris rei, uel econuerso res excedat pretium, tollitur iustitie equalitas." Hec Tomas. Et commictitur consequenter iniquitas, iniquitas enim dicitur quasi inequitas, id est inequalitas. Sed, *qui diligit iniquitatem, odit animam eius*, secundum aliam translationem inquit Ps. 10, et loquitur de anima Dei, que est uoluntas eius. Vnde et 10 q. 2ª *Hoc ius*, dicitur quod si in uenditione rei ecclesiastice plus offeratur, quam res ualeat, ecclesia recipere

---

320 emptio … **321** econuerso] ARIST. *Polit.* 1, 9 (1257a10ff.).
324 Quantitas … **326** numisma] ARIST. *Ethica Nic.* 5, 5 (1133a19).
325 quod … **328** equalitas] THOM. AQ. *Sum. th.* 2a 2ae q. 77 a. 1.
329 qui … **330** eius] *Ps* 10.6: Dominus interrogat justum et impium; qui autem diligit iniquitatem, odit animam suam. Cfr *Glossa ord.* ad idem (3:509–10): diligentem iniquitatem odio habuit anima eius.
331 10 … ius] C. 10 q. 2 c. 2 (*Hoc ius porrectum*): Quo subsecuto, per uiginti dies rem ecclesiae esse uenalem sit publice notum, ut plus offerenti detur, precio modis omnibus pro debito dando.
331 dicitur … **335** tuas] Textus ex BERN. SEN. *Evang. aet.* 35, 1, 2 (4:192), quibusdam mutatis.

---

311 Sicut … **314** uendentibus] *in marg. super. add.* **325** mensuratur] -antur *cod.* **328** Hec Tomas] *s.l.* **330** secundum] + Psal- *a.c.* | inquit … 10] *in marg. sin. add.*

in that they lack communion. Hence Cassiodorus says on the cited verse of the Psalm: "Those traders are abominable," namely "who, not considering God's justice, pollute their merchandise by immoderate ambition for money," D. 88.[83] Now just as God's justice, that is justice according to God, is served in trading when the price is just, not excessive, and the whole good is handed over in the expected condition, not counterfeited, and/or in a barter the exchange is equitable; so also by contrast, traders – taking the word in a wide sense for buyers and sellers – transgress against God's justice in three ways:

1. By wrongful appraisal;
2. By various tricks and frauds; or
3. By illicit exchange.

3.1. Wrongful appraisal. As to the first, it must be understood, according to blessed Thomas, 2a 2ae q. 77 a. 1,[84] that "buying and selling seem to be established for the common advantage of both parties, namely when one has need of that which belongs to the other, and vice versa, as the Philosopher states in the first book of the *Politics*.[85] Now whatever is established for the common advantage should not be of more advantage to one party than to another, and therefore the contract ought to be established between them in accordance with equality. Now, the value of a thing that comes into human use is measured by the price given for it, for which purpose money was invented, as stated in the first book of the *Ethics*.[86] Therefore if the price exceeds how much the thing is worth, or, conversely, the thing exceeds the price, the equality of justice is destroyed." Thus Thomas. And consequently iniquity is committed, for it is called "iniquity" as if it were "inequity," that is inequality. But, *he that loveth iniquity, hateth his soul*, Psalm 10 says according to the other translation,[87] and it is speaking of God's soul, which is His will. Hence also in C. 10 q. 2 c. 2,[88] "it is said that if

---

83 Cass. in D. 88 c. 13 (*Quid est aliud*): see above.
Antoninus's text of this canon as quoted here, differing somewhat from the text given by Friedberg and the Roman edition, agrees with his quotation of the same canon in 3.8.1 (below), section 3.2.2.

84 Thom. Aq. *Sum. th.* 2a 2ae q. 77 a. 1. The text in quotation marks is from this passage, nearly verbatim.

85 Arist. *Polit.* 1, 9 (1257a10ff.; McKeon, 1138).

86 Arist. *Ethica Nic.* 5, 5 (1133a19; McKeon, 1011). I discuss this text above in ch. 3.

87 *Ps* 10.6: "The Lord trieth the just and the wicked: but he that loveth iniquity hateth his own soul." Cfr *Glossa ordinaria* to *Ps* 10.6 for an alternative translation.

88 C. 10 q. 2 c. 2 (*Hoc ius porrectum*): "This having been done, notice of the sale of the Church property shall be given for twenty days, and it shall then be sold to the person who offers the most; and the price must, by all means, be employed for the payment of the debt."

non debet, sed tantum iustum pretium. Et ratio est secundum Archidyaconum super dicto capitulo quia ecclesia non debet dolum facere in contractibus suis, *Extra, De donationibus, Per tuas*. Sic igitur res non possunt licite uendi plusquam ualeant, nec etiam minus emi, pensato earum ualore in respectu ad usum nostrum et probabile iudicium humane extimationis mensurantis ualorem rei infra limites latitudinis competentis. Et pro pleniori declaratione materie tria uidenda sunt.

1°. Vnde accipiendus sit debitus ualor rei.
2°. Que sit latitudo competens ualoris rei.
3°. Quid dicendum quando fit excessus ualoris rei.

3.1.1. Debitus ualor rei.

Et pro declaratione primi oportet tria considerare diligenter. Et primum est quod secundum Scotum in 4° d. 15, duplex est ualor rerum. Primus est ualor naturalis, secundus est ualor usualis. Valor naturalis rei est secundum bonitatem nature a Deo in re creata, et hoc modo mus uel formicha uel pulex plus ualent quam panis, quia illa habent uitam animam et sensum, et non panis uel etiam margarita. Secundus ualor dicitur usualis, secundum quod assummitur in respectu ad usum nostrum, et hoc modo quanto aliqua sunt usibus nostris utiliora, tanto plus ualent; et secundum hoc, plus ualet panis quam mus uel bufo. Quia igitur actus emendi et uendendi ad usus humane uite merito ordinatur, ideo rerum que sunt ad usum humane uite uenalium, ualor sumendus est secundo modo, non primo. Secundum considerandum est quod ipse

---

333 secundum Archidyaconum] Immo *Glossa ord.* ad C. 10 q. 2 c. 2 (*Hoc ius porrectum*) s.v. *ut plus*: Quid si offerat plus quam valet? tunc tantum iustum pretium recipiet, licet lex dicat quod contrahentes possunt se invicem fallere. ff. de minori. in causae. sed ecclesia in suis contractibus non debet dolum facere, ut extra de dona. per tuas.

Haec glossa non signata est in ed. Romae 1582, sed Archidiacono tribuit Bern. Sen. Sed cfr Archid. *Rosarium* ad C. 10 q. 2 c. 2 (fol. 184v).

335 Extra … tuas] X 3.24.5 (*Per tuas*): Nos igitur attendentes, quod ecclesia in actibus suis, fraudem non debet aliquam adhibere.

335 res … **338** competentis] Textus ex Bern. Sen. *Evang. aet.* 35, 1, 2 (4:191–2), quibusdam mutatis.

344 duplex … **345** usualis] Io. Scot. *In quartum* d. 15 q. 2 n. 14 (18:283b).

344 duplex … **353** primo] Textus, paucis mutatis, ex Bern. Sen. *Evang. aet.* 35, 1, 1 (4:190), qui transmittit Petr. Olivi *Tr. contr.* 1 q.1 (94–109).

---

345 Valor] + re *a.c.* **346** Deo] + creata *a.c.* **347** quia … habent] + uel margarita *s.l. a.c.*

in the sale"[89] of ecclesiastical property "more is offered than the property is worth, a church should not receive it, but only the just price. And the reason is, according to the Archdeacon on the said chapter,[90] that a church must not commit fraud in its contracts, as at *Extra, On gifts*."[91] Thus therefore "a good cannot licitly be sold for more than it is worth, neither can it be bought for less, with their value reckoned with respect to our use and a probable judgment of human estimation measuring the value of the thing within the limits of the applicable latitude."[92] And for the fuller explanation of this matter there are three questions to be considered:

1. From where does a thing get its due valuation;
2. What is the applicable latitude in the valuation of a thing; and
3. What must be said when an excess is perpetrated in the valuation of a thing.

3.1.1. Valuation of things. To answer the first we must diligently consider three things.[93] The first is that, according to Scotus in book 4 d. 15, things have value in two ways.[94] The first is natural value, the second is use-value. The natural value of a thing is based on the goodness of a thing's nature as created by God, and in this way a mouse or an ant or a flea is worth more than bread, because the former have life, soul, and sense, and bread does not, nor even does a pearl. The second value is called use-value, based on what we gain by use, and in this way things are worth more to the extent that they offer greater utility when we use them. Based on this, bread is worth more than a mouse or a toad. Consequently, since the act of buying and selling is ordered, rightly, towards the uses of human life, therefore the value of things which are for the use of human life, when they are put up for sale, must be obtained in the second way and not in the first. The second thing to be considered is that this value

89 The text in quotation marks here is copied from Bern. Sen. *Evang. aet.* 35, 1, 2 (4:192).

90 Rather *Glossa ord.* ad C. 10 q. 2 c. 2 (*Hoc ius porrectum*) s.v. *ut plus*: "What if he offers more than its worth? Then he shall receive only the just price, although the law says that the contracting parties are allowed to lead each other into error, *Digest* 4.4.16, but a church must not commit fraud in its contracts, as at *Decretals* 3.24.5."

This gloss is not signed in the Roman edition of 1582. Bernardino attributes this gloss to the Archdeacon; but cfr Archid. *Rosarium* ad C. 10 q. 2 c. 2 (fol. 184v).

This is the only decretist gloss of which I am aware citing the maxim, derived from Roman law, *licet contrahentibus sese invicem decipere*, "it is lawful for contracting parties to get the better of one another." This maxim was in common currency among decretalists by the time of Innocent IV's *Commentaria* (circa 1245), if not earlier.

91 *X* 3.24.5 (*Per tuas*).

92 The previous two sentences are copied from Bern. Sen. *Evang. aet.* 35, 1, 2 (4:191–2).

93 This whole section from 3.1.1 to 3.1.2 is an essentially complete reproduction, with a few small changes of wording, of Bern. Sen. *Evang. aet.* 35, 1, 1 (4:190–1), transmitting Petr. Olivi *Tr. contr.* 1 q. 1 (94–109).

94 Io. Scot. *In quartum* d. 15 q. 2 n. 14 (18:283b).

ualor rerum secundo modo acceptus, id est secundum quod sunt ad usum nostrum in re uenali, tripliciter pensatur. Primo ex eius uirtuositate, secundo ex eius raritate, tertio ex eius complacibilitate.

3.1.1.1. Ex virtuositate.

Et uirtuositas quidem rei attenditur, secundum quod res ex suis realibus uirtutibus et proprietatibus est nostris utilitatibus uirtuosior et effichacior, et hoc modo bonus panis triticeus plus ualet ad usum nostrum quam ordeaceus, et fortis equus ad uecturam uel ad bellum plus ualet quam asinus uel ronzinus.

3.1.1.2. Ex raritate.

Secundo pensatur rei uenalis ualor ex raritate, id est secundum quod res ex sue inuentionis raritate et difficultate magis neccessarie sunt, pro quanto uidelicet ex earum penuria maiorem ipsarum indigentiam, et minorem facultatem habendi et utendi habemus. Vnde Ieronimus, "Omne rarum charum," D. 93 *Legimus*. Et secundum hoc, bladum plus ualet tempori famis et charistie quam tempori quo multum habundat apud omnes. Sic quattuor elementa, ignis aer aqua et terra, uilioris pretii apud nos extimantur propter eorum copiam quam balsamum uel aurum, quamuis illa de se sint magis neccessaria magisque utilia uite nostre.

3.1.1.3. Ex complacibilitate.

Tertio pensatur in re uenali eius complacibilitas, id est secundum quod magis uel minus beneplacitum est uoluntati nostre habere talem rem et uti ea. Vti enim, prout hic summitur, est rem in facultatem uoluntatis assummere uel habere, et ideo non modicha pars | ualoris uenalium rerum ex beneplacito fol. 69r uoluntatis pensatur, siue plus siue minus complacentie in usu huius rei uel illius, iuxta quod unus equus gratior est uni et alter alteri, et unum ornamentum uni et aliud alteri. Et hoc modo unus rem alteri uiliorem multum appretiatur, et sibi reputat pretiosam et charam, et econuerso.

Tertium considerandum circa ualorem rei est quod ualor rerum uenalium uix aut numquam potest a nobis determinari nisi per coniecturalem et probabilem oppinionem, et hoc non punctaliter sub indiuisibili ratione aut mensura in plus et minus, sed sub aliqua latitudine competenti respectu temporum lochorum et personarum. Circa quam latitudinem diuersi homines in extimando differre

---

357 uirtuositas … **361** ronzinus] Textus ex Bern. Sen. *Evang. aet.* 35, 1, 1 (4:191).
362 Secundo … **370** nostre] Textus ex Bern. Sen. ibid.
365 Omne … charum] Hier. in D. 93 c. 24 (*Legimus*): Omne quod rarum est plus appetitur.
371 Tertio … **378** econuerso] Textus ex Bern. Sen. *Evang. aet.* 35, 1, 1 (4:191).
379 Tertium … **384** probantur] Textus ex Bern. Sen. ibid.

---

359 plus] *s.l.* : pretiositate *a.c.* **361** ronzinus] ronçinus *cod.* **366** D. 93] D. 92 *cod.* | Legimus] *p.c.* : Diaconus *a.c. ut vid.* **367** omnes] + uel multos *a.c.* **368** aqua] ignis *a.c.* **369** aurum] + magis quam illa illa de se in *a.c.* **370** magisque] magni *a.c.* **375** complacentie] *ut vid.* | huius] *in marg. sin. add.* : illius *a.c.* **378** appretiatur] + et econuerso *a.c.*

obtained in the second way, that is, based on what is useful for us in a thing for sale, is assessed on three bases: first, its efficacy; second, its scarcity; third, its desirability.

3.1.1.1. From efficacy. Now the efficacy of a thing is measured based on its potency and efficaciousness for our uses as a result of its real powers and properties, and in this way good wheat bread is worth more than barley bread, and a strong horse for transport or war is worth more than an ass or a nag.[95]

3.1.1.2. From scarcity. Second, the value of a thing for sale is assessed from its scarcity, that is, based on things being more necessary because of the rarity and difficulty of finding them. In other words, their value is increased to the extent that we have a greater need for them when they are scarce and a lesser ability to obtain and use them. Hence Jerome says, "Everything rare is dear," D. 93 c. 24.[96] According to this, grain is worth more in a time of famine and dearth than in a time when it is very abundant for all. Thus the four elements, fire, air, water, and earth, are accounted as of lower price among us because of their plenty than balsam or gold, although the former are in themselves more necessary and more useful for our life.

3.1.1.3. From desirability. Third, the desirability of a thing for sale is assessed on the basis of it being more or less pleasing to our will to have this sort of thing and to use it. For "to use," as it is understood here, is to take or have a thing in the power of the will, and therefore no small part of the value of things for sale is weighed based on how pleasing they are to the will: whether there is more or less desirability in the use of this thing or that. In this way one horse is more agreeable to one, another to someone else, and one ornament to one, and another to another. And in this way one person appraises a thing as quite worthless for another person, and regards it as precious and dear for himself, and vice versa.

The third thing to be considered in relation to the value of a thing is that the value of things for sale can rarely or never be determined by us except as a matter of conjecture and probable opinion. Even then it cannot be determined down to an exact point on an unchanging standard or measure which can be applied at all levels, but rather there is an appropriate range of values applicable for any given time, place, and set of persons. In relation to this latitude, different men are known to differ in their estimations. And blessed Thomas also

95 See *DMLBS* s.v. *runcinus*.

96 Hier. in D. 93 c. 24 (*Legimus*): "Whatever is rare is the more desired."

probantur. Et hoc etiam dicit beatus Tomas, ubi supra, quod ualor rerum non consistit in puncto indiuisibili. Vnde aliquantulum plus uel aliquantulum minus emere uel uendere non tollit equalitatem uel iustitiam, dummodo non fiat excessus notabilis uel contra conscientiam.

3.1.2. Latitudo ualoris rei.

Quantum ad secundum, scilicet que sit competens latitudo ualoris rerum, infra cuius limites possit pretium extendi, dicendum quod tripliciter hoc innotescere potest: ex iure, ex consuetudine, ex discretione.

3.1.2.1. Ex iure.

Et primo ex iure. Quia si pretium quo uenditur res excedat medietatem iusti pretii, seu pretium quo emitur deficiat a medietate iusti pretii, puta ualet res X florenos prout communiter extimatur, et tamen uenditor petit et recipit XVI, uel cum ualeat X, emptor emit pro quattuor cum dimidio: tunc secundum iura contractus est nullus, *Extra*, *De empt. et uen.*, *Cum dilecti*, per iudicem irritandus uel facere supplere defectum commissum. Verum etiam si esset minor excessus quam medietas iusti pretii, si sit notabilis, utique secundum beatum Tomam 2^a 2^e q. 77 et Scotum in 4° d. 15, est ibi iniustitia, et per consequens peccatum mortale, et restitutio facienda quantum ad eum, per quem fit deceptio aduertenter in pretio multum excessiuo uel defectiuo. Sed si fiat deceptio ignoranter, quia scilicet emptor uel uenditor existimat tantum ualere, tunc non est ibi mortale, ex quo ipse decipitur per erorem, sed tamen cum perpendit uel sibi ostenditur, tenetur ad satisfactionem, alias tunc peccaret mortaliter, si non uellet satisfacere. Quod totum intelligitur quando defraudatur iusto pretio emptor uel uenditor ex errore seu ignorantia. Nam si sciens et aduertens quantitatem excessus uel defectus libere consensit in tale pretium et contractum, in nullo tenetur alter cum eo contrahens, cum sciat illum aduertere de excessu uel defectu pretii. Et ratio est quia "scienti et consentienti non

---

384 ualor … **385** indiuisibili] Thom. Aq. *Sum. th.* 2a 2ae q. 77 a. 1 ad 1: Iustum pretium rerum quandoque non est punctaliter determinatum, sed magis in quadam aestimatione consistit, ita quod modica additio vel minutio non videtur tollere aequalitatem iustitiae.

388 Quantum … **412** iniustitia] Textus, quibusdam mutatis, ex Bern. Sen. *Evang. aet.* 35, 1, 2 (4:191–2), qui transmittit Petr. Olivi *Tr. contr.* 1 q. 1 (94–109) et Io. Scot. *In quartum* d. 15 q. 2 n. 15 (18:283b). Cfr Bern. Sen. *Chr. rel.* 37, 2, 1 (1:470–2).

391 si … **395** nullus] *X* 3.17.3 (*Cum dilecti*): vide supra. Cfr Hostien. *Sum.* 3.17 *De emptione et venditione* §. 7 (3:943).

396 Verum … **400** defectiuo] Thom. Aq. *Sum. th.* 2a 2ae q. 77 a. 1; Io. Scot. *In quartum* d. 15 q. 2 n. 15 (18:283b).

408 scienti … **409** dolus] *VI* 5.[13.]27 (*Scienti*): Scienti et consentienti non fit iniuria neque dolus. Cfr Ant. Flor. *Summa* 1.20.1.94 (apud *N* fol. 323r, Ballerini 1:899, Mamachi 1:1422): *scienti et consentienti.*

---

389 limites] + se *a.c. ut vid.* **391** quo] + emitur uel *a.c.* **393** florenos] + et uenditur *a.c.* **395** Cum dilecti] *in spatio quattuor litterarum add. Antoninus* **396** uel … commissum] *in marg. sin. add.* **399** quantum … **404** satisfacere] *in marg. super. add.* **400** aduertenter] *s.l.* **403** peccaret] peccare *cod.*

says at the place cited above that the value of things does not consist of a single unchanging quantity. Hence buying or selling for some little more or some little less does not destroy equality or justice, provided that a notable excess is not perpetrated, nor is it done against conscience.[97]

3.1.2. Latitude in valuation. As to the second question, that is, what is the applicable latitude in the valuation of a thing – the latitude within whose limits the price can extend – we must say that this can be known in three ways: from law, from custom, and from discretion.[98]

3.1.2.1. From law. First from law. For if the price at which a thing is sold exceeds half of the just price, or the price at which it is bought fails by half of the just price – say, a thing is worth 10 florins as it is commonly estimated, and nevertheless the seller demands and receives 16, or when a thing is worth 10 florins and the buyer buys it for four and a half: then according to the laws the contract is null, *Extra, On buying and selling*, c. 3,[99] and to be voided by a judge, or the party who perpetrated the wrongful price is to be compelled to make up the difference. But even if there should be a lesser excess than half the just price, if it is notable, at any rate according to blessed Thomas in 2a 2ae q. 77 and Scotus in book 4 d. 15,[100] there is injustice present and by consequence mortal sin, and restitution must be made by whoever knowingly deceived the other through an excessive or deficient price. But if the deception was done in ignorance, in other words the buyer or seller who benefited estimated that it was really worth that much, then a mortal sin is not present, because the opposite party is misled by mistake. But nevertheless when the one who benefited recognizes the error or it is shown to him, he is bound to make satisfaction, otherwise he would then sin mortally if he chose not to make satisfaction. All of this is understood as applying to when a buyer or seller is defrauded of the just price out of error or ignorance. For if both parties, knowing and realizing that the price is high or low by however much, freely consent to this price and contract, the one who benefits from the contract does not owe the other anything, knowing as he does that the other is aware of the excessive or defective price. And the reason is that "to one who knows and consents no injury nor fraud is done," as the rule says

97 Thom. Aq. *Sum. th.* 2a 2ae q. 77 a. 1 ad 1: "The just price of things is not fixed with mathematical precision, but depends on a kind of estimate, so that a slight addition or subtraction would not seem to destroy the equality of justice."

98 This section 3.1.2 follows generally, though not exactly, Bern. Sen. *Evang. aet.* 35, 1, 2 (4:191–2), transmitting Petr. Olivi *Tr. contr.* 1 q. 1 (94–109) and Io. Scot. *In quartum* d. 15 q. 2 n. 15 (18:283b). Cfr Bern. Sen. *Chr. rel.* 37, 2, 1 (1:470–2).

99 *X* 3.17.3 (*Cum dilecti*): see above. Cfr Hostien. *Sum.* 3.17 *De emptione et venditione* §. 7 (3:943).

100 Thom. Aq. *Sum. th.* 2a 2ae q. 77 a. 1; Io. Scot. *In quartum* d. 15 q. 2 n. 15 (18:283b).

fit iniura neque dolus," ut dicit regula, *De re. iur., libro 6°*. Sicut enim potest rem suam absque omni pretio dare et donare, ita etiam potest pro centesima parte iusti pretii rem suam uendere secundum beneplacitum suum, et alteri pro 5^{a} parte, et alteri pro iusto pretio tantum. Nec in hoc fit iniustitia ex parte alterius, nisi cogeretur uenditor ad uendendum aliqua magna neccessitate ad hoc inducente cui non potest sibi aliter prouidere, uellet tamen iustum pretium, sed inuenire non potest; uel etiam magna leuitate ad hoc mouente, ut prodighus et leuis. Tunc enim sechus dicendum.

3.1.2.2. Ex consuetudine.

Secundo ipsa latitudo pretii potest innotescere ex consuetudine. Nam, ut dicit Scotus in 4° ubi supra, per experientiam satis patet, quod consuetudinarie relinquitur ipsis permutantibus ut, pensata mutua neccessitate, reputent se mutuo dare equiualens, et hinc inde accipere. Durum quippe uidetur inter homines contractus esse, in quibus contrahentes non intendant aliquid de rigore iudiciali, qui est ut tantum res ematur uel uendatur quantum ualet, sibi mutuo relaxare; ut sic communem contractum commitetur aliqua donatio uera. Et hic modus commutantium fundatur quasi super lege nature dicente: *Fac alteri quod tibi uis fieri*. Satis igitur est probabile quod quando contrahentes mutuo sunt contenti, mutuo sibi remictere uelint, si aliquo modo, dum tamen non enormi, deficiunt a perfecta iustitia.

3.1.2.3. Ex discretione.

Tertio innotescit latitudo pretii rerum ex discretione. Dictat enim discretio quod cum res in se ualens X tamen habenti est chara et utilis ut XII, si uolo eam habere, dem sibi non tantum X sed quantum sibi ualet, ex quo ipse retinere uolebat quia utilis ut XII. Vnde et beatus Tomas, 2^{a} 2^{e} q. 77, dicit quod uendere

---

417 Secundo … **427** iustitia] Textus, paucis mutatis, ex Bern. Sen. *Evang. aet.* 35, 1, 2 (4:193).
418 Scotus … supra] Io. Scot. *In quartum* d. 15 q. 2 n. 15 (18:283b–284a).
425 Fac … fieri] *Lc* 6.31: Et prout vultis ut faciant vobis homines, et vos facite illis similiter. *Mt* 7.12: Omnia ergo quaecumque vultis ut faciant vobis homines, et vos facite illis. Haec est enim lex, et prophetae.
Cfr Hostien. *Comm.* ad *X* 3.17.1 (3:57a).

---

411 iusti] *in marg. sin. add.* **412** fit] fiat *a.c.* **414** potest] + aliter *a.c.* **417** Secundo] Secundo dico quod ista *a.c.* **429** quod] *s.l.*

in *The rules of law, Liber Sext.*[101] For just as he could give or donate his property without any price at all, so also he can sell his property for a hundredth of the just price according to his good pleasure; and he can sell it to another person for a fifth, and to another only for the just price. Nor is any injustice done in this by the other party, unless the seller was compelled to sell, induced by some extreme necessity in which he could not otherwise provide for himself – though he wanted a just price, he cannot find it – or if the contracting party was carried away by extreme frivolity, like a prodigal or fickle person. For in those cases a different answer must be given.

3.1.2.2. From custom. Second, the latitude of a price may be known from custom.[102] For, as Scotus says in book 4 at the place already cited,[103] by experience it is evident enough that customarily it is left up to the exchanging parties if, taking account of the need on either side, they consider themselves to give equivalent value and hence to receive equivalent value from the transaction. For it seems harsh for there to be contracts among men in which the contracting parties do not intend to allow each other any slack at all from legal rigour, which says that a thing should only be bought or sold for exactly what it is worth. And thus an element of free gift truly accompanies the usual contract. And this method of the contracting parties is founded, as it were, on the law of nature that says: *Do to another what you would have done to you.*[104] Therefore it is probable enough that when the contracting parties are mutually content, they wish to mutually remit to each other whatever small amount, provided it is not gross, may depart from perfect justice.

3.1.2.3. From discretion. Third, the latitude in the price of things may be known from discretion.[105] For discretion dictates that when a thing is worth 10 in itself, yet to the possessor it is dear and useful enough to be worth 12, if I want to have it I should give him not only 10, but as much as it is worth to him, because of which he wants to retain the thing since it is useful to the extent of 12. Hence also blessed Thomas, 2a 2ae q. 77, says that to sell a thing for more than it is worth "is unjust, unless it yields a detriment to the seller," namely in selling the thing at its current value, say because this thing is very useful or necessary to himself. For then he may sell for more than the thing is worth in itself, as much namely

---

101 *VI* 5.[13.]27 (*Scienti*): "No injury or malice is done to the one who knows and approves." English trans. from Gauthier, *Roman Law and … Canon Law*, 110. Cfr Ant. Flor. *Summa* 1.20.1.94 (apud *N* fol. 323r, Ballerini 1:899, Mamachi 1:1422): *scienti et consentienti.*

102 This section draws on Bern. Sen. *Evang. aet.* 35, 1, 2 (4:193).

103 Io. Scot. *In quartum* d. 15 q. 2 n. 15 (18:283b–284a).

104 *Lc* 6.31: "And as you would that men should do to you, do you also to them in like manner." *Mt* 7.12: "All things therefore whatsoever you would that men should do to you, do you also to them. For this is the law and the prophets."
Cfr Hostien. *Comm. X* 3.17.1 (3:57a).

105 This paragraph is largely copied from Bern. Sen. *Evang. aet.* 35, 1, 2 (4:193).

rem plus quam ualeat, "est iniustum, nisi in detrimentum cederet uenditoris," uendere scilicet quantum ualet, puta quia multum sibi est utilis illa res uel neccessaria: tunc enim uendere poterit plus quam res in se ualeat, quantum scilicet ualet ipsi uenditori. Sed quamuis emptor multum iuuetur ex re quam uult emere, si uenditor inde non damnificatur ex charentia ipsius rei, non propterea potest plus uendere rem quam ualeat in se: quia utilitas, que superuenit emptori, non est ex condictione uendentis nec ex condictione rei in se, sed ex condictione ementis; unde non debet uendere illi quod non est suum. Idem Schotus in 4°. Si tamen sua liberalitate emptor uult aliquid plus dare quam ualeat res, quia inde multo iuuatur, potest recipi, ar. 1 q. 2 *Sicut episcopum.*

3.1.3. Excessus ualoris rei.

Quantum ad tertium prime partis, scilicet quando fit excessus in pretio, quid iuris? Ad hoc dicendum, quod tripliciter potest fieri excessus in pretio rerum uenalium uel defectus.

3.1.3.1. Excessus ultra dimidiam iusti pretii.

Primo quidem ultra dimidiam iusti pretii: et sic contractum potest rescindere deceptus, uel restaurationem dampni sui petere, ut dictum est. Nec obstat si dicatur quod "unusquisque in re sua est moderator et iudex" secundum iura, ergo rei mee possum imponere quod pretium uolo, nec aliquis potest me cogere ad pretaxatum pretium, sicut nec etiam ad uendendum, sicut etiam emptor non cogitur ad emendum nisi pretio sibi beneplacito; sicut igitur contractus emptionis et uenditionis est mere uoluntarius, sic etiam | taxatio fol. 69v
pretii uenalium rerum debet esse uoluntaria secundum uoluntatem uendentis et ementis, iuxta illud prouerbium legale: "Res tantum ualet quantum uendi potest." Ad illud enim respondeo: quamuis quis non cogatur ad uendendum

434 uendere … **435** uenditori] Thom. Aq. *Sum. th.* 2a 2ae q. 77 a. 1 co.

428 Tertio … **439** suum] Textus, paucis mutatis, ex Bern. Sen. *Evang. aet.* 35, 1, 2 (4:193).

439 Idem … **440** 4°] Io. Scot. *In quartum* d. 15 q. 2 n. 16 (18:289a).

440 Si … **441** recipi] C. 1 q. 2 c. 4 (*Sicut episcopum*): Ab ordinato non debet aliquid exigi, sed nec uoluntarie oblata respui oportet. … [Gratianus:] Auctoritate uero Gregorii datur intelligi, quod pro ingressu ecclesiae non licet pecuniam exigere, sed spontanee oblatam suscipere licet.

447 unusquisque … iudex] *Cod.* 4.35.21 (*In re mandata*): Nam suae quidem quisque rei moderator atque arbiter non omnia negotia, sed pleraque ex proprio animo facit.
Cfr Io. Andr. *Novella* ad *X* 3.17.1 s.v. *possunt* (3:79b–79va); Ant. Butr. *Comm.* ad *X* 3.17.1 §. 7 *Vendere quando quis compellatur rem suam iusto pretio* (3:75r–v); Panorm. *Comm.* ad *X* 3.17.1 §. 6 (1583 ed., 3:95v–96r).

448 ergo … **460** equitatem] Textus, quibusdam mutatis, ex Bern. Sen. *Evang. aet.* 35, 1, 3 (4:194), qui transmittit Petr. Olivi *Tr. contr.* 1 q.1 (94–109).

453 Res … **454** potest] Vide *Glossa ord.* ad *X* 5.19.6 s.v. *non valent*: Immo videtur quod tantum valeat: res enim tantum valet, quantum vendi potest. Pretia enim rerum non ex affectu singulorum, sed communiter aestimantur. Vide etiam Inno. IV *Comm.* ad *X* 5.19.6 s.v. *non valent* (517); Hostien. *Comm.* ad *X* 5.19.6 s.v. *non valent* (5:57).

439 non[1]] *bis* | in 4°] + p. *a.c.* **446** uel] dicendum *a.c.* | petere] *in marg. sin. add.* **453** prouerbium] uulgare *a.c.*

as it is worth to him, the seller.[106] But however much the buyer may be helped by the thing which he wants to buy, if the seller does not suffer loss from the lack of the thing, he may not on that account sell the thing for more than it is worth in itself. This is because the extra utility which the buyer gains does not come from the condition of the seller, nor the condition of the thing in itself, but from the condition of the buyer; hence the seller ought not to sell him what is not his own. And Scotus says the same in book 4.[107] However, if in his liberality the buyer wants to give something more than the thing is worth, because he is helped very much by it, then it may be received, by the argument of C. 1 q. 2 c. 4.[108]

3.1.3. Excess in valuation. As for the third item of the first part, namely when an excess is committed in the price, what is the law? To this it must be answered, that an excess or deficiency in the price of a thing for sale can be committed in three ways.

3.1.3.1. Excess beyond half the just price. First of all, when the price departs by more than half from the just price: and here the deceived party may rescind the contract or sue for a restoration of his loss, as was said.[109] Notwithstanding that someone might argue, "each person is the moderator and judge of his own property" according to the laws,[110] therefore I may impose on my own thing whatever price I wish, nor can anyone compel me to accept a price fixed for me, just as they also cannot compel me to sell, in the same way as the buyer is not compelled to buy except at a price which satisfies him; therefore, just as the contract of buying and selling is purely voluntary, so also the establishment of the price of things for sale ought to be voluntary based on the will of the seller and the buyer, according to that legal maxim: "A thing is worth as much as it can be sold for."[111] For to that I answer: although one should not be compelled to sell his own property, nevertheless in the act and contract of sale, if he wants to sell, he is obliged to observe the legal form and the rule of justice and equity. Therefore in the act of selling it is not

---

106 Thom. Aq. *Sum. th.* 2a 2ae q. 77 a. 1 co.

107 Io. Scot. *In quartum* d. 15 q. 2 n. 16 (18:289a).

108 C. 1 q. 2 c. 4 (*Sicut episcopum*): "Nothing is to be exacted from an ordinand, but neither is it fitting to reject anything which is offered voluntarily … [Gratian:] And by the authority of Gregory, it is given to be understood that, for entry into a Church, it is not lawful to exact money, but it is lawful to receive it, if it is offered freely."

109 This section 3.1.3.1 follows generally, though not exactly, Bern. Sen. *Evang. aet.* 35, 1, 3 (4:194), transmitting Petr. Olivi *Tr. contr.* 1 q. 1 (94–109).

110 *Cod.* 4.35.21 (*In re mandata*): "Each man is governor and arbiter of his own affairs, and he carries on, not all, but most of his business as he lists."

Cfr Io. Andr. *Novella X* 3.17.1 s.v. *possunt* (3:79b–79va); Ant. Butr. *Comm. X* 3.17.1 §. 7 *Vendere quando quis compellatur rem suam iusto pretio* (3:75r–v); Panorm. *Comm. X* 3.17.1 §. 6 (1583 ed., 3:95v–96r).

111 See *Glossa ord. X* 5.19.6 s.v. *non valent*; Inno. IV *Comm. X* 5.19.6 s.v. *non valent* (517); Hostien. *Comm.* ad *X* 5.19.6 s.v. *non valent* (5:57). I discuss this legal maxim extensively above in ch. 3.

rem suam, tamen in actu et contractu uendendi, si uendere uult formam iuris et regulam iustitie seruare debet et equitatis: et ideo in actu uendendi non licet sibi rei sue statuere iniustum pretium et accipere, quia tunc non imponit rei ut simpliciter sue pretium, sed ut in alterum commutande. Huius autem impositio commutatiue includit acceptionem pretii preualentis, accipere autem preualens pretium, est iniustum et contra equitatem. Insuper secundum Hostiensem, quamuis non possit quis cogi ab initio rem suam uendere uel alienare, ut patet *Cod. De contrahenda emptione*, l. *Dudum*, si tamen exposuerit uenalem, et pretium offeratur, si pro iusto pretio uendere non uult potest cogi per iudicem quod iusto pretio uendat, *Ff. De offitio prefecti urbi*, l. 1. Et cum dicitur, "res tantum ualet quantum uendi potest," intelligitur de iure non de facto, secundum extimationem communem, secundum Antonium de Butrio.

3.1.3.2. Excessus notabilis infra dimidiam iusti pretii.

Secundus excessus est in contractu huiusmodi quando utique notabilis est, non tamen pertingens ad medietatem iusti pretii. Et tunc aliqui dicunt

---

461 non … **462** alienare] *Cod.* 4.38.14 (*Dudum*): Dudum proximis consortibusque concessum erat, ut extraneos ab emptione removerent neque homines suo arbitratu vendenda distraherent. Sed quia gravis haec videtur iniuria, quae inani honestatis colore velatur, ut homines de rebus suis facere aliquid cogantur inviti, superiore lege cassata unusquisque suo arbitratu quaerere vel probare possit emptorem, nisi lex specialiter quasdam personas hoc facere prohibuerit.

461 quamuis … **464** uendat] Hostien. *Sum.* 3.17 §. 1 (935): Imo et si ab initio invitus distrahere vel emere nemo cogatur: ut C. e. invitum. [*Cod.* 4.38.11] et l. dudum. [*Cod.* 4.38.14] si tamen rem exponas venalem et precium, quo vendere vis, fit iniustum, potes cogi per iudicem ut temperes. infra e. c.1 [X 3.17.1] ff. de offi. praefec. urbi. l. 1 §. cura carnis [*Dig.* 1.12.1.11].

462 si … **464** uendat] *Dig.* 1.12.1.11 (§. *Cura carnis*): Cura carnis omnis ut iusto pretio praebeatur ad curam praefecturae pertinet, et ideo et forum suarium sub ipsius cura est.

465 res … **466** communem] Fortasse Ant. Butr. *Comm.* ad *X* 5.19.6 §. 10 (4:63r–63v): Valet res tantum, quantum vendi potest. … Opp. quod res vendita tantum valet, quantum est vendita: et sic non posset hoc dici peccatum, quod plus sit vendita, quam valeat res. Res enim tantum valet, quantum vendi potest, arg. ff. ad Trebel. l. j. §. si haeres. ff. ad legem Falci. l. pretia. Sol. dicit gl. quod res tantum valet, quantum vendi potest: tamen habito respectu ad communem aestimationem, non habito respectu ad singularem, maxime quae fit per dilationem temporum in solvendo.

Cfr ibid. ad *X* 3.17.1 §. 3 (3:75r–v): Vendere quod liceat rem quantum potest, aut valet, intelligitur quantum vendi solet in mercato. … No. quod res tantum valet, quantum vendi potest. Intelligitur id est quantum vendi potest in mercato, vel ubi consuevit vendi. vide l. pretia rerum. ff. ad leg. Fal.

---

457 sibi rei] mihi re- *a.c.* | statuere] *scripsi cum* F_2 *fol. 48va* : statuem *cod. ut vid.* **458** rei] + sue *a.c.* **464** prefecti] presi *cod.* **468** utique] *ut vid. in rasura*

lawful for him to establish and receive an unjust price on his thing, because then he does not impose it on his thing simply as the price of his own thing, but as of a thing to be exchanged for another. The imposition of this in an exchange involves taking a overvalued price, but to take an overvalued price is unjust and against equity. Moreover according to Hostiensis,[112] although one may not be compelled from the outset to sell or alienate his own property, as is evident in the *Code*, *On contracts of purchase*, l. 14,[113] if one nevertheless has put an item up for sale and a price is offered, if he does not wish to sell for a just price, he may be compelled by a judge to sell it at the just price, according to *Digests*, *Duties of the prefect of the city*, l. 1.[114] And when it is said, "a thing is worth as much as it can be sold for," this means from the point of view of the law, not in actual fact, <and> based on common estimation, according to Antonio da Budrio.[115]

3.1.3.2. Excess notable but less than half. The second sort of excess in a contract of this kind is when it is indeed notable, but not reaching half of the just price. And then some say that it is licit, and one <who benefits from such a deception> is not bound to restitution, because the laws permit this, as in the cited chapter, *Extra*, *On buying and selling*, c. 3.[116] Durandus of the Franciscan Order seems to have followed this opinion in his *Summa*.[117] But blessed Thomas, 2a 2ae q. 77, and Scotus, in book 4 d. 15,[118] reprove this opinion as erroneous and dangerous to the salvation of souls, saying that such a one, who deceives knowingly, commits an injustice, and consequently sins mortally and is bound to make restitution of

112 Hostien. *Sum.* 3.17 §. 1 (935).

113 *Cod.* 4.38.14 (*Dudum*): "Formerly relatives and consorts had the right to keep outsiders from purchasing property (belonging to a relative or consort), nor could men sell property which they had for sale at their discretion. But since this has only the appearance of being proper, and it seems to be a grave wrong, that men should be compelled to handle their property in a manner contrary to their wish, the ancient law is abrogated and everyone my seek and approve of his own purchaser as he pleases, unless the law specially forbids certain persons to do this."

114 *Dig.* 1.12.1.11 (§. *Cura carnis*): "Supervision of the whole meat trade to secure that meat is on offer at just prices is another matter in the care of the prefecture ..."

115 Perhaps Ant. Butr. *Comm. X* 5.19.6 §. 10 (4:63r–63v). Cfr ibid. *X* 3.17.1 §. 3 (3:75r–v).

116 *X* 3.17.3 (*Cum dilecti*); see Hostien. *Sum.* 3.17 §. 7 (3:944).

117 Dur. Camp. *Sum. conf.*, perhaps book 2 tit. *de avaritia* (fol. 77rb–va); see Langholm, *Merchant in the Confessional*, 78–9.

118 Thom. Aq. *Sum. th.* 2a 2ae q. 77 a. 1 ad 1; Io. Scot. *In quartum* d. 15 q. 2 n. 15 (18:283b).

licitum esse, nec teneri ad restitutionem, quia iura hoc permictunt, ut in dicto capitulo *Cum dilecti*, *De emptione et uenditione*. Quam oppinionem sequi uidetur Durandus ordinis Minorum in *Summa* sua. Sed hanc oppinionem tamquam eroneam et periculosum saluti animarum reprobant beatus Tomas, 2^a 2^e q. 77, et Schotus, in 4° d. 15, dicentes quod talis scienter decipiens iniustitiam facit, mortaliter per consequens peccat, et tenetur ad restitutionem eius in quo decepit. Si autem ignoranter et ex errore, scilicet exstimans tantum illam ualere et huiusmodi, tunc non peccat, sed cum aduertit errorem tenetur ad satisfactionem dampni leso seu decepto, alias tunc peccaret si non disponeret se ad emendam. Ad rationem ab illis inductam de lege, respondet beatus Tomas, ubi supra, quod lex "datur populo, in quo sunt multi deficientes a uirtute," unde solum prohibet ea mala que habent destruere humanum conuictum pacificum ea puniendo, ut furta adulteria, notabiles deceptiones in contractibus ut deceptio ultra dimidiam iusti pretii; et hoc, cum punire potest absque maiori scandalo, alias etiam illa tollerat, ut 1. q. 7 *Quotiens*, 23 q. 4 *Ipsa pietas*, D. 50 *Vt constitueretur*. "Alia autem permictit," non quia licita, sed in quantum "non punit ea," et hoc, ne puniendo sequerentur maiora mala. "Sed lex diuina," que datur omnibus, "nil dimictit impunitum" in hac uita uel alia quod sit uirtuti contrarium. Vnde

---

470 quia … permictunt] *X* 3.17.3 (*Cum dilecti*); vide Hostien. *Sum.* 3.17 §. 7 (3:944): Emptio et venditio qualiter rescindatur. … Sed si deceptio non excedit ultra dimidiam iusti precii, et utraque contrahentium maior est et privatus toleratur, quia licitum ad contrahentibus sese ad invicem decipere naturaliter, id est, bona fide.

471 Quam … **472** uidetur] Dur. Camp. *Sum. conf.* fortasse 2 tit. *de avaritia* (fol. 77rb–va).

472 hanc … **476** decepit] Thom. Aq. *Sum. th.* 2a 2ae q. 77 a. 1 ad 1; Io. Scot. *In quartum* d. 15 q. 2 n. 15 (18:283b).

479 Ad … **491** excessus] Textus, quibusdam mutatis, ex Bern. Sen. *Evang. aet.* 35, 1, 2 (4:192), qui exponit Thom. Aq. *Sum. th.* 2a 2ae q. 77 a. 1 ad 1.

484 1. … **485** Quotiens] C. 1 q. 7 c. 14 (*Quotiens a populis*): Quociens a populis aut a turba peccatur, quia in omnes propter multitudinem vindicari non potest, inultum solet transire.

485 23 … pietas] C. 23 q. 4 c. 24 (*Ipsa pietas*): Verum in huiusmodi causis, ubi per graues dissensionum scissuras non huius aut illius hominis est periculum, sed populorum strages iacent, detrahendum est aliquid seueritati, ut maioribus malis sanandis sincera karitas subueniat.

485 D. … constitueretur] D. 50 c. 25 (*Ut constitueretur*) praebet eumdem canon cum C. 23 q. 4 c. 24 citato.

---

471 De … uenditione] *in marg. sin. add.* | oppinionem] oppi *cod.* **472** Summa] + de casibus *a.c. ut vid.* **474** dicentes] + ut dictum est supra *a.c.* **475** mortaliter … peccat] *in marg. dext. add.* **476** restitutionem] + ut dictum est *a.c.* **483** deceptiones] + scilicet *a.c.* | pretii] pretii *scr. sed postea del. et iterum scr. in marg. dext. et hic inserendum notavit cod.* | et … **485** constitueretur] *in marg. super. add.* **485** Quotiens] Quia *a.c. ut vid.* **486** non[1] … sed] *in marg. sin. add.* | quantum] + scilicet *a.c.* **488** alia] aliam *a.c.*

the amount in which he deceived the other. If, however, he did this ignorantly and out of error, in other words he estimated that the thing was only worth so much and what have you, then he does not sin, but when he realizes his error he is bound to make satisfaction for the loss to the one injured or deceived; otherwise he would then commit a sin if he were not disposed to amend it. To the argument from law invoked by the opponents, blessed Thomas responds at the cited place[119] that the law "is given to the people, in whom there are many deficient in virtue," hence it only prohibits through punishment those evils which are destructive of peaceful human fellowship, such as theft, adultery, notable deception in contracts like deception beyond half the just price; and only when the law can punish without greater scandal, otherwise it tolerates even these evils, as in C. 1 q. 7 c. 14,[120] C. 23 q. 4 c. 24,[121] D. 50 c. 25.[122] "The law permits other evils," not as licit but in as much as "it does not punish them," and only lest in punishing them greater evils should follow. "But the divine law," which is given to everyone, "leaves nothing unpunished," in this life or the next, which is contrary to virtue. Hence according to divine law it is regarded as illicit if in contracts "equality is not observed," which is

119 This discussion of human law versus divine law is drawn, with some changes, from BERN. SEN. *Evang. aet.* 35, 1, 2 (4:192), expounding THOM. AQ. *Sum. th.* 2a 2ae q. 77 a. 1 ad 1.

120 C. 1 q. 7 c. 14 (*Quotiens a populis*): "Whenever a sin is committed by the peoples or a crowd, because it cannot be avenged in all due to their multitude, it is usually passed over unpunished."

121 C. 23. q. 4 c. 24 (*Ipsa pietas*): "Punishment is not always to be applied to those who sin … But in cases of this kind, when, because of the grave divisions of dissensions, the danger is not only to this or that person, but the slaughter of nations are at issue, something is to be taken from our severity, that sincere charity may aid in healing the greater evils."

122 D. 50 c. 25 (*Ut constitueretur*) provides the same text as C. 23 q. 4 c. 24 (just cited).

secundum diuinam legem illicitum reputatur, si in contractibus "equalitas non seruetur," quod fit plus uendendo rem quam ualeat, uel minus emendo, cum fit precipue notabilis excessus. In hoc cum beato Toma concordant Iohannes de Lignano et Iohannes Calderinus et plures alii canoniste, dicentes illam decretalem habere locum "iure fori, non iure poli," et hoc ad uitanda multa litigia que de leui possent cotidie fieri.

3.1.3.3. Excessus minor.

Tertius excessus est quando in huiusmodi contractibus parum fit dampnificatio, ut quia paulo plus uenditur res, uel paulo minus emitur iusto pretio. Et tunc, quamuis quidam dicant indistincte non commicti peccatum nec teneri ad restitutionem, eo quod pretia rerum non consistant in puncto indiuisibili sed habeant quamdam latitudinem in plus et minus; uerius tamen uidetur dicendum quod quia latitudo illa debet esse competens, et sic habet limites suos, qui tamen difficulter sciri possunt, ideo si quis in emendo uel uendendo excedat aliquantulum limites, non agens contra conscientiam, quia scilicet credit illud esse satis iustum pretium, etsi rigidum: non peccat, nec tenetur ad restitutionem, quamuis aliquantulum excedat limites iusti pretii. Et tunc habet locum quod illi dicunt, scilicet omnem contractum concomitari aliqualem donationem, et sibi inuicem partes remittere modicum plus uel

---

491 In … **494** fieri] Io. et Gasp. Cald. *Repet.* ad *X* 5.19.19 (fol. 281v–282r); Io. Lig. *Comm.* ad *X* 5.19.19 (fol. 99v).

Vide etiam Laur. Rod. *Tr. usur.* 2 op. 6 (Armstrong, 161): Oppone .vi.o ad idem quod iuris dispositione permictente attentatur non est iudicandum male agi. Sed iuris dispositione permissum est contrahentibus se decipere usque ad dimidiam iusti pretii, supra de emp. et ven., Cum dilecti [X 3.17.3] et c. penultimo [X 3.17.6] et C. de rescin. vendi. l. .ii. [*Cod.* 4.44.2] et finali [*Cod.* 4.44.18], ergo et cetera. Solutio: Innocentius in c. In civitate supra eodem in quadam sua additione [Innocent IV, Commentaria ad X 5.19.6 n.1 (ed. cit. fol. 517ra–b)], ut refert etiam Iohannes Calderinus in c. finali infra eodem in .3. oppositione [op. cit.], et dominus meus ibidem [op. cit.] dicebant quod illud habet locum iure fori, non iure poli, pro qua facit ista decretalis Consuluit cum sua glosa finali.[X 5.19.10; gl. ord. ad X 5.19.10, v. Male agere].

492 illam decretalem] Scilicet *X* 3.17.3 (*Cum dilecti*).

503 rigidum] Cfr Ant. Flor. *Summa* 2.1.8.1 (apud Ballerini 2:126c–d; 2.1.7.1 apud Mamachi 2:171; sed hoc locum non exstat in cod. M_1): Proinde advertendum est, quod huiusmodi primi pretii iustificati et limitati potest etiam distingui triplex limitationis gradus etiam iustus. Primus potest nominari pius, secundus discretus, tertius vero rigidus. Primus est pretii minoris, secundus est mediocris, tertius est maioris.

---

491 In … **494** fieri] *in marg. infer. add.* **495** contractibus] *p.c.* : *haud. leg. a.c.* **496** plus] + iusto iusto pretii *a.c.* **497** tunc] si quis *a.c.* **500** illa] + pret- *a.c.* | debet] -eat *a.c.* | habet] -eat *a.c.* **501** limites] tamen *a.c. ut vid.*

committed in selling a thing for more than it is worth, or in buying for less, especially when a notable excess is committed. In this Giovanni da Legnano and Giovanni Calderini and many other canonists agree with blessed Thomas, saying that this decretal[123] has force "by the law of the forum and not the law of heaven" – and its purpose is to avoid the excessive lawsuits which could otherwise lightly be brought daily.[124]

3.1.3.3. Minor excess. The third kind of excess is when in such contracts a small injury is committed, so that the thing is sold for a little more, or bought for a little less, than the just price. And then, although some say without distinction that no sin is committed nor is one bound to restitution, because the price of things does not consist of an unchanging quantity but has an appropriate range of higher and lower values, nevertheless it seems more true that we must say that, because there is this applicable latitude, so it must have its limits, even if they can only be defined with difficulty. Therefore if someone in buying and selling exceeds the limits by a little, not going against conscience, in other words he believes it to be a just enough price, though rigid,[125] then he does not sin, nor is he required to make restitution, even though he exceeds by a little the limits of the just price. And in that case what they say is valid, namely that an element of free gift accompanies every contract, and the parties mutually remit to each other the little bit more or less than the just price. But if someone sells for more or buys for less than the just price against conscience, that is, believing that it exceeds the highest degree of the price's latitude, even by a small amount, then

123 I.e. *X* 3.17.3 (*Cum dilecti*).

124 Io. et Gasp. Cald. *Repet.* ad *X* 5.19.19 (fol. 281v–282r); Io. Lig. *Comm.* ad *X* 5.19.19 (fol. 99v).

See also Laur. Rod. *Tr. usur.* 2 op. 6 (Armstrong, 161). Armstrong's summary (303): "The provisions of *laesio enormis* permit deception up to half the just price, but according to Innocent IV, although such deception may pass in the external forum, it will be condemned in the internal forum if it is intentional, as Bernard of Parma notes in the gloss to X 5.19.10."

125 Cfr Ant. Flor. *Summa* 2.1.8.1 (apud Ballerini 2:126c–d; 2.1.7.1 apud Mamachi 2:171; but this passage does not exist in the autograph codex M_l).

minus iusto pretio. Sed si quis contra conscientiam uendat plus uel emat minus iusto pretio, id est credens excedere suppremum gradum latitudinis pretii, etsi in modicho, non potest excusari a peccato saltim ueniali, cum omnis deceptio et fraus sit peccatum, et etiam tenetur ad satisfactionem. Ex quo minutie tales sunt innumere, et parum inde etiam leditur proximus, debet illud sic iniuste acquisitum pauperibus erogari, 14 q. 5 *Qui habetis.*

Declarantur predicta per Geraldum ordinis Herimitarum et Iohannes de Rip., quod si fiat diminutio uel excessus iusti pretii in contractibus in modicho, non est neccesse restitutionem fieri, ad quod probandum inducunt triplicem rationem.

3.1.3.3.1. Ratione pacis et saluationis.

Primo quidem ratione pacis et saluationis. Quod enim ex consensu et statuto communi et pro communi omnium utilitate procedit, eo ipso obtinet equitatem et robur iuris communis; sed communis consensus ac recta et discreta consuetudo uult, quod non omnis excessus in talibus restitui sit neccesse. Et hoc ideo, quia expedit temporali paci et saluti spirituali. Expedit quidem temporali paci quia alias infinite querimonie et litigia ex huiusmodi orirentur. Spirituali etiam saluti hoc expedit, scilicet communitatis et partium eius, quia cum difficillimum | sit ab huiusmodi contractuum excessibus se totaliter depurare, et maxime in hominibus imperfectis inhiantibus lucris, ex quibus et in quibus maior pars communitatis hominum consistit, periculosissimum omnibus esset si huiusmodi excessum sibi uendicare et retinere non liceret.

3.1.3.3.2. Ratione mutue concordationis.

Secundo hoc idem probatur ratione mutue concordationis. Propria namque forma et ratio commutatiui contractus ex utriusque partis libero ac pleno consensu inchoatur et rectificatur, ita quod emptor uult sibi rem emptam potius quam pretium eius, et uenditor econuerso; uterque etiam ex pleno consensu a se alienare intendit proprium dominium rei sue, illud in alium totaliter transferendo. Et si in aliquo preter intentionem et propriam extimationem defraudatur, citra tamen excessum enormem lege diuina uel humana

---

507 Sed … **512** erogari] C. 14 q. 5 c. 14 (*Qui habetis*): Qui habetis aliquid de malo, facite inde bonum. … De malo ergo bonum facit qui pauperibus dispensat quod cum labore et sollicitudine acquisiuit, iuxta illud euangelii: "Facite uobis amicos de mammona iniquitatis." … De peccato etiam aliqua nonnumquam acquiruntur, que pauperibus iuste erogantur.

513 Declarantur … **515** fieri] Fortasse, Langholm secutus, Ger. Odon. *Tr. contr.* q.4 (fol.81v); Io. Reg. *Quodl.* 4.18 (fol.64va–65ra).

517 Primo … **582** proni] Textus in his sectionibus usque finem, paucis mutatis, ex Bern. Sen. *Chr. rel.* 37, 2, 1 (1:470–2), quit transmittit Petr. Olivi *Tr. contr.* 1 q.5 n.52–61 (126–35).

---

507 contra] consc- *a.c.* **510** Ex quo] Verum quia *a.c.* **511** debet] pret- *a.c. ut vid.* **512** erogari] + urbe *a.c. ut vid.* | 5] 6 *a.c. ut vid.* **513** Declarantur] *in marg. sin. add.* : Confirmant *a.c. ut vid.* | Iohannes … **514** Rip] Io. de Rip(re?)- *cod. ut vid.* **514** in modicho] *in marg. sin. add.* **526** communitatis] *s.l.* **533** intendit] consentit *a.c.*

he cannot be excused from at least venial sin, for every deception and fraud is a sin, and he is also required to make satisfaction. Because minute deviations like this are innumerable, and also because they injure one's neighbour only a little, the small amount unjustly acquired should be bestowed on the poor <as satisfaction>, according to C. 14 q. 5 c. 14.[126]

The aforesaid things are explained by Gerald of the order of Hermits and John of Rip.,[127] that if in contracts there is a departure from the just price by a little less or a little more, it is not necessary that restitution be made, and they introduce three arguments to prove this.[128]

3.1.3.3.1. Argument from peace and salvation.

The first argument is based on peace and salvation.[129] For what proceeds from common consent and institution, and provides for the common utility of all, by that very fact obtains the equity and firmness of a general principle of justice; but common consent and upright and discreet custom see fit that not every excess in such things must necessarily be restored. And this is so because it is expedient for temporal peace and spiritual safety. Indeed it is expedient for temporal peace because otherwise infinite quarrels and lawsuits would be born from this sort of thing. It is expedient for spiritual safety, namely that of the community and its parts, because since it is extremely difficult to totally purify oneself from every excess in contracts of this kind, and most of all in imperfect men who covet profits, of whom and in whom the greater part of the human community consists, it would be extremely perilous for everyone if it were illicit to claim for oneself and retain such excess.

3.1.3.3.2. Argument from mutual agreement.

Second, the thesis is argued based on mutual agreement. For the proper form and rule of a commutative contract begins and is governed by the free and full consent of both parties, such that the buyer wants for himself the thing purchased more than its price, and the seller vice versa; each one also with full consent intends to alienate from himself his own ownership of his thing, by transferring it totally to the other party. And if someone is defrauded in something outside his own intention and estimation, but within the limits of gross excess prohibited by divine and human law, he wills nonetheless that the

126 C. 14 q. 5 c. 14 (*Qui habetis*): "If you have something out of evil, do something good with it … And so, he does good from evil who gives to the poor what he has acquired with labour and care, according to that text of the Gospel: Make friends for yourselves from the mammon of iniquity (Lc. 16.9) … Also, some things are acquired by sin which may justly be distributed to the poor."

127 The best conjecture, put forward by Langholm (see above, ch. 4), is Ger. Odon. *Tr. contr.* q. 4 (fol. 81v); Io. Reg. *Quodl.* 4.18 (fol. 64va–65ra).

128 At this sentence, beginning at the word *Declarantur*, the look of the writing changes slightly: the ink is darker and the letters are sharper at the top and bottom, with greater distinction between heavy and fine lines. However, the letter-forms appear the same. It seems likelier that Antoninus wrote this section later, or at least changed pens and perhaps ink, than that another scribe wrote it.

129 The next four sections are copied essentially verbatim from Bern. Sen. *Chr. rel.* 37, 2, 1 (1:470–2), transmitting Petr. Olivi *Tr. contr.* 1 q. 5 n. 52–61 (126–35).

prohibitum, uult nichilominus contractum initum ratum esse et firmum. Ac si libere et expresse omni tali legi renuntiaret in contrarium facienti, pro quanto pro sua temporali indempnitate id facit. Alter sibi nichil inde reddere obligatur, quia ibi iam non est enormis, ymmo forte nec ullus excessus: quia sicut potuit totum absque omni pretio donare, sic potuit pro minori pretio iuste uendere uel dare.

3.1.3.3.3. Ratione humane extimationis.

Tertio hoc probatur ratione humane extimationis, que quidem incerta est ad mere iusta pretia pretaxanda, et ad precise discernendum excessus et defectus iusti pretii. Propter quod, licet pretium [licet] in aliquo minuatur uel excedatur, nichilominus nulli proprio uel communi iudicio censetur aut censeri debet pro enormi, nec sic respectu iudicii nostri recedit a moderantia iusti pretii sub competenti latitudine mensurandi, quin ipsum aliqualiter includatur, sicut mustum uel uinum acerbum uel aliqualiter acetosum non sic recedit a specie uini, quin includatur in ipsa. Et secundum Scotum in 4° d. 15, equalitas commutationum et contractuum non consistit in indiuisibili medio, ymmo in medio illo quod iustitia commutatiua respicit magna est latitudo, et intra illam latitudinem non attingere indiuisibilem punctum equiualentie rei. In quocumque gradu citra extrema fiat, iuste fit.

3.1.3.3.4. Contra quoddam obiectionum.

Si quis autem obstaret et diceret, quod quicquid in contractibus est illicitum et peccatum, contra ius diuinum esse uidetur, et sic nullum robur ab eo obtinere uidetur, ymmo potius oppositum, propter quod nullus illicitus excessus pretii potest a iure diuino acquiri peccanti in illo: respondeo dicendum quod in huiusmodi contractibus sunt duo precipue attendenda, scilicet intrinsecha affectio, et extrinsecha operatio. Et quantum ad primum, scilicet intrinsecham affectionem, sciendum quod pro quanto uult in proximum scienter aliquam inequalitatem, ut scilicet in huiusmodi contractibus meliorem partem habeat quam ille, pro tanto aliquid de inustitia habet: que si non est mortale, quia scilicet non notabilis, sufficit aut per contritionem et penitentialem satisfactionem aut per purgatorii ignem, sicut et cetera uenialia, expiari. Quantum ad secundum, scilicet operationem extrinsecham et commutationem, licet secundum ueridicam extimationem pretii sui contineat aliquantulam inequalitatem, respectu tamen ad commune statutum et ad condescensiuam legem Dei, que permictit aliquos minores defectus, ita scilicet quod per eos non punit ad mortem ecternam, et

549 equalitas … **553** fit] Io. Scot. *In quartum* d. 15 q. 2 n. 15 (18:283ff.).

538 facit] faceret *a.c.* **544** licet^{2}] *delevi* **550** medio] + *spatium unius litterae* **564** ignem] *ut vid.* **567** Dei] + que p- *a.c.* | que permictit] *bis a.c.* **568** defectus] *ut vid.*

contract entered into be fixed and firm. And if he should freely and expressly renounce all such law to the other party, who does the reverse, he does it even just for his own temporal indemnity. The other is obliged to render nothing to him thence, because there is not present a gross excess, perhaps not even any excess: because just as he was able to freely give the whole thing for free, thus he can sell or give it justly for a lesser price.

3.1.3.3.3. Argument from human estimation. Third, the thesis is argued based on human estimation, which indeed is uncertain at fixing purely just prices, and at precisely discerning excesses and deficiencies from the just price. On account of this, although the price may be too low or too high by some amount, none the less it is not reckoned nor ought to be reckoned as a gross departure by anybody's particular judgment nor by common judgment, nor is it removed with respect to our judgement from the moderation of the just price which must be measured against the applicable latitude. Rather it is to some extent included within the latitude of the just price, just as must or bitter or somewhat acidic wine is not removed from the category "wine," but rather is included in it. And according to Scotus in book 4 d. 15,[130] equality in commutations and contracts does not consist in a precise mean, but rather within that mean which commutative justice regards there is a great latitude, and within that latitude one does not attain a precise point of equivalence to a thing. In whatever grade within those extremes it is done, it is done justly.

3.1.3.3.4. Against an objection. But if someone should object and say that whatever is illicit and sinful in contracts seems to be contrary to divine law, and thus would seem to attain no firmness from it, actually quite the opposite, on account of which no illicit excess of price can be acquired by divine law for the one sinning in it, I answer, it must be said that in contracts of this kind two things principally demand attention, namely the inner intention and the outer act. And as to the first, namely the inner intention, one must understand that to the extent that one wants knowingly some inequality against a neighbour, in other words to have the better part in such contracts than he, to that extent it has something of injustice. If the injustice is not mortal, that is, because it is not notable, it suffices that it be expiated either by contrition and penitential satisfaction or by purgatorial fire, just like with other venial sins. As for the second, namely the outer act and exchange: although according to a truthful estimation of its price it may contain some small inequality, with respect however to common statute and to the condescending law of God, which permits some lesser defects, namely so that because of them he does not punish to the extent of eternal death, and with respect to the free consent of the contracting parties, it does not have inequality, actually it really has benign and concessive and salutary equity. And therefore as to this, it obtains force and firmness as much

130 Io. Scot. *In quartum* d. 15 q. 2 n. 15 (18:283ff.).

ad liberum consensum contrahentium, non habet inequalitatem, ymmo potius benignam et concessoriam et salutiferam equitatem. Et ideo quantum ad hoc, tam diuino iure quam humano robur obtinet firmitatis. Aliter omnes huiusmodi excessus pretii illiciti erunt in acquirentibus mortalis culpa, quia esset usurpatio rei aliene in quantum aliene. Teneretur etiam quilibet uenditor siue emptor omnem talem excessum restituere, et sic omnes qui hic non restituerent, dampnarentur: quod quidem nequissimum et durissimum est pensare. Verum propter puritatem humani affectus ad talia temporalia inclinati, ac propter inequalitatem talium commutationum, securius et iustius esset, omnem talem excessum scienter factum, si alicuius quantitatis appretiabilis foret, satisfacere; aut si parui ualoris sunt, pro animabus illorum pauperibus erogare, quia in hoc plus proficeret fraudato nisi et ipse graui inopia laboraret. Hec tamen predicanda cum magna discretione, cum populi ad dilatandum conscientiam sint proni. Et ideo que tutiora sunt, dicenda sunt.

Quantum ad fraudes quas faciunt homines in negotiando, et illicitas permutationes, dicetur in sequentibus sub alio sermone.

---

582 proni] Hic finit textus ex Bern. Sen.

---

572 pretii] + erunt *a.c.* **576** temporalia] tporalia *cod.*

by divine law as by human law. Otherwise all such illicit excess of price will be a mortal fault for those who acquire it, since it would be a usurpation of another's property in as much as it belongs to the other. Every seller or buyer would also be bound to restore every such excess, and thus everyone who did not restore it would be damned, which is indeed an extremely evil and harsh thought. But because of the intensity of human desire inclined to such temporal things and because of the inequality of such commutations, it would be safer and more just to make satisfaction for every such excess knowingly committed, if it is of any appreciable quantity; or if it is of little value, to bestow it on the poor for the good of souls, because from this the one defrauded would get more benefit, unless he himself should labour under grave poverty. These things, however, must be preached with great discretion, since the people are prone to loosening their consciences.[131] And therefore the safer things are the ones we must say.[132]

As to those frauds which men commit in trade, and illicit exchanges, they will be discussed in the following pages in another sermon.

131 Here Antoninus ceases to repeat Bern. Sen.

132 At this point the pen begins to look more like it did before commencing this section from Bern. Sen. Nevertheless the letter-forms and abbreviations appear the same.

Antoninus Florentinus, *Summa*, 2.1.17
De uariis fraudibus que commictuntur in negotiando

Summarium ab editore confectum

Thema. ***Tota die iniustitiam cogitauit lingua tua; sicut nouacula acuta fecisti dolum*** (*Ps* 51.4).

1. **Astutia.**
2. **Malitia.**
    - 2.1. **De dolo et fraude.**
    - 2.2. **Dolus dans causam contractui.**
    - 2.3. **Dolus incidens in contractum.**
3. **Fraudulentia.**
    - 3.1. **In rei quiditate.**
    - 3.2. **In sui quantitate.**
        - 3.2.1. **In pondere.**
        - 3.2.2. **In mensura.**
        - 3.2.3. **In numero.**
        - 3.2.4. **De more in dando ad filandum.**
        - 3.2.5. **De tabernariis.**
        - 3.2.6. **De lanificibus et factoribus caligarum.**
        - 3.2.7. **De laninis deferentibus ad filandum.**
    - 3.3. **In eius qualitate.**
        - 3.3.1. **Quando defectus rei debet manifestari.**
        - 3.3.2. **De uendentibus pannos uel uestes defectuosos.**
        - 3.3.3. **De remendatoribus pannorum.**
    - 3.4. **In soluendi tarditate.**
        - 3.4.1. **De campsoribus.**
        - 3.4.2. **De officialibus communitatis.**
    - 3.5. **In pretii ad res mutabilitate.**
    - 3.6. **In bono opere cum intentionis prauitate.**
        - 3.6.1. **A corde.**
        - 3.6.2. **Ab ore.**
        - 3.6.3. **Ab opere.**
4. **De permutationibus seu baracti.**

St Antoninus, *Summa*, 2.1.17
On the various frauds which are committed in trading

Summary prepared by the editor

Thema. *All the day long thy tongue hath devised injustice: as a sharp razor, thou hast wrought guile* (*Ps* 51.4).

1. Craftiness.
2. Malice.
   - 2.1. Guile and fraud.
   - 2.2. Guile giving rise to a contract.
   - 2.3. Guile incidental in a contract.
3. Fraudulence.
   - 3.1. Fraud in a thing's essence.
   - 3.2. Fraud in a thing's quantity.
     - 3.2.1. In weight.
     - 3.2.2. In measure.
     - 3.2.3. In number.
     - 3.2.4. The customary practice when giving material to be spun.
     - 3.2.5. Tavern keepers.
     - 3.2.6. Wool merchants and shoemakers.
     - 3.2.7. *Lanini* putting out material to be spun.
   - 3.3. Fraud in a thing's quality.
     - 3.3.1. When a thing's defect ought to be revealed.
     - 3.3.2. Selling defective cloth or clothing.
     - 3.3.3. Cloth menders.
   - 3.4. Fraud in late payment.
     - 3.4.1. Bankers.
     - 3.4.2. Civic officials.
   - 3.5. Fraud in payment of the price in kind.
   - 3.6. Fraud in a good work with crooked intention.
     - 3.6.1. From the heart.
     - 3.6.2. From the mouth.
     - 3.6.3. From the work.
4. Exchanges of goods or barter.

17^m capitulum: de uariis fraudibus que commictuntur in negotiando.

M_1 fol. Vr

Thema. De uaria fraudatione loquitur Psalmista dicens, Ps. 51, *Tota die iniustitiam cogitauit lingua tua; sicut nouacula acuta fecisti dolum.* Vbi ultra frequentiam mali operis quam signat dicens *Tota die*, sententiam dampnationis insinuat dicens: *Propterea Deus dextruet te in finem* et *euellet te* etc. Vnde et Apostolus Thessal., *Neque quis circumueniat*, id est decipiat, *in negotio fratrem suum*, quia *uindex est Deus de omnibus hiis.* Et de bestia quam uidit Ioannes Apoc. 13 dicitur quod *faciet, ne quis possit uendere uel emere, nisi qui habuerit characterem ac nomen bestie.* Bestia, que dicitur a uastando, diabolus est; character eius, que est ymago eius, est fraus et dolus; nomen eius est falsitas, quia mendax est. Absque ista ymagine, scilicet fraudis, dicuntur mercatores non posse uendere uel emere. Sed ibi subditur quod qui *acceperit* hunc *karacterem, bibet de uino ire Dei.* Et notat tria mala que facit dolosus seu deceptor in negotiando seu uendendo.

fol. 70v

Primum est astutia in modos ad decipiendum exquirendo, ibi *Tota die iniustitiam cogitauit lingua tua.*

Secundum est malitia in decipiendos liniendo, ibi *Sicut nouacula acuta.*

Tertium est fraudulentia in excogitatos exequendo, ibi *Fecisti dolum.*

---

2 Tota … **3** dolum] *Ps* 51.4: Tota die injustitiam cogitavit lingua tua; sicut novacula acuta fecisti dolum.

5 Propterea … te[2]] *Ps* 51.7: Propterea Deus destruet te in finem; evellet te, et emigrabit te de tabernaculo tuo, et radicem tuam de terra viventium.

5 Vnde … **14** uendendo] Cfr Bern. Sen. *Evang. aet.* 33, 2, 7 (4:151–5).

6 Neque … 7 hiis] *1 Th* 4.6: et ne quis supergrediatur, neque circumveniat in negotio fratrem suum : quoniam vindex est Dominus de his omnibus, sicut praediximus vobis, et testificati sumus.

8 faciet … **9** bestie] *Apc* 13.16–17: Et faciet omnes pusillos, et magnos, et divites, et pauperes, et liberos, et servos habere caracterem in dextera manu sua, aut in frontibus suis : et ne quis possit emere, aut vendere, nisi qui habet caracterem, aut nomen bestiae, aut numerum nominis ejus.

---

2 De] *in marg. sin. scr. Antoninus* dominicha 3 in XL[a] *vel* 4L[a] | loquitur] pal- *a.c.* **4** signat] no(tat) *a.c.* | die] + et *a.c.* | insinuat … **5** dicens] quam preca- *a.c.* **5** Vnde … **13** Dei] *in marg. super. add.* **6** Thessal.] Ephe. *cod.* **9** uastando] *ut vid.* **11** dicuntur] dicunt *cod.* **13** Dei] *ut vid.* | Et] *ut vid.* **15** Primum … **18** dolum] *tr. per litteras* a (astutia …) c (fraudulentia …) b (malitia …) *cod.* | ad decipiendum] *in marg. sin. add.* **17** decipiendos] *in marg. sin. add.* : decipiendo *a.c. ut vid.*

Chapter 17: On the various frauds which are committed in trading.

Thema. The[1] Psalmist speaks about all different sorts of fraudulence when he says in Psalm 51: *All the day long thy tongue hath devised injustice: as a sharp razor, thou hast wrought guile.*[2] There, in addition to the frequency of evil work, which he signifies when he says *All the day long*, he also introduces a sentence of condemnation when he says *Therefore will God destroy thee for ever*, and *he will pluck thee out* etc.[3] Hence the Apostle also says in Thessalonians: *and that no man circumvent*, that is deceive, *his brother in business, because the Lord is the avenger of all these things.*[4] And about the beast which John sees in Apocalypse 13 it is said that *he shall make … that no man might sell or buy, but he that shall have the character or the name of the beast.*[5] The beast, which is named after desolation, is the devil; his character, which is his image, is fraud and guile; his name is falsehood, because he is a liar. Without that image, namely of fraud, merchants are said not to be able to sell or buy. But it is added there that whoever *shall receive* this *character, shall drink of the wine of the wrath of God.*[6] Now the Psalmist notes three evils which the guileful man or deceiver commits in trading or selling.[7]

The first is craftiness in seeking out methods for deceiving, at *All the day long thy tongue hath devised injustice.*

The second is malice in coaxing people to be deceived, at *As a sharp razor.*

The third is fraudulence in executing methods contrived, at *Thou hast wrought guile.*[8]

---

1 In the left margin beside the opening of this chapter, Antoninus has written: "3rd Sunday in Lent."

2 *Ps* 51.4: "All the day long thy tongue hath devised injustice: as a sharp razor, thou hast wrought deceit."

3 *Ps* 51.7: "Therefore will God destroy thee for ever: he will pluck thee out, and remove thee from thy dwelling place: and thy root out of the land of the living."

4 *1 Th* 4.6: "And that no man overreach, nor circumvent his brother in business: because the Lord is the avenger of all these things, as we have told you before, and have testified."

5 *Apc* 13.16–17: "And he shall make all, both little and great, rich and poor, freemen and bondmen, to have a character in their right hand, or on their foreheads. And that no man might buy or sell, but he that hath the character, or the name of the beast, or the number of his name."

6 *Apc* 14.9–11: "And the third angel followed them, saying with a loud voice: If any man shall adore the beast and his image, and receive his character in his forehead, or in his hand; he also shall drink of the wine of the wrath of God, which is mingled with pure wine in the cup of his wrath, and shall be tormented with fire and brimstone in the sight of the holy angels, and in the sight of the Lamb. And the smoke of their torments shall ascend up for ever and ever: neither have they rest day nor night, who have adored the beast, and his image, and whoever receiveth the character of his name."

7 For this whole introductory paragraph, contrast Bern. Sen. *Evang. aet.* 33, 2, 7 (4:151–5).

8 Antoninus originally placed craftiness first, fraudulence second, malice third; but afterwards reordered them as set out above, indicating their intended order with the letters **a**, **c**, and **b**. The printed editions do not incorporate the author's transposition: in Ballerini and even Mamachi, the original order of craftiness, fraudulence, malice is reproduced.

1. Astutia. Quantum ad primum, sciendum quod licet astutia fraus et dolus possint in actibus aliorum peccatorum reperiri, communius tamen in uitio auaritie circa acquisitionem temporalium consueuerunt exerceri. Et ut dicit beatus Tomas, 2^{a} 2^{e} q. 55, astutia proprie est cum quis "ad consequendum aliquem finem bonum uel malum utitur non ueris uiis," seu mediis, "sed simulatis et apparentibus." Hoc autem est peccatum, quia contra rationem rectam, unde et contra prudentiam. "Neque," enim etiam "ad bonum finem oportet falsis uiis et simulatis peruenire, sed ueris," et realibus; quod facit prudentia. Et quia similitudinem habet cum ea, in eo scilicet quod utitur ad perueniendum ad finem intentum illis mediis que conducunt ad ipsum, sed prudentia debitis et iustis mediis utitur et ad bonum finem, astutia indebitis mediis uel ad malum finem; ideo ipsa astutia aliquando dicitur prudentia propter dictam similitudinem, sed improprie. Vnde Prouerb. 1 dicitur, *ut paruulis detur astutia*, id est prudentia; et Prouerb. 13: *Astutus*, id est prudens, *omnia facit cum consilio.* Sic ergo astutia consistit in excogitatione dictarum uiarum simulatarum ad aliquem finem querendum, puta ut in proposito ad decipiendum proximum in temporalibus. Et hoc est quod dicit Psalmista de iniquo: *Tota die iniustitiam cogitauit lingua tua*, lingua scilicet cordis exquirendo et inuestigando

---

19 astutia … **25** prudentiam] Thom. Aq. *Sum. th.* 2a 2ae q. 55 a. 3 resp.: Respondeo dicendum quod prudentia est recta ratio agibilium, sicut scientia est recta ratio scibilium. Contingit autem contra rectitudinem scientiae dupliciter peccari in speculativis, uno quidem modo, quando ratio inducitur ad aliquam conclusionem falsam quae apparet vera; alio modo, ex eo quod ratio procedit ex aliquibus falsis quae videntur esse vera, sive sint ad conclusionem veram sive ad conclusionem falsam. Ita etiam aliquod peccatum potest esse contra prudentiam habens aliquam similitudinem eius dupliciter. Uno modo, quia studium rationis ordinatur ad finem qui non est vere bonus sed apparens, et hoc pertinet ad prudentiam carnis. Alio modo, inquantum aliquis ad finem aliquem consequendum, vel bonum vel malum, utitur non veris viis, sed simulatis et apparentibus, et hoc pertinet ad peccatum astutiae. Unde est quoddam peccatum prudentiae oppositum a prudentia carnis distinctum.

25 Neque … **26** prudentia] Thom. Aq. *Sum. th.* 2a 2ae q. 55 a. 3 ad 2: Ad secundum dicendum quod astutia potest consiliari et ad finem bonum et ad finem malum, nec oportet ad finem bonum falsis viis pervenire et simulatis, sed veris. Unde etiam astutia si ordinetur ad bonum finem, est peccatum.

30 astutia … **31** improprie] Thom. Aq. *Sum. th.* 2a 2ae q. 55 a. 3 ad 1: Ad primum ergo dicendum quod, sicut Augustinus dicit, in IV *contra Iulian.*, sicut prudentia abusive quandoque in malo accipitur, ita etiam astutia quandoque in bono, et hoc propter similitudinem unius ad alterum. Proprie tamen astutia in malo accipitur; sicut et philosophus dicit, in VI *Ethic.*

31 ut … astutia] *Prv* 1.4: ut detur parvulis astutia, adolescenti scientia et intellectus.

32 Astutus … consilio] *Prv* 13.16: Astutus omnia agit cum consilio, qui autem fatuus est aperit stultitiam.

---

22 55] 54 *cod.* **29** astutia] prudentia *a.c.* **33** ergo] ibi *a.c.* **34** querendum] *vel* consequendum *cod.* **35** Et hoc] Ita dolus consistit in ex- *a.c.* **36** cordis] + si *a.c. ut vid.*

1. Craftiness. First, it must be understood that although craftiness, fraud, and guile may be found in the acts of other sins, nevertheless typically they tend to be exercised in the vice of avarice in connection with acquiring temporal things. And as blessed Thomas says, 2a 2ae q. 55, craftiness properly speaking is when someone "in order to obtain a certain end, whether good or evil, uses ways," or means, "that are not true but fictitious and counterfeit."[9] And this is a sin, because it is contrary to right reason, hence also contrary to prudence. For "neither should a good end be pursued by means that are false and counterfeit but by such as are true," and real; which is what prudence does.[10] And because craftiness has a resemblance to prudence, in that in order to reach the intended end it uses those means which conduce to it – but prudence uses proper and just means and for a good end, craftiness undue means or for a bad end – therefore craftiness itself is sometimes called prudence because of the aforementioned resemblance, but speaking loosely.[11] Whence it is said in Proverbs 1, *to give to little ones craftiness*,[12] that is, prudence; and in Proverbs 13: *the crafty man*, that is the prudent, *doth all things with counsel.*[13] Thus it follows that craftiness consists in thinking out the aforesaid counterfeit ways to pursue a certain end: say, as in the intention to deceive a neighbour in temporal things. And this is what the Psalmist says about the wicked man: *all the day long thy tongue hath devised injustice*, the tongue, namely, of the heart in seeking out, and of the mind in investigating, how he may commit injustices and deceive his neighbour. But the Lord says through the prophet Job, chapter 5, which the Apostle

9 Thom. Aq. *Sum. th.* 2a 2ae q. 55 a. 3 *resp.*: "Prudence is 'right reason applied to action,' just as science is 'right reason applied to knowledge.' In speculative matters one may sin against rectitude of knowledge in two ways: in one way when the reason is led to a false conclusion that appears to be true; in another way when the reason proceeds from false premises, that appear to be true, either to a true or to a false conclusion. Even so a sin may be against prudence, through having some resemblance thereto, in two ways. First, when the purpose of the reason is directed to an end which is good not in truth but in appearance, and this pertains to prudence of the flesh; secondly, when, in order to obtain a certain end, whether good or evil, a man uses means that are not true but fictitious and counterfeit, and this belongs to the sin of craftiness. This is consequently a sin opposed to prudence, and distinct from prudence of the flesh."

10 Thom. Aq. *Sum. th.* 2a 2ae q. 55 a. 3 *ad* 2: "Craftiness can take counsel both for a good end and for an evil end: nor should a good end be pursued by means that are false and counterfeit but by such as are true. Hence craftiness is a sin if it be directed to a good end."

11 Thom. Aq. *Sum. th.* 2a 2ae q. 55 a. 3 *ad* 1: "As Augustine observes (*Contra Julian.* iv, 3) just as prudence is sometimes improperly taken in a bad sense, so is craftiness sometimes taken in a good sense, and this on account of their mutual resemblance. Properly speaking, however, craftiness is taken in a bad sense, as the Philosopher states in *Ethic.* vi, 12."

12 *Prv* 1.4: "To give subtilty to little ones, to the young man knowledge and understanding."

13 *Prv* 13.16: "The prudent man doth all things with counsel: but he that is a fool, layeth open his folly."

mente quomodo iniusta possit facere et proximum decipere. Sed dicit Dominus per prophetam Iob, 5° capitulo, quod recitat Apostolus 1 Corinth. 3: *Comprehendam sapientes*, scilicet *mundi*, *in astutia eorum*, quia frequenter cum intendant decipere, ipsi decipiuntur.

2. Malitia. Quantum ad secundum, notandum secundum beatum Tomam, 2^{a} 2^{e} q. 55, quod dolus est executio astutie, unde consistit in executione dictarum uiarum falsarum que excogitantur per astutiam. Et "principaliter fit per uerba ad decipiendum," iuxta illud Ps.: *Lingua tua concinnabat*, id est multiplicabat, *dolos*; quamuis et ad malitias cordis cogitatas ad decipiendum extendatur etiam dolus, iuxta illud Ecclesiastici 1, *Cor tuum plenum est dolo*; et ad opera deceptoria, secundum illud Ierem. 6, *Cuncti faciunt dolum*.

2.1. De dolo et fraude. Fit ergo dolus per uerba et facta deceptoria, fraus autem proprie per facta. Et sic sumuntur cum dicitur, *Extra*, *De rescrip.*, *Ex tenore*, quod "fraus et dolus nemini debent patrocinari," ut fraus referatur ad facta deceptoria, ad uerba autem dolus.

---

39 Comprehendam ... eorum] *Iob* 5.13: qui apprehendit sapientes in astutia eorum, et consilium pravorum dissipat. *1 Cor* 3.19: Sapientia enim hujus mundi, stultitia est apud Deum. Scriptum est enim : Comprehendam sapientes in astutia eorum.

42 dolus ... **43** astutiam] Thom. Aq. *Sum. th.* 2a 2ae q. 55 a. 4 resp.: Respondeo dicendum quod, sicut supra dictum est (a.3), ad astutiam pertinet assumere vias non veras, sed simulatas et apparentes, ad aliquem finem prosequendum vel bonum vel malum. Assumptio autem harum viarum potest dupliciter considerari. Uno quidem modo, in ipsa excogitatione viarum huiusmodi, et hoc proprie pertinet ad astutiam, sicut etiam excogitatio rectarum viarum ad debitum finem pertinet ad prudentiam. Alio modo potest considerari talium viarum assumptio secundum executionem operis, et secundum hoc pertinet ad dolum. Et ideo dolus importat quandam executionem astutiae. Et secundum hoc ad astutiam pertinet.

43 principaliter ... **44** decipiendum] Thom. Aq. *Sum. th.* 2a 2ae q. 55 a. 4 ad 2: Ad secundum dicendum quod executio astutiae ad decipiendum primo quidem et principaliter fit per verba, quae praecipuum locum tenent inter signa quibus homo significat aliquid alteri, ut patet per Augustinum, in libro *de Doct. Christ.* Et ideo dolus maxime attribuitur locutioni. Contingit tamen esse dolum et in factis, secundum illud Psalm., *et dolum facerent in servos eius*. Est etiam et dolus in corde, secundum illud Eccli. XIX. *Interiora eius plena sunt dolo*. Sed hoc est secundum quod aliquis dolos excogitat, secundum illud Psalm., *dolos tota die meditabantur*.

44 Lingua ... **45** dolos] *Ps* 49.19: Os tuum abundavit malitia, et lingua tua concinnabat dolos.

46 Cor ... dolo] *Sir* 1.40: quoniam accessisti maligne ad Dominum, et cor tuum plenum est dolo et fallacia.

47 Cuncti ... dolum] *Ier* 6.13: a minore quippe usque ad majorem, omnes avaritiae student, et a propheta usque ad sacerdotem cuncti faciunt dolum.

49 fraus ... **50** patrocinari] *X* 1.3.16 (*Ex tenore*): ... quia fraus et dolus alicui patrocinari non debent.

---

40 decipiuntur] + pau- *a.c. ut vid.* **42** 55] 54 *cod.* **46** Ecclesiastici] Ecc^{i} *cod.* **49** sumuntur] sununtur *cod. ut vid.* **50** ad uerba] fraus *a.c.*

cites in 1st Corinthians 3: *I will catch the wise*, namely *of this world, in their own craftiness*;[14] because often when they intend to deceive, they are deceived themselves.

2. Malice. Second, it should be noted, according to blessed Thomas, 2a 2ae q. 55, that guile is the execution of craftiness, hence it consists in the execution of the aforementioned false ways which are thought out through craftiness.[15] And "it is effected first and foremost by words with the purpose of deceiving,"[16] according to that text of the Psalm: *thy tongue hath framed*, that is multiplied, *guiles*;[17] although guile is even extended to malicious plans in the heart which are thought out in order to deceive, according to that text in Sirach 1, *thy heart is full of guile*,[18] and to deceptive works, according to that text in Jeremiah 6, *all commit guile*.[19]

2.1. Guile and fraud. Guile is done therefore through deceptive words and acts, but fraud properly through acts. And they are so applied when it is said in the *Liber Extra*, *On rescripts*, c. 16, that "no one's fraud and guile ought to be defended,"[20] that fraud refers to duplicitous acts, but guile to words.

---

14 *Iob* 5.13: "Who catcheth the wise in their craftiness, and disappointeth the counsel of the wicked." *1 Cor* 3.19: "For the wisdom of this world is foolishness with God. For it is written: I will catch the wise in their own craftiness."

15 Thom. Aq. *Sum. th.* 2a 2ae q. 55 a. 4 *resp.*: "As stated above (a. 3), it belongs to craftiness to adopt ways that are not true but counterfeit and apparently true, in order to attain some end either good or evil. Now the adopting of such ways may be subjected to a twofold consideration; first, as regards the process of thinking them out, and this belongs properly to craftiness, even as thinking out right ways to a due end belongs to prudence. Secondly the adopting of such like ways may be considered with regard to their actual execution, and in this way it belongs to guile. Hence guile denotes a certain execution of craftiness, and accordingly belongs thereto."

16 Thom. Aq. *Sum. th.* 2a 2ae q. 55 a. 4 *ad* 2: "The execution of craftiness with the purpose of deceiving, is effected first and foremost by words, which hold the chief place among those signs whereby a man signifies something to another man, as Augustine states (*De Doctr. Christ.* ii, 3), hence guile is ascribed chiefly to speech. Yet guile may happen also in deeds, according to Ps. 104:25, 'And to deal deceitfully with his servants.' Guile is also in the heart, according to Ecclus. 19:23, 'His interior is full of deceit,' but this is to devise deceits, according to Ps. 37:13: 'They studied deceits all the day long.'"

17 *Ps* 49.19: "Thy mouth hath abounded with evil, and thy tongue framed deceits."

18 *Sir* 1.40: "Because thou camest to the Lord wickedly, and thy heart is full of guile and deceit."

19 *Ier* 6.13: "For from the least of them even to the greatest, all are given to covetousness: and from the prophet even to the priest, all are guilty of deceit."

20 *X* 1.3.16 (*Ex tenore*).

2.2. Dolus dans causam contractui.

Et nota secundum Petrum de Palude in 4° Goffredum et Bernardum, quod si dolus dat causam contractui, puta quis celat uitium equi quem exponit uenalem uel laudat ipsum ut indefectuosum, quem defectum si sciret emtor nullo modo emeret, ut equum cadentem periculosum; tunc quamuis res illa ualeret pretium, tamen quia uenditor celando uitium occultum rei illius uel laudando ut non habentem defectum, cum sciret, tenetur ad restitutionem pretii emptori reofferenti rem, quia propter talem dolum potest rescindi contractus secundum iura.

2.3. Dolus incidens in contractum.

Si autem dolus per uerba uel facta incidit in contractum, quia scilicet emptor emisset illam rem cuius defectum nesciebat, sed non tantum pretium, tunc si res illa tantum ualet, non tenetur ei uenditor in aliquo, quia ex quo uolebat emere, debebat emere iusto pretio. Sed si non tantum ualebat, debet restituere illud plus. Hos dolos facit iniustus auarus per uerba adulatoria plena fallaciis, alliciendo uerbis humanis et reuerentibus, ostendendo se amichum emptoris, et huiusmodi. Vnde Psalmista propter hoc assimilat eum barbitonsori et linguam suam nouacule cum qua radit pilos, quia antequam radat acuit nouaculam super lapidem oleo litum: ita auarus et fraudulentus oleo adulationis linguam acuit ad radendum pilos, id est auferendum temporalia. Dicit ergo: *Sicut nouacula acuta*, scilicet *lingua tua* fuit. Contra hos imprecatur Psalmista dicens: *Linguis suis dolose agebant, iudica illos*, id est condempna eos, *Deus*.

---

52 Petrum … 4°] Locum Petr. Pal. non inveni. Cfr Thom. Aq. *Sum. th.* 2a 2ae q. 77 a. 2–3.

52 Goffredum] Gauf. Tran. *Sum.* 3.17 *de emptione et venditione* §. 7 (135r–v).

52 Bernardum] Bern. Parm. in *Glossa ord.* ad *X* 3.17.3 (*Cum dilecti*) s.v. *deceptione* (2:1124): Cum dolus dat causam contractui, puta, dolo induxi te ad vendendam rem, alias non venditurus, non tenet contractus. ff. de dolo, et eleganter, arg. 12 q. 2 quisquis episcopus, in fine, et infra de re. permuta., cum universorum. Si vero incidit in contractum, quia venditurus eram, sed per dolum tuum minus vendidi, vel per dolum meum plus emisti: tenet quidem contractus, sed agitur ad supplementum residui. ff. de actio. emp. et ven., Iulianus, §. sed si venditor. Si vero dolus non dat causam contractui, nec incidit in contractum, sed deceptus sum ultra dimidiam iusti pretii in venditione, obtinet quod hic dicitur, et infra …

58 propter … **59** iura] E.g. in iure civili, *Dig.* 4.3.7 (*Et eleganter*) pr.: … aut nullam esse venditionem, si in hoc ipso ut venderet circumscriptus est. E.g. in iure canonico, C. 12 q. 2 c. 19 (*Quisquis episcopus*); *X* 3.19.8 (*Cum universorum*).

70 Linguis … **71** Deus] *Ps* 5.11: Sepulchrum patens est guttur eorum; linguis suis dolose agebant, judica illos, Deus. Decidant a cogitationibus suis; secundum multitudinem impietatum eorum expelle eos, quoniam irritaverunt te, Domine. Cfr *Rm* 3.13: Sepulchrum patens est guttur eorum, linguis suis dolose agebant : venenum aspidum sub labiis eorum.

---

52 Goffredum … Bernardum] Goff. et Ber. *cod. s.l.* | Et … **64** plus] *in marg. infer. add.* **63** restituere] supplere *a.c.* **64** dolos] *s.l.* : dum *a.c. ut vid.* | adulatoria] d(eceptoria?) *a.c.* **70** fuit] *ut vid.* | Psalmista] Ps. *cod.*

2.2. Guile giving rise to a contract. And note that according to Peter of la Palud in the fourth book,[21] Goffredo,[22] and Bernard,[23] if guile gives rise to the contract, as when someone conceals the fault of a horse which he puts up for sale or praises it as free of defects, when it has a defect and if the buyer of it knew he would by no means make the purchase, e.g., a horse that falls dangerously; then although the thing for sale is worth a price, nevertheless the seller, because he has concealed the hidden fault which he is aware of in the thing or has praised it as not having any defect, is bound to restore the price to the buyer who returns the item, because on account of such guile the contract can be rescinded according to the laws.[24]

2.3. Guile incidental in a contract. If, however, guile through words or acts is incidental within the contract, that is, because the buyer would have bought the same thing of whose defect he was ignorant, but not for the same price, then if the thing itself is worth that price, the seller does not owe the buyer anything; because from the fact that he wished to purchase, he was obliged to purchase at a just price. But if it was not worth so much, the seller ought to restore the excess. The unjust avaricious man commits these acts of guile through laudatory words full of falsehoods, coaxing with kindly and reverent words, making himself out to be the friend of the buyer and so forth. Hence because of this the Psalmist likens him to a barber, and his tongue to the razor with which he trims hair, because before he trims he sharpens his razor on an oiled stone: thus the avaricious and fraudulent man sharpens his tongue with the oil of flattery in order to trim hair, that is, to carry off temporal goods. Therefore the Psalmist says: it was *as a sharp razor*, namely *thy tongue*. The Psalmist curses against these saying: *they dealt deceitfully with their tongues: judge them*, that is, condemn them, *O God*.[25]

---

21 I have not found the *locus* in Petr. Pal. in his *Quartus sententiarum liber* (Paris, 1514). Cfr Thom. Aq. *Sum. th.* 2a 2ae q. 77 a. 2–3.

22 Gauf. Tran. *Sum.* 3.17 *de emptione et venditione* §. 7 (135r–v).

23 Bern. Parm. in *Glossa ord.* ad *X* 3.17.3 (*Cum dilecti*) s.v. *deceptione* (2:1124).

24 In civil law, e.g. *Dig.* 4.3.7 (*Et eleganter*) pr.: "… or there is no sale if he was deceived with respect to the very fact that he was selling." In canon law, e.g. C. 12 q. 2 c. 19 (*Quisquis episcopus*); *X* 3.19.8 (*Cum universorum*).

25 *Ps* 5.11: "Their throat is an open sepulchre: they dealt deceitfully with their tongues: judge them, O God. Let them fall from their devices: according to the multitude of their wickedness cast them out: for they have provoked thee, O Lord." Cfr *Rm* 3.13: "Their throat is an open sepulchre; with their tongues they have dealt deceitfully. The venom of asps is under their lips."

3. Fraudulentia. Notatur in tertio fraudulentia que consistit in factis, et comprehenditur in dolo dum dicitur: *Fecisti dolum*, id est operatus es fraudem. Sed ut dicitur Prouerb. 1: *Ipsi moliuntur fraudes contra animas suas*. Est enim ista fraudulentia aliquando mortale peccatum et ad restitutionem obligat, si sit notabilis deceptio. Vnde dicitur Leuitic. fit ergo fraudulentia: primo in rei quiditate, secundo in sui quantitate, tertio in eius qualitate, quarto in soluendi tarditate, quinto in pretii ad res mutabilitate, sexto in bono opere cum intentionis prauitate.

3.1. In rei quiditate. Primus ergo defectus fraudis est in quiditate seu specie et substantia rei, ut si uendatur auricalchum pro auro, unus lapis pretiosus pro altero, uinum limphatum pro puro et huiusmodi. De qua fraude contra eam facientes inuehit Deus per Ysaiam dicens primo capitulo, *Argentum tuum uersum est in scoriam: uinum tuum mixtum est aqua*, ubi alia translatio habet: *Caupones tui uinum aqua miscent.* Hanc fraudem commictunt, scilicet in specie rei: macellarii uendentes carnes hyrcinas uel caprinas pro castratinis; aromatarii uendentes unum aroma mixtum cum alio pro puro, ceram mixtam oleo pro pura cera, unum medicinale pro alio; et multi alii artificiis suis faciunt multas sophisticationes. Si quis ergo scienter aliquam fraudem facit in huiusmodi decipiens uel intendens decipere proximum, peccat, et tenetur ad restitionem si notabiliter

---

74 Ipsi … suas] *Prv* 1.18: Ipsi quoque contra sanguinem suum insidiantur, et moliuntur fraudes contra animas suas.

76 primo … **79** prauitate] Cfr Thom. Aq. *Sum. th.* 2a 2ae q. 77 a. 2 resp.; Bern. Sen. *Evang. aet.* 35, 3, 1 (4:199); ibid., 32, 3, 3 (4:138); ibid., 33, 2, 7 (4:155).

83 Argentum … **84** aqua] *Is* 1.22: Argentum tuum versum est in scoriam; vinum tuum mistum est aqua.

84 ubi … habet] Cfr Bern. Sen. *Evang. aet.* 33, 2, 7 (4:155): … *vinum tuum mixtum est aqua.* Alia littera ibi habet: *Caupones tui* et tabernarii tui *miscent vinum aqua.*

84 Caupones … **85** miscent] *Is* 1.22 in *Vetere Latina* (Gryson 12:80–1): Caupones tui miscent vinum aqua.

89 Si … **91** ledit] Thom. Aq. *Sum. th.* 2a 2ae q. 77 a. 2 resp.: Respondeo dicendum quod circa rem quae venditur triplex defectus considerari potest. Unus quidem secundum speciem rei. Et hunc quidem defectum si venditor cognoscat in re quam vendit, fraudem committit

---

74 Est enim] *ut vid.* | ista … **75** restitutionem] ista fraudulentia multiplex que aliquando est mortale aliquando ueniale et restitutionem *a.c.* **75** ad] *s.l.* **76** Vnde … Leuitic.] *cod. et* F_2 *fol. 49rb a.c.* : *om.* F_2 *p.c.* | fit … fraudulentia] *cod.* : *om.* F_2 *fol. 49rb a.c.* : fit autem fraus F_2 *p.c.* | fraudulentia] + in re *a.c.* **78** res] *ut vid.* | sexto … **79** prauitate] *ut vid., in marg. sin. add. cod* : in bon. intentionis pui[te] F_2 *fol. 49rb* : in bono pro intentionis prauitate *Mamachi* **82** et huiusmodi] *s.l.* **83** capitulo] + Vinum tuum mixtum est aqua *a.c.* **90** decipere] nocere *a.c.* | proximum] + notabiliter *a.c.*

3. Fraudulence. Third is fraudulence which consists in acts, and it is comprehended in guile when it is said: *thou hast wrought guile*, that is, you have worked fraud. But as is said in Proverbs 1: *They themselves practise frauds against their own souls.*[26] For that sort of fraudulence is sometimes a mortal sin and creates a requirement for restitution, if the deception is notable. From there it is said in Leviticus[27] that fraudulence happens: first in the essence of a thing, second in the quantity of it, third in its quality, fourth in late payment, fifth in payment of the price in kind, sixth in a good work with crooked intention.[28]

3.1. Fraud in a thing's essence. The first fraudulent defect then is in essence or species or substance of a thing, as when brass[29] is sold as gold, one precious stone as another, diluted wine as pure, and things of this sort. Concerning this fraud, God curses those committing it through Isaiah, saying in chapter 1, *Thy silver is turned into dross: thy wine is mingled with water,*[30] where the other translation has:[31] *Your innkeepers mix wine with water.*[32] Butchers[33] commit this fraud, namely in a thing's species, when they sell ram's or goat's meat as the meat of a wether; apothecaries[34] when they sell one perfume mixed with something else as pure perfume, wax mixed with oil as pure wax, one medicine as another; and many others with their artifices produce all sorts of counterfeits. If, then, someone knowingly commits some kind of fraud in this sort of thing, deceiving or intending to deceive a neighbour, he sins, and he is bound to restitution if he does a notable injury, according to blessed Thomas, 2a 2ae q. 77.[35] But

---

26 *Prv* 1.18: "And they themselves lie in wait for their own blood, and practise deceits against their own souls."

27 The words "from there it is said in Leviticus" may possibly be written by a hand other than Antoninus's.

28 Cfr Thom. Aq. *Sum. th.* 2a 2ae q. 77 a. 2 *resp.*; Bern. Sen. *Evang. aet.* 35, 3, 1 (4:199); ibid., 32, 3, 3 (4:138); ibid., 33, 2, 7 (4:155).

29 Lat. *auricalchum* for CL *orichalcum*: "copper alloy, brass, bronze." *DMLBS*, s.v.

30 *Is* 1.22: "Thy silver is turned into dross: thy wine is mingled with water."

31 Cfr Bern. Sen. *Evang. aet.* 33, 2, 7 (4:155).

32 *Is* 1.22 in the *Vetus Latina* (Gryson 12:80–1).

33 On butchers, see also Ant. Flor. *Summa* 3.8.3 (below), section 4.3.

34 On apothecaries, see also Ant. Flor. *Summa* 3.8.4 (below), section 9.

35 Thom. Aq. *Sum. th.* 2a 2ae q. 77 a. 2 *resp.*: "A threefold fault may be found pertaining to the thing which is sold. One, in respect of the thing's substance: and if the seller be aware of a fault in the thing he is selling, he is guilty of a fraudulent sale, so that the sale is rendered unlawful. Hence we find it written against certain people (Is. 1:22), 'Thy silver is turned into dross, thy wine is mingled with water': because that which is mixed is defective in its substance. … In all these cases not only is the man guilty of a fraudulent sale, but he is also bound to restitution. But if any of the foregoing defects be in the thing sold, and he knows nothing about this, the seller does not sin, because he does that which is unjust materially, nor is his deed unjust, as shown above (q. 59 a. 2). Nevertheless he is bound to compensate the buyer, when the defect comes to his knowledge. Moreover what has been said of the seller applies equally to the buyer. For sometimes it happens that the seller thinks his goods to be

ledit, secundum beatum Tomam, 2^{a} 2^{e} q. 77. Sed si ignoranter fieret talis deceptio, scilicet uendendo unam rem pro alia, cum scilicet credat talem esse, non peccat, sed tamen tenetur ad satisfactionem, cum percipit de errore: puta uendit quis anulum aurichalcheum pro aureo, credens esse aureum, tenetur | cum perpendit (fol. 71r) de errore illi emptori satisfacere; sicut etiam si quis daret alicui unum grossum argenteum deauratum pro uno floreno, tenetur dare florenum. Et ex hiis patet, dicit beatus Tomas ubi supra, quod illicitum est uendere aurum et argentum alchimichum pro uero: tum quia non est adeo purum sicut uerum, tum quia etiam non habet easdem proprietates, sicut proprietatem letificandi, aut quia non ualet contra certas infirmitates et huiusmodi. “Si autem per alchimiam fieret uerum aurum, non esset illicitum uendere pro uero; quia nichil prohibet artem uti aliquibus naturalibus causis ad producendum ueros et naturales effectus, sicut Augustinus dicit, in libro *de Trinitate*, de hiis que fiunt arte demonum.” Et quod dictum est de uenditore, idem intelligendum est de emptore, cum scilicet uenditor crederet rem suam minus pretiosam, puta esse aurichalchum quod est

---

in venditione, unde venditio illicita redditur. Et hoc est quod dicitur contra quosdam Isaiae I, argentum tuum versum est in scoriam; vinum tuum mixtum est aqua, quod enim permixtum est patitur defectum quantum ad speciem. … Et in omnibus talibus non solum aliquis peccat iniustam venditionem faciendo, sed etiam ad restitutionem tenetur. Si vero eo ignorante aliquis praedictorum defectuum in re vendita fuerit, venditor quidem non peccat, quia facit iniustum materialiter, non tamen eius operatio est iniusta, ut ex supradictis patet (q. 59 a. 2), tenetur tamen, cum ad eius notitiam pervenerit, damnum recompensare emptori. Et quod dictum est de venditore, etiam intelligendum est ex parte emptoris. Contingit enim quandoque venditorem credere suam rem esse minus pretiosam quantum ad speciem, sicut si aliquis vendat aurum loco aurichalci, emptor, si id cognoscat, iniuste emit, et ad restitutionem tenetur. Et eadem ratio est de defectu qualitatis et quantitatis.

96 ex … **105** pretiosam] Textus ex Bern. Sen. *Evang. aet.* 35, 3, 1 (4:199–200).

97 dicit … supra] Thom. Aq. *Sum. th.* 2a 2ae q. 77 a. 2 ad 1: Ad primum ergo dicendum quod aurum et argentum non solum cara sunt propter utilitatem vasorum quae ex eis fabricantur, aut aliorum huiusmodi, sed etiam propter dignitatem et puritatem substantiae ipsorum. Et ideo si aurum vel argentum ab alchimicis factum veram speciem non habeat auri et argenti, est fraudulenta et iniusta venditio. Praesertim cum sint aliquae utilitates auri et argenti veri, secundum naturalem operationem ipsorum, quae non conveniunt auro per alchimiam sophisticato, sicut quod habet proprietatem laetificandi, et contra quasdam infirmitates medicinaliter iuvat. Frequentius etiam potest poni in operatione, et diutius in sua puritate permanet aurum verum quam aurum sophisticatum. Si autem per alchimiam fieret aurum verum, non esset illicitum ipsum pro vero vendere, quia nihil prohibet artem uti aliquibus naturalibus causis ad producendum naturales et veros effectus; sicut Augustinus dicit, in III *de Trin.*, de his quae arte Daemonum fiunt.

103 Augustinus … demonum] Aug. *Trin.* 3, 8.

104 quod … **108** satisfactionem] Thom. Aq. *Sum. th.* 2a 2ae q. 77 a. 2 resp: vide supra.

105 puta … **108** satisfactionem] Cfr Bern. Sen. *Evang. aet.* 33, 2, 7 (4:157): Quinto insuper quidam sunt qui minus debito emunt et carius debito vendunt. Et circa hoc ponamus

---

104 uenditore] emp(tore) *a.c.*

if this kind of deception is done in ignorance, that is, selling one thing for another when the seller does believe it to be the proper thing, the seller does not sin, but nevertheless he is bound to satisfaction when he becomes aware of his error. Suppose for example someone sells a brass ring as gold, believing it to be gold, he is bound, when he becomes aware of his error, to make satisfaction to the buyer; just as, likewise, if someone should pay to another one gold-plated silver groat as one florin, he is bound to pay the florin. And from these it is evident, says blessed Thomas at the place cited,[36] that it is illicit to sell alchemical gold and silver as true gold: both because it is not as pure as true gold, and also because it does not have the same properties, such as the property of causing delight, or because it is not effective against certain maladies, and so forth. "If however real gold were to be produced by alchemy, it would not be unlawful to sell it as the genuine article, for nothing prevents art from employing certain natural causes for the production of natural and true effects, as Augustine says in the book *On the Trinity*[37] of things produced by the art of the demons." And what was said about the seller, the same must be understood as applying to the buyer, namely when the seller believes his thing to be less precious[38] – suppose he thinks a thing to be brass which is in fact gold, or a precious stone to be glass – for the buyer, when he perceives this, sins gravely if he does not give to the seller the price applicable for the value of the thing, moreover according to the seller's estimate, and he is bound to satisfaction.[39] But when some people counterfeit the things which they sell in order

---

specifically of lower value, as when a man sells gold instead of copper, and then if the buyer be aware of this, he buys it unjustly and is bound to restitution: and the same applies to a defect in quantity as to a defect in quality."

36 THOM. AQ. *Sum. th.* 2a 2ae q. 77 a. 2 *ad* 1: "Gold and silver are costly not only on account of the usefulness of the vessels and other like things made from them, but also on account of the excellence and purity of their substance. Hence if the gold or silver produced by alchemists has not the true specific nature of gold and silver, the sale thereof is fraudulent and unjust, especially as real gold and silver can produce certain results by their natural action, which the counterfeit gold and silver of alchemists cannot produce. Thus the true metal has the property of making people joyful, and is helpful medicinally against certain maladies. Moreover real gold can be employed more frequently, and lasts longer in its condition of purity than counterfeit gold. If however real gold were to be produced by alchemy, it would not be unlawful to sell it for the genuine article, for nothing prevents art from employing certain natural causes for the production of natural and true effects, as Augustine says (*De Trin.* iii, 8) of things produced by the art of the demons."

The next nine lines or so are quoting BERN. SEN. (see the note below), within which a quotation of Thomas Aquinas is embedded.

37 AUG. *Trin.* 3, 8.

38 The previous nine lines or so are copied by Antoninus from BERN. SEN. *Evang. aet.* 35, 3, 1 (4:199–200).

39 Cfr THOM. AQ. *Sum. th.* 2a 2ae q. 77 a. 2 *resp.* (see above); BERN. SEN. *Evang. aet.* 33, 2, 7 (4:157).

aurum, et lapidem uitreum qui est pretiosus; emptor enim cum hoc percipit, peccat grauiter si non dat sibi pretium competens ualori rei, sed secundum extimationem uendentis, et tenetur ad satisfactionem. Verum cum aliqui sophisticant ea que uendunt, ut se seruent indemnes et cum aliquo lucro congruo, quia si uenderent puras res emptores non uellent dare iustum pretium, quia alii uendunt talia sic sophisticata et mixta minori pretio: uidentur posse excusari, dummodo non fiant tales mixture quod noceant humanis corporibus, quod accidere potest in hiis que ueniunt in cibum et potum hominum, precipue medicinalibus. Similiter non uidetur illicitum cum per talem mixturam res redduntur magis amabiles et non nociue, sicut audiui contingere de uino grecho, quod aliquando cum est purum, quia nimis fumosum, minus placet, cum uero aqua misceatur amabilius redditur, et libentius emunt homines credentes tamen esse purum; debent tamen uenditores in huiusmodi casibus minus uendere quam si esset purum, alias uenderent aquam pro uino, et sic de aliis similibus.

3.2. In sui quantitate.

In quantitate fit fraus in pondere numero et mensura. Vnde Dominus Deutero. 25, *Non habebis in sachulo diuersa pondera, maius et minus*, et Leuit. 19, *Nolite facere iniquum aliquid in iudicio, in regula, in pondere, et in mensura*, et Osee 12, *Chanaan, in manu eius statera dolosa*. Chanaan interpretatur negotiator: hii enim commictunt dolos et fraudes in mensuris, quia etsi habeant iustas mensuras et pondera, tamen fraudulenter utuntur eis ad decipiendum.

---

aliquos casus. Primus casus. – Pone quod quidam simplex habet lapidem pretiosum, quem vitreum esse credit; lapidarius vero, cognoscens eum, emit illum pro vili pretio. Quid iuris? – Dicendum quod illicitum est, quia scienter decipit proximum suum qui de illo confisus est; unde usque ad iustum pretium restituere obligatur. Secus autem, si ille qui emit credebat etiam illum vitreum esse, quia tunc, secundum quosdam, restituere non tenetur, eo quod per emptionem bona fide factam lapidem acquisivit. Sed consulendum est ei quod de lapidis lucro provideat venditori plus vel minus, secundum indigentiam eius.

108 Verum … **109** indemnes] Cfr Thom. Aq. *Sum. th.* 2a 2ae q. 77 a. 3 resp: vide infra.

108 Verum … **114** medicinalibus] Cfr Bern. Sen. *Evang. aet.* 35, 3, 2 (4:200): … Si vero per hoc non intendunt nisi iustum pretium citius aut fortius extorquere, tunc ad satisfactionem non obligantur, si tamen certitudinaliter aut multum probabiliter sciunt iustum pretium non excessisse; si autem dubitant, tunc quidem tenentur, pro eo quod de fraude sua certi sunt. Cfr Petr. Olivi *Tr. contr.* 1 q.7 (148–9).

121 Non … minus] *Dt* 25.13: Non habebis in sacculo diversa pondera, majus et minus.

122 Nolite … **123** mensura] *Lv* 19.35: Nolite facere iniquum aliquid in judicio, in regula, in pondere, in mensura.

123 Chanaan[1] … dolosa] *Os* 12.7: Chanaan, in manu ejus statera dolosa, calumniam dilexit.

---

109 ut] cum *a.c. ut vid.* **121** sachulo] + tuo *a.c.* **125** et … **126** decipiendum] *in marg. super. add.*

to protect themselves from loss and receive some appropriate profit, because, were they to sell the things pure, the buyers would not want to give a just price, since others sell such things counterfeited and diluted as described at a lower price:[40] it seems that these sellers may be excused, provided that such mixtures are not made as do harm to the human body, as can happen in those things which come into people's food and drink, especially medicines.[41] Similarly it does not seem illicit when through such a mixture things are rendered more pleasant and not harmful: just as I have heard is the case with Greek wine, which sometimes when it is pure, because it is so rich,[42] is less pleasant, but mixed with water it becomes more pleasant, and men buy it more willingly, though believing it to be pure; sellers, nevertheless, ought in such cases to sell for less than if it were pure, otherwise they sell water for wine, and the same is true for other similar cases.

3.2. Fraud in a thing's quantity. Fraud in quantity happens in weight, number, or measure. Hence the Lord says in Deuteronomy 25, *Thou shalt not have divers weights in thy bag, a greater and a less*,[43] and in Leviticus 19, *Do not any unjust thing in judgment, in rule, in weight, or in measure*,[44] and in Hosea 12, *Chanaan, there is a guileful balance in his hand.*[45] *Chanaan*, we can interpret, means a trader. For they commit acts of guile and frauds using measures, because even if they have just measures and weights, they nevertheless use them to deceive.

40 Cfr Thom. Aq. *Sum. th.* 2a 2ae q. 77 a. 3 *resp.* (see below).

41 Cfr Bern. Sen.*Evang. aet.* 35, 3, 2 (4:200), incorporating material from Petr. Olivi *Tr. contr.* 1 q. 7 (148–9).

42 "Smoky, cloudy, odoriferous, fragrant." *DMLBS* s.v. *fumosus.*

43 *Dt* 25.13: "Thou shalt not have divers weights in thy bag, a greater and a less."

44 *Lv* 19.35: "Do not any unjust thing in judgment, in rule, in weight, or in measure."

45 *Os* 12.7: "He is like Chanaan, there is a deceitful balance in his hand, he hath loved oppression."

3.2.1. In pondere. Et in pondere quidem fraus est, cum dat quis undecim uncias pro una libra carnium aromatum piscium lane lini et aliarum rerum ponderabilium.

3.2.2. In mensura. In mensura, ut cum dant de panno laneo uel lineo, decem brachia uel ulnas cum dimidio panni pro undecim, uel sextarium uel minam uictualium diminutam, uel metretam uini olei uel alterius liquori non plenam.

3.2.3. In numero. In numero, ut cum quis debet aliquas res in certo numero dare, numerum diminutum tribuit. Omnes hii qui has scienter faciunt fraudes, inique agunt et contra Dominum, de quo dicitur Sapientie <11>: *Omnia constituisti in pondere, numero, et mensura*, scilicet debitis; et tenentur ad satisfactionem dampnificatis, uel si parum est dampni pauperibus.

3.2.4. De more in dando ad filandum. Nota tamen quod ubi est de more patrie quod qui dat lanam uel linum ad nendum seu filandum, accipiat et computet filatum ad rationem 13 unciarum pro libra, quando hoc scit qui laborat illa filando, si non soluitur sibi de 13 unciis nisi pro una libra non proprie ibi est fraus quia non decipitur, cum sciat sic sibi debere solui et sic intelligi pactum cum a principio sibi datur opus. "Scienti," enim, "et consentienti non fit iniuria neque dolus," *De re. iur., libro 6º*; quamuis turpis uideatur mos.

3.2.5. De tabernariis. Non autem sic excusantur tabernarii dantes mensuras uini diminutas, scilicet usque collum metrete uel alterius mensure, cum sit de more; nam ementes decipiuntur, cum intendant habere plenam mensuram et contra uoluntatem eorum diminuitur. Nec consuetudo excusat, que dicenda est corruptela, nisi hoc facerent ut se conseruent indempnes uel cum aliquo lucro rationabili, qui alias non lucrarentur si plenas mensuras darent, quia oporteret pretium augere in quo non inuenirent emptores, uel paucos.

---

134 Omnia … **135** mensura] *Sap* 11.21: Sed et sine his uno spiritu poterant occidi, persecutionem passi ab ipsis factis suis, et dispersi per spiritum virtutis tuae; sed omnia in mensura, et numero et pondere disposuisti.

142 Scienti … dolus] *VI* 5.[13.]27 (*Scienti*): Scienti et consentienti non fit iniuria neque dolus. Cfr Ant. Flor. *Summa* 1.20.1.94 (apud *N* fol. 323r, Ballerini 1:899, Mamachi 1:1422): *scienti et consentienti.*

147 Nec … corruptela] Cfr Raym. Penn. *Sum. paen.* 2.8.5 (Ochoa-Diez, 1B:563): Sed quid faciet iudex paenitentialis de mercatoribus, pellipariis et similibus qui de longa, non dico consuetudine sed corruptela, nec emere sciunt, nec vendere absque mendaciis et iuramentis incautis, necnon et interdum periuriis …

---

127 quis] *s.l.* **129** uel lineo] *s.l.* **131** liquori] *cod.* : -oris F_2 *fol. 49va* **132** certo] certlo *a.c. ut vid.* **133** fraudes] decipere *a.c. ut vid.* **134** 11] *spatium duarum litterarum praeb. cod.* **137** dat] conducit *a.c. ut vid.* **141** et … pactum] *in marg. dext. add.* **146** intendant] intendat *cod.* **148** rationabili] *in marg. dext. add.* **149** oporteret] *in marg sin. add.* : opperet *a.c. ut vid.*

3.2.1. In weight. And in weight indeed it is fraud when someone gives eleven ounces as one pound of meat, perfume, fish, wool, linen, or other things measured by weight.

3.2.2. In measure. In measure, as when people give of wool or linen cloth ten and a half yards[46] or ells of cloth as eleven, or a diminished sester[47] or mina[48] of food, or a less than full tun[49] of wine, oil, or other liquid.

3.2.3. In number. In number, as when someone is supposed to give some good in a specific number, but he hands over a reduced number. All those who knowingly commit these frauds deal unjustly and in opposition to the Lord, about whom it is said in Wisdom 11, *all things thou hast ordered in weight, number, and measure,*[50] namely the proper weights, numbers, and measures; and they are bound to make satisfaction to the ones who have been injured, or if the loss is very little, to the poor.

3.2.4. The customary practice when giving material to be spun. Note, however, that where it is the local custom that those who give wool or linen to be threaded or spun receive and reckon the spun material at a ratio of 13 ounces per pound, when the person who does the labour of spinning knows this, if for 13 ounces the spinner is only paid for a pound, there is no fraud present, properly speaking, because the spinner is not deceived, since he knows that it is supposed to be paid out to him in this way, and that the agreement was understood to be thus when the work was first given to him. For, "to one who knows and consents no injury or guile is done," *On the rules of law, Liber Sext*;[51] although this seems like a distasteful custom.

3.2.5. Tavern keepers. Tavern keepers,[52] however, are not excused by this principle when they give reduced measures of wine, namely up to the neck of the tun or other measure, notwithstanding that this is the practice among them; for the buyers are deceived, since they intend to have the full measure and it is diminished against their will. Nor does the custom, which must be described as corrupt,[53] excuse, unless the tavern keepers do this in order to protect themselves from loss or to receive some reasonable profit, when otherwise they would not make a profit if they gave full measures, because it would be necessary to increase the price, and then they would not find any buyers, or only a few.

---

46 "Braccio; a cloth measure, an arm's length, a yard (about 2/3 of an English yard, but it varied from place to place … In Florence and elsewhere the *braccio* was frequently used for cloth sold by the cut, and the *canna* for full-length cloths)." Edler, *Terms of Business*, 52. "Braccio: arm's length (in Italy) … *ca.* 22–26 inches." Ibid., 317.

47 "Sestiere: *ca.* 2 Florentine bushels (in S. France)." Ibid., 318.

48 "Mina: *ca.* 1 1/2–4 Florentine bushels (in Genoa and S. France). Ibid., 318.

49 Lat. *metreta*: "Tun, cask, jar." *LS*, s.v. "Metro: metre, 1/45–1/50 of a Neapolitan butt (in Constantinople, Tana, etc.)." Ibid., 319.

50 *Sap* 11.21: "Yea and without these, they might have been slain with one blast, persecuted by their own deeds, and scattered by the breath of thy power: but thou hast ordered all things in measure, and number, and weight."

51 *VI* 5.[13.]27 (*Scienti*): "No injury or malice is done to the one who knows and approves." English trans. from Gauthier, *Roman Law and … Canon Law*, 110. Cfr Ant. Flor. *Summa* 1.20.1.94 (apud *N* fol. 323r, Ballerini 1:899, Mamachi 1:1422): *scienti et consentienti*.

52 On tavern keepers, see also Ant. Flor. *Summa* 3.8.3 (below), section 4.2.

53 Cfr Raym. Penn. *Sum. paen.* 2.8.5 (Ochoa-Diez, 1B:563).

3.2.6. De lanificibus et factoribus caligarum.

Item lanifices qui faciunt trahere pannos ad tiratorium ultra debitum artis, unde postea madefactus et tonsus, ut moris est, retrahitur ad longe minorem mensuram quam debet: fraudem faciunt. Et multo magis qui uendunt caligas, cum faciunt pannum ex quo eas formant secundum rationem artis minus debito madefieri, ita quod postea ipsis futis cum utitur emptor, multum restringuntur et decurtantur; peccant non parum, et fraudatis tenentur ad satisfactionem, cum cito lacerentur et male deseruiant eis.

3.2.7. De laninis defentibus ad filandum.

Item lanini, id est deferentes lanam uel linum ad filandum, quibus pecunia datur a magistris suis ut soluant ad rationem tantum pro libra, puta 5 solidos: si minus soluunt, et istud sibi retinent, fraudem faciunt.

Et si a filatricibus auferunt minus conuento uel debito pretio soluentes, illis debent satisfacere in futurum supplendo illud minus datum eisdem, uel pauperibus erogando si parum est pro qualibet, uel non bene sciuntur persone; si uero eis soluunt conuentum et congruum pretium, quod eis remanet de peccunia, tenentur magistris restituere. |

3.3. In eius qualitate.

In qualitate rerum fit fraus, ut cum scilicet uenduntur carnes infecte pro fol. 71v sanis, aromata antiquata et sic uirtute debilitata pro recentibus, liber corruptus et falsus pro fideli, corium fragile pro durabili, uinum corruptum pro sano, animal infirmum pro sano, domus ruitura pro stabili et firma, pannus defectuosus pro indefectuoso et huiusmodi. De hiis dicitur Ysaie <32>, *Vasa fraudulenti pessima sunt*, uasa, id est, artificiata.

3.3.1. Quando defectus rei debet manifestari.

Et cum queritur si teneatur uenditor semper dicere defectum rei quam exponit uenalem, respondet beatus Tomas, 2^a 2^e q. 77, quod defectus rei aut est occultus aut manifestus. Si occultus, tunc aut talis defectus reddit usum illius rei uenalis impeditum uel noxium, aut non. Et siquidem talis defectus reddat

---

166 ut … **170** huiusmodi] Cfr Bern. Sen. *Evang. aet.* 33, 2, 7 (4:160).

170 Vasa … **171** sunt] *Is* 32.7: Fraudulenti vasa pessima sunt; ipse enim cogitationes concinnavit ad perdendos mites in sermone mendacii, cum loqueretur pauper judicium.

173 defectus … **180** recompensationem] Thom. Aq. *Sum. th.* 2a 2ae q. 77 a. 3 resp.: Respondeo dicendum quod dare alicui occasionem periculi vel damni semper est illicitum, quamvis non sit

---

152 retrahitur] *in marg. sin. add.* : reuertitur *a.c.* **153** uendunt] *s.l.* : faciunt *a.c. cum uno verbo haud leg.* **154** ex] mo- *a.c. ut vid.* | formant] faciunt *a.c.* | secundum … artis] *in marg. dext. add.* **155** cum] + eis *a.c.* | utitur] + eis *a.c.* **161** si] *s.l.* **166** uenduntur] uenditur *a.c. ut vid.* **169** domus ruitura] domum ruituram *cod.* | pannus defectuosus] pannum defectuosum *cod.* **170** 32] *spatium duarum litterarum praeb. cod.* **174** usum … **175** uenalis] rem illam uenalem *a.c.*

3.2.6. Wool merchants and shoemakers. Also wool merchants[54] commit fraud when they have wool stretched or tentered in the *tiratoi*[55] beyond what the craft requires, so that later when dampened and sheared, as is done, it shrinks down to a much smaller measure than it ought. And still more, those who sell footwear,[56] when they have the cloth they use to make it dampened less than required according to the method of the craft, such that afterwards when the buyer uses this footwear it becomes much tightened and shrunk; these sellers of footwear sin not a little, and are bound to make satisfaction to those defrauded, since the footwear splits easily and serves the buyers very badly.

3.2.7. *Lanini* putting out material to be spun. Also *lanini*,[57] that is, those putting out wool or linen to be spun, to whom money is given by their masters so that they may pay it at such-and-such rate per pound, say, five shillings; if they pay less, and keep the difference, they commit fraud.

And if they collect from the spinners and pay less than the agreed or due price, they ought to make satisfaction to them in the future by supplying the difference, or by giving it as alms to the poor if it is very little per whatever measure, or if they are not certain of the spinners' identities; but if they pay to them the agreed and applicable price, they are bound to return any money that is left over to their masters.

3.3. Fraud in a thing's quality. Fraud happens in things' quality, as when rotten meat is sold as fresh, old perfume much weakened in potency as new, a corrupt and false manuscript as a faithful one, fragile leather as durable, spoiled wine as good, an infirm animal as a healthy one, a collapsing house as one stable and firm, defective cloth as flawless, and so forth.[58] About these it is said in Isaiah 32: *The vessels of the deceitful are most wicked*,[59] understanding "vessels" as "products."

3.3.1. When a thing's defect ought to be revealed. And when it is asked if the buyer is always bound to state a defect in a thing which he puts up for sale, blessed Thomas replies, 2a 2ae q. 77,[60] that a thing's defect is

---

54 On wool merchants, see also Ant. Flor. *Summa* 3.8.4 (below), section 3.

55 "Tiratore; cloth-stretcher, tenterer (small master workman who stretched cloth after it came from the fuller, usually using rented tenters in one of the large open buildings containing tenters or large wooden frames for stretching and drying cloth [*tiratoi*]." Edler, *Terms of Business*, 299.

56 On shoemakers, see also Ant. Flor. *Summa* 3.8.4 (below), section 4.

57 "Lanino; originally (in Florence) an independent intermediary who bought carded wool (*lana*) and had it spun by women spinners, then sold the yarn to the industrial entrepreneurs who gave it to their weavers to be used as weft threads. By the 15th century the *lanini* had lost their independence …" Edler, *Terms of Business*, 149.

On *lanini*, see also Ant. Flor. *Summa* 3.8.4 (below), section 3.9.

58 Cfr Bern. Sen. *Evang. aet.* 33, 2, 7 (4:160).

59 *Is* 32.7: "The vessels of the deceitful are most wicked: for he hath framed devices to destroy the meek, with lying words, when the poor man speaketh judgment."

60 Thom. Aq. *Sum. th.* 2a 2ae q. 77 a. 3 *resp.*: "It is always unlawful to give anyone an occasion of danger or loss, although a man need not always give another the help or counsel which would be for his advantage in any way; but only in certain fixed cases, for instance when someone is subject to him, or when he is the only one who can assist him. Now the seller who offers goods for sale, gives the buyer an occasion of loss or danger, by the very fact that he offers him defective goods, if such defect may occasion loss or danger to the buyer – loss,

usum rei impeditum uel noxium, puta cum quis "uendit equum claudicantem pro ueloci, uel domum ruinosam pro firma, uel cibum corruptum pro sano," peccat grauiter iniustitiam committendo in dolosa et fraudulenta uenditione et proximum damnificando ex hoc; unde et tenetur ad dampni recompensationem per regulam illam, "Qui occasionem dampni dat, dampnum quoque dedisse uidetur," *Extra*, *De iniur. et damp.*, *Si culpa*. Tenetur ergo manifestare uitium rei, nec potest celare. Si autem defectus rei non impedit totaliter usum eius nec reddit noxium, sed minus reddit rem utilem: si demat de pretio quantum importat ille defectus, celando defectum non peccat, dum tamen non dicat mendacium; nec tenetur manifestare uitium rei, si tunc nec iustum pretium inueniret, uel etiam emptorem. Potest enim adhuc talis res esse utilis ad plura, etsi non ad omnia ad que ualeret existens sine defectu. Multo magis si defectus sit de se manifestus, puta quia equus est monoculus, non tenetur manifestare, sed tenetur pretium diminuere pro illo defectu quem emptor ignorat, nisi usus eius esset periculosus uel noxius: tunc enim tenetur dicere emptori illud ignoranti, ymmo nec deberet exponere uenditioni, precipue <si> extimet emptorem ex leuitate et presumptione non curare, se periculo persone exponere, uel alium in uendendo decepturum.

---

necessarium quod homo alteri semper det auxilium vel consilium pertinens ad eius qualemcumque promotionem, sed hoc solum est necessarium in aliquo casu determinato, puta cum alius eius curae subdatur, vel cum non potest ei per alium subveniri. Venditor autem, qui rem vendendam proponit, ex hoc ipso dat emptori damni vel periculi occasionem quod rem vitiosam ei offert, si ex eius vitio damnum vel periculum incurrere possit, damnum quidem, si propter huiusmodi vitium res quae vendenda proponitur minoris sit pretii, ipse vero propter huiusmodi vitium nihil de pretio subtrahat; periculum autem, puta si propter huiusmodi vitium usus rei reddatur impeditus vel noxius, puta si aliquis alicui vendat equum claudicantem pro veloci, vel ruinosam domum pro firma, vel cibum corruptum sive venenosum pro bono. Unde si huiusmodi vitia sint occulta et ipse non detegat, erit illicita et dolosa venditio, et tenetur venditor ad damni recompensationem. Si vero vitium sit manifestum, puta cum equus est monoculus; vel cum usus rei, etsi non competat venditori, potest tamen esse conveniens aliis; et si ipse propter huiusmodi vitium subtrahat quantum oportet de pretio, non tenetur ad manifestandum vitium rei. Quia forte propter huiusmodi vitium emptor vellet plus subtrahi de pretio quam esset subtrahendum. Unde potest licite venditor indemnitati suae consulere, vitium rei reticendo.

180 per regulam] Cfr Bern. Sen. *Evang. aet.* 35, 3, 3 (4:201).

180 Qui … **181** uidetur] *X* 5.36.9 (*Si culpa*): Si culpa tua datum est damnum vel iniuria irrogata, … iure super his satisfacere te oportet, nec ignorantia te excusat, si scire debuisti, ex facto tuo iniuriam verisimiliter posse contingere vel iacturam. … Sane, licet qui occasionem damni dat damnum videatur dedisse: secus est tamen in illo dicendum, qui, ut non accideret, de contingentibus nil omisit.

181 Tenetur … **190** noxius] Cfr Bern. Sen. *Evang. aet.* 35, 3, 3 (4:201–2); Petr. Olivi *Tr. contr.* 1 q.4 (126–7).

185 nec[1] … **186** emptorem] Cfr Thom. Aq. *Sum. th.* 2a 2ae q. 77 a. 3 ad 2.

---

181 Tenetur … **182** celare] *in marg sin. add.* **184** dum] nondum *a.c. ut vid.* **188** de se] *s.l.*
191 si] *supplevi cum F_2 p.c. fol. 49vb et Mamachi et Ballerini*

either hidden or manifest. If it is hidden, then the defect either renders the use of that thing for sale impeded or harmful, or it does not. And supposing such defect renders the thing's use impeded or harmful, for instance when "a man sells a lame for a fleet horse, a tottering house for a safe one, rotten food for wholesome," the seller sins gravely by committing an injustice in a guileful and fraudulent sale and by injuring a neighbour through it; hence the seller is also bound to give compensation to the buyer for the loss incurred, according to that rule, "Who gives the occasion of injury, seems also to have given the injury," *Liber Extra, On injuries and losses*, c. 9.[61] The seller is bound, therefore, to reveal the thing's fault, nor can he conceal it. But if a thing's defect does not totally impede its use nor render it harmful, but does render the thing less useful, then if he deducts from the price as much as the defect entails, he does not sin by concealing the defect, provided, however, that he does not lie; nor is he bound to manifest the thing's fault, if then he would not find a just price, or even a buyer.[62] For such a thing can still be useful enough for many things, even if not for everything that it could do were it truly free of defect. Much more, if the defect is self-evident, for instance that a horse has but one eye, the seller is not bound to state it outright, but he is bound to reduce the price on account of that defect of which the buyer is ignorant, unless its use is dangerous or harmful:[63] for then he is bound to inform a buyer who does not notice it, and actually he should not even put it out for sale, especially if he gathers that the buyer is not careful because of shallowness or presumption, is putting himself in danger, or is going to deceive another by reselling it.

---

if, by reason of this defect, the goods are of less value, and he takes nothing off the price on that account – danger, if this defect either hinder the use of the goods or render it hurtful, for instance, if a man sells a lame for a fleet horse, a tottering house for a safe one, rotten or poisonous food for wholesome. Wherefore if such like defects be hidden, and the seller does not make them known, the sale will be illicit and fraudulent, and the seller will be bound to compensation for the loss incurred. On the other hand, if the defect be manifest, for instance if a horse have but one eye, or if the goods though useless to the buyer, be useful to someone else, provided the seller take as much as he ought from the price, he is not bound to state the defect of the goods, since perhaps on account of that defect the buyer might want him to allow a greater rebate than he need. Wherefore the seller may look to his own indemnity, by withholding the defect of the goods."

61 *X* 5.36.9 (*Si culpa*). Cfr Bern. Sen. *Evang. aet.* 35, 3, 3 (4:201).

62 Cfr Thom. Aq. *Sum. th.* 2a 2ae q. 77 a. 3 *ad* 2.

63 Cfr Bern. Sen. *Evang. aet.* 35, 3, 3 (4:201–2), drawing upon Petr. Olivi *Tr. contr.* 1 q. 4 (126–7).

Nec ex hoc quod aliquis fuit deceptus in emendo rem defectuosam credens bonam, potest ipse similiter alium decipere uendendo iniusto pretio, ac si defectum non haberet, postquam defectum nouit: sicut nec licet furari alteri, uel ledere, puta Petro, ex eo quod Martinus furatus est sibi. Pena enim tenere debet suos auctores, non alios: unde uendendo plus iusto pretio scienter propter defectum, tenetur ultra peccatum satisfacere emptori ignoranti defectum illum.

3.3.2. De uendentibus pannos uel uestes defectuosos.

Quid de lanificibus uendentibus pannos laceratos ad tiratorium sed remendatos ac si non haberent dictum defectum, aut etiam pannos intextos uel tinctos male pro bonis, uel uestes ueteres renouatas et cardatas ac si essent quasi noue, ut righatterii faciunt? Respondeo dicendum: si tales non diminuant de pretio quantum importat ille defectus, fraudem et dolum perpetrant et tenentur ad satisfactionem. Mediatores quoque seu sensales qui sciunt tales defectus, et pro bonis et in defectuosis uendere faciunt, participes sunt fraudis et peccati et sunt obligati ad restitutionem, ut *De iniur. et dampn.*, *Si culpa*. Idem de facientibus fieri pannos lineos uel de sericho intextos, cum eueniunt notabiles defectus in eis siue ratione materie siue forme seu texture, qui tamen non percipi de facili possunt ab emptoribus. Secus autem dicendum in omnibus predictis casibus quando emptor percipiens tales defectus uel non percipiens uoluntarie emit et illo pretio, peritus in negotiando: quia intendit inde bene lucrari, puta in alio locho ubi chare uenduntur etiam cum talibus defectibus. "Scienti," enim "et consentienti non fit iniuria neque dolus," *De re. iu., libro 6º*.

3.3.3. De remendatoribus pannorum.

Sed quid de ipsis remendatoribus pannorum, qui uidentur ex opere sue artis esse occasio illius fraudis, quia ita subtiliter agunt quod non percipi de facili possunt scissure pannorum? Respondeo, quod cum ars illa sit publica

208 De … culpa] *X* 5.36.9 (*Si culpa*): vide supra.
215 Scienti … dolus] *VI* 5.[13.]27 (*Scienti*): vide supra.

197 puta] ex eo *a.c.* **201** laceratos] d(efectuosos?) *a.c.* **204** Respondeo dicendum] *in marg. dext. add.* | diminuant] d'māt *cod.* : demāt *F_2 fol. 50ra* : diminuant *Mamachi et Ballerini* **209** Idem … **216** 6°] *in marg. infer. add.* **213** peritus … negotiando] *in marg. sin. add.* **215** enim] et *a.c.* **219** publica] pu^{ca} *cod. et F_2 fol. 50ra*

Nor can someone use the fact that he was deceived himself, in buying a defective thing which he believed to be good, to justify himself similarly deceiving another by selling at an unjust price as if it had no defect, after he has become aware of the defect; just as it is not permitted for you to steal from or injure another, say Peter, just because Martin has stolen from you. For the penalty ought to bind the perpetrators, not others: and hence in knowingly selling for more than the just price because of a hidden defect, as well as incurring the sin you are also bound to make satisfaction to the one who purchases unaware of that defect.[64]

3.3.2. Selling defective cloth or clothing. What about wool merchants selling cloth damaged during stretching but repaired,[65] as if it did not have the aforesaid defect, or indeed badly woven or badly dyed cloth as good cloth, or old garments restored and napped[66] as if they were like new, as the second-hand dealers do?[67] I answer: we must say that if such vendors do not subtract from the price as much as the defect entails, they perpetrate fraud and guile and are bound to satisfaction. Mediators also or brokers[68] who are aware of such defects and have the items sold as good and undamaged are participants in the fraud and sin, and are obliged to restitution, as in *On injuries and losses*, c. 9.[69] It is the same for those who have this done with linen cloth or cloth woven of silk when it turns out to have notable defects either in material or shape or weaving, which nevertheless cannot easily be perceived by buyers. However, the answer must be otherwise in all the aforesaid cases when the buyer, perceiving such defects or not perceiving them, purchases voluntarily and at that price as an experienced practitioner in trade, because he intends to profit well from it, for example in another place where the items sell at a high price even with such defects. For, "to one who knows and consents no injury nor guile is done," *On the rules of law, Liber Sext.*[70]

3.3.3. Cloth menders. But what about the cloth menders themselves,[71] who seem, in the work of their own craft, to be the occasion of that fraud, since they work so subtly that rents in the cloth cannot easily be perceived? I answer that since this is a public

64 This paragraph becomes ambiguous or awkward when translated literally using third-person verbs. I have changed the phrasing to second-person for clarity: thus "for you," "from you," "you are," where the Latin literally says "for him," "from him," "he is," etc.

65 The Latin reads: *pannos laceratos ad tiratorium sed remendatos*. A *tiratorium* (Italian *tiratoio*) is a large open building containing tenters or large wooden frames for stretching and drying cloth (after it has been fulled). See Edler, *Terms of Business*, 298–9; and for the steps involved in the manufacture of woollen cloth in Italy, see ibid., 324–9.

66 Lat. *cardare*, presumably from Ital. "Cardare; to nap or teasel cloth (i.e., to raise up the loose fibres of woolen yarn into a nap on the surface of the cloth by scratching it with teasels." Ibid., 64. Napping was part of the process of finishing woven cloth. Ibid., 328–9.

67 On second-hand dealers, see also Ant. Flor. *Summa* 3.8.4 (below), section 4.1.

68 On mediators and brokers, see also Ant. Flor. *Summa* 3.8.4 (below), section 2.

69 *X* 5.36.9 (*Si culpa*): see above.

70 *VI* 5.[13.]27 (*Scienti*): see above.

71 On cloth menders, see also Ant. Flor. *Summa* 3.8.4 (below), section 3.10.

in ciuitate et tolleretur et rationabiliter, quia si non fieret illa emendatio, nec etiam iustum pretium uellent emptores dare, uel etiam forte non ita de facili inuenirent emptores; unde et homines possunt intelligere pannos aliquando habere tales defectus, lanifices insuper possunt iuste uendere diminuendo de pretio secundum quantitatem defectus, quod utrum faciant uel non faciant, non habent ipsi diiudichare: ideo non uidetur posse condempnari, sed tollerari.

3.4. In soluendi tarditate.

In solutionis diminutione <et> tarditate fit fraus seu dampnum, quando non soluitur laboranti pro opere suo termino debito: quod faciunt multi non tam ex impotentia quam ex auaritia, quia cum illa peccunia debita solui mercenariis uel aliis uolunt aliquo tempore negotiari et lucrari. Sed hoc est expresse contra Domini mandatum dicentis, <Leu. 19>, *Non morabitur opus mercenarii tui apud te usque mane*, et Prouerb. <3>, *Ne dicas amicho tuo: uade, reuertere cras, cum statim possis dare*. Cum enim tales indigent, substinent inde plura incommoda quorum illi sunt causa. Et hoc, nisi nondum terminus aduenisset solutionis fiende secundum pactum et conuentionem. Vnde et Dominus uinee dixit in fine diei procuratori suo: *Voca operarios, et da illis mercedem*, secundum conuentionem factam. Aliquando etiam dant eis falsas monetas pro bonis, aliquando etiam eis subtrahunt de debito diuersis uiis. |

3.4.1. De campsoribus.

fol. 72r

Sed quid, cum Petrus uolens soluere creditori, puta Ioanni, pro re empta uel opere facto sibi uel uectura rerum uel alia causa, mictit eum ad campsorem uel mercatorem, qui habet suas peccunias uel sibi eas mutuat, ut ipsi soluatur; et capserius uel alius gerens negotia ipsius merchatoris, pro

---

230 Non … **231** mane] *Lv* 19.13: Non facies calumniam proximo tuo nec vi opprimes eum. Non morabitur opus mercenarii tui apud te usque mane.

231 Ne … **232** dare] *Prv* 3.28: Ne dicas amico tuo : Vade, et revertere, cras dabo tibi, cum statim possis dare.

235 Voca … **236** mercedem] *Mt* 20.8: Cum sero autem factum esset, dicit dominus vineae procuratori suo : Voca operarios, et redde illis mercedem incipiens a novissimis usque ad primos.

---

221 uellent] uolunt *vel* uult *a.c. ut vid.* **223** diminuendo] de- *a.c.* **226** diminutione] *in marg. sin. add. cod. : del. p.c.* F_2 *fol. 50ra* | et] *supplevi cum Mamachi* **228** debita] ne- *a.c. ut vid.* **229** aliis] *ut vid.* **230** Leu. 19] *spatium quinque litterarum praeb. cod.* **231** 3] *spatium unius litterae praeb. cod.* | uade] *s.l.* **235** procuratori] procurati *cod.* **238** Petrus] *s.l.* | puta Ioanni] *s.l.* **240** campsorem uel] banchum uel *a.c.* **241** capserius] *sic cod.*

craft in the city and is tolerated – and reasonably, because if the mending was not done, the buyers would not want to give even a just price, or buyers might not even be found so easily – and hence men can understand that cloth sometimes has such defects – besides, wool merchants can sell justly by subtracting from the price according to the amount of defect, which, whether they should do it or not, they must not themselves judge[72] – therefore it does not seem that this can be condemned, but can be tolerated.

3.4. Fraud in late payment. Fraud or injury is committed in reduced or late payment, when a worker is not paid for his work at the proper time: which many employers do, not so much from inability to pay as from avarice, because with that money, which ought to be paid to hired workers or others, they want to trade for some time and make a profit. But this is expressly contrary to the command of the Lord, who says, in Leviticus 19, *The wages of him that hath been hired by thee shall not abide with thee until the morning*,[73] and in Proverbs 3, *Say not to thy friend: Go, and come again tomorrow, when thou canst give at present.*[74] For when workers lack their wages, they sustain many inconveniences as a consequence, of which those who pay late are the cause. And this applies unless the time for making payment has not yet arrived according to the pact and agreement. Hence also the Lord of the vineyard said at the end of the day to his steward: *Call the labourers and give them their wage*,[75] according to the agreement which they made. Sometimes employers even give counterfeit coinage as good, sometimes they also make subtractions from that which is due to the workers by various means.[76]

3.4.1. Bankers. Now what about when Peter, wanting to pay his creditor, e.g., John, for a thing which he has bought or work done for him or transport of goods or some other reason, sends him to a banker[77] or merchant who has his money or is lending

72 The sense here is obscure. A footnote to this sentence by the Florentine editors (Mamachi 2:353) reads: "Nempe, pro subito suo, sed prudentum virorum et in ea re peritorum existimatione."

73 *Lv* 19.13: "Thou shalt not calumniate thy neighbour, nor oppress him by violence. The wages of him that hath been hired by thee shall not abide with thee until the morning."

74 *Prv* 3.28: "Say not to thy friend: Go, and come again: and tomorrow I will give to thee: when thou canst give at present."

75 *Mt* 20.8: "And when evening was come, the lord of the vineyard saith to his steward: Call the labourers and pay them their hire, beginning from the last even to the first."

76 On defrauding employees, see also Ant. Flor. *Summa* 3.8.4 (below), section 3.9.

77 "Cambiatore; a banker (who did a local business in loans, deposits, bills of exchange, etc., in contrast to the international banking activities of a *banchiere*, in Bologna, Florence, Siena, etc. The term originally meant money-changer, but in the available sources of the 13th and later centuries, it apparently means more than a simple money-changer)." Edler, *Terms of Business*, 56.

eo soluit Ioanni ad instantiam et uoluntatem ipsius Petri, retinet tamen duos denarios pro libra pro mercatore [capserius eius]: numquid est licitum? Respondeo, si hoc habet consuetudo ciuitatis in huiusmodi, et creditor hoc sciens non contradicit, uidetur posse tollerari ratione consuetudinis, que legem facit cum est rationabilis, ut D. 1 *Consuetudo*. Non autem uidetur irrationabilis dicta consuetudo, cum introducta sit respectu laboris numerantis peccuniam et scribentis et expensarum quas facit campsor uel mercator pensionis exercentium artem pro eo; ratio enim expensarum et laboris habenda est, ar. *De uoto, Magne*, et nullus stipendiis suis cogitur militare, 13 q. 1. §. 1. Si autem ultra consuetum acciperet, fraudem commicteret, uel etiam si creditor hoc nesciens contra uoluntatem suam et intentionem recipit illam diminutionem; nam tunc mercedem laboris sui, si uult campsor, ab eo scilicet Petro, cuius nomine soluit, recipiat, non a creditore Ioanne, qui integre debet recipere ius suum.

3.4.2. De officialibus communitatis.

Sed quid de camerariis uel depositariis communitatis in diuersis officiis, ut montis uel gabellarum et huiusmodi, habentibus uel recipere peccunias a personis uel tradere uariis hominibus pro communitate; a quolibet dante uel recipiente peccuniam, ab eis exigant aliquid, puta unum denarium pro floreno uel libra: numquid est licitum, si hoc habet consuetudo loci a diu seruata? Respondeo dicendum, saluo meliori iudicio, hoc uidetur distinguendum: quia

---

245 consuetudinis … **246** rationabilis] D. 1 c. 5 (*Consuetudo*): Consuetudo autem est ius quoddam moribus institutum, quod pro lege suscipitur, cum deficit lex. §. 1. Nec differt, an scriptura, an ratione consistat, quoniam et legem ratio commendat.

249 ratio … **250** est] *X* 3.34.7 (*Magnae*): … licentiam concedimus, votum peregrinationis taliter commutare, ut expensas, quas fueras in eundo, morando et redeundo facturus, alicui religioso committas, in necessarios usus terrae illius sine diminutione qualibet transferendas. Laborem etiam laboribus recompenses, sollicitius instando vigiliis, devotius vacans orationibus, et in ieiuniis fortius te exercens.

250 nullus … militare] C. 13 q. 1 c. 1 Gr. p. §. 4 (1:719): Item: "Quis umquam suis militat stipendiis? quis pascit gregem, et de lacte eius non edit [*1 Cor* 9.7]?"

---

242 Ioanni] *s.l.* | Petri] *in marg. dext. add.* **243** eius] + quia sic est de *a.c.* | numquid] s- *a.c.* **244** ciuitatis] + que *a.c.* **246** cum … rationabilis] *in marg. sin. add.* **249** exercentium] gerentium *a.c.* **250** nullus] + de *a.c.* | 13 … **251** 1] + Gratianus §. Si item quis *add.* F_2 *in marg. sin. fol. 50ra* **251** §.] G *a.c. ut vid.* **252** si] + ab *a.c.* **253** scilicet Petro] *s.l.* **258** tradere] + per *a.c.*

money to him,[78] to have it paid out to John; and the merchant's cashier[79] or other party administering that merchant's business pays John on the merchant's behalf at the request and will of Peter, but retains two pence per pound for the merchant who employs him: is this licit? I answer, if the custom of the city has it work this way in this sort of transaction, and the creditor, knowing this, does not contradict it, it seems that it can be tolerated on account of custom, which creates law when it is reasonable, as in D. 1 c. 5.[80] Nor does the said custom appear unreasonable, since it is introduced in consideration of the labour of the one counting the money and writing, and of the expenses which the banker or merchant spends as a salary for those who practise a trade for him; for an account must be taken of expenses and labour, by the argument of *On vows*, c. 7,[81] and no one is compelled to soldier at his own charges, C. 13 q. 1 c. 1 Gr. p. §. 4.[82] But if he were to take something beyond what is customary, he would commit fraud; and also if the creditor, ignorant of this practice, against his will and intention accepts that diminution – for then if the banker wants, he should receive the wage of his labour from the other in whose name he pays, namely Peter, not from the creditor John, who ought to receive the whole of what is rightfully his.

3.4.2. Civic officials. But what about chamberlains or civic depositaries in various offices, e.g., of the *monte*, taxes,[83] and so forth, who have to receive money from people or transfer money to various people on behalf of the community; from anyone who pays or receives money they exact something, say one penny per florin or pound: is this licit, if longstanding local custom has it work this way? I answer that, with due respect for a better judgment, it seems that we must make some distinctions: because such officials either are salaried by the community, and at a sufficient rate in relation to the work and quality of their duty; or they are not salaried, or are salaried to a limited extent and insufficiently. In the first case, I do not believe that they may exact or receive anything: because in that case the custom does not seem to have any valid purpose, since it is unreasonable, introduced from pure and boundless cupidity, and hence must rather be called

78 Or: "is borrowing it from him."

79 Lat. *capserius*. "Gall. Caissier, Ital. Cassiere, Capsae seu arcae publicae custos." Du Cange s.v. "Cassiere; cashier (salaried, in a mercantile firm or bank)." Edler, *Terms of Business*, 70.

80 D. 1 c. 5 (*Consuetudo*): "Custom is in some way a law (*ius*) instituted by usages (*mores*); it is received as law when a written law (*lex*) is lacking. 1. Nor does it matter whether it is known by writing or by reason alone because it is reason itself which points out the law."

81 *X* 3.34.7 (*Magnae*).

82 C. 13 q. 1 c. 1 Gr. p. §. 4: "Also: What soldier ever fights at his own expense? Who tends a flock, and does not feed on its milk (*1 Cor.* 9.7)?"

83 "Gabella (Ar. qabāla, tax); tax on imports and exports (in Tuscany and elsewhere)." Edler, *Terms of Business*, 130.

aut tales sunt salariati a communitate et sufficienter secundum laborem offitii et qualitatem; aut non sunt salariati uel diminute et insufficienter salariati. In primo casu, non credo posse exigere uel recipere: quia ibi non uidetur habere locum consuetudo, cum irrationabilis sit, introducta ex mera et immensa cupiditate, unde potius dicenda corruptela, D. 8 *Consuetudo*; et sic credo talia sic extorta seu acquisita ex debito pauperibus eroganda, ut 14 q. 5 c. *Non sane*. In secundo casu, uidetur eos posse exigere, et consuetudinem eos excusare que rationabilis est, cum seruiat illis personis, et nemo de suo cogitur facere beneficium, ar. 10 q. 2; sed *Dignus est mercenarius mercede sua.*

3.5. In pretii ad res mutabilitate.

Quinto fit fraus in peccunie ad res mutabilitate, et ex hoc diminuitur pretium debitum promissum: quia non indigentes aliquando talibus rebus conducti in aliquo opere, cum uendunt, minus pretium inueniunt quam id quod constitit eis. Et contra hos ait Iacobus, 5° capitulo, *Ecce merces mercenariorum uestrorum, que fraudata est a uobis, clamat contra uos* etc. Sciendum igitur quod cum pacta debeant seruari, *Extra, De pac., Antigonus*, et pacta

---

266 potius … corruptela] D. 8 c. 8 (*Consuetudo*): Consuetudo, que apud quosdam irrepserat, impedire non debet, quo minus ueritas preualeat et uincat. Nam consuetudo sine ueritate uetustas erroris est: propter quod relicto errore sequamur ueritatem, scientes, quia et apud Esdram ueritas uicit, ut scriptum est: "Veritas ualet et inualescit in eternum, et uiuit et obtinet in secula seculorum."

267 talia … eroganda] C. 14 q. 5 c. 15 (*Non sane*): Non sane quicquid ab inuito sumitur iniuriose aufertur. Nam plerique nec medico uolunt reddere honorem suum, nec operario mercedem; nec tamen hec qui ab inuito accipiunt, per iniuriam accipiunt, que potius per iniuriam non darentur. … Isti, si uiam uitae mutauerint, aut excellentioris conscenderint sanctitatis gradum, facilius ea, que hoc modo acquisierunt, tanquam sua pauperibus largiuntur, quam eis, a quibus accepta sunt, tamquam aliena restituant. §. 4. Qui uero contra ius societatis humanae furtis, rapinis, calumpniis, obpressionibus, inuasionibus aliqua abstulerit, reddenda potius quam donanda censemus, Zachei publicani exemplo [*Lc* 19.1–10].

269 nemo … **270** beneficium] C. 10 q. 2 c. 4 (*Precariae*[1]): Decrevit etiam sancta synodus, et imperialis auctoritas denuntiavit, ut a nulla potestate quis cogatur facere precariam de rebus proprie Deo et sanctis eius dicatis, cum ratio et usus obtineat neminem cui non vult contra utilitatem et rationem cogi de proprio facere beneficium.

270 Dignus … sua] *Lc* 10.7: In eadem autem domo manete, edentes et bibentes quae apud illos sunt : dignus est enim operarius mercede sua. Nolite transire de domo in domum. *1 Tim* 5.18: Dicit enim Scriptura : Non alligabis os bovi trituranti. Et : Dignus est operarius mercede sua.

274 Ecce … **275** clamat] *Iac* 5.4: Ecce merces operariorum, qui messuerunt regiones vestras, quae fraudata est a vobis, clamat : et clamor eorum in aures Domini sabbaoth introivit.

276 pacta … seruari] *X* 1.35.1 (*Antigonus*): Aut inita pacta suam obtineant firmitatem, aut conventus, si se non cohibuerit, ecclesiasticam sentiat disciplinam. Dixerunt universi: Pax servetur, pacta custodiantur. Vide etiam *Glossa ord.* ad idem. Cfr *X* 3.18.8 (*Cum universorum*).

---

266 unde] de *a.c.* **268** et] + locum habere *a.c.* **270** 10 … 2] + Precarie *add. F_2 in marg. dext. fol. 50rb* **271** in peccunie] in pret(ii) *a.c.* **272** debitum] *s.l.* **273** conducti … opere] *in marg. sin. add.*

a corrupt custom, D. 8 c. 8.[84] Thus I believe that things extorted or acquired in this way from the money that is due should be bestowed on the poor, as in C. 14 q. 5 c. 15.[85] In the second case, it seems that the officials may make this exaction, and that the custom, which is reasonable, excuses the officials, since it supports them, and no one is compelled to provide a benefit out of his own property, by the argument of C. 10 q. 2;[86] but *the wage-labourer is worthy of his wage.*[87]

3.5. Fraud in payment of the price in kind.

Fifth, fraud is committed through paying in kind rather than money, and through this the due price promised is diminished: because sometimes the people hired for some sort of work, not needing such goods, when they sell them, receive a price lower than that which they agreed to.[88] And against these James says, in chapter 5: *Behold the wages of your wage-labourers, which by fraud has been kept back by you, crieth against you* etc.[89] Therefore it must be understood that since agreements must

---

84 D. 8 c. 8 (*Consuetudo*): "Custom, which had crept in among some, ought not to impede truth from prevailing and conquering. Custom without truth is error made ancient; leaving error behind, let us follow truth, knowing that in Esdras also the truth conquered, as it is written: Truth endures and grows in strength in eternity, and lives and prevails forever and ever (*3 Esd.* 4.38)."

85 C. 14 q. 5 c. 15 (*Non sane*): "It is not the case that all that is taken from one unwilling is wrongfully taken. Indeed, many do not wish to give his honorary to their physician, nor his salary to a worker. Yet, when these take their due from one unwilling, they do not do so by an injury; indeed, it would rather be an injury if they were not given to them ... These, if they change their manner of life, or rise to a greater degree of holiness, are more easily disposed to distribute to the poor, as if they were their own, the resources which they have acquired in this manner, than to restore them to those from whom they took them, as if they were not their own. By the example of Zacchaeus the tax-collector (*Lc.* 19.1–10), we adjudge that he who has breached the law of human fellowship by theft, plunder, calumny, oppression, or break-in, is to return rather than to give away goods acquired in these ways."

86 C. 10 q. 2 c. 4 (*Precariae*[1]): "The holy Synod also decreed, and imperial authority published it, that no one is to be compelled by any power to lease possessions properly dedicated to God and his saints, since law and usage obtain by which no one is to be compelled to render a benefit to one to whom he does not wish to do so, out of his own property against usefulness and reason."

87 *Lc* 10.7: "And in the same house, remain, eating and drinking such things as they have: for the labourer is worthy of his hire. Remove not from house to house." *1 Tim* 5.18: "For the scripture saith: Thou shalt not muzzle the ox that treadeth out the corn: and, The labourer is worthy of his reward."

88 On payment in kind and Antoninus's censures of the truck system, see also ANT. FLOR. *Summa* 3.8.3 (below), section 3, and *Summa* 3.8.4 (below), section 3.9 and section 5.1.

89 *Iac* 5.4: "Behold the hire of the labourers, who have reaped down your fields, which by fraud has been kept back by you, crieth: and the cry of them hath entered into the ears of the Lord of Sabaoth."

ex conuentione legem accipiunt: ideo cum quis conducitur ad aliquod opus, si <conductor> promictit sibi dare peccuniam, non debet illi dare uictualia uel pannum uel alias res, nisi in quantum uelit ipse conductus sua sponte uoluntate, uel nisi alio modo non possit sibi soluere ex defectu peccunie. Sed tunc si ille non indiget usu illius rei, puta panni, sed oportet ipsum uendere ut habeat peccuniam pro aliis rebus emendis, illud dampnum quod inde substinet in minus uendendo, debet conductor resarcire, ex quo pactum fuit de peccunia et inuoluntarius alias res recepit. Sed si a principio operis pactum in soluendo sibi de labore suo certo pretio <partim> in rebus, puta panni uictualium, et partim in peccunia: tunc si illas res quas sibi dat pro parte solutionis secundum conuentionem, uendit iusto pretio secundum quod alius uendit, quamuis ipse non indigens eis reuendendo multum perdat, quia quod sibi datum fuit pro 20 solidis non potest uendere nisi pro XVI uel minus, in nullo committit fraudem conductor, quia "Scienti et consentienti non fit iniuria neque dolus," *De re. iu.* in *6°*. Sed si ipse uel alius pro eo, puta ritagliator pro setaiuolo, dat pannum textori conducto a setaiuolo maiori pretio quam aliis uendatur, de illo pluri certe tenetur, puta ritagliator uendit pannum aliis ad rationem 30 solidorum pro bracchio, sed textori serici dat ad rationem 33 uel plus, quem pannum reuendens reperit 25 solidos: certe setaiuolus tenetur textori de tribus solidis pro quolibet brachio panni, quia plus iusto pretio tantum uendidit sibi ritagliator ad petitionem setaiuoli; sed de illis quinque quibus minus uendit quam emit, non tenetur, ex quo iusto pretio uenditum fuit, et conuentio inter illos talis fuit, ut scilicet in panno sibi solueret in totum uel partem pro suo labore.

Sed etsi ipse textor serici ab initio, cum pactum facit cum setaiuolo de panno sibi dando pro labore suo, scit quod ritagliator uendet sibi plus iusto pretio, quia sic communiter fit et alias expertus est, non uidetur sibi setaiuolus

---

290 Scienti … **291** dolus] *VI* 5.[13.]27: vide supra.

---

278 conductor] *supplevi cum* F_2 *s.l. fol. 50rb* **280** uoluntate] *in marg. dext. add.* : om. F_2 *fol. 50rb et Mamachi et Ballerini* **283** uendendo] + quam *a.c.* | resarcire] resarciri *cod.* **284** inuoluntarius] + conductus *add.* F_2 *in marg. dext. fol. 50rb* **285** soluendo] dando *a.c. ut vid.* | certo pretio] *in marg. dext. add.* | partim] *supplevi* **288** alius] ał *cod. et* F_2 *fol. 50rb* : aliis *Mamachi et Ballerini* | ipse] + conductus *add.* F_2 *in marg. dext. fol. 50rb* **293** uendit] *ut vid.* **297** petitionem] inst(antiam?) *a.c.* **302** suo] + et *a.c.* | sibi] *in rasura* **303** fit] *s.l.* | alias] ałs *cod.*

be kept, *Extra, On agreements*, c. 1,[90] and pacts take the force of law from agreement, it follows that when someone is hired for some sort of work, if the hirer promises to pay him money, he should not pay him in foodstuffs or cloth or other things, except to the extent that the one hired himself desires it by his own free will, or unless the hirer is not able to pay him in any other way for want of money. But then, if the one hired does not need the use of the goods, such as cloth, but it is necessary for him to sell them so that he may have money to buy other goods, the hirer ought to make up the loss which he thence sustains in selling for less, because the pact was made for money and the one hired received other goods involuntarily. But if from the beginning of the work the agreement was that payment would be made to him for his labour at a fixed price <partly> in goods, for instance cloth or foodstuffs, and partly in money: then if he sells those things which the hirer pays him as part of his pay, as agreed, at a just price like what another seller would charge, even though not needing the things himself he takes much loss in reselling them, because he can only sell what was given to him as 20 shillings' worth for 16 shillings or less: the hirer commits no fraud, because "To one who knows and consents no injury nor guile is done," *On the rules of law* in the *Sext*.[91] But if the hirer himself or another on his behalf, say, a retail cloth merchant on behalf of a silk merchant, pays cloth to a weaver[92] hired by the silk merchant at a greater price than it is sold to others, the merchant certainly owes the weaver that additional amount. For instance, the retail cloth merchant sells cloth to others at a rate of 30 shillings per yard, but he pays it to the silk weaver at a rate of 33 or more, but when the weaver resells this cloth he obtains 25 shillings: certainly the silk merchant owes the weaver the three shillings for every yard of cloth, because it was only at the request of the silk merchant that the retail merchant sold to him at more than the just price; but the silk merchant does not owe the weaver those five by which the weaver sells for less than he bought, because the cloth was sold at a just price and such was the agreement between them, that is, that the hirer would pay him in cloth in whole or in part for his labour.

But moreover if the silk weaver himself, from the beginning, when he makes the pact with the silk merchant about the cloth to be given to him for his labour, knows that the retail merchant will sell to him at more than the just price, because it is commonly done that way and he has prior experience, it does not seem that the silk merchant owes him, because the transaction amounts to the same thing as if from the beginning the silk merchant had made the pact with the weaver to pay him only as much as he would get for selling the cloth given to him. For instance, he is supposed to pay him 10 florins for his labour,

90 *X* 1.35.1 (*Antigonus*). See also *Glossa ord.* ad idem. Cfr *X* 3.18.8 (*Cum universorum*).

91 *VI* 5.[13.]27 (*Scienti*): see above.

92 "Tessitore; master weaver (under the dependent wholesale handicraft system, who wove cloth at home from material furnished by an entrepreneur who paid him by the piece and who frequently furnished the loom)." Edler, *Terms of Business*, 295, 329–31.

teneri, quia in idem reuertitur ac si setaiuolus a principio faceret pactum cum textore dandi sibi tantum quantum uendet pannum sibi datum: puta debet sibi dare X florenos pro suo labore, sed in panno, de quo scit textor quod non inueniet de ipso panno uendens ipsum nisi sex florenos; unde ita est sicut faceret pactum cum eo dare sibi sex florenos, non obstante quod dicatur de X, quia non in peccunia X promisit sed in panno, sibi computando taliter quod sex florenos habebit. Unde etsi textor peteret tantum sex florenos a setaiuolo, quia sic credit habiturum per pannum sic uenditum, non uidetur setaiuolus malefacere. Est tamen satis turpis talis modus utrique et setaiuolo et ritagliatori.

Nota tamen, quod si ex | hoc non accipit textor debitum lucrum de labore fol. 72v
suo secundum communem extimationem sed diminutum, putatur autem debitum lucrum illud in quo conueniunt in peccunia, puta X florenos, sed quia pauper est et oportet eum accipere etiam multominus ut se et familiam substentet: tunc utique setaiuolus sibi teneretur dare supplementum usque ad decem uel circa, si dat sibi pannum quem non uendit nisi 6; quia sicut *dignus est operarius mercede sua* ex debito iustitie, ita et conuenienti mercede. Alias esset contra equalitatem iustitie, sicut in contractu emptionis et uenditionis est iniustitia et peccatum cum res emitur minus iusto pretio ex necessitate uenditoris. Sed si quantitas sex florenorum reputatur congrua merces sui laboris, uidetur posse illud, etsi turpiter inuentum, admicti. Verum quia talia communiter inuenta sunt ad decipiendum et opprimendum pauperes, ideo inducendi sunt setaiuoli et ritagliatores quod abstineant a talibus, et ex factis huiusmodi fraudibus satisfaciant lesis, uel pauperibus erogent si non grauauerunt notabiliter textores, ar. 14 q. 5 *Qui habetis* et c. *Non sane*. Et idem dicendum de aliis conducentibus laborantes ad alias artificia et exercitia. Sed de setaiuolis et textoribus dictum est, quia hoc multum Florentie practichatur.

---

318 dignus … **319** sua] *Lc* 10.7; *1 Tim* 5.18.

327 ar. … habetis] C. 14 q. 5 c. 14 (*Qui habetis*): Qui habetis aliquid de malo, facite inde bonum. … Gratianus: Sed hoc multipliciter intelligitur. Facit enim de malo bonum qui reddit quod illicite abstulit. … De malo ergo bonum facit qui pauperibus dispensat quod cum labore et sollicitudine acquisivit, iuxta illud evangelii: Facite vobis amicos de mammona iniquitatis (*Lc* 16.9).

327 c. … sane] C. 14 q. 5 c. 15 (*Non sane*): vide supra.

---

308 cum] apud *a.c. ut vid.* **312** ritagliatori] *cod.* : F_2 *fol. 50va add.* reprobandus ut iniustus : *Ballerini scr.* et potius est reprobandus ut iniustus. **313** textor] *s.l. ut vid.* **319** Alias] *in marg. dext. add.* **320** esset … **322** uenditoris] *in marg. super. add.* **321** iniustitia] iniustitiam *cod.* **327** ar.] *p.c.* : *haud leg. a.c.*

but in cloth, and the weaver is aware that from that cloth, on reselling it, he will only make at most 6 florins: and so it is just as if the merchant were to make a pact with the weaver to pay him 6 florins, notwithstanding what may be said about 10, because he did not promise 10 in money but in cloth, computing it such that he will end up with 6 florins. For if the weaver were to ask only 6 florins from the silk merchant, because he believes that he will end up with this amount through selling the cloth this way, it does not seem that the silk merchant does anything wrong. Such a method is nevertheless distasteful enough when used by either sort, whether a silk merchant or a retail merchant.[93]

Note, however, that if because of this the weaver does not receive a proper profit for his labour according to common estimation, but a diminished one – and his due profit is reckoned to be what they agreed to in money, e.g., 10 florins – but because he is poor he has to accept less, even a lot less, just to sustain himself and his family: then without a doubt the silk merchant would be bound to pay a supplement up to 10 or thereabouts, if he pays him cloth which he only sells for 6; because just as *the labourer is worthy of his wage* as a matter of justice,[94] so he is also worthy of an appropriate wage. Otherwise the contract would go against the equality of justice; just as in a contract of purchase and sale it is injustice and a sin when a thing is bought for less than the just price due to the seller's need. But if the quantity of 6 florins is considered an appropriate wage for a weaver's labour, it seems that this practice can be allowed, even if it is distastefully devised. But because such devices are commonly invented to deceive and oppress the poor, silk merchants and retail merchants should be induced to abstain from them, and to make satisfaction to those injured from frauds of this kind, or to bestow alms on the poor if they did not notably burden the weavers, by the argument of C. 14 q. 5 c. 14[95] and c. 15.[96] And the same must be said about those hiring labourers in other crafts and occupations. But silk merchants and weavers were discussed because this is very much practised in Florence.

93 Ballerini's edition adds here: "and rather must be reprobated as unjust" (2:269).

94 *Lc* 10.7; *1 Tim* 5.18.

95 C. 14 q. 5 c. 14 (*Qui habetis*): "If you have something out of evil, do something good with it … Gratian: But this is understood in a variety of ways. For he does good from evil who returns what he had stolen unlawfully … And so, he does good from evil who gives to the poor what he has acquired with labour and care, according to that text of the Gospel: Make friends for yourselves from the mammon of iniquity (*Lc.* 16.9)."

96 C. 14 q. 5 c. 15 (*Non sane*): see above.

3.6. In bono opere cum intentionis prauitate.

Sexta fraus est in operibus de genere bonorum, cum scilicet quis in eis querit aliud quam gloriam Dei, iuxta illud apostoli, *Omnia in gloriam Dei facite*: puta remunerationem in mundo, propter quod dicitur Ierem. <48>, *Maledictus omnis, qui facit opus Dei fraudulenter, et desidiose*. Quod exponens Gregorius in 9° libro *Moralium* dicit quod triplex fraus commictitur in bono opere, quod est opus Dei, cum scilicet intenditur remuneratio ex eo ab homine.

3.6.1. A corde.

Et hoc primo a corde, ut scilicet habeat amicitiam et gratiam hominum, ideo aliquid boni operatur: sed *fallax gratia*, dicitur Prouerb. ultimo. Qui enim hoc querit, sepe, ut ait Augustinus, ab eo offenditur <Deus> ne

---

331 Omnia … facite] *1 Cor* 10.31: Sive ergo manducatis, sive bibitis, sive aliud quid facitis : omnia in gloriam Dei facite.

332 Maledictus … **333** desidiose] *Ier* 48.10: Maledictus qui facit opus Domini fraudulenter (*Glossa ord.*: vel desidiose), et maledictus qui prohibet gladium suum a sanguine. Vide Greg. M. *Moral.* 9, 53 (PL 75:888): Unde et per prophetam apud vetustam translationem dicitur: *Maledictus omnis qui facit opus Dei fraudulenter et desidiose.*

333 Quod … **356** transitoria] Greg. M. *Moral.* 9, 53 (PL 75:888–9): *Maledictus omnis qui facit opus Dei fraudulenter et desidiose* (Jerem. XLVIII, 10). Sed sciendum magnopere est, quia desidia per torporem nascitur, fraus per privatam dilectionem. Illam namque minor Dei amor exaggerat, hanc autem male mentem possidens proprius amor creat. Fraudem quippe in Dei opere perpetrat quisquis, semetipsum inordinate diligens, per hoc quod recte egerit, ad remunerationis transitoria bona festinat. Sciendum quoque est quod tribus modis fraus ipsa committitur, quia per hanc procul dubio aut tracita cordis humani gratia, aut favoris aura, aut res quaelibet exterior desideratur. Quo contra recte de justo per prophetam dicitur: *Beatus qui excutit manus suas ab omni munere* (Isai. XXXIII, 15). Quia enim non solum fraus in acceptione pecuniae est, munus procul dubio unum non est. Tres vero sunt acceptiones munerum, ad quas ex fraude festinatur. Munus namque a corde est captata gratia a cogitatione. Munus ab ore est gloria per favorem. Munus ex manu est praemium per dationem. Sed justus quisquis ab omni munere manus excutit, quia in eo quod recte agit, nec ab humano corde inanem gloriam, nec ab ore laudem, nec a manu recipere dationem quaerit. Solus ergo in Dei opere fraudem non facit, qui cum ad studia bonae actionis invigilat, nec ad corporalis rei praemia, nec ad laudis verba, nec ad humani judicii gratiam anhelat.

337 fallax gratia] *Prv* 31.30: Fallax gratia, et vana est pulchritudo : mulier timens Dominum, ipsa laudabitur.

338 Qui … **339** amichus] Aug. *Gen. ad litt.* 11, 42.59: Ita et Adam, posteaquam de ligno prohibito seducta mulier manducavit … Non quidem carnis victus concupiscentia, quam nondum senserat in resistente lege membrorum legi mentis suae; sed amicali quadam benevolentia, qua plerumque fit ut offendatur Deus, ne homo ex amico fiat inimicus: quod eum facere non debuisse, divinae sententiae iustus exitus indicavit. Cfr Petr. Abael. *Sic et non* q.55.

---

332 48] *spatium duarum litterarum praeb. cod.* **336** Et … primo] *in marg. sin. add.* : uel ab *a.c.* **338** Deus] *supplevi secutus* F_2 *fol. 50va et Mamachi et Ballerini*

3.6. Fraud in a good work with crooked intention. A sixth type of fraud is committed when a person does works which are good in their nature, but in doing them seeks something other than the glory of God, according to the apostle's statement, *Do all to the glory of God.*[97] For example, he seeks recompense in this world, on account of which it is said in Jeremiah 48, *Cursed be all that doth the work of the Lord deceitfully and negligently.*[98] Expounding this verse, Gregory says in book 9 of the *Morals*[99] that a threefold fraud is committed in a good work, which is the work of God, when compensation from men is aimed at from it.

3.6.1. From the heart. The first form of fraud is fraud of the heart, that is, when some good work is done in order to have the friendship and favour of men: but *favour is deceitful*, it is said in the final Proverb.[100] For the one who seeks this, often, as Augustine says, by him <God> is offended so that his friend be not offended.[101] But *God*, the Psalm says, *hath scattered the bones*, i.e. the works of a virtuous nature, *of them that please men.*[102]

---

97 *1 Cor* 10.31: "Therefore, whether you eat or drink, or whatsoever else you do, do all to the glory of God."

98 *Ier* 48.10: "Cursed be he that doth the work of the Lord deceitfully (the *Glossa ord.* adds: "or negligently"): and cursed be he that withholdeth his sword from blood."

Gregory the Great cites an older translation of this verse: "Cursed be he that doeth the work of the Lord deceitfully and negligently." Greg. M. *Moral.* 9, 53 (trans. Parker, 1:534).

99 Greg. M. *Moral.* 9, 53 (trans. Parker, 1:534–5): "*Cursed be he that doeth the work of the Lord deceitfully and negligently* (*Ier* 48.10). Now it is to be carefully noted, that sloth comes of insensibility, deceit of self-love, for over little love of God gives magnitude to the first, while self-love, miserably possessing the mind, engenders the other. For he is guilty of deceit in the work of God, whosoever loving himself to excess, by that which he may have done well, is only making the best of his way to transitory good things in compensation. We must bear in mind too that there are three ways in which deceit itself is practised, in that, surely, the object aimed at in it is either the secret interest of our fellow creatures' feelings, or the breath of applause, or some outward advantage; contrary to which it is rightly said of the righteous man by the prophet, *Blessed is he that shaketh his hands clear of every favour* (*Is* 33.15). For as deceit does not consist only in the receiving of money; so, no doubt, a favour is not confined to one thing, but there are three ways of receiving favours after which deceit goeth in haste. For a favour from the heart, is interest solicited in opinion, a favour from the mouth is glory from applause, a favour from the head (sic) a reward by gift. Now every righteous man 'shaketh his hands clear of every favour,' in that in whatever he does aright, he neither aims to win vainglory from the affections of his fellow-creatures, nor applause from their lips, nor a gift from their hands. And so he alone is not guilty of deceit in doing God's work, who while he is energetic in studying right conduct, neither pants after the rewards of earthly substance, nor after words of applause, nor after favour in man's judgment."

100 *Prv* 31.30: "Favour is deceitful, and beauty is vain: the woman that feareth the Lord, she shall be praised."

101 Aug. *Gen. ad litt.* 11, 42.59. Cfr Petr. Abael. *Sic et non* q. 55.

102 *Ps* 52.6: "They have not called upon God: there have they trembled for fear, where there was no fear. For God hath scattered the bones of them that please men: they have been confounded, because God hath despised them."

offendatur amichus. *Deus* autem, ait Psalm., *dissipauit ossa eorum*, id est opera in genere uirtuosa, *qui hominibus placent.*

3.6.2. Ab ore. Secundo ab ore, cum scilicet ex bono opere queritur laus humana, quod prohibuit Christus dicens: *Cum facis elemosinam, noli tuba canere ante te*, Matth. 6, id est noli publicare ut lauderis. Quamuis enim dicatur quod *Memoria iusti cum laudibus*, non tamen ipse eam requirit: sed Deus illi eam tribuit, ut non solum a Deo sed etiam ab hominibus uiuens et mortuus laudetur.

3.6.2. Ab opere. Tertio ab opere, cum scilicet quis bonum aliquod facit, ut a Deo remuneretur temporaliter, id est, ut prosperetur seu ieiunat orat et huiusmodi facit, ut consequatur elemosinas uel ecclesiasticham dignitatem, uel alios confidentes de sua bonitate decipiat temporaliter uel spiritualiter: talis ypocrita est, et de huiusmodi Dominus dicit: *Ve uobis ypocrite, qui similes estis sepulchris dealbatis, que parent hominibus spetiosa* etc., Matth. 23.

Omnes ergo tales, qui fraudes faciunt in opere Dei, id est de genere bonorum, maledictionem Dei incurrunt. E contra de uiro iusto dicitur Ysaie <33>, beatus, *qui excutit manus suas,* id est opera, *ab omni munere*, id est cordis oris et operis, nil scilicet querens ab hominibus ut finem ipsorum operum: nec gratiam hominum nec laudem nec transitoria.

---

339 Deus … **340** placent] *Ps* 52.6: Deum non invocaverunt; illic trepidaverunt timore, ubi non erat timor. Quoniam Deus dissipavit ossa eorum qui hominibus placent : confusi sunt, quoniam Deus sprevit eos.

342 Cum … te] *Mt* 6.2: Cum ergo facis eleemosynam, noli tuba canere ante te, sicut hypocritae faciunt in synagogis, et in vicis, ut honorificentur ab hominibus. Amen dico vobis, receperunt mercedem suam.

343 Memoria … **344** laudibus] *Prv* 10.7: Memoria justi cum laudibus, et nomen impiorum putrescet.

350 Ve … **351** spetiosa] *Mt* 23.27: Vae vobis scribae et pharisaei hypocritae, quia similes estis sepulchris dealbatis, quae a foris parent hominibus speciosa, intus vero pleni sunt ossibus mortuorum, et omni spurcitia.

354 qui … munere] *Is* 33.15: Qui ambulat in justitiis et loquitur veritatem, qui projicit avaritiam ex calumnia, et excutit manus suas ab omni munere, qui obturat aures suas ne audiat sanguinem, et claudit oculos suos ne videat malum.

---

343 enim] *s.l.* **345** non] etiam *a.c.* **347** ieiunat] operatur *a.c. ut vid.* **348** alios] + in se *a.c.* **353** 33] *spatium duarum litterarum praeb. cod.*

3.6.2. From the mouth. The second form of fraud is fraud of the mouth, that is, when human applause is sought from a good work, which Christ prohibited, saying: *when thou dost an almsdeed, sound not a trumpet before thee*, Matthew 6,[103] that is, do not publicize it in order to be praised. For although it is said that *the memory of the just is with praises*,[104] nevertheless the just man does not himself seek praise: but God bestows it on him, so that alive and dead he should be praised not only by God but also by men.

3.6.3. From the work. The third form of fraud is fraud of the work, that is, when one does some good deed in order to be rewarded by God in this world. For instance, for the sake of prosperity a person fasts, prays, or does things like this, in order to obtain alms or ecclesiastical dignity or to deceive others temporally or spiritually who trust in one's goodness. Such a person is a hypocrite, and about such ones the Lord says: *Woe to you hypocrites, who are like to whited sepulchres, which appear to men beautiful* etc., Matthew 23.[105]

Therefore all such people, who commit frauds in the work of God, that is works good in their nature, incur God's curse. By contrast, about the just man it is said in Isaiah 33, blessed is *he that shaketh his hands*, that is, his works, *from all bribes*,[106] that is, of the heart and of the mouth and of the work. In other words, he seeks nothing from men as the end of the works themselves: neither men's favour, nor applause, nor transitory things.

103 *Mt* 6.2: "Therefore when thou dost an almsdeed, sound not a trumpet before thee, as the hypocrites do in the synagogues and in the streets, that they may be honoured by men. Amen I say to you, they have received their reward."

104 *Prv* 10.7: "The memory of the just is with praises: and the name of the wicked shall rot."

105 *Mt* 23.27: "Woe to you scribes and Pharisees, hypocrites; because you are like to whited sepulchres, which outwardly appear to men beautiful, but within are full of dead men's bones, and of all filthiness."

106 *Is* 33.15: "He that walketh in justices, and speaketh truth, that casteth away avarice by oppression, and shaketh his hands from all bribes, that stoppeth his ears lest he hear blood, and shutteth his eyes that he may see no evil."

4. De permutationibus seu baracti.

De permutationibus rerum ad res in negotiando, que uulgariter dicuntur baracti, puta dat lanifex setaiuolo duos pannos laneos extimatos ab eo C florenis, et pro hiis setaiuolus dat lanifici pannum serichum extimatum ab ipso C florenis; siue merchator dat lanifici lanam, et setaiuolo serichum, et pro hiis lanifex dat sibi non peccuniam sed pannos laneos, et setaiuolus dat pannos serichos, in tali extimatione in quanta receperunt lanam uel serichum: numquid est licitum? Respondeo: si pure, et absque fraude partium fiat quantitatis pretii uel qualitatis rerum, est contractus permutationis, et licitus, quia a iure approbatus simpliciter in temporalibus, *Extra, De rerum permutatione*, per totum.

Si autem fiat fraus: aut hoc est in ipsis mercimoniis quoad qualitatem aut in extimatione pretii. Si in qualitate rerum permutatarum, tunc si est fraus ex parte unius tantum, quia scilicet dat alteri pannum laneum uel serichum, seu lanam uel serichum, multum defectuosa contra intentionem eius, cum tamen ipse recipiat res ab eo non uitiatas, utique peccat mortaliter, et tenetur satisfacere notabiliter ledens, *Extra, De iniur. et damp.*, *Si culpa*. Et similiter mediator qui nouit huiusmodi fraudem seu sensalis, cooperatur fraudi, 2 q. 1 *Notum*. Si autem uterque intendit alterum decipere, et | ab utroque datur alteri res defectuosa pro bona, utroque ignorante fraudem alterius, utique uterque peccat mortaliter propter malam intentionem, 22 q. 5. *Qui periurare*. Quantum autem ad satisfactionem, potest hic habere locum compensatio, ut unus alteri non teneatur, si in tanto deceptus est unus contra intentionem suam, quantum alter. Si uero uterque ut pratici scirent defectus rerum permutandarum, non uidetur ibi esse fraus, quia "Scienti et consentienti non fit iniuria neque dolus," *De re. iu., libro 6º*, et alter alteri non tenetur.

fol. 73r

---

365 Extra … permutatione] *X* 3.19 *De rerum permutatione*.

372 Extra … culpa] *X* 5.36.9 (*Si culpa*): vide supra.

373 cooperatur fraudi] C. 2 q. 1 c. 10 (*Notum*): … quia facientem et consentientem par pena constringit.

376 peccat … intentionem] C. 22 q. 5 c. 13 (*Qui periurare*): Qui periurare paratus est, ante, quam periuret, iam periurus uidetur, quia Deus non ex operibus iudicat, sed ex cogitationibus et ex corde.

377 potest … compensatio] Cfr *Dig.* 16.2.1 (*Compensatio est*): Compensatio est debiti et crediti inter se contributio.

380 Scienti … **381** dolus] VI 5.[13.]27 (*Scienti*): vide supra.

---

357 rerum] + in negotiando *a.c.* | in negotiando] *in marg. sin. add.* **358** setaiuolo] et la- *a.c. ut vid.* | laneos] *s.l.* **361** laneos] *p.c.* : *haud leg. a.c.* **363** pure] ab(sque) *a.c.* | partium] *in marg. sin. add.* **364** est] licitus est *a.c.* **365** simpliciter … temporalibus] *in marg. sin. add. ut vid.* **368** extimatione] pretio *a.c.* **369** laneum] uel *a.c.* **371** mortaliter] *in marg. dext. add.* **372** Extra … culpa] *in marg. sin. add.* **373** sensalis] + quia *a.c.* **374** ab utroque] utriusque *a.c.* **376** intentionem] + et mal- *a.c.* **377** ad] *bis a.c.* **381** alter] alteri *a.c.*

4. Exchanges of goods or barter. About the exchange of goods for other goods in trading, which is called barter in the vernacular, suppose that a wool merchant gives to a silk merchant two wool cloths appraised by him at 100 florins, and for these the silk merchant gives to the wool merchant silk cloth appraised by himself at 100 florins, or a trader gives wool to a wool merchant, and silk to a silk merchant, and for this the wool merchant gives to him not money but wool cloths, and the silk merchant gives silk cloths, appraised at an equal value to the amount of wool or silk he received: is this licit? I answer: if it is done pure and free of fraud in relation to the price or to the quality of the goods, it is a contract of exchange of goods, and is licit, because it is straightforwardly approved by the law concerning temporal things, in the whole title *On the exchange of goods* in the *Liber Extra*.[107]

However, if fraud happens, this is either in the merchandise itself with regard to quality, or in the appraisal of the price. If in the quality of the goods exchanged, then if there is fraud by one party only, that is, because contrary to the other's intention he gives to the other wool or silk cloth or wool or silk which is seriously defective, when he himself nevertheless receives unspoiled goods from the other, without a doubt he sins mortally, and, notably injuring another, he is bound to make satisfaction, *Extra*, *On injuries and losses*, c. 9.[108] And the same goes for a mediator or broker who knows of such a fraud or cooperates in it, C. 2 q. 1 c. 10.[109] If each party, however, intends to deceive the other, and each gives to the other defective goods as quality ones, each party being ignorant of the other's fraud, certainly each one sins mortally because of evil intent, C. 22 q. 5 c. 13.[110] As to satisfaction, a set-off[111] can apply here, so that one is not bound to the other, if he was deceived contrary to his intention by the same amount as the other. But if both parties, as practitioners, were cognizant of the defects of the goods they were going to exchange, there does not seem to be fraud present, because "To one who knows and consents no injury nor guile is done," *On the rules of law*, *Liber Sext*,[112] and the one is not bound to make any satisfaction to the other.

---

107 *X* 3.19 *De rerum permutatione.*

108 *X* 5.36.9 (*Si culpa*): see above.

109 C. 2 q. 1 c. 10 (*Notum*): "... because an equal penalty binds the one who commits a deed and the one who consents to it."

110 C. 22 q. 5 c. 13 (*Qui periurare*): "He who is ready to commit perjury seems to be a perjurer even before he swears, because God does not judge from deeds, but from thoughts and from the heart."

111 Cfr *Dig.* 16.2.1 (*Compensatio est*): "Set-off is the adjustment of a debt and a claim one with the other."

Dicussing *dolus* and its remedies, Zimmermann notes: "Where both parties have acted fraudulently, a kind of compensatio doli takes place; an application of the more general principle that an action cannot be brought by a person who has himself been guilty of behaviour tinged with turpitudo (nemo auditur turpitudinem suam allegans). Cf. Marc. D. 4, 3, 36: 'Si duo dolo malo fecerint, invicem de dolo non agent.'" Zimmermann, "*Metus* and *Dolus*," ch. 21 in *Law of Obligations*, 670 n147.

112 *VI* 5.[13.]27 (*Scienti*): see above.

Si autem fit deceptio in pretio, quia excessiuum ponitur suis mercimoniis: tunc si unus eorum excedit in pretio, et non alter, qui excedit ille peccat, et obligatur satisfacere si notabilis est excessus, nisi hoc alter perpendat et tamen sic uelit facere permutationem; tunc non uidetur teneri per regulam, "Scienti," *De re. iu.* in *6º*. Si autem scienter uterque excedit in pretio in extimando suas res, quia alter de altero hoc credit et cognoscit, cum cotidie hoc praticent, puta mercator de lana quam dat lanifici ualentem 90 florenos secundum currens pretium, exigit C uel circa, et lanifex de pannis laneis quos dat mercatori pro sua lana, exigit centum, cum non ualeant nisi 90 uel circa; cum alter probabiliter sciat de altero, quod iniustum pretium exigunt de sua re: uidetur hic habere locum compensatio, nec proprie esse ibi fraudem, cum intendant se conseruare indempnes, non alterum grauare. Tales tamen adinuentiones sunt ex cupiditate inuente, et ideo uitande.

---

383 qui] ille qui *a.c.* **384** si] + illud *a.c.* **388** puta] + uel *a.c.* | de] *s.l.* **389** uel circa] *in marg. sin. add.* : et non minus *a.c.* | laneis] + et setaiuolus de sericis *a.c.* **391** cum alter] cum ex hoc alteri *a.c.* | iniustum] immoderatum *a.c. ut vid.*

If, however, deception was committed in the price, that is, an excessive price is placed on the merchandise, then if one of them charges an excessive price and not the other, the one who charges the excessive price commits a sin and is obliged to make it good to the other if the excess is notable. An exception must be made, however, if the other recognized the excessive price and nevertheless wanted to make this exchange; then the one who charged the excessive price does not seem to owe anything, following the rule "To one who knows," *On the rules of law* in the *Sext*. But what about if each party knowingly charges an excessive price for his goods, that is, they both expect this and are aware of it, since they practise this daily? For instance, a trader trading wool to a wool merchant charges 100 or thereabouts for wool valued at 90 florins by the current price, and the wool merchant charges 100 for the wool cloth which he exchanges for the trader's wool, when the cloth is only worth 90 or thereabouts. When each one knows with a high probability that the other is demanding an unjust price for the goods, it seems that a set-off applies here, and fraud is not, properly speaking, present, since they both intend to protect themselves from loss, not to burden the other party. Nevertheless devices like this are devised out of cupidity, and therefore should be shunned.

Antoninus Florentinus, *Summa*, 3.8.1
De merchatoribus et artificibus per modum sermonis

Summarium ab editore confectum

Thema. *Exibit homo ad opus suum, et ad operationem suam usque ad uesperam* (*Ps* 103.23).

1. **Ad opus uirtuale.**
2. **Ad opus criminale.**
3. **Ad opus manuale.**
   - **3.1. Bona conscientia.**
     - **3.1.1. Rectum in intentione.**
     - **3.1.2. Licitum ex improhibitione.**
     - **3.1.3. Congruum in discretione.**
   - **3.2. Apta conuenientia.**
     - **3.2.1. Operatio ad quam cogit necessitas.**
     - **3.2.2. Operatio quam inuenit cupiditas.**
       Exemplum.
     - **3.2.3. Operatio quam induxit uanitas.**
   - **3.3. Debita permanentia.**

St Antoninus, *Summa*, 3.8.1
On merchants and workers, arranged for a sermon

Summary prepared by the editor

Thema. ***Man shall go forth to his work, and to his labour until the evening* (*Ps* 103.23)**

1. **To virtuous work.**
2. **To criminal work.**
3. **To manual work.**
    - **3.1. Good conscience.**
        - **3.1.1. Right intention.**
        - **3.1.2. Liceity.**
        - **3.1.3. Appropriateness.**
    - **3.2. Apt suitability.**
        - **3.2.1. Work which necessity compels.**
        - **3.2.2. Work which cupidity invented.**
          Example.
        - **3.2.3. Work which vanity introduced.**
    - **3.3. Necessary perseverance.**

OCTAVUS TITULUS: DE STATU MERCATORUM ET ARTIFICORUM. *M*₂ fol. IIr

1^m capitulum: per modum sermonis. Titulus de merchatoribus et artificibus.

fol. 69r

Thema. *Exibit homo ad opus suum, et ad operationem suam usque ad uesperam*, Ps. 103. Prima perfectio cuiuslibet creature est primus actus eius, id est forma substantialis, ut in homine anima rationalis; secunda uero perfectio seu secundus actus est operatio eius que ab ea procedit, per quam manifestatur uirtus eius. Nec enim creatura aliqua est que non aliquid operetur uel operari possit. Et frustra est potentia que non reducitur ad actum; "Deus autem et natura nichil frustra" operantur, secundum Philosophum. Vnde et Commentator dicit quod si quis aufert operationes a rebus aufert essentias rerum. Vltima etiam felicitas hominis in operatione consistit per optima. Et de primo homine dicitur quod *posuit eum* Deus *in paradiso uoluptatis, ut operaretur*, Genes. 2. Et licet opus eius esset principaliter spirituale, de quo Christus, Io. 6, *Operamini non cibum qui periit, sed qui permanet in uitam ecternam*, scilicet

---

4 Exibit … uesperam] *Ps* 103.23: Exibit homo ad opus suum, et ad operationem suam usque ad vesperum.

5 Prima … **7** eius[2]] Cfr Arist. *Anim.* 2, 1 (412a10–27; *AL* 12.2:67); Thom. Aq. *sup. Sent.* 1.33.1.1 ad 1; Ant. Flor. *Summa* 1.1.4 pr. (apud *N* fol. 22r, Ballerini 1:38, Mamachi 1:82 para. 8).

9 Deus … **10** operantur] Arist. *Cael.* 1, 4 (271a25ff.; *AL* 8.2): Si quidem enim equales essent, non utique esset motus ipsarum; si autem alter motus dominaretur, alter utique non esset. Itaque, si ambo essent, frustra utique esset alterum corpus non motum eodem motu; frustra enim calciamentum hoc dicimus cuius non est calciatio. Deus autem et natura nichil frustra faciunt.

11 si … rerum] Locum Averr. non inveni. Cfr Thom. Aq. *Sum. th.* 1a q. 13 a. 8: Utrum hoc nomen Deus sit nomen naturae vel operationis … Non est semper idem id a quo imponitur nomen ad significandum, et id ad quod significandum nomen imponitur. Sicut enim substantiam rei ex proprietatibus vel operationibus eius cognoscimus, ita substantiam rei denominamus quandoque ab aliqua eius operatione vel proprietate, sicut substantiam lapidis denominamus ab aliqua actione eius, quia laedit pedem; non tamen hoc nomen impositum est ad significandum hanc actionem, sed substantiam lapidis. … Quia igitur Deus non est notus nobis in sui natura, sed innotescit nobis ex operationibus vel effectibus eius, ex his possumus eum nominare, ut supra dictum est. Unde hoc nomen Deus est nomen operationis, quantum ad id a quo imponitur ad significandum. … Ex hac autem operatione hoc nomen Deus assumptum, impositum est ad significandum divinam naturam.

11 Vltima … **12** optima] Cfr Arist. *Ethica Nic.* 1, 7–13; ibid. 10, 7–8.

13 posuit … operaretur] *Gen* 2.15: Tulit ergo Dominus Deus hominem, et posuit eum in paradiso voluptatis, ut operaretur, et custodiret illum.

15 Operamini … ecternam] *Io* 6.27: Operamini non cibum, qui perit, sed qui permanet in vitam aeternam, quem Filius hominis dabit vobis. Hunc enim Pater signavit Deus.

---

7 que … procedit] *in marg. sin. add.* **8** operari] opari *cod.* **13** operaretur] + Et *a.c.*

TITLE EIGHT: ON THE STATE OF MERCHANTS AND WORKERS.

Chapter 1: Arranged for a sermon. Title on merchants and workers.

Thema. *Man shall go forth to his work, and to his labour until the evening*, Psalm 103.[1] The first perfection of any creature is its first act, that is, its substantial form, for instance the rational soul in man; and the second perfection or second act is its work, which proceeds from its substantial form, through which its virtue is manifested.[2] For there is not any creature which does not or is not able to perform any work. And potential which is not reduced to act is without purpose; "but God and nature work nothing without purpose," according to the Philosopher.[3] Hence also the Commentator says that if one withdraws the operations from things, he withdraws the things' essences.[4] Likewise man's final happiness consists in work towards the best things.[5] And about the first man, it is said that God *took man, and put him into the paradise of pleasure, to work it*, Genesis 2.[6] And although his work was principally spiritual, about which Christ says in John 6, *Work not for the meat which perisheth, but for that which endureth unto life everlasting*,[7] namely by meditating and contemplating divine

1 *Ps* 103.23: "Man shall go forth to his work, and to his labour until the evening."

2 Cfr Arist. *Anim.* 2, 1 (412a10–27; McKeon, 555); Thom. Aq. *sup. Sent.* 1.33.1.1 ad 1; Ant. Flor. *Summa* 1.1.4 pr. (apud *N* fol. 22r, Ballerini 1:38, Mamachi 1:82 para. 8).

3 Arist. *Cael.* 1, 4 (271a25ff.; McKeon, 404): "For if the two motions were of equal strength, there would be no movement either way, and if one of the two were preponderant, the other would be inoperative. So that if both bodies were there, one of them, inasmuch as it would not be moving with its own movement, would be useless, in the sense in which a shoe is useless when it is not worn. But God and nature create nothing that has not its use."

4 I have not found the place in Averroës. One difficulty in interpreting this sentence is deciding what Antoninus means by *auferre*: the usual meaning is "remove, take away, destroy" (*DMLBS*; Deferrari, *Lexicon*, s.v.); but in classical Latin the meaning is also recorded "obtain, get, acquire," and trop. "to learn, to understand" (*LS* s.v. *aufero*, 2C). Employing the latter sense, cfr Thom. Aq. *Sum. th.* 1a q. 13 a. 8: "Whence a name is imposed, and what the name signifies are not always the same thing. For as we know substance from its properties and operations, so we name substance sometimes for its operation, or its property; e.g. we name the substance of a stone from its act, as for instance that it hurts the foot; but still this name is not meant to signify the particular action, but the stone's substance … Because therefore God is not known to us in His nature, but is made known to us from His operations or effects, we name Him from these, as said in Article [1]; hence this name 'God' is a name of operation so far as relates to the source of its meaning … But taken from this operation, this name 'God' is imposed to signify the divine nature."

5 Cfr Arist. *Ethica Nic.* 1, 7–13; ibid. 10, 7–8.

6 *Gen* 2.15: "And the Lord God took man, and put him into the paradise of pleasure, to dress it, and to keep it."

7 *Io* 6.27: "Labour not for the meat which perisheth, but for that which endureth unto life everlasting, which the Son of man will give you. For him hath God, the Father, sealed."

meditando et contemplando diuina; erat tamen et aliquando opus corporale, non quidem ad necessitatem sed ad delectationem mentalem, ad experiendum uires nature et exinde magis cognoscendum res ipsas et Creatorem in eis. Sed de paradiso expulsus propter peccatum necessitatus est ad operandum terram, dictumque est illi: *In sudore uultus tui uesceris pane* tuo, Genes. 3; id est fit ut conserues te in uita, oportet te operari unde uiuas et procures tibi cibum, *donec reuertaris in terram*. Et sic *exibit homo ad opus suum et ad operationem suam usque ad uesperam*, id est usque ad mortem, que est sero et finis uite sue.

Et ita in hiis operibus exterioribus immergitur ut raro sciat reuerti ad opus suum proprium ad quod est factus, scilicet ad Deum cognoscendum et diligendum et fruendum. Nam ut dicit Magister Sententiarum in secundo libro, d. 1, "fecit Deus rationalem creaturam ut summum bonum intelligeret, intelligendo amaret, amando frueretur." Et hoc est summum et perfectum opus. Vbi sciendum quod homo exiit ad opus suum in mundo isto tribus modis:

Ad opus uirtuale, Deo principaliter mouente.
Ad opus criminale, diabolo internaliter suggerente.
Ad opus manuale, ingenio naturaliter agente.

1. Ad opus uirtuale.

De primo dicit Ysaie <26>, *Omnia opera nostra operatus es in nobis*, scilicet tu Deus, et loquitur de operibus uirtuosis; de quibus etiam Christus ait, Io. 15, *Sine me nichil potestis facere*, scilicet boni. Dicitur tamen opus uirtuosum, hominis opus, quia ibi cooperatur liberum arbitrium eius, non enim inuitus trahitur animus sed amore, secundum Augustinum, scilicet ad bonum opus.

---

20 In … **22** terram] *Gen* 3.19: In sudore vultus tui vesceris pane, donec revertaris in terram de qua sumptus es: quia pulvis es et in pulverem reverteris.

28 fecit … **29** frueretur] Petr. Lomb. *Sent.* 2.1.4.1 (1:332): Quare rationalis creatura facta sit. Et quia non valet eius beatitudinis particeps exsistere aliquis nisi per intelligentiam, quae quanto magis intelligitur, tanto plenius habetur, fecit Deus rationalem creaturam, quae summum bonum intelligeret, et intelligendo amaret, et amando possideret, et possidendo frueretur. Cfr Ant. Flor. *Summa* 1.1.4.2 (apud *N* fol. 23r in marg. dext., Ballerini 1:40e, Mamachi 1:92 para. 4).

34 Omnia … nobis] *Is* 26.12: Domine, dabis pacem nobis: omnia enim opera nostra operatus es nobis.

36 Sine … facere] *Io* 15.5: Ego sum vitis, vos palmites: qui manet in me, et ego in eo, hic fert fructum multum, quia sine me nihil potestis facere.

37 ibi … **38** amore] Aug. *Grat.* 17[33]: Mandata Dei implentur magna voluntate, hoc est magna caritate … Quando enim martyres magna illa mandata fecerunt, magna utique voluntate, hoc est, magna caritate fecerunt. … Et quis istam etsi parvam dare coeperat caritatem, nisi ille qui praeparat voluntatem, et cooperando perficit, quod operando incipit? Quoniam ipse ut velimus operatur incipiens, qui volentibus cooperatur perficiens.

---

21 fit] *ut vid.* **22** cibum] + et hoc *a.c.* **27** fruendum] *s.l.* : laudandum *a.c.* **30** quod] + ad *a.c.* | modis] + quia *a.c.* **34** 26] *spatium duarum litterarum praeb. cod.*

things; nevertheless, there was also sometimes corporal work, not indeed out of necessity, but for delighting the mind, for experiencing the forces of nature and thence considering things in themselves and in them the Creator. But when he was expelled from paradise because of sin, he was compelled to work the earth, and it was said to him: *In the sweat of thy face shalt thou eat* thy *bread*, Genesis 3; that is, it was brought about that, to maintain yourself in life, you must do work from which to live and to procure your food, *till thou return to the earth.*[8] And thus *man shall go forth to his work, and to his labour until the evening*, that is until death, which is the evening and end of his life.

And he is so immersed in these exterior works that he seldom knows how to return to his own proper work for which he was made, namely knowing and loving and enjoying God. For as the Master of Sentences says in book 2, d. 1, "God made the rational creature, so that it might understand the highest good, and by understanding it, love it, and by loving it, enjoy it."[9] And this is the highest and perfect work. At which point it must be understood that man goes forth to his work in this world in three ways:

To virtuous work, with God principally moving.

To criminal work, with the devil internally suggesting.

To manual work, with one's disposition naturally working.

1. To virtuous work. About the first it says in Isaiah 26, *Thou hast wrought all our works for us*,[10] namely thou God, and this is speaking about virtuous works; about which Christ also says in John 15, *Without me you can do nothing*, that is, nothing good.[11] Nevertheless virtuous work is called a man's work, because his free will cooperates in it, for the soul is not dragged unwilling, but by love, according to Augustine, namely to the good work.[12] And hence they are made

8 *Gen* 3.19: "In the sweat of thy face shalt thou eat bread till thou return to the earth, out of which thou was taken: for dust thou art, and into dust thou shalt return."

9 Petr. Lomb., *Sent.* 2.1.4.1 (Silano, *Sentences*, 2:5): "Why the rational creature was made. But no one can be a sharer of his blessedness, which is had so much more fully the more it is understood, except through intelligence. And so God made the rational creature, which might understand the highest good, and love it by understanding it, and possess it by loving it, and enjoy it by possessing it." Cfr Ant. Flor. *Summa* 1.1.4.2 (apud *N* fol. 23r in marg. dext., Ballerini 1:40e, Mamachi 1:92 para. 4).

10 *Is* 26.12: "Lord, thou wilt give us peace: for thou hast wrought all our works for us."

11 *Io* 15.5: "I am the vine: you the branches: he that abideth in me, and I in him, the same beareth much fruit: for without me you can do nothing."

12 Aug. *Grat.* 17[33] (trans. Holmes and Wallis): "Operating and Co-Operating Grace … When the martyrs did the great commandments which they obeyed, they acted by a great will, – that is, with great love … He operates, therefore, without us, in order that we may will; but when we will, and so will that we may act, He co-operates with us."

Et inde efficiuntur *nostra* propter meritum, Apocal. <14>, *Opera illorum*, scilicet bonorum hominum, *sequuntur illos*. Cum enim Deus remunerat merita nostra, "coronat munera sua," id est opera bona que ut faceremus ab eo accepimus.

2. Ad opus criminale. De secundo ait Dominus Noster, Io. 8, *Vos facitis opera patris uestri*, scilicet diaboli, scilicet faciendo que ipse suggerit mala: diaboli enim sunt propter suggestionem. Vnde Ieronymus, "Sicut in bonis operibus nostris perfector est Deus, quia non est uolentis" etc., "ita in malis," scilicet operibus, "et in peccatis semina nostra sunt incentiua et perfectio diaboli," *De pen.* D. 2 *Si enim inquit*. Quod tamen sane intelligendum, quia non eo modo diabolus operatur in malis nostris quo Deus in bonis operibus nostris. Nam Deus efficaciter mentem mouendo, diabolus mentem per ymaginationem et sensualitatem incitando, sicut qui porrigeret alicui pomum delectabile ad edendum. Nostra autem sunt propter spontaneam uoluntatem, unde Ambrosius: "Quod possumus non facere si uolumus, huius electionem mali potius debemus nobis ascribere quam aliis," 15 q. 1 *Illa*. Et quia opera *nostra*, propter illa dampnatur et punitur quis, secundum illud Ro. 2, *Tribulatio et angustia in omnem animam operantis malum, Iudeo primum et Grecho*.

---

39 Opera … **40** illos] *Apc* 14.13: Et audivi vocem de caelo, dicentem mihi: Scribe: Beati mortui qui in Domino moriuntur. Amodo jam dicit Spiritus, ut requiescant a laboribus suis: opera enim illorum sequuntur illos.

41 coronat … sua] Aug. *Epist.* 194, 5, 19 in Petr. Lomb. *Sent.* 2.27.6[178] (1:484): De muneribus virtutum et de gratia, quae non est sed facit meritum. … Unde Augustinus, *Ad Sixtum Presbyterum*: "Cum coronat merita nostra, nihil aliud coronat quam munera sua." Cfr Aug. *in Evang. Ioh.* 3, 10 (PL 35:1400); *in Psalm.* 70 serm. 2, 5 (PL 36); *Glossa ord.* ad *Rm* 6.23.

43 Vos … uestri] *Io* 8.41: Vos facitis opera patris vestri. Dixerunt itaque ei: Nos ex fornicatione non sumus nati: unum patrem habemus Deum.

45 Sicut … **47** diaboli] Hier. in *De pen.* D. 2 c. 40 (*Si enim*): Sicut in bonis operibus perfector est Deus (non est enim volentis, neque currentis, sed miserentis, et adiuvantis Dei, ut pervenire valeamus ad calcem) sic in malis, atque peccatis semina nostra sunt incentiva, et perfectio diaboli. Cfr *Glossa ord.* ad idem s.v. *calx*.

49 Nam … **51** edendum] Cfr Thom. Aq. *Sum. th.* 1a q. 111 a. 2; Aug. *Grat.* 1, 41; ibid. 1, 43.

52 Quod … **54** aliis] Ambr. in C. 15 q. 1 c. 6 (*Illa cavenda*): Reus voluntate, non necessitate constringitur. … Quod enim possumus non facere, si volumus; huius electionem mali nobis potius debemus, quam aliis adscribere.

55 Tribulatio … **56** Grecho] *Rm* 2.9: Tribulatio et angustia in omnem animam hominis operantis malum, Judaei primum, et Graeci.

---

39 14] *spatium duarum litterarum praeb. cod.* **40** illos] illorum *a.c.* **43** Noster] *ut vid.* **44** mala] + nostra quidem sunt propter consens *a.c.* | enim sunt] *in marg. dex. add.* **47** peccatis] + incentiva *a.c.* | Si … **48** inquit] *in marg. dex. add.*

our works by merit, as in Apocalypse 14: *Their works*, namely of good men, *follow them*.[13] For when God rewards our merits, "he crowns his own gifts,"[14] that is, the good works which we have received from him in order that we might do them.

2. To criminal work. About the second Our Lord says in John 8, *You do the works of your father*,[15] that is the devil, namely by doing the evil things which he suggests: for these are the devil's works by suggestion. Hence Jerome says, "As in our good works, God is the one who grants perfection, for it is not of him that wills" etc., "so also in our wickedness," namely wicked works, "and sins, our seeds are the incentives, and their perfection is the devil's," D. 2 c. 40.[16] Which nevertheless must be rightly understood, since the devil does not work in our wicked works in the same way God works in our good ones. For God works by moving the mind efficaciously, the devil by inciting the mind through the imagination and the sense faculty, just like the person who holds out to someone an apple delicious to eat.[17] But they are our works by free will; hence Ambrose says, "We ought to attribute to ourselves, rather than ascribe to others, the choice of an evil which we are able not to do, if we wish," C. 15 q. 1 c. 6.[18] And because they are *our* works, we are damned by them and punished, according to that statement in Romans 2: *Tribulation and anguish upon every soul that worketh evil, the Jew first, and also the Greek*.[19]

---

13 *Apc* 14.13: "And I heard a voice from heaven, saying to me: Write: Blessed are the dead, who die in the Lord. From henceforth now, saith the Spirit, that they may rest from their labours; for their works follow them."

14 Aug. *Epist.* 194, 5, 19 in Petr. Lomb., *Sent.* 2.27.6[178] (Silano, *Sentences*, 2:135–6): "Hence Augustine, in *To the Priest Sixtus:* 'When he crowns our merits, he crowns nothing other than his own gifts.'"

There are numerous parallel passages repeating or echoing St Augustine's phrase *coronat munera sua*. Cfr Aug. *in Evang. Ioh.* 3, 10 (PL 35:1400); *in Psalm.* 70 serm. 2, 5 (PL 36); *Glossa ord.* ad *Rm* 6.23.

15 *Io* 8.41: "You do the works of your father. They said therefore to him: We are not born of fornication: we have one Father, even God."

16 Hier. in *De pen.* D. 2 c. 40 (*Si enim*): "As in good works, God is the one who grants perfection: So then it is not of him that wills, nor of him that runs, but of God that shows mercy and gives help that we may be able to reach the goal (Cfr Rom. 9.16), so also in our wickedness and sins, our seeds are the incentive, and their perfection is the devil's." Cfr *Glossa ord.* ibid. s.v. *calx*.

17 Antoninus's discussion of the action of God and the devil participating in human acts is clearly indebted to St Thomas Aquinas, particularly Thomas's discussion of the action of angels upon men: Thom. Aq. *Sum. th.* 1a q. 111 a. 2; cfr Aug. *Grat.* 1, 41; ibid. 1, 43.

18 Ambr. in C. 15 q. 1 c. 6 (*Illa cavenda*): "One who is guilty is bound by his own will and not by necessity ... We ought to attribute to ourselves, rather than ascribe to others, the choice of an evil which we are able to avoid, if we had wished it."

19 *Rm* 2.9: "Tribulation and anguish upon every soul of man that worketh evil, of the Jew first, and also of the Greek."

3. Ad opus manuale.

De tertio opere dicitur, *Exibit homo ad opus suum* etc. Aliis quidem animalibus natura prouidit de uictu et uestitu et armis ad se defendendum sine eorum opere; | homini uero dedit rationem ex qua exeundo per discursum fol. 69v ad actum considerationis et inuestigationis, per opera exteriora diuersorum exercitiorum sibi prouidere possit de uictu et uestitu et defensione a nociuis. Et quasi omnia opera exteriora hominum ad hec ordinantur. *Exibit* ergo etc. Vbi de ipsis operibus corporalibus tria nota.

1. Bonam conscientiam, ibi *Exibit homo ad opus suum.*
2. Aptam conuenientiam, ibi *Ad operationem suam.*
3. Debitam permanentiam, ibi *Vsque ad uesperam.*

3.1. Bona conscientia.

Quantum ad primum. In operibus exterioribus artium debet homo exire de potentia intellectus ad opus suum interius, scilicet ad actum discussionis mentalis de qualitate operationis artis sue; ut non solum operationem faciat exteriorem secundum regulam artis illius, sed etiam secundum regulam conscientie bone. Vnde Apostolus, Galatis 6, *Probet autem unusquisque opus suum*, id est examinet:

Si est rectum in intentione,
Si est licitum ex improhibitione,
Si est congruum in discretione.

57 Aliis … **61** nociuis] Cfr Thom. Aq. *Sum. th.* 1a 2ae q. 5 a. 5 ad 1.
71 Probet … **72** suum] *Gal* 6.4: Opus autem suum probet unusquisque, et sic in semetipso tantum gloriam habebit, et non in altero.

57 dicitur] + *a.c. Antoninus scr.:* Prover. <12.11>, Qui operatur terram, scilicet cultiuando, replebitur panibus, scilicet recolligit fructum. Et de muliere nobili dicitur Prouer. ultimo <31.27; 31.13>, Panem otiosa non comedit, sed [panem] operata est consilio manuum suarum. Harum autem operationum extraneorum, ut dicit Hug. de Sancto Vic., ad quedam opera cogit necessitas, quedam adinuenit cupiditas, quedam induxit uanitas. Ad necessitatem est opus [g] agriculture, unde dicitur Ecclesiastici <7.16>, Non oderis opera rustichana. Et sicut ad uictum necessarium est opus agriculture, propter quod dicitur Prouerb. <12.11> Qui operatur terram replebitur panibus. Et alibi <10.4>, Egestatem operata est manus remissa. Ita ad uestitum opus lanificii et linificii et alie que hiis deseruiunt, unde dicitur Prouerb. ultimo <31.13> de muliere sapienti, Quesiuit lanam et linum et operata est consilio manuum suarum. Et econtra dicitur Prouerb. <10.4>, Egestatem operata est manus remissa, que scilicet non operatur aliquod exercitium corporale, uel negligenter. Nam [suo] artium in unoquoque suo opere mater inuenitur instantia, id est sollicitudo et frequentia, [ita nouercha est neglig eruditionis, scientie scilicet uel artis, est negligentia, dicit Anacletus] D. 83 Nichil. Et ideo si uult uiue- *haec paulatim del. auctor et demum hoc totum indicavit vacandum* **59** opere] *in marg. infer. add. Antoninus:* Ecclesiastes <9.10>, Quodcumque potest manus tua, instanter operare. *sed non notavit quo inserendum* **60** exteriora] + sibi *a.c.* **65** Aptam] *p.c.* : *haud leg. a.c.* **68** potentia] + ratio *a.c.* **71** Apostolus] + 1 Corin. *a.c.* | Galatis 6] *in marg. sin. add.*

3. To manual work. About the third work it is said, *Man shall go forth to his work* etc.[20] For nature has provided the other animals with means of sustenance and garment and weapons for defending themselves without their labour; but to man she gave reason, so that by proceeding from it through thinking to the act of deliberation and investigation, through the exterior works of different occupations he may provide himself with means of sustenance and garment and defence from harmful things.[21] And practically all the exterior works of man are ordered towards these. Therefore *man shall go forth to his work* etc. In that text, three things are to be noted about these corporal works.

1. Good conscience: *Man shall go forth to his work.*
2. Apt suitability: *To his labour.*
3. Necessary perseverance: *Until the evening.*

3.1. Good conscience. First, in the exterior works of the crafts, man ought to proceed from the potential of the intellect to his interior work, namely to the act of mental discourse about the quality of the work of his craft; so that he carry out the exterior work not only following the rule of that craft, but also following the rule of a good conscience. Hence the Apostle says in Galatians 6, *But let every one prove his own work*;[22] that is, let him examine:

If it is right in intention,
If it is licit in non-prohibition,
If it is appropriate in discretion.

---

20 At this place in the autograph (M_2), Antoninus initially drafted 11 lines of text, parts of which he deleted by striking through, finally deleting the whole by indicating these lines with *vacat*. Just below this place, at the foot of fol. 69r, Antoninus has made an addition: "Ecclesiastes: *Whatsoever thy hand is able to do, do it earnestly.*" *Ecl* 9:10. There is no indication where this was meant to be added to the text, though it seems to answer to the final lines of the deletion just mentioned.

21 Cfr Thom. Aq. *Sum. th.* 1a 2ae q. 5 a. 5 ad 1.

22 *Gal* 6.4: "But let every one prove his own work, and so he shall have glory in himself only, and not in another."

3.1.1. Rectum in intentione. De primo dicit Ambrosius: intentio "operi tuo nomen imponit." Nam cuius finis bonus est, id est intentio que respicit finem, ipsum quoque bonum est, scilicet opus inde sequens. Quod uerum est in hiis que de se mala non sunt; nam talibus nullus bonus finis seu intentio potest opus reddere bonum, sicut nec intentio dandi elemosinam in furto de eo excusat a peccato. Debet ergo in omni exercitio artis haberi recta intentio, ut finis remotus et ultimus sit Deus, secundum illud Apostoli, *Omnia que facitis in uerbo uel opere in gloriam Dei facite*; finis propinquus sit aliquid rationabile, ut subuentio sue necessitatis uel proximorum, secundum illud Apostoli, *Operetur manibus suis, ut habeat unde necessitatem tribuat patienti.* Cum enim omnia agant propter finem, homo qui facit opus agriculture, lanificii, artis fabrilis, et huiusmodi, finis propinquus intentus est fructus seu lucrum. Et recte ait Christus et Apostolus, *Dignus est enim operarius mercede sua.* Finis mercedis sue debet esse ut ex ea possit se et alios gubernare et prouidere secundum statum suum; finis substentationis sui et suorum debet esse ut possint uiuere uirtuose; finis uirtuose uiuendi est consequutio glorie: ut enim dicit Augustinus super Io., "Ad hoc debet quisque bene uiuere ut detur semper uiuere." Et sic de primo ad ultimum debet *homo exire ad opus suum in gloriam Dei.*

---

76 intentio … imponit] AMBR. *Off.* 1, 30, 147 in PETR. LOMB. *Sent.* 2.40.1 (1:557–61): Unde Ambrosius ait: "Affectus tuus nomen operi tuo imponit." … Sed Augustinus evidentissime docet in libro *Contra mendacium* omnes actus secundum intentionem et causam iudicandos bonos vel malos, praeter quosdam qui ita sunt mali ut nunquam possint esse boni, etiam si bonam videantur habere causam. … Ex quo consequi videtur quod non semper ex fine iudicatur voluntas sive actio mala, sicut in illis quae per se peccata sunt. … Omnia igitur hominis opera secundum intentionem et causam iudicantur bona vel mala, exceptis his quae per se mala sunt, id est quae sine praevaricatione fieri nequeunt.

76 intentio … **80** peccato] Cfr PETR. LOMB. ibid.

82 Omnia … **83** facite] *Col* 3.17: Omne, quodcumque facitis in verbo aut in opere, omnia in nomine Domini Jesu Christi, gratias agentes Deo et Patri per ipsum. *1 Cor* 10.31: Sive ergo manducatis, sive bibitis, sive aliud quid facitis: omnia in gloriam Dei facite.

84 Operetur … **85** patienti] *Eph* 4.28: Qui furabatur, jam non furetur: magis autem laboret, operando manibus suis, quod bonum est, ut habeat unde tribuat necessitatem patienti.

88 Dignus … sua] *Lc* 10.7: In eadem autem domo manete, edentes et bibentes quae apud illos sunt: dignus est enim operarius mercede sua. Nolite transire de domo in domum. *1 Tim* 5.18: Dicit enim Scriptura: Non alligabis os bovi trituranti. Et: Dignus est operarius mercede sua.

91 Ad … **92** uiuere] AUG. *in Evang. Ioh.* 45, 2: Ad hoc enim debet unicuique prodesse bene vivere, ut detur illi semper vivere: nam cui non datur semper vivere, quid prodest bene vivere? Quia nec bene vivere dicendi sunt, qui finem bene vivendi vel caecitate nesciunt, vel inflatione contemnunt.

---

76 intentio] + tua *a.c.* **87** ait … **88** Apostolus] *in marg. sin. add.* **90** finis] + uite *a.c.*

3.1.1. Right intention. About the first, Ambrose says: intention "attaches a name to your work."[23] For that which has a good end, that is, the intention which looks to an end, the same also is good, namely the work following therefrom. Which is true in those things which are not evil in themselves; for with evil things no good end or intention can render the work good, just as in the case of theft the intention of giving alms from it does not excuse a person from the sin.[24] Therefore a right intention is required in every exercise of a craft, so that the remote and ultimate end be God, according to what the Apostle says, *All whatsoever you do in word or in work, do to the glory of God*;[25] and the proximate end be some rational thing, for instance the support of one's need or that of neighbours, according to what the Apostle says, *Let him work with his hands, that he may have something to give to him that suffereth need.*[26] For since all men who work work for an end – a man who does the work of agriculture, of wool working, of crafting and smithing, and so forth – the proximate end which they aim at is produce or profit. And rightly spoke Christ and the Apostle, *For the labourer is worthy of his wage.*[27] The end of his wage ought to be that, from it, he may take care and provide for himself and others in accordance with his state; the end of sustaining himself and his own ought to be that they may live virtuously; the end of virtuous living is the attainment of glory: for as Augustine says on John, "For to this end ought every one to live well, that it may be given him to live for ever."[28] And thus from first to last, *man* must *go forth to his work to the glory of God.*

---

23 Ambr. *Off.* 1, 30, 147 in Petr. Lomb., *Sent.* 2.40.1 (Silano, *Sentences*, 2:198–202): "Hence Ambrose says: 'Your disposition gives a name to your deed' … But Augustine most clearly teaches in the book, Against Lying, that all actions are to be judged good or evil according to intention and cause, except for some which are so evil that they can never be good, even if they seem to have a good cause … From this it seems to follow that a will or action is not always judged to be evil from its end, as is the case with those things which are sins in themselves … And so all the works of man are judged good or evil according to intention and cause, except for those which are evil in themselves, that is, which cannot be done without transgression."

24 Cfr Petr. Lomb. ibid.

25 *Col* 3.17: "All whatsoever you do in word or in work, do all in the name of the Lord Jesus Christ, giving thanks to God and the Father by him." *1 Cor* 10.31: "Therefore, whether you eat or drink, or whatsoever else you do, do all to the glory of God."

26 *Eph* 4.28: "He that stole, let him now steal no more; but rather let him labour, working with his hands the thing which is good, that he may have something to give to him that suffereth need."

27 *Lc* 10.7: "And in the same house, remain, eating and drinking such things as they have: for the labourer is worthy of his hire. Remove not from house to house." *1 Tim* 5.18: "For the scripture saith: Thou shalt not muzzle the ox that treadeth out the corn: and, The labourer is worthy of his reward."

28 Aug. *in Evang. Ioh.* 45, 2 (trans. Gibb): "For to this end ought good living to benefit every one, that it may be given him to live for ever: for to whomsoever eternal life is not given, of what benefit is the living well? For they ought not to be spoken of as even living well, who either from blindness know not the end of a right life, or in their pride despise it."

3.1.2. Licitum ex improhibitione.

Secundo debet attendere ut opus illud sit licitum non prohibitum. *Odisti omnes qui operantur iniquitatem*, ait Psalmista ad Dominum. Iniquitatem operatur qui facit artem uel operationem illicitam a Deo uel Ecclesia prohibitam, ut opus meretricium, usurarium, taxillatorium faciendo taxillos uel utendo, negotiatio quoad clerichos. Vnde Augustinus: “Fornichari nunquam licet, negotiari aliquando licet aliquando non licet: antequam clerichus fias, licet; postquam clerichus factus es, non licet.” D. 88 *Fornichari*.

3.1.3. Congruum in discretione.

Tertio debet *probare opus suum*, si est cum discretione. Nullum enim est uirtuosum opus nisi debitis circumstantiis uestiatur, ut scilicet fiat debito tempori et locho et modo. Non enim omni tempori licet operari, unde Dominus, Exo. 20, *Sex diebus operaberis, septima die sabbatum Domini est. Omne opus* seruile *non facietis in eo* etc. Et sic de aliis circumstantiis, ut debite obseruetur et impleatur illud Apostoli, *In omni opere bono fructificantes*. Fructificat quis in opere bono quando illud cum debito modo agit. *Si* enim *recte offeras et non recte diuidas, peccasti*, dixit Dominus ad Chayn, Genes. 4, secundum tamen translationem Septuaginta non nostram; id est si facias opus de se bonum, ut sacrificium et huiusmodi, et non cum debita circumspectione, peccatum est, ut exponit Gregorius.

3.2. Apta conuenientia.

Nota secundo aptam conuenientiam in operibus exterioribus mechanicis de quibus loquitur, quia dicit, *Ad operationem suam*. Operatio exterior hominis potest dici *sua* que scilicet sibi conuenit propter inclinationem et aptitudinem

---

94 Odisti … **95** iniquitatem] *Ps* 5.7: Odisti omnes qui operantur iniquitatem; perdes omnes qui loquuntur mendacium. Virum sanguinum et dolosum abominabitur Dominus.

98 Fornichari … **100** licet] Aug. in D. 88 c. 10 (*Fornicari*): Fornicari omnibus semper non licet: negotiari vero aliquando licet; aliquando non licet. Antequam enim ecclesiasticus quis sit; licet ei negotiari: facto iam, non licet.

104 Sex … **105** eo] *Ex* 20.9–10: Sex diebus operaberis, et facies omnia opera tua. Septimo autem die sabbatum Domini Dei tui est: non facies omne opus in eo, tu, et filius tuus et filia tua, servus tuus et ancilla tua, jumentum tuum, et advena qui est intra portas tuas.

106 In … fructificantes] *Col* 1.10: Ut ambuletis digne Deo per omnia placentes: in omni opere bono fructificantes, et crescentes in scientia Dei.

107 Si … **108** peccasti] *Gen* 4.7 *in Septuaginta* (*El Octàteuco*, ed. Ayuso, 88): Nonne si recte offeras recte autem non dividas peccasti. Cfr *Gen* 4.7 *in Vulgata*: Nonne si bene egeris, recipies: sin autem male, statim in foribus peccatum aderit? sed sub te erit appetitus ejus, et tu dominaberis illius.

107 Si … **110** est] Greg. M. *Moral.* 3, 13: Scriptum quippe est: si recte offeras, recte autem non diuidas peccasti. Recte namque offertur cum recta intentione quid agitur. Sed recte non diuiditur, si non hoc quod pie agitur, etiam subtiliter discernatur. Oblata enim recte diuidere est quaelibet bona nostra studia sollicite discernendo pensare. Quod nimirum qui agere dissimulat, etiam recte offerens peccat. Cfr *Glossa ord. ad Gen* 4.7.

---

109 Septuaginta] LXX *cod.*

3.1.2. Liceity. Second, one must take care that that work be licit and not prohibited. *Thou hatest all the workers of iniquity*, the Psalmist says to the Lord.[29] He is a worker of iniquity who exercises an illicit craft or work prohibited by God or the Church, such as the work of prostitutes, usury, gaming by making or by using dice, or if one is a cleric, trade. Hence Augustine: "To fornicate is never lawful, to engage in trade is at times lawful, at times unlawful: before you become a cleric, it is lawful; after you have become a cleric, it is no longer lawful," D. 88 c. 10.[30]

3.1.3. Appropriateness. Third, one must *prove his own work*, if it is to be carried out with discretion. For there is no virtuous work unless it is clothed with the right circumstances, so that it is done in the proper time and place and manner. For it is not lawful to work at all times, hence the Lord said in Exodus 20, *Six days shalt thou work; the seventh day is the sabbath of the Lord: thou shalt do no* servile *work on it*, etc.[31] And so it is for the other circumstances, so that that statement of the Apostle may be duly observed and fulfilled: *Being fruitful in every good work*.[32] One is fruitful in good work when one carries it out in the proper manner. For, *If thou offerest rightly, and dividest not rightly, thou hast sinned*, the Lord said to Cain in Genesis 4, yet according to the Septuagint translation, not ours.[33] That is, if you do a work good in itself, such as sacrifice and things of that sort, and without the proper circumspection, it is a sin, as Gregory expounds.[34]

3.2. Apt suitability. Second, note the apt suitability of exterior mechanical works about which the Psalmist speaks, when he says *To his labour*. The exterior work of a man may be called *his* when it suits him by a natural inclination and aptitude for it. "Pleasure,"

29 *Ps* 5.7: "Thou hatest all the workers of iniquity. Thou wilt destroy all that speak a lie. The bloody and the deceitful man the Lord will abhor."

30 Aug. in D. 88 c. 10 (*Fornicari*): "To fornicate is always unlawful for everyone, but to engage in trade is at times lawful, at times unlawful. Before someone becomes an ecclesiastic, it is lawful for him to be in trade; once he has become one, it is no longer lawful."

31 *Ex* 20.9–10: "Six days shalt thou labour, and shalt do all thy works. But on the seventh day is the sabbath of the Lord thy God: thou shalt do no work on it, thou nor thy son, nor thy daughter, nor thy manservant, nor thy maidservant, nor thy beast, nor the stranger that is within thy gates."

32 *Col* 1.10: "That you may walk worthy of God, in all things pleasing; being fruitful in every good work, and increasing in the knowledge of God."

33 The reading cited by St Antoninus is transmitted in the *Glossa ord.* to *Gen* 4.7, together with the exposition by St Gregory quoted below. Cfr *Gen* 4.7 (Vulgate): "If thou do well, shalt thou not receive? but if ill, shall not sin forthwith be present at the door? but the lust thereof shall be under thee, and thou shalt have dominion over it."

34 Greg. M. *Moral.* 3, 13 (trans. Parker): "For it is written, If thou offerest rightly, but dividest not rightly, thou hast sinned. For it is rightly offered, when the thing that is done is done with a right intention. But it is not 'rightly divided,' unless that which is done with a pious mind be made out with exact discrimination. For to 'divide the offering aright' is to weigh all our good aims, carefully discriminating them; and whoso puts by doing this, even when we offer aright, is guilty of sin."

naturalem ad illam. "Delectatio," secundum Philosophum, "perficit opus." Cum ergo quis inclinatur ad unum opus non malum naturaliter, cum natura delectabiliter operetur applicando se ad illud exercitium, peruenit ad perfectionem illius artis. Sicut enim a natura habemus inclinationes ad uirtutes, unus magis ad unam ut iustitiam, alius ad humilitatem, alius ad misericordiam, magis quam ad alias, propter quod dixit Iob c. <31>, *Ab infantia creuit mecum miseratio, et de utero matris egressa est mechum*, et *Moral.* Senec., "Semina in nobis uirtutum [in nobis] sparsa, sed exercitio nostro postea perficiuntur," et sic etiam secundum Albertum Magnum, homines a natura dociles inclinantur ad scientias uarias secundum qualitatem complexionum: nam malenchonici ad poetichas, flemmantici ad morales, sanguinei ad naturales, collerici ad mathematichas uel metafisichas. Ita et ad cetera opera mechanicha et artes unus inclinatur magis ad unam, alius ad aliam, et naturali instinctu et diuina prouidentia etiam disponente ad pulcritudinem uniuersi et ostensionem sue sapientie, que tantas et tam uarias operationes artificium inspirauit mentibus hominum. Exeat ergo *homo ad operationem suam*, id est ad eam artem quam iudicat sibi magis conuenire et complacere. | fol. 70r Et dicit Hugo de sancto Victore quod operationum humanarum exteriorum triplex differentia inuenitur. Nam:

Ad quedam cogit necessitas;
Quedam inuenit cupiditas;
Quedam induxit uanitas.

---

115 Delectatio … opus] Arist. *Ethica Nic.* 10, 4 (1174b30ff.; 1175a20ff.); cfr Thom. Aq. *Sum. th.* 1a 2ae q. 33 a. 4: Utrum delectatio perficiat operationem. … Et secundum hoc dicit philosophus, in X Ethic., quod delectatio perficit operationem sicut quidam superveniens finis, inquantum scilicet super hoc bonum quod est operatio, supervenit aliud bonum quod est delectatio, quae importat quietationem appetitus in bono praesupposito.

120 Ab … **121** mechum] *Iob* 31.18: Quia ab infantia mea crevit mecum miseratio, et de utero matris meae egressa est mecum. Cfr Thom. Aq. *Sum. th.* 1a 2ae q. 63 a. 1.

121 Semina … **122** perficiuntur] Sen. *Epist.* 108, 8 (LCL 77:234): Facile est auditorem concitare ad cupidinem recti; omnibus enim natura fundamenta dedit semenque virtutum. Omnes ad omnia ista nati sumus; cum inritator accessit, tunc illa anima bona veluti soluta excitatur. Cfr Thom. Aq. *sup. Sent.* 1.17.1.3 co.

123 homines … **126** metafisichas] Alb. M. *Animal.* 20.1.11; *Metaph.* 1.1.5. Vide etiam Ant. Flor. *Summa* 1.1.6 (apud *N* fol. 25v, Ballerini 1:49d–e, Mamachi 1:119), ubi Iohanni Dominici in *Dialogo* suo (non exstante) sententiam tribuit Antoninus. Cfr Boeth. (pseud.) *Disc. schol.* 4.1–4; 4.34–5.

131 operationum … **132** inuenitur] Hugo S. Vict. *sup. Eccles.* 14 (PL 175:217a): Talia sunt omnia opera hominum, quae fiunt super terram, ex quibus multa mortalis vitae necessitas cogit, multa suadet cupiditas, multa vanitas operatur.

---

119 iustitiam] misericordiam *a.c.* **120** 31] *spatium duarum litterarum praeb. cod.* **122** in nobis] *delevi* **125** flemmantici] *ut vid.* **126** uel metafisichas] *s.l.* | cetera] *ut vid.* **129** hominum] + et hoc est quod dicit Sapiens *a.c.* **131** complacere] com- *p.c.* : p- *a.c.* **132** differentia] *s.l.* : est differentia *a.c.*

according the Philosopher, "perfects work."[35] When therefore someone is inclined to some work not naturally evil, when his nature works with pleasure in applying itself to that occupation, he arrives at the perfection of that craft. For just as by nature we are inclined to the virtues, one person more to one, such as justice, another to humility, another to mercy, more than to the others, because of which Job said in ch. 31, *For from my infancy mercy grew up with me: and it came out with me from my mother's womb*,[36] and Seneca in the *Moral epistles* said, "The seeds of virtue are sown in us, but after they are brought to perfection by our exercise,"[37] in just the same way, according to Albert the Great, men who are studious by nature are inclined to different sciences according to the quality of their temperaments: for melancholics are inclined to the poetic sciences, phlegmatics to the moral sciences, sanguines to the natural sciences, cholerics to the mathematical or metaphysical sciences.[38] Thus also with the other mechanical works and crafts, one man is inclined more to one, another to another; natural instinct and Divine Providence likewise disposing towards the beautification of the whole world and the exhibiting of Her wisdom, Who inspired the minds of men with such great and so various occupations of workers. Therefore let *man go forth to his labour*, that is to that craft which he judges to be more suitable and pleasing to him. And Hugh of St Victor says that a threefold distinction is found of the exterior human works.[39] For:

Some necessity compels;
Some cupidity invented;
Some vanity introduced.

---

35 Arist. *Ethica Nic.* 10, 4 (1174b30ff.; 1175a20ff.; McKeon, 1099–1100); cfr Thom. Aq. *Sum. th.* 1a 2ae q. 33 a. 4: "And in this sense the Philosopher says (Ethic. x, 4) that 'pleasure perfects operation … as some end added to it': that is to say, inasmuch as to this good, which is operation, there is added another good, which is pleasure, denoting the repose of the appetite in a good that is presupposed."

36 *Iob* 31.18: "For from my infancy mercy grew up with me: and it came out with me from my mother's womb." Cfr Thom. Aq. *Sum. th.* 1a 2ae q. 63 a. 1.

37 Sen. *Epist.* 108, 8 (trans. Gummere, 3:235): "It is easy to rouse a listener so that he will crave righteousness; for Nature has laid the foundations and planted the seeds of virtue in us all. And we are all born to these general privileges; hence, when the stimulus is added, the good spirit is stirred as if it were freed from bonds." Cfr Thom. Aq. *sup. Sent.* 1.17.1.3 *co.*

38 Alb. M. *Animal.* 20.1.11; *Metaph.* 1.1.5. See also Ant. Flor. *Summa* 1.1.6 (apud *N* fol. 25v, Ballerini 1:49d–e, Mamachi 1:119), where the author attributes this opinion to his master Giovanni Dominici, in a work (*Dialogue*) which is not extant. On a similar theme, cfr Boeth. (pseud.) *Disc. schol.* 4.1–4; 4.34–5 (Sanford, "A Medieval Handbook," 91).

39 Hugo S. Vict. *sup. Eccles.* 14 (PL 175:217a).

3.2.1. Operatio ad quam cogit necessitas.

Cogit utique necessitas ad opera agriculture, quia si uult fructus terre colligere unde comedat et bibat, oportet quod operetur colendo terram per se uel alium, unde dicitur Prouerb. 12, *Qui operatur terram, saturabitur panibus*, et econtra, *egestatem operata est manus remissa*, scilicet ad operandum. Et Ecclesiastici <7> dicitur, *Ne oderis opera rustichana.* Nam Deus eam instituit quia, ut dicitur Genes. 3, *Emisit Deus Adam de paradiso uoluptatis, ut operaretur terram de qua sumptus est.* Et post diluuium, ut dicitur Genes. 9, *Noe uir agrichola cepit exercere terram et plantauit uineam*, ut uinum colligeret quod prius ignorabatur. Sed ut ait Ambrosius: "Nec uinum suo pepercit auctori, sed ebrietas illius suadet sobrietatem," D.35 *Sexto die.* Cogit etiam necessitas uite humane ad opera pastorum ac etiam lanificii et linificii et opera que hiis deseruiunt, pro uestitu humano necessario. Et primas quidem uestes Deus fecit, ut haberi Genes. 3, quia *fecit Deus Adae et Eue* in hoc exilio positis *tunichas pelliceas.* "Non," inquit Ambrosius, "serichas sed pelliceas," habitum scilicet humilitatis et penitentie, non uanitatis et iactantie. Et de sapienti muliere dicitur Prouerb. ultimo, *Quesiuit lanam et linum, et operata est consilio manuum suarum*, scilicet uestes, nam subdit *stragulatam uestem fecit sibi.* Et primus

---

138 Qui … panibus] *Prv* 12.11: Qui operatur terram suam satiabitur panibus; qui autem sectatur otium stultissimus est. Qui suavis est in vini demorationibus, in suis munitionibus relinquit contumeliam.

139 egestatem … remissa] *Prv* 10.4: Egestatem operata est manus remissa; manus autem fortium divitias parat. Qui nititur mendaciis, hic pascit ventos; idem autem ipse sequitur aves volantes.

140 Ne … rustichana] *Sir* 7.16: Non oderis laboriosa opera, et rusticationem creatam ab Altissimo.

141 Emisit … **142** est] *Gen* 3.23: Et emisit eum Dominus Deus de paradiso voluptatis, ut operaretur terram de qua sumptus est.

142 Noe … **143** uineam] *Gen* 9.20: Coepitque Noe vir agricola exercere terram, et plantavit vineam.

144 Nec … **145** sobrietatem] Ambr. in D. 35 c. 8 (*Sexto die*): In principio generis humani ignorabatur ebrietas; primus Noe uineam plantauit, dedit naturam, sed ignorauit potentiam. Itaque uinum nec suo pepercit auctori. Sed illius ebrietas nobis suadet sobrietatem.

148 fecit … **149** pelliceas] *Gen* 3.21: Fecit quoque Dominus Deus Adae et uxori ejus tunicas pelliceas, et induit eos.

149 Non … **150** iactantie] Locum Ambr. non inveni.

151 Quesiuit … **152** sibi] *Prv* 31.13: Quaesivit lanam et linum, et operata est consilia manuum suarum. *Prv* 31.22: Stragulatam vestem fecit sibi; byssus et purpura indumentum ejus.

152 Et … **153** Abel] *Gen* 4.2: Rursumque peperit fratrem ejus Abel. Fuit autem Abel pastor ovium, et Cain agricola.

---

138 saturabitur] satura- *p.c.* : reple- *a.c.* **140** 7] *quattuor puncta praeb. cod.* | instituit] instuit *cod.* **141** paradiso] + ut *a.c.* **142** est] + Et primus filius eius, scilicet Chayn, agrichola fuit *a.c.* | Et] + Noe *a.c.* **147** humano] + sibi *a.c.* **148** Adae] Adam *cod.* **152** subdit] *ut vid.*

3.2.1. Work which necessity compels. Necessity certainly compels the works of agriculture, because if a person wants to collect the produce of the earth from which to eat and drink, it is necessary that he work in tilling the earth by his own labour or by relying on another's labour, whence it said in Proverbs 12, *He that worketh the land shall be satisfied with bread,*[40] and on the other hand, *The slothful hand*, namely at working, *hath worked poverty.*[41] And in Ecclesasticus 7 it is said, *Hate not the works of husbandry.*[42] For God instituted them because, as is said in Genesis 3, *God sent Adam out of the paradise of pleasure, to work the earth from which he was taken.*[43] And after the flood, as is said in Genesis 9, *Noah, a husbandman, began to till the ground, and planted a vineyard,*[44] so that he could gather from the vine of which he was ignorant before. But as Ambrose says, "Wine did not spare its own inventor; but his drunkenness encourages sobriety," D. 35 c. 8.[45] The needs of human life also compel the work of shepherds, those who work with wool and linen, and those doing various supportive tasks, to produce the clothing humans require. And indeed God made the first clothes, as it is written in Genesis 3 that *God made for Adam and Eve*, placed in their exile, *garments of skins.*[46] "Not," says Ambrose, "of silk but of skins," the dress namely of humility and penance, not of vanity and ostentation.[47] And about the wise woman it is said in the last chapter of Proverbs, *She hath sought wool and flax, and hath worked by the counsel of her hands*, namely clothes, for the Proverb tells us, *she hath made for herself clothing of tapestry.*[48] And the first pastor was Abel; and the

40 *Prv* 12.11: "He that tilleth his land shall be satisfied with bread: but he that pursueth idleness is very foolish. He that is delighted in passing his time over wine, leaveth a reproach in his strong holds."

41 *Prv* 10.4: "The slothful hand hath wrought poverty: but the hand of the industrious getteth riches. He that trusteth to lies feedeth the winds: and the same runneth after birds that fly away."

42 *Sir* 7.16: "Hate not laborious works, nor husbandry ordained by the most High."

43 *Gen* 3.23: "And the Lord God sent him out of the paradise of pleasure, to till the earth from which he was taken."

44 *Gen* 9.20: "And Noe, a husbandman, began to till the ground, and planted a vineyard."

45 Ambr. in D. 35 c. 8 (*Sexto die*): "In the beginning of humankind, drunkenness was not known. Noah was the first to plant a vineyard; he made a gift of its nature, but proved ignorant of its power. Thus, wine did not spare its own inventor. But his drunkenness leads us to sobriety."

46 *Gen* 3.21: "And the Lord God made for Adam and his wife, garments of skins, and clothed them."

47 I have not found the cited place in Ambrose.

48 *Prv* 31.13: "She hath sought wool and flax, and hath wrought by the counsel of her hands." *Prv* 31.22: "She hath made for herself clothing of tapestry: fine linen, and purple is her covering."

pastor fuit Abel, quem sequuti in hoc opere sunt Iacob Patriarcha cum filiis suis. Primus hedifichator habitationum et ciuitatum fuit Chayn, qui *hedificauit ciuitatem nomen* imponens *filii sui*, scilicet *Enoch*, Genes. 4. Nam patriarche Habraam, Ysaach, et Iacob non in ciuitatibus uel palatiis sed in tabernaculis habitabant; quorum tabernaculorum seu tentoriorum primus operator fuit Iabel. Primus autem *malleator et faber in omnia opera ferri et eris* fuit Tubalchayn, ut dicitur Genes. 4. Et sic paulatim artes necessarie inuente sunt.

3.2.2. Operatio quam inuenit cupiditas.

Operatio exterior inuenta a cupiditate est negotiatio. Vnde et Philosophus dicit <Polit.>, habere in se turpitudinem quia deseruit cupiditati cum fiat propter lucrum, que cupiditas in immensum crescit et finem nescit. Verum est tamen quod etsi in se turpis sit, potest tamen aliquo bono fine honestari et licita fieri, puta propter substentationem familie sue uel subuentionem pauperum ex moderato et iusto lucro. Primi negotiatores quos inuenio in Sacra Scriptura fuerunt Hismaelite, qui scilicet descenderunt ex Ismael filio Agar, unde dicuntur Agareni, id est Saraceni. Dicitur enim Genes. 37, quod *transeuntibus negotiatoribus Madianitis*, qui scilicet *portabant aromata et alia in*

---

155 hedificauit … Enoch] *Gen* 4.17: Cognovit autem Cain uxorem suam, quae concepit, et peperit Henoch: et aedificavit civitatem, vocavitque nomen ejus ex nomine filii sui, Henoch.

156 patriarche … **157** habitabant] Vide *Gen* 12.8; *Gen* 26.17; *Gen* 33.18; *Hbr* 11.8–10.

157 tabernaculorum … **158** Iabel] *Gen* 4.20: Genuitque Ada Jabel, qui fuit pater habitantium in tentoriis, atque pastorum.

158 malleator … **159** Tubalchayn] *Gen* 4.22: Sella quoque genuit Tubalcain, qui fuit malleator et faber in cuncta opera aeris et ferri. Soror vero Tubalcain, Noema.

162 habere … **163** nescit] Arist. *Polit.* 1, 10 (1258a15–1258b10); cfr Thom. Aq. *Sum. th.* 2a 2ae q. 77 a. 4: Quarto, utrum licitum sit aliquid, negotiando, plus vendere quam emptum sit. … Ad negotiatores pertinet commutationibus rerum insistere. Ut autem philosophus dicit, in I Polit., duplex est rerum commutatio. Una quidem quasi naturalis et necessaria, per quam scilicet fit commutatio rei ad rem, vel rerum et denariorum, propter necessitatem vitae. Et talis commutatio non proprie pertinet ad negotiatores, sed magis ad oeconomicos vel politicos, qui habent providere vel domui vel civitati de rebus necessariis ad vitam. Alia vero commutationis species est vel denariorum ad denarios, vel quarumcumque rerum ad denarios, non propter res necessarias vitae, sed propter lucrum quaerendum. Et haec quidem negotiatio proprie videtur ad negotiatores pertinere. Secundum philosophum autem, prima commutatio laudabilis est, quia deservit naturali necessitati. Secunda autem iuste vituperatur, quia, quantum est de se, deservit cupiditati lucri, quae terminum nescit sed in infinitum tendit. Et ideo negotiatio, secundum se considerata, quandam turpitudinem habet, inquantum non importat de sui ratione finem honestum vel necessarium.

169 transeuntibus … **171** Egiptum] *Gen* 37.25–8: Et sedentes ut comederent panem, viderunt Ismaelitas viatores venire de Galaad, et camelos eorum portantes aromata, et resinam, et

---

153 in hoc] *in marg. dex. add.* | opere] *in marg. sin. add.* **155** Nam] Primus *a.c.* **156** patriarche] patriar- *bis a.c* **162** Polit.] *quattuor puncta praeb. cod.* **166** Primi] -us *a.c.*

patriarch Jacob and his sons followed him in this work.[49] The first builder of dwelling-places and cities was Cain, who *built a city*, imposing *the name of his son*, namely *Enoch*, Genesis 4.[50] For the patriarchs Abraham, Isaac, and Jacob did not live in cities or palaces but in tabernacles;[51] of which tabernacles or tents the first maker was Jabal.[52] But the first *hammerer and artificer in every work of iron and brass* was Tubalcain, as is said in Genesis 4.[53] And thus step by step all the necessary crafts were invented.

3.2.2. Work which cupidity invented.

The exterior work invented by cupidity is trade. And hence the Philosopher says <in the *Politics*>[54] that trade has a certain distastefulness in itself because it serves cupidity when it is carried out for profit; and this cupidity increases into immensity and knows no limit. Nevertheless, it is true that although it is distasteful in itself, it may nevertheless be made respectable and licit by some good end, for instance support of one's family or assistance of the poor out of a moderate and just profit. The first traders whom I find in Sacred Scripture were the Ishmaelites, namely those descended from Ishmael the son of Hagar, whence they are called Agarenes, that is, Saracens.[55] For it is said in Genesis 37 that *when the Midianite merchants passed by*, namely who were *carrying spices, and other things to Egypt, his brethren sold* Joseph *to the Ishmaelites, and they,*

---

49 *Gen* 4.2: "And again she brought forth his brother Abel. And Abel was a shepherd, and Cain a husbandman."

50 *Gen* 4.17: "And Cain knew his wife, and she conceived, and brought forth Henoch: and he built a city, and called the name thereof by the name of his son Henoch."

51 See *Gen* 12.8; *Gen* 26.17; *Gen* 33.18; *Hbr* 11.8–10.

52 *Gen* 4.20: "And Ada brought forth Jabel: who was the father of such as dwell in tents, and of herdsmen."

53 *Gen* 4.22: "Sella also brought forth Tubalcain, who was a hammerer and artificer in every work of brass and iron. And the sister of Tubalcain was Noema."

54 Arist. *Polit.* 1, 10 (1258a15–1258b10; McKeon, 1140–1); cfr Thom. Aq. *Sum. th.* 2a 2ae q. 77 a. 4: "A tradesman is one whose business consists in the exchange of things. According to the Philosopher (Polit. i, 3), exchange of things is twofold; one, natural as it were, and necessary, whereby one commodity is exchanged for another, or money taken in exchange for a commodity, in order to satisfy the needs of life. Such like trading, properly speaking, does not belong to tradesmen, but rather to housekeepers or civil servants who have to provide the household or the state with the necessaries of life. The other kind of exchange is either that of money for money, or of any commodity for money, not on account of the necessities of life, but for profit, and this kind of exchange, properly speaking, regards tradesmen, according to the Philosopher (Polit. i, 3). The former kind of exchange is commendable because it supplies a natural need: but the latter is justly deserving of blame, because, considered in itself, it satisfies the greed for gain, which knows no limit and tends to infinity. Hence trading, considered in itself, has a certain debasement attaching thereto, in so far as, by its very nature, it does not imply a virtuous or necessary end."

55 See *DMLBS* and Du Cange s.v. *agarenus, agareni.*

Egiptum, uendiderunt Ismaelitis Ioseph *fratres sui, qui* Ismaelite *uendiderunt eum in Egiptum.* De hiis dicitur Baruch 3, *Filii quoque Agar,* id est Saraceni, *qui exquisierunt prudentiam que de terra est, negotiatores Merrhe, uiam sapientie non intellexerunt.* Et quem ut summum prophetam et quasi Deum ueneran-tur Saraceni, maledictum Machomethum, primo fuit negotiator; sed in pro-cessu temporis, malitiis suis quodam heretícho Iacobita adiutus, illos rudes et bestiales homines [illos] sua pessima et fatua doctrina decepit. Et quia inimici sunt Christianorum facientes negotiationem de eis, quando capere possunt uel peruertere ad eorum perfidiam; ideo Ecclesia statuit per extrauagantes Nicholai 4 Clementis 5 Ioannis 22 quod negotiatores uel alii quicumque "non deferant" ad terras eorum "quecumque mercimonia," sub penis exchommunicatio-nis papalis et aliarum penarum. Operatio hec plena periculis est et frau-dibus et aliquando mixta usuris, ut notatur *Extra, De usur., In ciuitate* et c. *Nauiganti.* Et ideo oculos aperi. Vnde et Crisostomus dicit super Matheum: "Nullus Christianus debet esse merchator," quia "merchator numquam potest

---

stacten in Aegyptum. Dixit ergo Judas fratribus suis: Quid nobis prodest si occiderimus fratrem nostrum, et celaverimus sanguinem ipsius? Melius est ut venundetur Ismaelitis, et manus nostrae non polluantur: frater enim et caro nostra est. Acquieverunt fratres ser-monibus illius. Et praetereuntibus Madianitis negotiatoribus, extrahentes eum de cisterna, vendiderunt eum Ismaelitis, viginti argenteis: qui duxerunt eum in Aegyptum.

171 Filii … **173** intellexerunt] *Bar* 3.23: Filii quoque Agar, qui exquirunt prudentiam quae de terra est, negotiatores Merrhae et Theman, et fabulatores, et exquisitores prudentiae et intelligentiae: viam autem sapientiae nescierunt, neque commemorati sunt semitas ejus.

179 negotiatores … **181** penarum] Nic. IV *Reg.* 6789 (28 December 1289) (*Registres*, ed. Langlois, 2:641–2): Presentium tenore statuimus ut nullus arma, equos, ferrum, lignamina, victualia et alia quecumque mercimonia in Alexandriam vel alia loca Sarracenorum terre Egipti deferre, mittere vel portare seu de portibus eorum ut eisdem deferantur extrahere vel extrahi permittere aut eis alias auxilium vel favorem prestare quoquo modo presumant. Cfr. ibid. 4402–3, 6784–8; *Extrav.Com.* 5.2.1; *Extrav.Jo.* 8.1; *X* 5.6.6; *X* 5.6.11; *X* 5.6.12; *X* 5.6.17.

181 Operatio … **182** usuris] *X* 5.19.6 (*In civitate*): Vendens rem plus, quam valeat, quia solu-tionem differt, peccat … Licet autem contractus huiusmodi ex tali forma non possit censeri nomine usurarum, nihilominus tamen venditores peccatum incurrunt, nisi dubium sit, merces illas plus minusve solutionis tempore valituras.

X 5.19.19 (*Naviganti*): Non est usurarius emptor rei minus iusto pretio, si tunc verisi-militer dubitetur, an tempore solutionis plus vel minus sit res valitura.

184 Nullus … **185** placere] Chrys. (pseudo) *Opus imperf.* in D. 88 c. 11 (*Eiciens*): Eiciens Dominus uendentes et ementes de templo, significauit, quia homo mercator uix aut numquam potest Deo placere. Et ideo nullus Christianus debet esse mercator, aut, si uolu-erit esse, proiciatur de ecclesia Dei.

---

172 Merrhe] terre *cod.* **174** negotiator] *bis a.c.* **175** suis] + cum *a.c.* **176** illos] *delevi* **181** penarum] *ut vid.* | Operatio] *scilicet* negotiatio **183** aperi] *bis a.c.* | Vnde … **192** granum] *in marg. infer. add.*

the Ishmaelites, sold *him into Egypt*.[56] About them it is said in Baruch 3, *The children of Hagar also*, that is the Saracens, *that have sought after the wisdom that is of the earth, the merchants of Merran; the way of wisdom they have not known*.[57] And the one whom the Saracens venerate as the highest prophet and almost as God, the accursed Mohammed, was a trader at first; but as time went on, having been encouraged in his wickedness by a certain Jacobite heretic, he duped those rough and bestial men with his most debased and foolish doctrine. And because they are enemies of Christians, trading in them when they can capture them or pervert them to their perfidy, therefore the Church established, through decretals of Nicholas IV, Clement V, and John XXII, that traders or whosoever else "must not deliver" to their lands "any kind of merchandise" under pain of papal excommunication and other penalties.[58] This work <i.e. trade> is full of dangers and frauds and is sometimes mingled with usury, as is warned in *Extra*, *On usury*, c. 6 and c. 19.[59] And therefore open your eyes! Hence also Chrysostom says on Matthew: "No Christian must be a merchant," because "a merchant can never please God," D. 88 c. 11.[60] Which

---

56 *Gen* 37.25–8: "And sitting down to eat bread, they saw some Ismaelites on their way coming from Galaad, with their camels, carrying spices, and balm, and myrrh to Egypt. And Juda said to his brethren: What will it profit us to kill our brother, and conceal his blood? It is better that he be sold to the Ismaelites, and that our hands be not defiled: for he is our brother and our flesh. His brethren agreed to his words. And when the Madianite merchants passed by, they drew him out of the pit, and sold him to the Ismaelites, for twenty pieces of silver: and they led him into Egypt."

57 *Bar* 3.23: "The children of Agar also, that search after the wisdom that is of the earth, the merchants of Merrha, and of Theman, and the tellers of fables, and searchers of prudence and understanding: but the way of wisdom they have not known, neither have they remembered her paths."

58 Nicholas IV (r. 1288–92), *Reg.* 6789 (28 December 1289); cfr ibid. 4402–3 (1:641–2); 6784–8 (2:901); Clement V (r. 1305–14) in *Extrav.Com.* 5.2.1 (2:1289–90); John XXII (r. 1316–34) in *Extrav.Io.* 8.1 (2:1214–15); Lateran III in *X* 5.6.6; Clement III in *X* 5.6.11; X 5.6.12; Lateran IV in *X* 5.6.17.

59 *X* 5.19.6 (*In civitate*); *X* 5.19.19 (*Naviganti*).

60 CHRYS. (pseudo) *Opus imperf.* in D. 88 c. 11 (*Eiciens*): "In casting sellers and buyers from the Temple, the Lord signified that a man who engages in trade can rarely or never please God. And so no Christian must be a merchant, or, if he should wish to be one, let him be cast out of God's Church."

Deo placere," D. 88 *Eiciens.* Quod dicit beatus Tomas, 2^{a} 2^{e} q. 77, esse intelligendum de hiis qui ponunt finem suum ultimum in acquisitione lucri seu peccunie; uel de illicitas negotiationes exercentibus, scilicet cum usuris fraudibus et periuriis et huiusmodi. Vnde et Cassiodorus dicit D. eadem, "Negotiatores illi" de templo eiciuntur, qui "per immoderatum peccunie ambitum merces suas polluunt plus onerantes periuriis quam pretiis." Ponuntur illa, c. *Eiciens* et c. *Quoniam*, pro palea, unde et aliqui libri non habent, sed sunt optimum granum. Dicit etiam Crisostomus in dicto c. *Eiciens*, "Quemadmodum qui ambulat inter duos inimichos uolens ambobus placere, sine alloquio mali esse non potest, sic" merchator "sine mendacio et periurio esse non potest." "Sed substantia talium stabilis" esse non potest, "nec proficit ad bonum quod de malo congregatur. Quemadmodum si tritichum aut aliquid tale cernas in cribro, dum huc illucque iactatur omnia grana paulatim

---

185 esse ... **188** huiusmodi] Thom. Aq. *Sum. th.* 2a 2ae q. 77 a. 4 ad 1: Verbum Chrysostomi est intelligendum de negotiatione secundum quod ultimum finem in lucro constituit, quod praecipue videtur quando aliquis rem non immutatam carius vendit. Si enim rem immutatam carius vendat, videtur praemium sui laboris accipere. Quamvis et ipsum lucrum possit licite intendi, non sicut ultimus finis, sed propter alium finem necessarium vel honestum.

189 Negotiatores ... **190** pretiis] Cass. in D. 88 c. 13 (*Quid est aliud*): Negotiatores ergo illi abhominabiles existimantur, qui iustitiam Dei minime considerantes per inmoderatum pecuniae ambitum polluuntur, merces suas plus periuriis onerando quam preciis. Tales eiecit Dominus de templo.

191 Quoniam] Aug. in D. 88 c. 12 (*Quoniam non*): "Quoniam non cognoui litteraturam:" Aliqui codices habent "negotiationes:" in quo diuersitas interpretum sensum ostendit, non errorem inducit. Ergo si propterea iste tota die laudem Dei dicit, quia non cognouit negotiationes, corrigant se Christiani, non negotientur.

191 pro palea] Vide notitiam correctorium Romanorum ad D. 88 c. 11–13 (Friedberg 1:307–8): Haec Palea (quemadmodum et sequens) est in aliquot vetustis exemplaribus, in quibus Paleae raro habentur. Est autem sumta ex auctore operis imperfecti (cuius multae sententiae partim reiiciendae, partim in bonam partem interpretandae sunt) et quidem multis locis de industria, quod ibi plenius, hic in summam redactum est, incolumi fere sententia. Quamobrem ea tantum mutata aut locupletata sunt, quae valde conducere visum est. Quod etiam in sequenti capite est observatum.

Cfr *Glossa ord.* ad D. 88 c. 4 (*Perlatum*) s.v. *perlatum* (1:561): Sequentia capitula plana sunt usque ad paleam illam, *Eiiciens*, quae in scholis non legitur: sed in ea ratio adsignatur quare in domo, vel re consimili non est usura, sed pecunia sic.

196 Quemadmodum ... **199** peccatum] Chrys. (pseudo) *Opus imperf.* in D. 88 c. 11 (*Eiciens*): Quemadmodum enim qui ambulat inter duos inimicos, ambobus placere uolens et se

---

187 peccunie] peccunia *cod.* **195** nec] + ad malum *a.c.* **196** Quemadmodum] + al *a.c.* **197** illucque] + grana *a.c.* | iactatur] *vel* iactantur

blessed Thomas says, 2a 2ae q. 77, must be understood as applying to those who place their ultimate end in the acquisition of profit or money; or those exercising illicit types of trade, namely involving usury, frauds, perjury, and things of this sort.[61] Hence Cassiodorus also says in D. 88, "Those traders" are cast out from the temple, who "pollute their merchandise by immoderate ambition for money, burdening it more with perjuries than prices."[62] These canons, c. 11 and c. 12,[63] are counted as chaff, and hence some manuscripts do not have them; but they are the best grain.[64] Chrysostom also says in the aforesaid c. 11: "For just as one who walks between two enemies, in wishing to please both, cannot fail to engage in slander; so also" a merchant "cannot be free of lying and perjury." "But the wealth of such as these" cannot be "permanent, nor does that profit for good which is gathered from evil. For just as if you sift wheat or suchlike in a sieve, while it is cast back

61 Thom. Aq. *Sum. th.* 2a 2ae q. 77 a. 4 ad 1: "The saying of Chrysostom refers to the trading which seeks gain as a last end. This is especially the case where a man sells something at a higher price without its undergoing any change. For if he sells at a higher price something that has changed for the better, he would seem to receive the reward of his labor. Nevertheless the gain itself may be lawfully intended, not as a last end, but for the sake of some other end which is necessary or virtuous."

62 Cass. in D. 88 c. 13 (*Quid est aliud*): "And so those traders are esteemed to be abominable who, with no consideration of God's justice, are polluted by their immoderate desire for money, burdening their merchandise more with perjuries than prices. The Lord cast out such people from the Temple."

63 I expect that Antoninus meant to refer to the two canons just cited: D. 88 c. 11 (*Eiciens*) and c. 13 (*Quid est aliud*); but he provides the incipit *Quoniam*, which corresponds to D. 88 c. 12 (likewise marked as a *palea*).

Aug. in D. 88 c. 12 (*Quoniam*): "*Because I have not known learning.* Some manuscripts have *tradings*, in which the difference shows the sense of the interpreters, and does not induce error. And so, if this man gives praise to God all day because he did not know tradings, let Christians correct themselves and not trade … "

64 On these chapters' standing as *paleae* (D. 88 c. 11–13), see the Roman correctors' note (Friedberg 1:307–8). Cfr *Glossa ord.* ad D. 88 c. 4 (*Perlatum*) s.v. *it has been reported*: "The next chapters are plain, until the palea at c. 11, which is not read in the schools, but in it a reason is given for why there is no usury in a house or a similar thing, but there is in money."

deorsum cadunt et tandem in cribro nil remanet nisi sterchus; sic de substantia negotiatori nil remanet nisi peccatum."

Exemplum. Nam etsi legatur in uitis Patrum de quodam merchatore, quod fuit uisus a beato Pannusio ei equiparandus in gloria, qui tamen Pannusius hermita sanctissimus magni meriti fuit apud Deum: attende quia ipse Pannusius examinans uitam eius inuenit quia totum lucrum expendebat in pauperes Christi ut pater pauperum, ab usuris et periuriis et aliis illicitis abstinebat, cum magna deuotione uacans diuinis tempori suo; qui demum etiam dimisit opus illud. *Quis est hic, et laudabimus eum*?

3.2.3. Operatio quam induxit uanitas.

Operatio autem tertia que deseruit uanitati est illa que deseruit ornatui iactantie, ut ars serici in magna parte. Nam et si dominos deceat tales uestes et reginas, ut Hester sancta, et sancti aliqui reges se ornantes; | sed multi (fol. 70v) abutuntur quos non decet. Vnde Petrus in 1ª chanonicha ait: *Non in ueste pretiosa auri* et argenti *et margharitis*. Ars reticellorum et rechamature in uestibus et perforature seu stampature et purpure cerusse ad colorandum faciem et huiusmodi, ad quid deseruiunt nisi uanitati, ut dici possit illud Iere. <51>, *Opera eorum uana, et risui digna*? Vnde et Crisostomus dicit super Mattheum quod ab arte calceorum et textorum multa abscidere opportet.

---

commendare, sine maliloquio esse non potest (necesse est enim, ut isti male loquatur de illo, et illi male de isto), sic qui emit et uendit sine mendacio et periurio esse non potest. … Sed est nec stabilis substantia eorum, neque ad bonum proficit, quod de malo congregatur. Quemadmodum enim, si triticum aut aliud tale cernas in cribro, dum huc et illuc iactatur, grana omnia paulatim deorsum cadunt, et tandem in cribro nichil remanet, nisi stercus solum: sic de substantia negotiatorum nouissime nil remanet, nisi solum peccatum.

200 quodam … **201** gloria] *Vitae Patrum*, de Paphnutio (ed. Roseyde, 2, 16).

205 Quis … **206** eum] *Sir* 31.9: Quis est hic? et laudabimus eum: fecit enim mirabilia in vita sua.

209 Hester sancta] Vide *Est* passim, praecipue *Est* 2.15–17; 5.1–2; 15.4–7.

210 Non … **211** margharitis] Potius *1 Tim* 2.9: Similiter et mulieres in habitu ornato, cum verecundia et sobrietate ornantes se, et non in tortis crinibus, aut auro, aut margaritas, vel veste pretiosa: Sed quod decet mulieres, promittentes pietatem per opera bona. Sed cfr *1 Pt* 3.

214 Opera … digna] *Ier* 51.18: Vana sunt opera, et risu digna: in tempore visitationis suae peribunt.

214 Vnde … **217** commiscentes] Textus ex Thom. Aq. *Sum. th.* 2a 2ae q. 169 a. 2 ad 4.

214 Crisostomus … **215** Mattheum] Chrys. *in Mt hom.* 49, 5 (fol. 162vb): Propter hoc et ab arte calcei sutorum et textorum multa abscidere oporteret. Etenim ad luxuriam plura eius deduxerunt necessitatem eius, corrumpentes artem male arti commiscentes.

---

192 Dicit … **198** sterchus] *in marg. super. add.* **199** negotiatori] merchatori *a.c.* | peccatum] *in marg. sin. add.* **211** auri] -t *a.c.* **212** stampature] *vel* scampature **214** 51] *spatium duarum litterarum praeb. cod.*

and forth all the grains gradually fall outside and finally nothing is left in the sieve except waste; so also no wealth is left for the trader except sin."[65]

Example. For although we read in the lives of the Fathers about a certain merchant, whom blessed Paphnutius saw as rivalling himself in glory, even though Paphnutius was an extremely holy hermit of great merit in God's sight: consider that this same Paphnutius, examining the merchant's life, found that he bestowed the whole of his profit upon Christ's poor as a father of the poor, he abstained from usury and perjuries and other illicit deeds, with great devotion spending his time on divine things; in the end he even set aside that very work.[66] *Who is he, and we will praise him?*[67]

3.2.3. Work which vanity introduced. Now the third work, which serves vanity, is that which produces ostentatious attire, for instance the craft of silk making in large part. For even if such clothes befit lords and queens, such as Saint Esther and some saint-kings, in dressing themselves,[68] nevertheless many, whom they do not befit, misuse them. Hence Peter says in the first canonical epistle: *Not with costly attire of gold* or silver *or pearls*.[69] The craft of lace[70] and embroidery[71] on clothing, and beading or textile printing,[72] and purple cosmetic for making up the face, and things of this sort: what do they serve except vanity? As that text of Jeremiah 51 could say:

65 CHRYS. (pseudo) *Opus imperf.* in D. 88 c. 11 (*Eiciens*): "For just as one who walks between two enemies, in wishing to please and commend himself to both, cannot fail to engage in slander (for it is necessary that he speak ill of the first to the second, and of the second to the first), so also one who buys and sells cannot be free of lying and perjury ... But neither is their wealth enduring, nor does that profit for a good end which is gathered from evil. For just as, if you sift wheat and suchlike in a sieve, while it is cast back and forth, all the grains gradually fall outside, and finally nothing is left in the sieve, apart from ordure, so also in the end nothing is left of the wealth of traders, apart from sin."

66 *Vitae Patrum*, ed. Heribert Roseyde (Antwerp, 1628), 2, 16 *Paphnutius*.

67 *Sir* 31.9: "Who is he, and we will praise him? for he hath done wonderful things in his life."

68 See *Est* passim. Beauty and splendour are running themes in the book of Esther. Particular instances which evoke the beauty of Esther and her garments include *Est* 2.15–17; 5.1–2; 15.4–7.

69 Rather *1 Tim* 2.9–10: "In like manner women also in decent apparel: adorning themselves with modesty and sobriety, not with plaited hair, or gold, or pearls, or costly attire, But as it becometh women professing godliness, with good works."

Cfr *1 Pet* 3, where the Apostle admonishes wives to adorn themselves not with the attire of ostentation but with subjection to their husbands; St Antoninus attributes the text quoted from 1 Timothy to this chapter instead.

70 See *DMLBS* s.v. *reticulum*: net, hairnet, veil; tissue with a net-like structure.

71 See Du Cange s.v. *recamatura*.

72 I have not been able to determine decisively what craft *stampatura* describes. In *GDLI* the word *stampator* is recorded as referring to either textile printers or fabric decorators. In the 1580 *Statuti dell'Arte di Por Santa Maria, seconda parte*, the list of members of the guild includes "Ricamatori et Stampatori di Drappi e Panni." Ital. *ricamator* means "embroiderer." It could be that Antoninus uses *stampator* simply as a synonym for *ricamator*.

For further references, see my footnote in ANT. FLOR. *Summa* 3.8.4 (below), section 4.1.

Etenim ad luxuriam deduxerunt necessitatem eius, corrumpentes artem mali arti commiscentes.

3.3. Debita permanentia.

Demum quantum ad tertium, opportet habere in operibus et artibus instantiam et perseruerantiam. Nam ut dicit Anacletus papa, "In unoquoque artium opere mater inuenitur instantia," D. 83 *Nichil.* Et hoc est quod dicit Psalmista: *Vsque ad uesperam*, id est usque sero continuando, non parum operando et subito dimittendo; uel *usque ad uesperam*, id est terminum uite. Quod est contra aliquos instabiles, qui omni die mutant unam artem. Hii sunt similes filio inconstantie de quo dicit Boetius, de eo narrans in libro *De scolarium disciplina* quod cum pater eius posuisset ad opera diuerse artis, quia subito attediabatur cum unam inchoabat, demum omnes renuens; interrogante patre quid facere uellet, respondit se uelle fieri asinum ut salmam ferret. Sed cum aliquis in operibus alicuius licite artis bene uiuendo perseuerat *usque ad uesperam*, id est finem; tunc facto sero, id est uita deficiente, dicit Dominus: *Voca operarios, et da illis mercedem*, Matth. 20, scilicet glorie.

---

219 In … **220** instantia] Anacl. (pseudo) in D. 83 c. 6 (*Nihil illo*): Sicut autem artium in suo quoque opere inuenitur mater instantia, ita nouerca erudicionis est negligentia.

225 disciplina … **227** ferret] Boeth. (pseud.) *Disc. schol.* 3 (Weijers, 104–8): Inprobo corruptas, lectos detestor aniles, / nil michi cum feda virgine: solus ero. … Miserum est me hominem esse. Utinam humanitatem possem exuere, asinitatem possem induere specie mutata!

230 Voca … mercedem] *Mt* 20.8: Cum sero autem factum esset, dicit dominus vineae procuratori suo: Voca operarios, et redde illis mercedem incipiens a novissimis usque ad primos.

---

221 Psalmista] Ps. *cod.* **230** glorie] *in marg. sin. add. Antoninus* hic pone §. de contractibus *et in marg. sin. add. Iulianus de Lapaccinis* quere infra ad cartam 125

Their works are vain, and worthy to be laughed at.[73] And hence, Chrysostom on Matthew says that it is necessary to set limits on the craft of shoemakers and weavers,[74] for they have gone beyond necessity into luxury, corrupting the craft, mingling it with an evil craft.[75]

3.3. Necessary perse-verance.

Finally, as to the third, one must have constancy and perseverance in works and crafts. For as Pope Anacletus says, "Diligence is the mother of the works of each craft," D. 83 c. 6.[76] And this is what the Psalmist says: *Until the evening*, that is, keeping at it until the evening, not working a little and quickly forsaking it; or *until the evening*, that is, the end of life. This is said against some unsteady people, who turn to another craft every day. These are like the son of inconstancy about which Boethius speaks, narrating about him in his book *On the Discipline of Scholars* that when his father had placed him in the works of different crafts, when starting one he quickly became bored,[77] in the end refusing all; when his father asked him what he wanted to do, he replied that he wanted to be made into an ass and carry a saddle.[78] But when someone by living well perseveres in the works of any good art *until the evening*, that is, the end; then, when the evening has arrived, that is when life is ending, the Lord says: *Call the labourers and give them their wage*, Matthew 20, namely of glory.[79]

73 *Ier* 51.18: "They are vain works, and worthy to be laughed at, in the time of their visitation they shall perish."

74 Chrys. *in Mt hom.* 49, 5 (trans. Prevost and Riddle): "For this same cause the sandal-makers too, and the weavers, should have great retrenchments made in their art. For most things in it they have carried into vulgar ostentation, having corrupted its necessary use, and mixed with an honest art an evil craft."

75 This sentence is copied from Thom. Aq. *Sum. th.* 2a 2ae q. 169 a. 2 ad 4.

76 Anacl. (pseudo) in D. 83 c. 6 (*Nihil illo*): "Just as diligence is the mother of the works of each art, so is negligence the step-mother of learning."

77 Cfr *DMLBS* s.v. *attaediare.*

78 Boeth. (pseud.) *Disc. schol.* 3. The tale of the "son of inconstancy" became proverbial, according to Weijers.

79 *Mt* 20.8: "And when evening was come, the lord of the vineyard saith to his steward: Call the labourers and pay them their hire, beginning from the last even to the first."

Antoninus Florentinus, *Summa*, 3.8.2
De diuersis generibus contractuum

Summarium ab editore confectum

1. **De translatione rerum.**
   - **1.1. Donatio.**
   - **1.2. Permutatio.**
   - **1.3–4. Emptio-uenditio.**
   - **1.5–6. Mutui datio-acceptio.**
   - **1.7. Isti sex contractus liciti uel illiciti.**
2. **De translatione usus.**
   - **2.1. Commodatum.**
   - **2.2. Accomodatio.**
   - **2.3–4. Conductio-locatio.**
   - **2.5–6. Pignus-ypotheca.**
3. **De fraude legi.**
   - **3.1. De re ad rem.**
   - **3.2. De persona ad personam.**
   - **3.3. De uno contractu ad alium.**
   - **3.4. De uno contractu ad alium alio modo.**

St Antoninus, *Summa*, 3.8.2
On the various kinds of contracts

Summary prepared by the editor

1. Transfer of ownership.
- **1.1. Gift.**
- **1.2. Exchange of goods.**
- **1.3–4. Purchase and sale.**
- **1.5–6. Giving and receiving a loan.**
- **1.7. Liceity of these six conveyances.**

2. Transfer of use.
- **2.1. Loan for use.**
- **2.2. Accommodation.**
- **2.3–4. Hire and lease.**
- **2.5–6. Pledge and mortgage.**

3. Evasion of law.
- **3.1. From thing to thing.**
- **3.2. From person to person.**
- **3.3. From contract to contract.**
- **3.4. From contract to contract in a different fashion.**

2^{m} capitulum: de diuersis generibus contractuum.

M$_2$ fol. IIr

1. De translatione rerum. Notandum quod in translatione rerum de una persona ad aliam que fit per priuatas personas, aliquando transfertur dominium rei, aliquando solum usus rei retento dominio. Et primum fit sex modis. fol. 115v

1.1. Donatio. Primo per liberalem dationem, cum scilicet nichil expectatur retributionis ex tali datione rei nisi beniuolentia, et dicitur donatio, de qua infra dicetur post sequentem titulum c. de testamentis.

Aliis quinque modis fit per dationem illiberalem, qua uidelicet transferens unam rem expectat ab alio aliquid equiualens ei quod transfert.

1.2. Permutatio. Et primus modus dicitur permutatio, cum uidelicet transfertur dominium alicuius rei utilis pro alia re utili, puta frumentum pro uino, uel pannus meus cum lana tua uel panno sericho tuo, uel peccunia mea aurea, puta unus florenus, pro peccunia tua argentea, puta pro grossis XVII uel circa. Istud tamen ultimum solet dici cambium communiter, alie uero permutationes uulgariter dicuntur baracti.

1.3–4. Emptio-uenditio. Alius modus dicitur in uno transferente dominium rei cum altero uenditio, et in altero emptio, quando scilicet transfertur dominium rei utilis, puta frumenti uini animalium domorum agrorum et huiusmodi, pro numismate uel econuerso. Quia enim difficile erat semper res usuales immediate commutare in alias res, ideo inuentum est medium, per quod talis commutatio fiat; et hoc medium dicitur numisma seu peccunia numerata. Et commutatio rei utilis pro numismate dicitur uenditio; commutatio numismatis pro re utili dicitur emptio.

---

2 Notandum … **4** modis] In hoc cap. plura desumpsit Antoninus ex Io. Scot. *In quartum* 4 d. 15 q. 2 a. 2 (271–320). Cfr Bern. Sen. *Evang. aet.* 32, 3 (4:134–9).

6 dicetur … **7** testamentis] Ant. Flor. *Summa* 3.10.3: *de testamentis*; vide etiam ibid. 3.10.4: *de donationibus*.

18 pro … **21** numisma] Textus ex Io. Scot. *In quartum* 4 d. 15 q. 2 a. 2 n. 12 (*Opera omnia*, 18:282), paucis mutatis. Cfr *Dig.* 18.1.1 (*Origo*); Arist. *Ethica Nic.* 5 (1133a15–35).

---

2 de … aliam] *s.l.* **7** titulum] *in marg. sin. add. Antoninus vel Iul. de Lapacc.* **8** Aliis] Secundo fit *a.c.* **9** ab alio] *in marg. dext. add.* **12** aurea] argentea puta *a.c.* **13** pro] + quod *a.c.* **15** baracti] + Secundus modus rei *a.c.* **16** transferente] transferentium *cod.* | uenditio] emptio *cod.* **17** emptio] uenditio *cod.* **18** et huiusmodi] *in marg. dext. add.* **20** medium] *in marg. sin. add.* : numisma *a.c.*

Chapter 2: On the various kinds of contracts.

1. Transfer of ownership. One[1] must observe that in the transfer of things from one person to another which is carried out by private persons, sometimes ownership of the thing is transferred, sometimes only the use of the thing with ownership being retained. And the first is carried out in six ways.[2]

1.1. Gift. First, through a liberal conveyance, namely when no recompense is expected for conveying the thing apart from goodwill, and this is called a gift, which will be discussed below after the next title in the chapter on wills.[3]

In the other five ways, transfer of ownership is carried out through an illiberal conveyance, in other words, when the one transferring a thing expects from the other party something equivalent to that which he transfers.

1.2. Exchange of goods. And the first method is called exchange of goods; that is, when the ownership of some useful thing is transferred in exchange for another useful thing: for instance grain for wine, or my cloth for your wool or silk cloth, or my gold money – say one florin – for your silver money – say for 17 groats or thereabouts. Yet this last type of exchange is by custom usually called "moneychanging," while the other sorts of exchange are called in the vernacular "barter."

1.3–4. Purchase and sale. The second method is called, as applied to the one transferring ownership of a thing to someone else, sale, and as applied to the other person, purchase;[4] namely, when ownership is transferred of a useful thing – for instance grain, wine, animals, houses, fields, and so forth – "in exchange for money, or vice versa. For since it was always difficult to exchange useful things directly for other things, therefore a medium was invented through which such exchange could be carried out; and this medium is called money" or coinage.[5] The exchange of a useful thing for money is called "sale," and the exchange of money for a useful thing is called "purchase."

---

1 Immediately above the body of this chapter, a note added by Giuliano Lapaccini reads: "This chapter ought to be placed above, in the title on merchants, at fol. 70 at the following symbol." The symbol is a ladder. There are also numbers 1–6 added in the left and right margins of this chapter, corresponding to two sets of six types of contract. The hand which wrote these numbers cannot be definitely identified.

2 This chapter draws much material from from Io. Scot. *In quartum* 4 d. 15 q. 2 a. 2 (*Opera Omnia*, 18:271–320; Wolter, 35–60). Cfr Bern. Sen. *Evang. aet.* 32, 3 (4:134–9).

3 Ant. Flor. *Summa* 3.10.3: *de testamentis*; see also ibid. 3.10.4: *de donationibus*.

4 I have emended the Latin text here, conjecturing what appears to be necessary both for grammar and sense. The autograph reads: "Alius modus dicitur in uno transferentium dominium rei cum altero emptio, et in altero venditio."

5 The words in quotation marks are copied, with a few changes, from Io. Scot. *In quartum* 4 d. 15 q. 2 a. 2 n. 12 (*Opera Omnia*, 18:282; Wolter, 42–3).

On the origins of money, cfr *Dig.* 18.1.1 (*Origo*); Arist. *Ethica Nic.* 5 (1133a15–35; McKeon, 1011).

1.5–6. Mutui datio-acceptio.

Vltimus modus est cum fit permutatio numismatis pro numismate, sed cum expectatione temporis, et in eo qui dat peccuniam dicitur mutui datio, in eo qui recipit peccuniam et expectatur ad reddendam peccuniam dicitur mutui acceptio; per mutuum enim transfertur dominium peccunie in accipientem.

1.7. Isti sex contractus liciti uel illiciti.

Et isti contractus sex sunt liciti cum debito modo fiunt; illiciti cum iniuste fiunt. Nam donatio, si fiat per eum qui non potest donare, ut est religiosus, iniusta est, et non tenet; et si fiat iniusta causa, ut ob turpitudinem, peccatum est, ar. D. 86 *Donare*.

Permutatio rerum cum fit sine fraude licita est, ut patet *De rerum permutatione* per totum; si cum fraude peccatum est. Et uidentur ad hanc reduci contractus innominati, scilicet do ut des, et do ut facias uel facio ut des.

Emptio et uenditio licita sunt nisi fiat excessus pretii in uendente notabilis, uel diminutio in emente, uel fraus, uel usura implicita propter expectationem temporis, ut *Extra*, *De usur.*, *In ciuitate*, et c. *Nauiganti*.

Datio mutui que est circa res | que usu consumuntur, ut frumentum uinum et huiusmodi, uel distrahuntur, ut peccunia numerata: cum fit gratis, ut nil expectetur nisi suum capitale et beniuolentia ex obsequio, licita est et pium opus. Si autem aliquid temporalis utilitatis expectetur, unde principaliter

fol. 116r

---

29 Et … **30** fiunt] Cfr Raym. Penn. *Sum. paen.* 2.8 (1B:557–8): Alia plura [negotia] sunt quae non sunt inhonesta sui natura, sed ex causa, vel ex tempore, vel ex persona, vel ex loco, ut emptio-venditio, locatio-conductio et similes contractus; similiter et quasi contractus, ut tutela, cura, negotiorum gestorum iudicium et similia.

32 D. 86 Donare] D. 86 c. 7 (*Donare*): Inmane peccatum est res suas istrionibus donare. Cfr *Glossa ord.* ad idem.

Cfr D. 86 c. 8 (*Qui venatoribus*): Qui donant istrionibus qui donant meretricibus, quare donant? numquid non et ipsa hominibus donant: Non tamen naturam ibi attendunt operis Dei, sed nequitiam operis humani.

33 patet … **34** totum] *X* 3.19 *De rerum permutatione.*

38 Extra … ciuitate] *X* 5.19.6 (*In civitate*): Vendens rem plus, quam valeat, quia solutionem differt, peccat … Licet autem contractus huiusmodi ex tali forma non possit censeri nomine usurarum, nihilominus tamen venditores peccatum incurrunt, nisi dubium sit, merces illas plus minusve solutionis tempore valituras.

38 Nauiganti] *X* 5.19.19 (*Naviganti*): Non est usurarius emptor rei minus iusto pretio, si tunc verisimiliter dubitetur, an tempore solutionis plus vel minus sit res valitura.

---

30 est] *s.l.* **33** ut … **34** totum] *in marg. sin. add.* **34** si] uel *a.c.* | uidentur] uidetur *cod.* **35** do[2] … uel] *bis.* **39** mutui] cum non *a.c.*

1.5–6. Giving and receiving a loan.

The final method is when there is an exchange of money for money, but with a delay of time; and with regard to the one who gives the money it is called giving a loan, and with regard to the one who accepts the money and is expected to return the money it is called receiving a loan. For through a loan, ownership of the money is transferred to the one receiving the loan.

1.7. Liceity of these six conveyances.

And these six contracts are licit when they are carried out in the proper manner; they are illicit when they are carried out in an unjust manner.[6] For a gift, if made by one who is unable to make a gift, such as a religious, is unjust and invalid; and if carried out for an unjust cause, as in for the sake of indecency, it is a sin, by the argument of D. 86 c. 7.[7]

Exchange of things, when it is carried out without fraud, is licit, as evident from the whole title *On exchange of things*;[8] when carried out with fraud, it is a sin. And the innominate contracts seem to reduce to this category of exchange, namely the innominate contracts "I give so that you give" and "I give so that you do" or "I do so that you give."

Purchase and sale are licit unless the seller charges a notably excessive price or the buyer pays a price too low, or there is fraud or implicit usury because of a time delay, as in *Extra*, *On usury*, c. 6 and c. 19.[9]

Giving a loan involving things which are consumed in their use, such as grain, wine, and so forth, or are paid out, such as coinage, when the loan is provided free of charge so that nothing is expected except the return of the principal and goodwill motivated by a sense of duty, then it is licit and a pious

---

6 Cfr Raym. Penn. *Sum. paen.* 2.8.1 (1B:557–8).

7 D. 86 c. 7 (*Donare*): "It is a very great sin to give one's possessions to actors." Cfr *Glossa ord.* ad idem.

Cfr D. 86 c. 8 (*Qui venatoribus*): "Those who give to actors, or who give to charioteers, or who give to prostitutes, why do they give? It is not to human beings that they give. For it is not the nature of God's work to which they attend, but to the iniquity of the human work."

8 *X* 3.19 *De rerum permutatione.*

9 *X* 5.19.6 (*In civitate*); *X* 5.19.19 (*Naviganti*).

mouetur ad mutuandum, illicita est et usura, ar. 14 q. 3 *Si feneraueris*, et *Extra, De usur., Consuluit.*

Mutui acceptio licita est non solum cum fit gratis, sed etiam cum fit sub usuris, quando scilicet ad hoc neccessitate mouetur, nec inducit mutuantem ad usuram faciendum, ut quia ad hoc paratus erat.

2. De translatione usus. Aliquando uero transfertur solum usus rei, retento sibi dominio eius rei. Et huius translationis sunt sex modi quasi correspondentes predictis sex modis quibus transfertur dominium rerum.

2.1. Commodatum. Nam primo modo, scilicet donationi, correspondet contractus dictus commodatum, quod proprie est rei que utendo non consumitur uel distraitur, ut cum quis commodat alicui gratis equum librum domum et huiusmodi, ut utatur ad certum tempus. Et licitus contractus est de se, sicut dictum est de donato.

2.2. Accomodatio. Permutationi correspondet mutua accomodatio predictarum rerum, puta tu commodas mihi equum tuum et ego bouem meum, uel tu unum librum et ego tibi alium librum, tu unam domum et ego unum agrum; et totum [et] sine fraude immixta licitum erit.

2.3–4. Conductio-locatio. Emptioni correspondet conductio, et uenditioni lochatio, que possunt esse de rebus mobilibus et immobilibus que tamen non consumuntur usu. Et ista non fiunt gratis sed cum dato pretio pro tali usu, puta cum accipitur equus ad uecturam pro tali pretio, uel domus ad pensionem, uel ager ad collendum pro medietate uel ad affictum, uel cum quis lochat operas suas personales et alter eum conducit ad laborandum. Totum est licitum, dummodo iustum pretium statuatur et fraus omnis tollatur. Nam "fraus et dolus nemini debent patrocinari," *Extra, De rescrip., Sedes.*

---

43 ar. … feneraueris] C. 14 q. 3 c. 1 (*Si foeneraveris*): Quod autem preter summam emolumenta sectari sit usuras exigere, auctoritate Augustini probatur … Si feneraueris hominem, id est si tu mutuum dederis pecuniam tuam, a quo plus quam dedisti expectes, non pecuniam solam, sed aliquid plus quam dedisti, siue illud triticum sit, siue uinum, siue oleum, siue quodlibet aliud, si plus quam dedisti expectes accipere, fenerator es, et in hoc inprobandus, non laudandus.

44 Extra … Consuluit] *X* 5.19.10 (*Consuluit*): Mutuans ea mente, ut ultra sortem aliquid recipiat, tenetur in foro animae ad illud restituendum, si ex hoc aliquid consecutus est … Verum quia, quid in his casibus tenendum sit, ex evangelio Lucae manifeste cognoscitur, in quo dicitur: "Date mutuum, nihil inde sperantes:" huiusmodi homines pro intentione lucri, quam habent, quum omnis usura et superabundantia prohibeatur in lege, iudicandi sunt male agere, et ad ea, quae taliter sunt accepta, restituenda, in animarum iudicio efficaciter inducendi.

65 fraus … Sedes] *X* 1.3.15 (*Sedes apostolica*): Fraus et dolus ei patrocinari non debent.

---

48 retento] rentento *cod.* **52** quod] que *a.c.* **57** totum] + gratis *a.c.* | et[3]] *delevi* **61** cum[1]] + peccunia *a.c.* **62** collendum] affictum *a.c.* **65** patrocinari] *ut vid.*

act. But if something of temporal utility is expected, which is the lender's primary motive for lending, then it is illicit and usury, by the argument of C. 14 q. 3 c. 1,[10] and *Extra, On usury*, c. 10.[11]

Receiving a loan is licit not only when it is free of charge but even when it bears usury, that is, when the borrower is motivated by necessity and is not inducing the lender to commit usury, as in, because he had been planning to do it.

2. Transfer of use. But sometimes only the use of a thing is transferred, with the ownership of one's thing retained for oneself. And there are six methods of transferring use, as it were corresponding to the aforesaid six methods by which ownership of a thing is transferred.

2.1. Loan for use. For to the first method, namely a gift, corresponds the contract called "loan for use," which is, properly speaking, a loan of a thing which is not consumed or paid out in its use, such as when someone loans to another free of charge a horse, a book, a house, and things of this sort, so that it may be used for a certain time. And this is in itself a licit contract, as was said about the gift of a thing.

2.2. Accommodation To an exchange of goods corresponds mutual accommodation of the aforesaid things: for instance, you lend me your horse and I lend you my ox, or you lend one book and I lend you another book, you lend one house and I lend one field; and the whole thing, without any hidden fraud, will be licit.

2.3–4. Hire and lease. To a purchase corresponds leasing or hiring, and to a sale corresponds leasing out or hiring out, which may be of mobile or immobile things when they are not consumed in use. And these are not done free of charge but with a price given for the use: for instance when a horse is taken as a means of transport for a set price, or a house for rent, or a field to be cultivated for a half portion or a regular revenue,[12] or when someone hires out his personal services and the other hires him to work. The whole is licit, provided that a just price is established, and all fraud is precluded. For "no one's fraud and guile ought to be defended," *Extra, On rescripts*, c. 15.[13]

---

10 C. 14 q. 3 c. 1 (*Si foeneraveris*): "That it is an exaction of usury to seek gains beyond the sum given is proven by the authority of Augustine … If you have lent to a man at interest, that is, if you have given your money in loan, and you expect to receive something more than what you gave, and not the money alone, but something more than you gave, whether you receive it in wheat, or in wine, or in oil, or in anything else, if you expect to receive more than you gave, you are a lender at interest, and in this you are to be condemned, and not to be praised."

11 *X* 5.19.10 (*Consuluit*).

12 Lat. *affictus* or *affictum*: "Affictus, Census, Reditus. … Vocabularium utriusque iuris: Affictus penes vulgare Lumbardorum et Thuscanorum…. dicitur census qui datur ratione praediorum, etc." Du Cange, s.v.

13 *X* 1.3.15 (*Sedes Apostolica*).

2.5–6. Pignus-ypotecha. Mutuo non respondet proprie aliquis alius contractus; habet tamen aliquam similitudinem licet modicam ad pignus, in quantum restituta peccunia ab eo qui dedit pignus, ille qui acceperat restituit pignus. Et in pignoratione potest ibi esse et non esse peccatum: nam si solum pignus quis recipiat ut de suo sit securus, ita quod de pignore non consequatur aliam utilitatem, licitum est. Si autem de eo consequatur utilitatem, siue sit rei mobilis que proprie dicitur pignus, siue rei immobilis, ut domus et ager, quod magis proprie dicitur ypotecha, puta quia utitur equo uel ueste quam habet in pignus, utitur domo habitando uel habendo de ea pensionem, agro recipiendo fructum eius, que habet pro pignore: ibi est usura expressa, *Extra*, *De pigno.*, *Illo nos*. Tenetur enim omnem fructum quem habet ex pignore computare in sortem. De huiusmodi contractibus habes supra in secunda parte titulo primo c. de usura.

3. De fraude legi. Item nota quod facere fraudem legibus iniustum est, unde et peccatum, et ut dicit glossa Io. super c. *Plerique*, "facit fraudem legi qui uerba legis seruat, sed mentem eius circumuenit, ut *Ff.*, *De legi.*, *Fraus*." Sed ut dicit regula iuris ultima in *6°*, "Certum est quod is commictit in legem qui uerba legis amplectens contra legis nititur uoluntatem."

Fit autem quattuor modis fraus legi.

3.1. De re ad rem. Vno modo de re ad rem, quando datur in fraudem una res pro alia, ut 14 q. 3 *Plerique*, ubi ponitur exemplum de eo qui ratione peccunie mutuate, ne

---

75 ibi … nos] *X* 3.21.4 (*Illo vos*): Si usurarius emit rem eo pacto, quod post tempus restituat eam venditori, recipiendo aliquid ultra sortem, fructibus tamen in ea computatis, iudicatur contractus foeneratitius. … Verum quia ambigitis, utrum pura sit et absoluta venditio, an praefatus contractus pignus debeat iudicari, respondemus, quod, qualiscunque fuerit intentio contrahentium, et ex forma contractus venditio non appareat conditionalis, sed pura, quamvis per conditionem possit resolvi, ex duobus tamen, quae in pacto fuerunt expressa, videlicet, quod fructus percepti deberent in solvenda pecunia numerari, et quod ultra summam receptam LX. solidi deberent persolvi, contra ipsum emptorem praesumitur vehementer, praesertim quum usuras consueverit exercere.

77 secunda … usura] Ant. Flor. *Summa* 2.1.6–10 (apud M_1 fol. Vr et Ballerini; 2.1.5–9 apud Mamachi): *de usura*, etc.

78 ut … **80** Fraus] *Glossa ord.* ad C. 14 q. 3 c. 3 (*Plerique*) s.v. *precepta*: Nolunt quidam facere contra legem, sed faciunt fraudem legi. Ille vero facit fraudem legi, qui observat verba legis, sed mentem eius circumvenit, ut ff. de legib. fraus.

80 Ff. … Fraus] *Dig.* 1.3.30 (Fraus): Fraus enim legi fit, ubi quod fieri noluit, fieri autem non vetuit, id fit: et quod distat hryton apo dianoias, hoc distat fraus ab eo, quod contra legem fit.

80 regula … **82** uoluntatem] *VI* 5.[13.]88 (*Certum est*): Certum est, quod is committit in legem, qui, legis verba complectens, contra legis nititur voluntatem.

83 Fit … **102** Mulierem] Textus ex *Glossa ord.* ad C. 14 q. 3 c. 3 (*Plerique*) s.v. *precepta*, quibusdam mutatis.

---

72 siue] siue equ- *a.c.* **76** ex] in sortem *a.c.* **77** supra] in secunda *a.c.* **79** Io.] *ut vid.* **83** legi] legis *cod.* **84** Vno] P- *a.c.*

2.5–6. Pledge and mortgage. To a loan there is no other precisely corresponding contract; it has, nevertheless, some similarity, though small, to pledge, in as much as when the money is returned by the one who gave the pledge, the one who had received it returns the pledge. In pledging there may or may not be sin present: for if someone accepts a pledge solely so that from his possession of it he may be secure, such that from the pledge he does not derive any utility, it is licit. If, however, he derives utility from it – whether it is a mobile thing, which is called "pledge" properly speaking, or an immobile thing like a house or a field, which is more properly called "mortgage" – for instance, he uses the horse or clothing which he has in pledge, he uses the house which he holds as a pledge by living in it or getting a rent from it, the field which he holds as a pledge by taking its produce: then there is express usury, *Extra*, *On pledges*, c. 4.[14] For he is bound to count all the profit which he has from the pledge towards the principal. There is a discussion of contracts of this sort above in the second part, title 1, in the chapter on usury.[15]

3. Evasion of law. Also, note that to evade the laws is unjust, and hence also a sin, and as John's gloss on the canon *Plerique* says: "he evades the law who respects the words of the law but circumvents its intention, as in the *Digest*, *On Statutes*, l. 30."[16] But as the last rule of law in the *Sext* states: "it is certain that he contravenes the law, who, embracing the words of the law, strives against the will of the law."[17]

Now evasion of the law is committed in four ways.[18]

3.1. From thing to thing. In one way, from thing to thing, when one thing is given in place of another to evade the law, as in C. 14 q. 3 c. 3, where there is set out the example of one who, on account of money lent, lest he should appear to commit usury, does not seek more money than was lent but rather a bribe[19] of meat or wine and

---

14 *X* 3.21.4 (*Illo vos*).

15 Ant. Flor. *Summa* 2.1.6–10 (apud M_l fol. Vr et Ballerini; 2.1.5–9 apud Mamachi): *de usura*, etc.

16 *Glossa ord.* ad C. 14 q. 3 c. 3 (*Plerique*) s.v. *precepta*. "Some people do not wish to act against the law, but they defraud the law. He defrauds the law who observes the words of the law, but circumvents its intent, as at *Digest* 1.3.30."

Dig. 1.3.30 (*Fraus*). "Fraud on the statute is practiced when one does what the statute does not wish anyone to do yet which it has failed expressly to prohibit. And what separates 'words from meaning' separates cheating from what is done contrary to law."

17 *VI* 5.[13.]88 (*Certum est*): "It is certain that he transgresses the law, who, while observing its letter, goes against its spirit." English trans. from Gauthier, *Roman Law and … Canon Law*, 117.

18 The rest of this chapter, from this sentence to the end, is based on the *Glossa ord.* ad C. 14 q. 3 c. 3 (*Plerique*) s.v. *precepta*. The gloss lists the four ways of evading the law; for each of the four ways, Antoninus quotes a sentence of the gloss, with few changes, as the leading sentence of a paragraph, expanding the gloss's points with his own explanation of the relevant cases.

19 Lat *ensenia*, cfr CL *exenium*.

uideatur commictere usuram, non plus peccunie quam mutuatam sed querit ex hoc ensenia carnium uel uini et huiusmodi que peccunia extimantur. Iste fraudem facit legi unde et contra legem, quia usura est, ut ibi dicitur et 1 q. 1 *Sunt non nulli*; et talis est fraus Macedoniani, *Ff.*, *ad Macedon.*, l. *Iul.*

3.2. De persona ad personam.

Item fit fraus de persona ad personam, ut cum quis sub persona alterius exercet usuram, quasi ipse non sit usurarius, cum in ueritate sit peccator usurarius, et teneatur ad restitutionem ex quo de pecunia sua sit, D. 46 *Sicut non suo.* Et cum maritus non potest aliquid dare uxori, supponit aliam personam cui det, ut *Ff.*, *De donat. inter uirum et uxo.*, *Hec ratio*, §. ultima.

3.3. De uno contractu ad alium.

Item fit fraus de uno contractu ad alium, ut cum mulier non possit aliquid dare uiro, fingit se uendere ei, ut *Ff.*, *De dona. inter uirum et uxor.*, l. *Si sponsus.* Sic 16 q. 3 *Si sacerdotes*, ubi ponuntur casus; secundum unam lecturam, cum episcopus uel sacerdos uolens dare nepotibus de rebus ecclesie, fingit litem habere cum eis pro ecclesia, et facit transactionem cum eis.

---

88 ut ... **89** nulli] C. 1 q. 1 c. 114 (*Sunt nonnulli*): Sunt nonnulli, qui quidem nummorum premia ex ordinatione non accipiunt, et tamen sacros ordines pro humana gratia largiuntur, atque de ipsa largitate laudis solummodo retributionem querunt. ... Aliud est munus ab obsequio, aliud a manu, aliud a lingua. Munus ab obsequio est seruitus indebite inpensa. Munus a manu pecunia est; munus a lingua fauor.

89 Ff. ... Iul.] *Dig.* 14.6.19 (*Iulianus*), sed potius *Dig.* 14.6.7.3 (*Sed Iulianus adicit*, §. *Mutui*): Sed si fraus sit senatus consulto adhibita, puta frumento vel vino vel oleo mutuo dato, ut his distractis fructibus uteretur pecunia, subveniendum est filio familias.

92 D. ... suo] D. 46 c. 10 (*Sicut non suo*): Sicut non suo, ita nec alieno nomine aliquis clericorum exercere fenus attemptet. Indecens enim est crimen suum commodis alienis inpendere et exercere.

94 Ff. ... ultima] *Dig.* 24.1.3.13 (*Haec ratio et*, §. ult.): Si donaturum mihi iussero uxori meae dare: ait enim Iulianus nullius esse momenti, perinde enim habendum, atque si ego acceptam et rem meam factam uxori meae dedissem.

94 Ff. ... **95** sponsus] *Dig.* 24.1.5.5 (*Si sponsus sponsae*, §. *Circa*): Venditionem donationis causa inter virum et uxorem factam nullius esse momenti, si modo, cum animum maritus vendendi non haberet, idcirco venditionem commentus sit, ut donaret.

97 16 ... sacerdotes] *Glossa ord.* ad C. 16 q. 3 c. 10 (*Si sacerdotes*) s.v. *si sacerdotes*: Triplex casus solet hic poni. ... Vel, secundum alium casum, expone, scripto decreverunt, idest, scripto transegerunt, et in fraudem: cum enim non poterat dare nepotibus suis, fingebat se habere litem cum eis de illo, et transigebat cum eis.

---

91 cum in] *in marg. sin. add.* : cum aliter peccat *a.c.* **92** sit] *vel* fit | 46] 47 *cod.* **99** eis^{2}] *ut vid. propter detrimentum cod.*

other such things which are valued in money. That man commits evasion of law, and hence also breaks the law because this is usury, as is said there and at C. 1 q. 1 c. 114;[20] and such is the fraud of the Macedonian, *Digest*, *Macedonianum*, l. *Iulianus*.[21]

3.2. From person to person. Also the law is evaded from person to person, such as when someone exacts usury while representing himself as someone else, as though he himself were not a usurer, when in truth he is a usurious sinner, and is bound to make restitution of what he gets for his money, D. 46 c. 10.[22] And when a husband is not legally able to make a gift of something to his wife, he substitutes another person to whom he may give, as in *Digest*, *Gifts between husband and wife*, l. 3 §. 13.[23]

3.3. From contract to contract. Also the law is evaded from one contract to another, for instance, since a woman is not legally able to make a gift of something to her husband, she represents herself as selling to him, as in *Digest*, *Gifts between husband and wife*, l. 5.[24] This is the situation in C. 16 q. 3 c. 10,[25] where the cases are set out; according to one reading, when a bishop or a priest, wishing to give to his nephews out of the goods of the church, contrives that he has a lawsuit with them on behalf of the church, and makes a settlement with them.

---

20 C. 1 q. 1 c. 114 (*Sunt nonnulli*): "There are some who do not accept a gift of money for ordination, yet they bestow sacred orders for some human favour, and from this bestowal they seek only the reward of praise … One gift is by deference, another by the hand, and another by the tongue. A gift by deference is one of undue servility; a gift by hand is money; a gift by tongue is flattery."

21 *Dig.* 14.6.7.3 (*Sed Iulianus adicit*, §. *Mutui*): "But if a loan of, say, corn or wine or oil is made so that the son-in-power may sell it and use the proceeds, this is a fraud on the *senatus consultum* and he should be given relief."

Antoninus's citation points to *Dig.* 14.6.19 (*Iulianus*), but this fragment does not answer to the subject at hand. The *Glossa ord.*, Antoninus's source, cites the fragment I have just given.

22 D. 46 c. 10 (*Sicut non suo*). "No cleric should attempt to engage in money-lending, either in his own name or in another's, for it is indecent to cover up one's crime under another's gains."

23 *Dig.* 24.1.3.13 (*Haec ratio et*, §. ult.): "If I order someone who is about to give something to me to give it to my wife, the transaction will be void; for the position would be held to be the same as if I had received it myself and when it became mine, I had given it to my wife."

24 *Dig.* 24.1.5.5 (*Si sponsus sponsae*, §. *Circa*): "A sale between husband and wife for the purpose of making a gift will only have no effect if the husband did not intend to sell the property at all, but pretended to sell it so as to make a gift of it."

25 *Glossa ord.* ad C. 16 q. 3 c. 10 (*Si sacerdotes*) s.v. *si sacerdotes*: "It is usual to pose a threefold case here … According to another case, expound 'they decreed such things in writing,' that is, they entered into a written out of court settlement, and did so fraudulently; for being unable to give those things to his nephews, he feigned a controversy with them as to those goods and made the agreement with them."

3.4. De uno contractu ad alium alio modo.

Item fit fraus de uno contractu ad alium <sed alio modo>, ut cum mulier non possit fideiubere, constituit se principalem debitricem, ut *Ff.*, *Ad Vell.*, *Quamuis*, et 33 q. 5 *Mulierem.*

---

101 Ff. … **102** Quamuis] *Dig.* 16.1.8 pr. (*Quamvis pignoris*): Redditionem pignoris, si creditrix mulier rem, quam pignori acceperat, debitori liberaverit, non esse intercessionem.

102 33 … Mulierem] C. 33 q. 5 c. 17 (*Mulierem*): Mulierem constat subiectam dominio viri esse, et nullam auctoritatem habere: nec docere enim potest, nec testis esse, neque fidem dare nec iudicare: quanto magis non potest imperare?

Cfr *Glossa ord.* ad C. 33 q. 5 c. 17 (*Mulierem*) s.v. *neque fidem*: Obligatur tamen si dolose fideiubeat, ut creditorem decipiat.

---

100 fit] sit *ut vid. cod.* | sed … modo] *addidi Glossam ordinariam secutus* **101** Ad Vell.] *bis a.c.*

3.4. From contract to contract in a different fashion.

Also the law is evaded from one contract to another <but in a different fashion,> for instance, since a woman cannot stand surety, she sets herself up as the principal debtor, as in *Digest*, *Velleianum*, l. 8,[26] and in C. 33 q. 5 c. 17.[27]

26 *Dig.* 16.1.8 pr. (*Quamvis pignoris*): "The return of a pledge does not constitute an intercession if a woman, who is the creditor, releases to the debtor the property which she has received on pledge."

27 C. 33 q. 5 c. 17 (*Mulierem*): "It is clear that the woman is subject to her husband's dominion, and to have no authority; she can neither teach, nor be a witness, nor give faith, nor judge; how much more is she unable to command?" Cfr *Glossa ord.* ad C. 33 q. 5 c. 17 s.v. *neque fidem*.

Antoninus Florentinus, *Summa*, 3.8.3
De negotiatoribus et campsoribus

Summarium ab editore confectum

Pr. Negotiator proprie qui dicitur.

1. **Cambium.**
   - **1.1. Cambium minutum.**
   - **1.2. Cambium per litteram.**
   - **1.3. Cambium sichum.**
   - **1.4. Cambium mixtum quod usuram sapere uidetur.**
   - **1.5. De usura in cambiis.**
   - **1.6. De usura mentali.**
   - **1.7. Cambium in curia Romana quod uidetur magis illicitum.**
2. **Securitates.**
   - **2.1. Securitas in mercimoniis.**
   - **2.2. Securitas in peccuniis.**
   - **2.3. Securitas in personis.**
3. **Permutatio uel baractum.**
4. **Emptio et uenditio.**
   - **4.1. De ritagliatoribus et righatteriis.**
   - **4.2. De merchatoribus uictualium.**
   - **4.3. De macellariis et pizicangnolis.**

St Antoninus, *Summa*, 3.8.3
On traders and bankers

Summary prepared by the editor

Pr. Who is properly called a trader?

1. **Exchange.**
    1.1. **Petty exchange.**
    1.2. **Exchange by bill.**
    1.3. **Dry exchange.**
    1.4. **Mixed exchange which seems to savour of usury.**
    1.5. **Usury in exchanges.**
    1.6. **Mental usury.**
    1.7. **Particularly illicit exchange carried out in the Roman curia.**
2. **Assurance.**
    2.1. **Assurance on merchandise.**
    2.2. **Assurance on money.**
    2.3. **Assurance on persons.**
3. **Exchange of goods or barter.**
4. **Purchase and sale.**
    4.1. **Retail cloth merchants and second-hand dealers.**
    4.2. **Food merchants.**
    4.3. **Butchers and small retail dealers.**

3^{m} capitulum: de negotiatoribus et campsoribus.

M_2 fol. IIr

Pr. Negotiator proprie qui dicitur.

fol. 70v

Incipiendo ergo ab opere negotiationis, que uidetur honorabilior in ciuilitate humana inter mechanica. Negotiator proprie dicitur qui rem comparat ut integram et immutatam uendendo lucretur, dicit Crisostomus D. 88 *Eiciens*. Et potest dici esse triplex genus negotiationis, quia uel de peccunia ad peccuniam, uel de mercimonio ad mercimonium, uel de mercimonio ad peccuniam. Et prima dicitur campsio uel cambitio. Secunda permutatio uel barattum. Tertia emptio et uenditio.

1. Cambium.

Et cambium fit multis modis.

1.1. Cambium minutum.

Primum dicitur cambium minutum, ut de moneta argentea uel aurea ad eream et econuerso. Vt cum quis dat campsori unum florenum aureum et recipit pro eo 4^{or} libras et solidos XIIII uel quindecim si est largus, uel grossos argenteos 17 et solidos unum cum dimidio uel circa, et sic campsor retinet sibi IIII^{or} denarios uel duos quatrenos uel unum solidum secundum consuetudinem loci. Et sic econuerso, quando uult quis habere florenum largum a campsore dabit pro eo sibi 4^{or} libras et solidos sexdecim uel circa. Illud igitur plus quod recipit campsor, non capit ratione mutui quia ibi non est mutuum, nec quia peccunia uendatur, que est inuendibilis ut dicit Archidiaconus, sed ratione laboris quem subit in numerando peccuniam et expensarum quas facit

---

3 Negotiator … **4** lucretur] D. 88 c. 11 (*Eiciens*): … Sed omnes homines uidentur esse mercatores; ostendam ergo, quis non est negotiator, ut qui talis non fuerit, eum intelligas esse negotiatorem. Quicumque rem conparat, non ut ipsam rem integram et inmutatam uendat, sed ut materia sibi sit inde aliquid operandi, ille non est negotiator; qui autem conparat rem, ut illam ipsam integram et inmutatam dando lucretur, ille est mercator, qui de templo Dei eicitur.

10 Primum … **11** econuerso] Cfr Laur. Rod. *Tr. usur.* 2, q. 26 (no. 8 in TUI 7:22vab); 3, q. 1 (TUI 7:37vb)

18 que … Archidiaconus] Archid. *Rosarium*, fortasse ad C. 14 q. 3 c. 1 (fol. 221v): Respondeo quia pecunia tantum ad emendum disposita est ut in illa palea eiiciens secundum Io. de F. … in glo. per Io. F. quod non possit proprie vendi usus pecunie sic nec locari. Vide etiam Laur. Rod. *Tr. usur.* 2, q. 26 (no. 8 in TUI 7:22va): quia attento subiecto pecuniae est invendibilis; quia omnium rerum aestimatio est. ff. de fideiussori. l. si ita. nisi propter concursum monetae. … vendens pecuniam quae est invendibilis, ut supra dictum est et firmavit Archi. etiam in C. 14 q. 3 super glo. Cfr Bern. Sen. *Evang. aet.* 39, 3, 1 (4:289); Thom. Aq. *sup. Sent.* 3, 37, 1, 6.

---

3 qui] s(cilicet) *a.c.* | comparat] comperat *cod.* **4** uendendo … Eiciens] *in marg. dext. add.* **6** mercimonio^{1}] mer- *ut vid.* **10** Primum] Primo *cod.* **12** grossos … **13** solidos] gross. argent. 17 et solid. *cod.* **14** consuetudinem] consud- *a.c.* **15** quando] + de uul quis *a.c*

3: On traders and bankers.

Preamble. Who is properly called a trader?

We begin then with trade, a type of work which, among the mechanical arts, appears to be most esteemed in human society. A trader properly so called is one who buys a thing in order to make a profit by selling it whole and unchanged, Chrysostom says in D. 88 c. 11.[1] And one can describe three kinds of trade: of money for money, of merchandise for merchandise, or of merchandise for money. And the first is called banking or exchange (i.e., moneychanging), the second exchange of goods or barter, and the third purchase and sale.

1. Exchange.

Now exchange is carried out in many different ways.[2]

1.1. Petty exchange.

The first is called petty exchange,[3] as of silver or gold coinage for copper and vice versa. For example, when someone gives one gold florin to a banker[4] and receives in return 4 pounds and 14 or 15 shillings (if it is a large gold florin),[5] or 17 silver groats and one and a half shillings or thereabouts, and thus the banker keeps for himself 4 pence or 2 *quattrini*[6] or one shilling according to the local custom. And so in reverse, when someone wants to have a large florin from the banker, he will give for it 4 pounds and 16 shillings or thereabouts. Therefore, the additional amount which the banker receives, he does not get on account of a loan, because there is no loan here, nor because money is sold, which is incapable of being sold as the Archdeacon says,[7] but on account of the labour which he undergoes in counting money and because of his expenses on rent

---

1 Chrys. (pseudo) *Opus imperf.* in D. 88 c. 11 (*Eiciens*): "But all men seem to be merchants. And so I will show who is not a trader, so that you will understand anyone to be a trader who does not fit my description. Whoever purchases a thing, not in order to sell it whole and unchanged, but in order to have matter to work into something else, he is not a trader. But he who buys a thing in order to gain something by alienating it whole and unchanged, he is a trader who is cast out of God's Temple."

2 This section on exchange draws much material from Laur. Rod. *Tr. usur.* 3, 1–4 (TUI 7:37r–38v). Cfr Bern. Sen. *Evang. aet.* 39, 3, 1–3 (4:289–95), relying on Laur. Rod. *Tr. usur.*

For background and summary of other scholastic writers on this subject, see Noonan, *Scholastic Analysis of Usury*, 175–93; Langholm, "The Medieval Schoolmen," 493–4.

3 Cfr Edler, *Terms of Business*, 57: "Cambio (manesco) a contanti; actual or manual exchange of money from one currency to another."

4 "Cambiatore; a banker (who did a local business in loans, deposits, bills of exchange, etc., in contrast to the international banking activities of a *banchiere*, in Bologna, Florence, Siena, etc. The term originally meant money-changer, but in the available sources of the 13th and later centuries, it apparently means more than a simple money-changer)." Ibid., 56.

5 "Largo (shortened form of *fiorino largo*); large gold florin (in Florence)." Ibid., 150.

6 "Quattrino; 1. a small copper coin, worth 4 *denari* (in Florence)." Ibid., 233.

7 Although Antoninus here does not give a specific reference for the quote he attributes to the Archdeacon (Guido de Baysio), in *Sum.* 2.1.7 he cites the Archdeacon commenting on C. 14 q. 1 c. 1 (given as C. 14 q. 4 c. 1 in Mamachi's edition). In the Archdeacon's *Rosarium*, however, I have found nothing relevant at either of those places. Lorenzo Ridolfi and

pro pensione et ministris. Ratio enim laboris et expensarum habenda est, *Extra, De uoto, Magne*. Vnde de se tale cambium est licitum: sed fit illicitum, uel quia plus accipiunt quam sit communiter consuetum uel quia dant monetas diminutas in pondere uel numero; et tenentur ad satisfactionem uel pauperibus erogandum.

1.2. Cambium per litteram.

Est aliud cambium quod dicitur per litteram, quod sic celebratur. Dat quis campsori uel merchatori Florentie centum florenos restituendos sibi uel alteri pro eo Rome ubi illis indiget, et hoc ut securius et aptius illos habeat, pro quo litteram cambii campsor facit, scribens alteri campsori Rome ut ad requisitionem portantis talem litteram tali det centum florenos Florentie receptos. Et sic Rome centum florenos sibi assignantur secundum litteram. Et inde campsor lucratur, siue propter uarietatem ualoris monetarum quia centum florenos quos Florentie recipit campsor plus ualent quam ualeant Rome, siue quia etiam Rome dabuntur sibi centum minus aliquibus solidis. Aut etiam econuerso, quando de Roma sibi faceret transmicti peccuniam quam quis ibi habet et per campsorem cum littera cambii, ex quo campsor lucratur. Et cum hoc non sit mutuum nec uenditio peccunie, sed contractus innominatus do ut des, deseruiens utilitati hominum rationabiliter, quod inde lucretur ratione laboris et expensarum et periculorum de se licitum uidetur, sequestratis fraudibus. Nemo enim cogitur de suo facere beneficium, 10 q. 2 *Precarie*, et 1 Cor. 9: *Quis umquam militat suis stipendiis?*

---

20 Ratio … **21** Magne] *X* 3.34.7 (*Magnae devotionis*), fortasse *Glossa ord.* s.v. *sine diminutione* (2:1284): praeter illam diminutionem, quae fieret in pecunia transferenda: quia ille qui eam portabit, suis expensis non militabit.

38 Nemo … **39** Precarie] C. 10 q. 2 c. 4 (*Precariae*[1]): Decrevit etiam sancta synodus, et imperialis auctoritas denuntiavit, ut a nulla potestate quis cogatur facere precariam de rebus proprie Deo et sanctis eius dicatis, cum ratio et usus obtineat neminem cui non vult contra utilitatem et rationem cogi de proprio facere beneficium.

39 Quis … **40** stipendiis] *1 Cor* 9.7: Quis militat suis stipendiis umquam? quis plantat vineam, et de fructu ejus non edit? quis pascit gregem, et de lacte gregis non manducat?

---

20 ministris] s- *a.c.* | Ratio … **21** Magne] *in marg super. add.* **21** illicitum] + multipliciter *a.c.* **23** satisfactionem] *ut vid.* **29** Florentie] Florent. *cod.* **34** habet] *ut vid.* **39** 9] 6 *cod.*

and employees. For one must take account of labour and expenses, *Extra*, *On vows*, c. 7.[8] Hence in itself this kind of exchange is licit; but it becomes illicit, either because the bankers take more than is the common custom or because they give coinage which has been reduced in weight or number, and they are bound to make satisfaction or to bestow it on the poor.

1.2. Exchange by bill. There is a second kind of exchange which is called exchange by bill, which is conducted in the following way. Someone gives to a banker or merchant in Florence 100 florins, to be returned to him or to a third party on his behalf in Rome where he needs them, and this is done so that he may have them more safely and conveniently; for which the banker prepares a bill of exchange, writing to another banker in Rome that at the request of the person carrying the bill he should give to the person the 100 florins which he received in Florence. And so in Rome 100 florins are granted to him in accordance with the bill. And the banker gains a profit from this, either because of the variation in the value of the currency, since the 100 florins which the banker receives in Florence are worth more <there> than they are worth in Rome, or also because in Rome 100 will be given minus a certain number of shillings. Or on the other hand, someone can order the money which he has in Rome transferred to him, again through a banker with a bill of exchange, from which the banker makes a profit. And since this is not a loan or a sale of money, but an "I give so that you give" innominate contract which serves human utility in a reasonable way, it seems in itself licit for someone to make a profit from this on account of labour and expenses and risk, assuming all frauds are excluded. For no one is compelled to provide a benefit out of his own property, C. 10 q. 2 c. 4,[9] and 1st Corinthians 9: *Who ever soldiers at his own expense?*[10]

Bernardino of Siena cite the Archdeacon on C. 14 q. 3 c. 1 (*Si foeneraveris*), at which place in the *Rosarium* there is mention of the impossibility of selling the use of money (fol. 221v).

The closest match I have found to Antoninus's wording here is in Lorenzo Ridolfi (Laur Rod.) *Tr. usur.*, part 2, q. 26 (no. 8 in TUI 7:22va), as well as at other places in the same work: 2, q. 18 (Armstrong, p. 205; no. 54 in TUI 7:21); 3, q. 1 (no. 4 in TUI 7:37vb). Indeed, Antoninus closely follows Lorenzo Ridolfi here.

On the notion that money is nonvendible, compare also Bern. Sen. *Evang. aet.* 39, 3, 1 (4:289); Thom. Aq. *sup. Sent.* 3, 37, 1, 6 (discussed by Noonan, *Scholastic Analysis of Usury*, 51–3).

8 *X* 3.34.7 (*Magnae devotionis*).

9 C. 10 q. 2 c. 4 (*Precariae*[1]): "The holy Synod also decreed, and imperial authority published it, that no one is to be compelled by any power to lease possessions properly dedicated to God and his saints, since law and usage obtain by which no one is to be compelled to render a benefit to one to whom he does not wish to do so, out of his own property against usefulness and reason."

10 *1 Cor* 9.7: "Who serveth as a soldier at any time, at his own charges? Who planteth a vineyard, and eateth not of the fruit thereof? Who feedeth the flock, and eateth not of the milk of the flock?"

1.3. Cambium sichum.

Est tertium genus cambii quod dicitur sichum seu sine littera seu ad | libras fol. 71r grossorum. Et una libra grossorum sunt X ducati. Fit autem sic tale cambium. Accipit quis X libras grossorum Florentie, id est centum ducatos, a campsore seu merchatore, quos sibi restituere debet inde ad mensem Florentie, et eo ualore quo ualebunt Venetiis centum ducati inde ad decendium a die celebrati contractus, id est acceptionis dicte peccunie. Et si plus uult tenere dictam quantitatem centum ducatos de mense in mensem, renouatur contractus modo predicto. Contingit autem quod centum ducati in X[a] die a receptione pecunie ualent Venetiis tantum, quantum tunc ualebant Florentie quando illos recepit, et sic campsor nil lucratur; aliquando minus ualent, et sic campsor uel merchator perdit quia illud minus sibi redditur de centum ualore, quo minus ualent; aliquando plus ualent, et tunc campsor lucratur illud plus. Et communiter ut in pluribus casibus plus ualent quando reddit quam cum accepit, quamuis aliquando, ut dictum est, <ualeant> minus: unde in capite anni semper reperitur in lucro et magno. Istud communiter censetur usurarium, quia ibi <est> mutuum et spes lucri in campsore, ex quibus duobus perficitur usura, 14 q. 3 *Si feneraueris*. Et hoc sentire uidetur Laurentius de Ridolfis in *Tractatu de usuris*. Nec excusat periculum uel dubium amictendi, id est quia minus possunt ualere illa centum tempore redditionis: tum quia in mutuo cum spe lucri, ar. *De usuris*, *Nauiganti*, tum quia raro contingit quod perdat.

---

41 Est … **55** magno] Cfr Laur. Rod. *Tr. usur.* 3, q. 1 (TUI 7:37v–38r).

56 mutuum … **57** feneraueris] C. 14 q. 3 c. 1 (*Si foeneraveris*): Quod autem preter summam emolumenta sectari sit usuras exigere, auctoritate Augustini probatur … Si feneraueris hominem, id est si tu mutuum dederis pecuniam tuam, a quo plus quam dedisti expectes, non pecuniam solam, sed aliquid plus quam dedisti, siue illud triticum sit, siue uinum, siue oleum, siue quodlibet aliud, si plus quam dedisti expectes accipere, fenerator es, et in hoc inprobandus, non laudandus.

57 Laurentius … **58** usuris] Laur. Rod. *Tr. usur.* 3, q. 1 (TUI 7:37v–38r): Et quia sub spe lucri et intentione plus percipiendi quam sit quod tunc mutuatur; quia ut plurimum sic contingit, et alias non mutuaret ipse mutuans, talia perpetrantur, consulo ut omnes abstineant, arg. supra eo. in civitate. in fi. bene facit quod not. Hosti. in summa eo. tit. §. an aliquo. ver. 4. et infra eo. c. fi. ubi ponit etiam Ioan. And. et facit text. cum glo. sua in decre. naviganti. in 2. responsio. infra eo.

59 tum … **60** Nauiganti] *X* 5.19.19 (*Naviganti*): Usurarius est, qui a debitore recipit aliquid ultra sortem, etiamsi suscipiat in se periculum. … Naviganti vel eunti ad nundinas certam mutuans pecuniae quantitatem, pro eo, quod suscipit in se periculum, recepturus aliquid ultra sortem, usurarius est censendus.

---

42 libra] libr. *cod.* **43** libras] libr. *cod.* | ducatos] ducat. *cod. et similiter passim* **45** Venetiis] Venet. *cod.* : Venetias F_3 *fol. 68vb* **54** ualeant] aliquando *cod.* | aliquando … minus] *scripsi cum Ballerini* : aliquando, ut dictum est, aliquando minus *cod. et* F_3 *fol. 68vb a.c.* : aliquando plus, ut dictum est, aliquando minus F_3 *fol. 68vb p.c. s.l.* **56** est] *supplevi cum Ballerini* **57** Ridolfis] Ridol. *cod.* : Ridolfis F_3 *fol. 68vb* **58** Nec] Et *a.c.* **59** tum … **60** lucri] *cod.* : F_3 *fol. 68vb in marg. dext. add.* aliquid sperare non licet : *Ballerini scr.* tum quia in mutuo aliquid sperare non licet

1.3. Dry exchange. There is a third kind of exchange which is called dry or bill-less or exchange into pounds of groats.[11] And one pound of groats equals 10 ducats. Now this sort of exchange occurs in the following way. Someone receives 10 pounds of groats in Florence, i.e., 100 ducats, from a banker or merchant, which he is obliged to repay in Florence a month from then, and at the value which 100 ducats were worth in Venice ten days after the contract was concluded, i.e., when the said money was received. And if he wants to hold the said quantity of 100 ducats from month to month, the contract is renewed in the way just described. Now it happens that 100 ducats on the tenth day after the money was accepted are worth in Venice the same amount as they were then worth in Florence when they were accepted, and thus the banker makes no profit; sometimes they are worth less, and thus the banker or merchant takes a loss, because by however much the value of 100 ducats is reduced, that much less is paid back to him; sometimes they are worth more, and then the banker takes that much profit. And commonly, more often than not, they are worth more at the time of repayment than when received, although sometimes, as was said, they are worth less; hence at year-end[12] it is always turned into a profit, and a large one. This is commonly considered usurious, because there <is> a loan with the hope of profit on the part of the banker, from which two elements usury is effected, C. 14 q. 3 c. 1.[13] And Lorenzo Ridolfi seems to be of this opinion in his *Treatise on Usury*.[14] Nor is it excused by the risk or possibility of loss, i.e., because the 100 may be worth less at the time of repayment: both because this is within a loan with hope of profit, by the argument of *On usury*, c. 19,[15] and because it rarely

11 In the whole paragraph that follows, Antoninus appears to be again drawing on Lorenzo Ridolfi, expanding on *Tr. usur.* 3, q. 1 (TUI 7:37v–38r).

12 Lat. *caput anni.* "Capo d'anno; end of the (fiscal) year." Edler, *Terms of Business*, 62.

13 C. 14 q. 3 c. 1 (*Si foeneraveris*): "That it is an exaction of usury to seek gains beyond the sum given is proven by the authority of Augustine … If you have lent to a man at interest, that is, if you have given your money in loan, and you expect to receive something more than what you gave, and not the money alone, but something more than you gave, whether you receive it in wheat, or in wine, or in oil, or in anything else, if you expect to receive more than you gave, you are a lender at interest, and in this you are to be condemned, and not to be praised."

14 Laur. Rod. *Tr. usur.* 3, q. 1 (TUI 7:37v–38r).

15 *X* 5.19.19 (*Naviganti*).

De hiis tamen tribus generibus cambii habes in secunda parte titulo primo c. de cambiis.

1.4. Cambium mixtum quod usuram sapere uidetur.

Est et quartum genus cambii quod frequenter modernis temporibus celebratur, quod dicitur per litteram, dissimile tamen a secundo quod dicitur etiam per litteram. Et uidetur quoddam mixtum ex secundo et tertio, et magis trahi ad naturam tertii. Vnde et usuram sapere uidetur. Et fit hoc modo. Petrus indigens peccunia Florentie uel alibi existens petit a Martino campsore uel merchatore centum florenos, sibi tunc dandos ad rationem cambii per Venetias uel Barchinonam uel Neapolim et huiusmodi, quod intelligitur quod Petrus faciet restituere ipsi Martino illa centum Venetiis Barchinone uel Neapoli prout conuentum est inter eos eo ualore quo ualebunt ipsa centum de illa moneta que ibi currit, quando littera cambii presentabitur ibi, in capite uidelicet quindene uel mensis uel pluris temporis, secundum distantiam loci a ciuitate ubi recipitur peccunia ad ciuitatem ubi redditur: et sic mictitur littera cambii. Et ipsa recepta peccunia redditur per factorem illius qui peccuniam acceperat, sed de illa moneta ibi currente: et ex hoc campsor seu merchator lucratur, quia communiter plus ibi recipit quam dederit, et hoc ratione uariationis ualoris dicte monete in ibi, licet etiam aliquando non lucretur uel aliquid perdat ipse mercator.

Queritur utrum hoc sit licitum: et uidetur quod sic. Nam simile uidetur ac si quis procuraret magnam quantitatem habere bononenorum Florentie, ubi unus ualet 24 denarios, et deferret eos Bononiam uel alio ubi ualeret 26 denarios. Sed hoc nullus illicitum assereret tale lucrum industrie, quia hic tantum dat de bononenis quantum ualent Florentie, scilicet 24 denarios, et Bononie uel alibi tantum permutando cum alia moneta quantum ibi ualet, scilicet 26 denarios, accipit. Quod autem accipiat plus duos denarios de uno quam sibi constiterit, hoc facit uarietas ualoris monete magis in uno locho quam alio, sicut et de quibuscumque mercibus constat quod ualent plus in uno locho quam alio, sic et in dicto cambio uidetur. Sed responderi potest

---

61 in … **62** cambiis] Ant. Flor. *Summa* 2.1.7.47–50 (apud M_1 fol. Vr, 30rff. et Ballerini 2: 122b–125; 2.1.6.47–50 apud Mamachi 2:165–70): *de cambiis* (vel *canbiis*).

---

62 de cambiis] de usuris *a.c.* **69** Neapolim] Neapol. *cod.* **76** moneta] *bis a.c. ut vid.* **78** monete] *cod.* : + date F_3 *fol. 68vb s.l. ut vid.* **81** bononenorum] *cod.* : bonenorum F_3 *fol. 68vb* **82** denarios] denar. *cod. et similiter passim* **83** assereret] *ut vid.* **84** bononenis] *cod.* : bonenis F_3 *fol. 68vb* | denarios] *in marg. sin. add.* **87** ualoris] monete *a.c.* **87** locho] + magis *a.c.* **88** plus] *in marg. dext. add.*

happens that the banker loses. However, there is a treatment of these three kinds of exchange in the second part, title 1, the chapter on exchanges.[16]

1.4. Mixed exchange which seems to savour of usury.

There is also a fourth kind of exchange which is frequently conducted in modern times, which is called exchange by bill, yet it differs from the second kind of exchange which is also called exchange by bill. And it seems a kind of mixture of the second and third kinds, and drawn more to the nature of the third. Hence it also seems to savour of usury. And it is done in the following way. Peter, who is in Florence or some other city and needs money, asks for 100 florins from Martin, a banker or merchant, to be paid to him then at the rate of exchange "through Venice" (or Barcelona or Naples or what have you). This is understood to mean that Peter will have that 100 florins repaid to this Martin in Venice (or Barcelona or Naples) as was agreed between them, at the value which that 100 will have in terms of the currency which circulates there when the bill of exchange is presented there, namely at the end of 15 days or a month or a longer period corresponding to the distance from the city where the money was received to the city where it is repaid. And thus a bill of exchange is sent. And the money originally received is repaid through an agent of the one who received the money, but in the currency that circulates there: and from this the banker or merchant makes a profit, because commonly he receives there more than he gave, and this is because of the variation in value of the said currency there, although sometimes the merchant does not make a profit or takes some loss.

It is asked whether this is licit: and it appears that it is. For it seems comparable to someone arranging to buy a great quantity of *bolognini*[17] in Florence, where one is worth 24 pence, and then conveying them to Bologna or another place, where one is worth 26 pence. But no one would assert that this kind of profit from one's industry is illicit, because he only pays for *bolognini* the amount they are worth in Florence, namely 24 pence, and in Bologna or elsewhere when he exchanges them for another currency he only receives the amount they are worth there, namely 26 pence. Now, that he receives for one *bolognino* two more pence than it cost him, this is produced by the variation in the value of money, higher in one place than in another. This is a well-known fact in relation to merchandise of whatever sort – that it is worth more in one place than in another – and so also seems to be the case in the aforesaid kind of exchange. But one can reply that it is not comparable. For in the case of merchandise, there is no loan, as is self-evident, but a real exchange of goods, in which it is licit to hope for and seek a profit. In the aforesaid exchange, however, although it is called an "exchange," nevertheless

16 ANT. FLOR. *Summa* 2.1.7.47–50 (apud M_1 fol. Vr, 30rff. et Ballerini 2:122b–125; 2.1.6.47–50 apud Mamachi 2:165–70): *de cambiis* (or *canbiis*).

17 On the *bolognino*, see Spufford, *Money and Its Use*, 326–7 (*b. grosso*); ibid., 322, 407 (*b. d'oro*).

quod non est simile. Nam ibi nullum est mutuum, ut patet de se, sed realis permutatio in qua licet sperare et querere lucrum. In cambio autem predicto, quamuis sic nominetur tamen realiter uidetur esse mutuum. Nam Petrus indigens Florentie peccuniis ut sibi prouideat, accipit sub mutuo a Martino illa centum sub nomine cambii per Venetias uel Barchinonam et huiusmodi, ibi restituenda, cum ibi non habeat aliquando mercimonium facere uel inde peccunias ad se retrahere. Ex quo mutuo ibi sibi restituendo Martinus sperat inde lucrari, unde usuram sapere uidetur, ar. 14 q. 3 *Plerique*. Ad quod satisfacit quod habetur in *Directorio iuris*. Vbi querit Petrus quid iuris, cum quis mutuat peccuniam recepturus ad certum terminum alterius generis monetam uel aurum uel argentum uel aliam speciem? Et respondet dicendum secundum Hostiensem et Goffredum quod si hoc faciat ut in expectatione lucretur, usurarius est, ex quo fraudulenter uel mala intentione fit et aliquid inde sorti accedit, 14 q. 3 *Plerique*, et sic uidetur esse in proposito. Vnde male possunt excusari ab | usura mentali. fol. 71v

1.5. De usura in cambiis.

Et licet in *Summa Astensi* dicantur licita esse cambia, quia ars campsoria a quibusdam teologis in 4° dicitur licita, tum etiam quia utilis et necessaria rei publice sicut et negotiatio, tum etiam quia curia romana, ubi etiam

97 ar. … Plerique] C. 14 q. 3 c. 3 (*Plerique*): Et esca usura est; et uestis usura est, et quodcumque sorti accedit, usura est; quod uelis ei nomen imponas, usura est.

98 Directorio iuris] Petr. Ques. *Direct. iur.*, fortasse 3, 44 (fol. 264ra–269vb).

101 Hostiensem] Hostien. *Sum.* 5.19 *De usuris* §. 8 (1627): Quid si quis pecuniam mutuet, recepturus ad certum terminum, alterius generis monetam, vel aurum, vel argentum, vel aliam speciem? Respondeo, si ideo hoc facit, ut in aestimatione lucretur, usurarius est, secundum Goff.

101 Goffredum] Gauf. Tran. *Sum.* 5.19 *De usuris* §. 13 (221v): Quid si quis pecuniam mutuat recepturus in termino aurum vel argentum vel alterius generis monetam. Respondeo si ideo facit ut in estimatione lucratur usurarius est.

103 14 … Plerique] C. 14 q. 3 c. 3 (*Plerique*): vide supra.

105 Summa … cambia] Astes. *Sum.* 3.9 *De permutatione* a.5 (1:320–1): Sequitur videre de quinto, scilicet de arte campsoria, in qua commutatur pecunia pro pecunia, et quaeritur utrum sit licita? Respondetur secundum Alex. Lombardum in quolibet. q. de usuris, quod sic. Cuius signum est, quod Ecclesia damnat, et persequitur usurarios, non autem campsores, sed potius eis favet, ut patet in Ecclesia Romana. Ad cuius evidentiam sciendum, quod oportuit esse campsores, tum propter diversitatem nummismatum in diversis Regionibus, sicut in eadem diversifacantur; tum pro utilitate Legatorum diversae regiones circumeuntium; tum pro commutatione rerum necessariarum vitae hominum: Rerum enim commutatio est necessaria, quae non potest fieri commode sine nummismate, quia res commode ferri non possent ad loca remota pro commutatione facienda, et ideo necessarium fuit nummisma; Necessaria igitur fuit ars campsoria.

106 quibusdam … 4°] Ut Astes. ibid. et Alex. Lomb. *Tr. usur.* c. 7 (fol. 167ra–168rb).

96 se] + reuochare seu *a.c. ut vid.* | mutuo] + Mar- *a.c.* **97** Ad] V(t) *a.c.* **98** querit] queritur *a.c. ut vid.* **101** Goffredum] Goff. *cod.* **105** Astensi] Astens. *cod.* : Astensis F_3 *fol. 69ra*

in reality it seems to be a loan. For Peter, needing money in Florence in order to provide for himself, receives that 100 as a loan from Martin in a so-called "exchange through Venice or Barcelona" or what have you, to be repaid there, when he does not ever have any business to carry out there or money to bring back to himself from there. From this loan to be repaid there, Martin hopes to make a profit; hence it seems to savour of usury, by the argument of C. 14 q. 3 c. 3.[18] On this point what is written in the *Directory of Law* seems to suffice.[19] There, Peter <Quesnel> asks what is the law when one lends money, expecting to receive at an established term coinage of another kind, whether gold or silver or other *specie*? And he answers that, following Hostiensis[20] and Goffredo,[21] if he does this so that he may make a profit on account of the delay, he is a usurer, for the reason that it is done fraudulently or with a bad intention, and something is added therefrom to the capital, C. 14 q. 3 c. 3,[22] and thus it seems to be in this case. Hence he can hardly be excused from mental usury.

1.5. Usury in exchanges. And although in the *Summa Astensis* exchange transactions are said to be licit,[23] reasoning that the bankers' craft is described as licit by certain theologians commenting on the fourth book,[24] both because this craft is useful and necessary for the commonwealth, just like trade, and because the Roman curia, where banking is also done, tolerates it; nevertheless those arguments do not seem sufficient to excuse usury. For we concede that the bankers' craft is in itself licit, as was said in relation to the first and second kinds of exchange; but not everything which is called an "exchange" is licit, because in the aforesaid case there does not appear to be an exchange but a loan. In the same way trade too, although in itself it can be carried out licitly, can also be carried out in a usurious way, as in c. 6, *On usury*,[25] and then it is not licit. That

18 C. 14 q. 3 c. 3 (*Plerique*): "And food is usury, dress is usury, and whatever is added to the capital [or principal] is usury; whatever name you wish to use for it, it is usury."

19 Petr. Ques. *Direct. iur.*, perhaps book 3 tit. 44 (fol. 264ra–269vb); see Langholm, *Merchant in the Confessional*, 66–8.

20 Hostien. *Sum.* 5.19 *De usuris* §. 8 (1627).

21 Gauf. Tran. *Sum.* 5.19 *De usuris* §. 13 (221v).

22 C. 14 q. 3 c. 3 (*Plerique*): see above.

23 Astes. *Sum.* 3.9 *De permutatione* a. 5 (1:320–1).

24 Such as Astes. and Alex. Lomb. *Tr. usur.* c. 7 (fol. 167ra–168rb); see Noonan, *Scholastic Analysis of Usury*, 183–4.

25 *X* 5.19.6 (*In civitate*).

exercetur, tollerat: ista non uidentur sufficere ad excusandum usuram. Nam conceditur quod ars campsoria de se sit licita, ut in primo et secundo genere cambii dictum est; sed non in omni eo quod dicitur cambium, quia in dicto casu non uidetur cambium sed mutuum; sicut et negotiatio, quamuis licite de se fieri possit, potest etiam fieri cum usura, ut in c. *In ciuitate*, *De usuris*, et tunc non licita. Quod etiam dicatur utilis et necessaria rei publice, etiam non excusat, quia et rei publice etiam est utile haberi prostibula ad obuiandum maioribus malis, et publichos feneratores ad subueniendum indigentiis multorum, ne si eis non prouideretur uel sic machinentur malum contra ciuitatem; et tamen nullus dicit propter hec illa non esse mortalia et dampnabilia facientibus ea. Sic et in proposito, quamuis multis sit hoc utile non tamen excusat facientes talia cum usura uideatur. Quod curia romana tollerat etiam non ualet, quia non propter hoc intelligitur approbare, cum non declarauerit hoc licere. Nam et tollerat concubinatus multorum curialium, quia forte male posset auferre; nec tamen dubium <est> quod non approbat. Vnde Crisostomus: "Quod permictimus, nolentes precipimus," id est "permictimus" secundum glossam, "quia malas hominum uoluntates ad plenum prohibere non possumus," 31 q. 1 *Hac ratione*. Et *Extra*, *De preben.*, *Cum iam dudum*, dicitur: "Multa per patientiam tolleramus, que" si ad iudicium reduceremus, cassarentur. Vnde saluo meliori iudicio, uidetur tale cambium sapere usuram, quod tamen multum frequentatur. Et multos doctissimos et Deum timentes audiui sic tenere.

---

111 negotiatio … **112** usuris] *X* 5.19.6 (*In civitate*): Vendens rem plus, quam valeat, quia solutionem differt, peccat …

123 permictimus … **124** glossam] *Glossa ord.* ad idem s.v. *precipimus* (1:2083–4): id est, permittimus.

123 Crisostomus … **125** ratione] CHRYS. (pseudo) *Opus imperf.* in C. 31 q. 1 c. 9 (*Hac ratione*): Quod enim permittimus nolentes precipimus, quia malas hominum uoluntates ad plenum prohibere non possumus.

125 Extra … **127** cassarentur] *X* 3.5.18 (*Cum iam dudum*): … quum multa per patientiam tolerentur, quae, si deducta fuerint in iudicium, exigente iustitia non debeant tolerari.

---

114 prostibula] prostribula *cod. et* F_3 *fol. 69ra* **116** ciuitatem] *cod.* : *Ballerini scr.* caritatem **118** in] + casu *a.c.* **121** concubinatus] concubinat. *cod.* : concubinatus F_3 *fol. 69ra* : concubinatum *Ballerini* | curialium] + uel *a.c. ut vid.* **122** posset] poss. *cod.* | est] *supplevi cum Ballerini* **125** 31] 30 *cod.* **127** uidetur] + puta *a.c. ut vid.*

this exchange transaction may well be described as useful and necessary to the commonwealth also does not excuse it, because it is likewise useful to the commonwealth that brothels[26] be maintained to prevent worse evils, and public moneylenders be allowed to assist the needs of many people, lest, were this not provided for them, they might even plot some evil against the city; and yet nobody says on this account that these are not mortal sins and condemnable in those who carry them out. Thus also in the case under discussion, although this type of exchange is useful for many people, nevertheless that does not excuse those carrying out such activity, since it seems to be usury. That the Roman curia tolerates it also does not suffice, since the curia is not on this account to be understood as approving, when it has not declared this to be licit. For the curia also tolerates the concubinage of many of its members, because perhaps it could hardly get rid of all concubinage; yet there is no doubt that the curia does not approve of it. Whence Chrysostom: "What we allow, we unwillingly command," that is "we permit" according to the gloss, "because we cannot fully forbid the wicked wills of men," C. 31 q. 1 c. 9.[27] And in *Extra*, *On prebends*, c. 18, it is said: "We tolerate many things through patience, which," were we brought to judgment, should be made to cease.[28] Hence, with due respect for a better judgment, this kind of exchange seems to savour of usury, although it is nevertheless used very frequently. And I have heard many very learned and God-fearing men hold this opinion.

26 Or "prostitutes."

27 Chrys. (pseudo) *Opus imperf.* in C. 31 q. 1 c. 9 (*Hac ratione*): "For what we allow, we command unwilling, because we cannot fully forbid the wicked wills of men." See also *Glossa ord.* ad idem s.v. *precipimus*.

28 *X* 3.5.18 (*Cum iam dudum*).

1.6. De usura mentali.

Videtur tamen talis campsor usurarius mentalis censendus, de quo usurario, scilicet qui est mentalis, dicunt Bernardus Innocentius Goffredus et Hostiensis, ut refertur in *Directorio iuris*, quod inducendus est in foro penitentiali ut restituat, per c. *Consuluit, De usuris*. Et inducendus est non compellendus, scilicet in iudicio contentioso, ut restituat, nec tamquam usurarius est puniendus. Sed quoad Deum uere est usurarius et sic accepta tenetur restituere, quia sola intentio facit usurarium, quod intellige cum effectu

---

131 Bernardus] Bern. Parm. in *Glossa ord.* ad *X* 5.19.10 (*Consuluit*) s.v. *male agere* (2:1739): ibi quo ad formam contractus usurarii non dicuntur: sed isti propter intentionem quam habuerunt, iudicandi sunt in iudicio animae male agere: et inducendi sunt, sed non compellendi, ut sic recepta restituant: nec tamquam usurarii puniendi sunt, sed reuera quo ad Deum usurarii uidentur, quia restituere tenentur sic accepta. Et hic habes manifeste, quod intentio facit hominem usurarium: intellige cum effectu. sic et expectatio. 14. q. 3. c. 1. et q. 4. si quis clericus. B. Vel fortasse Bern. Pap. *Sum.* 5.15 *De usuris* n. 7–9 (236–8).

131 Innocentius] Inno. IV. *Comm.* ad *X* 5.19.10 s.v. *pro intentione* (517v): si creditor principaliter intentionem habet ad lucrum, usura est, vel malum lucrum, alias si secundario aliquid sperat, secus 61. di. quid proderit. 59. di. si officia. Item recipere ex tali spe secundario, non est malum. 2. q. 2. quam pio. quia tenetur ei ad antidora. ff. de pet. haere. si lega. infra de testa. cum in officiis. sed et qui principalem habent intentionem ad usuram, licet usurarius sit, non tenetur restituere. arg. infra de simo. c. ult. nisi forte aliquid faceret, quare debitor, et si non voluntarie, tamen necessario ei daret, puta quia negat sibi terminum, nisi det aliquid, et ibi plus vendidit propter dilationem, quia tunc restituere tenetur. 14. q. 5. non sane. in fi. Alii tamen dicunt, quod semper tenetur restituere, et est tutus (inducendi) si autem agere posset conditione, ex hoc canone, quaeritur?

131 Goffredus] Gauf. Tran. *Sum.* 5.19 *De usuris* §. 12–13 (221r–222r).

132 Hostiensis] Hostien. *Sum.* 5.19 *De usuris* §. 8 (5:1620–1): An aliquo casu ultra sortem quicquam licite exigatur. … Tertio, quando sine omni pacto datur gratis oblatum. caueas tamen de intentione praua, quia si illam haberes, principaliter in foro poenitentiali, inducendus es, ut illud, quod ultra sortem accepisti, reddas, ut infra eodem consuluit. et c. in ciuitate. et no. supra de simo. §. quid sit simonia, et supra §. i. ver. pactione. Sed cfr Hostien. *Comm.* ad *X* 5.19.10 s.v. *pro intentione* (4:57v): Quid si principalem intentionem ad usuram habuit? Dicunt quidam, quod licet talis usurarius sit, non tamen tenetur restituere, nisi forte aliquid faceret, quare debitor et si non sponte tamen necessario ei det, puta, quia negat terminum, nisi plus vendat, vel aliquid ultra donet, quia tunc tenetur restituere, ut patet ex praemissis. et 24. q. v. non sane. in fine. secundum istos igitur non nocet mentalis usura, sicut nec simonia, quantum ad restitutionem sic receptorum, sed alias per solam poenitentiam aboletur, ut supra de simo. c. fi. Alii dicunt, quod semper tenetur restituere, ex quo hac intentione ducitur principali, quod tutius est secundum d. n. Immo hoc ultimum verissimum est, et aliud falsissimum, ut patet in praece. gl. et infra eodem c. in fi. Nec obstat supra de simonia. c. fi. aliud enim est in usura, ut hic, et aliud in simo. ut ibi. et quae sit diversitatis ratio. ibi. no.

132 ut … iuris] Petr. Ques. *Direct. iur.*, fortasse 3, 44 (fol. 264ra–269vb).

133 Consuluit … usuris] *X* 5.19.10 (*Consuluit*): Mutuans ea mente, ut ultra sortem aliquid recipiat, tenetur in foro animae ad illud restituendum, si ex hoc aliquid consecutus est.

---

130 usurarius] + mag(is) *a.c. ut vid.*

1.6. Mental usury. It seems that a banker who engages in this kind of exchange must be considered a mental usurer, about whom, namely the sort of usurer who commits it mentally, Bernard,[29] Innocent, Goffredo, and Hostiensis say, as is reported in the *Directory of Law*,[30] that he is to be urged in the penitential forum to make restitution, with reference to c. 10, *On usury*.[31] And he is to be urged not compelled, i.e., in a contentious judgment, to make restitution, but he is not to be punished as a usurer. But in the eyes of God he is truly a usurer and thus is bound to restore what he has received, because the intention alone makes a usurer – and understand that this has the effect of obliging him to make restitution, namely when he has received something beyond the principal, as in the

29 Most likely Bern. Parm. in *Glossa ord.* ad *X* 5.19.10 (*Consuluit*), but possibly Bern. Pap. *Sum.* 5.15 *De usuris* n. 7–9 (236–8).

30 Petr. Ques. *Direct. iur.*, perhaps book 3 tit. 44 (fol. 264ra–269vb); see Langholm, *Merchant in the Confessional*, 66–8.

31 Bern. Parm. in *Glossa ord.* ad *X* 5.19.10 (*Consuluit*) s.v. *male agere* (2:1739); Inno. IV *Comm.* ad *X* 5.19.10 s.v. *pro intentione* (517v); Gauf. Tran. *Sum.* tit. *De usuris* §. 12–13 (221r–222r); Hostien. *Sum.* 5.19 *De usuris* §. 8 (5:1620–1). Sed cfr Hostien. *Comm.* ad *X* 5.19.10 s.v. *pro intentione* (4:57v).

quantum ad obligationem restitutionis, cum scilicet accepit ultra sortem, ut 14 q. 3 per totum. Sic talis in tali mutuo, quod cambium dicitur, intendit lucrum, alias non facturus.

Alii forte dicerent non esse mutuum sed cambium realiter; sed utrum uerum sit, ipsi uiderint. Nam si appellant contractum innominatum, do ut des, etiam ibi potest esse implicitum mutuum, ut aliquando contingit in contractu emptionis et uenditionis, et potest ibi esse usura, *De usuris*, c. *In ciuitate*.

1.7. Cambium in curia Romana quod uidetur magis illicitum.

In romana curia fit aliud genus cambii per campsores seu merchatores quod uidetur magis etiam illicitum et usurarium. Nam beneficia uel dignitates inibi accipientes cum habeant soluere annatam seu primos fructus beneficii, ut dicitur pro medietate chamere apostolice, infra breue tempus secundum taxam que ibi habetur, accipiunt prelati seu beneficiati ipsi sub nomine cambii a campsoribus soluenda apostolice chamere, obligantes se ad restituendum ipsa in partibus illis ubi sunt benficiati et de illa moneta ibi currente. Et ultra lucrum quod consequuntur ex uarietate monetarum ibi restituendarum, uolunt sibi dari tantum pro centenario, puta V uel VII uel plus et minus secundum diuturnitatem temporis, maiorem uel minorem, qua habent expectare redditionem peccunie sue. Et instrumentum fieri faciunt obligationis debiti, non solum peccunie mutuate sed etiam usure addite, tamquam totum sit de

---

137 14 … **138** totum] C. 14 q. 3 c. 1–4. Vide C. 14 q. 3 c. 1 Gr.a.: Quod autem preter summam emolumenta sectari sit usuras exigere…. Cfr *Glossa ord.* ad idem s.v. *quod autem*: Hic intitulatur tertia quaestio, in qua quaeritur utrum sit usura, si aliquid praeter sortem exigatur? Et certum est quod sic, nisi cum ecclesia mutuat pecuniam laico, ad hoc ut praedium ecclesiasticum de manu laici redimatur, quo casu fructus ecclesiastici fundi praeter sortem retinebit, ut dicit Innocentius III in prima decretali, de feu., Alexander, de usu., in prima decretali, in fine. Similiter non licet aliquid expectare praeter sortem, ut infra ead. c. 1. Spes enim facit usurarium, sicut simoniacum, arg. 1 q. 3 c. Non solum.
143 De … ciuitate] *X* 5.19.6 (*In civitate*): vide supra.

---

143 ciuitate] *hic add.* F_3 *fol. 69rb haec verba in novo paragrapho* Dominus Lau. de Ridolfis in tractatu prolixo quem edidit de usuris, et multum eleganti super decretali *Consuluit*, *De usuris*, in 3a parte operis mouet istam questionem, et postquam disputando rationes induxit ad ostendendum talem contractum licitum siue cambium dicatur mutuum siue permutatio. In fine sic concludit: respondeo unico uerbo secundum ea que supra scripsi, q. 27, ubi ista dilucidantur, et infra q. 4or illam sequenti. Et subdit: quia sub spe lucri et intentione plus percipiendi quam sit illud quod mutuatur, et quia ut plurimum sic contingit et aliter (*vel* alias) mutuans non mutuaret, talia perpetrantur, consulo ut omnes abstineant, ar. *In ciuitate*, *De usuris* in fi. Et bene facit ad hoc quod no(tat?) Hosti. in *Summa*. In illis autem questionibus ad quas remittit, uidetur ex similibus dictum contractum cambiorum predictorum esse usurarium. **145** beneficia] p- *a.c.* | uel dignitates] *in marg. sin. add.* **149** soluenda] -ns *a.c. ut vid.* **150** ipsa] -m *a.c.* **151** ex] + cambio *a.c.* **153** temporis] + qua *a.c.* **154** obligationis debiti] mutui *a.c.*

whole of C. 14 q. 3.[32] And just so, such a person in this sort of loan, which is called an exchange, intends a profit, otherwise he would not do it.

Some may perhaps say that it is not a loan but in reality an exchange; but whether this is true, they themselves shall see. For if they call it an "I give so that you give" innominate contract, even in such a contract there can be an implicit loan, as sometimes happens in a contract of buying and selling, and there can be usury present, *On usury*, c. 6.[33]

1.7. Particularly illicit exchange carried out in the Roman curia.

In the Roman curia another kind of exchange is carried out by bankers or merchants which seems even more illicit and usurious. For those receiving benefices or dignities there, when they have to pay the first year's revenue or first fruits of the benefice, "for the portion of the apostolic treasury," as is said, within a short time according to the tax which is in force there, the prelates or beneficed clerics themselves receive as a so-called "exchange" from the bankers the amount they need to pay to the apostolic treasury, obliging themselves to repay it in the regions where they are beneficed and in the currency which circulates there. And beyond the profits which follow from the difference of currencies to be repaid there, they want also so much per cent to be given to them, say 5 or 7 or more or less according to the length of time, greater or smaller, during which they have to await repayment of their money. And they have an instrument prepared of the debt owed, not only of the money lent but also of the added usury, as though the whole thing represented the capital: so that if they lend 1000 and the bankers want in the regions <of the benefice> to have 1050 on account of the loan, the instrument specifies 1050 lent to be repaid at such time. Hence, since on account of the interval of time they seek that additional amount, i.e., 50, it is not evident how this sort of contract can be defended from the charge of usury, by the argument of C. 14 q. 3 c. 1 along with c. 2, and *On usury*, c. 10 and c.

32 C. 14 q. 3 c. 1–4. See C. 14 q. 3 c. 1 Gr. a.: "That it is an exaction of usury to seek gains beyond the sum given …"

Cfr *Glossa ord.* ad idem s.v. *that it is an exaction*: "Here begins the third question, in which it is asked whether it is usury if something more than the sum given is exacted? And it is certain that it is, except when a Church lends money to a layman so that an ecclesiastical estate may be redeemed from the hand of a layman, in which case he shall retain the fruits of the ecclesiastical estate beyond the sum lent, as Innocent III says in the decretal at Decretals 3.20.1, and Alexander in the decretal at Decretals 5.19.1, toward the end. Similarly, it is not licit to expect anything beyond the sum lent, as below, C. 14 q. 3 c. 1. Indeed, mere hope makes a usurer, just as is the case with a simoniac, as is argued at C. 1 q. 3 c. 11."

33 *X* 5.19.6 (*In civitate*).

At this point in the manuscript F_3 (fol. 69rb) there is another paragraph, presented as part of Antoninus's original text. It praises Lorenzo Ridolfi's treatment of the topic of mental usury in these sorts of exchanges, and recommends his conclusion that people should be counselled to avoid them, since they appear to be usurious.

capitali: ut si mutuant mille et campsores uolunt in partibus habere mille et quinquaginta ratione mutui, instrumentum continet mille quinquaginta mutuata tali tempore restituenda. Vnde cum ratione dilationis temporis illud plus petant, scilicet 50, quomodo ab usura possit defendi contractus talis, non uidetur, ar. 14 q. 3 *Si feneraris* cum c. sequen., et *De usuris*, *Consuluit* et c. *In ciuitate*, et D. 88 *Eiciens*. Solent autem tales campsores excusare tale lucrum ratione periculi, dicentes quia si prelatus moreretur in uia amicterent totam peccuniam mutuatam, uel etiam sine casu mortis posset contingere quod in partibus sibi non restitueretur. Sed hoc non uidetur uerum. Nam | nisi essent fol. 72r prius in curia bene securi de peccunia mutuata per satisdationem aliquorum ibi existentium, non mutuarent. Etsi obiciatur per exemplum a simili. Nam concedunt doctores quod cum quis uolens et intendens actu de peccunia quam habet negotiari sperans inde sibi lucrum uerisimiliter euenire, quidam hoc sciens et indigens peccunia illum rogat quod illam peccuniam cum qua est paratus negotiari et lucrari sibi mutuet, et propter hoc dabit sibi lucrum quod in illo dubio potest rationabiliter extimari, licite posse mutuare et lucrum illud accipere; nec est usura sed ut interesse petitur, id est uitatio sui dampni, cum non moueatur intentione lucrandi ex mutuo quod est usura, sed seruiendi proximo cum uitatione tamen sui dampni. Nemo enim debet cum iactura

---

160 ar. … **161** Eiciens] C. 14 q. 3 c. 1 (*Si foeneraveris*); C. 14 q. 3 c. 2 (*Putant quidam*); *X* 5.19.10 (*Consuluit*); *X* 5.19.6 (*In civitate*); D. 88 c. 11 (*Eiciens*).

167 concedunt doctores] Ut Hostien. *Comm.* ad *X* 5.19.16 (*Salubriter*) n. 4–5 (4:58v–59r): In eo enim quod sorti accedit, non prohibetur petitio interesse, sed tantum turpis lucri, vel alterius illiciti incrementi, ut patet. 14. q. ini. si quis oblitus. Ideo puto ex mente praemissorum iurium, quod si aliquis sit mercator, qui consueuit sequi mercata et nundinas, et ibi multa lucrari, mihi multum indigenti, ex charitate mutuaret pecuniam, cum qua negotiaturus erat, quod ego exinde sibi ad suum interesse remaneo obligatus, dummodo nihil fiat hic in fraudem usurarum, ut patet in eo, quod notatur. supra eo. tuas. in fin. Et dummodo dictus mercator non consueuerit pecuniam suam taliter tradere ad usuram. argu. in eo quod legitur, et no. supra e. consuluit. §. i. Dominus tamen noster scripsit contrarium, ut no. infra eod. ca. fina. respon. primo. Vide etiam Petr. Olivi *Quodl.* 1, 17, co. (398); Astes. *Sum.* 3.11 *De usuris* a.4 (1:330); Laur. Rod. *Tr. usur.* 2, 24 (no. 6 in TUI 7:22v); Bern. Sen. *Evang. aet.* 42, 2, 2 (4:358–9). Sed contra cfr Io. And. *Novella* ad *X* 5.19.19 (*Naviganti*) n. 5 (4:77v), Inno. IV° citato. Cfr Thom. Aq. *Sum. th.* 2a 2ae q. 78 a. 2 ob. 1 et ad 1; *De malo* q. 13 a. 4 ad 14.

174 Nemo … **175** 6°] *VI* 5.[13.]48 (*Locupletari*): Locupletari non debet aliquis cum alterius iniuria vel iactura.

---

156 campsores uolunt] campsor uult *a.c.* | partibus] *cod.* : + illis F_3 *fol. 69rb s.l. et Ballerini* **157** et] *s.l.* **161** et … Eiciens] *in marg. sin. add.* **161** campsores] + se *a.c.* **167** quod] *p.c.* : + licitum *a.c. ut vid.* **168** euenire] + exaduerso *a.c. ut vid.*

6, and D. 88 c. 11.[34] But such bankers are accustomed to excuse such profit on account of risk, saying that if the prelate were to die on the road they would lose all of the money lent, or even apart from the case of death it could happen that in the regions <of the benefice> the money is not repaid to them. But this does not appear to be true. For unless they were well secured beforehand at the curia for the money lent, through some people present there standing surety, they would not lend. However, an objection is made through an example from a similar case. For the doctors concede that when a person wants and intends to engage in trade through making use of money which he has, hoping that a profit will genuinely be produced for himself from it, and someone, knowing this and needing money, asks that he lend him that money with which he was prepared to engage in trade and to make a profit, and because of this he will pay him the profit which can reasonably be estimated in the state of uncertainty, the trader is able to lend and receive that profit licitly; nor is this usury, but it is sought as interest, that is, the avoidance of his loss, since he is not moved by the intention of making a profit from a loan, which is usury, but of serving his neighbour, yet while avoiding his own loss.[35] For, "no one ought to obtain an advantage to the detriment of another," *On the rules of law, Liber Sext.*[36] Nevertheless the doctors say that although when this is really the case and is done without fraud <it is not usurious>,[37] it must not be recommended lest through this a road should be

34 C. 14 q. 3 c. 1 (*Si foeneraveris*); C. 14 q. 3 c. 2 (*Putant quidam*); *X* 5.19.10 (*Consuluit*); *X* 5.19.6 (*In civitate*); D. 88 c. 11 (*Eiciens*).

35 Hostien. *Comm.* ad *X* 5.19.16 (*Salubriter*) n. 4–5 (4:58v–59r): "For, in what is added to the principal, the seeking of interest is not prohibited, but only the seeking of shameful gain or of other illicit increment, as appears in C. 14 q. 4 *Si oblitus*. Therefore, I think from the intention of the above laws, that if some merchant, who is accustomed to pursue trade and the commerce of the fairs and there profit much, has, out of charity to me, who needs it badly, lent money with which he would have done business, I remain obliged from this to his *interesse*, provided that nothing is done in fraud of usury, as appears in what is noted in *Supra eo tuas, in fine*, and provided that said merchant will not have been accustomed to give his money in such a way to usury." English trans. from Noonan, *Scholastic Analysis of Usury*, 118. See also Petr. Olivi *Quodl.* 1, q. 17, co. (398); Astes. *Sum.* 3.11 *De usuris* a. 4 (1:330); Laur. Rod. *Tr. usur.* 2, 24 (no. 6 in TUI 7:22v); Bern. Sen. *Evang. aet.* 42, 2, 2 (4:358–9).
Disapproving any interest from the beginning of a loan, cfr Io. And. *Novella* ad *X* 5.19.19 (*Naviganti*) n. 5 (4:77v), citing Inno. IV. Cfr Thom. Aq. *Sum. th.* 2a 2ae q. 78 a. 2 ob. 1 and ad 1; *De malo* q. 13 a. 4 ad 14.

36 VI 5.[13.]48 (*Locupletari*): "No one ought to obtain an advantage to the detriment of another." English trans. from Gauthier, *Roman Law and … Canon Law*, 112.

37 The words I have angle-bracketed are not present in the autograph manuscript, but some such sense seems to be required in order to complete the thought; I have taken them from the place in *Summa* 2.1.7.15 where Antoninus discusses *lucrum cessans* (profit ceasing) as a title to interest (M_1 fol. 25r et Ballerini 2:98c–d; 2.1.6.15 apud Mamachi 2:136–8), paragraph beginning *quid si haberem peccuniam*. Note that the paragraphs which follow in Ballerini's edition, cols 98d–99b (from the words *quod enim licitus sit talis contractus* up to

alterius loquupletari, *De re. iu.*, *libro 6º*. Dicunt tamen etsi cum realiter fit et sine fraude <non usurarium sit>, non consulendum ne per hoc aperiatur uia fraudibus. Ergo a simili licitum uidetur in casu nostro: nam campsor ex carentia peccunie quam mutuat pro illo tempore, non potest cum ea negotiari et sic patitur iacturam. Respondeo quod non est simile: quia ille de quo positus est casus intendebat principaliter dare se negotiationi et peccuniam exercere in negotiatione licita. A casu autem est quod mutuet postea petenti sibi ut seruiat amicho, in quo tamen uult se indempnem seruare. Sed campsor principaliter intendit exercere tale mutuum quod cambium uocat, nec illi prelato mutuat ut seruiat, sed ut magis lucretur, quia magis per uiam illam lucratur quam per uiam negotiationis; et intentio lucri ex mutuo explicito uel implicito facit usurarium, ut in dicto c. *Si feneraueris*, 14 q. 3.

Hii etiam aliquando sunt mediatores in simoniis que fiunt in curia, offerentes munera intercedentibus pro beneficiis obtinendis pro prelatis suis amicis, unde et grauiter offendunt. Et hii sunt numularii de templo eiecti Io. 2, de quibus etiam dicitur 1 q. 1, *Si quis episcopus*: "Si quis mediator tam turpibus

---

176 non[2] … **177** fraudibus] Vide ANT. FLOR. *Summa* 2.1.7.15 (apud M_1 fol. 25r et Ballerini 2:98c–d; 2.1.6.15 apud Mamachi 2:136–8): Respondet Inno. in c. fi. e. ti. dicens quod licet quidam contrarium dicant, ipse putat hunc contractum usurarium, nec scit sic contrahentem excusare. Hosti. uero in c. *Salubriter* dicit quod talis est mihi obligatus ad interesse illius lucri quod facturus eram uerisimiliter ex peccunia, dummodo nil fiat in fraudem usurarium. Io. An. approbat dictum Inno. Et quod dicitur de interesse habet locum post moram debitoris, contrarium dicendo pararetur uia aperta ad fenus. Et hoc etiam placet Io. Cald. Sed Io. de Lig. dicit quod quamuis communiter teneatur cum Inno., ne uia fraudibus aperiatur; ipse tamen credit ueram oppinionem Hosti., dummodo nil fiat in fraudem. Tutum tamen est ab hoc abstinere, Lau. de Ridol. Quod etiam dicit Hosti. de lucro uidetur intelligendum deducto etiam dubio lucri, cum scilicet potuisset etiam non lucrari uel perdere. Et ante factum prohibendum est, post factum uero in foro conscientie ubi credendum est pro se sicut contra se, cum asserit sine fraude egisse uidetur posse pertransire.

186 dicto … 3] C. 14 q. 3 c. 1 (*Si foeneraveris*): vide supra.

189 numularii … eiecti] *Io* 2.14–16: et invenit in templo vendentes boves, et oves, et columbas, et numularios sedentes. Et cum fecisset quasi flagellum de funiculis, omnes ejecit de templo, oves quoque, et boves, et numulariorum effudit aes, et mensas subvertit. Et his qui columbas vendebant, dixit : Auferte ista hinc, et nolite facere domum patris mei, domum negotiationis.

190 Si[1] … **191** anathematizetur] C. 1 q. 1 c. 8 (*Si quis episcopus*): Si quis uero mediator tam turpibus et nefandis datis uel acceptis extiterit, siquidem clericus fuerit, proprio gradu decidat, si uero laicus anathematizetur.

---

175 loquupletari] + contra *a.c.* **176** sine fraude] *cod.* : *scr. F_3 fol. 69va et Ballerini* sine fraude possit tolerari post factum, tamen ante factum non est consulendum | non[1] … sit] *scripsi Antoninum secutus in Summa c. 2.1.7.15 de lucro cessante, M_1 fol. 25r* | non[2]] + multam *a.c.* **180** negotiationi] *in marg. sin. add.* **188** suis] *vel* siue **189** offendunt] + et sunt exchomuni- *a.c.* **190** 1[1]] *ut vid.*

opened to frauds. Therefore arguing by analogy with this example, the loan with interest in the case we are discussing seems licit: for the banker, as a result of not having the money which he lends for that period of time, is not able to engage in trade with it and thus suffers a loss. I answer that the analogy fails: because the trader described in the example was intending principally to devote himself to trade and to make use of his money in licit commerce. It is only by chance[38] that he subsequently lends to his friend who asks him, in order to do him a favour, and yet he nevertheless wants to protect himself from loss. But the banker intends principally to make use of this kind of loan (which he calls an "exchange"), and he does not lend to the prelate in order to do him a favour, but in order to make a greater profit, because he makes more profit this way than through using his money in commerce; and the intention of profiting from a loan, whether explicit or implicit, makes one a usurer, as in the aforesaid canon C. 14 q. 3 c. 1.[39]

These bankers also are sometimes mediators in the simonies which are carried out in the curia, offering rewards to those who intercede to obtain benefices for their prelate friends, and in this also they offend gravely. And these are the changers of money driven out of the temple in John 2,[40] about whom also it is said in C. 1 q. 1 c. 8: "And if anyone should be found to be the mediator in such shameful and nefarious transactions … if he is a layman, let

---

the words *etiam cum piam haberent intentionem*), are not found in the autograph manuscript, as Mamachi notes (see col. 126, note m); the majority of the text printed by Ballerini here appears to have been copied originally from Bern. Sen. *Evang. aet.* 42, 2, 2 (4:358–9). In the autograph manuscript, c. 2.1.7.15 ends with these words: "Also what Hostiensis says about profit, it seems must be understood as excluding doubtful profit, namely when he could also have not profited or taken a loss. And before the fact, this should be prohibited, but after the fact in the court of conscience, where one must be believed in favour of oneself just as against oneself, when one has asserted that he did this without fraud, it seems it can be overlooked." A marginal note has been added beside these words, barely legible today and probably not written by Antoninus, which refers to Bernardino, sermon 41 or 42, a. 2, c. 1–2.

At this sentence in c. 3.8.3, where I have inserted the bracketed words, the manuscript F_3 fol. 69va and Ballerini read: "when this is really the case and is done without fraud, it can be tolerated after the fact, nevertheless beforehand it should not be advised."

38 Or "because of circumstance" or "fortuitously."

39 C. 14 q. 3 c. 1 (*Si foeneraveris*): see above.

40 *Io* 2.14–16: "And he found in the temple them that sold oxen and sheep and doves, and the changers of money sitting. And when he had made, as it were, a scourge of little cords, he drove them all out of the temple, the sheep also and the oxen, and the money of the changers he poured out, and the tables he overthrew."

et nephandis datis et acceptis extiterit, si laychus est, anathematizetur." Sed per extrauagantem tales sunt exchommunicati.

2. Securitates.

Negotiatores insuper in securitatibus aliquando se exercent ut inde lucrentur, quod cum debite fiunt non uidetur illicitum. Et fieri potest securitas in mercimoniis in peccuniis et in personis.

2.1. Securitas in mercimoniis.

Et in mercimoniis quidem siue per mare siue per terram deferendis. Puta Petrus habet mille florenorum ualorem in mercimoniis in naui de Flandria Anglia uel Yspania Pisas deferenda, dubitat uel timet de submersione nauis uel captura a piratis, offert Martino quinque uel X pro centenario plus uel minus secundum quod plus uel minus timetur de periculo, pro securitate sibi super hiis fienda, cui assentit sumens in se periculum ratione dicti lucri. Ille igitur Martinus acceptis illis quinque uel X pro centenario, si merces salue conducuntur, sibi remanet illud lucrum ratione dicte securitatis; sed si nauis periret uel caperetur ab hostibus, Martinus tenetur Petro mille florenorum pro securitate facta. Licitum reputatur tale lucrum ratione periculi quod subiit. Nec enim potest dici ibi esse mutuum cum nil mutuetur, nec turpe lucrum cum non inueniatur prohibitum et utilitati deseruiens hominum. Nec obstat c. *Nauiganti*, *De usuris*, quia illud habet lochum cum scilicet suscipiens in se periculum mercium, si aliquid percipit de mercibus dicitur usura, quando uidelicet illud petit non ratione periculi sed ratione mutui facti ei cuius sunt merces, ut notat Ioannes Calderinus. Et idem dicendum de mercibus deferendis per terram per locha periculosa.

---

192 extrauagantem ... exchommunicati] Decretalem extravagantem non inveni, sed exstat Pauli II[i] papae *Extrav.Com.* 5.1.2 (*Cum detestabile*) et *Extrav.Com.* 5.9.3 (*Etsi dominici*[1]). Vide etiam Ant. Flor. *Summa* 3.25.65 (apud M_2 fol. VIIr; 3.24.65 apud Ballerini): *de excommunicatione contra symoniacos in ordine uel beneficio.*

193 Negotiatores ... **195** personis] Cfr Bern. Sen. *Evang. aet.* 39, 1, 3 (4:272–5).

208 Nauiganti ... usuris] *X* 5.19.19 (*Naviganti*): Naviganti vel eunti ad nundinas certam mutuans pecuniae quantitatem, pro eo, quod suscipit in se periculum, recepturus aliquid ultra sortem, usurarius est censendus.

211 ut ... Calderinus] Io. et Gasp. Cald. *Repet.* ad *X* 5.19.19 (fol. 282v). Cfr Laur. Rod. *Tr. usur.* 2 op. 8 (Armstrong, 165–6 et 307; TUI 7:18r).

---

192 extrauagantem] *vel* extrauagantes **187** mediatores ... **192** exchommunicati] *in marg. super. add.* **197** florenorum ualorem] *cod.* : florenos F_3 *fol. 69va* **198** deferenda] *sic cod.* : deferendis *Ballerini* **199** offert] dat *a.c.* **201** super] *vel* sunt *cod.* : super F_3 *fol. 69va et Ballerini* **204** Petro] + ipso *a.c. ut vid.* **209** si] *s.l.*

him be anathematized."[41] But through a decretal letter those doing this are excommunicated.[42]

2. Assurance. Traders moreover sometimes operate in assurances to make a profit, which does not seem illicit when they are carried out in a proper manner. And an assurance can be applied to merchandise, to money, and to persons.

2.1. Assurance on merchandise. Now an assurance can be applied to merchandise whether it is to be transported by sea or by land. Suppose Peter has the value of 1000 florins in merchandise on a ship to be transported to Pisa from Flanders, England, or Spain, and he is concerned or fears that the ship may sink or be captured by pirates. He offers Martin 5 or 10 per cent – more or less in proportion to the greater or lesser risk anticipated – for Martin to provide him insurance on those things; Martin assents to this, taking on himself the risk in exchange for the aforesaid profit. This Martin therefore, having received the 5 or 10 per cent, if the merchandise is conducted safely, keeps the profit in exchange for the aforementioned insurance; but if the ship should be lost or be captured by enemies, Martin owes Peter 1000 florins as the insurance which he provided. This kind of profit is considered licit on account of the risk which the insurer assumes. For this can be called neither a loan, since nothing is lent, nor shameful gain, since nothing prohibited is found in it, and it provides a useful service for people. Notwithstanding the canon *Naviganti, On usury*,[43] because that applies specifically when someone takes upon himself the risk of the merchandise; if he gains something from the merchandise it is called usury, namely when he seeks it not on account of the risk but on account of the loan he has made to the one who owns the merchandise, as Giovanni Calderini notes.[44] And the same must be said about merchandise to be transported by land through dangerous places.

---

41 C. 1 q. 1 c. 8 (*Si quis episcopus*): "And if anyone should be found to be the mediator in such shameful and nefarious transactions, let him also, if he is a cleric, fall from his rank, and if he is a layman or monk, let him be anathematized."

42 I have not succeeded in identifying the exact decretal letter to which Antoninus refers here; however, two later decretals of Paul II (1464 and 1468 AD) declare simoniacs as well as mediators in simony excommunicated, with absolution reserved to the Roman Pontiff: *Extrav.Com.* 5.1.2 (*Cum detestabile*) and *Extrav.Com.* 5.9.3 (*Etsi dominici*[1]). See also ANT. FLOR. *Summa* 3.25.65 (apud M_2 fol. VIIr; 3.24.65 apud Ballerini): *de excommunicatione contra symoniacos in ordine uel beneficio*.

43 *X* 5.19.19 (*Naviganti*). In this canon Pope Gregory IX condemns the so-called sea loan (*foenus nauticum*), also known as maritime interest or bottomry. This is a type of loan used to finance a trade voyage, with the lender assuming the risk of losing the investment if the ship or merchandise is lost, but taking a profit if it succeeds.

44 IO. ET GASP. CALD. *Repet.* ad *X* 5.19.19 (fol. 282v). Cfr LAUR. ROD. *Tr. usur.* 2 op. 8 (Armstrong, 165–6 and commentary 307; TUI 7:18r).

2.2. Securitas in peccuniis.

In peccuniis nota exemplum. Petrus petit a Martino centum sub mutuo siue gratis si potest siue sub usura cum indiget, et cum non confidat de Petro Martinus, exigit securitatem seu satisdationem pro eo. Albertus negotiator uel campsor qui habet magnum creditum uel quicumque alius satisdat pro eo de illis centum sed pro hac satisdatione uult duo pro centenario: utrum licite accipiat illa duo pro scripta satisdatione? Videtur dicendum quod si non est omnino securus satisdator, ut quia potest fallere, tunc uidetur licitum ratione periculi, quia si ille non solueret, scilicet principalis, haberet satisdator soluere; sed si est omnino securus, ut quia certum est illum habere tot bona quod satisdator non habebit ipse reddere uel laborare, non uidetur tutum lucrum quia uidetur implicitum mutuum et ratione illa recipere duo. Et quando idem esset creditor, id est mutuator peccunie, et satisdator, sed alium fingit esse mutuantem alium satisdantem, esset usura manifesta. De hiis habes per Laurentium de Ridofis in secunda parte, titulo primo, c. De securitatibus.

2.3. Securitas in personis.

De securitate personarum, que fit multipliciter. Vno modo per saluiconducta, ut cum dubitatur de transitu per aliquem lochum sibi suspectum, | uel accessum ad locum ubi sibi imminet periculum uite uel capture, et datur sibi saluiconductum pro quo soluit certum quid: licite quidem accipitur illud, si tamen faciens sibi securitatem seruet promissum, pacta enim "ex conuentione legem accipiunt," *De re. iu.* Et "fides etiam hosti, cum promittitur, seruanda est," 23 q. 1 *Noli.* Sed de hiis non hic agitur principaliter, nec est hoc exercitium merchatorum sed dominorum. fol. 72v

Est et alia securitas personarum, qua uidelicet quis cum alio contendens de uita uel morte alicuius principis, unus eorum assecurat de uita per tantum temporis, puta per annum, obligans se alteri in X florenos uel in centum sibi dandos si usque ad annum non superuiuat. Alius econtra se sibi obligat in tantumdem uel aliam quantitatem maiorem uel minorem si non moriatur. Et cum alterum eorum opporteat euenire, queritur si illud est licitum lucrum?

---

225 De … **226** securitatibus] Ant. Flor. *Summa* 2.1.7.45–6 (apud M_1 fol. Vr, 29v–30r et Ballerini 2:121–2; 2.1.6.45–6 apud Mamachi 2:164–5): *de securitatibus.*

231 pacta … **232** iu.] *VI* 5.[13.]85 (*Contractus*): Contractus ex conventione legem accipere dinoscuntur.

232 Et … **233** Noli] C. 23 q. 1 c. 3 (*Noli existimare*): Fides enim, quando promittitur, etiam hosti seruanda est, contra quem bellum geritur; quanto magis amico, pro quo pugnatur?

---

216 illis] ill. *cod.* **218** pro scripta] *vel* proscripta **219** periculi] + Sed si est securus, quia sat illum habere tot bona quod nullo modo potest perdere seu quia *a.c.* **225** Ridofis] *sic cod.* **238** si … annum] *cod.* : *Ballerini scr.* suique ad damnum **239** si non] *cod.* : *Ballerini scr.* si **240** euenire] + si *a.c.*

2.2. Assurance on money. For an assurance on money, note this example. Peter asks 100 from Martin as a loan, whether for free if he can or bearing usury because he is in need, and since Martin does not have confidence in Peter, he demands security for the loan or a surety. Albert, a trader or banker who has large credit or whoever else it may be, stands surety for him for that 100, but for this surety he wants 2 per cent: is it licit for him to receive this 2 per cent for being registered as his surety? It seems we must say that if the one acting as surety is not entirely secure, for instance because the debtor could default,[45] then it seems licit on account of the risk, because if he, i.e., the debtor, were not to pay, the one acting as surety would have to pay. But if the one acting as surety is entirely secure, for instance because he is certain that the debtor has enough goods that he will not have to pay or work himself, then this profit does not seem safe, because it appears to be an implicit loan and the 2 per cent seems to be taken on account of the loan. And when the same person is the creditor, that is the lender of the money, as well as the one standing surety, but he feigns that there is one person lending and a different person standing surety, then this is manifest usury. About these there is a discussion following the lead of Lorenzo Ridolfi in the second part, title 1, in the chapter on assurances.[46]

2.3. Assurance on persons. Assurance on persons is carried out in many ways. In one way, through a safe-conduct, such as when someone is concerned about travelling through a place which seems suspicious or approaching a place where there is imminent danger of being killed or captured, and he pays a fixed amount to receive a safe-conduct. The one providing the assurance certainly receives this payment licitly, if, mind you, he keeps his promise, for pacts "receive their rule from the agreement of the parties," *On the rules of law*.[47] And "faith, when it is pledged, is to be kept even with the enemy," C. 23 q. 1 c. 3.[48] But safe-conducts are mainly dealt with elsewhere, nor is this a practice of merchants but of lords.

There is another type of assurance on persons, namely when someone bets with another party about the life or death of some prince, one of them "insuring" his life for some length of time, say for a year, committing himself to give the other party 10 florins or 100 if the prince does not survive to the end of the year. The other party, vice versa, commits himself for the same amount or another larger or smaller amount if the prince does not die. And since it is necessary that one of the two results comes to pass, it is asked: is this profit licit? And it seems evident enough that it is not, because it serves no useful purpose,

---

45 Or "fall short," "fail."

46 Ant. Flor. *Summa* 2.1.7.45–6 (apud M_1 fol. Vr, 29v–30r et Ballerini 2:121–2; 2.1.6.45–6 apud Mamachi 2:164–5): *de securitatibus*.

47 *VI* 5.[13.]85 (*Contractus*): "Contracts are known to receive their rule from the agreement of the parties." English trans. from Gauthier, *Roman Law and … Canon Law*, 116.

48 C. 23 q. 1 c. 3 (*Noli existimare*): "Faith, when it is pledged, is to be kept even with the enemy against whom the war is waged; how much more with the friend, for whom it is fought?"

Et satis uidetur quod non, quia nulli deseruit utilitati, sed solum cupiditati. Vnde et turpe lucrum dici potest, et ideo illicitum. Datur etiam per hoc uia ad optandum mortem aliorum, quod est illicitum. Vnde et pauperibus uidetur erogandum, 14 q. 5 *Qui habetis* cum §. sequenti, de consilio tamen non de necessitate. Et idem uidetur dicendum de contentionibus que fiunt non solum inter merchatores sed alios quoscumque de aliquo euentu rei preterite presentis uel future, puta quod talis est mortuus uel non mortuus, quod tale negotium fuit uel non fuit, quod in anno futuro erit penuria uel pestis uel aduentus alicuius exercitus. Etiam inter scolares uel doctores super decisione alicuius questionis fiunt huiusmodi pacta que dicuntur a quibusdam inuadiationes. Et omnia uana et turpia lucra uidentur. De turpi lucro habes in secunda parte titulo primo c. de turpi lucro.

3. Permutatio uel baractum.

De permutationibus que fiunt a mercatoribus. Cum merchatores non possunt ita cito et apte expedire mercimonia sua per contractum uenditionis ut uellent, transeunt ad contractum permutationis quem uocant baractum, qui contractus de se est licitus: possunt tamen et ibi fieri fraudes sicut et in quibuscumque aliis contractibus de se licitis. Sed ut dicit Augustinus, "hec sunt uitia hominum non rerum." Fit ergo commutatio aliquando de pannis ad lanam uel de pannis laneis ad serichos uel de sericho ad aromata et huiusmodi diuersi generis rerum que hodie multum frequentantur propter penuriam denariorum. In huiusmodi autem remouende sunt fraudes, que hodie ubique habundant. Si quis autem in permutando pretium ponit excedens iustum ualorem rei sue permutande secundum conscientiam suam, sed ex eo quia nouit aperte et indubie quod ille cum quo permutat similiter apponit pretium excessiuum rei sue, huiusmodi excessus pari compensatione tolluntur; turpis tamen est usus.

243 Vnde … **245** necessitate] C. 14 q. 5 c. 14 (*Qui habetis*) et Gr. p.: Qui habetis aliquid de malo, facite inde bonum. … De malo ergo bonum facit qui pauperibus dispensat quod cum labore et sollicitudine acquisiuit, iuxta illud euangelii: "Facite uobis amicos de mammona iniquitatis." … De peccato etiam aliqua nonnumquam acquiruntur, que pauperibus iuste erogantur.

251 in … **252** lucro] Ant. Flor. *Summa* 2.1.23 (apud M_1 fol. Vr, 86r–92v et Ballerini et Mamachi): *de turpi lucro.*

257 Augustinus … **258** rerum] Aug. in D. 88 c. 12 (*Quoniam non*): De mendacio, de periurio agitur, non de negotio. Ego enim mentior, non negotium. … Omnia ista [sc. vitia] hominum, non rerum peccata sunt.

244 de … **245** necessitate] *in marg. sin. add.* **248** quod] uel *a.c.* **250** huiusmodi] *vel* huius *cod.* : huiusmodi F_3 *fol. 69vb* **254** et apte] *s.l.* **261** que] qui *a.c.* **265** compensatione] *cod.* : recompensione F_3 *fol. 70ra* : recompensatione *Ballerini*

but only greed.[49] Hence also it may be called shameful gain, and therefore illicit. This also can lead to desiring the death of others, which is illicit. Hence also it seems that any such gain should be bestowed on the poor, C. 14 q. 5 c. 14 and the section which follows;[50] nevertheless this is of counsel, not of necessity. And it seems the same must be said about the betting which is done not only between merchants but whoever else about the outcome of some matter whether past, present, or future: say, that so-and-so is dead or not dead, or that such-and-such business has happened or not, or that in a future year there will be a shortage or a plague or the arrival of some army. Even between scholars or doctors pacts of this kind are made, which by some are called "wagers,"[51] about how some question will be decided. And all these appear to be vain and shameful kinds of gain. About shameful gain there is in the second part, title 1, the chapter on shameful gain.[52]

3. Exchange of goods or barter. About exchanges of goods which are done by merchants. When merchants are not able to expedite their merchandise as quickly and conveniently as they wish through a contract of sale, they switch over to the contract of exchange of goods, which they call barter; this contract is in itself licit, nevertheless frauds can be committed therein just as in any of the other contracts which are in themselves licit. But as Augustine says, "All these are sins of the men, not of the things."[53] Exchange of goods, therefore, is done sometimes by exchanging cloth for wool, or woollen cloth for silk, or silk for aromatics, and so forth with various kinds of things; exchanges are very frequently made use of today because of the shortage of coins.[54] In this sort of thing, however, frauds, which today are abundant everywhere, must be kept out. But if someone sets a price for his thing to be exchanged which exceeds the just value according to his conscience, but on the grounds that he knows plainly and without doubt that the person with whom he is exchanging goods is likewise setting an excessive price on his own thing, these sorts of excesses can be nullified by their being equalized; nevertheless it is a distasteful practice. But in the exchange of goods, just as in

---

49 Or "the desire for money," "cupidity."

50 C. 14 q. 5 c. 14 (*Qui habetis*) and Gr. p.: "If you have something out of evil, do something good with it ... And so, he does good from evil who gives to the poor what he has acquired with labour and care, according to that text of the Gospel: *Make friends for yourselves from the mammon of iniquity* (Lc. 16.9) ... Also, some things are acquired by sin which may justly be distributed to the poor."

51 Lat. *invadatio*, cfr *invadiare*: "3 a (~*iare duellum*) to wage judicial combat. b (~*are legem* or *juramentum*) to wage one's law." *DMLBS*, s.v.

52 Ant. Flor. *Summa* 2.1.23 (apud M_1 fol. Vr, 86r–92v et Ballerini et Mamachi): *de turpi lucro*.

53 Aug. in D. 88 c. 12 (*Quoniam non*): "But what is at issue is lying and perjury, and not trading. For I am the one to lie, and not the trade ... All these are sins of men, not of things."

54 Lat. *denarii*, literally "pennies."

In permutatione autem sicut et in aliis quibuscumque contractibus et actibus "fraus et dolus nemini debent patricinari," *Extra, De rescriptis, Sedes.*

Hic etiam aduertere oportet quod in hiis permutationibus tertia persona non ledatur. Nam, ut dicit Ambrosius, "cum non potest alteri subueniri nisi alterum grauando, commodius est neutrum iuuari quam alterum grauari," 14 q. 5 *Denique*. Verbi gratia: cum permutat lanifex uel retagliator pannos laneos cum setaiuolo dante sibi pro eis pannos serichos, frequenter fit ut setaiolus dimictat pannos laneos in eum permutatos penes ritagliatorem, ea de causa et pacto ut de ipso panno ritagliator uendat textoribus serichorum seu det pro parte mercedis quam debent habere ipsi textores a magistris suis setaiuolis, et communiter pro maiori pretio ipsis dant quam aliis uendant. Vnde recipiunt textores diminutionem sue mercedis, in quo et setaioli male faciunt defraudando mercedem et ritagliatores eis in hoc seruiendo ut satellites eorum.

4. Emptio et uenditio.

De negotiatione que fit emendo aliqua ut ipsa immutata maiori pretio ab eodem uendantur, quod contingit fieri de omni genere rerum, scilicet de animalibus diuersi generis, de uictualibus uariis, frumento uino oleo et huiusmodi, de libris, de pannis laneis lineis sericis, de metallis, lapidibus pretiosis et aliis. Que quidem omnia predicta illicitum est clericis et religiosis, ut D. 88 *Fornichari*, et *Extra, Ne clerici uel mo.*, c. ultimo. Laycis licet, remotis tamen fraudibus periuriis mendaciis et aliis iniustitiis, quibus communiter pleni sunt moderni negotiatores.

4.1. De ritagliatoribuset righatteriis.

Superflui autem uidentur qui dicuntur ritagliatores et righatterii, et quod eodem tempori et eodem locho possint uendere retagliatores pannos uel

---

267 fraus … Sedes] *X* 1.3.15 (*Sedes apostolica*): Fraus et dolus ei patrocinari non debent.

269 Ambrosius … **271** Denique] Ambr. in C. 14 q. 5 c. 10 (*Denique*): Denique, si non potest alteri subueniri, nisi alter ledatur, commodius est neutrum iuuari quam alterum grauari.

283 D. … **284** Fornichari] D. 88 c. 10 (*Fornicari*): Fornicari omnibus semper non licet: negotiari vero aliquando licet; aliquando non licet. Antequam enim ecclesiasticus quis sit; licet ei negotiari: facto iam, non licet.

284 Extra … ultimo] *X* 3.50.10 (*Super specula*): Contra regiosas personas, de claustris exeuntes ad audiendum leges vel physicam, Alexander praedecessor noster olim statuit in concilio Turonensi, ut, nisi infra duorum mensium spatium ad claustrum redierint, sicut excommunicati ab omnibus evitentur, et in nulla causa, si patrocinium praestare voluerint, audiantur. Vide etiam *X* 3.50.6 (*Secundum*).

---

267 Sedes] + dol- *a.c. ut vid.* **270** 5] 4 *cod.* **271** pannos … **272** serichos] *cod.* : pannos serichos *Ballerini* **277** male faciunt] *vel* malefaciunt **281** huiusmodi] *ut vid.* **287** et righatterii] *cod.* : id est sondacharii et rigatterii *Ballerini* **288** tempori] *sic cod.* | et … locho] *in marg. sin. add.*

other contracts and acts of whatever sort, "no one's fraud and malice ought to be defended," *Extra*, *On rescripts*, c. 15.[55]

Here also it is necessary to observe that in these exchanges of goods a third party should not be injured. For, as Ambrose says, "when it is impossible to help one without burdening the other, it is better to help neither than to burden one," C. 14 q. 5 c. 10.[56] For example: when a wool merchant or retail cloth merchant exchanges wool cloth with a silk merchant who gives him silk cloth for it, it frequently happens that the silk merchant remits the wool cloth exchanged to him into the hands of the retail cloth merchant, because it has been agreed that the retail cloth merchant should sell or pay some of that cloth to the silk weavers as part of the wages which those weavers are supposed to get from their masters the silk merchants, and commonly they pay it to these at a greater price than they sell to others. Hence the weavers receive a reduction of their wage, in which both the silk merchants do wrong by defrauding them of their wage, and the retail cloth merchants do wrong by serving as their accomplices in this.

4. Purchase and sale. About trade which is carried out by buying things in order for the same person to sell them unchanged for a greater price, which is done on occasion with all sorts of things, namely animals of diverse kinds, various foodstuffs like grain, wine, oil and so forth, books, wool, linen, or silk cloth, metals, precious stones, and other things. Now <trading in> all of the things just named is illicit for clerics and religious, as in D. 88 c. 10,[57] and *Extra*, *That clerics and monks not involve themselves in secular affairs*, c. 10.[58] It is licit for laypeople, provided however that frauds, perjuries, lies, and other injustices are kept out, which modern traders are commonly replete with.

4.1. Retail cloth merchants and second-hand dealers. Now those who are called retail cloth merchants[59] and second-hand dealers[60] appear to be superfluous, and that retail cloth merchants may licitly sell cloth or second-hand dealers may sell furniture[61] immediately and in the same place for a higher price than they bought them is not clearly apparent, because if

55 *X* 1.3.15 (*Sedes apostolica*).

56 Ambr. in C. 14 q. 5 c. 10 (*Denique*): "If it is impossible to help one without injuring another, it is better to help neither than to burden one."

57 D. 88 c. 10 (*Fornicari*): "To fornicate is always unlawful for everyone, but to engage in trade is at times lawful, at times unlawful. Before someone becomes an ecclesiastic, it is lawful for him to be in trade; once he has become one, it is no longer lawful."

58 *X* 3.50.10 (*Super specula*). See also *X* 3.50.6 (*Secundum*), where monks and clerics are prohibited from engaging in business for profit.

59 "Ritagliatore; retail cloth merchant (in Florence)." Edler, *Terms of Business*, 247.

60 "Rigattiere; second-hand clothes dealer, who 1. made over clothing and who 2. sold new articles of linen (such as handkerchiefs, towels and sheeting, in Florence, where the linen merchants and the *rigattieri* were united in the same gild from the 14th century)." Ibid., 243.

61 Or more broadly "property," "possessions," "stuff." See *DMLBS* s.v. *supellex*.

rigatteri superlectilia maiori | pretio quam emerint licite, non clare apparet, fol. 73r quia si iusto pretio emerunt, plus uendendo quam dederint excessiuo pretio uendunt et sic illicitum uidetur. Si iusto pretio uendunt tunc minus iusto pretio emerunt et sic illicitum, nisi sic excusetur ars eorum quod ipsi emunt in notabili quantitate pannos uel superlectilia, et ipsi postea ut plurimum uendunt, non statim sed de tempori in tempus et per partes, unde aliquando diu expectant antequam aliqua uendant, quanto tempori non possent expectare uendentes eis, et in huiusmodi laborare habent in discurrendo, exigendo, reuidendo, scribendo, et ministros tenere oportet et pensiones soluere. "Dignus est" autem "mercenarius mercede sua," 12 q. 2 *Quicumque*. Vnde lucrum moderatum in huiusmodi querendo non uidetur illicitum. Sed in mendaciis et periuriis non euadent dampnationem, cum dicunt *malum bonum*, scilicet esse, puta pannum uel aliud, hii faciunt monstras in locis obscuris ut decipiant; contra quos dicitur Ysaie 5: *Ve qui dicitis bonum malum, ponentes tenebras lucem.*

Hic etiam sigillanda fraudulentia rigatteriorum, quia cum datur eis aliquid ad uendendum, cum dominus uestis superlectilis uel cuiuscumque rei exprimit ultimum pretium pro quo uult rem suam uendi, rigatterius si potest plus habere laborat et illud plus sibi retinet, assignans domino rei illud quod condixerat quasi sit satisfactum uoluntati eius. Sed certe fur est et latro quia etsi dominus contentus remanebat de minori pretio, hoc intendebat ubi plus haberi non posset; sed cum maiori pretio uendiderit, totum illi debet consignare. Alias si quid sibi retinet, restituere tenetur, nisi forte in casu ubi dominus non uellet ei soluere pro labore suo secundum morem artis illius: nam quantum mercedis meretur retinere potest, sed non plus. Vel nisi dominus rei dicat expresse quod quicquid plus habet de illa re sua in uendendo eam ultra tantum pretium, illud sit suum: quod rarum est. Vel nisi ipse rigatterius emat pro se,

---

297 Dignus … **298** Quicumque] C. 12 q. 2 c. 66 (*Quicumque*[2]): Quicumque suffragio cuiuslibet aliquid ecclesiasticae utilitatis prouiderint, et pro eo quodcumque commodum in remuneratione promiserint, promissi solutionem eos absoluere oportebit, ita ut ad concilium conprouinciale deferatur, ut eorum conuentu confirmetur, quia (sicut Paulus ait) dignus est mercenarius mercede sua [*1 Tim* 5.19].

302 Ysaie … **303** lucem] *Is* 5.20: Vae qui dicitis malum bonum, et bonum malum; ponentes tenebras lucem, et lucem tenebras; ponentes amarum in dulce, et dulce in amarum!

---

291 Si] + minus *a.c.* | Si … **292** illicitum] *cod.* : *F_3 fol. 70ra haec verba in marg. infer. add.* **296** in] *fortasse del. p.c.* **297** pensiones] *vel* pensionem **298** mercenarius] *s.l.* : operarius *a.c.* | 12 … Quicumque] *in rasura ut vid.* **299** Sed … **303** lucem] *in marg. super. add.* **302** bonum malum] *cod.* : + et malum bonum *F_3 fol. 70ra s.l. et Ballerini* **305** superlectilis] *vel* superlectilium **308** condixerat] *ut vid.* **309** intendebat] agebat *a.c.* **312** nam] *cod.* : + tunc *F_3 fol. 70rb s.l. et Ballerini*

they bought for a just price, then in selling for more than they paid, they sell at an excessive price and thus this seems illicit. If they sell at the just price, then they bought the goods for less than the just price, and thus illicitly, unless their craft is excused because they buy cloth or furniture in significant quantity and then, in order to sell as much as possible, they do not sell them immediately but from time to time and in portions, and hence sometimes they wait a long time before they sell some things, during which time those selling to them cannot wait, and in this sort of business they have to labour in running around, collecting, reviewing, writing, and it is necessary for them to keep employees and to pay salaries. But "the wage-labourer is worthy of his wage," C. 12 q. 2 c. 66.[62] Hence seeking a moderate profit in such things does not seem illicit. But in lies and perjuries they do not escape condemnation, when they *call bad good*, i.e., they say that something bad is good, such as cloth or anything, they set up their displays[63] in dim places in order to deceive; against these it is said in Isaiah 5: *Woe to you that call bad good, and good bad: that put darkness for light.*[64]

Here also the fraudulence of second-hand dealers must be marked out, because when something is given to them to be sold, and the owner of the clothing or furniture or whatever thing it may be states the highest price for which he wants his item to be sold, the second-hand dealer works to see if he can get more, and keeps for himself that additional amount, granting to the owner of the thing the amount which he had established as if this fulfilled his intention. But he is certainly a thief and a robber, because even if the owner remained content with a lesser price, this was his intention when he could not get more; but since the second-hand dealer sold the thing for a greater price, he ought to pass it all on to the owner. Otherwise, if he keeps something for himself, he is bound to repay it, unless perhaps in a situation when the owner did not want to pay him for his labour according to the custom of the craft: for he may keep the amount of wage which is owed him, but not more. Or unless the thing's owner expressly said that whatever additional amount he gets for his thing in selling it for more than such and such price may be his: which is rare. Or unless that second-hand dealer buys it for himself, for a just price mind you, and later sells it for more to another, seeking, however, a moderate profit from this – otherwise it would entail deceiving the one

62 C. 12 q. 2 c. 66 (*Quicumque*[2]): "If any of the bishops, with someone's aid, have provided something of utility to the Church, and they have promised some advantage in reward, it shall be fitting for them to satisfy their promise, so that it is brought before the provincial council to be confirmed by its agreement, because (as Paul says) the labourer is worthy of his hire (1 Tim. 5.19)."

63 Lat. *monstra*, pl. *-ae*, presumably for CL *monstrum*, pl. *-a*: "act of showing, displaying, demonstrating ... something that is shown, displayed, or demonstrated, sample." *DMLBS*, s.v.

64 *Is* 5.20: "Woe to you that call evil good, and good evil: that put darkness for light, and light for darkness: that put bitter for sweet, and sweet for bitter."

iusto tamen pretio, et postea plus uendat alteri, moderatum tamen lucrum inde querendo: alias opporteret quod deciperet uenditorem ei in diminutione iusti pretii uel emptorem ab eo in excessu pretii. Quod etiam cardent uestes ut uideantur quasi noue et quasi pro nouis uendant, fraus et dolus est, que neminem a peccato excusant in dampnum proximi, quia "nemo cum iactura alterius debet locupletari," *De re. iur., libro 6°*.

4.2. De merchatoribus uictualium.

Merchatores uictualium, sub quibus continentur bladaioli et tabernarii seu caupones, ex hoc solum quod ementes blada tempori messium et uina tempore uindemiarum quando communiter minus ualent, postea in processu temporis carius uendant quia tunc sunt in chariori foro, et hoc siue in magna quantitate simul siue in parua minutatim ut tabernarii, etiam si exspectent per annos quousque magno pretio uendant, dummodo non intendant charistiam inducere ex maxima talium rerum congregatione: non est illicitum uendendo pretio currenti, nec est contra quod dicitur 14 q. 4 *Quicumque*, ubi dicitur hoc esse turpe lucrum. Nam hoc est uerum cum hoc fit causa cupiditatis, ut ibi dicitur in textu: puta cum quis est diues uel habet alia exercitia unde multum lucratur, et nichilominus non ex causa alia nisi ut magis diuitias augeat, etiam talia lucra querit. Sechus autem cum hoc facit ut inde ex lucro subueniat sibi et familie uel pauperibus prouideat uel communitati talibus indigenti. Et hoc quidem clericis prohibetur ut alie negotiationes, D. 88 *Negotiatorem*. Sed non prohibetur eis fructus possessionum suarum uel ecclesie retinere usque ad tempus quo charius uendantur et multo minus laycis.

Sed prohibetur bladaiolis uendere quisquilias et mixturas immunditiarum pro bonis bladis et facere iniustas mensuras, contra quos dicit Dominus, Amos 8 c., *Audite qui conteritis pauperem et deficere facitis egenos terre dicentes: Quando transibit messis, et uenundabimus merces? et sabbathum*

320 nemo … **321** locupletari] *VI* 5.[13.]48 (*Locupletari*): vide supra.

329 14 … **330** lucrum] C. 14 q. 4 c. 9 (*Quicumque*): Quicumque tempore messis uel uindemiae non necessitate, sed propter cupiditatem conparat annonam uel uinum, uerbi gratia de duobus denariis conparat modium unum, et seruat, usque dum uendatur denariis quatuor aut sex, aut amplius, hoc turpe lucrum dicimus.

335 clericis … **336** Negotiatorem] D. 88 c. 9 (*Negotiatorem*): Negotiatorem clericum, ex inope diuitem et ex ignobili gloriosum, quasi quasdam pestes fuge.

340 Amos … **344** eorum] *Am* 8.4–7: Audite hoc, qui conteritis pauperem, et deficere facitis egenos terrae, dicentes : Quando transibit mensis, et venundabimus merces? et sabbatum,

317 ei] *ut vid.* **318** cardent] *cod.* : re- *F_3 fol. 70rb s.l. et Ballerini* **319** fraus] fur *a.c.* **321** locupletari] lop- *a.c.* **323** tempori … **324** tempore] *sic cod.* **326** tabernarii] + de se non *a.c. ut vid.* **327** magno] car- *a.c.* **331** ibi] *bis a.c.* **335** prohibetur] + qu- *a.c.* **338** bladaiolis] eis *a.c.* | quisquilias] quisquiliquias *cod. et F_3 fol. 70rb* | et] pro bonis *a.c.* **339** facere] + mensuras *a.c.* **341** messis] *sic cod. et F_3 fol. 70rb*

who sells to him through a reduction from the just price, or deceiving the one who buys from him through an excess of price. Now, when they nap[65] garments so that they look like new and sell them as new, this is fraud and guile, which excuse no one from sin in harming a neighbour, because "no one ought to obtain an advantage to the detriment of another," *On the rules of law, Liber Sext.*[66]

4.2. Food merchants. Food merchants, among whom are counted grain merchants[67] and tavern keepers or innkeepers, from the sole fact that they buy grain at the time of reaping and wine at the time of the grape harvest, when they are commonly worth less, and later in the course of time sell it more dear because then they are in a dearer market,[68] and this whether they sell in great quantity all at once or in small quantities a little at a time as tavern keepers do, even if they wait for years until they can sell for a very high price, provided that they do not intend to create a shortage[69] by accumulating as much as possible of the goods: this is not illicit when they sell at the current price, nor is it contrary to what is said in C. 14 q. 4 c. 9, where this is described as shameful gain.[70] For this is true when this is done because of greed, as is said within the text: say, when someone is rich or has other activities from which he makes plenty of profit, and nonetheless, for no other reason than to increase his wealth even more, he also seeks these sorts of profits. But it is different when a person does this so that from the profit he may support himself and his family or provide for the poor or for a community which needs these goods. And this indeed is prohibited to clerics, as are other sorts of trade, D. 88 c. 9.[71] But it is not prohibited to them to hold back the produce of their properties or church until a time when they can be sold more dear, and much less is this prohibited to laypeople.

But it is prohibited to grain merchants to sell chaff[72] or maslins[73] of waste as good grain and to make unjust measures, against whom the Lord says in Amos ch. 8:[74] *Hear, you that crush the poor, and make the needy of the land to fail, say-*

65 Lat. *cardare*, presumably from Ital. "Cardare; to nap or teasel cloth (i.e., to raise up the loose fibres of woolen yarn into a nap on the surface of the cloth by scratching it with teasels." Edler, *Terms of Business*, 64.

66 *VI* 5.[13.]48 (*Locupletari*): see above.

67 "Biadaiuolo – *biadaiuolus*: litt. = marchand d'avoine, mais, de fait, de céréales en général." Stella, *La révolte des Ciompi*, 298.

68 Lat. *in c(h)ariori foro*.

69 This Latin phrase (*caristiam inducere*) is often translated "induce dearth."

70 C. 14 q. 4 c. 9 (*Quicumque*): "Whoever, at the time of harvest of wheat or grapes, buys wheat or wine, not by any need, but out of cupidity, so that, for example, he buys a measure for two pennies and keeps it until it is sold for four, or six, or more pennies, we say that he is engaging in a shameful gain."

71 D. 88 c. 9 (*Negotiatorem*): "As for a cleric who engages in trade, and from poor becomes rich, and from obscure to renowned, avoid him as you would the plague."

72 Or "rubbish," "refuse."

73 Or "mixtures."

74 *Am* 8.4–7: "Hear this, you that crush the poor, and make the needy of the land to fail, Saying: When will the month be over, and we shall sell our wares: and the sabbath, and we

et aperiemus frumentum? ut imminuamus mensuram et augeamus siclum, et supponamus stateras dolosas, et quisquilias frumenti uendamus? Et infra: *Si oblitus fuero usque ad finem omnis opera eorum*, quasi dicat, puniam pro talibus excessibus. De inducentibus caristiam dicit Ieronymus: "Exurientibus plurimis reseruare omnium predonum uincit crudelitatem," 12 q. 2 *Gloria.*

Reprehenduntur caupones de mixtura quam faciunt aque cum uino, uendentes aquam pro uino, contra quos dicitur, Ysaie 1° c., *Caupones tui aquam uino miscent*, secundum aliam translationem. Sed non minus malum est cum immiscent uinis aliqua nociua corporibus hominum, ut faciant clariora uel suauiora. Mensuras quoque diminutas tribuunt quia non plenas. Nec a graui peccato excusari possunt quando, ut uendant frequentantibus tabernas, scienter administrant hiis qui se inebriant; defraudant communitates in gabellis frequenter uendendo minutatim in taberna. De mane diebus festis cum celebrantur misse publice tenere tabernam, incongruum est.

4.3. De macellariis et pizi cagnolis.

Macellarii quoque fraudibus utuntur cum uendunt carnes pecudinas pro castratis et huiusmodi, et grauius offendunt cum infectas, uel propter dilationem temporis uel propter infirmitatem animalis, carnes uendunt pro sanis, unde nocumentum corporibus hominum sequitur. Stateras in se uel in ponderando falsificant, pro libra una dando XI uel X uncias, cum tamen dicatur, Prouerb. XI, *Statera dolosa abhominabilis est apud Dominum.* Et cum non

---

et aperiemus frumentum, ut imminuamus mensuram, et augeamus siclum, et supponamus stateras dolosas, ut possideamus in argento egenos et pauperes pro calceamentis, et quisquilias frumenti vendamus? Juravit Dominus in superbiam Jacob : Si oblitus fuero usque ad finem omnia opera eorum.

345 Exurientibus … **346** Gloria] Hier. in C. 12 q. 2 c. 71 (*Gloria*) §. 2: Amico rapere quippiam furtum est, ecclesiam fraudare sacrilegium est; accepisse pauperibus erogandum et esurientibus plurimis illud reseruare, uel cautum uel timidum est aut, quod apertissimi sceleris est, exinde aliquid subtrahere, omnium predonum crudelitatem superat.

348 Ysaie … **349** translationem] *Is* 1.22 in *Vetere Latina* (Gryson 12:80–1): Caupones tui miscent vinum aqua.

361 Prouerb. … Dominum] *Prv* 11.1: Statera dolosa abominatio est apud Dominum, et pondus aequum voluntas ejus.

---

343 quisquilias] quisquiliquias *cod. et F_3 fol. 70rb a.c.* : quisquilias *F_3 fol. 70rb p.c.* **345** excessibus] + ¶ *cod. a.c.* **349** secundum … translationem] *in marg. sin. add.* **353** defraudant] + aliquando *a.c.*

ing: when will the harvest[75] *be over, and we shall sell our wares? and the sabbath, and we shall offer the wheat? that we may lessen the ephah, and increase the shekel, and may deal with deceitful balances ... and may sell the refuse of the wheat?* And further on: *Surely I will never forget all their works*, as if to say, I will punish such excesses. About those who create shortages Jerome says: "To have received what was to be distributed to the poor surpasses the cruelty of all robbers," C. 12 q. 2 c. 71.[76]

Innkeepers are censured for mixing water with wine, selling water as wine, against whom it is said in Isaiah ch. 1: *Your innkeepers mix wine with water*, according to the other translation.[77] But no less evil is it when they mix with their wines other sorts of things which are harmful to the human body, in order to make it clearer or sweeter.[78] They also offer reduced, i.e., less than full, measures. Nor can they be excused from grave sin when, in order to sell to people frequenting taverns, they knowingly serve those who get themselves drunk. They frequently defraud communities in their taxes[79] by selling a little at a time in the tavern. It is improper to open a tavern from the morning on feast days when public masses are celebrated.

4.3. Butchers and small retail dealers.

Butchers also use frauds when they sell sheep's meat[80] as the meat of a wether[81] and so forth, and it is a graver offence when as healthy meat they sell rotten meat, whether it is rotten because of long delay or because the animal was ill, whence there results harm to people's bodies. They falsify scales by altering them or, while weighing, giving 11 or 10 ounces for a pound, when however it is said in Proverbs 11: *A deceitful balance is abominable before the*

---

shall open the corn: that we may lessen the measure, and increase the sicle, and may convey in deceitful balances, That we may possess the needy for money, and the poor for a pair of shoes, and may sell the refuse of the corn? The Lord hath sworn against the pride of Jacob: surely I will never forget all their works."

75 Antoninus wrote *messis*, "harvest," here, while the Vulgate text of Amos reads *mensis*, "month."

76 Hier. in C. 12 q. 2 c. 71 (*Gloria*) §. 2: "To steal a thing from a friend is theft, but to defraud the Church is sacrilege. To have received what was to be distributed to the poor, to be cautious or timid while many are starving, or, what is a most wicked crime, to subtract something of it for yourself, surpasses the cruelty of all robbers."

77 *Is* 1.22 in the *Vetus Latina* (Gryson 12:80–1).

78 Or "more agreeable," "more pleasant."

79 "Gabella (Ar. qabāla, tax); tax on imports and exports (in Tuscany and elsewhere)." Edler, *Terms of Business*, 130. The best-known such tax was the French salt tax, but Italian cities levied *gabelle* on a wide variety of products, such as textiles, metals, cheese, fish, grain, wine, oil, dyestuff, and spices. See Jamison, "Fiscal Policy in an Italian Commune," 84, table 2.3.

80 Lat. *carnes pecudinas*, cfr Ital. *pecorino*: "of sheep," *Oxford-Paravia Italian Dictionary*, s.v.

Cfr Ant. Flor. *Summa* 2.1.17 (above), section 3.1: "Butchers commit this fraud, namely in a thing's species when they sell ram's or goat's meat (*carnes hyrcinas uel caprinas*) as the meat of a wether."

81 Lat. *(carnibus) castratis*, i.e., the meat of a castrated animal (wether). Cfr Ital. *carne di castrato*: "mutton," *Oxford-Paravia Italian Dictionary*, s.v.

possunt per dies carnes conseruari, ut in estate, quod preparent diebus festiuis eas uidentur excusati, et etiam in uendendo talibus diebus, sed non in dimictendo propter hoc diuina ut auditionem misse. | fol. 73v

Pizicangnoli quoque pollarioli et trichones uendentes caseum et oua, pisces sallitos uel recentes, aues oleum minutis mensuris aut fructus, cum excessiuo pretio uendunt, uel diminutis mensuris quoad mensurabilia, uel res infectas seu coruptas, uel diebus festiuis, nisi fructus et aliqua magis necessaria uel etiam huiusmodi, dimictentes missam: sine peccato graui non sunt, etiam fraudantes gabellas.

364 misse] *cod.* : *add.* F_3 *fol. 70va in marg. sin. et Ballerini* Hi etiam usuram aliquando commictunt, dando scilicet animalia agricolis ad socidam saluo capitali et uariis aliis modis usurariis, de quibus habes supra in 2a parte, de usuris. Vadunt insuper diebus festiuis ad diuersos foros ad emendum animalia sine auditione misse et absque ieiuniorum preceptorum obseruatione, necnon et rusticos a quibus animalia emunt sepe decipiunt, quorum fraudes super ipsorum capita in fine reuertuntur. **365** Pizicangnoli] piçicangnoli *cod.* : picicangnoli F_3 *fol. 70va* | Pizicangnoli … **370** gabellas] *in marg. super. add.* **369** sunt] + non autem ex h- *a.c.* **370** gabellas] *cod.* : *add.* F_3 *fol. 70va in marg. sin. et Ballerini* Vadunt et ipsi diebus festis ad forum, de ieiuniis et auditione misse parum curantes, periuria et iuramenta et mendacia pro nichilo reputantes.

Lord.[82] And since they are not able to store meat for days, for instance in summer, if they prepare it on feast days and even if they sell it on such days, they seem to be excused from sin, as long as they do not for this reason omit divine services such as hearing Mass.[83]

Small retail dealers[84] and poulterers[85] and produce dealers[86] selling cheese and eggs, salted or fresh fish, birds, or oil in small amounts, or produce, when they sell at an excessive price, or sell measurable things with reduced measures, or sell infected or rotten goods, or sell on feast days – apart from selling produce and other necessities and things of that kind – and omit Mass: they are not without grave sin, and so are those who defraud taxes.[87]

---

82 *Prv* 11.1: "A deceitful balance is an abomination before the Lord: and a just weight is his will."

83 The manuscript F_3 (fol. 70va, in the left margin) and Ballerini's edition add two sentences here: "These also sometimess commit usury, namely by giving animals to farmers in agistment with the capital safe, and by various other usurious means, about which you have above in the second part, on usury. They go moreover on feast days to different markets to buy animals without hearing Mass and without observing the precepts of fasting, and indeed they also deceive the rustics from whom they buy animals; their frauds in the end are turned back onto their own heads."

84 "Pizzicaiuolo; small retail dealer in spices, drugs, wax, etc. (in Siena)." Edler, *Terms of Business*, 216.

85 "Pollaiuolo/a – *pollaiuolus*: volailler." Stella, *La révolte des Ciompi*, 312.

86 "Trecca – *triccula, ... di cacio e uova* (1), ... *ad cellam* (3), ... *ad stincas* (1): revendeuse de fruits et légumes, et parfois de paille, oeufs et herbes médicinales. Treccone – *tricculus*: cf. *trecca*." Ibid., 315.

87 The manuscript F_3 (fol. 70va, in the left margin) and Ballerini's edition add a sentence here: "These also go to the market on feast days, caring little about fasting and hearing Mass, accounting perjuries and oaths and lies as nothing."

Antoninus Florentinus, *Summa*, 3.8.4
De diversis generibus artificum

Summarium ab editore confectum

1. **De merciariis aurificibus et gioielleriis.**
   1.1. **De aurificibus.**
   1.2. **Non uendant aurum et argentum alchimiatum pro uero.**
   1.3. **De mixtura eris in auro uel argento.**
2. **De prosenetis seu sensalibus.**
   2.1. **Si est mediator in contractibus.**
   2.2. **Si est mediator in emptione iurium montis.**
   2.3. **Idem de omnibus qui sunt mediatores.**
3. **De lanificibus.**
   3.1. **De emptione ad terminum.**
   3.2. **De moderato lucro.**
   3.3. **De lanifice in casu usurario.**
   3.4. **De ponentibus peccunias apud lanifices.**
   3.5. **Si lanifex peccunias accipiat ad discretionem.**
   3.6. **De ministris in apotheca.**
   3.7. **De consulibus.**
   3.8. **De officialibus.**
   3.9. **De ministris artis lane.**
   3.10. **De arte emendatorum.**
   3.11. **De retaliatoribus.**
4. **De sartoribus et caligarum uel chalceorum factoribus et huiusmodi.**
   4.1. **De arte stampatorum.**
   4.2. **Qui commodant uestimenta pretiosa uel iocalia.**
   4.3. **De cerdonibus et planellariis.**
   4.4. **De pellipariis.**
5. **De serificibus seu setaiuolis.**
   5.1. **De textoribus et tintoribus.**
   5.2. **De aliquibus fraudantibus gabellas uel pedagia.**
   5.3. **De emendo serichum ab furatis.**
   5.4. **De uendendo ad terminum uel faciendo permutationes.**
6. **De architectis seu hedificatoribus.**
   6.1. **Caueant a fraudibus.**
   6.2. **De lathomariis et cementariis.**
   6.3. **De lapicidinariis.**

St Antoninus, *Summa*, 3.8.4
On the various kinds of workers

Summary prepared by the editor

1. **Outfitters, goldsmiths, and gem dealers.**
   1.1. **Goldsmiths.**
   1.2. **Let them not sell alchemical gold and silver for the real thing.**
   1.3. **On mixing copper into gold or silver.**
2. **Agents and brokers.**
   2.1. **If one is a mediator in contracts.**
   2.2. **If one is a mediator in the purchase of credits in the *monte*.**
   2.3. **The same applies to all those who are mediators.**
3. **Wool merchants.**
   3.1. **Purchase on credit.**
   3.2. **On moderate profit.**
   3.3. **The wool merchant in a case of usury.**
   3.4. **Depositing money with wool merchants.**
   3.5. **If a wool merchant receives money at his discretion.**
   3.6. **Employees in the workshop.**
   3.7. **Consuls.**
   3.8. **Officials.**
   3.9. **Employees in the wool craft.**
   3.10. **The craft of menders.**
   3.11. **Retail cloth dealers.**
4. **Tailors, makers of boots and shoes, and so forth.**
   4.1. **The craft of fabric decorators.**
   4.2. **Those who lend precious garments and jewelled items.**
   4.3. **Cobblers and slipper makers.**
   4.4. **Furriers.**
5. **Silk makers or silk merchants.**
   5.1. **Weavers and dyers.**
   5.2. **Those who defraud taxes or tolls.**
   5.3. **Buying silk from those who have stolen it.**
   5.4. **Selling on credit or making exchanges.**
6. **Architects and builders.**
   6.1. **Let them beware of frauds.**
   6.2. **Masons and bricklayers.**
   6.3. **Stonecutters.**

7. De fabris.
  7.1. De maniscallis, id est fabris facientibus ferramenta iumentis.
  7.2. De armaiolis, id est fabris facientibus arma.
  7.3. De fabris ad alia opera deditis.
8. De carpentariis.
  8.1. De facientibus galeas naues et nauiculas.
  8.2. De marinariis.
9. De aromatariis.
  9.1. De ministris talis artis.
  9.2. De barbitonsoribus.
  9.3. De operando in sabbatho.
10. De artificibus circa scripturas et picturas.
  10.1. De chartulariis.
  10.2. Quomodo scriptores offendunt.
  10.3. De pictoribus.
11. De ministerio musichorum in cantando et pulsando.
  11.1. De laycis pulsantes instrumenta ob recreationem.
  11.2. De arte histrionum.
12. De agricolis.
  12.1. Si laborant terras aliorum.
  12.2. Si tenent animalia ad soccidam.
  12.3. Offendunt in non soluendo decimas.
  12.4. Quomodo communiter offendunt.

7. Smiths.
    7.1. Farriers, that is, smiths who make shoes for oxen.
    7.2. Armourers, that is, smiths who make arms.
    7.3. Craftsmen devoted to other sorts of work.
8. Carpenters.
    8.1. On those who make galleys, ships, and boats.
    8.2. Mariners.
9. Apothecaries.
    9.1. Employees in this craft.
    9.2. Barber-surgeons.
    9.3. Working on the sabbath.
10. Artisans whose work relates to writings and pictures.
    10.1. Booksellers.
    10.2. How scribes do wrong.
    10.3. Painters.
11. The occupation of musicians in singing and playing.
    11.1. Laypeople playing instruments recreationally.
    11.2. The craft of performing.
12. Farmers.
    12.1. If they work the lands of others.
    12.2. If they hold animals in agistment.
    12.3. They do wrong in not paying tithes.
    12.4. How they commonly do wrong.

4ᵐ capitulum: de diuersis generibus artificum.

M_2 fol. IIr

1. De merciariis aurificibus et gioielleriis.

fol. 73v

De merciariis aurificibus et gioielleriis, sciendum quod hii in aliquibus se habent ut merchatores, in aliis ut artifices. Nam emendo diuersa mercimonia in magna quantitate et postea uendendo ea immutata in magna quantitate, uel parua paulatim, ut communiter accidit, et in prolixitate temporis, ac exinde moderatum lucrum querendo, reprehendi non potest cum *militare* non debeat *suis stipendiis*, ar. 13 q. 1 §. 2. Et hoc nisi emat ut reuendat ea quorum usus communiter est ad peccatum et graue, ut taxillos naybos seu cartas fuchos et huiusmodi. Vt enim dicit Gregorius, sunt pleraque negotia que uix aut numquam sine peccato exerceri possunt. Ea ergo que sine peccato exerceri non possunt, ad ea post conuersionem, scilicet ad penitentiam, necesse est ut animus non recurrat, De pen. D. 5 *Negotium*. Et multo magis qui talia faciunt, scilicet taxillos et cartas et huiusmodi, sunt in malo statu anime sue. Si autem merciarii ad dictas merces adiungunt aliqua alia ad ornandum, tunc se habent ut artifices, et de labore ibi apposito et materia iustum est eos inde lucrari.

1.1. De aurificibus

Aurifices cum emunt uasa aurea uel argentea et huiusmodi ut ea immutata reuendant maiori tamen pretio sed moderato, non est illicitum si aliquid lucrentur moderate, dummodo tamen <non> ex eo quod non cognoscit uendens pretiositatem rei, ut puta lapidem pretiosum, multo minori pretio emat notabiliter quam ualeat. Et econuerso non uendat ipse aurifex rem minus pretiosam, puta uitrum in anulo inclusum, pro lapide pretioso. Hoc enim generaliter tenendum est secundum Tomam in *Sum.*, quod quamuis iura

---

6 militare … **7** 2] C. 13 q. 1 c. 1 Gr. p. §. 4 (1:719): Item [*1 Cor* 9.7]: "Quis umquam suis militat stipendiis? quis pascit gregem, et de lacte eius non edit?" Nos militamus: et uos stipendia nostrae miliciae uobis queritis? Nos gregem pascimus: et uos lac eius et lanam accipere uobis uultis? Sapere est de alieno labore uictum querere, si sapere est uelle quod non possis.

9 Gregorius … **12** recurrat] Greg. M. in *De pen.* D. 5 c. 7 (*Negotium*): Sunt enim pleraque negotia, que sine peccatis exhiberi aut uix, aut nullatenus possunt. Que ergo ad peccatum inplicant, ad hec necesse est ut post conuersionem animus non recurrat.

21 Hoc … **22** Tomam] Thom. Aq. *Sum. th.* 2a 2ae q. 77 a. 1 ob. 1 et ad 1: Sed secundum eas [leges civiles] licitum est emptori et venditori ut se invicem decipiant, quod quidem fit inquantum venditor plus vendit rem quam valeat, emptor autem minus quam valeat. … Sic igitur [lex humana] habet quasi licitum, poenam non inducens, si absque fraude venditor rem suam supervendat aut emptor vilius emat, nisi sit nimius excessus, quia tunc etiam lex humana cogit ad restituendum, puta si aliquis sit deceptus ultra dimidiam iusti pretii quantitatem [cfr *Cod.* 4.44.8; *Cod.* 4.44.15]. Sed lex divina nihil impunitum relinquit quod sit virtuti contrarium. Unde secundum divinam legem illicitum reputatur si in emptione et venditione non sit aequalitas iustitiae observata. Et tenetur ille qui plus habet recompensar ei qui damnificatus est, si sit notabile damnum.
Cfr Ant. Flor. *Summa* 2.1.16 (supra).

---

18 non[1]] *supplevi* **20** emat] + quam *a.c.*

Chapter 4: On the various kinds of workers.

1. Outfitters, goldsmiths, and gem dealers. About outfitters,[1] goldsmiths, and gem dealers,[2] it must be recognized that they conduct themselves in certain affairs as merchants, in others as artisans. For when they buy a variety of merchandise in large quantities and later sell these goods unchanged in large quantities or in small quantities a little at a time, as commonly occurs, and over a long period of time, and they seek a moderate profit from this, they cannot be censured, since one is not obliged *to soldier at his own expense*, by the argument of C. 13 q. 1 c. 1 Gr. p. §. 4.[3] And this is so unless one buys, in order to sell again, things whose use commonly leads to grave sin, such as dice, games or cards, cosmetics, and so forth.[4] For as Gregory says, there are many kinds of business which can scarcely or never be exercised without sin. Therefore such things as cannot be exercised without sin, it is necessary after conversion, namely to penance, that one's mind not return to them, *De pen.* D. 5 c. 7.[5] And much more are those who make such things, namely dice and cards and so forth, in a bad state in their souls. But if outfitters add something else on to the aforesaid merchandise to decorate it, then they conduct themselves as artisans, and for the labour therein applied and the material it is just that they make a profit from it.

1.1. Goldsmiths. Goldsmiths, when they buy vessels of gold or silver and so forth in order to sell them again unchanged for a greater – but nevertheless moderate – price, this is not illicit if they make some moderate profit, apart from the situation, however, that because the seller does <not> know how precious the item is, say a precious stone, the goldsmith buys it for a notably smaller price than it is worth. And vice versa, the goldsmith himself should not sell a thing which is less precious, say glass set in a ring, as a precious stone. For this is to be held as a general rule, according to Thomas in the *Summa*, that although <human> laws permit the parties in a contract of buying and selling to mutually deceive each other up to half the just price, the divine law does not allow any fraud at all, and in the court of conscience a person deceiving another is bound to make satisfaction to the injured party in a

---

1 "Merciaio; mercer, merchant who sold a great variety of articles, including arms and armor, hardware, saddles, straps, belts, and other leather goods, dry goods, millinery, notions, jewelry, etc." Edler, *Terms of Business*, 178.

2 "Gioiellieri: Gem dealers, who were retailers of gemstones (diamonds, emeralds, garnets, rubies, sapphires, spinels) and most impressively in the Quattrocento, of pearls." Frick, *Dressing Renaissance Florence*, 229.

3 C. 13 q. 1 c. 1 Gr. p. §. 4: "Also: What soldier ever fights at his own expense? Who tends a flock, and does not feed on its milk (1 Cor. 9.7)? We serve as soldiers, and you seek for yourselves the rewards of our service? We feed the flock, and you wish to take for yourselves its milk and wool? It is wisdom to want to feed on another's labour; if this is wisdom, then go on wishing the impossible."

4 Cfr Ant. Flor. *Summa* 2.1.16 (above), section 2.7.

5 Greg. M. in *De pen.* D. 5 c. 7 (*Negotium*): "For there are many kinds of business which can scarcely or never be performed without sins. But as for those things which involve one in sin, it is necessary that one's mind not turn to these after conversion."

permictant in contractu emptionis et uenditionis partes se inuicem decipere usque ad dimidiam iusti pretii, lex diuina nullam fraudem admictit et in foro conscientie tenetur talis satisfacere leso in modicha deceptione, dum certa est. Si autem aurifex conflat uas argenteum uel aureum uel aliam rem et inde facit aliquod artificium, iustum est ut inde reportet lucrum de suo labore. Quantum autem possit petere pro lucro non bene potest dari regula certa, sed arbitrio boni uiri statur, secundum laborem ibi habitum et ingenium etiam seu industriam facientis et morem patrie. Nam in quacumque arte attenditur nobilitas materie et industria facientis et periculum etiam: puta si lapidem pretiosum includendo uel laborando, circa eum esset periculum fractionis et emendare haberet, plus licite reciperet quam si non esset ibi periculum. Et maius etiam decet lucrum operando in auro et argento quam in chorio et ferro. Et plus ei debetur qui melius opera artis agit. Sicut etiam in pictoria arte in faciendo similem figuram, multo plus petet in duplo uel triplo magnus magister quam rudis. Caueat autem, ne furata emat quia inde habet bonum forum, quia restituere opportebit cum postea de furto perpenditur. Quamuis enim si ignorauit excusatus sit tunc a peccato, cum postea nouerit, nec rem ipsam retinere potest nec pretium repetere quod soluit a domino rei. Calices et huiusmodi emere non debet ad conflandum nisi prius fracta fuerint, unde consecrationem amiserint.

1.2. Non uendant aurum et argentum alchimiatum pro uero.

Aurum et argentum alchimiatum non uendat pro uero quia fraus est et illicitum secundum Thomam 2^{a} 2^{e} q. 77, quia non est adeo purum sicut uerum, nec habet illas proprietates aurum alchimichum sicut uerum quia non habet proprietatem letificandi cor, uel quod ualet contra certas infirmitates et huiusmodi. Et subdit Thomas quod si "per alchimiam fieret uerum aurum non esset illicitum uendere pro uero, quia nichil prohibet artem uti aliquibus naturalibus causis ad producendos ueros et naturales effectus, sicut Augustinus dicit in libro *de Trinitate* de hiis que fiunt arte demonum." Aduertendum tamen

---

43 secundum … **49** demonum] THOM. AQ. *Sum. th.* 2a 2ae q. 77 a. 2 ad 1: Et ideo si aurum vel argentum ab alchimicis factum veram speciem non habeat auri et argenti, est fraudulenta et iniusta venditio. Praesertim cum sint aliquae utilitates auri et argenti veri, secundum naturalem operationem ipsorum, quae non conveniunt auro per alchimiam sophisticato, sicut quod habet proprietatem laetificandi, et contra quasdam infirmitates medicinaliter iuvat. Frequentius etiam potest poni in operatione, et diutius in sua puritate permanet aurum verum quam aurum sophisticatum. Si autem per alchimiam fieret aurum verum, non esset illicitum ipsum pro vero vendere, quia nihil prohibet artem uti aliquibus naturalibus causis ad producendum naturales et veros effectus; sicut Augustinus dicit, in III de Trin., de his quae arte Daemonum fiunt.

48 Augustinus … **49** Trinitate] AUG. *Trin.* 3, 8 (875).

---

25 in modicha] *vel* immodicha *cod.* **47** uti] + ad *a.c.* **48** dicit] + de h(iis?) *a.c.*

small deception, when the deception is a matter of certainty.[6] But if a goldsmith melts down a silver or gold vessel or another thing and makes from it some item, it is just that he receive a profit from his labour. As to how much he may seek as a profit, however, it is not possible to give readily a definite rule, but it stands on the judgment of a good man, according to the labour the craftsman put into it, and also the ability or diligence of the craftsman and the custom of the country. For in any kind of craft the excellence of the material and the diligence of the craftsman are considered, and risk as well: for suppose that in setting and working a precious stone there is involved a risk of breaking it and the artisan would have to repair it, then he may licitly receive more than if there was no risk in the work. And more profit is also fitting in working in gold and silver than in leather and iron. And more is owed to one who better executes the works of the craft. Just as also in the art of painting, when painting the same image a great master seeks much more, twofold or threefold, than an untrained one. Let him beware, however, that he not buy stolen goods because he gets a good deal on them, since he will be obliged to restore them later when the theft becomes known. For although if he was unaware he is then excused from sin, when he becomes aware of it later, he may neither keep the thing itself nor seek a refund from the thing's owner of the price which he paid. Chalices and such things a goldsmith should not buy in order to melt down unless they were previously broken, and hence have lost their consecration.

1.2. Let them not sell alchemical gold and silver for the real thing.

One should not sell alchemically produced gold and silver as the real thing, because this is fraud and unlawful according to Thomas, 2a 2ae q. 77,[7] since they are not pure to the same degree as the real thing, nor does alchemical gold have the same properties as true gold, because it does not have the property of making the heart joyful or being effectual against certain ailments and so forth. And Thomas adds that

---

6 Thom. Aq. *Sum. th.* 2a 2ae q. 77 a. 1 ob. 1 et ad 1: "Now according to these [civil] laws it is just for buyer and seller to deceive one another: and this occurs by the seller selling a thing for more than its worth, and the buyer buying a thing for less than its worth … Accordingly, if without employing deceit the seller disposes of his goods for more than their worth, or the buyer obtain them for less than their worth, the law looks upon this as licit, and provides no punishment for so doing, unless the excess be too great, because then even human law demands restitution to be made, for instance if a man be deceived in regard to more than half the amount of the just price of a thing [cfr *Cod.* 4.44.8; *Cod.* 4.44.15]. On the other hand the Divine law leaves nothing unpunished that is contrary to virtue. Hence, according to the Divine law, it is reckoned unlawful if the equality of justice be not observed in buying and selling: and he who has received more than he ought must make compensation to him that has suffered loss, if the loss be considerable."
Cfr Ant. Flor. *Summa* 2.1.16 (above).

7 Thom. Aq. *Sum. th.* 2a 2ae q. 77 a. 2 ad 1: "Hence if the gold or silver produced by alchemists has not the true specific nature of gold and silver, the sale thereof is fraudulent and unjust, especially as real gold and silver can produce certain results by their natural action, which the counterfeit gold and silver of alchemists cannot produce. Thus the true metal has the property of making people joyful, and is helpful medicinally against certain maladies. Moreover real gold can be employed more frequently, and lasts longer in its condition of purity than counterfeit gold. If however real gold were to be produced by alchemy, it would not be unlawful to sell it for the genuine article, for nothing prevents art from employing certain natural causes for the production of natural and true effects, as Augustine says (De Trin. iii, 8) of things produced by the art of the demons."

quod de hiis qui uacant huiusmodi exercitio alchimie communiter uerificatur illud Apostoli in secunda ad Thim.: *Semper addiscentes et numquam ad scientiam ueritatis peruenientes*. Experientias multas faciunt et quasi numquam ad perfectum effectum deueniunt, multa consumunt in huiusmodi et tempus et peccunias et laborem et famam et semper pauperiores inueniuntur, unde se ditari exspectant. Vnde et si abstinendum sit omnibus, ne decipiant uendendo sophistichum aurum et argentum pro uero, permaxime clericis et religiosis.

1.3. De mixtura eris in auro uel argento.

Fraudem quoque artifices commictunt, quando opera argenteorum que uendunt ipsum argentum non reperitur in tot ligis ut iuxta uulgare loquar, uel opera aurea in tot charatis quot rationabiliter esse debet ita quod est ibi plus de mixtura eris quam esse debeat, secundum statuta ciuitatis uel communem morem. Dicitur enim argentum omnino purum et sine aliqua mixtura, quando est XII ligarum, et aurum omnino purum quando est 24 carathorum. Et quando est huiusmodi puritatis, quantumcumque in igne permaneat non diminuitur in pondere suo seu quantitate. Sed si est infra dictos gradus ligarum uel charatorum, in igne proiectum minoratur in quantitate, quia materia alia ibi admixta eris uel stagni et alterius metalli paulatim consumitur <et> in fumum euanescit. Si ergo statutum est in ciuitate, quod opera argentea debeant esse X ligarum cum dimidio, scilicet argenti in una libra operis argentei, si esset ibi argentum X ligarum ita quod residuum est mixtura eris fraudem utique commicteret, quia mediam illam ligam eris, que in illo opere est, pro argento uendit. |

2. De prosenetis seu sensalibus.

fol. 74r

De prosenetis seu sensalibus. Hii sunt mediatores in multis generibus contractuum. Et si sunt mediatores in cambiis illicitis et usurariis, exercere non ualent nisi cum dampnatione artem illam in ea parte, nisi forte cum facerent intendendo ut prouideatur necessitati accipientis sub cambio. Sed sechus si in sui ipsius utilitatem ut inde lucretur ut fit. Si uero sit mediator in matrimoniis

---

51 illud … **52** peruenientes] *2 Tim* 3.7: semper discentes, et numquam ad scientiam veritatis pervenientes.

---

50 de] *add. p.c.* **51** illud … Thim.] *in rasura* **55** se ditari] *ut vid. cod.* : si ditari F_3 *fol. 70vb* : se divites *Ballerini* **58** opera argenteorum] *cod. p.c. ut vid. cum* F_3 *fol. 70vb* : operum argentea(?) *a.c.* **63** 24] + qu- *a.c.* **71** eris] arg- *a.c.* **77** ut fit] + communiter *add. s.l.* F_3 *fol. 71ra et item Ballerini*

if "real gold were to be produced by alchemy, it would not be unlawful to sell it for the real thing, for nothing prevents art from employing certain natural causes for the production of natural and true effects, as Augustine says in the book *On the Trinity*[8] of things produced by the art of the demons." It should be noted nevertheless that, speaking about those who spend time on this practice of alchemy, the saying of the apostle in the second epistle to Timothy is commonly proven true: *ever learning, and never attaining to knowledge of the truth.*[9] They perform many experiments and practically never arrive at the perfect effect, they expend many things in this affair, time and money and labour and reputation, and are always found poorer from that which they expect to enrich them. And hence, if it is the case that all should abstain from this practice to avoid deceiving people by selling counterfeit gold and silver as the real thing, this goes most of all for clerics and religious.

1.3. On mixing copper into gold or silver. Artisans likewise commit fraud when <in> the works of silver which they sell, the silver itself is not found in as many *lege*[10] (to use the vernacular term) or works of gold in as many carats[11] as they are reasonably supposed to be, such that there is more mixture of copper[12] present than should be there, according to the statutes of the city or common custom. For silver is called entirely pure and free of any mixture when it is of twelve *lege*, and gold is called entirely pure when it is of twenty-four carats. And when it is of this level of purity, however long it stays in a fire it is not diminished in its weight or quantity. But if it is below the aforesaid level of *lege* or carats, cast into a fire it is reduced in quantity, because the other material of copper or tin[13] or other metal mixed therein is gradually consumed and disappears into smoke. If therefore there is a statute in the city that works of silver must be of ten and a half *lege*, namely of silver in one pound of silver work, if there were present silver of ten *lege* such that the rest is a mixture of copper, certainly one would commit fraud, because the half *lega* of copper in that work is being sold as silver.

2. Agents and brokers. About agents and brokers. These are mediators in many kinds of contracts. And if they are mediators in illicit and usurious kinds of exchange <i.e., moneychanging or bills of exchange>, then their practice of this craft on behalf of the usurious lender must necessarily be condemned, except perhaps when they do

---

8 Aug. *Trin.* 3, 8 (875).

9 *2 Tim* 3.7: "Ever learning, and never attaining to the knowledge of the truth."

10 Lat. *liga, -ae*, Ital. *lega* or *legha*. "Lega; … 2. alloy; the relation between the precious and base metal in a coin." Edler, *Terms of Business*, 151–2. See also Du Cange, s.v. *Liga*.

11 "Carata; the weight of a precious stone in carats." "Carato … 1. a variable unit of weight for gold, silver, and precious stones, sometimes 4 grains (in Venice, Paris, the Levant, and elsewhere)." Edler, *Terms of Business*, 63.

12 Lat. *aes, aeris* (spelled *es, eris* by Antoninus): "1 copper, bronze, or brass." *DMLBS*, s.v. Since bronze and brass are both alloys of copper, I have chosen "copper" for my translation.

13 Med. Lat. *stagnum, -i* (CL *stannum, -i*). Cf. "Stagniere*; tinsmith." Edler, *Terms of Business*, 279.

tractandis inter partes, quod pro labore suo accipiat a partibus secundum morem patrie, non improbatur. Sed caueat a mendaciis, puta referendo uni partium aliam: puta mulieri nubere uolenti uel propinquis eius hoc tractantibus, illum esse diuitem qui nil uel parum habet, esse modestum et bonum quem nouit esse discolum dissolutum et lusorem et huiusmodi. Sunt enim hec mendacia mortalia, cum sint in magnum detrimentum proximi. Et de huiusmodi mendacio intelligitur dictum Crisostomi, scilicet, "utrumque et periurium et mendacium diuini iudicii pena dampnatur, dicente scriptura, *Os quod mentitur occidit animam,"* 22 q. 5 *Iuramenti*.

2.1. Si est mediator in contractibus.

Si est mediator in contractibus emptionis et uenditionis uel permutationis, uel locationis et conductionis domorum agrorum merchationum, et huiusmodi, licite recipit lucrum a partibus secundum morem patrie. Abstineat tamen a fraudibus. Nam cum percipit partem unam ex eis grauare alteram, puta uendere uelle uel permutare mercimonia defectuosa pro bonis et huiusmodi, illicite agit mediatorem se faciendo seu cooperatorem huius fraudis, et teneri uidetur ad dampnum, *Extra, De iniuriis et dampno*, c. ult.

2.2. Si est mediator in emptione iurium montis.

Si est mediator in emptione iurium montis que quis ibi habet, distinguendum: quia si emptor hoc agit non ad faciendum negotiationem de huiusmodi iuribus, id est intentione reuendendi et inde lucrandi ex augmento pretii, sed ad prouidendum sue necessitati et gubernationi familie secundum decentiam sui status, tunc si contractus illius emptionis talium iurium seu creditorum montis dicatur esse licitus ut quidam asseuerant, erit et lucrum licitum quod consequitur proseneta ex tali mediatione; si illicitus ut ab aliis iudicatur, erit et lucrum illud illicitum, et cooperatio prosenete ad illud. De qua materia, scilicet emptionis talium iurium, habes diffuse supra in secunda parte titulo primo,

---

84 utrumque … **86** Iuramenti] Imo Chrom. in C. 22 q. 5 c. 12 (*Iuramenti*): … sicut in iuramento nullam conuenit esse perfidiam, ita quoque in uerbis nostris nullum debet esse mendacium, quia utrumque, et periurium et mendacium, diuini iudicii pena dampnatur, dicente scriptura [*Sap* 1.11]: "Os, quod mentitur, occidit animam."

93 teneri … ult] *X* 5.36.9 (*Si culpa*): Si culpa tua datum est damnum vel iniuria irrogata, seu aliis irrogantibus opem forte tulisti, aut haec imperitia tua sive negligentia evenerunt: iure super his satisfacere te oportet, nec ignorantia te excusat, si scire debuisti, ex facto tuo iniuriam verisimiliter posse contingere vel iacturam.

101 De … **102** primo] Ant. Flor. *Summa* 2.1.11 (apud M_I fol. Vr et Ballerini; 2.1.10 apud Mamachi 2:213–59): *de materia montis de Florentia et inprestitarum Venetiis et locis Ianuensium.*

this with the motive of enabling the one who receives the loan to provide for his necessities by means of this exchange transaction. But it is otherwise if the mediator is motivated by his own utility, aiming to make a profit from the transaction, as is <commonly> done.[14] Now if someone is a mediator between two parties in contracting a marriage, that he should receive <something> from the parties for his labour, in keeping with the custom of the country, is not disapproved. But let him beware of lies, such as in representing one of the parties to the other: for example, to a woman desiring to wed or to her relatives contracting the marriage, representing someone as rich who possesses nothing or little, or representing someone as modest and good whom he knows to be of bad temper, dissolute, and a gambler and so forth. For these are mortal sins, since they are to the great harm of a neighbour. And about this sort of lie the statement of Chrysostom applies, namely: "each of perjury and lying is condemned by the punishment of divine judgment, as Scripture says: *The mouth which lies kills the soul*," C. 22 q. 5 c. 12.[15]

2.1. If one is a mediator in contracts.

If someone is a mediator in contracts of purchase and sale or of exchange, or of lease and hire of houses, fields, or markets, and so forth, he licitly receives a profit from the parties according to the custom of the country. Nevertheless let him abstain from frauds. For when he perceives that one of the parties is burdening the other, say he wants to sell or exchange defective merchandise as good or things of this kind, he acts illicitly, making himself a mediator or cooperator in this fraud, and he seems to be bound <to make satisfaction> for the loss, *Extra*, *On injuries and losses*, c. 9.[16]

2.2. If one is a mediator in the purchase of credits in the *monte*.

If someone is a mediator in the purchase of credits in the *monte* which people have there, we must make distinctions. For if the buyer does this not in order to trade in these sorts of credits, that is, with the intention of reselling them to make a profit from increasing the price, but rather in order to provide for his needs and for the governance of his family according to the character of his state, then if the contract to purchase such credits of the *monte* is considered licit, as some affirm, the profit which the agent obtains from acting as mediator will also be licit. If it is illicit, as it is judged by others, that profit will also be illicit, and so will be the cooperation of the agent in the same. About this subject, namely purchasing such credits, there is an extensive discussion above

---

14 The autograph codex says merely "as is done," but F_3 fol. 71ra adds "commonly" above the line, which helps the sense and seems plausible as an interpretation of Antoninus's intended meaning; this addition is also transmitted by Ballerini.

On the different types of exchange transaction to which Antoninus alludes here, see Ant. Flor. *Summa* 3.8.3 (above), section 1.

15 Rather Chrom. in C. 22 q. 5 c. 12 (*Iuramenti*): "… as it is not fitting that there be any perfidy in the oath, so also there is to be no lying in our words, because each of perjury and lying is condemned by the punishment of divine judgment, as Scripture says: The mouth which lies kills the soul (*Sap* 1.11)."

16 *X* 5.36.9 (*Si culpa*).

et quia dubium, ideo dimictendum exercitium in huiusmodi. Si autem emptor talium iurium hoc facit negotiando, id est intendendo ad reuendendum et inde lucrandum, etiam si de se foret licitus contractus talis emptionis, cum sit turpe lucrum quia non utilitati hominum rationabili sed cupiditati deseruiat, illicita uidetur talis emptio, ar. 14 q. 4 *Quicumque*, et per consequens illicitum est cooperari tali contractui mediando, 11 q. 3: "Qui consentit peccantibus, maledictus erit apud Deum et homines," ubi dicit glossa super uerbo *consentit*, scilicet "per cooperationem."

2.3. Idem de omnibus qui sunt mediatores.

Idem dicendum de omnibus qui sunt mediatores in quocumque contractu etiam si non sint prosenete. Solent enim mercatores unius ciuitatis frequenter esse mediatores merchatoribus aliarum ciuitatum ad procurandum uenditionem suorum mercimoniorum que ad eos transmictunt secundum commissionem quam eis faciunt per litteras suas. Et tales mediatores communiter retinent sibi unum florenum pro centenario quasi pro suo labore cooperationis, sine alia conuentione facta ad inuicem. Et sic uice uersa, fit eis, quando sua mercimonia uenduntur ab aliis in ciuitatibus eorum. Cum ergo hoc sit de communi more merchatorum in ratione fundatum, quia omnis labor optat premium, non apparet illicitum, ar. D. 8 *Que contra mores*. Verum si ostendunt tales mediatores per litteras uel uerba uelle gratis et ratione amicitie in huiusmodi seruire mercatoribus aliorum lochorum, cum et ipsi etiam seruiant gratis uice uersa in similibus, tunc non liceret occulte aliquid ut pretium laboris accipere, puta dicendo se mercimonia eorum uendidisse centum, cum uendiderint centum et unum florenum, illud unum sibi retinendo pro suo labore. Fraus enim est et dolus ex amicitia ostendere gratis uelle pro aliquo laborare, et occulte exinde pretium laboris extorquere.

---

103 Si … **107** Quicumque] C. 14 q. 4 c. 9 (*Quicumque*): Quicumque tempore messis uel uindemiae non necessitate, sed propter cupiditatem conparat annonam uel uinum, uerbi gratia de duobus denariis conparat modium unum, et seruat, usque dum uendatur denariis quatuor aut sex, aut amplius, hoc turpe lucrum dicimus.

108 11 … **109** homines] C. 11 q. 3 c. 100 (*Qui consentit*): Qui consentit peccantibus, et defendit alium delinquentem, maledictus erit apud Deum et homines, et corripietur increpatione seuerissima.

109 glossa … **110** cooperationem] *Glossa ord.* ad idem, s.v. *consentit*: per cooperationem, et auctoritatem, ut 2 q. 1 notum sit, in fine.

120 ar. … mores] D. 8 c. 2 (*Que contra mores*): … ut pactum gentis inter se aut consuetudine ciuitatis, uel lege firmatum, nulla ciuis aut peregrini libidine uioletur.

---

108 peccantibus] *in rasura*

in part 2, title 1,[17] and because it is doubtful, therefore this kind of practice should be set aside. Now if the buyer of such credits is trading in them, that is, he is intending to resell and to make a profit, even if in itself this sort of contract of purchase should turn out to be licit, nevertheless since the profit is shameful because it does not serve reasonable human utility, but rather greed, such purchase seems to be illicit, by the argument of C. 14 q. 4 c. 9.[18] And by consequence it is illicit to cooperate by mediating this sort of contract, C. 11 q. 3 c. 100: "He who consents to sinners shall be cursed before God and men."[19] And the gloss says there on the word "consents," namely "by cooperation."[20]

2.3. The same applies to all those who are mediators.

The same must be said about all who are mediators in whatever kind of contract, even if they are not agents. For the merchants of one city are accustomed to act frequently as mediators for the merchants of other cities in order to provide for the sale of their merchandise, which they send over to them according to a commission[21] which they make with them by writing letters to each other. And such mediators commonly keep one florin per 100 for themselves as if for the labour of their cooperation, without any agreement made between the two. And thus vice versa this is done for them, when their merchandise is sold by others in their cities. Since therefore this is part of the common custom of merchants and founded in reason, because all labour desires its reward, it does not seem illicit, by the argument of D. 8 c. 2.[22] But if such mediators present themselves through letters or words as wanting to act free of charge or on account of friendship in serving the merchants of other places in these matters, and when the others also will vice versa act free of charge in similar affairs, then it would not be licit to secretly take something as the price of labour, say, stating that one had sold their merchandise for 100 when they had actually sold for 101 florins, keeping that one florin for oneself for one's labour. For it is fraud and malice to present oneself as wanting to work for another free of charge because of friendship, and then to secretly extract a price for one's labour.

---

17 Ant. Flor. *Summa* 2.1.11 (apud M_1 fol. Vr, 31v–36v, Ballerini 2:159–91; 2.1.10 apud Mamachi 2:213–59): *de materia montis de Florentia et inprestitarum Venetiis et locis Ianuensium.*

18 C. 14 q. 4 c. 9 (*Quicumque*): "Whoever, at the time of harvest of wheat or grapes, buys wheat or wine, not by any need, but out of cupidity, so that, for example, he buys a measure for two pennies and keeps it until it is sold for four, or six, or more pennies, we say that he is engaging in a shameful gain."

19 C. 11 q. 3 c. 100 (*Qui consentit*): "He who consents to sinners and defends another in his sin shall be cursed before God and men, and he will be corrected with a most severe reproof."

20 *Glossa ord.* ad idem, s.v. *consentit*: "*He who consents.* By cooperation and approval, as at C. 2 q. 1 c. 10, toward the end."

21 Lat. *commissio*, Ital. *commessione*: "commission (to buy or sell merchandise given to someone who is not a member or employee of the company)." Edler, *Terms of Business*, 80.

22 D. 8 c. 2 (*Que contra mores*): "And so a common pact, confirmed by the custom of city or nation or by law, is not to be violated by any caprice of a citizen or of a foreigner."

3. De lanificibus.

De lanificibus. Huiusmodi ars satis necessaria est uite humane, pro uestitu ad arcendum frighus nuditatem tegendam lasciuiam prouochantem et decentem ornatum persone. Habet autem hoc artificium multa membra sibi deseruienta.

3.1. De emptione ad terminum.

Et primo quidem communiter consueuerunt emere lanas a mercatoribus, termino sex mensium uel anni dato ad soluendum pretium lane. Pariformiter lanifices ipsi pannos inde perfectos uendunt merchatoribus uel retagliatoribus plures simul cum termino mensium uel anni ad soluendum pretium, et retagliator ipse pannos uendit de tempore in tempus, et per partes, puta tot cannas uni, tot alteri, sed cum termino solutionis simili. Hoc autem communiter obseruatur, quia uendens lanam uel pannos, uendit plus uendendo in termino quam uendendo peccunia tunc sibi numerata, seu iuxta uulgare a chontanti, ad rationem X pro centenario. Exempli gratia: uendit lanifex pannum finem seu pretiosum, florenis 45 si sibi tunc datur peccunia, ubi autem non detur, sed terminum uult consuetum, scilicet sex mensium uel anni, uendit cum 50 florenis. In quo contractu merito dubitatur, utrum sit contractus usurarius cum scilicet uendit lanifex uel retagliator pannum illum 50 florenis ratione termini sibi dati sex mensium uel anni. Equidem certum est quod uendere pannos uel alias res plus iusto pretio ratione dilationis solutionis fiende | contrac- fol. 74v
tus decernitur usurarius, *Extra*, *De usuris*, *Consuluit*, et c. *In ciuitate*. Et hoc nisi illa mercimonia esset reseruaturus ad tempus, quo ipsa tali pretio quo tunc uenduntur uel maiori essent ualitura, quia tunc licitum ut ibi dicitur. Ista ergo exceptione ablata que licitat contractum, cum scilicet illa non esset reseruaturus, opportet uidere, quid iudicetur iustum pretium. Nam terminus ipse seu dilatio data ad soluendum de se non facit contractum usurarium, ymmo

---

145 Equidem … **147** Consuluit] *X* 5.19.10 (*Consuluit*): … an negotiator poena consimili debeat condemnari, qui merces suas longe maiori pretio distrahit, si ad solutionem faciendam prolixioris temporis dilatio prorogetur, quam si ei in continenti pretium persolvatur. Verum quia, quid in his casibus tenendum sit, ex evangelio Lucae manifeste cognoscitur, in quo dicitur: “Date mutuum, nihil inde sperantes:” huiusmodi homines pro intentione lucri, quam habent, quum omnis usura et superabundantia prohibeatur in lege, iudicandi sunt male agere, et ad ea, quae taliter sunt accepta, restituenda, in animarum iudicio efficaciter inducendi.

147 In ciuitate] *X* 5.19.6 (*In civitate*): In civitate tua dicis saepe contingere, quod, quum quidam piper, seu cinamomum, seu alias merces comparant, quae tunc ultra quinque libras non valent, et promittunt, se illis, a quibus illas merces accipiunt, sex libras statuto termino soluturos. Licet autem contractus huiusmodi ex tali forma non possit censeri nomine usurarum, nihilominus tamen venditores peccatum incurrunt, nisi dubium sit, merces illas plus minusve solutionis tempore valituras. Et ideo cives tui saluti suae bene consulerent, si a tali contractu cessarent, quum cogitationes hominum omnipotenti Deo nequeant occultari.

---

129 frighus] + ad *s.l.* F_3 *fol. 71rb* **135** mensium] *scilicet* sex(?) **139** uendendo] + cum F_3 *fol. 71rb s.l. et item Ballerini* **140** finem] *i.e.* finum(?) **141** florenis] flor. *cod. et similiter passim* **149** quia … dicitur] *in rasura*

3. Wool merchants. About wool merchants. This sort of craft is quite necessary to human life, for clothing to ward off the cold, to cover nakedness because it provokes lasciviousness, and for the decent attire of the person. Now this craft has many members who serve it.

3.1. Purchase on credit. First of all, wool merchants are commonly accustomed to buy wool from other merchants on credit,[23] with six months or a year to pay the price of the wool. Equally the wool merchants themselves sell a great deal of the finished wool cloth all at once to merchants or retail cloth dealers[24] on credit, with so many months or a year to pay the price, and then the retail cloth dealer sells the cloth from time to time and piecemeal, say so many ells[25] to one person, so many to another, but likewise on credit, with deferred payment. Now this is commonly observed, that someone selling wool or cloth sells it for more when selling on credit than when selling for money counted out to him right then (or "for cash"[26] in the vernacular), at a rate of 10 per cent. For example: a wool merchant sells fine or valuable cloth for 45 florins if the money is paid to him right then; however, when it is not paid but instead the buyer wants to buy on credit in the usual way, namely for six months or a year, he sells it for 50 florins. When it comes to this contract, people are rightfully in doubt about whether it is a usurious contract, that is, when the wool merchant or retail cloth dealer sells the cloth for 50 florins because he gives credit for six months or a year. Indeed it is certain that a sale of cloth or other goods for more than the just price because of delayed payment has been ruled a usurious contract, *Extra, On usury*, c. 10 and c. 6.[27] And this is the case unless the merchandise was intended to be stored until such goods would be worth the price for which they are now being sold <on credit>, or worth even more, because then this would be licit, as is said in the canons just cited. Therefore, having set aside this exception which makes the contract licit, that is, when the merchandise was not intended to be held onto, it is necessary to observe what is judged to be the just price. For the fact of giving credit or deferring payment does not in itself make the contract

23 "Termine, a or al; 1. on time, on credit; cf. a tempo. 2. at maturity (of a loan or a bill of exchange)." Edler, *Terms of Business*, 293. "Termine, per lo; for the [usual] term (one year being always understood). Found in the Medici ledgers of the 15th century." Ibid., 294. On the credit practices of the wool, silk, and *calimala* guilds, see ibid., appendix 3.

24 "Ritagliatore; retail cloth merchant (in Florence)." Ibid., 247.

25 Lat. *canna, -ae*, Ital. *canna*: "a cloth measure, an ell (about 2 1/3–3 Eng. yards; 3–4 *braccia* equal 1 *canna*. The most widely used cloth measure in Italy and other countries)." Ibid., 59, 317.

26 "Contanti, a; for cash." Ibid., 86.

27 *X* 5.19.10 (*Consuluit*); *X* 5.19.6 (*In civitate*). "X 5.19.6 deals with a contract of sale. In this decretal and in the third question of X 5.19.10, we have cases of mental usury because the buyer on credit is effectively granted a loan that is repayable with profit." Armstrong, *Usury and Public Debt*, 302–3, see also 59n26.

si gratis facit karitas est. Sed uendere plus iusto pretio ratione temporis dilati, hoc facit usuram.

3.2. De moderato lucro.

Et cum nullus faciat aliquod artificium gratis sed ea intentione, ut ex moderato lucro exinde sibi prouideat, quod utique licet: si lanifex, deductis omnibus expensis factis, puta lane manufacture ministrorum pensionum et huiusmodi, de dicto panno lucretur V uel sex secundum commune iudicium artis quod debent inde lucrari, quia illa omnia sibi constant 43 uel 44 uel 45 et uendendo pannum ad terminum 50 florenis remanent in lucro 5 uel sex uel circa, non uidetur immoderatum lucrum nec iniustum pretium, etiam si uenderet ad contantos, cum cogatur uendere ad terminum ratione communis consuetudinis. Si enim solum uellet uendere ad contantos pauchos inueniret emptores. Nec obstat si dicatur quia res tantum ualet quantum uendi potest ut dicit lex; sed non potest uendi ad contantos nisi pro 45 ergo illud uidetur esse iustum pretium, et si plus petit uidetur usura. Nam res ualet quantum uendi potest, sed secundum commune iudicium sapientum in arte extimata et nisi impediatur ut in casu nostro quia communis consuetudo dat talem terminum cum tamen communis ratio uenditionis sit ut data re recipiatur pretium. Et precium eciam non consistit in pretio id est in puncto indiuisibili sed habet quosdam terminos latitudinis. Et inde recipiunt ex illa expectatione precii multa incommoda et pericula perdendi, quibus opportet eos se exponere si uolunt continuare negotium artis. Hec omnia simul et si non aliqua de per se ex hiis uidentur, tollerabilem reddere talem modum uendendi ad terminum. Non autem uidetur facere talem contractum illicitum hoc solum quia uendendo ad contantos dat pannum pro minori pretio, scilicet 45, quia tale pretium currit in uenditione ad contantos; quia ex hoc quod de uno et eodem genere mercimonii uendat uni pro 10 ut iusto pretio, alteri ratione amicitie uel quia indiget peccuniis det pro 8 uel 5, non potest dici usurarius propterea in primo contractu. Si enim lanifex uellet uendere pannos suos ad terminum eo pretio quo uendit ad contantos in capite anni, reperiret se in suo capitali et frustra suum laborem pro aliis exposuisset ut dicunt, uel minutissimum et indecens lucrum consequeretur, et hoc non esset solum una uice uel in uno anno sed quasi semper.

---

164 res … lex] Cfr *Dig.* 36.1.1.16; *Dig.* 36.2.63; *Dig.* 9.2.33; *Glossa ord.* ad *X* 5.19.6 s.v. *non valent.*
169 precium … **171** latitudinis] Cfr Io. Scot. *In quartum* d. 15 q. 2 n. 15 (18:283b); Bern. Sen. *Evang. aet.* 35, 1, 2 (4:191–2).

---

157 huiusmodi] + deductis omnibus expensis factis eciam extraordinariis F_3 *fol. 71va* **158** panno] pannos *cod.* **159** 45] *p.c.* : *haud leg. a.c.* **160** remanent] remanet *cod.* **164** Nec … **170** est] *in marg. infer add. sed post verba* in casu nostro quia *attritum est folium, et reliqua verba collegi ex* F_3 *fol. 71va* **170** in² … **174** terminum] *in marg. super. add.* **171** inde] *ut vid. vel* tamen *secundum* F_3 *fol. 71va* **172** opportet] *ut vid.* **182** uel minutissimum] et hoc non esset *a.c.*

usurious; actually if it is granted free of charge then it is charity. But to sell for more than the just price because of a time delay, this makes it usury.

3.2. On moderate profit. Now no one practises any craft for free, but with the intention that with the moderate profit one makes from it one may provide for oneself, which is entirely licit. And therefore if a wool merchant, after deducting all his expenses – such as for the manufacture of wool and employee salaries and so forth – makes a profit from the aforesaid cloth of the 5 or 6 that he ought to make from it (following the common judgment of the craft), because all those expenses amount to 43 or 44 or 45 and, since he sells the cloth on credit for 50 florins, there remain 5 or 6 or thereabouts as profit, this does not seem to be an immoderate profit or an unjust price even if he were selling for cash, although he is compelled to sell on credit because of the common custom. For if he wanted to sell only for cash he would find few buyers. Nor would it suffice to object that "a thing is worth as much as it can be sold for," as the law says;[28] but it can only be sold for cash at the price of 45, therefore that appears to be the just price, and if one seeks more it seems to be usury. For a thing is worth as much as it can be sold for, but estimated according to the common judgment of wise people in the craft, and unless there is an obstacle, as in our case, because this sort of credit is a part of standard custom, notwithstanding the common principle of sale that the price should be received when the goods are delivered. And also the <just> price does not consist in an unchanging price, that is, an exact point, but has a latitude within a range of values.[29] And wool merchants receive many inconveniences and dangers of loss that arise out of having to wait for payment of the price, yet they are required to expose themselves to these if they want to continue the business of the craft. All these put together, even if no one of them in and of itself, seem to render tolerable this mode of selling on credit. Now this alone does not seem to make this contract illicit, that when they sell for cash they offer the cloth for a lower price, namely 45, which is the price current in sales for cash. Because the fact that someone sells one and the same type of merchandise to one person for 10 as the just price and to another person he offers it for 8 or 5, because of friendship or because the person is short of money, does not entail that his conduct in the first contract can be called usurious. For if a wool merchant wanted to sell his cloth on credit at the price at which he sells for cash, at the end of the year[30] he would find himself in his capital and he would have put his labour out for others in vain, as they say, or he would obtain an extremely minute and unsuitable profit, and this not only one time or in one year but

28 Cfr *Dig.* 36.1.1.16; *Dig.* 36.2.63; *Dig.* 9.2.33; *Glossa ord.* ad *X* 5.19.6 s.v. *non valent.* On this maxim, see above, ch. 3, and see also Ant. Flor. *Summa* 2.1.16 (above), section 3.1.3.1.

29 Cfr Io. Scot. *In quartum* d. 15 q. 2 n. 15 (18:283b); Bern. Sen. *Evang. aet.* 35, 1, 2 (4:191–2).

30 Lat. *caput anni.* "Capo d'anno; end of the (fiscal) year." Edler, *Terms of Business*, 62.

Vendendo autem pannum talem ad contantos 45 florenis, quamuis parum uel nichil de illo lucrentur, tamen sic oportet eos aliquos pannos uendere ut habeant peccunias paratas ad dandum ministris de die in diem, cum habeant expectare solutionem pannorum uenditorum ad terminum per mensem et annum. Vnde etiam ex hoc substinent laborem ad mictendum ad exigendum pluries, et multotiens etiam in termino conuento non soluunt unde incommodum patiuntur, et aliquando fallendo non soluunt. Que omnia cessarent si numerata sibi peccunia cum uendunt, daretur. Et ut dicunt, libentius ipsi uenderent tales pannos tali pretio, scilicet 45 uel sex ad contantos si omnes uel maiorem partem sic possent uendere, quam pro 50 ad terminum, quia peccuniam tunc habitam cito reinuestirent pluries in anno pannos faciendo, et quod minus de pretio cuiuslibet panni acciperent ad contantos uendendo quam ad terminum, recompensaretur ex multiplicatione factionis plurium pannorum, quia facerent centum pannos ubi faciunt 50 propter carentiam peccunie quam exspectare habent ex termino.

3.3. De lanifice in casu usurario.

Sed si lanifex in casu proposito uendendo ad contantos pannum pro 45 florenis, quia tale pretium currit, inde lucratur competenter, puta ad rationem 10 pro centenario uel circa, quia ipse expense in eo facte sunt 40 unde quinque uel sex lucratur, et nichilominus ut plus lucretur non uult uendere ad contantos eo pretio, quod posset, sed uult potius ad terminum uendere, ubi superlucrabitur ad rationem 20 pro centenario: male potest excusari ab usura, quia tunc ratione termini seu temporis quod uendi non potest, uult plus iusto pretio, illa 5 de panno uendendo ipsum ad terminum. Et hoc improbatur ut usura ibi in dicta decret. *Consuluit* et *In ciuitate*. Est tamen materia ista multum intrichata nec bene clara, et ideo non amplianda, cum et tales etiam aliquando decipiant seipsos in tractando huiusmodi negotia et intentionem suam obumbrent. De hiis multa habes supra in secunda parte titulo primo c. de emptione et uenditione. Ibi uide.

---

210 De … **211** uenditione] Ant. Flor. *Summa* 2.1.8 (apud M_I fol. Vr et Ballerini; 2.1.7 apud Mamachi 2:169–92): *de usura in emtione et venditione* (vel *de venditione ad terminum*); *Summa* 2.1.16 et 2.1.17 supra.

---

188 exigendum] + scilicet *a.c.* **193** quia] + ex *a.c. ut vid.* **206** ut usura] *in marg. sin. add.* **208** nec] et ideo *a.c.*

practically always. Now although the merchants may take little or no profit from selling their cloth for 45 florins in cash, nevertheless it is necessary for them to sell some cloth for cash so that they have money available to pay their employees from day to day, while they are forced to await payment for a month or a year for the cloth they have already sold on credit. And from this practice of giving credit the merchants also sustain the labour of constantly sending people to collect the debts, and often enough the purchasers do not pay on time, causing inconvenience to the merchants, and sometimes the purchasers default and do not pay at all. All of this would cease if the money were counted out and paid when the sale was made. And the merchants themselves, as they say, would sell their cloth much more willingly at a price of 45 or 46 for cash if they could sell all of it or the greater part in this way, than for 50 on credit, because then with the money in hand they would be quick to reinvest it regularly throughout the year in making cloth, and the difference in price they receive by selling however much cloth for cash rather than on credit would be made up for by the increased amount of cloth manufactured, because they would make 100 cloths where they make 50 for lack of the money which they are stuck waiting for on a term of credit.

3.3. The wool merchant in a case of usury.

But if we take this case of a wool merchant who sells cloth for 45 florins cash because that is the current market price and makes a suitable profit therefrom, say at a rate of 10 per cent or thereabouts, because his costs for the cloth amounted to 40 and thus he makes 5 or 6 in profit, and nevertheless in order to make more profit he does not want to sell for cash at that price, as he could do, but rather wants to sell on credit which will yield greater profits at a rate of 20 per cent: such a merchant can hardly be excused from usury, since in that case, when he sells the cloth for 5 more on credit, he wants 5 more than the just price for the credit or for time, which cannot be sold. And this is rejected as usury in the previously cited decretals *Consuluit* and *In civitate*.[31] This present matter is extremely involved and not fully clear, and therefore it should not be widely disseminated, and also because people who carry out this sort of trade sometimes deceive even themselves, concealing their intention. About these matters there is much written above in part 2, title 1, the chapter on buying and selling.[32] See there.

---

31 *X* 5.19.10 (*Consuluit*); *X* 5.19.6 (*In civitate*).

32 Ant. Flor. *Summa* 2.1.8 (apud M_1 fol. Vr et Ballerini; 2.1.7 apud Mamachi 2:169–92): *de usura in emtione et venditione* (or *de venditione ad terminum*); *Summa* 2.1.16 and 2.1.17 (above).

3.4. De ponentibus peccunias apud lanifices.

De ponentibus peccunias apud lanifices. Et illi quidem qui ponunt peccuniam in huiusmodi artificio per modum societatis iuste, scilicet licite exercendo cum debitis pactis, participando in lucro et dampno proportionaliter, non peccant. Et pacta iusta seruari debent, *Extra*, *De pactis*, c. 1.

3.5. Si lanifex peccunias accipiat ad discretionem.

Si autem accipiat lanifex peccunias aliorum non per modum societatis, sed ad discretionem secundum uulgare, id est ut saluo capitali secundum discretionem suam lanifex det sibi de lucro prout sibi uidetur: cum hoc sit usurarium, *Extra*, *De usuris*, *Consuluit*, peccat lanifex accipiendo talem peccuniam ad usuram, quia dat illi occasionem talis peccati. Et *digni sunt morte non solum qui faciunt sed etiam qui consentiunt facientibus*, Ro. 1, et 2 q. 1 *Notum*. Et hoc nisi lanifex indigeret peccuniis: tunc enim sicut liceret sibi mutuo accipere ad usuram, sic in tali casu; ab eo tamen qui est paratus ad faciendum talia lucra usuraria scienter. Vnde a persona simplici que hoc putaret iustum lucrum, alias non facturus, non liceret sic peccuniam accipere. |

3.6. De ministris in apotheca.

fol. 75r

Item cum quis est minister in apothecha alicuius laborans, et certam partem peccunie ponit in exercitio artis, saluo capitali ipso, et propter dictam peccuniam puta centum florenos percipit salarium a magistro pro suo labore 50 florenos, ubi sine illa peccunia sic exposita non recepisset nisi 40, utique usura est: nam illa X intelliguntur dari sibi propter centum mutuatos, ar. 14 q. 3 *Si*

215 Et … 1] *X* 1.35.1 (*Antigonus*): Aut inita pacta suam obtineant firmitatem, aut conventus (si se non cohibuerit) ecclesiasticam sentiat disciplinam. Universi dixerunt, pax servetur, pacta custodiantur. Vide *Glossa ord.* ad idem: … Nota quod pacta seruari debent. … Pactum vero quod dolo initum est, non valet. Cfr *X* 3.19.8 (*Cum universorum*).

220 digni … **221** facientibus] *Rm* 1.32: Qui cum justitiam Dei cognovissent, non intellexerunt quoniam qui talia agunt, digni sunt morte: et non solum qui ea faciunt, sed etiam qui consentiunt facientibus.

221 2 … Notum] C. 2 q. 1 c. 10 (*Notum sit*): … et nullatenus canonica instituta alicuius temeritate contempni permittas, quia facientem et consentientem par pena constringit.

230 nam … **231** feneraueris] C. 14 q. 10 c. 1 (*Si feneraveris*): Qui plus quam dederit expetit usuras accipit. Si feneraueris hominem, id est si tu mutuum dederis pecuniam tuam, … si plus quam dedisti expectes accipere, fenerator es, et in hoc inprobandus, non laudandus.

213 iuste] F_3 *fol. 71va* : *haud leg. cod.* **213** scilicet … **214** exercendo] *in marg. sin. add.* **215** pactis … 1] F_3 *fol. 71va* : *spatium dimidiae lineae praeb. cod.* **218** uidetur] *ut vid.* : uidebitur F_3 *fol. 71va* : *om. Ballerini* **228** florenos] flor. *cod. et similiter passim*

3.4. Depositing money with wool merchants. About those depositing money with wool merchants. And indeed those who deposit money in this sort of craft in the form of a just partnership, that is, engaging in a partnership licitly with the appropriate agreements and participating proportionately in the profit and loss, certainly they commit no sin. And just agreements must be kept, *Extra, On agreements*, c. 1.[33]

3.5. If a wool merchant receives money at his discretion. Now if a wool merchant receives money from others not in the form of a partnership but "at his discretion"[34] (using the vernacular), that is, with the principal safe, according to his discretion the wool merchant should give to the lender some profit as seems good to him: since this is usurious (*Extra, On usury*, c. 10),[35] the wool merchant sins in receiving this money at usury, because he gives to the other party the occasion of this sin. And *they are worthy of death, not only they that do them, but also they that consent to them that do them*, Romans 1, and C. 2 q. 1 c. 10.[36] And so it is, unless the wool merchant should be in need of money: for then, just as it would be licit for him to receive a loan at usury, so in this sort of case; yet only from one who is knowingly prepared to make these usurious profits. Hence it would not be lawful to receive money on these terms from a simple person who supposes this to be a just profit, and who would not do it if he knew otherwise.

3.6. Employees in the workshop. Also when someone is an employee working in someone's workshop,[37] and this employee places a certain amount of money into the business of the craft, with the principal itself safe, and because of the aforesaid money, say 100 florins, he receives from the employer a salary of 50 florins for his labour, when without the money being lent in this way he would only receive 40, this is certainly usury: for those 10 are understood to be given to him because of the 100 he

33 *X* 1.35.1 (*Antigonus*). See also *Glossa ord.* ad idem. Cfr *X* 3.18.8 (*Cum universorum*).

34 Lat. *ad discretionem*, Ital. *a discrezione*. On *a discrezione* contracts: "The Church forbade usury, but it did not forbid bankers to be generous toward depositors and to pay them a return on their deposits 'as a free gift.' Such deposits were called *depositi a discrezione* because they yielded a return payable at the discretion of the banker. There are many examples of this practice in the Medici Bank's records but it dates back to the twelfth century. The characteristic of *depositi a discrezione* was that there existed no contractual obligation to pay interest on the part of the banker, but he was impelled to do so if he wanted to stay in business and retain his customers." De Roover, *Great Economic Thinkers*, 31–2.

35 *X* 5.19.10 (*Consuluit*).

36 *Rm* 1.32: "Who, having known the justice of God, did not understand that they who do such things, are worthy of death; and not only they that do them, but they also that consent to them that do them."

C. 2 q. 1 c. 10 (*Notum sit*): "Do not in any way allow anyone, by any sort of temerity, to hold in contempt canonical institutes, because an equal penalty binds the one who commits a deed and the one who consents to it."

37 Lat. *apotheca*, Ital. *apoteca*. "Apoteca, see Bottega." "Bottega; 1. shop (for displaying and selling goods). 2. workshop (of a master artisan)." Edler, *Terms of Business*, 51. Antoninus uses this word *apotheca* both to describe workshops where manufacturing is carried out (as in the current paragraph) and shops for displaying and selling goods (as in the paragraph on apothecaries).

feneraueris; 40 autem iuste recipit ex quo labor exercitii sui 40 extimatur, et illa X restituere tenetur.

3.7. De consulibus. Sed et consules artis lane siue alterius artis, cum uniuersitas ipsius artis ex introitibus suis habundans peccunia mutuat eam ministris artis seu lanificibus, ut exercentes eam in arte, de lucro inde sequuto tantum dent pro centenario puta quinque expendenda in pios nichilominus usus, ut pauperibus: usuram commictunt, quamuis nichil ipsi participerent de tali lucro, 14 q. 3 *Vsura*. Et quia ipsi sunt auctores talis contractus, si disponere non ualent, ut de peccunia uniuersitatis que illud lucrum usurarium habuit, restitutio fiat hiis qui usuras soluerunt, tenentur ipsi de suo restituere, ar. *De iniur. et damp.*, *Si culpa*, et D. 46, *Sicut non suo*.

3.8. De officialibus. Item consules artis lane uel officiales mercantie, uel alii quicumque officiales, cum ante eos defertur causa usuraria, et usuras quidem immoderatas restituere cogunt non tamen in totum sed cum quadam apparenti equitate, puta ad rationem quinque pro centenario; uel cogunt ad compromictendum in aliquos cum clare perpendunt de usura; uel sententiant ut tanto tempore qui usuras recepit teneat tantumdem peccunie eius qui usuras soluit, quanto tempore ipse tenuit peccunias usurarii: omnia ista illicita sunt et tenentur ad satisfactionem lesis, non obstante quod statutum sic decerneret, quod nullius roboris extat, ymmo facientes talia statuta quod usure non possint repeti sunt exchommunicati et seruantes ea, *De usuris*, *Ex graui*, in Clem. Et multo magis cum statuta

---

237 14 … **238** Vsura] C. 14 q. 3 c. 4 (*Usura est*): Usura est, ubi amplius requiritur quam quod datur.

240 De … **241** culpa] *X* 5.36.9 (*Si culpa*): vide supra.

241 D. … suo] D. 46 c. 10 (*Sicut non suo*): Sicut non suo, ita nec alieno nomine aliquis clericorum exercere fenus attemptet. Indecens enim est crimen suum commodis alienis inpendere et exercere.

250 quod … **251** Clem.] *Clem.* 5.5.1 (*Ex gravi*): Officiales communitatem, facientes, dictantes vel scribentes statuta super usuris solvendis, non repetendis, vel non restituendis, vel iudicantes secundum illa, vel non delentes illa, si possunt, infra tres menses de libris communitatum, vel illa servantes, excommunicati sunt. (Ioann. Andr.).

---

234 eam] eas *a.c.* **237** participerent] *vel* participeret *cod.* | 3] 4 *cod.* **241** 46] 47 *cod.*
247 ipse] + usurarius *a.c.*

lent, by the argument of C. 14 q. 10 c. 1.[38] But he justly receives 40, since the labour of his job is estimated at 40; and he is bound to repay the additional 10.

3.7. Consuls. But also consuls[39] of the wool craft or of another craft commit usury when the craft guild,[40] abounding in money from its receipts,[41] lends money to the craft's employees or to the wool merchants, such that the borrowers use it for the craft, and of the profits arising therefrom they only pay, say, 5 per cent, to be spent, however, on pious uses such as the poor. The consuls commit usury even though they themselves share in none of the profits, C. 14 q. 3 c. 4.[42] And because they are the originators of this contract, if it does not suffice to use the guild's money which was made as usurious profit to make restitution to those who have paid usury, they are bound themselves to make restitution from their own property, by the argument of *On injuries and losses*, c. 9,[43] and D. 46 c. 10.[44]

3.8. Officials. Also consuls of the wool craft or officials of the mercantile court[45] or whatever other kind of officials, when a case of usury is brought before them and they do indeed compel immoderate usuries to be restored, yet not in full but with a certain only apparent equity, say at a rate of 5 per cent; or they force a compromise upon some parties when they clearly recognize usury; or they pronounce that one who took usuries should retain the sum of money belonging to the one who paid usuries for the same amount of time as he borrowed the usurer's monies: all the aforesaid are illicit, and these consuls or officials are bound to make satisfaction to the injured parties, notwithstanding that this has been decreed by a statute, since it is of no force, and actually those who create these statutes that usuries cannot be reclaimed are excommunicated as well as those who observe them, *On*

38 C. 14 q. 10 c. 1 (*Se feneraveris*): "He who receives more than he has given seeks usury. If you have lent to a man at interest, that is, if you have given your money in loan ... if you expect to receive more than you gave, you are a lender at interest, and in this you are to be condemned, and not to be praised."

39 "Console; consul or commercial agent (appointed by a government or a powerful mercantile gild, e.g., the Calimala Gild of Florence, to protect the interest of its citizens or the gild members in a foreign country)." Edler, *Terms of Business*, 85.

40 I interpret the Lat. *universitas ipsius artis* as referring to the wool guild proper, the Arte di Lana.

41 "Entrata e uscita; 1. receipt and expenditure." Edler, *Terms of Business*, 112.

42 C. 14 q. 3 c. 4 (*Usura est*): "It is usury, where more is required than is given."

43 *X* 5.36.9 (*Si culpa*).

44 D. 46 c. 10 (*Sicut non suo*): "No cleric should attempt to engage in money-lending, either in his own name on in another's, for it is indecent to cover up one's crime under another's gains."

45 Lat. *mercantia*. "Mercanzia; ... 3. Gild of merchants and the court for mercantile cases (in Pisa, Siena, and esp. in Florence, where from 1319 on the *Mercanzia* was the judicial organ of the 12 major gilds for cases between Florentines and between Florentines and foreigners)." Edler, *Terms of Business*, 176.

disponunt quod in huiusmodi contractibus qui usuram sapiunt, non possit haberi recursos ad iudicium ecclesiastichum, quod est expresse contra libertatem ecclesie, cum hoc spectet ad iudicium ecclesie. Vnde exchommunicati sunt et qui ea seruant, *Extra, De sententia excommunicationis, Nouerit.* De quo uide infra in titulo de exchommunicatione.

3.9. De ministris artis lane.

De ministris artis lane. Et primo de schardasseriis. Hii immodestissimi in uerbis et factis sunt. Quorum animarum et si curam magistri eorum non habeant aut inquirere de uita eorum, sed solum ad laborem conducuntur sub certa mercede, tamen ab insolentiis eorum iniuriis et lasciuiis in apotecis suis et domibus debent cohercere quantum ualent et permaxime a uitio turpissimo. Mercedem autem quesitam secundum conuentionem eis reddere tardare non debent secundum illud Tob. 4: *Quicumque tibi aliquid operatus fuerit, statim ei mercedem tribue. Nec merces mercenarii omnino apud te maneat.* Et multo minus fraudare uel diminuere, dando eis monetas diminutas, uel pannum aut uictualia cum debeant habere peccuniam unde decipiuntur, contra quos inuehitur Iacobi 5: *Ecce merces operariorum uestrorum que fraudata est a uobis clamat* contra uos *et clamor in aures Domini introiuit.* Ipsi autem laborantes scardassarii fideliter operari debent et sollicite, non tempus amictere in otio et truphis, uel inepte que pertinent ad artem peragere. Alias et ipsi tenentur magistris suis, et peccant.

---

254 exchommunicati … **255** Nouerit] *X* 5.39.49 (*Noverit*): Noverit fraternitas tua, … Excommunicamus omnes haereticos utriusque sexus, quocunque nomine censeantur, et fautores et receptatores et defensores eorum, nec non et qui de cetero servari fecerint statuta edita et consuetudines introductas contra ecclesiae libertatem, nisi ea de capitularibus suis infra duos menses post huiusmodi publicationem sententiae fecerint amoveri. Item excommunicamus statutarios et scriptores statutorum ipsorum, nec non potestates, consules, rectores et consiliarios locorum, ubi de cetero huiusmodi statuta et consuetudines editae fuerint vel servatae, nec non et illos, qui secundum ea praesumpserint iudicare, vel in publicam formam scribere iudicata.

255 uide … **256** exchommunicatione] Ant. Flor. *Summa* 3.25.17 (apud M_2 fol. Vv; 3.24.17 apud Ballerini): *de excommunicatione contra seruantes uel facientes seruare statuta contra libertatem ecclesiastica*; *Summa* 3.25.23 (apud M_2 fol. Vv; 3.24.23 apud Ballerini): *de excommunicatione contra impedientes litigare in foro ecclesiastico in causis que de iure uel consuetudine possunt ibi tractari*; *Summa* 3.25.29 (apud M_2 fol. VIr; 3.24.29 apud Ballerini): *de excommunicatione contra facientes statuta uel seruantes quibus compellantur soluere usuras, uel solutas non repetere.*

263 Tob. … **264** maneat] *Tb* 4.15: Quicumque tibi aliquid operatus fuerit, statim ei mercedem restitue, et merces mercenarii tui apud te omnino non remaneat.

266 Iacobi … **268** introiuit] *Iac* 5.4: Ecce merces operariorum, qui messuerunt regiones vestras, quae fraudata est a vobis, clamat : et clamor eorum in aures Domini sabbaoth introivit.

---

255 sententia excommunicationis] *a.c.* : immunitate ecclesie *p.c. cod.* **258** Quorum] quos *a.c.* **263** Quicumque … **264** maneat] *postea add. Antoninus in spatio praebito* **265** monetas] + unde- *a.c.* **266** 5] 4 *cod.* **268** scardassarii] *sic cod.*

usury, c. 1, in the *Clementines*.[46] And much more when the statutes provide that in these sorts of contracts which savour of usury, one cannot have recourse to an ecclesiastical judgment, which is expressly contrary to the liberty of the Church, since this pertains to the Church's judgment. Hence they and those who observe these statutes are excommunicated, *Extra, On sentence of excommunication*, c. 49.[47] About this see below in the title on excommunication.[48]

3.9. Employees in the wool craft. About employees in the wool craft. And first about wool carders.[49] These are very undisciplined in their words and acts.[50] And even if their employers do not have to take care of their souls or investigate their lives, as they are only hired to work for a set wage, nevertheless the employers should restrain them to the extent that they can from their outrages, wrongs, and lecheries in their workshops and homes, and most of all from the filthiest vice. Now the employers must not delay paying them the wages they seek according to their agreement, in accordance with that statement in Tobit 4: *If any man hath done any work for thee, immediately pay him his wage, and let not the wages of thy hired servant remain with thee at all.*[51] And much less should they defraud or diminish their wages, by paying them in diminished currency, or in cloth or foodstuffs when they are supposed to get money, from which they are deceived;[52] those doing this are inveighed against in James 5: *Behold the wage of your labourers which has been defrauded by you, cries* against you *and the cry has entered into the ears of the Lord.*[53] Now the wool carders themselves as employees ought to work faithfully and attentively, not wasting time in idleness and distractions,[54] nor performing the tasks that pertain to this craft incompetently. Otherwise they owe their employers <for this>, and commit sin.

---

46 *Clem.* 5.5.1 (*Ex gravi*).

47 *X* 5.39.49 (*Noverit*).

48 Ant. Flor. *Summa* 3.25.17 (apud M_2 fol. Vv; 3.24.17 apud Ballerini): *de excommunicatione contra seruantes uel facientes seruare statuta contra libertatem ecclesiastica*; *Summa* 3.25.23 (apud M_2 fol. Vv; 3.24.23 apud Ballerini): *de excommunicatione contra impedientes litigare in foro ecclesiastico in causis que de iure uel consuetudine possunt ibi tractari*; *Summa* 3.25.29 (apud M_2 fol. VIr; 3.24.29 apud Ballerini): *de excommunicatione contra facientes statuta uel seruantes quibus compellantur soluere usuras, uel solutas non repetere.*

49 "Scardazziere; wool-carder (who worked for day wages in the central workshop of an industrial entrepreneur, in Tuscany). Cf. *scardassatore, scarteggino*." Edler, *Terms of Business*, 260.

50 Cfr Raymond de Roover's paraphrase of this passage in *Great Economic Thinkers*, 27: "Wool-beaters, carders, and combers were a rowdy lot, vile in language, loose in morals, if not addicted to filthy vices."

51 *Tb* 4.15: "If any man hath done any work for thee, immediately pay him his hire, and let not the wages of thy hired servant stay with thee at all."

52 On payment in kind and Antoninus's censures of the truck system, see also Ant. Flor. *Summa* 2.1.17 (above), section 3.5, and *Summa* 3.8.3 (above), section 3.

53 *Iac* 5.4: "Behold the hire of the labourers, who have reaped down your fields, which by fraud has been kept back by you, crieth: and the cry of them hath entered into the ears of the Lord of Sabaoth."

54 Lat. *trufa, ae* (or *trupha*).

Secundo de laninis, qui scilicet dant lanam ad nendum seu filandum, uel extendunt lanam ad solis radium. Et si hoc faciunt diebus festiuis indifferenter, cum apte possint sibi aliis diebus prouidere sine aliquo periculo, male faciunt, cum multum de tempore ibi ponunt. Si autem hoc agunt ex causa rationabili, ut puta quia lana destrueretur et huiusmodi, excusantur. Isti etiam lanini solent cum detur eis certa quantitas peccunie quam debent filatricibus dare pro labore suo, puta solidos octo pro libra, unum pro se retinere. Vnde cum recipiant sa- | -larium a magistris pro labore suo, non possunt pro se illud fol. 75v
quod subtrahunt retinere, sed filatricibus tenentur restituere, si minus iusto uel conuento pretio dederunt, alias magistris suis quod superfluit eis assignare. Et si filatricibus tenentur, cum perseuerant in dando eisdem ad nendum, debent satisfacere plus dando in posterum quam mereatur earum labor quousque satisfacere compleuerint. Vel si ignorantur persone uel difficulter inueniuntur et quantitas modicha est, pauperibus erogetur, 14 q. 5 *Non sane*.

Multi per uaria exercitia deseruiunt huic arti, ut filatrices, textores, qui si in exercitio suo commictunt defectus unde pannus patiatur detrimentum in ualore, tenentur. Vnde si propter hoc minus soluitur eis quam conuentum pretium, non fit eis iniustitia. Purgatores, qui si suis uerendis honorem habundantiorem tribuerent eas uelando, decentius agerent. Fullones, tinctores, qui

---

284 pauperibus … sane] C. 14 q. 5 c. 15 (*Non sane*): Isti, si uiam uitae mutauerint, aut excellentioris conscenderint sanctitatis gradum, facilius ea, que hoc modo acquisierunt, tanquam sua pauperibus largiuntur, quam eis, a quibus accepta sunt, tamquam aliena restituant. Cfr Gr.a. idem: De peccato etiam aliqua nonnumquam acquiruntur, que pauperibus iuste erogantur.

---

271 uel … **276** solent] *in marg. infer. add.* **272** extendunt] ex- *s.l.* | solis] *ut vid. cod. p.c. cum* F_3 *fol. 72ra* : soles *vel* solens *a.c.* **277** retinere] -erent *a.c. ut vid.* **282** labor] *in marg. sin. add. Iulianus de Lapacc. ut vid.* **284** erogetur] *p.c.* : *haud leg. a.c.* **288** iniustitia] -iam *cod.*

Second, about *lanini*,[55] namely those who give out <carded> wool to be spun and spread out wool as far as the sun shines. And if they do this on feast days without a care, when they are quite able to provide for themselves on other days without any danger, they do ill, when they spend a lot of time on this. But if they do this for a reasonable cause, as for example to avoid the wool being ruined and so forth, they are excused. Now these *lanini* are accustomed, when a certain quantity of money is given to them which they are supposed to pay to the spinners for their labour, say 8 shillings per pound, to keep one shilling for themselves. About which: since they receive a salary from the employer for their labour, they may not keep that amount which they subtract for themselves, but they are bound to hand it on to the spinners, if they have paid less than the just or agreed price, otherwise they are bound to return to their employers whatever they have left over. And if they owe something to the spinners, while they continue to give wool to them to be spun, they ought to make satisfaction by paying them more in the future than their labour entitles them to until they have made complete satisfaction. Or if the individuals are not known or are difficult to find and the quantity is small, it should be bestowed on the poor, C. 14 q. 5 c. 15.[56]

Many serve this craft through various occupations, such as spinners[57] and weavers,[58] who are responsible for it if they commit defects in their work which cause the cloth to suffer loss of value. And so if because of this less is paid out to them than the agreed price, an injustice is not done to them. Washers,[59] if they confer greater honour on those who are to be held in reverence by clothing them,

---

55 "Lanino; originally (in Florence) an independent intermediary who bought carded wool (*lana*) and had it spun by women spinners, then sold the yarn to the industrial entrepreneurs who gave it to their weavers to be used as weft threads. By the 15th century the *lanini* had lost their independence ... The amount that the spinners were to receive from the *lanini* was also established by law; for example, an ordinance of 1547, renewed in 1556 and 1557, provided that for each pound of yarn to be used for rash (*lana da rascie*) the entrepreneur (*lanaiuolo*) must pay his *lanino* s.14 *piccioli*, out of which sum, the *lanino* had to pay s.12 per pound to the spinner, in money, never in kind, leaving a profit of 2 soldi per pound to the *lanino*, plus the customary commission." Edler, *Terms of Business*, 149. See also ibid., 413–18, where the functions of the *lanini* in the 1550s are explained.

56 C. 14 q. 5 c. 15 (*Non sane*): "... These, if they change their manner of life, or rise to a greater degree of holiness, are more easily disposed to distribute to the poor, as if they were their own, the resources which they have acquired in this manner, than to restore them to those from whom they took them, as if they were not their own." Cfr Gr.a. idem: "Also, some things are acquired by sin which may justly be distributed to the poor."

57 "Filatrice; female spinner (of wool, more common in Italy, than men spinners; worked more or less independently at home for piece wages)." Edler, *Terms of Business*, 122.

58 "Tessitore; master weaver (under the dependent wholesale handicraft system, who wove cloth at home from material furnished by an entrepreneur who paid him by the piece and who frequently furnished the loom)." Ibid., 295, 329–31.

59 "Purgatore; washer, scourer (of woolen cloth)." Ibid., 228.

et ipsi si minus diligenter in tintura operantur, unde pretiositas minuatur, si in pena peccuniaria luant conqueri non ualent. Tiratores qui cum ultra decentiam trahunt et morem artis ut ex quantitate augmentata lucrentur, non sunt mundi a peccato.

3.10. De arte emendatorum.

Ex hac autem sequitur scissura panni, ad quod remediandum est inducta ars emendatorum, qui scilicet subtiliter tales consuant, ut non uideantur, propter quod posset dubitari de licitatione talis artis cum operentur ad deceptionem. Sed posset responderi quod si non occultaretur talis defectus, nec etiam iusto pretio emptor uellet emere cum tali defectu cum tamen ex hoc non reddatur usus talis panni noxius uel omnino inutilis, et si forte non ita duratiuus et apparens. Vnde lanifex si ratione talis defectus minuit de quantitate quantum importat talis defectus non uidetur comdempnari posse ut elici potest ex dictis beati Tome 2^{a} 2^{e} q. 77, ubi loquitur de fraude que commictitur in qualitate rerum. Et cum lanifex possit et debeat sic agere, deseruiens emendator illi operi non dat illi occasionem mali sed conseruandi se indempnem, cum etiam inspiciantur postea per reuenditores. Qui si non fideliter agunt detrahentes de pretio panni ut decet sed simulantes, ac si non haberet talem defectum, tenentur de tali dampno emptoribus ipsi cum lanificibus, uel pauperibus erogentur, 14 q. 5 *Non sane.*

---

302 beati … **303** rerum] THOM. AQ. *Sum. th.* 2a 2ae q. 77 a. 2 co. et ad 3: Tertius defectus est ex parte qualitatis, puta si aliquod animal infirmum vendat quasi sanum. Quod si quis scienter fecerit, fraudem committit in venditione, unde est illicita venditio. … Ad tertium dicendum quod, sicut Augustinus dicit, in XI de Civ. Dei, pretium rerum venalium non consideratur secundum gradum naturae, cum quandoque pluris vendatur unus equus quam unus servus, sed consideratur secundum quod res in usum hominis veniunt. Et ideo non oportet quod venditor vel emptor cognoscat occultas rei venditae qualitates, sed illas solum per quas redditur humanis usibus apta, puta quod equus sit fortis et bene currat, et similiter in ceteris. Has autem qualitates de facili venditor et emptor cognoscere possunt. Cfr ibid. a.3.

307 pauperibus … **308** sane] C. 14 q. 5 c. 15 (*Non sane*): vide supra.

---

292 trahunt et] F_3 *fol. 72rb add. s.l.* secundum **295** tales] + resarciunt uel potius *a.c. ut vid.* | ut] *vel* uti *cod.* **298** defectu] defectum *cod. ut vid.* **305** inspiciantur] *sic cod.* : -atur F_3 *fol. 72rb*

they do very fittingly. Fullers[60] and dyers,[61] they also if they work with little diligence in dyeing and cause the wool's quality to be diminished are in no position to complain if they pay for it through a monetary penalty. Cloth stretchers,[62] when they stretch beyond what is suitable and the method of the craft, so that they may make a profit from the increased quantity, they are not clear of sin.

3.10. The craft of menders. Now from this there follow rents in the cloth, and to remedy these the craft of menders[63] was introduced, that is, those who sew them up with such subtlety that they cannot be seen, because of which one can be in doubt about the liceity of this craft when they do their work in order to deceive. But one can answer that if this sort of defect were not concealed, the buyer would not want to buy items with such defects even for a just price, even though these defects do not render the use of such cloth harmful or altogether worthless, even if perhaps it is not as durable or nice looking.[64] Hence if a wool merchant because of these defects reduces <the price> in proportion to the defect, it does not seem that this can be condemned, as can be elicited from blessed Thomas's words, 2a 2ae q. 77, where he talks about fraud which is committed in things' quality.[65] And since the wool merchant can and should behave thus, the mender serving in this task does not give to him an occasion of evil, but of protecting himself from loss, since the cloth is also inspected later by resellers.[66] If these latter do not behave faithfully by subtracting from the price of the cloth as is appropriate, but pretend that it does not have this defect, they themselves along with the wool merchants owe the buyers for this loss, or it should be be bestowed on the poor, C. 14 q. 5 c. 15.[67]

60 "Fullo [CL], -onus, fuller." *DMLBS*, s.v.

61 "Tintore; dyer (a master with his own dyehouse)." Edler, *Terms of Business*, 297.

62 "Tiratore; cloth-stretcher, tenterer (small master workman who stretched cloth after it came from the fuller, usually using rented tenters in one of the large open buildings containing tenters or large wooden frames for stretching and drying cloth. Originally such establishments were owned by private families, but gradually, as in the case of the fulling etablishments, the wool gilds in the different towns acquired their own *tiratoi*)." Ibid., 299.

63 "Rimendatori: Menders of woolen cloth, who repaired tiny imperfections in newly woven and sheared cloth." Frick, *Dressing Renaissance Florence*, 230. "Rimendatore; mender, drawer (of woolen cloth, usually a small master working in his own workshop, but sometimes a worker in the central workshop of an industrial entrepreneur. Cf. emendatore, mendatore." "Rimendare; to mend, to draw, to correct defects (in new woolen cloth, either after burling, dyeing, or first shearing of cloth) … Cf. emendare." Edler, *Terms of Business*, 244.

64 It is also possible that *apparens* here means "serviceable."

65 Thom. Aq. *Sum. th.* 2a 2ae q. 77 a. 2 co. et ad 3: "A third defect is on the part of the quality, for instance, if a man sell an unhealthy animal as being a healthy one: and if anyone do this knowingly he is guilty of a fraudulent sale, and the sale, in consequence, is illicit … As Augustine says (De Civ. Dei xi, 16) the price of things salable does not depend on their degree of nature, since at times a horse fetches a higher price than a slave; but it depends on their usefulness to man. Hence it is not necessary for the seller or buyer to be cognizant of the hidden qualities of the thing sold, but only of such as render the thing adapted to man's use, for instance, that the horse be strong, run well and so forth. Such qualities the seller and buyer can easily discover." Cfr ibid. a. 3.

66 "Rivenditore; middleman, a jobber, one who buys to resell (to merchants or dealers)." Edler, *Terms of Business*, 251.

67 C. 14 q. 5 c. 15 (*Non sane*): see above.

3.11. De retaliatoribus.

Demum ueniunt communiter ad retagliatores qui minutatim uendunt ad mensuram canne uel brachii, et si diminutam mensuram tribuunt ut multi faciunt, fraudem faciunt. Hii etiam aliquando solent facere quosdam contractus illicitos, ipsi uel lanifices, qui dicuntur barochola, cum uidelicet uendunt alicui pannum ad terminum anni, certo pretio, et cum emptor non egeat panno sed peccunia, pannum ipsum reuendat peccunia sibi numerata sed minori pretio quam emerit, V uel 7 floren., eidem lanifici uel retaliatori, que utique usura est cum habeat implicitum mutuum cum lucro, 14. q. 3 *Vsura*. Sed de hoc contractu habes plenius in secunda parte titulo primo, de barocholis.

4. De sartoribus et caligarum uel chalceorum factoribus et huiusmodi.

De sartoribus et stampatoribus et cerdonibus, qui in arte sua uitia perpetrant. Primo cum postulant 20 solidos pro repe uel sericho, cum sciant decem solidos in huiusmodi non posituros. Excusare tamen se solent ex eo quod diminutam mercedem recipiant sui laboris, quod si uerum esset, admicti posset hec compensatio, alias sechus. Secundo cum partem et non modicam sibi retinent panni supereffluentis, sine scitu domini eius, et tunc sunt fures et latrones et tenentur ad satisfactionem. Tertio quia promictunt opera perfecta reddere certa die aliquando hoc iuramento etiam firmantes, cum tamen sciant se non posse ita cito perficere propter alia opera etiam sic promissa et sic infideliter agunt. Quarto si non diligenter, sed defectuose faciunt ut citius se expediant. Quinto quia per totas quasi noctes festiuas operantur et suis ministris operari faciunt quia in festis persone uolunt ea habere, quod est uiolare festa. Sexto quia de mane in festis accedunt ad domos ad primo ad induendum uestes mulieribus uel uiris pluribus, et propter hoc dimictunt auditionem misse contra mandatum ecclesie. Et sub hiis comprehenduntur | caligarum et fol. 76r

315 usura … **316** Vsura] C. 14 q. 3 c. 4 (*Usura est*): vide supra.
317 secunda … barocholis] Ant. Flor. *Summa* 2.1.8.5 *de baroccolis* (apud Ballerini 2:131–3; 2.1.75. apud Mamachi 2:177–9; sed non exstat in cod. M_1).

309 minutatim] + per cannas *a.c.* **316** 3] 4 *cod.* **317** barocholis] + Hiis sequuntur pannorum sutores seu sartores *a.c.* **318** De … **319** perpetrant] *p.c. in marg. sin. add.* : *a.c.* De artificibus sericii seu setaiuoli, hec ars honorabilis haberi in ciuitati et quamuis de se licita, tamen deseruiens in multis uanitati potius quam neccesitati uel utilitati | sciant] + cum *a.c.* **320** solidos] + non *a.c.* | posituros] *ut vid. cod. cum* F_3 *fol. 72rb* **329** faciunt] + ut *a.c.*

3.11. Retail cloth dealers. Finally, wool merchants commonly come to retail cloth dealers who sell in small amounts to the measure of ells or yards,[68] and if they provide a diminished measure, as many do, they commit fraud. These also sometimes are in the habit of making certain illicit contracts, they themselves or the wool merchants, which are called *baroccole*,[69] that is, when they sell to someone cloth on credit for the term of a year, for a set price, and since the buyer does not need cloth but money, he resells that cloth to the same wool merchant or retail cloth dealer and the money is paid out to him but at a lower price than when he bought, by 5 or 7 florins; this practice is certainly usury, since it has an implicit loan with profit, C. 14 q. 3 c. 4.[70] But about this contract there is a fuller treatment in the second part, title 1, on *baroccole*.[71]

4. Tailors, makers of boots and shoes, and so forth. About tailors and fabric decorators and cobblers who perpetrate vices in their craft. First, when they ask for 20 shillings for thread[72] or silk, when they know that at most 10 shillings of thread or silk will be used. Nevertheless they are accustomed to excuse themselves because they receive a reduced wage for their labour; if true, this compensation could be allowed, otherwise not. Second, when they keep a part, and not a small one, of the superfluous cloth for themselves, without its owner's knowledge, and then they are thieves and robbers and are bound to make satisfaction. Third, when they promise to provide the finished products on a certain day, sometimes even affirming this with an oath, but on the contrary they know that they cannot complete them so quickly because of the other jobs they have also promised in the same way, and thus they behave dishonestly. Fourth, when they do not work diligently but defectively in order to dispatch their work more quickly. Fifth, when they work and make their employees work through practically the whole night during feasts because people want to have the products on feast days, which violates the feasts. Sixth, when in the morning on feast days they go to houses at Prime[73] to deliver clothes to many women and men, and because of this they omit hearing Mass, which is against the Church's commandment. And under these are included makers of boots and shoes, who sometimes commit fraud in this

68 "Braccio; a cloth measure, an arm's length, a yard (about 2/3 of an English yard, but it varied from place to place; usually 1/3 or ¼ of a *canna*, ell. In Florence and elsewhere the *braccio* was frequently used for cloth sold by the cut, and the *canna* for full-length cloths)." Edler, *Terms of Business*, 52.

69 "Barochum, usurae species, lucrum illicitum, ab Ital. Barocco, eadem notione." Du Cange, s.v.

70 C. 14 q. 3 c. 4 (*Usura est*): see above.

71 Ant. Flor. *Summa* 2.1.8.5 *de baroccolis* (apud Ballerini 2:131–3; 2.1.7.5 apud Mamachi 2:177–9; but this passage does not exist in the autograph codex M_1).

72 Lat. *repe* (abl.). "Repum, Filum." "Reppus, Italis Reffo, Gallis Fil, Filum." Du Cange, s.v.

73 The canonical hour or office of Prime, "(generally) first hour of the day, usu. to coincide with sunrise." *DMLBS*, s.v.

chalceorum factores, qui in hoc aliquando fraudem committunt quod cum non madefaciunt pannum ut minus de eo in ipsis ponant, postea pannus contrahitur, precipue cum balneatur, et propter arcitudinem earum cito lacerantur.

4.1. De arte stampatorum.

Est autem ad superfluitatem et uanitatem ars stampatorum perforantium pannos et cincinnantium uel lingulantium. Verum quia de se non uidetur mortale talis uanitas uel prodigalitas communiter non de facili debet ut dampnatum reprobari tale ministerium, sed persuaderi ad dimictendum, ar. *De pe.* D. 5 *Negotium.* Et multo magis exercitium facientium serta uel coronas seu mitras cum multa pompa mulieribus, qui etiam in aliquibus predictorum offendunt.

4.2. Qui commodant uestimenta pretiosa uel iocalia.

Qui uero commodant uestimenta pretiosa, uel torques de perlis uel alia iocalia ad tempus certum, uiris uel mulieribus, et inde percipiunt certum pretium secundum conuentionem eorum, de se non est illicitum quia non est hic mutuum sed commodatum et per modum locationis datum, sicut etiam licet lochare animalia ad uecturam et uasa etiam aurea et argentea secundum Tomam in *Summa.* Talia enim ex usu paulatim deteriorantur, unde licite

339 De … **340** Negotium] *De pen.* D. 5 c. 7 (*Negotium*): Sunt enim pleraque negotia, que sine peccatis exhiberi aut uix, aut nullatenus possunt. Que ergo ad peccatum inplicant, ad hec necesse est ut post conuersionem animus non recurrat.

346 secundum … **347** Summa] Thom. Aq. *Sum. th.* 2a 2ae q. 78 a. 1 co.: Quaedam vero sunt quorum usus non est ipsa rei consumptio, sicut usus domus est inhabitatio, non autem dissipatio. Et ideo in talibus seorsum potest utrumque concedi, puta cum aliquis tradit alteri dominium domus, reservato sibi usu ad aliquod tempus; vel e converso cum quis concedit alicui usum domus, reservato sibi eius dominio. Et propter hoc licite potest homo accipere pretium pro usu domus, et praeter hoc petere domum commodatam, sicut patet in conductione et locatione domus. Vide etiam ibid. a. 3 co.

335 lacerantur] *ut vid. cod. cum F_3 fol. 72rb* **337** lingulantium] + unde dimictenda *a.c.* **339** dimictendum] + de pe. *a.c.* **341** etiam] + in predictis *a.c.* **342** commodant] + aliis *a.c.* **345** hic] *ut vid. cod.* : hoc *F_3 fol. 72va* **346** uecturam] *ut vid. cod.* : uecturas *F_3 fol. 72va* | secundum … **347** Summa] *in marg. sin. add.*

way: they do not dampen the cloth so that they can use less of it in the boots or shoes, and later the cloth shrinks, especially when it is washed, and because of their tightness the boots or shoes are quickly split.

4.1. The craft of fabric decorators.

Now the craft of fabric decorators,[74] embroidering and ruffling[75] or fringing[76] cloths, is directed to excess and vanity. However since in itself this vanity or prodigality does not seem to be usually mortal, this occupation should not be facilely censured as condemned, but people should be persuaded to set it aside, by the argument of *De pen.* D. 5 c. 7.[77] And much more the work of those who make head garlands[78] and crowns[79] and very ostentatious headdresses[80] for women, who also do wrong in some of the aforesaid.

4.2. Those who lend precious garments and jewelled items.

Now those who lend precious garments, or torques of pearls or jewellery[81] for a fixed time to men or women, and take for this a price determined according to their agreement, in itself this is not illicit, since there is not here a loan for consumption[82] but a loan for use[83] given through the form of a lease,[84] just as it

74 The word *stampator* (Ital. *stampatore*) which Antoninus uses here is recorded in *GDLI* as referring to either textile printers or fabric decorators: "Che stampa tessuti," "Che pratica decorazioni e fregi su tessuti." In the 1580 *Statuti dell'Arte di Por Santa Maria, seconda parte*, the list of members of the guild includes "Ricamatori et Stampatori di Drappi e Panni." Ital. *ricamator* means "embroiderer." In the current context it appears that Antoninus is describing decorating fabric through beading or embroidery, ruffling, and fringing. It could be that he is using *stampator* simply as a synonym for *ricamator*; or he may be referring to one who prints on fabrics.

Block printing on cloth is described by the Florentine writer Cennino Cennini, though using different Italian terms, in his *Libro dell'arte*, c. 173 in Milanesi's edition: *Il Libro dell'Arte*, 126–9. The English translation I have consulted is *The Craftsman's Handbook*, trans. Daniel V. Thompson, Jr, 115–18.

The term *stampator* is not included in the list of categories of clothier or in Frick's glossary in *Dressing Renaissance Florence*, 228–319. Nor is it found in Edler's *Terms of Business*, nor in the *Oxford–Paravia Italian Dictionary*, Du Cange, the *DMLBS*, or Goldthwaite, *Economy of Renaissance Florence*. Stella includes the term in his glossary and defines it as "faiseur de moules à chaussures" (*La révolte des Ciompi*, 314), but I do not think that "shoe-mould makers" are what Antoninus is describing here. I have similarly been unable to find satisfactory definitions of the verbs *perforare*, *cincinnare*, and *lingulare* in the aforementined Latin and Italian dictionaries.

75 I have translated the Lat. *cincinnare* assuming a relation to *cincinnus*, "curl, ringlet." *DMLBS* and *LS*, s.v. See also *GDLI*, s.v., "Acconciare i capelli con cura."

76 Translating based on Lat. *lingula*, sense 3 d in *DMLBS*: "tail or forked banner, or strip or fringe of cloth."

77 *De pen.* D. 5 c. 7 (*Negotium*): "For there are many kinds of business which can scarcely or never be performed without sins. But as for those things which involve one in sin, it is necessary that one's mind not turn to these after conversion."

78 Lat. and Ital. *sertum*, "head garland (from the Latin)." Frick, *Dressing Renaissance Florence*, 317.

79 "Corona: A crown; popular head ornament for women in early Trecento. Later outlawed by sumptuary laws." Ibid., 306.

80 "At that time elaborate high headdresses were being worn." Origo, *World of San Bernardino*, 47.

81 "Iocalia, Monilia, gemmae, annuli, aliaque id genus pretiosa, Gall. Joyaux, Anglis Jewells." Du Cange, s.v. Cfr Ital. *gioiello*.

82 Lat. *mutuum*.

83 Lat. *commodatum*.

84 Lat. *locatio*.

pro commodatione eorum pretium recipitur; posset tamen esse excessus pretii, unde et quantitas in huiusmodi debita est attendenda secundum pretiositatem rei commodate, et secundum diuturnitatem temporis, et secundum periculum deteriorationis, et secundum morem patrie et arbitrio boni uiri iudicanda, nec potest dari regula certa.

4.3. De cerdonibus et planellariis.

Cerdones et planellarii uestes faciunt pedibus, qui fraudem commictunt cum aluctas seu sutilares uel ocreas de chorio uitulino uendunt pro chorio hyrcino, et huiusmodi, uel cum male et indebite suunt ut citius se expediant, uel nimis charo pretio uendunt. Nam planellarii ultra predicta uitia in hoc uidentur offendere adiuuantes uanitates et fictiones mulierum, dum nimis altas planellas faciunt, ut mulieres inde magne appareant que parue stature sunt. Et ad maiorem uanitatem aliquando etiam deaurant, unde moneri debent et argui de huiusmodi uanitate.

4.4. De pellipariis.

Pelliparii quoque satis sunt necessarii ad arcendum frighus. Vnde et Dominus primis parentibus *fecit tunichas pelliceas*, ut habetur Gen. 3. Vnde et licitum est eorum lucrum nisi cum pelles malas pro bonis uendunt uel ultra

---

361 Dominus … **362** 3] *Gen* 3.21: Fecit quoque Dominus Deus Adae et uxori ejus tunicas pelliceas, et induit eos.

---

349 huiusmodi] + est *a.c.* | attendenda] + arbitrium boni uiri *a.c.* **354** seu sutilares] *in marg. sin. add.* | sutilares] *ut vid. cod.* : sotulares F_3 *fol. 72va* **356** predicta] predictam *cod.* : predicta F_3 *fol. 72va*

is also lawful to lease animals for transportation and even gold and silver vessels according to Thomas in the *Summa*.[85] For such things gradually wear out from use, and hence a price is taken for lending them; there can, however, be an excessive price, hence also in such things the proper value must be appraised according to the preciousness of the item lent, and the duration of time, and the risk of wear and tear, and this should be judged in accordance with the custom of the country and by the judgment of a good man, nor can a definite rule be given.

4.3. Cobblers and slipper makers. Cobblers[86] and slipper makers[87] make garments for feet, and they commit fraud when they sell soft leather[88] or shoes[89] or boots[90] made of calfskin as goatskin,[91] and so forth, or when they sew badly and improperly in order to work quicker, or when they sell at far too dear a price. Indeed slipper makers beyond the aforesaid vices seem to do wrong in this, that they help the vanities and pretences of women, when they make excessively high slippers[92] so that they make women who are of short stature appear tall. And for greater vanity they sometimes even gild them, and so they should be warned and argued away from this sort of vanity.

4.4. Furriers. Furriers[93] are also quite necessary for warding off the cold. Hence even the Lord *made garments of skins* for our first parents, as is said in Genesis 3.[94] Hence also their profit is licit except when they sell poor furs for good ones, or beyond

85 Thom. Aq. *Sum. th.* 2a 2ae q. 78 a. 1 co.: "On the other hand, there are things the use of which does not consist in their consumption: thus to use a house is to dwell in it, not to destroy it. Wherefore in such things both may be granted: for instance, one man may hand over to another the ownership of his house while reserving to himself the use of it for a time, or vice versa, he may grant the use of the house, while retaining the ownership. For this reason a man may lawfully make a charge for the use of his house, and, besides this, revendicate the house from the person to whom he has granted its use, as happens in renting and letting a house." See also ibid., a. 3 co.

86 Lat. *cerdo*, "leatherworker, cobbler." *DMLBS*, s.v.

87 "Pianellaio; slipper-maker (small independent master with a shop)." Edler, *Terms of Business*, 213.

88 Lat. *aluta* (CL), also *alutum* (ML), "a kind of soft leather," "tawed leather," *LS* and *DMLBS*, s.v.

89 Lat. *subtalaris* [CL = *not reaching as high as the ankle*] or *sotularis*, "sort of shoe, slipper." *DMLBS*, s.v.

90 Lat. *ocrea*, "leather legging or boot." *DMLBS*, s.v.

91 Lat. *corium*, "hide, skin; leather." *DMLBS*, s.v.

92 "Pianelli: Slippers that did not cover the heel of the foot, usually made of cloth and worn indoors by both men and women. Outside, high wooden clogs – zoccoli or chopine – were added. Pianelli could, however, be made double-soled, or *assuole doppie*, which increased their durability. Alternatively, scarpe, that is, soft shoes with thin leather soles, were substituted for the pianelli." Frick, *Dressing Renaissance Florence*, 315.

93 "Pellicciaio/a – pelliparius – pellicciarius : fourreur." Stella, *La révolte des Ciompi*, 312. "Pellicciai: Furriers, who were either fur dealers or dressers of fur. In the fourteenth century, they dealt especially with fox and wildcat; in the fifteenth, marten was added." Frick, *Dressing Renaissance Florence*, 229.

94 *Gen* 3.21: "And the Lord God made for Adam and his wife, garments of skins, and clothed them."

iustum pretium, uel diebus festiuis in nocte laborantes in hyeme cum opus eorum multum requiritur. Variarii autem satis uidentur superflui, cum uarie pelles murium ad ornatum sint inuente; et si aliquando decentem frequenter tamen uanum et pomposum, quo etiam aliquando prelati utuntur contra quos inuehitur Amos 6: *Ve qui opulenti estis in Syon*, id est in ecclesia, *optimates capita populorum pompatice ingredientes domui Israel*. Possunt tamen et ipsi tollerari in arte sua sicut et multi alii in superfluis operibus, dummodo abstineant et ipsi a fraudibus.

5. De serificiis seu setaiuolis.

De serificiis seu setaiuolis, hec ars honorabilis est in humana ciuilitate, et quamuis de se non illicita, tamen in multis deseruiens uanitati cum sericis utantur hodie et uellutis et chermusinis stipendiarii et mulieres non solum uxores baronum principum et militum sed etiam merchatorum et artifichum quod est satis indecens, et magis secundum abusionem quam consutudinem lochorum. Et in signum detestationis talis uanitatis legitur Luc. 16 quod *diues epulo, qui induebatur purpura et bisso sepultus est in infernum*. Et quod dicitur D. 41 *Quisquis*, quod in huiusmodi debet quis <se> conformare mori patrie, intelligitur salua semper honestate et decentia. Ad setaiuolos tamen non spectat discernere si uellutum uel brochatum emat quis ab eo, ad congruentiam sui status uestem faciendam, uel ad excessum et uanitatem,

---

368 Amos … **369** Israel] *Am* 6.1: Vae qui opulenti estis in Sion, et confiditis in monte Samariae : optimates capita populorum, ingredientes pompatice domum Israel!

377 Luc. … **378** infernum] *Lc* 16.19–22: Homo quidam erat dives, qui induebatur purpura et bysso, et epulabatur quotidie splendide. … Mortuus est autem et dives, et sepultus est in inferno.

378 D. … **380** patrie] D. 41 c. 1 (*Quisquis*): Quisquis rebus pretereuntibus restrictius utitur quam sese habent mores eorum, cum quibus uiuit, aut intemperans, aut supersticiosus est. Quisquis uero sic eis utitur, ut metas consuetudinis bonorum, inter quos uersatur, excedat, aut aliquid significat, aut flagitiosus est. … Quid igitur locis, et temporibus, et personis conueniat, diligenter adtendendum est, nec temere flagitia reprehendamus.

---

369 Israel] Isrl *cod.* : Israel F_3 *fol. 72va* **379** debet] *bis scr. cod.* | se] *supplevi cum* F_3 *fol. 72va* | conformare] + p(atrie?) *a.c.* **380** Ad] *s.l.* | setaiuolos] setaiuolo *a.c.* **381** si] + petit *a.c. ut vid.* | uellutum … brochatum] F_3 *fol. 72va* : uelluti uel brochati *cod.* | emat] emptor *a.c.* **382** status] + uel *a.c.* | uel] + excess- *a.c.*

the just price, or work during the night on feast days in winter when their work is greatly sought after. However, multi-coloured furs[95] seem quite superfluous, when for adornment mouse furs of different colours are found; even if sometimes they are suitable, nevertheless frequently they are vain and pompous, and even prelates sometimes wear them, against whom it is inveighed in Amos 6: *Woe to you that are wealthy in Sion*, that is in the Church, *ye great men, heads of the people, that go with pomp into the house of Israel.*[96] Nevertheless even these can be tolerated in their craft, and many others in superfluous works, provided that they abstain from frauds.

5. Silk makers or silk merchants. About silk makers or silk merchants,[97] this craft is esteemed in human refinement, and although it is not in itself illicit, nevertheless among many it serves vanity, since today mercenaries and women wear silks and velvets[98] and crimsons,[99] and not only the wives of barons, princes, and knights, but even the wives of merchants and artisans, which is quite unbecoming, and is more in accordance with local malpractice than local practice. And to signify the repudiation of such vanity we read in Luke 16 that *a rich man, a feaster, who was clothed in purple and fine linen, was buried in hell.*[100] And what is said in D. 41 c. 1,[101] that in these sorts of things one should conform himself to the custom of the country, is understood to mean with due respect for honesty and decency. Nevertheless it does not belong to the silk merchants to discern whether someone is buying velvet or brocade from him in order to make clothing to suit his

95 My best interpretation of Lat. *variarii*, based on *variare*, "to colour in two or more colours, to variegate." *DMLBS*, s.v.

96 *Am* 6.1: "Woe to you that are wealthy in Sion, and to you that have confidence in the mountain of Samaria: ye great men, heads of the people, that go in with state into the house of Israel."

97 "Setaiuolo; silk merchant." Edler, *Terms of Business*, 270.

98 "Velluto: Velvet, a silk-based fabric characterized by a surface pile created by the use of an extra warp. During the late medieval period, many types of luxury velvet were developed, and also forbidden by 1346 sumptuary legislation." Frick, *Dressing Renaissance Florence*, 318.

99 "Chermisi: The highest quality, most brilliant, and longest-lasting crimson dyestuff in the fifteenth century; called 'kermes' in English (from Spanish *quermes*, Arabic *qirmizī*, Persian *kirm*, Sanscrit *kr̥mih*, all meaning vermin, worm, or insect) because made from the dessicated bodies of pregnant females of kermes lice … This dye was used in Florence in the fifteenth century for both silk velvets and wool. When a garment was referred to as chermisi, Jacqueline Herald says, fine woolen fabric is meant." Ibid., 305.

100 *Lc* 16.19–22: "There was a certain rich man, who was clothed in purple and fine linen; and feasted sumptuously every day … And the rich man also died: and he was buried in hell."

101 D. 41 c. 1 (*Quisquis*): "Whoever uses perishable goods more sparingly than is the custom of those among whom he lives is either intemperate or superstitious. Whoever, however, uses them so as to exceed the limits of the custom of the good men among whom he lives, either he means something else, or is sinful … Therefore, we must diligently attend to what is suitable to places, times, and persons, lest we rashly reprove [people with] sins."

dummodo iusto pretio uendat, et si aliquem defectum habeat non perceptibilem, et si notabilem, tantum minori pretio | uendat, quantum importat ille defectus. fol. 76v

5.1. De textoribus et tintoribus.

Verum si defectus ille processit ex textore uel tintore sete, ab eo potest petere emendam talis defectus et sic minus sibi dare de mercede conuenta. Quibus textoribus, si facto opere soluere pro eorum labore differant, contra iustitiam agunt. Et multo magis, si cum debeant peccuniam dare ex conuentione facta, dant eis uictualia uel pannos laneos uel serichos, cum ipsi textores uel tintores talia uendendo eis data, minus pretium semper recipiunt, quam illud pro quo fuit eis datum. Sechus autem ubi sic est conuentum inter eos ut pro suo labore soluatur eis de pane uino panno et huiusmodi totum uel pars mercedis debite secundum pretium commune concurrens, quia, ut dicitur *De re. iur., libro 6º*, “Scienti et consentienti non fit iniuria neque dolus,” quod tamen intelligitur in hiis que de se non sunt illicita. Nam et si quis sciens et consentiens soluat usuras, fit utique ei iniuria, quia contra ius est diuinum unde et iniuria est accipere usuram. Sic etiam in proposito: si ex illo pacto grauatur textor, quia plus mercedis debetur ei de labore suo secundum commune iudicium artis, tamen assentit ne sit otiosus sed aliquid lucretur et si parum, non excusatur setaiuolus ab iniustitia.

5.2. De aliquibus fraudantibus gabellas uel pedagia.

Delinquunt autem aliqui fraudando gabellas uel pedagia portare facientes serichum occultatum inter lanam uel linum uel alias merces, ut non perpendatur, et tenentur ad restituendum dictas gabellas et pedagia fraudata primo ipsi fieri facientes et secundo per quos facta est. Sed et aliquando emunt serichum ab hiis quos sciunt fraudasse gabellam. Si autem super hoc extat prohibitio statuti ciuitatis qua cauetur ut nullus emat serichum, nisi de ipso sit gabella soluta, tunc male faciunt emendo a talibus quos sciunt fraudasse gabellas cum contra statutum agant satis rationabile, D. 8 *Que contra morem*. Et cum per hoc

---

394 De … **395** dolus] *VI* 5.[13.]27 (*Scienti*): Scienti et consentienti non fit iniuria neque dolus.
409 D. … morem] D. 8 c. 2 (*Que contra mores*): vide supra.

---

383 dummodo] *p.c.* : ¶ *a.c.* **397** est[2]] *s.l.* **394** quia … **401** iniustitia] *in marg. super. add.* **409** D. … morem] *in marg. sin. add.*

status or to excess or vanity, provided that the merchant sell at a just price, even if the fabric has some imperceptible defect, and if it is a noteworthy defect, that he sell at a price reduced by the value of that defect.

5.1. Weavers and dyers. But if the defect is caused by the silk weaver or the dyer,[102] the merchants may claim compensation from him for this defect and thus in paying him may deduct from the agreed wage. Now if, when the work has been done, they delay paying these weavers for their labour, they act contrary to justice. And much more so if, although a merchant is supposed to pay a weaver or dyer in money based on the agreement made between them, he pays them in foodstuffs or wool or silk cloth, when these weavers or dyers in selling these things paid to them always receive a lower price than the amount in place of which they were paid. However, it is otherwise when it was so agreed between them that the weaver or dyer should be paid the whole or part of his due wage for his labour in bread, wine, cloth, or what have you, according to the usual current price, because, as is said in the *On the rules of law* in the *Liber Sext*, "To one who knows and consents no injury or fraud is done."[103] This, however, is understood to apply to those things which are not in themselves illicit. For even if someone pays usuries knowing and consenting, without a doubt an injury is done to him, because it is against divine law, and hence it is an injury to take usury. So also in the case under discussion: if from this agreement the weaver is burdened because a greater wage is due him for his labour according to the common judgment of the craft, yet he agrees in order to avoid being unemployed and to make some kind of profit, even if small; then the silk merchant is not excused from injustice.

5.2. Those who defraud taxes or tolls. Now some commit crime by defrauding taxes[104] or tolls,[105] having silk transported hidden between wool or linen or other merchandise, so that it is not recognized, and these are bound to make restitution of the aforesaid defrauded taxes and tolls: first of all, those who have this done, and second, those by whom it is done. But they also sometimes buy silk from those whom they know to have defrauded the tax. Now if there exists a prohibition on this in a city statute, which warns that no one may buy wool except from one who has paid the tax, then they do wrong in buying from those whom they know to have defrauded the taxes, since they act in violation of a quite reasonable statute, D. 8 c. 2.[106] And since by this means they can buy for less than the common just

102 "Tintore; dyer (a master with his own dyehouse)." Edler, *Terms of Business*, 297.

103 *VI* 5.[13.]27 (*Scienti*): "No injury or malice is done to one who knows and approves." English trans. from Gauthier, *Roman Law and … Canon Law*, 110.

104 "Gabella (Ar. qabāla, tax); tax on imports and exports (in Tuscany and elsewhere)." Edler, *Terms of Business*, 130.

105 "Pedaggio; transit toll (on merchandise or persons) or place where toll was collected." Ibid., 207.

106 D. 8 c. 2 (*Que contra mores*): see above.

minus iusto communi pretio emant, ex quadam equitate uidentur teneri de illa parte qua minus iusto pretio emunt gabelle. Si autem fuissent cooperati ad fraudem puta iuuantes eos ad inducendum in ciuitatem occulte tenerentur ad totam fraudem gabelle, *Extra, De iniur.*, *Si culpa.* Si autem nulla extat prohibitio per statutum, emendo a talibus non uidentur in aliquo teneri, sed solum ipsi fraudatores.

5.3. De emendo serichum ab furatis.

Emendo autem serichum ab hiis quos uerisimiliter credunt fuisse furatos ut filatores uel textores aut textrices, eo modo tenentur quo et illi qui emunt rapta ab aliis de quibus in secunda parte titulo primo c. de furto. Nec excusaret eos si illi dicant se iuste habuisse illud serichum quia magister seu setaiuolus tenebatur ei in tantum, quia hoc non est ei notum et in huiusmodi multotiens homines seipsos decipiunt. Excusarentur tamen ipsi textores uel alii in hac arte operarii, quando certi sunt de hoc; puta quia cum debeat dare XX ex manifesta conuentione, et non dat sibi nisi X, nec se potest aliter iuuare, accipiendo ab illo X siue de sericho quod peruenit ad manus eius, siue de aliis rebus, amotis scandalis: non tenetur illi, nec peccat, ar. D. 1 *Ius naturale* cum glossa. Caueat tamen ne se decipiat, nec in dubio hoc agat.

5.4. De uendendo ad terminum uel faciendo permutationes.

Vendunt etiam hii ad terminum frequenter ut lanifices. Vnde idem iuris quoad licitationem uel illicitationem contractus seu usurariam prauitatem, quod est dictum supra de lanificibus. Faciunt etiam permutationes frequenter cum lanificibus et ritagliatoribus in quibus communiter grauant textores et

---

413 Extra … culpa] *X* 5.36.9 (*Si culpa*): vide supra.

418 secunda … furto] Ant. Flor. *Summa* 2.1.12–15 (apud M_1 fol. Vr et Ballerini; 2.1.11–15 apud Mamachi 2:259–331): *de rapina; diffuse de rapina et participantibus in ea et talliis seu prestantis que imponuntur iniuste …; de furto; de multis speciebus seu modis furti.*

425 ar. … **426** glossa] D. 1 c. 7 (*Ius naturale*). Fortasse hoc locum in canone citato: Ius naturale est commune omnium nationum, eo quod ubique instinctu naturae, non constitutione aliqua habetur, ut … depositae rei uel commendatae pecuniae restitutio, uiolentiae per uim repulsio. *Glossa ord.* ad idem, s.v. *per vim*: quod cuilibet licet, ut ff. de ius. et iur. ut vim. in fi. extra de sent. excom. c. 3. §. si vero. in fin. De illa materia habes not. 23. q. 1. in summa. Ioan.

---

411 gabelle] *add. Ballerini* uel illi qui emunt a communitate ipsam gabellam **412** inducendum] mict(endum?) *a.c.* **413** Extra … culpa] *in marg. sin. add.* **416** furatos] *ut vid. cod.* : furatum *F_3 fol. 72vb* **417** aut textrices] *cod.* : *om. F_3 fol. 72vb* **418** aliis] + iniuste *a.c.* **419** dicant] *vel* dicunt *cod. et F_3 fol. 72vb* **425** rebus] + non pecca(n)t *a.c.*

price, by a certain sort of equity they seem to owe the difference to the tax. But if they cooperated in fraud, say, helping transporters to surreptitiously bring goods into the city, they would owe the whole amount gained by fraud to the tax, *Extra*, *On injuries*, c. 9.[107] However, if no prohibition exists by statute, then when they buy from such people they do not seem to owe anything, but only those do who commit fraud themselves.

5.3. Buying silk from those who have stolen it.

Now <silk merchants> buying silk from those whom they plausibly believe to have stolen it, such as throwsters[108] or male or female weavers, they are bound in the same way as those who buy things stolen by others, about which there is the chapter on theft in the second part, title 1.[109] Nor would it excuse them if they should say that they acquired that silk justly because the employer or silk merchant owed them the value of it, because this is not known to them,[110] and in this sort of thing people oftentimes deceive themselves. Nevertheless these weavers or other workers in this craft would be excused when they are certain about this. For instance, say that an employer was supposed to pay 20 by open agreement, and only paid the worker 10, and the worker is not able to assist himself otherwise than by taking 10 from the employer either in the silk which comes into his hands or in other things; if every occasion of scandal is avoided, the worker <who compensates himself by keeping some silk> does not owe the employer, nor does he sin, by the argument of D. 1 c. 7 with the gloss.[111] Nevertheless let him take care that he not deceive himself, or do this when in doubt.

5.4. Selling on credit or making exchanges.

These <silk merchants> also frequently sell on credit just like wool merchants. Hence the same norms apply in relation to the liceity or illicitness of contracts and to usurious misconduct as was described above in the section on wool merchants. They also frequently make exchanges with wool merchants and retail cloth dealers, in which they commonly burden the weavers and their other

107 *X* 5.36.9 (*Si culpa*).

108 "Filatoiaio, filatore, filatrice, and torcitore: throwster." These workers throw the silk to make thread (corresponds to the spinning of wool, flax, etc.). Edler, *Terms of Business*, 330.

109 Ant. Flor. *Summa* 2.1.12–15 (apud M_1 fol. Vr et Ballerini; 2.1.11–15 apud Mamachi 2:259–331): *de rapina; diffuse de rapina et participantibus in ea et talliis seu prestantis que imponuntur iniuste …; de furto; de multis speciebus seu modis furti.*

110 The syntax in the preceding part of this sentence is awkward to translate; I have adapted it slightly.

111 D. 1 c. 7 (*Ius naturale*). It is not entirely clear what passage of this canon and the gloss Antoninus is referring to, but my interpretation is that he refers to the repelling of violence by force: "Natural law is common to all nations because it is found everywhere by the instinct of nature and not by any constitution. Thus, there is … the restitution of a thing deposited or of money entrusted and the repelling of violence by force. And this, or anything similar to this, is never to be held as unjust, but always as natural and equitable." *Glossa ord.* ad idem: "*By force.* Which is lawful for anyone, as in *Digest* 1.1.3, toward the end; *Decretals* 2.27.3, toward the end. Concerning this topic you will find a discussion at the beginning of C. 23 q. 1. Ioan."

alios operarios suos, facientes eis dari pannum quo non egent, unde et reuendendo multum de iusto etiam pretio perdunt, ut dictum est supra. |

6. De architectis seu hedificatoribus.

De architectis seu hedificatoribus. Huius ars satis necessaria est uite humane fol. 77r
pro domibus et habitationibus fiendis que nos defendant a pluuiis et uentis frigoribus et caumatibus et ut quiescere ualeat et secrete operari que expedit. Primus *Cayn* reprobus legitur *hedificasse ciuitatem* unde et domos, *post diluuium* autem *Menroth* primus tyrannus, alios ad turrim hedificandum *Babel* induxit, ubi *confusis* ob superbiam illorum *linguis* opportuit hedificium imperfectum dimictere. Lata enim palatia et excessiua hedificia ultra conuenientiam sui status ad ostentationem facta Deo non placent. Patriarche autem in tentoriis habitabant, ut Habraam Ysach et Iacob, scientes se *hic non habere ciuitatem manentem* sed *domum non manufactam in celis* amplissimam expectare.

---

436 Primus … ciuitatem] *Gen* 4.17: Cognovit autem Cain uxorem suam, quae concepit, et peperit Henoch: et aedificavit civitatem, vocavitque nomen ejus ex nomine filii sui, Henoch.

436 post diluuium] *Gen* 10.1: Hae sunt generationes filiorum Noe, Sem, Cham et Japheth : natique sunt eis filii post diluvium.

437 Menroth … **438** induxit] *Gen* 10.8–10: Porro Chus genuit Nemrod : ipse coepit esse potens in terra, et erat robustus venator coram Domino. Ob hoc exivit proverbium : Quasi Nemrod robustus venator coram Domino. Fuit autem principium regni ejus Babylon, et Arach et Achad, et Chalanne, in terra Sennaar.

438 confusis … **439** dimictere] *Gen* 11.5–9: Descendit autem Dominus ut videret civitatem et turrim, quam aedificabant filii Adam, et dixit : Ecce, unus est populus, et unum labium omnibus : coeperuntque hoc facere, nec desistent a cogitationibus suis, donec eas opere compleant. Venite igitur, descendamus, et confundamus ibi linguam eorum, ut non audiat unusquisque vocem proximi sui. Atque ita divisit eos Dominus ex illo loco in universas terras, et cessaverunt aedificare civitatem. Et idcirco vocatum est nomen ejus Babel, quia ibi confusum est labium universae terrae : et inde dispersit eos Dominus super faciem cunctarum regionum.

440 Patriarche … **441** Iacob] Cfr *Gen* 12.8; *Gen* 26.17; *Gen* 33.18; *Hbr* 11.8–10.

442 hic … manentem] *Hbr* 13.14: Non enim habemus hic manentem civitatem, sed futuram inquirimus.

442 domum … celis] *2 Cor* 5.1: Scimus enim quoniam si terrestris domus nostra hujus habitationis dissolvatur, quod aedificationem ex Deo habemus, domum non manufactam, aeternam in caelis.

---

432 perdunt] + cum etiam et ultra iustum pretium eis uendiderunt *a.c.* **435** ualeat] + homo F_3 *fol. 73ra* **436** reprobus] *in marg. dext. add.* | domos] + Gen. 4(?) F_3 *fol. 73ra s.l.* **438** induxit] + Ge. 12(?) F_3 *fol. 73ra s.l.* **440** Patriarche autem] Patres autem *a.c.* **441** Iacob] *p.c.* : Ysae *a.c. ut vid.*

workers, having them be given cloth which they do not need, and hence when they resell it they lose a great deal also of the just price,[112] as was said above.

6. Architects and builders. About architects or builders.[113] Their art is quite necessary for human life, for we must make homes and dwellings to protect ourselves from rain and wind, cold and heat, and so that we may enjoy quiet and may do what is suitable privately. *Cain* the reprobate is the first whom we read to have *built a city* and hence also houses,[114] but *after the flood*,[115] *Nimrod*, the first tyrant, induced others to build the tower of *Babel*,[116] and after their *tongues were confounded* there because of pride it was necessary to abandon the building unfinished.[117] For wide palaces and extensive buildings, made beyond what is in harmony with one's state and passing into ostentation, do not please God. But the patriarchs lived in tents, like Abraham, Isaac, and Jacob,[118] knowing that they *had no lasting city here*,[119] but that they awaited the largest *house, not made with hands, in heaven*.[120]

---

112 This portion of the sentence is ambiguous in the Latin: it could also be translated "hence when they resell it even for a just price they take a great loss."

113 "Out of all this building activity that got under way in the fifteenth century emerges the new figure of the architect, but these men did not come out of the ranks of construction workers strictly speaking. In the cities of the Po valley, an area of brick architecture, the first generation of Renaissance architects … were trained as bricklayers. In Florence, however, not one architect is known to have been a waller, literally *muratore*, the Florentine term for a man who laid bricks and stones and could go on to supervise building projects as a foreman … In the fifteenth century the ranks of architects were filled with men trained as goldsmiths, stone sculptors, or woodcarvers …" Goldthwaite, *Economy of Renaissance Florence*, 387.

114 *Gen* 4.17: "And Cain knew his wife, and she conceived, and brought forth Henoch: and he built a city, and called the name thereof by the name of his son Henoch."

115 *Gen* 10.1: "These are the generations of the sons of Noe: Sem, Cham, and Japheth: and unto them sons were born after the flood."

116 *Gen* 10.8–10: "Now Chus begot Nemrod: he began to be mighty on the earth. And he was a stout hunter before the Lord. Hence came a proverb: Even as Nemrod the stout hunter before the Lord. And the beginning of his kingdom was Babylon, and Arach, and Achad, and Chalanne in the land of Sennaar."

117 *Gen* 11.5–9: "And the Lord came down to see the city and the tower, which the children of Adam were building. And he said: Behold, it is one people, and all have one tongue: and they have begun to do this, neither will they leave off from their designs, till they accomplish them in deed. Come ye, therefore, let us go down, and there confound their tongue, that they may not understand one another's speech. And so the Lord scattered them from that place into all lands, and they ceased to build the city. And therefore the name thereof was called Babel, because there the language of the whole earth was confounded: and from thence the Lord scattered them abroad upon the face of all countries."

118 Cfr *Gen* 12.8; *Gen* 26.17; *Gen* 33.18; *Hbr* 11.8–10.

119 *Hbr* 13.14: "For we have not here a lasting city, but we seek one that is to come."

120 *2 Cor* 5.1: "For we know, if our earthly house of this habitation be dissolved, that we have a building of God, a house not made with hands, eternal in heaven."

6.1. Caueant a fraudibus.

Artem igitur huiusmodi ut licitam exercentes cauere debent a fraudibus et periculosis seu ruinosis operibus magis, quod contingit multipliciter. Nam si conducuntur ad operas dietim data eis mercede secundum conuentionem, fraudem faciunt et peccant si non fideliter operantur diligentiam adhibentes prout opus requirit, et si tempus debitum subtrahunt in truffis et otiositatibus et pigritiis. Si eis soluitur ex pacto ad mensuram cannarum hedificii facti data eis omni materia necessaria a conducente, fraudem commictunt si ad hoc ut plus operis faciant unde plus lucrentur, non congrue laborant sed incurie, propter quod hedificium debile et ineptum redditur. Tertio quando accipiunt aliquod hedificium faciendum ad expensas suas materiam omnem ponentes pro certo pretio conuento inter eos, et tunc fraudem aliquando commictunt in non ponendo calcem ad sufficientiam uel alia opportuna, ut minus expendant pro materia quam ibi habent de suo ponere, unde hedificium non sufficiens redditur. Nec excusaret eos, quia si uellent ponere quod requiritur et diligenter operari, ualde modichum lucrarentur, ita paruum salarium inde recipiunt; quia debent ipsi in principio hoc aduertere, sed hoc ideo faciunt, ut citius eis quam aliis opus locetur. Verum est tamen quod quando conductor talium percipit quod nimis parum lucrantur ex tali pacto, eo non obstante debet supplere ad competentem mercedem, et precipue quando in tali opere superuenit casus qui bene non potuit preuideri, et ut ille diligentius agat opus. Debet etiam cauere talis patronus, ne differat mercedem soluere quando tempus aduenit solutionis, uel diminute soluat dando res pro peccunia uel malas monetas et huiusmodi.

6.2. De lathomariis et cementariis.

Hiis subseruiunt lathomarii et cementarii, qui peccant quando lateres uel calcem non bene cocta et conditionata tribuunt, uel cum mensuras uel numerum diminutum concedunt uel cum in diebus festis laborant, quando commode et sine magno detrimento sui ab hiis abstinere ualent.

---

450 eis] ei *cod.* : eis F_3 *fol. 73ra* | omni] *cod.* : omnis F_3 *fol. 73ra* **451** operis] operi *a.c.* | laborant] *cod. ut vid.* : laborando F_3 *fol. 73ra* **454** ponentes] + et t(unc?) *a.c.* **456** habent] *vel* haberent *cod.* : habent F_3 *fol. 73ra* **458** ita] + par- modichum *a.c.* | ita … **459** recipiunt] *cod.* : *om.* F_3 *fol. 73ra* **460** citius] + quam aliis *a.c.* **469** diminutum] *p.c.* **470** ualent] + id est aliis diebus faciendo *add. Ballerini*

6.1. Let them beware of frauds. Therefore these sorts <of workers>, practising this craft as licit, must avoid frauds and especially dangerous or shoddy works, which occur in many ways. For if they are hired for projects and their agreed wages are paid day by day, they commit fraud and sin if they do not work faithfully, applying the diligence which the work requires, and if they waste the working hours with trifles, idleness, and laziness. If it is agreed that they are paid by the number of ells of the building constructed, with all the necessary material provided to them by the hirer, they commit fraud if in this project, in order to make the building bigger and gain more profit, they do not work properly but carelessly, because of which the building is rendered defective and unfit. Third, when they take on some building to be constructed at their own expense, providing all material for a price determined by mutual agreement, even then they sometimes commit fraud by not providing lime[121] in sufficient amount or other things that are required, in order to spend less on the material which they have to provide at their own cost, thus rendering the building inadequate. Nor would it excuse them that if they wanted to provide what is required and work diligently they would make such a tiny profit that they receive a small salary for the work, because they themselves ought to realize this at the outset; but they do it this way for this reason, so that the work would be hired out to themselves sooner than to others. Nevertheless it is true that when the one who hires them perceives that they are making much too small a profit from this agreement, notwithstanding what they have agreed, he should make it up to an appropriate wage, and especially when in such a project a situation comes up which could not be foreseen clearly in advance, and when the worker does the work very diligently. Such a patron should also beware that he not delay paying the wage when the time of payment arrives, and that he not pay a diminished wage by paying in goods rather than money or by paying bad currency and so forth.

6.2. Masons and bricklayers. Serving these are the masons[122] and bricklayers,[123] who sin when they provide bricks[124] or lime[125] not well prepared[126] or conditioned, or when they offer a reduced measure or number, or when they work on feast days, when they could abstain from these things conveniently and without great detriment to themselves.

121 I have interpreted the Lat. *calx, calcis* here and in the next paragraph as referring to lime (i.e., as key ingredient in mortar or plaster). Other possible meanings of the word include limestone, some other sort of mineral, or the foundation or foot of a building. See *LS* and *DMLBS*, s.v.

122 Lat. *latomus*: "stone-cutter, mason; b (dist. as freemason, stone-layer, 'ligier')." *DMLBS*, s.v. "Lathomare, Sectis lapidibus instruere, sepire, munire." Du Cange, s.v.

123 Lat. *caementarius*: "a stone-cutter, a mason, a builder of walls." *LS*, s.v.

124 Lat. *later, -eris*, "brick, tile." *DMLBS*, s.v.

125 Lat. *calx, calcis*, as above.

126 Lat. *coctum* from *coquere*: "to cook … steep, melt, heat … to prepare by fire, burn, parch, etc." *LS*, s.v.

6.3. De lapicidinariis.

Lapicidinarii quoque predictis adnectuntur, quorum aliqui lapides cedunt et ad rudem formam trahunt. Alii diuersa inde opera exacta perficiunt, alii statuas et figuras sculpunt, ut etiam marmorarii, qui in operibus suis multas fraudes facere non possunt quia manifesta sunt opera eorum, possunt tamen nimis pretium exigere sui laboris; sed si sic existimatur a peritis in arte eis credendum. Post pactum etiam factum de mercede, si negligenter operaretur ut citius expediret malum esset. In hac arte periti fuerunt sancti quattuor coronati.

7. De fabris.

De fabris. Horum aliqui sunt fabri ferrarii, alii carpentarii, quorum primus fuit Tubalchain, ut patet Gen. 4. Inter fabros autem ferrarios primi in opere sunt, qui ferrum a schoria separantes, ad formam masse uel uirgarum adducunt.

7.1. De maniscallis, id est fabris facientibus ferramenta iumentis.

Exinde facientes ferramenta iumentis qui dicuntur maniscalli, qui non solum | offendunt imponendo praua ferramenta pro bonis, sed etiam quia (fol. 77v) aliquando male ferrant, unde iumentum efficitur clauatum, quod equitanti inducit aliquando magnum dampnum quia opportet propter hoc supersedere in hospitiis et expectare uel aliam equitaturam sumere; unde uidentur teneri de tali dampno, quando per incuriam eorum hoc contingit. Isti maniscalli solent se intromictere in medichatione ipsorum iumentorum equorum et aliorum, quod de se licitum est dummodo sciant artem et diligenter exerceant, sequestratis tamen omnibus incantationibus, quia hoc omnino illicitum. Et iuste mercedem inde petunt, quia *dignus est operarius mercede sua.* Hii

---

479 Tubalchain … 4] *Gen* 4.22: Sella quoque genuit Tubalcain, qui fuit malleator et faber in cuncta opera aeris et ferri. Soror vero Tubalcain, Noema.

491 dignus … sua] *Lc* 10.7: In eadem autem domo manete, edentes et bibentes quae apud illos sunt: dignus est enim operarius mercede sua. Nolite transire de domo in domum. *1 Tim* 5.18: Dicit enim Scriptura: Non alligabis os bovi trituranti. Et: Dignus est operarius mercede sua.

---

475 a] ab *a.c.* **476** negligenter] + et n- *a.c.* **479** 4] 5 *cod.* | Inter] E- *a.c.* **486** sumere] *vel* summere *cod.* **487** eorum] *in marg sin. add.* **490** quia] *in marg. sin.* Nota bene *scr. Iul. de Lapacc. ut vid.*

6.3. Stone cutters. Stonecutters[127] also are joined with the aforesaid, some of whom cut stones and bring them to their rough shape. Others from there complete various exact works, others sculpt statues and figures, as the marble workers also do, who in their works are not able to commit many frauds since their works are clearly visible, yet they can, however, exact an excessive price for their labour. But if it is assessed by experts in the craft, then they should be believed. Also after an agreement on a wage has been made, it would be wicked if one should work negligently in order to finish it more quickly. The Four Crowned Saints were practitioners of this art.[128]

7. Smiths. About craftsmen.[129] Some of these are smiths, others are carpenters.[130] The first of these was Tubalcain, as Genesis 4 reveals.[131] Now among smiths those whose work comes first are the ones who, separating iron from slag, shape it into a block or rods.

7.1. Farriers, that is smiths who make shoes for oxen. Next are those who make shoes[132] for beasts of burden, who are called farriers,[133] who not only do wrong in applying poor shoes for good ones, but also sometimes they fit them badly so that the animal is pierced with a nail, which sometimes leads to great loss for the rider since because of this it is necessary to let the animal rest in the hospital and to wait, or to take up another mount; hence the farriers seem to be obliged to pay for this loss, when it came about through their carelessness. These same farriers are also accustomed to occupy themselves in the medical treatment of these same oxen, horses, and others, which in itself is licit provided that they are knowledgeable in the craft and practise it diligently, abstaining, however, from any incantations, since this is entirely illicit. And they justly claim a wage from this, because *the labourer is*

---

127 Lat. *lapicidinarius*: "a superintendant of stone-quarries." *LS*, s.v. Cfr Lat. *lapicidarius*, "stone-cutter." *DMLBS*, s.v.

128 Four (or five) martyrs, reported in early Christian sources to have been sculptors put to death under Diocletian for refusing to make a statue of Aesculapius for a pagan temple. They were popular as patrons of masons, carpenters, and builders. In 1413 the Guild of Masons and Builders (*Arte di maestri de pietra e legname*) of Florence commissioned a statue of the Four Crowned Saints for Orsanmichele, executed by Nanno di Banco; this is the best-known artistic representation of the group. "Coronati, Quattro Santi"; Kirsch, "Four Crowned Martyrs"; E.G. Ryan, "Four Crowned Martyrs," in *New Catholic Encyclopedia*.

129 Lat. *faber, -bri*: "craftsman, usu. smith. … (w. *ferarrius*) blacksmith." *DMLBS*, s.v.

130 Lat. *carpentarius*: 2 b "carpenter, woodworker." *DMLBS*, s.v.

131 *Gen* 4.22: "Sella also brought forth Tubalcain, who was a hammerer and artificer in every work of brass and iron. And the sister of Tubalcain was Noema."

132 Lat. *ferramentum*, "iron implement, tool … horse-shoe … plough-iron, iron tyre for wheel cart." *DMLBS*, s.v.

133 Lat. *maniscallus*, presumably equiv. to *marescalcus, marescallus*: "farrier, servant who cares for horses." *DMLBS*, s.v.

aliquando solent esse mediatores ad uendendum et emendum talia animalia, tales tamen uulgariter dicuntur cozones, qui si commendant et consilio et persuasione inducunt ad emendum animal defectuosum pro sano, et in pretio notabiliter decipiunt plus iusto existimantes, scienter, tenentur leso de omni dampno; recte autem procedendo licite recipiunt pretium sue mediationis. Et isti uel alii quicumque qui locant equos ad uecturam offendunt cum commodant equos defectuosos pro bonis, unde conducenti sequitur dampnum in persona uel rebus, uel cum nimium de hoc pretium exigunt, quia ultra communem estimationem.

7.2. De armaiolis, id est fabris facientibus arma.

Alii sunt fabri ferrarii facientes diuersa artificia ex ferro uel aliis metallis, ut armaioli facientes galeas celatas thoraces lorichas, pectoralia brachialia et huiusmodi, lanceas sagiptas balistas bonbardas et huiusmodi. Et quia horum omnium potest esse licitus usus de se talis ars non est inlicita, quia in bello iusto si licet occidere multo magis et hiis uti, 23 q. 2 *Dominus Deus*, et q. 1 *Quid culpatur*. Nec obstat *Extra*, *De sagiptariis*, c. 1, quia illud exponitur

---

505 23 … Deus] C. 23 q. 2 c. 2 (*Dominus Deus*): Dominus Deus noster iubet ad Iesum Naue, ut constituat sibi retrorsum insidias, id est insidiantes bellatores ad insidiandum hostibus. Hinc admonemur, hoc non iniuste fieri ab his, qui iustum bellum gerunt, ut nichil iustus precipue cogitet in his rebus, nisi ut bellum suscipiat cui bellare fas est. Non enim fas est omnibus. Cum autem iustum bellum susceperit, utrum aperte pugnet, an ex insidiis, nichil ad iusticiam interest.

505 q.[2] ... **506** culpatur] C.23 q.1 c.4 (*Quid culpatur*): Quid culpatur in bello? An quia morituri quandoque moriuntur, ut domentur in pace uicturi? Hoc reprehendisse timidorum est, non religiosorum. Nocendi cupiditas, ulciscendi crudelitas, inplacatus atque inplacabilis animus, feritas rebellandi, libido dominandi, et si qua similia, hec sunt, que in bellis iure culpantur. Que plerumque ut etiam iure puniantur, aduersus uiolentias resistentium (siue Deo, siue aliquo legitimo inperio iubente) gerenda ipsa bella suscipiuntur a bonis, cum in eo rerum humanarum ordine inueniuntur, ubi eos uel iubere aliquid tale, uel in talibus obedire iuste ipse constringit.

506 Extra … 1] *X* 5.15.1 (*Artem illam*): Artem illam mortiferam et odibilem ballistariorum et sagittariorum adversus Christianos et catholicos exerceri de caetero sub anathemate prohibemus.

506 illud … **507** utitur] *Glossa ord.* ad idem s.v. *Christianos*: secus de Sarracenis, a contrario sensu. et intellige de bello iniusto, arg. supra de iureiur., sicut si constiterit 3. quoniam si iustum esset, licitum esset pugnare, 23 q. 2 dominus et q. ult. ut pridem.

---

497 locant] *s.l. p.c.* : commodant *a.c.* **501** uel … metallis] *in marg. dext. add.* **503** balistas] *in marg. sin. add.* **505** et[2]] *cod.* : et 10 F_3 *fol. 73rb* | Dominus … **506** culpatur] *postea add. Antoninus in spatio praebito ut vid.* | culpatur] -patur *in marg. sin. add.*

worthy of his wage.[134] These sometimes are in the habit of acting as mediators for selling and purchasing such animals, though such mediators are called in the vernacular animal brokers,[135] who, if they recommend a deficient animal as healthy and induce one to buy it by counsel and persuasion, and perpetrate a notable deception in price through assessing it above the just price, knowingly, they are obliged to the injured party for all losses; but proceeding uprightly they do licitly receive a price for their mediation. And these same or any others who lease out horses for transport do wrong when they hire out deficient horses as good ones, from which a loss ensues for the hirer in his person or his goods, or when they exact for this a price that is excessive because it goes beyond the common estimation.

7.2. Armourers, that is smiths who make arms.

Another sort are smiths who make diverse products of iron or other metals, such as armourers[136] who make helmets, sallets,[137] cuirasses, hauberks, armour for the chest and arms and so forth, lances, arrows, crossbows,[138] cannons,[139] and so forth. And because there can be a licit use for all of these, this craft is not in itself illicit, because in a just war if it is permissible to kill, much more so is it also permissible to use these things, C. 23 q. 2 c. 2,[140] and q. 1 c. 4.[141]

---

134 *Lc* 10.7: "And in the same house, remain, eating and drinking such things as they have: for the labourer is worthy of his hire. Remove not from house to house." *1 Tim* 5.18: "For the scripture saith: Thou shalt not muzzle the ox that treadeth out the corn: and, The labourer is worthy of his reward."

135 Ital. *cozzone*: "animal broker." Edler, *Terms of Business*, 94. Lat. *cosso*: "horse-coper." *DMLBS*, s.v.

136 "Armaiuolo – armaiuolus: armurier." Stella, *La révolte des Ciompi*, 297.

137 Ital. *celata*: "sallet." *Oxford-Paravia Italian Dictionary*, s.v. "Italis Celata, est cassis, unde nostri Salade effinxerunt : sic dicta, quod ea caput indutus miles celetur, et occultetur, ut a nemine agnoscatur." Du Cange, s.v.

138 Lat. *ballista*: "1 siege-catapult; 2 crossbow." *DMLBS*, s.v.

139 Lat. *bombardus, -a*: "bombard, cannon, fire-arm."

140 C. 23 q. 2 c. 2 (*Dominus Deus*): "Our Lord commands Joshua of Nave to set up ambushes behind him (Jos. 8.2), that is, fighters lying in ambush to take the enemies. By this, we are admonished that this is not done unjustly by those who wage a just war, so that the just man is not to consider anything more than that a just war is waged by one who has the right to do so. For this is not everyone's right. But when he has taken up a just war, it is not relevant to the issue of justice whether he wins by open warfare, or by ambush."

141 C. 23 q. 1 c. 4 (*Quid culpatur*): "What is to be faulted in war? Is it that some die, who would soon die in any case, so that others may live in peaceful subjection? To reprove this is timidity, not religion. The things which are faulted by right in war are desire to do harm, vengeful cruelty, fierce and implacable enmity, wild rebellion, the lust for power, and other such things. And it is generally to punish these things by right that (in obedience to the command of God or some lawful authority) good men undertake wars against the violence of resisters, when they find themselves in such a position in human affairs that either they must command such a thing, or a just order constrains them to obey in such matters."

communiter quando in bello iniusto his utitur. Ex hiis ergo iustum pretium petere de huiusmodi artificiis de se non est illicitum. Sed cum manifestum est aliquod bellum esse illicitum et iniustum, tunc talibus iniuste manifeste bellantibus uendentes talia uidentur cooperari peccato eorum et precipue quoad arma offensiua, ut gladios lanceas balistas bonbardas et huiusmodi, 11 q. 3 *Qui consentit*; forte non sic de defensiuis tantum ut galea torace loricha et huiusmodi. Vbi etiam dubium esset de iustitia belli forte possent excusari.

7.3. De fabris ad alia opera deditis.

Alii sunt fabri ad alia opera dediti, ut instrumenta ad culturam, uomeres zappas uangas sarculos falces secures et huiusmodi. Alii pertinentia ad coquinam, ut cachabos patellas urceolos tripodes chalderias chatinos et huiusmodi. Alii pertinentia ad fabricham uel carpenteriam, ut malleos incudes forcipes terebra ferras leuigas ascias celtes et huiusmodi. Qui omnes fraudem facere possunt in faciendo opera debilia, propter malam materiam, uel nimio pretio uel in diminuto pondere.

8. De carpentariis.

De carpentariis. Hii in faciendo ligna incidere secundum augmentum uel decrementum lune sine alia obseruatione dierum, non peccant, quia cum luna ut propinquior planeta multum influat in corpora inferiora, secundum rationem naturalem est quod potius incidantur, cum luna est in decremento quam in augmento. In faciendo autem diuersa opera ex lignis licitum est ex tali exercitio lucrum expetere secundum quantitatem laboris et industriam operis et morem patrie; sed fraude utuntur cum ligna parum durabilia tradunt pro solidis et diu permansuris. Ex hiis aliqui tarsias seu tarsiata lignamina faciunt quod magis pertinere uidetur ad quemdam ornatum seu ostentationem quam ad utilitatem. Qui uero ligna secant, cum multum laborent digni sunt mercede

---

511 11 … **512** consentit] C. 11 q. 3 c. 100 (*Qui consentit*): vide supra.

---

509 esse] *in marg. sin.* Nota bene *scr. Iul. de Lapacc. ut vid.* **511** bonbardas] *vel* bombardas *cod.* **516** chalderias] *cod.* : chalderios F_3 *fol. 73va* **523** inferiora] + rationale est *a.c.* **524** cum … **525** augmento] *in rasura ut vid.* **525** augmento] *in marg sin. add.* | licitum] licita *a.c.*

Notwithstanding *Extra*, *On archers*, c. 1,[142] because this canon is commonly expounded as applying when these are used in an unjust war.[143] From the foregoing therefore it is not illicit in itself to claim a just price for these sorts of products. But when it is manifest that a particular war is illicit and unjust, then selling such things to those who are manifestly making war unjustly seems to be cooperation in their sin, and especially in relation to offensive arms, such as swords, lances, crossbows, cannons, and so forth, C. 11 q. 3 c. 100.[144] It may not be so for purely defensive arms, such as helmets, cuirasses, hauberks, and the like. And where there was doubt about the justice of a war perhaps they could be excused.

7.3. Craftsmen devoted to other sorts of work. Another sort are craftsmen devoted to other sorts of work, such as farming implements, ploughshares, hoes,[145] spades, mattocks, sickles, hatchets, and so forth. Others make things pertaining to cooking, such as cooking pots, dishes, pitchers, trivets, cauldrons,[146] serving vessels, and so on. Others make things pertaining to forging or carpentry, such as hammers, anvils, tongs, bores, bars,[147] planes, adzes, chisels, and so on. All of these can commit fraud through making defective products because of poor material, or through too high a price, or through using a reduced weight.

8. Carpenters. About carpenters. These in felling wood according to the waxing or waning of the moon without observing any other days do not sin, for since the moon, as the nearest planet, exercises much influence on lower bodies, it is in accordance with natural reason that they should be felled rather when the moon is waning than when it is waxing. Now in making various products out of wood it is licit to seek out a profit from this type of employment according to the amount of labour and the diligence of the work and the custom of the country; but carpenters use fraud when they provide undependable wood as solid and long-lasting wood. From these some make timber marquetry or veneers,[148] which seems to pertain more to a certain decoration or display than utility. But those who cut wood, since they work very hard, are worthy of a good wage

142 *X* 5.15.1 (*Artem illam*). This canon prohibits the employment of crossbowmen (Lat. *ballistarius*) and archers (Lat. *sagittarius*) against Christians under penalty of anathema.

143 *Glossa ord.* ad idem s.v. *Christianos*.

144 C. 11 q. 3 c. 100 (*Qui consentit*): see above.

145 Ital. *zappa*: "hoe." *Oxford-Paravia Italian Dictionary*, s.v.

146 Lat. *caldaria* or *caldarium*: "metal pot for hot water, cauldron." *DMLBS*, s.v.

147 Lat. *ferra, -ae*: "Ferra, Instrumenta ferrea, quæ ad molendinum pertinent, et maxime ferrum, quod in media mola statuitur." Du Cange, s.v. Cf *ferrum, -i*: "1 iron … 5 c chisel … 9 iron implement: a (for branding) … 14 iron bar or sim. … 15 iron part of a mill." *DMLBS*, s.v. It is not certain what sort of implement Antoninus means here.

148 Cf Ital. *tarsia*: "marquetry." *Oxford-Paravia Italian Dictionary*, s.v.

bona fideliter operando. Huius artis fuit Ioseph Marie sponsus, dicit enim Crisostomus in sermone de Epiphania, quod fuit carpentarius. |

8.1 De facientibus galeas naues et nauiculas. Ad hoc genus ministerii spectat galeas facere naues et nauiculas, et alia per que nauigatur, quod opus multum est utile et necessarium humane conuersationi ad negotiandum. Qui tamen ista operarentur pro eis quos sciunt uti uelle ad pirrateriam, id est ad predandum quoscumque per mare, uel ad deferendum Saracenis ipsas, grauiter peccarent, quia cooperarentur in malo. fol. 79r

8.2. De marinariis. Marinarii autem et alii qui sunt directores talium lignorum per mare, scienter utique peccant mortaliter cum sciunt ad predam seu iniustum bellum se duci. Alias et opus licitum et merces debita. Et cum substineant ibi immensos labores et pessimam uitam, tamen dimictere nesciunt tale exercitium et ita periculosum, nec tenenter dimictere. Et communiter sunt homines pessimi, blasfematores frequentes Dei et sanctorum, et sine aliquo Dei timore. In periculis tamen deuotissime uidentur ad Deum recurrere, quos etiam Deus mirabiliter iuuat, sed timore seruili magis quam amore filiali apparet eos moueri cum quasi semper *ad uomitum reuertantur*, non curantes de Deo et salute sua. |

9. De aromatariis. De aromatariis. Hoc ministerium quoad medicinalia, uite humane conseruationi deseruit ad esse, quoad alia ad bene esse. Dicitur autem multas sophistichationes in ea fieri et fraudes. Et in conficiendis medicinis, aliquando ponunt aromata multum uetusta unde et uirtutem modicham habentia, uel si non habent illa que exiguntur, aliqua alia non ita conferentia locho illorum, unde et infirmo parum prosunt uel forte nocent. Quod cum fieret esset graue peccatum. fol. 78r

---

532 Crisostomus … carpentarius] Sermonem Ioannis Chrysostomi non inveni. Cfr *Mt* 13.53–5.

536 ad[1] … **537** peccarent] Cfr Ant. Flor. *Summa* 3.25.30–1 (apud M_2 fol. VIr; 3.24.30–1 apud Ballerini): *de excommunicatione contra deferentes arma uel lignamina ad Saracenos uel quecumque mercimonia; de excommunicatione contra piratas et expoliantes Romipetas euntes ad Curiam.*

545 ad … **546** reuertantur] *Prv* 26.11: Sicut canis qui revertitur ad vomitum suum, sic imprudens qui iterat stultitiam suam. Cfr *2 Pt* 2.22.

---

532 carpentarius] *in marg. infer.* Quere residuum huius §. in capite faciei post unam cartam, et incipit Ad hoc genus. *scr. Iul. de Lapacc.* **533** Ad] *in marg. sin.* pone hec ante precedentem (*unum uerbum haud leg.*) in fine faciei. *scr. Antoninus* | Ad … **546** sua] *in fol. 79r add.* **536** pirrateriam] *vel* pirreriam *cod.* : pirreriam F_3 *fol. 73va* **539** duci] *add.* F_3 *fol. 73va in marg. sin.* et sunt excommunicati utique cum depredantur per mare indifferenter quoscumque Christianos, et etiam cum deferunt uictualia et mercimonia ad partes infidelium, uide infra ti. 25 de censuris. **546** sua] *add. Ballerini* De piratis et poenis illorum habes supra in secunda parte titulo de auaritia cap. de furto, et infra titulo de excommunicatione. Ibi uide diffusius et clarius.

when they work faithfully. Joseph the spouse of Mary belonged to this craft, for Chrysostom says in a sermon on the Epiphany that he was a carpenter.[149]

8.1. On those who make galleys, ships, and boats. To this category belong workers who make galleys, ships and boats, and other things with which one sails; and this work is very useful and necessary for the human way of life in order to trade. Nevertheless those who should craft such things for people who they know want to use them for piracy,[150] that is to plunder indiscriminately at sea, or want to convey them to Saracens,[151] would gravely sin because they would be cooperating in evil.

8.2. Mariners. Now mariners and others who are overseers of such fleets at sea certainly commit mortal sin in full knowledge when they knowingly go off to plunder or to unjust war. Otherwise both the work is licit and a wage is due. And although mariners sustain immense labours and a terrible life, nevertheless they are unwilling to give up this so dangerous employment, nor are they obliged to give it up. And commonly they are terrible men, frequent blasphemers of God and the saints, and lacking any fear of God. In danger, however, they seem to run back to God most devoutly, and God even miraculously helps them; but it appears that they are moved by servile fear more than by filial love, since they almost always *return to their vomit*,[152] not taking thought for God and their salvation.

9. Apothecaries. About apothecaries. This occupation serves the preservation of human life: in relation to medical things for life itself, in relation to other things for living well. But it is said that many scams and frauds are practised in this. And in preparing medicines, sometimes they use aromatics that are very old, and hence have little potency, or if they do not have what is required they use some other less beneficial stuff instead, and hence they are of little help to the infirm, or possibly they are harmful. If this were done, it would be a grave sin.

---

149 I have not found the relevant sermon of John Chrysostom. Cfr *Mt* 13.53–5.

150 Ital. *pirateria*: "piracy." *Oxford-Paravia Italian Dictionary*, s.v.

151 Cfr Ant. Flor. *Summa* 3.25.30–1 (apud M_2 fol. VIr; 3.24.30–1 apud Ballerini): *de excommunicatione contra deferentes arma uel lignamina ad Saracenos uel quecumque mercimonia*; *de excommunicatione contra piratas et expoliantes Romipetas euntes ad Curiam.*

152 *Prv* 26.11: "As a dog that returneth to his vomit, so is the fool that repeateth his folly." Cfr *2 Pt* 2.22.

In candelis formandis aliquando ponunt ibi oleum uel lupinos seu fabas fractas bene maceratas, ut sic similis coloris existentes cere incorporentur.

In spetiebus componendis miscentes que minus ualent plus debito. Et in confectionibus etiam non seruando debitum modum.

In sirupiis cum parum in eis expendant quia aque sunt distillate corpus carum, nimium pretium apponunt.

In ponderibus diminutis offendunt dantes XI uncias eorum que ad pondus uenduntur pro libra; et ipsi, cum emunt ab aliis talia uelint habere libram pro XI unciis, agentes contra illud Deutero. <25>: *Non habebis in sacculo diuersa pondera maius et minus,* unum scilicet in emendo, aliud in uendendo.

Peccant et in diebus festiuis uendendo non necessaria. Nam necessaria ut puta medicinas pro infirmis, et ipsas componendo et alia huiusmodi necessaria ut ceram pro funeralibus, excusantur. Super quo tamen ciuitates bene ordinate solent prouidere ut aliqui ex eis teneant apothecas apertas, puta unum pro quarterio et huiusmodi.

9.1. De ministris talis artis.

Aliqui etiam ex ministris talis artis dediti gule, sibi assumunt uel sotiis dant de confectionibus et similibus ad comedendum, in quo tenentur magistro satisfacere si sine consensu eius faciunt. Mendacia autem et periuria in tali arte sicut et aliis semper sunt; ut peccata et aliquando mortalia uitanda et reprehendenda.

9.2. De barbitonsoribus.

Et quia ad medicinalia pertinet minutio sanguinis seu flebotomia, quod opus fieri solet per barbitonsores, ideo de eis breuiter agendum. In tali siquidem ministerio fraudes male fieri possunt. Sed in hoc aliqui offendunt quod diebus festis sine aliqua necessitate radunt aliquos, hoc querentes, scilicet radi uel tonderi ob iuuenilem uanitatem ut iuniores et pulcriores appareant, quod male potest, ut uidetur, excusari a mortali cum uiolent festum uterque, ar. 2 q. 1. *Notum* in fin.

---

561 Deutero. … **562** uendendo] *Dt* 25.13: Non habebis in sacculo diversa pondera, majus et minus.

578 uiolent … **579** fin.] C. 2 q. 1 c. 10 (*Notum sit*): vide supra.

---

554 incorporentur] *cod.* : incorporent F_3 *fol. 73va* **555** ualent] *p.c.* : *haud leg. a.c.* **557** corpus] *ut vid. cod. cum* F_3 *fol. 73vb* **557** corpus carum] *in marg. dext. add.* **558** carum] *ut vid. cod.* : eorum F_3 *fol. 73vb* : earum *Ballerini* **560** ipsi] + ementes *a.c.* **561** XI] *sic cod.* : tredecim F_3 *fol. 73vb in rasura* | 25] *spatium duarum litterarum praeb. cod.* **566** ordinate] *add. Ballerini* ut Florentia **568** assumunt] *vel* assummunt *cod.* **569** magistro] + safa- *a.c.* **571** aliis] *p.c.* : alios *a.c.* **573** flebotomia] *vel* flebootomia *cod.* **574** eis] *p.c.* : *haud vid. a.c.* **575** male] *om. Ballerini*

In fashioning candles sometimes they use therein oil or lupine[153] or broken-up henbane[154] well mashed so that, thus appearing of similar colour, they may be incorporated into the wax.[155]

In making up spices[156] <they do wrong>, mixing in what is of less value more than is proper. And in confections also, not observing the proper method.

In syrups, they set a too high price although they spend little costly substance in them, since the liquids have been distilled.

They do wrong in using reduced weights when they give 11 ounces of things which are sold by weight as a pound; and they themselves, when they buy from others such things, want to have a pound as 11 ounces, going against what is in Deutoronomy 25: *You shall not have diverse weights in your bag, a greater and a less*,[157] namely one for buying and another for selling.

They sin also when they sell non-necessities on feast days. For necessities are excused, as for example medicines for the infirm, in compounding both them and other such necessary things, such as wax for funerals. On this, however, cities that are well administered are accustomed to provide that some of these should keep their shops open, say, one per quarter and so forth.

9.1. Employees in this craft. Also some of the employees in this craft, devoted to gluttony, take for themselves or give to their fellows some of the confections and such like to consume them; in which they are bound to make satisfaction to the employer if they do this without his consent. Lies, however, and perjuries are always present in this art just like in others; as sins, and sometimes mortal ones, they are to be shunned and reprehended.

9.2. Barber surgeons. And because bloodletting or venesection pertains to medical affairs, which operation is usually carried out by barber-surgeons, therefore we must treat of them briefly. In fact in this kind of occupation frauds can hardly be committed. But in this some do wrong: on feast days, without any real need, they shave people who ask to be shaved or trimmed because of juvenile vanity, wanting to look younger and fairer; which, as it seems, can hardly be excused from mortal sin, since they each violate the feast, by the argument of C. 2 q. 1 c. 10.[158]

---

153 Lat. *lupinus*: 4 c "(as sb. m.) lupine (*Lupinus*)." *DMLBS*, s.v.

154 Lat. *faba*: "2 b (w. *lupina*) ? henbane (*Hyoscyamus niger*)." *DMLBS*, s.v.

155 Ital. *cera*: "wax." *Oxford-Paravia Italian Dictionary*, s.v.

156 Lat. *speties* or *species*; cfr Ital. *spezia*: "spice." *Oxford-Paravia Italian Dictionary*, s.v. "Speziale; merchant who sells spices, drugs, medicines, sugar, wax, dyes, etc." Edler, *Terms of Business*, 277. The three examples which Edler provides from sources are spelled "spetiali," as the word is spelled by Antoninus.

157 *Dt* 25.13: "Thou shalt not have divers weights in thy bag, a greater and a less."

158 C. 2 q. 1 c. 10 (*Notum sit*): see above.

9.3. De operando in sabbatho.

Ex hoc autem quod in sabbatis uel uigiliis solempnitatum operentur, usque ad tertiam horam noctis et ultra usque quasi ad mediam, ex eo quod communiter persone plus eo tempore in hoc uolunt sibi seruiri quam alio, et nisi quis illo tempore laboraret ut ceteri, ammicteret in magna parte concursum personarum unde et lucrum: uidetur hoc posse tollerari, attento more generali patrie in huiusmodi. Quamuis enim statutum ecclesie in obseruatione cessationis ab operibus diebus festiuis sit de uespera ad uersperam, id est sero, *De cons.* D. 3 *Pronuntiandum*, tamen mos patrie multum habet modifichare inchoationem et terminationem festorum, cum etiam habeat et tollere et instituere ipsa festa, ar. *De cons.* D. 3 *Rogationes*, et D. 11 *In hiis*; et precipue attento, quod post sero diei festi possent laborare, secundum illud decretum *Pronuntiandum*, cum tamen non operentur communiter usque ad mediam noctem, et sic uidetur admictenda talis compensatio sero uigilie cum sero festiuitatis. Si ab offitialibus ad quos spectat tales regulare ordinaretur quod post primam horam noctis uel secundam sub certa pena nullus in tali arte operaretur, melius esset et tutius, et tunc omnes tenerentur seruare; et seruando, nulli eorum fieret preiudicium.

In minuendo autem peccarent, si non essent in eo periti.

Super omnia debent cauere, ne in apotecis eorum |

---

585 statutum … **587** Pronuntiandum] *De cons.* D. 3 c. 1 (*Pronunciandum*): Pronunciandum est, ut sciant tempora feriandi per annum, id est: omnem dominicam a uespera usque ad uesperam, ne a Iudaismo capiantur. Feriandi uero per annum isti sunt dies: Natalis Domini, S. Stephani, … et S. Martini, et illae festiuitates, quas singuli episcopi in suis episcopiis cum populo collaudauerint, que uicinis tantum circummorantibus indicendae sunt, non generaliter omnibus. Reliquae uero festiuitates per annum non sunt cogendae ad feriandum, nec prohibendae. Indictum uero ieiunium quando fuerit denunciatum, ab omnibus obseruetur.

589 De … Rogationes] *De cons.* D. 3 c. 3 (*Rogationes*): Rogationes, id est letanias, ante Ascensionem Domini placuit celebrari ita, ut premissum triduanum ieiunium in dominicae Ascensionis solempnitate soluatur. Per quod triduum serui et ancillae ab opere relaxentur, quo magis plebs uniuersa conueniat. Cfr D. 76 c. 11 (*Utinam*) cum *Glossa ord.*; D. 12 c. 11 (*Illa autem*).

589 D.[2] … **590** hiis] D. 11 c. 7 (*In his rebus*): In his rebus, de quibus nihil certi statuit diuina scriptura, mos populi Dei et instituta maiorum pro lege tenenda sunt.

591 decretum Pronuntiandum] *De cons.* D. 3 c. 1 (*Pronunciandum*): vide supra.

---

580 sabbatis] *vel* sabbathis *cod.* **581** usque[2]] + ad *a.c.* | mediam] *cod.* : + noctem *add.* F_3 *fol. 73vb* **582** tempore] *cod. ut vid.* : tempore F_3 *fol. 73vb* **585** obseruatione] + festi *a.c.* **588** modifichare] + in c- *a.c.* **589** ar.] ut *a.c.* | 11] *p.c.* : 10 *a.c. ut vid.* **596** tenerentur] teneretur *cod.* : tenerentur F_3 *fol. 73vb* **597** In … periti] *om.* F_3 *fol. 73vb* **598** ne … eorum] *hoc completum est nusquam in foliis proximis cod.* : F_3 *fol. 73vb scr.* a colloquutionibus inhonestis in apothecis eorum ne schandalizentur honesti et spirituales homines. : *Ballerini scr.* ne in apothecis eorum fiat congregatio iuuenum ad maleficiendum, ut hodie faciunt plurimi.

9.3. Working on the sabbath. However, if they work on sabbaths or vigils of solemnities until the third hour of the night and beyond up to almost the middle of the night, for the reason that people commonly want this service to be provided to them more at this time than at another time, because if one were not to work at that time just as the rest do, he would be deprived in great part of the concourse of persons and hence of profit: on that ground it seems that this can be tolerated, with attention paid to the general custom of the country in such matters. For although the legislation of the Church on observing the cessation from work on festival days is from Vespers to Vespers, that is the evening, *De cons.* D. 3 c. 1 (*Pronuntiandum*),[159] nevertheless the tradition of the country has much power to modify the beginning and end of feasts, since it also has the power both to remove and to institute these feasts, by the argument of *De cons.* D. 3 c. 3,[160] and D. 11 c. 7.[161] And we should attend especially to this, that although people are allowed to work after the evening of the feast day, according to that decree *Pronuntiandum*,[162] nevertheless usually they do no work until the middle of the night. And thus it seems that this compensation may be admitted in the evening of the vigil alongside the evening of the festival. If it were ordained by the officials to whom it belongs to regulate such things that after the first or second hour of the night no one in this craft may work, under a fixed penalty, it would be better and safer, and then all would be bound to observe it; and in observing it, no prejudice would come to any of them.

Now in bloodletting they would sin if they were not experts in this.

Above all they must beware lest in their shops ...[163]

---

159 *De cons.* D. 3 c. 1 (*Pronunciandum*): "It is to be announced to laymen that they must know the times of abstention from work throughout the year, that is, every Sunday, from vespers to vespers, lest they be seized by Judaizing. Throughout the year, these are days of abstention from work: the Lord's Nativity, St. Stephen ... St. Martin, and those festivities, which the several bishops have approved in their episcopacies with their people, which are to be proclaimed only to those who live near-by, and not generally to all. They are not to be compelled to abstain from work on other festivities throughout the year, nor to be forbidden. But as for an appointed fast, when it has been announced, it is to be observed by all."

160 *De cons.* D. 3 c. 3 (*Rogationes*): "It has pleased us that rogations, that is, litanies be celebrated before the Lord's Ascension, so that a fast of three days be completed on the solemnity of the Lord's Ascension. Through this three day period, serfs and bondswomen are to be freed form work, so that a greater assembly of people may come together for it." Cfr D. 76 c. 11 (*Utinam*) with the *Glossa ord.*; D. 12 c. 11 (*Illa autem*).

161 D. 11 c. 7 (*In his rebus*): "In these things, as to which nothing certain has been established by divine Scripture, the custom of the people of God and the institutes of the ancestors are to be kept as law."

162 *De cons.* D. 3 c. 1: see above.

163 This sentence breaks off here. It is not completed on any of the other folios which make up this chapter in the autograph manuscript M_2. The manuscript F_3 and Ballerini's edition each supply different conclusions for this sentence. F_3 fol. 73vb: "Above all they must beware of dishonourable conversations in their shops lest honest and spiritual people be scandalized." Ballerini: "Above all they must beware lest in their shops there arise a crowd of youths to do evil, as today very many do."

10. De artificibus circa scripturas et picturas.

De artificibus circa scripturas et picturas. Et cartas quidem facientes bonbicinas qui dicuntur cartarii, non ualent commictere multas fraudes, quia cito apparet defectus carte uel de ruditate eius et grossitie, uel de insufficientia colle, unde aliquando attramentum non seruat sed diffunditur sugando. Cartas autem facientes de pergameno seu pellibus animalium qui dicuntur pelachani, plures fraudes commictere ualent, que non cito deprehendi possunt, sed in processu, ut cum littera extinguitur, quod ex parte etiam attramenti prouenire potest sed magis ex defectu siccitatis talium cartarum uel rasure. Et quia ex hoc sequitur notabile dampnum libris, ideo cum hoc perpendunt grauiter peccant. fol. 79r

10.1. De chartulariis.

Et similiter qui dicuntur cartularii qui huiusmodi cartas reuendunt cum sciunt illos defectus, *Extra*, *De iniur. et damp.*, c. ultimo. In ligando libros etiam cartularii frequentius operantur quod diligenter agendo digni sunt mercede sua competenti. Quod enim cartas emptas ab aliis de bombice uel pergameno, reuendant maiori pretio, dummodo moderato, non est de se illicitum. Solent etiam esse mediatores ad emendum uel uendendum libros pro aliis, et quod pro tali opere mediationis moderatum lucrum querant non est iniustum. Sed si defectuosum librum sciunt ut multum falsum et tamen procurant dari pretium ac si defectum non haberet commendantes pro bono, peccant et tenentur ad satisfactionem cum scienter decipiunt emptorem. Idem, si faciunt emere ultra iustum pretium contra conscientiam suam uel uendere longe minori pretio. Et si maiori pretio uendunt quam quod petebat uel intendebat dominus libri, et illud plus sibi retinent fures sunt et latrones et tenentur.

10.2. Quomodo scriptores offendunt.

Scriptores uero librorum, in multis offendere possunt. Et primo cum scribunt cum multis falsitatibus, ex quo liber quasi nichil ualet. Secundo cum pretio statuto certo pro carta qualibet uel sexterno aut quaterno, faciunt

---

609 Extra … ultimo] *X* 5.36.9 (*Si culpa*): vide supra.

---

599 facientes] + de *a.c.* **602** sugando] *sic cod. et* F_3 *fol. 73vb* **604** processu] + temporis *add.* F_3 *fol. 74ra* **605** etiam] + scriptoris et *add.* F_3 *fol. 74ra* | sed … **606** rasure] F_3 *fol. 74ra scr.* cum ipse scriptor nescit gummare sufficienter attramentum uel cum est recens immediate scribit. **606** cartarum] cartal- *a.c. ut vid.* | uel] et *a.c.* **609** sciunt … ultimo] *cod.* : F_3 *fol. 74ra scr.* sciunt defectus in eis et nichilominus ut uendant multa mendacia dicunt et raro tenent quod promittunt grauiter peccant. **611** enim] *ut vid. cod. cum* F_3 *fol. 74ra* : si *Ballerini* **618** uel] *p.c.* : *haud leg. a.c.* | uendere] *cod.* : F_3 *fol. 74ra add.* libros **620** retinent] retinet *cod.* : retinent F_3 *fol. 74ra* | fures … tenentur] *cod. cum* F_3 *fol. 74ra* : *om.* Ballerini | tenentur] *cod.* : F_3 *fol. 74ra add.* ad satisfactionem **621** cum] *in marg. dext. add.* **622** falsitatibus] F_3 *fol. 74ra add.* ut solent **623** quaterno] *cod.* : quinterno F_3 *fol. 74ra*

10. Artisans whose work relates to writings and pictures. About artisans in relation to writings and pictures. And indeed those who make writing sheets of cotton paper,[164] who are called stationers, are not capable of committing many frauds, because the defects of the paper quickly appear, whether in its roughness or thickness or inadequate glue, whence sometimes it does not hold ink but it spreads out as the paper sucks it up.[165] However, those who make writing sheets of parchment or animal skins, who are called tanners,[166] are capable of committing more frauds, which cannot be detected quickly, but only in the course of use, as when the handwriting fades, which can also be produced on the part of the ink, but more from insufficient drying or scraping of the writing sheets. And because from this notable damage to books ensues, therefore when they are aware of this they sin gravely.

10.1. Booksellers. And likewise for those who are called booksellers,[167] who resell these sorts of writing sheets when they know their defects, *Extra*, *On injuries and losses*, c. 9.[168] Booksellers also very frequently work in binding books; when they do this diligently they are worthy of their suitable wage. Now, that they resell at a higher price the writing sheets of cotton paper or parchment which they have purchased from others, provided that it is a moderate price, is not in itself illicit. They are also accustomed to be mediators for the purchase or sale of books on behalf of others, and that they ask a moderate profit for this work of mediating is not unjust. But if they know a book to be defective, such as that it is very corrupt, and yet they arrange that a price be paid as if it had no defect, recommending it as of good quality, they sin and are bound to make satisfaction, since they knowingly deceive the buyer. The same if, against their conscience, they induce someone to buy for beyond the just price or to sell for a far lower price. And if they sell for a greater price than what the owner of the book sought or intended, and they keep that additional amount for themselves, they are thieves and robbers and they owe it <to the owner>.

10.2. How scribes do wrong. Now scribes of books, they can do wrong in many ways. First, they may write with many errors, because of which the book is practically worthless. Second, when a fixed price has been established for every page or sextern[169] or quire,[170] they make wide spaces between lines or letters, so that they can fill the page quickly, or from hurrying they do not write a competent enough script. They

---

164 Lat. *bonbicina*, cfr *bombycinus*, *-a*, *-um*: 2 a "cotton (or other fabric)." *DMLBS*, s.v.

165 Antoninus writes *sugando*, for *sugendo*(?) from Lat. *sugere*: "to suck (fluid in or up)." *DMLBS*, s.v.

166 "Pelacane: tanneur de peaux; débourreur (?)." Stella, *La révolte des Ciompi*, 312.

167 "Cartolaio – cartolarius: cette désignation comprend le fabricant de papier, de parchemins, de cahiers et de livres; papetier-libraire." Ibid., 299.

168 *X* 5.36.9 (*Si culpa*).

169 Lat. *sexternus*: "gathering or quire of six pieces of parchment or paper, folded in half to form twelve folios." *DMLBS*, s.v.

170 Lat. *quaternus*: "set of four sheets of parchment or paper folded to form eight leaves, quire, gathering." *DMLBS*, s.v.

lata spatia linearum uel licterarum, ut cito cartam impleant, uel cum ex festinantia non ita competentem litteram faciunt. Offendunt etiam cum diebus festis scribunt pro lucro: uiolant enim festum, quod ecclesia precipit celebrandum in cessando ab operibus seruilibus seu manualibus, quale est tale opus, *De cons.* D. 3 *Pronuntiandum.*

10.3. De pictoribus. Pictores non solum secundum quantitatem laboris, sed magis secundum industriam et maiorem peritiam artis de salario sui artificii magis uel minus rationabiliter postulant sibi solui. Qui in hoc offendunt, quando formant ymagines prouocatiuas ad libidinem, non ex pulcritudine earum sed ex dispositione earum ut mulieres nudas et huiusmodi. Reprehensibiles etiam sunt cum pingunt ea que sunt contra fidem, cum faciunt Trinitatis ymaginem unam personam cum tribus capitibus, quod mon- | -strum in rerum natura, uel in fol. 79v
Annuntiatione Virginis paruulum Yesum formatum micti in uterum Virginis quasi non esset de substantia Virginis eius corpus assumptum, uel paruulum Yesum cum tabula litterarum, cum non didicerit ab homine. Sed nec etiam laudandi sunt cum apocripha pingunt, ut obstetrices in partu Virginis, Tome apostolo cingulum suum a Virgine Maria in Assumptione sua propter dubitationem eius dimissum et huiusmodi. In historiis etiam sanctorum seu in ecclesiis pingere curiosa que non ualent ad deuotionem excitandam sed risum et uanitatem ut simias canes et insequentes lepores et huiusmodi, uel uanos ornatus uestimentorum, superfluum uidetur et uanum.

Hiis herent miniatores librorum siue cum calamo siue cum pennello, quibus etiam competit premium de labore suo.

11. De ministerio musichorum in cantando et pulsando. De ministerio musichorum in cantando et pulsando. Et cantus quidem firmus in diuinis offitiis a sanctis doctoribus institutus est ut Gregorio Magno et Ambrosio et aliis. Biscantus autem in officiis ecclesiasticis quis adinuenerit

---

628 De … Pronuntiandum] *De cons.* D. 3 c. 1 (*Pronunciandum*): vide supra.

---

624 uel[1]] *bis scr. a.c.* **624** cum] *s.l.* **626** quod] *bis scr. a.c.* **628** Pronuntiandum] *cod.* : *Ballerini add.* Vide etiam de hoc supra in 2 part. tit. 9 cap. de negligentia. **632** ex[2]] + actibus *ut vid. a.c.* **633** Reprehensibiles] P- *a.c.* **636** Yesum] Y^{m} *cod.* : Yhm F_3 *fol. 74ra* **640** apostolo] *vel* apostola *cod.* : apostolo F_3 *fol. 74ra* | dubitationem] *p.c.* : dubia *a.c.* **645** calamo] cl- *a.c.* **646** suo] *cod.* : F_3 *fol. 74rab add.* tales non modicum errant cum nesciunt temperare colores qui cito deficiunt, ideo caueant nec magistri appetant uocari nisi prius fuerint docti discipuli : *Ballerini add.* Offendunt et ipsi, si diebus festis hoc agunt, uel quando nimium pretium exigunt, et maxime quum non bona temperamenta in coloribus mittunt, propter quod cito delentur de libris, uel quando ut cito expleant, non diligenter facient, quando neque firmatum est pactum de tanto pretio. **647** De] + exercentibus *a.c.* | ministerio] ministerium *a.c.* | musichorum] *p.c.* : cantand- *a.c.* **648** firmus] *s.l.* **649** Biscantus] *ut vid. cod. p.c. cum* F_3 *fol. 74rb* : *haud leg. cod. a.c.*

do wrong also when they write for profit on feast days: for they violate the feast, which the Church has commanded be commemorated by ceasing from all servile or manual works, and such is this kind of work, *De cons*. D. 3 c. 1.[171]

10.3. Painters. Painters reasonably ask for more or less to be paid as a salary for their craft not only according to the amount of labour but more importantly according to their diligence and greater expertise in the art. They do wrong in this when they produce pictures that provoke to lust, not from their beauty but from their disposition, such as nude women and so forth. They are also blameworthy when they paint things which are against the faith, when they make as an image of the Trinity one person with three heads, which is a monster in the nature of things, or in <the scene of> the Annunciation of the Virgin they make the child Jesus placed fully formed in the womb of the Virgin as if his body was not assumed from the substance of the Virgin, or the child Jesus with a tablet of letters when he has not yet learned from man. But neither are they to be praised when they paint apocryphal things, such as midwives at the Virgin's childbirth, her girdle left behind by the Virgin Mary at her Assumption for the apostle Thomas because of his doubt, and so forth. In stories of the saints also or in churches, painting curiosities which do not serve to inspire devotion but laughter and vanity, such as monkeys, dogs, and chasing hares and so forth, or vain decorations of clothing, seems superfluous and vain.

To these are closely joined illuminators[172] of books whether with the pen or the brush,[173] to whom also a reward for their labour is fitting.[174]

11. The occupation of musicians in singing and playing. On the occupation of musicians who sing and play instruments. Chant indeed was firmly established in the divine offices by the holy doctors like Gregory the Great and Ambrose and others. But who first introduced *biscantus*[175] in the ecclesiastical offices I do not know. It seems more to serve for excitement[176] of the ears than for devotion, although a pious mind may gain

171 *De cons*. D. 3 c. 1 (*Pronunciandum*): see above.

172 "Miniatore – *miniator, miniator librorum* (1): enlumineur." Stella, *La révolte des Ciompi*, 311.

173 Lat. *pennellus*, cfr Ital. *pennello*: "brush; (per dipingere) paintbrush." *Oxford-Paravia Italian Dictionary*, s.v.

174 The manuscript F_3 and Ballerini's edition each add a sentence here. F_3 fol. 74rab: "These err not a little when they do not know how to mix colours, which quickly fade, therefore they should take care that they not claim to be called masters unless they have first been educated as students." Ballerini: "These do wrong also if they do this work on feast days, or when they exact an excessive price, and most of all when they do not put good mixtures into colours, because of which they quickly disappear from books, or when in order to finish the work more quickly they do not work diligently, and when a pact has not been established for such a price."

175 I have not found the Lat. *biscantus* in any dictionary. However, in context it can be interpreted as referring to counterpoint or polyphony. See Pietschmann, "The Sense of Hearing Politicized."

176 Lat. *pluritus*, presumably meaning *pruritus*: "itch, itching, irritation … (~us libidinis, carnis, or sim.) sexual excitement, urge, or craving." *DMLBS*, s.v.

ignoro. Pluritui aurium uidetur magis deseruire quam deuotioni quamuis pia mens in hiis etiam fructum referat audiendo. Qui tamen huic operi insistunt uideant ne "dum blanda uox queritur, congrua uita negligatur, et Deum irritet contra se dum populum delectat," ut ait Gregorius, D. 92 *In sancta.* Communiter tales solent esse leues et dissoluti. Precipue autem redarguendum est in offitiis diuinis ibi misceri cantiones seu ballatas et uerba uana contra quod etiam Ieronymus inuehit, D. 92 *Cantantes.* Sed et pulsatio organorum uel aliorum instrumentorum ad diuinam laudem initium uidetur habuisse a propheta Dauith, qui non solum cantores instituit in cultu templi seu tabernaculi, sed et ipse etiam ante archam Domini pulsabat in psalterio uel organis, uterque salarium recipiunt iuste, ut habetur 2 Reg. 6, et in Psalmo ait ultimo: *Laudate eum in tympano et choro* etc. In ergo organis tamen pulsare ballatas, ut frequenter fit, ualde detestabile est.

11.1. De laycis pulsantes instrumenta ob recreationem.

Layci uero extra diuina offitia pulsantes diuersa instrumenta musicha uel in nuptiis uel in conuiuiis uel in curiis dominorum, ut tibias bifferes et alia instrumenta, uel aliter ob recreationem, condempnari non possunt de re illicita, unde et certo pretio conduci possunt. Et similiter cantantes siue laudes in ecclesia siue hystorias palatinorum, uel alia dummodo honesta, et locis et temporibus debitis obseruatis cum aliis circumstantiis, ita quod per hec diuina offitia non negligantur. Audire autem cantus mulierum periculosum est et ad lasciuiam incitatiuum et ideo cauendum.

---

652 blanda … **653** sancta] Greg. M. in D. 92 c. 2 (*In sancta*): Unde fit plerumque ut in sacro ministerio, dum blanda uox queritur, congrua uita negligatur, et cantor minister Deum moribus stimulet, cum populum uocibus delectet.

655 contra … **656** Cantantes] Hier. in D. 92 c. 1 (*Cantantes*): "Cantantes et psallentes in cordibus uestris Domino." Audiant hec adolescentuli, audiant hi, quibus in ecclesia est psallendi offitium: Deo non uoce, sed corde cantandum, nec in tragediarum modum guttur et fauces medicamine liniendae sunt, ut in ecclesia teatrales moduli audiantur et cantica.

658 Dauith … **659** tabernaculi] Cfr *1 Par* 9.33; 16.1, 4, 37; 23.4–5; 25.1, 6–8.

659 ipse … **660** 6] *2 Rg* 6.5: David autem et omnis Israel ludebant coram Domino in omnibus lignis fabrefactis, et citharis et lyris et tympanis et sistris et cymbalis.

660 Psalmo … **661** etc.] *Ps* 150.4: Laudate eum in tympano et choro; laudate eum in chordis et organo.

---

652 blanda] banda *cod.* : blanda F_3 *fol. 74rb cum Gregorio Magno in can. citato* | et] *p.c.* : ut ait Gregorius *a.c.* **653** sancta] + Quos contra etiam iero. inuehit *a.c.* **656** Ieronymus] Iero. *cod.* **660** uterque … iuste] *in marg. sin. add.* : *eadem scr. postmodo* F_3 *fol. 74rb* : *om. Ballerini sed postmodo scr.* Pulsare ergo in organis uel aliis ad Dei laudem non est prohibitum, et iuste recipiunt salarium pulsantes. | Psalmo] Ps. *cod.* **661** In ergo] *vel* Ante ergo *ut vid. cod.* : In F_3 *fol. 74rb* **662** est] *Ballerini add.* De hoc etiam habes supra in 2. part. tit. 3. cap. de curiositate. **664** bifferes] *vel* bifferos *cod.* : bifferos F_3 *fol. 74rb* **665** aliter] *vel* alias *cod.* : alias F_3 *fol. 74rb* **670** incitatiuum] *ut vid. cod.* : incitancium F_3 *fol. 74rb*

fruit in hearing even these. Nevertheless those who occupy themselves with this work should take care lest "while a pleasing voice is sought, a suitable manner of life is neglected, and he provokes God against himself while he delights the people," as Gregory says, D. 92 c. 2.[177] These are commonly accustomed to be frivolous and dissolute. Now it is especially to be criticized that there in the divine offices songs or ballads[178] and vain words are mixed in, against which Jerome also inveighs, D. 92 c. 1.[179] But also the playing of organs or other instruments for divine praise seems to have had its beginning from the prophet David, who not only appointed singers in the worship of the temple or tabernacle,[180] but also even himself played before the ark of the Lord on stringed instrument or organs. And each of these justly receives a salary, as is read in 2nd Kings 6,[181] and in the last Psalm he says: *Praise him with timbrel and choir*, etc.[182] Therefore to play ballads on organs, as frequently is done, is extremely detestable.

11.1. Laypeople playing instruments recreationally. Now laypeople playing various musical instruments outside the divine offices, whether at weddings or banquets or in lords' courts, such as double pipes[183] and other instruments, or otherwise for recreation, cannot be condemned as doing something illicit, and hence they can also be hired for a set price. And similarly for those who sing, whether praises in church, or courtly stories, or other things provided they are honourable, and observing the due places and times along with other circumstances, such that through these songs the divine offices are not neglected. But to hear songs of women is dangerous and an incitement to lust and therefore should be avoided.

---

177 Greg. M. in D. 92 c. 2 (*In sancta*): "And so it often happens that, while a pleasing voice is sought for the sacred ministry, a suitable manner of life is neglected, and the serving singer, by his manner of life, rouses God's wrath, while he delights the people with his singing."

178 Ital. *ballata*: ballad or ballade. *Oxford-Paravia Italian Dictionary*, s.v.

179 Hier. in D. 92 c. 1 (*Cantantes*): "*Singing and making melody in your hearts to the Lord* (Eph. 5.19). Let the young adolescents hear these words; let them hear who have the office of singing in the Church: song to God is to issue from the heart, not from the voice; nor must we follow the manner of the tragedians and daub our throat and gullet with sweet medicine so that theatrical modulations and songs might be heard in the Church."

180 Cfr *1 Par* 9.33; 16.1, 4, 37; 23.4–5; 25.1, 6–8.

181 *2 Rg* 6.5: "But David and all Israel played before the Lord on all manner of instruments made of wood, on harps and lutes and timbrels and cornets and cymbals."

182 *Ps* 150.4: "Praise him with timbrel and choir: praise him with strings and organs."

183 It is not clear if Antoninus wrote *bifferes* or *bifferos* in the autograph manuscript – both F_3 and Ballerini transmit *bifferos* and thus treat it as a noun – but I have read it as *bifferes*, adj. modifying *tibias*, from Lat. *biforis*, *-e*: "having two openings or holes, double." *LS*, s.v. Cfr Verg. *Aen.* 9, 617–18 (LCL 64:156–7): "ubi adsuetis biforem dat tibia cantum." Frederick Ahl in his translation of the *Aeneid* (Oxford, 2007) describes the Latin *tibiae pares*, "double woodwind" (equivalent to the Greek *aulos*), as played in southern Italy until modern times (228, 417).

11.2. De arte histrionum. Histrionatus ars quia deseruit humane recreationi, que necessaria est uite hominis, secundum Tomam de se non est illicita. Vnde et de illa arte uiuere non est prohibitum, ita tamen quod fiat obseruatis debitis circumstantiis lochorum temporum et personarum. Non enim decet clericum talia exercere, ymmo nec talibus interesse, *De cons.* D. 5 *Non oportet.* Nec in ecclesia, nec tempore penitentie ut Quadragesimale. Et quia representationes que fiunt hodie de rebus spiritualibus miscentur cum multis ioculationibus et truffis et laruis, ideo non congruit eas in ecclesiis fieri, nec per clerichos, *Extra, De ui. et ho. cle., Cum decorem.* Sed cum hystriones utuntur indifferenter [utuntur] tali exercitio ad representandum etiam turpia, uel uituperandum et irridendum personas spirituales, uel sacramenta et diuinum cultum, uel immiscentur ibi superstitiones uel periculum uite, ut tendere archum super funem et huiusmodi: illicita est ars, et eam opportet dimictere. Et de tali intelligitur *De cons.* D. 2 *Pro dilectione.* Et peccatum est talia aspicere et talibus pro illo opere dare, ut dicit Augustinus D. 86 *Donare.*

---

672 secundum Tomam] THOM. AQ. *Sum. th.* 2a 2ae q. 168 a. 3 ad 3: Ad tertium dicendum quod, sicut dictum est, ludus est necessarius ad conversationem humanae vitae. Ad omnia autem quae sunt utilia conversationi humanae, deputari possunt aliqua officia licita. Et ideo etiam officium histrionum, quod ordinatur ad solatium hominibus exhibendum, non est secundum se illicitum, nec sunt in statu peccati, dummodo moderate ludo utantur, idest, non utendo aliquibus illicitis verbis vel factis ad ludum, et non adhibendo ludum negotiis et temporibus indebitis.

675 ymmo … oportet] *De cons.* D. 5 c. 36 (*Non oportet*[1]): Non oportet ministros altaris uel quoslibet clericos spectaculis aliquibus, que aut in nuptiis, aut in cenis, exhibentur, interesse, sed ante, quam thimelici ingrediantur, surgere eos de conuiuio, et abire debere.

678 ideo … **679** decorem] *X* 3.1.12 (*Cum decorem* vel *decorum*): … Interdum ludi fiunt in ecclesiis theatrales, et non solum ad ludibriorum spectacula introducuntur in eis monstra laruarum, verum etiam in aliquibus festiuitatibus diaconi, presbyteri, ac subdiaconi insaniae suae ludibria exercere praesumunt: et infra. Fraternitati vestrae mandamus, quatenus ne per huiusmodi turpitudinem, ecclesiae inquinetur honestas, praelibatam ludibriorum consuetudinem, vel potius corruptelam, curetis a vestris ecclesiis extirpare (ed. Rome, 1582, 2:997–8).

683 de … **684** dilectione] *De cons.* D. 2 c. 95 (*Pro dilectione*): Ystrionibus sacra non conmittantur misteria. … Pro dilectione tua consulendum me existimasti, frater karissime, quid michi uideatur de ystrione et mago illo, qui apud uos constitutus adhuc in suae artis dedecore perseuerat, et magister et doctor non erudiendorum, sed perdendorum puerorum, id, quod male didicit, ceteris quoque insinuat: an talibus debeat sacra conmunio cum ceteris Christianis dari aut debeat conmunicare uobiscum? Puto nec maiestati diuinae, nec euangelicae disciplinae congruere, ut pudor et honor ecclesiae tam turpi et infami contagione fedetur.

685 ut … Donare] AUG. in D. 86 c. 7 (*Donare*): Donare res suas istrionibus uitium est inmane, non uirtus. Et scitis de talibus, quam sit frequens fama cum laude, quia, "laudatur peccator in desideriis animae suae, et qui iniqua gerit benedicitur."

---

676 Quadragesimale] 4Le *vel* XLe cod. : LXe F_3 *fol. 74rb* **683** illicita] h- *a.c.* **684** Et] Nec *a.c.* | opere] *cod.* : + aliquid *s.l.* F_3 *fol. 74rb*

11.2. The craft of performing. The craft of performing,[184] because it serves human recreation, which is necessary for the life of man, according to Thomas, is not in itself illicit.[185] Hence also it is not prohibited to live by practising this art, in such a way, however, that in its practice the due circumstances of place and time and person are observed. For it is not fitting for a cleric to practise such things, and actually not even to be present at them, *De cons.* D. 5 c. 36.[186] Nor in a church, nor during a penitential time such as Lent. And because the portrayals which are staged today about spiritual things are mixed with many jocularities and trifles and mockery, therefore it is not appropriate that they be put on in churches, nor by clerics, *Extra*, *On the life and honesty of clerics*, c. 12.[187] But when performers indifferently use their occupation to portray even shameful things, or to castigate and mock spiritual persons or the sacraments or divine worship, or there are mixed therein superstitions, or acts that endanger people's lives, such as setting up a tower on a rope and so forth – this is an illicit craft, and it is necessary to abandon it. And *De cons.* D. 2 c. 95 is understood to apply to this kind of performing.[188] And it is a sin to watch such performances and to pay such performers for that work, as Augustine says, D. 86 c. 7.[189]

---

184 Lat. *histrionatus ars* from *histrio, -onis*: "player, pantomime actor, jester." *DMLBS*, s.v.

185 Thom. Aq. *Sum. th.* 2a 2ae q. 168 a. 3 ad 3: "As stated [a. 2], play is necessary for the intercourse of human life. Now whatever is useful to human intercourse may have a lawful employment ascribed to it. Wherefore the occupation of play-actors, the object of which is to cheer the heart of man, is not unlawful in itself; nor are they in a state of sin provided that their playing be moderated, namely that they use no unlawful words or deeds in order to amuse, and that they do not introduce play into undue matters and seasons."

186 *De cons.* D. 5 c. 36 (*Non oportet*[1]): "It is not fitting that ministers of the altar, or any clerics, be present at certain spectacles which are shown either at weddings, or on a stage, but, before the actors (*thymelici*) enter, they must arise from the banquet and depart." Note that in the Roman edition (1582) and in Silano's translation, this canon is c. 37 (*Non oportet*[2]).

187 *X* 3.1.12 (*Cum decorem* or *decorum*).

188 *De cons.* D. 2 c. 95 (*Pro dilectione*): "The sacred mysteries are not to be entrusted to actors ... From your love and our mutual reverence, you have thought to seek my counsel, dearest brother, as to my opinion regarding a certain actor who, while living among you, still perseveres in the dishonour of his art. As a master and teacher of children, who are to be lost rather than instructed, that which he wickedly learned he now imparts to others. You ask whether such a one ought to communicate with us. I believe that it is congruent neither with the divine majesty, nor with the discipline of the Gospel, that the modesty and honour of the Church be polluted by such a shameful and infamous contagion."

189 Aug. in D. 86 c. 7 (*Donare*): "To grant their due to actors is a great vice, and not a virtue. And you know how frequent is the praise and fame regarding such because, as it is written: For the sinner is praised in the desires of his soul: and the unjust man is blessed (Ps. 9.24)."

12. De agricolis.

De agricolis. Ars quidem licita et opus necessarium est uite humane, fol. 78v unde et primo parenti dictum fuit: *In sudore uultus tui uesceris pane* tuo, Gen. 3. Et *Noe uir agricola plantauit uineam* post diluuium, Gen. 9. Et cum terras proprias laborant, fraudes in suis commictere non ualent, nisi in uendendo fructus suos uel nimio pretio uel diminutis mensuris uel uitiatos pro bonis. Sed tanta est hodie subtilitas et astutia hominum ut potius ipsi decipiantur ab emptoribus. In eo scilicet quod emunt ab eis necessitate ductis fructus et quia anticipant tempus fructuum in soluendo pro minori pretio emunt quod pertinet ad usuram quantum ad ementem. De hoc tamen habes plenius in secunda parte titulo primo c. de usura.

12.1. Si laborant terras aliorum.

Si autem laborant terras aliorum uel ad medietatem uel ad affictum, primo modo solent offendere in non respondendo patronis suis integre de medietate, secundo modo possunt offendere non habendo diligentiam debitam circa possessionem ipsam sed magis ad utilitatem suam in preiudicium patroni. Quod autem plus redderent fructuum cultores patronis ratione mutui eis facti, usuram saperet, quod esset uitium patronorum.

12.2. Si tenent animalia ad soccidam.

Si autem tenent animalia ad soccidam potest ibi esse peccatum usure uel iniustitie, secundum uarium modum dandi de quo supra in secunda parte titulo primo in c. de usura in soccidis. Sed hoc uitium magis accidit in dantibus ad soccidam quam in comitatiuis accipientibus. Et similiter de bobus cum quibus colunt terras uel suas uel aliorum aut etiam patronorum pro quo dant certam quantitatem frumenti locantibus ipsos, et cum pacto participandi

---

687 In … **688** 3] *Gen* 3.19: In sudore vultus tui vesceris pane, donec revertaris in terram de qua sumptus es: quia pulvis es et in pulverem reverteris.

688 Noe … 9] *Gen* 9.20: Coepitque Noe vir agricola exercere terram, et plantavit vineam.

694 De … **695** usura] Ant. Flor. *Summa* 2.1.6–10 (apud M_1 fol. Vr et Ballerini; 2.1.5–9 apud Mamachi): *de usura*, etc.

703 supra … **704** soccidis] Ant. Flor. *Summa* 2.1.7.39 (apud Ballerini 2:115ff.; 2.1.6.39 apud Mamachi 2:156ff.): *de soccidis animalium* (M_1 fol. 27r et ff.).

---

686 De agricolis] *in marg super. add. Antoninus* Iste §. in fine huius capituli ponatur. | licita] *s.l.* **687** fuit] *bis scr.* | In … **688** 9] *in marg. super. add.* **690** uel[1] … mensuris] *in marg. sin. add.* | uitiatos] *vel* vitiatas *cod.* : vitiatas F_3 *fol. 74rb* **698** debitam] *in marg. sin. add.* **707** ipsos] + de quo etiam ibidem habes *a.c.*

12. Farmers. About farmers. This craft is certainly licit, and is a work necessary for human life, hence even to our first parent it was said: *In the sweat of thy face shalt thou eat* thy *bread*, Genesis 3.[190] And *Noah, a farmer, planted a vineyard* after the flood, Genesis 9.[191] And when farmers work their own lands, they are not capable of committing frauds in their own affairs, unless in selling their produce either for an excessive price or using reduced measures or selling spoiled produce as good. But such is the subtlety and craftiness of men today that the farmers themselves are rather deceived by buyers. This occurs when buyers purchase produce from farmers who are induced by necessity to sell, and because the buyers pay in advance of the time of yield they buy for a lower price, which involves usury on the part of the buyer. About this, however, there is more extensive material in part 2, title 1, the chapter on usury.[192]

12.1. If they work the lands of others. Now if they work the lands of others either for a half portion or for a regular revenue,[193] in the first mode they are accustomed to do wrong in not answering to the patrons in full concerning the half portion, in the second mode they can do wrong by not working with the sort of due diligence which they ought to apply to the property, preferring their own utility to the prejudice of the patron. But that the cultivators should render more of the produce to the patron by reason of a loan which he has made to them would savour of usury, which would be a vice of the patrons.

12.2. If they hold animals in agistment. Now if they hold animals in agistment,[194] there can be a sin of usury or injustice therein, according to the different modes of payment, about which see above in the second part, title 1, in the chapter on usury in agistments.[195] But this vice occurs more often in those giving out in agistment than in the associates who receive in agistment. And similarly about the oxen with which they till the land (whether their own lands or others' lands or even lords' lands), for which they pay a certain quantity of produce to the ones leasing them out, and with an agreement to share in the profit and loss, the lessor and hirer for half portions, which you also have discussed in the same place.[196] In addition

---

190 *Gen* 3.19: "In the sweat of thy face shalt thou eat bread till thou return to the earth, out of which thou was taken: for dust thou art, and into dust thou shalt return."

191 *Gen* 9.20: "And Noe, a husbandman, began to till the ground, and planted a vineyard."

192 Ant. Flor. *Summa* 2.1.6–10 (apud M_1 fol. Vr et Ballerini; 2.1.5–9 apud Mamachi): *de usura*, etc.

193 Lat. *affictus* or *affictum*: "Afflictus, Census, Reditus. … Vocabularium utriusque iuris: Affictus penes vulgare Lumbardorum et Thuscanorum…. dicitur census qui datur ratione praediorum, etc." Du Cange, s.v.

194 Ital. *soccida*: "agistment." *Oxford-Paravia Italian Dictionary*, s.v.

195 Ant. Flor. *Summa* 2.1.7.39 (apud Ballerini 2:115ff.; 2.1.6.39 apud Mamachi 2:156ff.): this section of c. 2.1.7 (*diffuse de materia usurarum*) begins in the autograph (M_1) on fol. 27r, at the words *de soccidis animalium.*

196 Ibid.

lucrum et dampnum, lochator et conductor pro medietate, de quo etiam ibi habes. Insuper et cum animalibus offendunt quando ex negligentia et multo peius cum ex certa scientia seu malitia, permictunt animalia ipsa depascere in agris seu bladis alienis, unde et proximos dampnificant in quo tenentur ad satisfactionem. Et cum animalia ipsa uitiata uendunt pro sanis non diminuendo de pretio secundum quantitatem defectus, non sunt immunes a peccato et a satisfactione persone lese, precipue cum notabile sequitur dampnum emptori.

12.3. Offendunt in non soluendo decimas.

Offendunt etiam cum decimas non soluunt ecclesiis saltim secundum morem patrie totum uel partem in quo et tenentur ad restituendum ecclesiis subtractas. Sed de materia decimarum quomodo homines teneantur uel excusentur habes diffuse in secunda parte, titulo 4°, c. de retentione decimarum. Vacantibus autem ecclesiis quarum sunt parrochiani, de bonis ecclesie seu sacerdotis ipsius, aliquando capiunt et distrahunt, et dissipant in comedendo et bibendo. Cogunt etiam ipsos sacerdotes suos seruare quasdam abusiones, ut in diebus Resurrectionis uel Natalis uel alterius festiuitatis, dent eis notabilem quantitatem panis et uini ad bibendum usque ad hebrietatem. In ecclesiis ipsis aliquando terpudiant et choreas ducunt cum mulieribus.

12.4. Quomodo communiter offendunt.

Diebus festiuis parum uacant diuinis et auditioni integre misse sed ludis uel in tabernis et contentionibus ante ecclesias. In ipsis diebus festius deferunt in iumentis blada ligna uel alia patronis suis, per quod festa uiolant, nisi maxima necessitate ducantur, non ualentes aliter uiuere. De facili blasfemant Deum et sanctos. Maledicunt irati animalia sua bruta. Mendaciis et periuriis pleni sunt. De fornichationibus non faciunt sibi conscientiam. Plurimi eorum non confitentur annuatim, et multo pauciores communicant, falso extimantes se non debere communicare nisi cum senescunt uel ad mortem infirmantur.

---

717 de … **719** decimarum] ANT. FLOR. *Summa* 2.4.3.6 (apud Ballerini 2:570–4.; 2.4.3.11 apud Mamachi 2:790–6): *de non dantibus decimas utrum excusentur a peccato.*

---

714 cum] + est *a.c.* **715** decimas] *vel* decimans *cod.* **719** ecclesiis] + de *a.c.* | parrochiani] *vel* parochiani *cod.* : parochiani F_3 *fol. 74va* **723** hebrietatem] hebrietam *cod.* : ebrietatem F_3 *fol. 74va* **724** terpudiant] *ut vid. cod.* : tripudiant F_3 *fol. 74va et Ballerini* | mulieribus] *hic Ballerini add. hoc paragraphum*: Quidam autem illorum uadunt ad piscationem, que ars de se non est illicita: offendunt tamen, quum hoc faciunt diebus festis, idest propter cupiditatem, capientes pisces et uendentes, eo quod contra illud preceptum faciunt: Opus seruile non facietis, Exod. 20. Secus, si caussa recreationis, uel ut habeant aliquos pisciculos ad comedendum; si tamen propter hoc non dimittunt auditionem misse etc. quando furantur ad inuicem pisces, tenentur ad restitutionem. Item deuastant aliquando aggeres prediorum aliorum, et quandoque ipsa predia, unde tenentur ad damnum, ut habes supra in 2. part. tit. 2. de restitutione. **726** In … **728** uiuere] *in marg. infer. add.* **730** fornichationibus] *cod.* : *Ballerini add.* et sodomiis

they also do wrong with animals when in negligence, or, much worse, when in certain knowledge or malice, they allow these animals to graze on others' fields or crops, hence also they cause loss to their neighbours, for which they are obliged to make satisfaction. And when they sell impaired animals as if they were healthy without making any reduction of the price according to the value of the defect, they are not immune from sin and from satisfaction to the injured person, especially when a notable loss follows for the buyer.

12.3. They do wrong in not paying tithes.

They do wrong also when they do not pay tithes to the churches, at the very least in accordance with the custom of the country, whether in whole or in part, for which also they are obliged to restore the withheld tithes to the churches. But about the matter of tithes, how people are obliged or excused, there is an extensive treatment in the second part, title 4, chapter 3, on the withholding of tithes.[197] Now when those churches of which they are parishioners are vacant, sometimes they take from the goods of the church or of its priest and disperse them and squander them in eating and drinking. They also drive their priests themselves to observe certain malpractices, such as, on the days of the Resurrection or the Nativity or another festivity, giving to them a significant quantity of bread and wine to drink to intoxication. In the churches themselves sometimes they make merry[198] and lead dances with women.[199]

12.4. How they commonly do wrong.

On feast days they take little time for divine things and for hearing the entire Mass, but instead <spend time> in games or in taverns or in quarrels outside churches. On those feast days they transport grain or wood or other goods on oxen to their patrons, through which they violate the feasts unless they are induced by the greatest necessity, not being capable of providing a living otherwise. They easily blaspheme God and the saints. When angry they curse their brute animals. They are full of lies and perjuries. They do not trouble their consciences about fornications. Very many of them do not confess annually, and many fewer receive communion, falsely thinking that they ought not to receive communion except when they are growing old or are near death with illness. They instruct their families little in the ways of the faithful. They frequently leave aside the penances enjoined on them by confessors and the vows they have made. They use incantations, on themselves and on their oxen. They think nothing of God or of their salvation.

---

197 Ant. Flor. *Summa* 2.4.3.6 (apud Ballerini 2:570–4; 2.4.3.11 apud Mamachi 2:790–6): *de non dantibus decimas utrum excusentur a peccato.* I have not yet located the text of this section in the autograph (M_1). A heavily revised version of it appears to be present in the second autograph volume of the third part (M_3), fol. 404r–406v.

198 Lat. *terpudiare*, cfr *tripudiare*: "1 to dance (esp. as part of revelry or celebration). 2 to celebrate, rejoice." *DMLBS*, s.v.

199 At this place Ballerini's edition contains an additional paragraph on fishing, both as an employment and as recreation. This paragraph does not exist in the autograph manuscript or in the manuscript F_3.

Familias suas parum instruunt in moribus fidelium. Penitentias sibi iniunctas a confessoribus et uota facta frequenter dimictunt. Incantationibus utuntur, in se et in iumentis suis. De Deo uel sua salute nil cogitant. Et cum communiter sint ignorantes, et parum curantes de anima sua et obseruatione mandatorum Dei que nesciunt, hoc est quod adiuuat eos duci ad perditionem per uiam latam uitiorum: ignorantia et incuria parrochialium suorum cum conscientia mala, qui non curantes de ouibus sibi commissis sed de lana et lacte, non eos instruunt in predicationibus in confessionibus et priuatis monitionibus; sed cum communi errore eorum transeuntes corruptelas sequuntur eorum, non corrigentes eos de uitiis eorum, propter quod contingit bestialiter uiuentes aliquando bestialiter moriantur.

---

737 duci … **738** latam] Cfr *Mt* 7.13.

---

734 Incantationibus … **735** cogitant] *in marg. infer. add.* **736** anima] *p.c. in marg. sin.* : salute *a.c.* **737** quod] *in marg. dext. add.* | eos] + perd- *a.c.* **738** parrochialium] sacer(dotum) *a.c.*

And since commonly they are ignorant, and take little care of their soul and the observance of God's commandments which they do not know, this is what helps them to be led to perdition through the wide way[200] of the vices: the ignorance and negligence of their pastors with bad conscience, who, not caring for the sheep committed to them but for their wool and milk, do not instruct them in preaching and confessions and private warning; but traversing with their common error, follow their corrupt practices, not correcting them from their vices, because of which it comes about that they live like beasts, and sometimes die like beasts.

200 Cfr *Mt* 7.13.

Appendix 1: Recensions

1. Table of substantial additions to the first recension of 2.1.16

Thema.

1. De negotiatione spirituali.

1.1. In regione celesti.

1.2. In regione terrestri.

1.3. In regione infera.

2. De negotiatione mundiali.

2.1. Ratione finis cupidi.

recensio prima	*additiones*
"Quicumque rem comparat ut integram immutamque uendendo lucretur, ille est qui de templo eicitur," ut habetur D. 88 c. Eiciens, quod uerum est quando "ultimum finem constituit in lucro," tunc enim est extra ecclesiam quoad meritum.	*in marg. sin. add.:* Nolite hoc modo facere domum meum domum negotiationis etc. Hic tamen summimus large negotiationem, et in sequentibus huiusmodi sectionibus.

2.2. Ratione persone clerici.

recensio prima	*additiones*
Secundo negotiatio est mala ratione persone, cum scilicet aliquibus personis specialiter aliquo iure prohibetur, quod fit cunctis clericis et multo magis religiosis, ~~unde~~	*in marg. super. add.:* Extra, Ne clerici uel mona., per totum, ubi non solum negotiatio sed plura negotia ibi ponuntur eis interdicta. Dicit etiam

recensio prima	*additiones*
Augustinus: "Negotiari aliquando licet, aliquando non licet: antequam sis clerichus, licet; postquam effectus es clerichus, non licet," D. 88 Fornichari. Ratio huius est, secundum B. Tomam, 2a 2e q. 77 articulo 4, quia "clerici abstinere debent non solum" a malis, "sed etiam ab hiis que habent speciem mali, quod in negotiatione contingit," et hoc tripliciter. Primo, quia negotiatio "est ordinata ad lucrum, cuius clerici debent esse contemptores."	*in marg. sin. add.:* Vnde Ieronymus: "clerichum negotiatorem ex inopi diuitem tamquam quamdam pestem deuita," D. 88.
Secundo, "propter frequentia negotiatorum uitia, quia difficulter exuitur negotiator a peccatis labiorum, ut dicitur Ecclesiastici 26." Et Leo Papa: "Difficile est inter uendentis ementisque commercium non interuenire peccatum," De pen. D. 5 Qualitas.	*in marg. dext. add.:* Sed clerichus debet se multum cauere a peccatis *in marg. dext. add. Iul. de Lapacc.:* iuxta illud: Ambulans in uia immaculata, seruabat mihi etc.
Tertio, "quia negotiatio nimis implicat mentem curis secularibus et per consequens a spiritualibus retrahit, unde Apostolus, 2 ad Thim., Nemo militans Deo implicat se negotiis secularibus," et ad idem D. 88 Consequens,	*in marg. sin. add.:* habent autem frequenter uacare diuinis.

2.3. Ratione temporis feriati.

2.4. Ratione loci sacrati.

Quid consulendum sit de lucris in hiis quattuor casibus.

2.5. Ratione consortii iniusti.

2.6. Ratione medii iniqui.

recensio prima	*additiones*
De mendaciis autem dicit Raymundus quod si hoc faciunt ut decipiant, etiam mortaliter peccant,	*in marg. sin. add.:* et tenentur ad restitutionem eius in quo deceperunt.

2.7. Ratione materie mali.

recensio prima	*additiones*
Septimo ratione materie mali: quedam enim negotia sunt, que sunt de se mala in "sui natura," ut usura, symonia, et huiusmodi.	*in marg. infer. add.:* Vnde Ambrosius: "Reperiuntur quamplurimi negotiatione muneris merchari uelle gratiam Spiritus Sancti," 1 q. 1 Reperiuntur.
Et horum negotiatio, id est exercitatio, omnibus prohibetur "clericis et laycis" secundum Raymundum. ... Quedam alia sunt dubia, ut emere prestantias solutas communitati ab aliis, seu denarios montis, et imprestita Venetorum, et loca Ianuensium, que quidam dicunt licita, quidam illicita et usuraria, et ab huiusmodi etiam abstinendum, quia: "In dubiis tutior uia est eligenda," Extra, De spons., Iuuenis. Et	*in marg. infer. add.:* de hac materia diffuse habes supra eodem tit. c. <9>. Ibi ponuntur rationes ad utramque partem: et ideo non de facili condempnandum, et sic consulendum quod tutius est, ut dictum est.

3. De negotiatione temporali modesta.

recensio prima	*additiones*
Vnde Cassiodorus super dicto uersiculo Psalmi: "Illi abhominabiles sunt," scilicet "qui iustitiam Dei minime considerantes, per nimium peccunie ambitum merces suas polluunt," D. 88.	*in marg. super. add.:* Sicut autem seruatur iustitia Dei, id est iustitia secundum Deum, cum in negotiando datur iustum pretium, non excessiuum, et res integra debita, non sophisticata, et aut permutatio equa: ita econtra negotiantes, largo sumpto uocabulo pro ementibus et uendentibus,
tripliciter faciunt contra iustitiam Dei: 1o. Ex iniqua appretiatione. 2o. Ex uaria sophisticatione uel fraudatione. 3o. Ex illicita permutatione.	

3.1. Ex iniqua appretiatione.

3.1.1. Debitus ualor rei.

3.1.1.1. Ex virtuositate.

3.1.1.2. Ex raritate.

3.1.1.3. Ex complacibilitate.

3.1.2. Latitudo ualoris rei.

3.1.2.1. Ex iure.

recensio prima	*additiones*
… tunc secundum iura "contractus est nullus," Extra, De empt. et uen., Cum dilecti, "per iudicem irritandus," Verum etiam si esset minor excessus quam medietas iusti pretii, si sit notabilis, utique secundum B. Tomam, 2a 2e q. 77, et Scotum in 4o D. 15, est ibi iniustitia, et per consequens peccatum mortale, et "restitutio facienda"	*in marg. sin. add.:* uel facere supplere defectum commissum. *in marg. super. add.:* quantum ad eum, per quem fit deceptio aduertenter in pretio multum excessiuo uel defectiuo. Sed si fiat deceptio ignoranter, quia scilicet emptor uel uenditor existimat tantum ualere: tunc non est ibi mortale, ex quo ipse decipitur per erorem, sed tamen cum perpendit, uel sibi ostenditur, tenetur ad satisfactionem, alias tunc peccaret mortaliter, si non uellet satisfacere.

3.1.2.2. Ex consuetudine.

3.1.2.3. Ex discretione.

3.1.3. Excessus ualoris rei.

3.1.3.1. Excessus ultra dimidiam iusti pretii.

3.1.3.2. Excessus notabilis infra dimidiam iusti pretii.

recensio prima	*additiones*
Quam oppinionem sequi uidetur Durandus ordinis Minorum in Summa sua. Sed hanc oppinionem tamquam eroneam et periculosum saluti animarum reprobant B. Tomas, 2a 2e q. 77, et Schotus in 4o D. 15, dicentes quod talis scienter decipiens iniustitiam facit, et tenetur ad restitutionem eius in quo decepit.	*in marg. dext. add.:* mortaliter per consequens peccat,

… Ad rationem ab illis inductam de lege, respondet B. Tomas, ubi supra, quod lex "datur populo, in quo sunt multi deficientes a uirtute: unde solum prohibet ea" mala que habent destruere "humanum conuictum" pacificum ea puniendo, ut furta, adulteria, notabiles deceptiones in contractibus ut deceptio ultra dimidiam iusti pretii:	*in marg. super. add.:* et hoc, cum punire potest absque maiori scandalo, alias etiam illa tollerat, ut 1. q. 7 Quotiens, 23 q. 4 Ipsa pietas, D. 50 Vt constitueretur.
"Alia autem permictit,"	*in marg. sin. add.:* non quia licita, sed
in quantum "non punit ea:" et hoc, ne puniendo sequerentur maiora mala. "Sed lex diuina," que datur omnibus, "nil dimictit impunitum" in hac uita, uel alia quod sit uirtuti contrarium. Vnde secundum diuinam legem illicitum reputatur, si in contractibus "equalitas non seruetur:" quod fit plus uendendo rem quam ualeat, uel minus emendo, cum fit precipue notabilis excessus.	*in marg. infer. add.:* In hoc cum B. Toma concordant Iohannes de Ligna., et Iohannes Calderinus, et plures alii canoniste, dicentes illam decretalem habere locum "iure fori, non iure poli," et hoc ad uitanda multa litigia, que de leui possent cotidie fieri.

3.1.3.3. Excessus minor.

3.1.3.3.1. Ratione pacis et saluationis.

3.1.3.3.2. Ratione mutue concordationis.

3.1.3.3.3. Ratione humane extimationis.

3.1.3.3.4. Contra quoddam obiectionum.

2. Table of substantial additions to the first recension of 2.1.17

Thema.

recensio prima	*additiones*
De uaria fraudatione loquitur Psalmista dicens, Ps. 51, Tota die iniustitiam cogitauit lingua tua; sicut nouacula acuta fecisti dolum. Vbi ultra frequentiam mali operis quam signat dicens Tota die, sententiam dampnationis insinuat dicens: Propterea Deus dextruet te in finem et euellet te etc.	*in marg. super. add.:* Vnde et Apostolus Thessal., Neque quis circumueniat, id est decipiat, in negotio fratrem suum, quia uindex est Deus de omnibus hiis. Et de bestia quam uidit Ioannes Apoc. 13 dicitur quod faciet, ne quis possit uendere uel emere, nisi qui habuerit characterem ac nomen bestie. Bestia, que dicitur a uastando, diabolus est; character eius, que est ymago eius, est fraus et dolus; nomen eius est falsitas, quia mendax est. Absque ista ymagine, scilicet fraudis, dicuntur mercatores non posse uendere uel emere. Sed ibi subditur quod qui acceperit hunc karacterem, bibet de uino ire Dei.
Et notat tria mala que facit dolosus seu deceptor in negotiando seu uendendo. …	

1. **Astutia.**
2. **Malitia.**
   2.1. De dolo et fraude.

recensio prima	*additiones*
Fit ergo dolus per uerba et facta deceptoria, fraus autem proprie per facta. Et sic sumuntur cum dicitur, Extra, De rescrip., Ex tenore, quod “fraus et dolus nemini debent patrocinari,” ut fraus referatur ad facta deceptoria, ad uerba autem dolus.	*in marg. infer. add.:* **2.2. Dolus dans causam contractui.** Et nota secundum Petrum de Palude in 4o Goffredum et Bernardum, quod si dolus dat causam contractui, puta quis celat uitium equi quem exponit uenalem uel laudat ipsum ut indefectuosum, quem defectum si sciret emtor nullo modo emeret, ut equum cadentem

recensio prima	*additiones*
Hos dolos facit iniustus auarus per uerba adulatoria plena fallaciis, alliciendo uerbis humanis et reuerentibus, ostendendo se amichum emptoris, et huiusmodi. …	periculosum; tunc quamuis res illa ualeret pretium, tamen quia uenditor celando uitium occultum rei illius uel laudando ut non habentem defectum, cum sciret, tenetur ad restitutionem pretii emptori reofferenti rem, quia propter talem dolum potest rescindi contractus secundum iura. **2.3. Dolus incidens in contractum**. Si autem dolus per uerba uel facta incidit in contractum, quia scilicet emptor emisset illam rem cuius defectum nesciebat, sed non tantum pretium, tunc si res illa tantum ualet, non tenetur ei uenditor in aliquo, quia ex quo uolebat emere, debebat emere iusto pretio. Sed si non tantum ualebat, debet restituere illud plus.

3. Fraudulentia.

recensio prima	*additiones*
Vnde dicitur Leuitic. fit ergo fraudulentia: primo in rei quiditate, secundo in sui quantitate, tertio in eius qualitate, quarto in soluendi tarditate, quinto in pretii ad res mutabilitate,	*in marg. sin. add.:* sexto in bono opere cum intentionis prauitate.

3.1. In rei quiditate.

3.2. In sui quantitate.

recensio prima	*additiones*
In quantitate fit fraus in pondere numero et mensura. Vnde Dominus Deutero. 25, Non habebis in sachulo diuersa pondera, maius et minus, et Leuit. 19, Nolite facere iniquum aliquid in iudicio, in regula, in pondere, et in mensura,	*in marg. super. add.:* et Osee 12, Chanaan, in manu eius statera dolosa. Chanaan interpretatur negotiator: hii enim commictunt dolos et fraudes in mensuris, quia etsi habeant iustas mensuras et pondera, tamen fraudulenter utuntur eis ad decipiendum.

3.2.1. In pondere.
3.2.2. In mensura.
3.2.3. In numero.
3.2.4. De more in dando ad filandum.
3.2.5. De tabernariis.
3.2.6. De lanificibus et factoribus caligarum.
3.2.7. De laninis deferentibus ad filandum.

3.3. In eius qualitate.

3.3.1. Quando defectus rei debet manifestari.

recensio prima	*additiones*
… unde et tenetur ad dampni recompensationem per regulam illam, "Qui occasionem dampni dat, dampnum quoque dedisse uidetur," Extra, De iniur. et damp., Si culpa. Si autem defectus rei non impedit totaliter usum eius nec reddit noxium, sed minus reddit rem utilem: …	*in marg. sin. add.:* Tenetur ergo manifestare uitium rei, nec potest celare.

3.3.2. De uendentibus pannos uel uestes defectuosos.

recensio prima	*additiones*
… Mediatores quoque seu sensales qui sciunt tales defectus, et pro bonis et in defectuosis uendere faciunt, participes sunt fraudis et peccati et sunt obligati ad restitutionem, ut De iniur. et dampn., Si culpa.	*in marg. infer. add.:* Idem de facientibus fieri pannos lineos uel de sericho intextos, cum eueniunt notabiles defectus in eis siue ratione materie siue forme seu texture, qui tamen non percipi de facili possunt ab emptoribus. Secus autem dicendum in omnibus predictis casibus quando emptor percipiens tales defectus uel non percipiens uoluntarie emit et illo pretio, peritus in negotiando: quia intendit inde bene lucrari, puta in alio locho ubi chare uenduntur etiam cum talibus defectibus. "Scienti," enim "et consentienti non fit iniuria neque dolus," De re. iu., libro 6o.

3.3.3. De remendatoribus pannorum.

3.4. In soluendi tarditate.

3.4.1. De campsoribus.

3.4.2. De officialibus communitatis.

3.5. In pretii ad res mutabilitate.

recensio prima	*additiones*
Quinto fit fraus in peccunie ad res mutabilitate, et ex hoc diminuitur pretium debitum promissum: quia non indigentes aliquando talibus rebus	*in marg. sin. add.:* conducti in aliquo opere,
cum uendunt, minus pretium inueniunt quam id quod constitit eis. Et contra hos ait Iacobus, 5o capitulo, Ecce merces mercenariorum uestrorum, que fraudata est a uobis, clamat contra uos etc. Sciendum igitur quod cum pacta debeant seruari, Extra, De pac., Antigonus, et pacta ex conuentione legem accipiunt: ideo cum quis conducitur ad aliquod opus, si <conductor> promictit sibi dare peccuniam, non debet illi dare uictualia uel pannum uel alias res, nisi in quantum uelit ipse conductus sua sponte	*in marg. dext. add.:* uoluntate,
uel nisi alio modo non possit sibi soluere ex defectu peccunie. Sed tunc si ille non indiget usu illius rei, puta panni, sed oportet ipsum uendere ut habeat peccuniam pro aliis rebus emendis, illud dampnum quod inde substinet in minus uendendo, debet conductor resarcire, ex quo pactum fuit de peccunia et inuoluntarius alias res recepit. Sed si a principio operis pactum in soluendo sibi de labore suo	*in marg. dext. add.:* certo pretio
<partim> in rebus, puta panni uictualium, et partim in peccunia: … […] Nota tamen, quod si ex | hoc non accipit textor debitum lucrum de labore suo secundum communem extimationem sed diminutum, putatur autem debitum lucrum illud in quo conueniunt in peccunia, puta X florenos, sed quia pauper est et oportet eum accipere etiam multominus ut se et familiam substentet: tunc utique setaiuolus sibi teneretur dare supplementum usque ad decem uel circa, si dat sibi pannum quem non uendit nisi 6; quia sicut dignus est operarius mercede sua ex debito iustitie, ita et conuenienti mercede.	*in marg. dext. add.:* Alias *in marg. super. add.:* esset contra equalitatem iustitie, sicut in contractu emptionis et uenditionis est iniustitia et peccatum cum res emitur minus iusto pretio ex necessitate uenditoris.

3.6. In bono opere cum intentionis prauitate.

3.6.1. A corde.

3.6.2. Ab ore.

3.6.3. Ab opere.

4. De permutationibus seu baracti.

recensio prima	*additiones*
… et licitus, quia a iure approbatus	*in marg. sin. add.:* simpliciter in temporalibus,
Extra, De rerum permutatione, per totum. […]	
… utique peccat mortaliter, et tenetur satisfacere notabiliter ledens,	*in marg. sin. add.:* Extra, De iniur. et damp., Si culpa.
Et similiter mediator qui nouit huiusmodi fraudem seu sensalis, cooperatur fraudi,	

3. First Draft of 3.8.1 on M_2 fol. 69r

recensio prima deleta	*sectiones correspondentes*
hoc totum del. auctor fol. 69r: De tertio opere dicitur, Prouer. <12.11>, *Qui operatur terram,* scilicet cultiuando, *replebitur panibus,* scilicet recolligit fructum. Et de muliere nobili dicitur Prouer. ultimo <31.27; 31.13>, *Panem otiosa non comedit,* sed [panem] *operata est consilio manuum suarum.*	*fol. 69r–69v:* De tertio opere dicitur, *Exibit homo ad opus suum* etc. Aliis quidem animalibus natura prouidit de uictu et uestitu et armis ad se defendendum sine eorum opere; | homini uero dedit rationem ex qua exeundo per discursum ad actum considerationis et inuestigationis, per opera exteriora diuersorum exercitiorum sibi prouidere possit de uictu et uestitu et defensione a nociuis. Et quasi omnia opera exteriora hominum ad hec ordinantur. *Exibit* ergo etc. Vbi de ipsis operibus corporalibus tria nota. 1. Bonam conscientiam, ibi *Exibit homo ad opus suum.* 2. Aptam conuenientiam, ibi *Ad operationem suam.* 3. Debitam permanentiam, ibi *Vsque ad uesperam.*
Harum autem operationum extraneorum, ut dicit Hug. de Sancto Vic., ad quedam opera cogit necessitas, quedam adinuenit cupiditas, quedam induxit uanitas.	*fol. 70r:* Et dicit Hugo de sancto Victore quod operationum humanarum exteriorum triplex differentia inuenitur. Nam: Ad quedam cogit necessitas; Quedam inuenit cupiditas; Quedam induxit uanitas.
Ad necessitatem est opus [g] agriculture, unde dicitur Ecclesiastici <7.16>, *Non oderis opera rustichana.* Et sicut ad uictum necessarium est opus agriculture, propter quod dicitur Prouerb. <12.11> *Qui operatur terram replebitur panibus.* Et alibi <10.4>, *Egestatem operata est manus remissa.*	**3.2.1. Operatio ad quam cogit necessitas.** Cogit utique necessitas ad opera agriculture, quia si uult fructus terre colligere unde comedat et bibat, oportet quod operetur colendo terram per se uel alium, unde dicitur Prouerb. 12, *Qui operatur terram, saturabitur panibus,* et econtra, *egestatem operata est manus remissa,* scilicet ad operandum. Et Ecclesiastici <7> dicitur, *Ne oderis opera rustichana.* Nam Deus eam instituit quia, ut dicitur Genes. 3, *Emisit Deus Adam de paradiso uoluptatis, ut operaretur terram de qua sumptus est.* Et post diluuium, ut dicitur Genes. 9, *Noe uir agrichola cepit exercere terram et plantauit uineam,* ut uinum colligeret quod prius ignorabatur. Sed ut ait Ambrosius: "Nec uinum suo pepercit auctori, sed ebrietas illius suadet sobrietatem," D.35 *Sexto die.*
Ita ad uestitum opus lanificii et linificii et alie que hiis deseruiunt,	Cogit etiam necessitas uite humane ad opera pastorum ac etiam lanificii et linificii, et opera que hiis deseruiunt pro uestitu humano necessario. Et primas quidem uestes Deus fecit, ut haberi Genes.

unde dicitur Prouerb. ultimo <31.13> de muliere sapienti, *Quesiuit lanam et linum et operata est consilio manuum suarum.* Et econtra dicitur Prouerb. <10.4>, *Egestatem operata est manus remissa,* que scilicet non operatur aliquod exercitium corporale, uel negligenter.	3, quia *fecit Deus Adae et Eue* in hoc exilio positis *tunichas pelliceas.* "Non," inquit Ambrosius, "serichas sed pelliceas," habitum scilicet humilitatis et penitentie, non uanitatis et iactantie. Et de sapienti muliere dicitur Proverb. ultimo, *Quesiuit lanam et linum, et operata est consilio manuum suarum,* scilicet uestes, nam subdit *stragulatam uestem fecit sibi.* Et primus pastor fuit Abel, quem sequuti in hoc opere sunt Iacob Patriarcha cum filiis suis. Primus hedifichator habitationum et ciuitatum fuit Chayn, qui *hedificauit ciuitatem nomen* imponens *filii sui,* scilicet *Enoch,* Genes. 4. Nam patriarche Habraam, Ysaach, et Iacob non in ciuitatibus uel palatiis sed in tabernaculis habitabant; quorum tabernaculorum seu tentoriorum primus operator fuit Iabel. Primus autem *malleator et faber in omnia opera ferri et eris* fuit Tubalchayn, ut dicitur Genes. 4. Et sic paulatim artes necessarie inuente sunt.
Nam [suo] artium in unoquoque suo opere mater inuenitur instantia, id est sollicitudo et frequentia, [ita nouercha est neglig eruditionis, scientie scilicet uel artis, est negligentia, dicit Anacletus] D.83 *Nichil.* Et ideo si uult uiue- Ecclesiastes <9.10>, *Quodcumque potest manus tua, instanter operare.*	*fol. 70v:* **3.3 Debita permanentia.** Demum quantum ad tertium, opportet habere in operibus et artibus instantiam et perseruerantiam. Nam ut dicit Anacletus Papa: "In unoquoque artium opere mater inuenitur instantia," D.83 *Nichil.* Et hoc est quod dicit Ps.: *Vsque ad uesperam,* id est usque sero continuando, non parum operando et subito dimittendo; uel *usque ad uesperam,* id est terminum uite. Quod est contra aliquos instabiles, qui omni die mutant unam artem; hii sunt similes filio inconstantie de quo dicit Boetius, de eo narrans in libro *De scolarium disciplina* quod cum pater eius posuisset ad opera diuerse artis, quia subito attediabatur cum unam inchoabat, demum omnes renuens; interrogante patre quid facere uellet, respondit se uelle fieri asinum ut salmam ferret. Sed cum aliquis in operibus alicuius licite artis bene uiuendo perseuerat *usque ad uesperam,* id est finem; tunc facto sero, id est uita deficiente, dicit Dominus: *Voca operarios, et da illis mercedem,* Matth. 20, scilicet glorie.

4. Table of substantial additions to the first recension of 3.8.1

Thema.

recensio prima	*additiones*
Prima perfectio cuiuslibet creature est primus actus eius, id est forma substantialis, ut in homine anima rationalis; secunda uero perfectio seu secundus actus est operatio eius per quam manifestatur uirtus eius.	*in marg. sin. add.:* que ab ea procedit,

1. Ad opus uirtuale.
2. Ad opus criminale.

recensio prima	*additiones*
De secundo ait Dominus Noster, Io. 8, Vos facitis opera patris uestri, scilicet diaboli, scilicet faciendo que ipse suggerit ~~nostra quidem sunt propter consens-equidem(?)~~ Vnde Iero., "Sicut in bonis operibus nostris perfector est Deus, quia non est uolentis etc., ita in malis," scilicet operibus, "et in peccatis semina nostra sunt incentiua et perfectio diaboli," De pen. D.2	*p.c.:* mala: diaboli propter suggestionem. *in marg. dext. add.:* ^ enim sunt *in marg. dext. add.:* Si enim inquit.

3. Ad opus manuale.

recensio prima	*additiones*
a.c.: De tertio opere dicitur, Prover. <12.11>, Qui operatur terram, scilicet cultivando, replebitur panibus, scilicet recolligit fructum. Et de muliere nobili dicitur Prover. ultimo <31.27;31.13>, Panem otiosa non comedit, sed [panem] operata est consilio manuum suarum. Harum autem operationum extraneorum, ut dicit Hug. de Sancto Vic., ad quedam opera cogit necessitas, quedam adinvenit cupiditas, quedam induxit vanitas. Ad necessitatem est opus [g] agriculture, unde dicitur Ecclesiastici <7.16>, Non oderis opera rustichana. Et sicut ad victum necessarium est opus agriculture, propter quod dicitur Proverb. <12.11>	*p.c.:* *Exibit homo ad opus suum* etc. Aliis quidem animalibus natura prouidit de uictu et uestitu et armis ad se defendendum sine eorum opere; | homini uero dedit rationem ex qua exeundo per discursum ad actum considerationis et inuestigationis, per opera exteriora diuersorum exercitiorum sibi prouidere possit de uictu et uestitu et defensione a nociuis. Et quasi omnia opera exteriora hominum ad hec ordinantur. *Exibit* ergo etc. Vbi de ipsis operibus corporalibus tria nota. 1. Bonam conscientiam, ibi *Exibit homo ad opus suum.*

Qui operatur terram replebitur panibus. Et alibi <10.4>, Egestatem operata est manus remissa. Ita ad vestitum opus lanificii et linificii et alie que hiis deserviunt, unde dicitur Proverb. ultimo <31.13> de muliere sapienti, Quesivit lanam et linum et operata est consilio manuum suarum. Et econtra dicitur Proverb. <10.4>, Egestatem operata est manus remissa, que scilicet non operatur aliquod exercitium corporale, vel negligenter. Nam [suo] artium in unoquoque suo opere mater invenitur instantia, id est sollicitudo et frequentia, [ita novercha est neglig eruditionis, scientie scilicet vel artis, est negligentia, dicit Anacletus] D.83 Nichil. Et ideo si vult vive- Ecclesiastes <9.10>, Quodcumque potest manus tua, instanter operare.	2. Aptam conuenientiam, ibi *Ad operationem suam.* 3. Debitam permanentiam, ibi *Vsque ad uesperam.*

3.1. Bona conscientia.

3.1.1. Rectum in intentione.

3.1.2. Licitum ex improhibitione.

3.1.3. Congruum in discretione.

3.2. Apta conuenientia.

recensio prima	*additiones*
a.c.: … que tantas et tam uarias operationes artificium inspirauit mentibus hominum. ~~Et hoc est quod dicit Sapiens~~	*p.c.:* Exeat ergo homo ad operationem suam, id est ad eam artem quam iudicat sibi magis conuenire et complacere.

3.2.1. Operatio ad quam cogit necessitas.

recensio prima	*additiones*
a.c.: Nam Deus eam instituit quia, ut dicitur Genes. 3, Emisit Deus Adam de paradiso uoluptatis, ut operaretur terram de qua sumptus est. ~~Et primus filius eius, scilicet Chayn, agrichola fuit~~ … Et primus pastor fuit Abel, quem sequuti sunt Iacob Patriarcha cum filiis suis.	*p.c.:* Et post diluuium, ut dicitur Genes. 9, Noe uir agrichola cepit exercere terram et plantauit uineam, ut uinum colligeret quod prius ignorabatur. *in marg. dex. add.:* in *in marg. sin. add:* hoc opere

3.2.2. Operatio quam inuenit cupiditas.

recensio prima	*additiones*
Operatio hec plena periculis est et fraudibus et aliquando mixta usuris, ut notatur Extra De usur., In ciuitate, et c. Nauiganti. Et ideo oculos aperi.	*in marg. infer. add.:* Vnde et Crisostomus dicit super Matheum: "Nullus Christianus debet esse merchator" quia "merchator numquam potest Deo placere," D.88 Eiciens. Quod dicit B. Tomas 2a 2ae q. 77 esse intelligendum de hiis qui ponunt finem suum ultimum in acquisitione lucri seu peccunie; uel de illicitas negotiationes exercentibus, scilicet cum usuris, fraudibus, et periuriis, et huiusmodi. Vnde et Cassiodorus dicit D. eadem, "Negotiatores illi" de templo eiciuntur, qui "per immoderatum peccunie ambitum merces suas polluunt plus onerantes periuriis quam pretiis." Ponuntur illa, c. Eiciens et c. Quoniam, pro palea, unde et aliqui libri non habent, sed sunt optimum granum. *in marg. super. add.:* Dicit etiam Crisostomus in dicto c. Eiciens, "Quemadmodum qui ambulat inter duos inimichos uolens ambobus placere, sine alloquio mali esse non potest, sic" merchator "sine mendacio et periurio esse non potest." "Sed substantia talium stabilis" esse non potest, "nec proficit ad bonum quod de malo congregatur. Quemadmodum si tritichum aut aliquid tale cernas in cribro, dum huc illucque iactatur, omnia grana paulatim deorsum cadunt et tandem in cribro nil remanet nisi sterchus. *in marg. super. M_2 fol. 69v add.:* Sic de substantia negotiatori nil remanet nisi peccatum."
Exemplum. Nam et si legatur in vitis Patrum de quodam merchatore, quod fuit uisus a Beato Pannusio ei equiparandus in gloria, qui tamen Pannusius hermita sanctissimus magni meriti fuit apud Deum: attende quia ipse Pannusius examinans uitam eius inuenit quia totum lucrum expendebat in pauperes Christi ut pater pauperum, ab usuris et periuriis et aliis illicitis abstinebat, cum magna deuotione uacans diuinis tempori suo; qui demum etiam dimisit opus illud. *Quis est hic, et laudabimus eum?*	

3.2.3. Operatio quam induxit uanitas. Operatio autem tertia que deseruit uanitati est illa que deseruit ornatui iactantie, ut ars serici in magna parte. Nam et si dominos deceat tales uestes, et reginas, ut Hester sancta, et sancti aliqui reges se ornantes; |	

3.3. Debita permanentia.

5. First Draft of 3.8.2 on M_2 fol. 114v–115r

recensio prima in fol. 114v–115r	*comparatio textui Iohannis Scoti*
Antoninus scr.: Haec pone in titulo de merchatoribus et artificibus *Iulianus de Lapaccinis scr. in eadem linea:* ad cart. 70 supra *hoc totum scr. alia manus:* De primo sit haec r.^{d} quod dominus alicuius rei nisi prohibeatur a iure uel a superiori a cuius uoluntate dependet in dando potest donare rem suam alii uolenti et potenti recipere. Probatur quia sicut per actum uoluntatis potest iste esse dominus, ita potest per actum uoluntatis cessare esse dominus et dominium suum in alterum transferre.	*textus* Io. Scot. *In quartum* 4 d.15 q.2 a.2 c.2 (Wolter, 40): De primo sit haec conclusio quae est articuli huius secunda: Dominus alicuius rei non probibitus a lege seu superiori, a cuius voluntate dependeat in dando vel transferendo vel donando, potest rem suam donare alii volenti recipere. Hoc probatur, quia ex quo per actum voluntatis suae fuit dominus, ergo per voluntatem potest cessare esse dominus, et alius vult recipere, ergo potest incipere dominus, et non prohibet aliqua causa superior istum desinere et illum incipere esse dominum; ergo per donationem istam fit vere et iuste translatio dominii.
Ex hoc patet quod de ratione liberalis donationis sunt 3^{ia}, scilicet ex parte donatoris requiritur quod sit dominus rei quam dat, quia 2° quod in donatione siue translatione ius rei non dependeat ab alio a quo prohibeatur, quemadmodum prohibiti sunt clerici uisitati suis uisitatoribus dare, *Extra*, *de censibus*, *Romana*. Ad cuius constitutionis obseruantiam posuit penam Gregorius decimus. ~~Et est hodie illud capitulum in 6° libro decretalium, *Exigit*, quod uisitantes a uisitatis nullam recipiant munuscula et si susceperint teneantur duplum restituere uel non absoluantur a maledictione quam ipso facto incurrunt, ut dicitur libro 4° in nouis constitutionibus.~~ Ex hoc patet et quod monachus uel filius familias non potest aliquid dare contra assensum expressum uel presumptum abbatis uel patris. Tertio requiritur ex parte recipientis uoluntas et facultas recipiendi. Ex quo patet quod nullus potest dare fratri minori peccuniam, cum receptio peccunie sit per regulam sibi totaliter interdictam, ita quod nec per se nec per interpositam personam recipere potest sicut plenius *Extra* habetur, *de uerborum signific.*, *Exiit qui seminat*, in 6° libro.	Ex hoc patet quid requiritur ad iustam donationem, quia liberalis traditio ex parte donantis, et voluntas recipiendi ex parte illius cui fit donatio, et libertas ex parte amborum, huius donandi et illius recipiendi, et quod nulla lege superiori prohibeatur iste vel ille, nec per actum alterius a quo dependeat in ista translatione. Et propter defectum primi non potest quis donare pecuniam Fratri Minori, quia ille non vult esse dominus. Propter defectum secundi non potest Monachus dare praeter Abbatis licentiam, nec filius familias sine voluntate parentis vel parentum; nec etiam clericus in aliquo casu sine voluntate, vel saltem contra voluntatem, domini Papae, ut habetur *Extra de Censibus*, *Romana*. Ad cuius capituli observationem poenam posuit Gregorius X, cuius capitulum est hodie in 6 libro *Decretalium*, *Exigit*, scilicet quod visitantes a visitatis nulla recipiant manuscula, et si receperint, duplum teneantur restituere, vel non absolvantur a maledictione, quam ipso facto incurrunt, ut dicitur in 6 libro, in novis constitutionibus. […]

	textus ibid. (Wolter, 42)
Translatio autem illiberalis, puta illa in qua aliquid expectatur, expectat enim transferens equivalens illi quod transfert. Et hoc dupliciter quia uel statim recipite equiualens, uel expectat post tempus recipere et utraque istarum dicitur contractus, quia ibi simul trahuntur uoluntates partium, trahitur ennim iste ad transferendum in alium a comodo quod expectat ab initio (*vel* illo). Sunt autem huiusmodi contractus quibus dominia transferuntur aliquando rei utilis pro re utili, ut bladum pro uino et similia, et dicitur rerum permutatio do ut des uel do si des. Aliquando rei utilis pro numismate uel econuerso, quia enim difficile erat res usuales immediate commutare, ideo fuit inuentum medium per quod talis commutatio fieret, quod uocatur numisma; et dicitur commutatio numismatis pro re usuali emptio, econuerso uero uenditio. Aliquando uero est numismatis pro numismate, et dicitur mutua (*sic*) datio et mutua acceptio. Sunt ergo sex contractus in quibus transfertur dominium, scilicet liberalis datio, rerum permutatio, emptio, uenditio, mutui datio, et mutui acceptio. Si autem sit translatio usus dominio retempto, sic sunt sex modi, modis | [fol. 115r] translationis dominii correspondentes. Nam liberali dationi dominii correspondet liberalis usus rei accomodatio, et ista accomodatio iusta est eodem modo quo liberalis donatio dicta est iusta. Rerum uero commutationi correspondet mutua accomodatio, emptioni conductio, uenditioni locatio, mutui acceptioni non correspondet aliquid proprie in translatione usus rei. Sic igitur patet a quibus possunt rerum dominia et usus earum transferri, uerum quia istis modis supra positis possunt iuste et iniuste usus rerum et dominia transferri ~~ideo(?) de istis ostendendum est in speciali~~ *hic Antoninus scr.:* per fraudes, uarias usuras, et huiusmodi, de quibus supra in secunda parti ti. primo c. 2.	Alia est translatio non mere liberalis, sed ubi transferens exspectat aliquid aequivalens ei quod transfert, et dicitur proprie contractus, quia ibi simul trahuntur voluntates partium; trahitur enim iste ad transferendum in illum a commodo quod exspectat ab illo vel quod exspectat transferendum in se. Huiusmodi contractus in quibus dominia transferuntur, quidam sunt rei utilis pro re utili immediate, sicut vini pro blado, et huiusmodi, et dicitur rerum permutatio do ut des vel do si des. Quidam rei utilis pro numismate, vel e converso, quia enim difficile erat res usuales immediate commutare; ideo inventum est medium per quod talis commutatio faciliter fieret, quod vocatur numisma; et dicitur commutatio numismatis pro re usuali emptio, e converso vero venditio. Quaedam vero numismatis pro numismate, et dicitur mutui datio et mutui acceptio. Sunt ergo quinque contractus, in quibus transfertur dominium, quibus correspondent aliqui contractus in quibus transfertur usus, vel ius utendi, retento dominio. Nam rerum permutationi correspondet mutua vel permutata accommodatio; emptioni correspondent conductio, et venditioni locatio; mutui acceptationi non corespondet aliquid proprie in translatione usus rei.

6. Table of substantial additions to the first recension of 3.8.2

1. De translatione rerum.

recensio prima	*additiones*
Notandum quod in translatione rerum	*s.l. add.:* de una persona ad aliam
que fit per priuatas personas, aliquando transfertur dominium rei, aliquando solum usus rei retento dominio.	

1.1. Donatio.

1.2. Permutatio.

1.3–4. Emptio-uenditio.

recensio prima	*additiones*
Quia enim difficile erat semper res usuales immediate commutare in alias res, ideo inuentum est ~~numisma~~	*in marg. sin. add.:* medium
per quod talis commutatio fiat;	

1.5–6. Mutui datio-acceptio.

1.7. Isti sex contractus liciti uel illiciti.

recensio prima	*additiones*
Permutatio rerum, cum fit sine fraude, licita est,	*in marg. sin. add.:* ut patet De rerum permut. per totum;
si cum fraude peccatum est.	

2. De translatione usus.

2.1. Commodatum.

2.2. Accomodatio.

2.3–4. Conductio-locatio.

2.5–6. Pignus-ypotheca.

3. De fraude legi.

3.1. De re ad rem.

3.2. De persona ad personam.

3.3. De uno contractu ad alium.

3.4. De uno contractu ad alium alio modo.

recensio prima	*additiones*
… et facit transactionem cum eis.	*in marg. super. add.:* "Item, fit fraus de uno contractu ad alium <sed alio modo>, ut cum mulier non possit fideiubere, constituit se principalem debitricem, ut Ff. Ad Vell., Quamuis, et 33 q.5 Mulierem."

7. Table of substantial additions to the first recension of 3.8.3

Pr. Negotiator proprie qui dicitur.

recensio prima	*additiones*
Incipiendo ergo ab opere negotiationis, que uidetur honorabilior in ciuilitate humana inter mechanica. Negotiator proprie dicitur qui rem comparat ut integram et immutatam Et potest dici esse triplex genus negotiationis, …	*in marg. dext. add.:* uendendo lucretur, dicit Crisostomus D. 88 *Eiciens*.

1. Cambium.

1.1. Cambium minutum.

recensio prima	*additiones*
Illud igitur plus quod recipit campsor, non capit ratione mutui quia ibi non est mutuum, nec quia peccunia uendatur, que est inuendibilis ut dicit Archidiaconus, sed ratione laboris quem subit in numerando peccuniam et expensarum quas facit pro pensione et ministris. Vnde de se tale cambium est licitum: …	*in marg. super. add.:* Ratio enim laboris et expensarum habenda est, *Extra*, *De uoto*, *Magne*.

1.2. Cambium per litteram.
1.3. Cambium sichum.
1.4. Cambium mixtum quod usuram sapere uidetur.
1.5. De usura in cambiis.
1.6. De usura mentali.
1.7. Cambium in curia Romana quod uidetur magis illicitum.

recensio prima	*additiones*
Nam beneficia inibi accipientes cum habeant soluere annatam … […]	*in marg. dext. add.:* uel dignitates
Vnde cum ratione dilationis temporis illud plus petant, scilicet 50, quomodo ab usura possit defendi contractus talis, non uidetur, ar. 14 q. 3 *Si feneraris* cum c. sequen., et *De usuris*, *Consuluit* et c. *In ciuitate*, Solent autem tales campsores excusare tale lucrum ratione periculi, … […]	*in marg. dext. add.:* et D. 88 *Eiciens*.

<table>
<tr>
<td>Sed campsor principaliter intendit exercere tale mutuum quod cambium uocat, nec illi prelato mutuat ut seruiat, sed ut magis lucretur, quia magis per uiam illam lucratur quam per uiam negotiationis; et intentio lucri ex mutuo explicito uel implicito facit usurarium, ut in dicto c. Si feneraueris, 14 q. 3.</td>
<td>Antoninus postea add. in fine lineae:
¶ Hii etiam aliquando sunt
in marg. super. add.:
mediatores in simoniis que fiunt in curia, offerentes munera intercedentibus pro beneficiis obtinendis pro prelatis suis amicis, unde et grauiter offendunt. Et hii sunt numularii de templo eiecti Io. 2, de quibus etiam dicitur 1 q. 1, Si quis episcopus: “Si quis mediator tam turpibus et nephandis datis et acceptis extiterit, si laychus est, anathematizetur.”
Sed per extrauagantem tales sunt exchommunicati.</td>
</tr>
</table>

2. Securitates.

2.1. Securitas in mercimoniis.

2.2. Securitas in peccuniis.

recensio prima	*additiones*
Videtur dicendum quod si non est omnino securus satisdator, ut quia potest fallere, tunc uidetur licitum ratione periculi. ~~Sed si est securus, quia sat illum habere tot bona quod nullo modo potest perdere seu quia~~	*p.c.:* quia si ille non solueret, scilicet principalis, haberet satisdator soluere; sed si est omnino securus, ut quia certum est illum habere tot bona quod satisdator non habebit ipse reddere uel laborare, non uidetur tutum lucrum quia uidetur implicitum mutuum et ratione illa recipere duo.

2.3. Securitas in personis.

recensio prima	*additiones*
Datur etiam per hoc uia ad optandum mortem aliorum, quod est illicitum. Vnde et pauperibus uidetur erogandum, 14 q. 5 Qui habetis cum §. sequenti, Et idem uidetur dicendum de contentionibus …	*in marg. sin. add.:* de consilio tamen non de necessitate.

3. Permutatio uel baractum.

4. Emptio et uenditio.

4.1. De ritagliatoribus et righatteriis.

recensio prima	*additiones*
… et in huiusmodi laborare habent in discurrendo, exigendo, reuidendo, scribendo, et ministros tenere oportet et pensiones soluere. “Dignus est” autem	*p.c. s.l.:*
“~~operarius~~	mercenarius
mercede sua,”	*in rasura:*
	12 q. 2 *Quicumque.*
Vnde lucrum moderatum in huiusmodi querendo non uidetur illicitum.	*in marg. super. add.:* Sed in mendaciis et periuriis non euadent dampnationem, cum dicunt *malum bonum*, scilicet esse, puta pannum uel aliud, hii faciunt monstras in locis obscuris ut decipiant; contra quos dicitur Ysaie 5: *Ve qui dicitis bonum malum, ponentes tenebras lucem.*

4.2. De merchatoribus uictualium.

recensio prima	*additiones*
Reprehenduntur caupones de mixtura quam faciunt aque cum uino, uendentes aquam pro uino, contra quos dicitur, Ysaie 1° c.,	*in marg. sin. add.:*
Caupones tui aquam uino miscent,	secundum aliam translationem.
Sed non minus malum est …	

4.3. De macellariis et pizicangnolis.

recensio prima	*additiones*
Et cum non possunt per dies carnes conseruari, ut in estate, quod preparent diebus festiuis eas uidentur excusati, et etiam in uendendo talibus diebus, sed non in dimictendo propter hoc diuina ut auditionem misse. |	*hic, sc. fol. 73r, finivit recensio prima capituli; sed postea Antoninus add. in marg. super. 73v:* Pizicangnoli quoque pollarioli et trichones uendentes caseum et oua, pisces sallitos uel recentes, aues oleum minutis mensuris aut fructus, cum excessiuo pretio uendunt, uel diminutis mensuris quoad mensurabilia, uel res infectas seu coruptas, uel diebus festiuis, nisi fructus et aliqua magis necessaria uel etiam huiusmodi, dimictentes missam: sine peccato graui non sunt, etiam fraudantes gabellas.

8. Table of substantial additions to the first recension of 3.8.4

1. **De merciariis aurificibus et gioielleriis.**
   - **1.1. De aurificibus.**
   - **1.2. Non uendant aurum et argentum alchimiatum pro uero.**
   - **1.3. De mixtura eris in auro uel argento.**
2. **De prosenetis seu sensalibus.**
   - **2.1. Si est mediator in contractibus.**
   - **2.2. Si est mediator in emptione iurium montis.**
   - **2.3. Idem de omnibus qui sunt mediatores.**
3. **De lanificibus.**
   - **3.1. De emptione ad terminum.**

recensio prima	*additiones*
Et hoc nisi illa mercimonia esset reseruaturus ad tempus, quo ipsa tali pretio quo tunc uenduntur uel maiori essent ualitura,	*in rasura:* quia tunc licitum ut ibi dicitur.

3.2. De moderato lucro.

recensio prima	*additiones*
... non uidetur immoderatum lucrum nec iniustum pretium, etiam si uenderet ad contantos, cum cogatur uendere ad terminum ratione communis consuetudinis. Si enim solum uellet uendere ad contantos pauchos inueniret emptores.	*in marg. infer. add.:* Nec obstat si dicatur quia res tantum ualet quantum uendi potest ut dicit lex; sed non potest uendi ad contantos nisi pro 45 ergo illud uidetur esse iustum pretium, et si plus petit uidetur usura. Nam res ualet quantum uendi potest, sed secundum commune iudicium sapientum in arte extimata et nisi impediatur ut in casu nostro quia communis consuetudo dat talem terminum cum tamen communis ratio uenditionis sit ut data re recipiatur pretium. Et precium eciam non consistit in pretio id est *in marg. super. add.:* in puncto indiuisibili sed habet quosdam terminos latitudinis. Et inde recipiunt ex illa expectatione precii multa incommoda et pericula perdendi, quibus opportet eos se exponere si uolunt continuare

Non autem uidetur facere talem contractum illicitum hoc solum quia uendendo ad contantos dat pannum pro minori pretio, scilicet 45, quia tale pretium currit in uenditione ad contantos; quia ex hoc quod de uno et eodem genere mercimonii uendat uni pro 10 ut iusto pretio, alteri ratione amicitie uel quia indiget peccuniis det pro 8 uel 5, non potest dici usurarius propterea in primo contractu.	negotium artis. Hec omnia simul et si non aliqua de per se ex hiis uidentur, tollerabilem reddere talem modum uendendi ad terminum.

3.3. De lanifice in casu usurario.

recensio prima	*additiones*
Et hoc improbatur ibi in dicta decret. *Consuluit* et *In ciuitate*.	*in marg. sin. add.:* ut usura

3.4. De ponentibus peccunias apud lanifices.

recensio prima	*additiones*
Et illi quidem qui ponunt peccuniam in huiusmodi artificio per modum societatis iuste, cum debitis pactis, participando in lucro et dampno proportionaliter, non peccant.	*in marg. sin. add.:* scilicet licite exercendo

3.5. Si lanifex peccunias accipiat ad discretionem.
3.6. De ministris in apotheca.
3.7. De consulibus.
3.8. De officialibus.
3.9. De ministris artis lane.

recensio prima	*additiones*
Secundo de laninis, qui scilicet dant lanam ad nendum seu filandum,	*in marg. infer. add.:* uel extendunt lanam ad solis radium. Et si hoc faciunt diebus festiuis indifferenter, cum apte possint sibi aliis diebus prouidere sine aliquo periculo, male faciunt, cum multum de tempore ibi ponunt. Si autem hoc agunt ex causa rationabili, ut puta quia lana destrueretur et huiusmodi, excusantur. Isti etiam lanini solent
cum detur eis certa quantitas peccunie quam debent filatricibus dare pro labore suo, puta solidos octo pro libra, unum pro se retinere.	

3.10. De arte emendatorum.

3.11. De retaliatoribus.

4. De sartoribus et caligarum uel chalceorum factoribus et huiusmodi.

4.1. De arte stampatorum.

4.2. Qui commodant uestimenta pretiosa uel iocalia.

recensio prima	*additiones*
Qui uero commodant uestimenta pretiosa, uel torques de perlis uel alia iocalia ad tempus certum, uiris uel mulieribus, et inde percipiunt certum pretium secundum conuentionem eorum, de se non est illicitum quia non est hic mutuum sed commodatum et per modum locationis datum, sicut etiam licet lochare animalia ad uecturam et uasa etiam aurea et argentea	*in marg. sin. add.:* secundum Tomam in *Summa*.

4.3. De cerdonibus et planellariis.

4.4. De pellipariis.

5. De serificibus seu setaiuolis.

5.1. De textoribus et tinctoribus.

recensio prima	*additiones*
Sechus autem ubi sic est conuentum inter eos ut pro suo labore soluatur eis de pane uino panno et huiusmodi totum uel pars mercedis debite secundum pretium commune concurrens,	*in marg. super. add.:* quia, ut dicitur *De re. iur.*, *libro 6°*, "Scienti et consentienti non fit iniuria neque dolus," quod tamen intelligitur in hiis que de se non sunt illicita. Nam et si quis sciens et consentiens soluat usuras, fit utique ei iniuria, quia contra ius est diuinum unde et iniuria est accipere usuram. Sic etiam in proposito: si ex illo pacto grauatur textor, quia plus mercedis debetur ei de labore suo secundum commune iudicium artis, tamen assentit ne sit otiosus sed aliquid lucretur et si parum, non excusatur setaiuolus ab iniustitia.

5.2. De aliquibus fraudantibus gabellas uel pedagia.

recensio prima	*additiones*
Si autem super hoc extat prohibitio statuti ciuitatis qua cauetur ut nullus emat serichum, nisi de ipso sit gabella soluta, tunc male faciunt emendo a talibus quos sciunt fraudasse gabellas cum contra statutum agant satis rationabile,	*in marg. sin. add.:* D. 8 *Que contra morem.*
Et cum per hoc minus iusto communi pretio emant, ex quadam equitate uidentur teneri de illa parte qua minus iusto pretio emunt gabelle. Si autem fuissent cooperati ad fraudem puta iuuantes eos ad inducendum in ciuitatem occulte tenerentur ad totam fraudem gabelle,	*in marg. sin. add.:* *Extra, De iniur., Si culpa.*

5.3. De emendo serichum ab furatis.

5.4. De uendendo ad terminum uel faciendo permutationes.

6. De architectis seu hedificatoribus.

6.1. Caueant a fraudibus.

6.2. De lathomariis et cementariis.

6.3. De lapicidinariis.

7. De fabris.

7.1. De maniscallis, id est fabris facientibus ferramenta iumentis.

7.2. De armaiolis, id est fabris facientibus arma.

recensio prima	*additiones*
Alii sunt fabri ferrarii facientes diuersa artificia ex ferro	*in marg. dext. add.:* uel aliis metallis,
ut armaioli facientes galeas celatas thoraces lorichas, pectoralia brachialia et huiusmodi, lanceas sagiptas	*in marg. sin. add.:* balistas
bonbardas et huiusmodi.	

7.3. De fabris ad alia opera deditis.

8. De carpentariis.

recensio prima	*additiones*
Hii in faciendo ligna incidere secundum augmentum uel decrementum lune sine alia obseruatione dierum, non peccant, quia cum luna ut propinquior planeta multum influat in corpora inferiora, secundum rationem naturalem est quod potius incidantur,	*in rasura et marg. sin.:* cum luna est in decremento quam in augmento.

8.1. De facientibus galeas naues et nauiculas.

Sections 8.1 and 8.2 are added on fol. 79r, with an indication to place them after section 8 on carpenters. Based on their order of placement in the folios, it appears that sections 9–9.3 and sections 12–12.4 were written first.

8.2. De marinariis.

recensio prima	*additiones*
Et communiter sunt homines pessimi, blasfematores frequentes Dei et sanctorum, et sine aliquo Dei timore. In periculis tamen	*in marg. super. add.:* deuotissime uidentur ad Deum recurrere, quos etiam Deus mirabiliter iuuat, sed timore seruili magis quam amore filiali apparet eos moueri cum quasi semper ad uomitum reuertantur, non curantes de Deo et salute sua.

9. De aromatariis.
9.1. De ministris talis artis.
9.2. De barbitonsoribus.
9.3. De operando in sabbatho.
10. De artificibus circa scripturas et picturas.

Sections 10–11.2 are written on fol. 79r–79v, after sections 12–12.4, which are written on fol. 78v. However, in the upper margin of 78v, just above the heading "De agrocolis," Antoninus has written: "Iste §. in fine huius capituli ponatur." Based on their location in the folios, it appears that sections 10–11.2 of this chapter were probably the last ones written.

10.1. De chartulariis.
10.2. Quomodo scriptores offendunt.
10.3. De pictoribus.
11. De ministerio musichorum in cantando et pulsando.

recensio prima	*additiones*
Sed et pulsatio organorum uel aliorum instrumentorum ad diuinam laudem initium uidetur habuisse a propheta Dauith, qui non solum cantores instituit in cultu templi seu tabernaculi, sed et ipse etiam ante archam Domini pulsabat in psalterio uel organis, ut habetur 2 Reg. 6, et in Psalmo ait ultimo: *Laudate eum in tympano et choro* etc.	*in marg. sin. add.:* uterque salarium recipiunt iuste,

11.1. De laycis pulsantes instrumenta ob recreationem.
11.2. De arte histrionum.
12. De agricolis.

recensio prima	*additiones*
Ars quidem licita et opus necessarium est uite humane, unde et primo parenti dictum fuit:	*in marg. super. add.:* *In sudore uultus tui uesceris pane tuo*, Gen. 3. Et *Noe uir agricola plantauit uineam* post diluuium, Gen. 9.
Et cum terras proprias laborant, fraudes in suis commictere non ualent, nisi in uendendo fructus suos uel nimio pretio	*in marg. sin. add.:* uel diminutis mensuris
uel uitiatos pro bonis.	

12.1. Si laborant terras aliorum.
12.2. Si tenent animalia ad soccidam.
12.3. Offendunt in non soluendo decimas.
12.4. Quomodo communiter offendunt.

recensio prima	*additiones*
Diebus festiuis parum uacant diuinis et auditioni integre misse sed ludis uel in tabernis et contentionibus ante ecclesias.	*in marg. infer. add.:* In ipsis diebus festius deferunt in iumentis blada ligna uel alia patronis suis, per quod festa uiolant, nisi maxima necessitate ducantur, non ualentes aliter uiuere.
De facili blasfemant Deum et sanctos. Maledicunt irati animalia sua bruta. Mendaciis et periuriis pleni sunt. De fornichationibus non faciunt sibi conscientiam. Plurimi eorum non confitentur annuatim, et multo pauciores communicant, falso extimantes se non debere communicare nisi cum senescunt uel ad mortem infirmantur. Familias suas parum instruunt in moribus fidelium. Penitentias sibi iniunctas a confessoribus et uota facta frequenter dimictunt.	*in marg. infer. add.:* Incantationibus utuntur, in se et in iumentis suis. De Deo uel sua salute nil cogitant.
Et cum communiter sint ignorantes, et parum curantes de ~~salute~~	*p.c. in marg. sin.:* anima
sua et obseruatione mandatorum Dei que nesciunt, hoc est	*in marg. dext. add.:* quod
adiuuat eos ~~perd-~~ duci ad perditionem per uiam latam uitiorum: ignorantia et incuria ~~sacer(dotum)~~	*p.c.:* parrochialium

suorum cum conscientia mala, qui non curantes de ouibus sibi commissis sed de lana et lacte, non eos instruunt in predicationibus in confessionibus et priuatis monitionibus; sed cum communi errore eorum transeuntes corruptelas sequuntur eorum, non corrigentes eos de uitiis eorum, propter quod contingit bestialiter uiuentes aliquando bestialiter moriantur.	

Appendix 2: Sources and Parallel Passages for 2.1.16

Summary

Dominicans

Iohannes de Regina (de Neapoli). *Quodlibeta.* Naples, Biblioteca Nazionale, VII.B.28.

Petrus de Palude. *Quartus sententiarum liber.* Paris, 1514.

Raymundus de Pennaforti. *Summa de paenitentia.* Edited by Xaviero Ochoa and Aloisio Diez. Universa Bibliotheca Iuris, vol. 1B. Rome: Instituto Iuridico Claretiano, 1976.

Raymundus de Pennaforti and Guillelmus Redonensis. *Summa sancti Raymundi de Peniafort … De poenitentia et matrimonio cum glossis Ioannis de Friburgo* (recte *Guillelmi Redonensis*). Rome, 1603.

Thomas de Aquino. *The Summa Theologica.* Translated by Fathers of the English Dominican Province. 3 vols. New York: Benziger, 1947. https://isidore.co/aquinas/summa/index.html.

Franciscans

Bernardinus Senensis. *Opera omnia.* 9 vols. Quaracchi: Collegio San Bonaventura, 1950–65.

– Vol. 1: *Quadragesimale de christiana religione (Sermones I–XL).* 1950.

– Vol. 4: *Quadragesimale de Evangelio aeterno (Sermones XXVII–LIII).* 1956.

Durandus Campanus. *Summa collectionum pro confessionibus audiendis.* Paris, Bibliothèque nationale, lat. 3264.

Gerhardus Odonis. *Tractatus de contractibus.* Siena, Biblioteca Comunale, U.V.8.

Iohannes Duns Scotus. *Quaestiones in librum quartum Sententiarum* (*Collationes Oxonienses*). Vol. 18 of *Opera omnia.* Paris: Vives, 1894.

Petrus Iohannis Olivi. *De emptionibus et venditionibus, de usuris, de restitutionibus.* In *Traité des contrats.* Edited by Sylvain Piron. Paris: Belles Lettres, 2012.

Canonists

Antonius de Butrio. *Commentaria in libros Decretalium*. 4 vols. Venice, 1578. Reprinted Turin, Bottega d'Erasmo: 1967. http://amesfoundation.law.harvard.edu/digital/AntoniusDeButrio/AntoniusDeButrioMetadata.html.

Henricus de Segusio (Hostiensis). *In Decretalium libros commentaria*. 4 vols. Venice, 1581. http://amesfoundation.law.harvard.edu/digital/Hostiensis/HostiensisMetadataPrelim.html.

– *Summa aurea*. Venice, 1574. http://web.colby.edu/canonlaw/2009/09/24/liber-extra-decretalists/.

Iohannes Andreae. *Novella in Decretales*. 5 vols. Venice, 1581. http://amesfoundation.law.harvard.edu/digital/JohannesAndreae/JohannesAndreaeMetadata.html.

Iohannes and Gaspar Calderinus senior. *Repetitiones et distinctiones in Decretales*. Vatican City, Biblioteca Apostolica Vaticana, Vat. lat. 2652.

Iohannes de Lignano. *Commentaria in Decretales*. Florence, Biblioteca Medicea-Laurenziana, Edili 54.

Laurentius de Rodulphis. *Tractatus de usuris*. In Lawrin D. Armstrong, *Usury and Public Debt in Early Renaissance Florence: Lorenzo Ridolfi on the "Monte Comune"*. Studies and Texts 144. Toronto: Pontifical Institute of Mediaeval Studies, 2003.

Nicolaus de Tudeschis (Panormitanus). *Commentaria in Decretales Gregorii IX et in Clementinas epistolas*. 5 vols. Venice, 1583. Reissued on CD-ROM with introduction by Kenneth Pennington: Il Cigno Galileo Galilei Edizioni Informatiche, 2000.

– *Commentaria in quinque Decretalium libros*. 4 vols. Venice, 1570–1. http://amesfoundation.law.harvard.edu/digital/Panormitanus/PanormitanusMetadata.html.

Table 11. Sources and parallel passages for 2.1.16

2.1.16: SECTION	*Dominicans*	*Franciscans*	*Canonists*
Thema. Because I have not known trade …		Bern. Sen. *Evang. aet.* 35, pr. (4:198)	
1. Spiritual trade.			
1.1. In the heavenly realm.			
1.2. In the terrestrial realm.			
1.3. In the infernal realm.			
2. Worldly trade.	Raym. Penn. *Sum. paen.* 2.8.1–7 (557–67) Thom. Aq. *Sum. th.* 1a 2ae q. 7 a. 3	Bern. Sen. *Evang. aet.* 33, 2, 1–7 (4:145–51)	Hostien. *Sum.* 5.38 §. 50 (1811); 5.38 §. 61 (1858)
2.1. End: greed.	Raym. Penn. *Sum. paen.* 2.8.1 (558–9) Thom. Aq. *Sum. th.* 2a 2ae q. 77 a. 4	Bern. Sen. *Evang. aet.* 33, 2, 2 (4:146–7)	
2.2. Person: cleric.	Raym. Penn. *Sum. paen.* 2.7.9 (547); 2.8.1–2 (559–62) Thom. Aq. *Sum. th.* 2a 2ae q. 77 a. 4 ad 3	Bern. Sen. *Evang. aet.* 33, 2, 1 (4:145–6)	Hostien. *Sum.* 5.38 §. 61 (1858–60) Panorm. *Comm.* *X* 5.19.19 §. 18–19 (1571 ed. 7:150va–51vb)
2.3. Time: holiday.	Raym. Penn. *Sum. paen.* 1.12.4 (398–9); 2.8.1 (558–9) Petr. Pal. *Quart. sent.* *locus* unknown	Bern. Sen. *Evang. aet.* 33, 2, 3 (4:147)	Hostien. *Sum.* 5.38 §. 61 (1859)
2.4. Place: sacred.	Raym. Penn. *Sum. paen.* 2.8.3 (562)	Bern. Sen. *Evang. aet.* 33, 2, 4 (4:148)	Hostien. *Sum.* 5.38 §. 61 (1859)
What should be counselled about such profits in these four cases.	Raym. Penn. *Sum. paen.* 2.5.44 (524–5); 2.7.11 (548–50); 2.8.7 (566–7)		Hostien. *Sum.* 5.38 §. 49 (1805); 5.38 §. 62 (1862–5)
2.5. Combination: unjust.		Bern. Sen. *Evang. aet.* 33, 2, 5 (4:148–9); 33, 2, 7 §. 5 (4:153–4)	Hostien. *Sum.* 5.38 §. 61 (1859) Panorm. *Comm.* *X* 3.17.1 n. 9 (1583 ed. 3:96r)

(*Continued*)

Table 11. (Continued)

2.1.16: SECTION	*Dominicans*	*FRANCISCANS*	*CANONISTS*
2.6. Means: wicked.	RAYM. PENN. *Sum. paen.* 1.9.4–5 (367–8); 2.8.5 (563–4); GUIL. RED. *Glossa* ibid. s.v. *in quantum* (247) THOM. AQ. *Sum. th.* 1a 2ae q. 88 a. 4–5; 2a 2ae q. 77 a. 2; 2a 2ae q. 98 a. 3 2a 2ae q. 150 a. 2	BERN. SEN. *Evang. aet.* 33, 2, 5 (4:148–9); 33, 2, 7 §. 1 (4:152)	HOSTIEN. *Sum.* 5.38 §. 41 (1792); 5.38 §. 49 (1808–9); 5.38 §. 61 (1843–4; 1859)
2.7. Matter: evil.	RAYM. PENN. *Sum. paen.* 2.8.1 (558); 2.8.6 (564–6)		HOSTIEN. *Sum.* 5.38 §. 61 (1860) LAUR. ROD. *Tr. usur.* 2 q. 7 (180); 3 conc. (249)
3. Modest temporal trade.			
3.1. Wrongful appraisal.	THOM. AQ. *Sum. th.* 2a 2ae q. 77 a. 1	BERN. SEN. *Evang. aet.* 35, 1, 2 (4:191–2)	
3.1.1. Valuation of things.		PETR. OLIVI *Tr. contr.* 1 q. 1 (94–109) IO. SCOT. *In quartum* d. 15 q. 2 n. 14 (283b) BERN. SEN. *Evang. aet.* 35, 1, 1 (4:190–1)	
3.1.1.1. From efficacy.		PETR. OLIVI *Tr. contr.* 1 q. 1 n. 9 (100) BERN. SEN. *Evang. aet.* 35, 1, 1 (4:190–1)	
3.1.1.2. From scarcity.		PETR. OLIVI *Tr. contr.* 1 q. 1 n. 10 (100) BERN. SEN. *Evang. aet.* 35, 1, 1 (4:190–1)	
3.1.1.3. From desirability.	THOM. AQ. *Sum. th.* 2a 2ae q. 77 a. 1	PETR. OLIVI *Tr. contr.* 1 q. 1 n. 11–12 (100–2) BERN. SEN. *Evang. aet.* 35, 1, 1 (4:190–1)	

2.1.16: SECTION	*Dominicans*	*Franciscans*	*Canonists*
3.1.2. Latitude in valuation.		Petr. Olivi *Tr. contr.* 1 q. 1 (94–109) Io. Scot. *In quartum* d. 15 q. 2 n. 15 (283b) Bern. Sen. *Chr. rel.* 37, 2, 1 (1:470–2); ibid. *Evang. aet.* 35, 1, 2–3 (4:191–4)	
3.1.2.1. From law.	Thom. Aq. *Sum. th.* 2a 2ae q. 77 a. 1	Bern. Sen. *Evang. aet.* 35, 1, 2–3 (4:191–4)	Hostien. *Sum.* 3.17 §. 1 (935); 3.17 §. 7 (943)
3.1.2.2. From custom.		Io. Scot. *In quartum* d. 15 q. 2 n. 15 (283b–284a) Bern. Sen. *Evang. aet.* 35, 1, 2–3 (4:191–4)	
3.1.2.3. From discretion.	Thom. Aq. *Sum. th.* 2a 2ae q. 77 a. 1	Io. Scot. *In quartum* d. 15 q. 2 n. 16 (289a) Bern. Sen. *Evang. aet.* 35, 1, 2–3 (4:191–4)	
3.1.3. Excess in valuation.			
3.1.3.1. Excess beyond half the just price.		Petr. Olivi *Tr. contr.* 1 q. 1 (94–109) Bern. Sen. *Evang. aet.* 34, 2, 2 (4:178–9); 35, 1, 3 (4:194)	Hostien. *Sum.* 3.17 §. 1 (935); 3.17 §. 7 (943) Io. Andr. *Novella X* 3.17.1 (3:79b–79va) Ant. Butr. *Comm. X* 3.17.1 §. 3 (3:75r–v); *X* 3.17.1 §. 7 (3:75r–v); *X* 5.19.6 §. 10 (4:63r–v) Panorm. *Comm. X* 3.17.1 §. 6 (3:95v–96r)

(*Continued*)

Table 11. (Continued)

2.1.16: SECTION	*Dominicans*	FRANCISCANS	CANONISTS
3.1.3.2. Excess notable but less than half.	THOM. AQ. *Sum. th.* 2a 2ae q. 77 a. 1	IO. SCOT. *In quartum* d. 15 q. 2 n. 15 (283b) DUR. CAMP. *Sum. conf.* 2 *de avaritia* (77rb–va) BERN. SEN. *Evang. aet.* 35, 1, 2 (4:192)	HOSTIEN. *Sum.* 3.17 §. 7 (944) IO. GASP. CALD. *Repet.* *X* 5.19.19 (281v–82r) IO. LIG. *Comm.* *X* 5.19.19 (99v) LAUR. ROD. *Tr. usur.* 2 op. 6 (161)
3.1.3.3. Minor excess.	IO. REG. *Quodl.* 4.18 (64va–65ra)	PETR. OLIVI *Tr. contr.* 1 q. 5 n. 52–61 (126–35) GER. ODON. *Tr. contr.* q. 4 (81v) BERN. SEN. *Chr. rel.* 37, 2, 1 §. 1 (1:470)	
3.1.3.3.1. Argument from peace and salvation.		PETR. OLIVI *Tr. contr.* 1 q. 5 resp n. 55 (128–9) BERN. SEN. *Chr. rel.* 37, 2, 1 §. 2 (1:470)	
3.1.3.3.2. Argument from mutual agreement.		PETR. OLIVI *Tr. contr.* 1 q. 5 resp n. 57 (130–1) BERN. SEN. *Chr. rel.* 37, 2, 1 §. 4 (1:470–1)	
3.1.3.3.3. Argument from human estimation.		PETR. OLIVI *Tr. contr.* 1 q. 5 resp n. 58 (132–3) IO. SCOT. *In quartum* d. 15 q. 2 (283ff.) BERN. SEN. *Chr. rel.* 37, 2, 1 §. 5 (1:471)	
3.1.3.3.4. Against an objection.		PETR. OLIVI *Tr. contr.* 1 q. 5 arg. n. 53 (126–9); 1 q. 5 ad 1 n. 59–61 (132–5) BERN. SEN. *Chr. rel.* 37, 2, 1 §. 6 (1:471–2)	

Appendix 3: Description of the Hand A's Letter-Forms

The Hand A at M_1 fol. 66v and M_2 fol. 69r

For facsimiles of these folios, see plates 1 and 2 in chapter 2. The general characteristics of the hand A are described there. Here is provided a detailed discussion of this hand's individual letter-forms, as well as samples of its majuscules, arabic numerals, and abbreviations.

Letter-forms

a. The letter a is always single-compartment. Two forms are visible on the page: an **a** with a bulb and a flat **a** with no discernible bulb (pl. 1: l. 1, *fraudulentia*; pl. 2: l. 2 *suam*, l. 3 *anima*). It seems likely that the ductus is the same: the latter flat **a** merely having been written in haste such that the bulb is not traced with a curving motion, but is instead formed by a simple motion of the pen down and to the left, then up and to the right. The **a** can commence joined with the preceding letter or not; this does not produce a change in form, and both bulbous and flat **a** are found in either case.

b. On the second line in plate 1 there is a **b** with looped ascender (pl. 1: l. 2, *introibo*) and a loopless **b** (pl. 1: l. 2, *memorabor*). Biting occurs when followed by **o**, as in the two examples just cited, and even with **e** (pl. 1: l. 30 *habes*; pl. 2: l. 24 *bonum*). The loop is counter-clockwise, coming upwards from the base of the previous letter (pl. 2: l. 2 *Exibit*). It seems likely that loopless **b** is written with the same ductus, but receives a clubbed shape from the up-and-down motion rather than being given a round curve: this is the same variation as we saw in **a**. The frequent combination **ab**, with looped or loopless **b** (pl. 1: l. 4 *ab eis*, l. 5 *ab eo*), shows that the presence or absence of a loop is not regular by position. The bulb of **b**, like the ascender, is written counter-clockwise; when joined with the following letter, the join begins from the point where the lobe meets the ascender, i.e., the headline; when not joined, the lobe is sometimes incompletely closed (pl. 1: l. 5 *abstulit*, l. 6 *abstinuisse*; pl. 2: l. 36 *replebitur*).

c. The letter **c** has basically one form, with a two-stroke ductus: a stroke beginning from the top left and descending down and to the right, followed by a nearly horizontal stroke along the headline. Sometimes the first stroke is rather straight (pl. 1: l. 3 *cum*), sometimes it forms a distinct circular curve (pl. 1: l. 24 *coronam, corona*). Joining with the preceding letter is inconsistent (pl. 1: l. 3 *dicat*, l. 4 *peccuniam*, l. 5 *peccuniam*); it does regularly join with the following letter, merely a continuation of the horizontal stroke along the headline.

d. The letter **d** shows the same variation as **b**, sometimes having a looped ascender (pl. 1: l. 1 *fraudulentia, uenditione*; pl. 2: l. 2 *ad*^{1}), sometimes loopless (pl. 1: l. 2 *domini, domine*; pl. 2: l. 11 *ad*^{1}, *delectationem*). That the use of a looped or loopless ascender was not regular but a matter of choice[1] is illustrated by A's treatment of three feminine singular gerundives ending in *-enda*: the first is loopless, the second looped, the third loopless again (pl. 1: l. 8 *cauenda*, l. 9 *exercenda*, l. 10 *permittenda*). Nevertheless A does show a preference for loopless **d** in initial position. Both forms can join with the following letter; loopless **d** seems regularly not to be joined with the preceding letter. The loopless form, by contrast with flat **a** and loopless **b**, does suggest a different ductus. Looped **d** is written in one continuous counter-clockwise motion: starting at the headline, forming the circular lobe, continuing still counter-clockwise up to the top of the ascender, then forming the loop in a rapid curving motion downward and to the right leading directly into the following letter, which commences from the headline. Some looped **d**s are larger in size and come closer in appearance to majuscule **d** (pl. 1: l. 9 *cauenda*).[2] Loopless **d** is formed in two strokes: a first, semicircular stroke forming an open lobe, followed by the ascender, which is drawn from top left to bottom right, closing the lobe, and often enough joining to the next letter. The connecting stroke from loopless **d** theoretically stands on the baseline, but often enough is really some height above it. Note a variant form, a heavily clubbed **d** (pl. 1: l. 11 *inchoando*; pl. 2: l. 38 *cupiditas*). Indeed, **d** sometimes forms a ligature with the following letter (pl. 1: l. 1 *fraudulentia*, l. 31 *possidetur*; pl. 2: l. 38 *quedam*^{2}).

e. The letter **e** has typical *cursiva* forms listed by Derolez: in general its form is "two curved strokes traced in the same direction, which can cause confusion with **c**."[3] It rarely has a true lobe, but is distinguished from **c** by the second stroke beginning slightly to the right of the first, leaving a gap between the two (pl. 1: l. 4 *peccuniam, rationem*; pl. 2: l. 13 *te*), though sometimes they do touch (pl. 1: l. 4 *exigens*; pl. 2: l. 8 *operaretur*).

f. This letter has two forms visible on these folios, a thin form whose vertical descender appears to be written in a single stroke from top to bottom (pl. 1: l. 1 *fraudulentia*, l. 21 *affectu*; pl. 2: l. 2 *perfectio*, l. 24 *efficiuntur*), and a thick form whose descender is made in two strokes, overlapping or slightly apart (pl. 1: l. 5 *fuisse*, l. 13

1 Derolez, *The Palaeography of Gothic Manuscript Books*, 163.

2 Cfr ibid., 145 fig. 21.

3 Ibid., 145, fig. 22–4.

fit, l. 15 *manifestat*; pl. 2: l. 5 *frustra*). Sometimes it is hard to distinguish the two (pl. 1: l. 13 *fidelibus*, l. 24 *finem*; pl. 2: l. 33 *facere*). In either case the letter is written vertically, without a notable slant, and with a pointed descender. The crossbar begins low, near the baseline, but tends to join with the next letter at the headline. In A's hand **f** tends to be a large spacious letter, and stands out in the overall mise-en-page.

g. The letter **g**, on these folios at least, is completely regular (pl. 1: l. 1 *negotiatione*).[4] It appears to be traced in two strokes, the first forming the tail in a clockwise direction, the second, again clockwise, forming the lobe and joining with the following letter (pl. 1: l. 32 *-garite*; pl. 2: l. 38 *cogit*). Sometimes the loop comes up high enough to touch the lobe, which may also descend somewhat in a leaf-shape reminiscent of flat **a** (pl. 1: l. 7 *genus*, l. 32 *genera*; pl. 2: l. 41 *Egestatem*, l. 44 *negligentur*). There is a doubled **g**, abbreviating *Gregorius*, where the second **g** is much smaller than the first (pl. 1: l. 30; cfr. pl. 2: l. 27 *suggerit*).

h. The letter **h** has a looped form which acquires its loop from a counter-clockwise stroke, which can be joined with the preceding letter or not (pl. 1: l. 11 *inchoando*, l. 12 *homini*; pl. 2: l. 6 *nichil*, l. 19 *homo*). The loopless form has a straight vertical back (pl. 1: l. 7 *habere*, l. 12 *hic*; pl. 2: l. 18 *hoc*). The lower portions of the letter are as a rule identical in the two forms: the bulb is formed with a clockwise stroke, which descends down and to the left and terminates in a point or hairline (pl. 1: l. 9 *honesta*, l. 30 *hinc*). Sometimes the descender is extended to greater length (pl. 1: l. 5 *dauith*; pl. 2: l. 22 *nichil*). Biting sometimes occurs with a following round letter, like **o** (pl. 1: l. 32 *honores*). The scribe A has a habit of inserting unclassical **h** following **c**, as in *locha* (pl. 1: l. 20) for classical Latin *loca*.

i. The short form of **i** is a simple downstroke or minim, whose angle changes depending on the speed of writing and the letters joined to it (pl. 1: l. 1 *in*, *uenditione*, *negotiatione*, l. 11 *inchoando*). The long form descends below the line, terminates in a point, and is used regularly in final position (pl. 1: l. 2 *cognoui*, *domini*, l. 4 *negotiari*, l. 26 *domini*; pl. 2: l. 41–2 *lanificii et linificii*) and following another **i** (pl. 2: l. 16 *hiis*). Either form is usually undotted but occasionally dotted, perhaps to avoid minim-confusion with nearby letters, though without consistency (compare pl. 1: l. 3 *dicat*, *Negotiamini*, *uenio*, l. 31 *Nil uilius*, l. 32 *diuitie*). Sometimes indeed minims, particularly in the combination **ui**, are indistinguishable (pl. 1: l. 5 *increpauit*, *peccuniam*; pl. 2: l. 25 *inde efficiuntur*).

k. The letter **k** does not occur on these folios.

l. The looped form of **l** is written counter-clockwise, like a looped **b** whose lobe is not completed (pl. 1: l. 1 *fraudulentia*, l. 30 *uoluntati*; pl. 2: l. 3 *substantialis*). The loop can be narrow or wide and triangular (pl. 1: l. 3 *loquens*, l. 10 *temporalis*). The unlooped form is a simple downstroke, joining with the next letter from the baseline (pl. 1: l. 3 *lu.*, l. 10 *solius*; pl. 2: l. 3 *cuiuslibe*), or simply standing on the baseline (pl. 1: l. 30

4 Cfr ibid., 146 fig. 33.

gloriam, l. 31 *Nil*). It can begin with a connecting stroke from the preceding letter, yet receive no loop (pl. 1: l. 11 *spirituali, saluator, Simile*, l. 31 *uilius*; pl. 2: l.3 *rationalis*).

m. The normal form is a typical *cursiva* **m**, apparently formed in a single stroke (pl. 1: l. 2 *memorabor*, l. 8 *mundialis*; pl. 2: l. 41 *manus remissa*).[5] It need not join with the preceding letter, but usually joins with the following one (pl. 1: l. 3 *Negotiamini*). Its third minim is not usually lengthened in final position, which permits distinction from long-**i** (pl. 1: l. 30 *tantum*). The alternate form in final position is the sideways 3-shaped **m**, very frequent (pl. 1: l. 4 *rationem*, l. 5 *peccuniam*; pl. 2: l. 11 *delectationem mentalem*, l. 19 *summum*, l. 25 *Cum*).[6]

n. The one form of **n** is two minims written in a single stroke; the lines are usually not parallel but slope at different angles (pl. 1: l. 1 *emptione, uenditione, negotiatione*; pl. 2: l. 4 *manifestatur*). The letter is sometimes, but not always, joined with the letters on either side (pl. 1: l. 2 *non, cognoui*).

o. There is a single form of **o**: a circle written with a counter-clockwise stroke, often slightly open at the top (pl. 1: l. 1 *emptione, uenditione, negotiatione*, l. 2 *non*, l. 5 *eo*; pl. 2: l. 2 *perfectio*). When joined with the following letter, it is more likely to be closed at the top (pl. 1: l. 3 *loquens*, l. 32 *pretiosior omnibus*). Biting in the combination **bo** has already been mentioned (pl. 1: l. 2 *introibo, memorabor*, l. 3 *parabola*).

p. The letter is completely regular, and is executed with a standard cursive ductus in one stroke: starting at the headline, drawing the descender, then forming the lobe with a clockwise loop ending at the baseline (pl. 1: l. 1 *emptione*, l. 2 *potentias*, l. 3 *parabola*, l. 5 *increpauit*, l. 10 *permittenda*, l. 31 *possidetur*; pl. 2: l. 2 *opus, operationem, uesperam, psalm., perfectio*, l. 13 *pane*).[7] There is often a gap at the headline between the top of the descender and the top of the lobe. The descender is not typically very pointed, and is vertical.

q. There is one form for **q**, written in a single stroke: first, a probably counter-clockwise curve for the lobe, then a straight descender (pl. 1: l. 1 *que*, l. 4 *qua*, l. 32 *que*). The **q** can be joined with the following letter by drawing the pen upwards from the point of the descender (pl. 1: l. 4 *quem*). The lobe of **q** exhibits the same potential for flattening as **a** (pl. 1: l. 3 *loquens*, l. 32 *quia*; pl. 2: l. 5 *que, aliquid*).

r. The letter **r** has a standard form, but within this form it shows some diversity. The most typical form is a basically *textualis* **r**, written, seemingly, in two strokes: the first a minim forming the body of the letter, the second beginning towards the middle of the minim and moving up and to the right, with a clockwise hook at the end (pl. 1: l. 3 *parabola, tra-*, l. 4 *reperit*, l. 5 *dure*, l. 6 *intraret*, l. 31 *regione*; pl. 2: l. 3 *rationalis*).[8] When it joins with the next letter, which is usual, the connecting stroke begins at the foot of the **r**. An unjoined **r** exhibits this *textualis* form best (pl. 1: l. 7

5 Ibid., 148 fig. 42.
6 Cfr ibid., 148 fig. 47.
7 Ibid., 148 fig. 48.
8 Cfr ibid., 149 fig. 57.

recte). This form can even appear to have a serif on the baseline (pl. 1: l. 4 *negotiari*, l. 9 *spiritualis*, l. 32 *-garite*; pl. 2: l. 2 *Prima*).[9] Sometimes the second stroke begins high, near or at the headline (pl. 1: l. 2 *introibo*, l. 4 *rationem*; pl. 2: l. 14 *procures*). A 2- or z-shaped **r** follows round letters, especially **o** (pl. 1: l. 2 *memorabor*, l. 10 *temporalis*, l. 32 *honores*, *pretiosior*; pl. 2: l. 3 *forma*, l. 6 *commentator*, *aufert*).

s. The hand A's letter **s** shows some departures from a typical *cursiva* script. For one, the round **s** form is infrequent except as an initial majuscule (pl. 1: l. 3 *Sed*, l. 16 *Sic*; pl. 2: l. 3 *Secunda*, l. 28 *Sicut*). Contrary to a typical *cursiva* – "straight **s** in final position does not occur, or at least is definitely exceptional"[10] – the hand A regularly uses straight **s** in final position (pl. 1: l. 2 *potentias*, l. 3 *dominus*, *loquens*, l. 4 *exigens*, *eis*, l. 6 *dicens*; pl. 2: l. 7 *operationes*, *essentias*, *felicitas*, l. 28 *nostris*); contrast this with the round **s** in final position in one marginal addition (pl. 1: l. 2 *Psalm. 70*, cfr. l. 1 *Ps.*). The straight **s** in final position sometimes ends with a tail coming to the left off of the descender (pl. 1: l. 7 *negotiationis*, l. 8 *mundialis*, 9 *spiritualis*, l. 10 *temporalis*, l. 33 *sapiens*; pl. 2: l. 3 *rationalis*, l. 12 *eis*).[11] The more regular straight **s** simply ends in a point, without a tail (pl. 1: l. 6 *suum*, l. 9 *spiritualis*, l. 11 *secunda*, l. 30 *scilicet*; pl. 2: l. 2 *suum*). The vertical stroke of **s** exhibits the same variations as **f**: a thin form, and a fat form whose two strokes are often separated (pl. 1: l. 1 *seu*, l. 8 *scelesta*, l. 9 *honesta*, l. 10 *modesta*, l. 30 *sue*, l. 32 *pretiosior*; pl. 2: l. 3 *suam usque*, *psalm.*). The form does not change when doubled; in double-**s** one sees especially clearly the very vertical angle (pl. 1: l. 4 *posset*, l. 5 *fuisse*). There is a ligature in **st** (pl. 1: l. 2 *iustitie*, l. 5 *abstulit*, l. 32 *sunt*) and **se** (pl. 1: l. 6 *se*).

t. The letter **t** has one form, very simple: a vertical stroke which begins above the headline, often joined with the preceding letter, crossed by a horizontal stroke at the headline, often joined with the following letter. Sometimes **t** is written quite straight (pl. 1: l. 1 *fraudulentia*, *emptione*; pl. 2: l. 13 *uita*), sometimes curved (pl. 1: l. 1 *commictitur*, *uenditione*; pl. 2: l. 13 *ultus tui*).

u. There is no distinction between **u** and **v**; indeed, apart from the occasional majuscule **V** (pl. 1: l. 1 *Vnde*), the form of **u** is invariable. It is formed of two joined minims (pl. 1: l. 1 *fraudulentia*, *uenditione*, l. 3 *dum uenio*, l. 24 *seu*, *iusti*, *spiritualis*, l. 26 *seruis suis*, l. 29 *paruulus*; pl. 2: l. 20 *uirtuale*, *mouente*).

x. The form is typical *cursiva* **x** written in one counter-clockwise stroke, with the curve extending well below the baseline (pl. 1: l. 4 *exigens*, l. 7 *exemplo*, l. 22 *iuxta*; pl. 2: l. 11 *experiendum*, l. 12 *expulsus*).[12] The **x** can be an especially large letter. A possibly two-stroke form is seen occasionally (pl. 1: l. 9 *exercenda*; pl. 2: l. 11 *exinde*).

y. The letter **y** does not occur on plate 1. On plate 2, it appears as a plain undotted letter written in two strokes (pl. 2: l. 20 *ysaeie*, l. 31 *ymaginationem*). Both instances show A replacing a classical initial **i** with **y**.

---

9 Cfr ibid., 150 fig. 63.

10 Ibid., 150.

11 Cfr ibid., 151 fig. 73.

12 Ibid., 152 fig. 84.

z. The letter **z**, in the one place it occurs on these folios, is replaced by the typical Italian **c**-caudata or **c** with cedilla: **ç** (pl. 1: l. 29 *baptiçatus*).

Majuscules

The majuscules of hand A are most easily dealt with by a simple visual summary. Thus also for arabic numerals and abbreviations.

Table 12. Sample majuscules of hand A

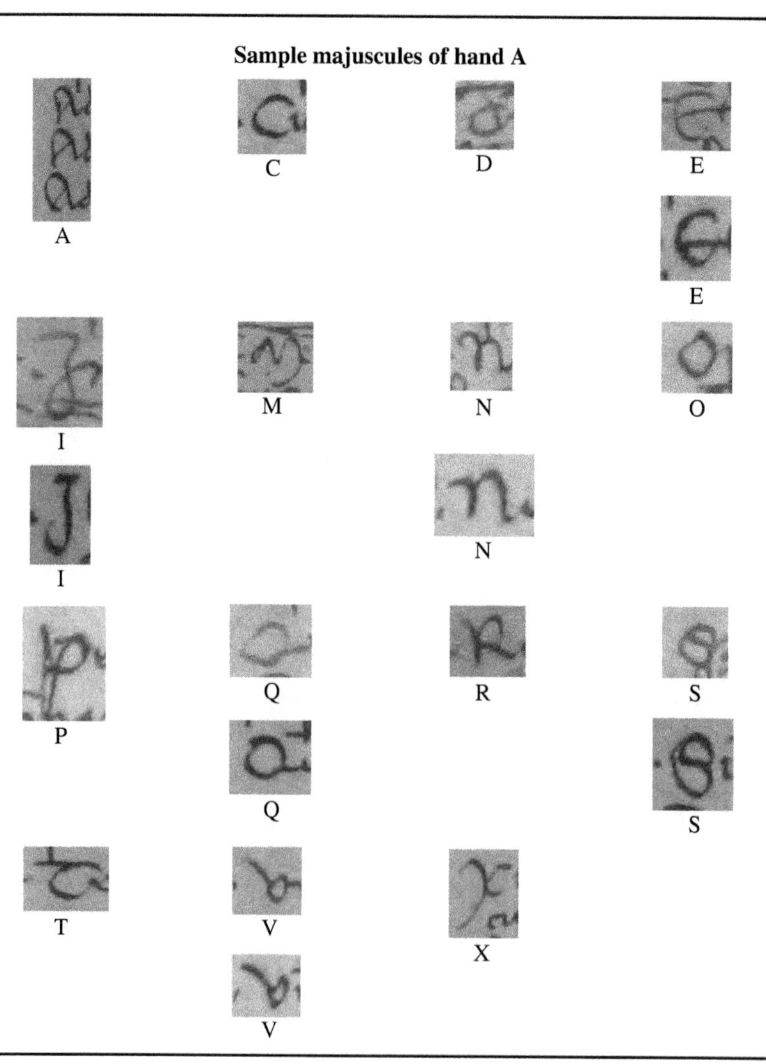

Arabic numerals

Table 13. Sample arabic numerals of hand A

Sample arabic numerals of hand A			
2	3	6	8
2[a]	3[a]		
15	70	83	103
15			

Abbreviations

Table 14. Sample abbreviations of hand A

Sample abbreviations of hand A			
-aliter	-bus	Christus	circa
	-ibus		
com-	de	et	etc
conser-		et	
licet	mer-	oportet	per
propter	-que	qui	quia
quod	-rum	scilicet	secundum
sed	-tur		

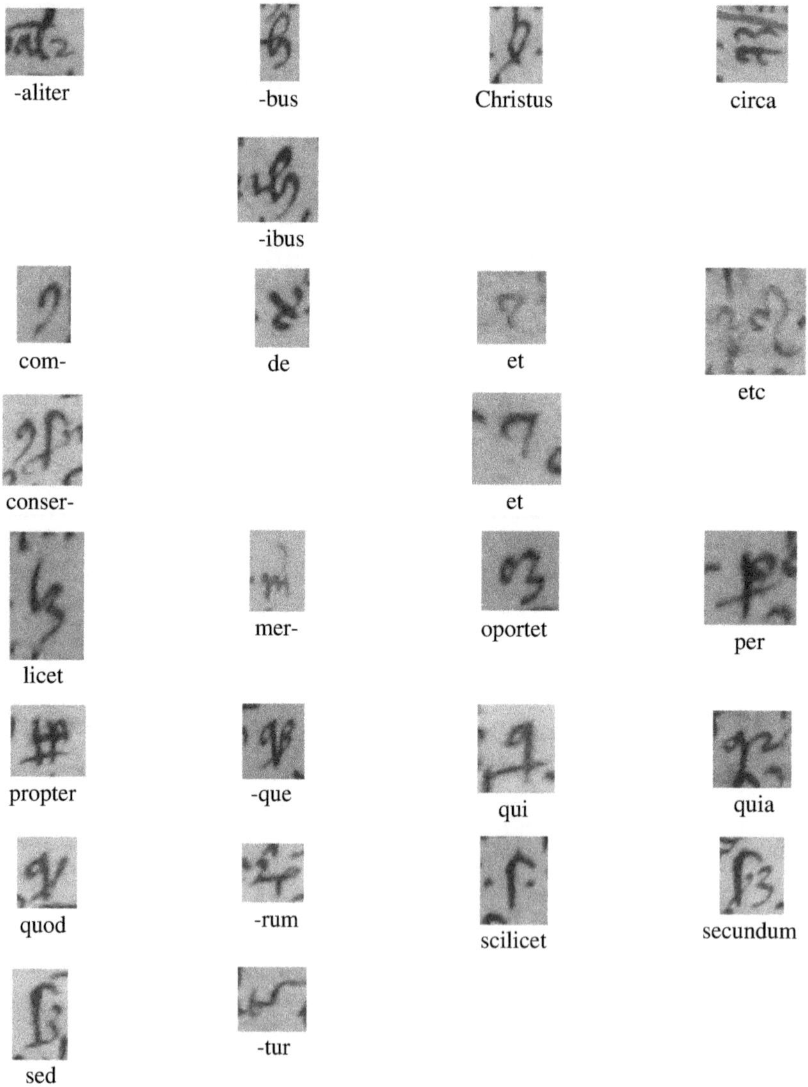

Bibliography

Pre-1600

Manuscript Sources

Alexander de Alexandria (Alexander Lombard). *Tractatus de usuris et de restitutionibus.* Vatican City, Biblioteca Apostolica Vaticana, Vat. lat. 1237, fol. 153–74.

Antoninus Florentinus. *Cronice.* Vol. 1. Florence, Museo di San Marco, Inventario n. 507.

– *Cronice.* Vol. 2. Florence, Museo di San Marco, Inventario n. 508.

– *Cronice.* Vol. 3. Florence, Biblioteca Santa Maria Novella, I.B.55.

– *Quadragesimale "Convertimini."* Florence, BNC, Conv. soppr. A. 8. 1750, fol. 1r–61v.

– *Summa.* Part 1. Florence, Biblioteca Santa Maria Novella, I.B.54. (= *N*)

– *Summa.* Part 2. Florence, Museo di San Marco, Inventario n. 504. (= M_1)

– *Summa.* Part 3, vol. 1. Florence, Museo di San Marco, Inventario n. 505. (= M_2)

– *Summa.* Part 3, vol. 2. Florence, Museo di San Marco, Inventario n. 506. (= M_3)

– *Summa.* Part 4. Florence, Museo di San Marco, Inventario n. 503. (= M_4)

– *Summa.* Part 1. Florence, BNC, Conv. soppr. A. 4. 2555 striscia 78. (= F_1)

– *Summa.* Part 2. Florence, BNC, Conv. soppr. A. 4. 2555 striscia 79. (= F_2)

– *Summa.* Part 3. Florence, BNC, Conv. soppr. A. 4. 2555 striscia 80. (= F_3)

– *Summa Sancti Antonini*: *Summa reverendi patris et domini fratris Antonini de Florentia* .... Florence, BNC, Cod. n. (57) Landau Finaly 68.

Durandus Campanus. *Summa collectionum pro confessionibus audiendis.* Paris, Bibliothèque nationale, lat. 3264.

Gerhardus Odonis. *Tractatus de contractibus.* Siena, Biblioteca Comunale, U.V.8.

Iohannes Chrysostomus. *In Matthaeum homiliae 90, interpretatio latina Iohannis Burgundo Pisani.* Vatican City, Biblioteca Apostolica Vaticana, Vat. lat. 383. https://digi.vatlib.it/mss/detail/2547.

Iohannes de Lignano. *Commentaria in Decretales.* Florence, Biblioteca Medicea-Laurenziana, Edili 54.

Iohannes de Regina (de Neapoli). *Quodlibeta.* Naples, Biblioteca Nazionale, VII.B.28.

Iohannes and Gaspar Calderinus senior. *Repetitiones et distinctiones in Decretales*. Vatican City, Biblioteca Apostolica Vaticana, Vat. lat. 2652.

Petrus de Quesnell. *Directorium iuris in foro conscientiae et iudiciali*. Oxford, Bodleian Library, Canon. Misc. 463.

Printed Sources

Abaelardus Petrus. *Sic et Non: A Critical Edition*. Edited by Blanche B. Boyer and Richard McKeon. Chicago: University of Chicago Press, 1977. http://individual.utoronto.ca/pking/resources/abelard/Sic_et_non.txt.

ALB. M. = Albertus Magnus.

Albertus Magnus. *Albertus Magnus e-Corpus*. Bruno Tremblay, University of Waterloo. Accessed 18 Sept 2017. http://albertusmagnus.uwaterloo.ca/.

– *De animalibus libri XIII–XXVI*. Edited by H. Stadler. Beiträge zur Geschichte der Philosophie des Mittelalters 16. Munster, 1920.

– *Metaphysicorum libri XIII*. Edited by A. Borgnet. Opera omnia 6. Paris, 1890.

– *Tratado sobre a prudência*. Sao Paolo: Editora Paulus, 2018.

ALEX. LOMB. = Alexander de Alexandria (Alexander Lombard). See above, manuscript sources.

AMBR. = Ambrosius Mediolanensis.

ANACL. = Anacletus I.

Annotated Justinian Code. Translated and annotated by Fred H. Blume. Edited by Timothy Kearley. Online hosted by the University of Wyoming. http://www.uwyo.edu/lawlib/blume-justinian/.

ANT. BUTR. = Antonius de Butrio.

ANT. FLOR. = Antoninus Florentinus.

Antoninus Florentinus. *Chroniques de Saint Antonin: Fragments originaux du titre XXII (1378–1459)*. Edited by Raoul Morçay. Paris: Librairie Gabalda, 1913.

– *Confessionale: Defecerunt scrutantes scrutinio. Add: Johannes Chrysostomus: Sermo de poenitentia*. Cologne, 1470.

– "Les 'consilia' de s. Antonin de Florence O.P." Edited by R. Creytens. *Archivum Fratrum Praedicatorum* 37 (1967): 203–342.

– *Divi Antonini Archiepiscopi Florentini … Chronicorum opus in tres partes divisum*. Lyon, 1586.

– *Eximii doctoris b. Antonini archiepiscopi Florentini ordinis praedicatorum Summae sacrae theologiae, iuris pontificii, et Caesarei pars prima[–quarta]* …. 4 vols. Venice: Giunta, 1581–2.

– *Gli autografi di S. Antonino Pierozzi e del B. Angelico nell'atto della separazione del convento di S. Marco in Firenze dal convento di S. Domenico di Fiesole concluso nel iuglio del 1445*. Edited by P. Vincenzo Chiaroni. Florence: Tipografia Giuntina, 1955.

– *Lettere di Sant'Antonino, Arcivescovo di Firenze, precedute dalla sua vita scritta da Vespasiano (da Bisticci) fiorentino*. Edited by T. Corsetti and D. Marchese. Florence: Tipoografia Barbèra, Bianchi e C., 1859.

– *Libellus de audientia confessionum Domini Antonini de Florentia ....* Venice, 1472.
– *Opera a ben vivere con altri suoi ammaestramenti.* Edited by Francesco Palermo. Florence: Cellini, 1858.
– *Sancti Antonini archiepiscopi Florentini ordinis praedicatorum Opera omnia ad autographorum fidem nunc primum exacta, vita illius, variis dissertationibus, et adnotationibus aucta.* Edited by Tommaso Maria Mamachi and Dionisio Remedelli. *Summa* parts 1 and 2 in 4 vols. Florence, 1741–56.
– *Sancti Antonini archiepiscopi Florentini ordinis praedicatorum Summa theologica in quattuor partes distributa ....* Edited by Pietro Ballerini. 4 vols. Verona, 1740. Facsimile reprint with prologue by Innocenzo Colosio. Graz: Akademische Druck- U. Verlagsanstalt, 1959.
– *Summa confessionalis Do. Antonini Archiepiscopi Florentini. Adiecta est tabula, praecipuas huius operis materias, et scitu digniores summatim complectens ....* Lyon: apud Theobaldum Paganum, 1546.
– *Une règle de vie au XVe siècle.* Translated by Thiérard-Baudrillart. Paris, 1921.
Antonius de Butrio. *Commentaria in libros Decretalium.* 4 vols. Venice, 1578; repr. Turin: Bottega d'Erasmo, 1967. http://amesfoundation.law.harvard.edu/digital/AntoniusDeButrio/AntoniusDeButrioMetadata.html.
Archid. = Guido de Baysio (Archidiaconus).
Arist. = Aristoteles.
Aristoteles. *Aristoteles Latinus Database.* Brepolis. Last modified 2016. www.brepolis.net.
– *The Basic Works of Aristotle.* Edited by Richard McKeon. Introduction by C.D.C. Reeve. New York: Modern Library, 2001.
– *De anima (translatio "nova" Guillelmi de Morbeka sive Iacobi Venetici translationis recensio).* AL 12.2. In Thomas de Aquino, *Sententia libri de anima.* Vol. 45.1 of *S. Thomae de Aquino opera omnia.* Rome: Commisio Leonina, 1984.
– *De caelo et mundo (Guillelmus de Morbeka translator Aristotelis).* Edited by F. Bossier. AL 8.2.
– *Ethica Nichomachea (Ethica Nichomachea: translatio Roberti Grosseteste Lincolniensis sive Liber ethicorum recensio pura).* Edited by René-Antoine Gauthier. AL 26.1–3, fasc. 4. Leiden: Brill, 1973.
– *Politica, Libri I–II.11: Translatio imperfecta interprete Guillelmo de Moerbeka(?).* Edited by Pierre Michaud-Quantin. AL 29.1. Bruges and Paris: Desclée de Brouwer, 1961.
Astes. = Astesanus ab Asta.
Astesanus ab Asta. *Summa astensis.* Edited by Giovanni Battista Lamberti. 2 vols. Rome, 1728–30.
– Vol. 1: https://books.google.ca/books?vid=IBNR:CR001137935&redir_esc=y.
– Vol. 2: https://books.google.ca/books?vid=IBNR:CR001137945&redir_esc=y.
Aug. = Augustinus Aurelius.
Augustinus Aurelius. *De genesi ad litteram libri duodecim.* PL 34.
– *De gratia et libero arbitrio liber unus.* PL 44.
– *De trinitate.* PL 42.

– *Enarrationes in Psalmos*. PL 36.
– *Epistolae*. PL 33.
– *In Evangelium Ioannis tractatus centum viginti quatuor*. PL 35.
– *On Grace and Free Will*. Translated by Peter Holmes and Robert Ernest Wallis. Revised by Benjamin B. Warfield. Nicene and Post-Nicene Fathers, 1st ser., vol. 5. Buffalo: Christian Literature Publishing Co., 1887. http://www.newadvent.org/fathers/1510.htm.
– *On the Trinity*. Translated by Arthur West Haddan. Nicene and Post-Nicene Fathers, 1st ser., vol. 3. Buffalo: Christian Literature Publishing Co., 1887. http://www.newadvent.org/fathers/1301.htm.
– *S. Aurelii Augustini opera omnia: editio latina*. Città Nuova Editrice; Nuova Biblioteca Agostiniana. Accessed 18 Sept 2017. http://www.augustinus.it/latino/index.htm.
– *Tractates on the Gospel of John*. Translated by John Gibb. Nicene and Post-Nicene Fathers, 1st ser., vol. 7. Buffalo: Christian Literature Publishing Co., 1888. http://newadvent.org/fathers/1701.htm.

"Autres documents." Edited by Raoul Morçay: Appendix 3-2 in *Saint Antonin* (see below, post-1600), 432–500.

Baldovino de Baldovini. *Vita di S. Antonino*. Edited by Raoul Morçay: Appendix 3-1 in *Saint Antonin* (see below, post-1600), 427–31.

Benedetto Cotrugli. *The Book of the Art of Trade, with Scholarly Essays from Niall Ferguson, Giovanni Favero, Mario Infelise, Tiziano Zanato and Vera Ribaudo*. Edited by Carlo Carraro and Giovanni Favero. Translated by John Francis Phillimore. Cham: Palgrave Macmillan, 2017.
– *Libro de l'arte de La Mercatura*. Edited by Vera Ribaudo. Venice: Edizioni Ca' Foscari, 2016.

Bern. Pap. = Bernardus Papiensis.

Bern. Parm. = Bernardus Parmensis.

Bern. Sen. = Bernardinus Senensis.

Bernardinus Senensis. *Opera omnia*. 9 vols. Quaracchi: Collegio San Bonaventura, 1950–65. Vol. 1: *Quadragesimale de christiana religione (Sermones I–XL)*. 1950. Vol. 4: *Quadragesimale de Evangelio aeterno (Sermones XXVII–LIII)*. 1956.

Bernardus Papiensis. *Summa decretalium*. Edited by Ernst A.T. Laspeyres. Regensburg: Josef Manz, 1860; repr. Graz: Akademische Druck-u. Verlagsanstalt, 1956. https://works.bepress.com/david_freidenreich/13/.

Bernardus Parmensis. *Glossa ordinaria ad Decretales Gregorii IX*. See below, *Corpus iuris canonici cum glossis*.

Biblia Sacra iuxta Vulgatam versionem. Edited by Robert Weber. 4th ed. prepared by Roger Gryson. Stuttgart: Deutsche Bibelgesellschaft, 1994. http://www.drbo.org/drl/index.htm.

Bibliorum sacrorum glossa ordinaria …. 7 vols. Venice, 1603.

"Blessèd city, heavenly Salem." Translated by John Mason Neale. In *The Stories of Hymns: The History behind 100 of Christianity's Greatest Hymns*, edited by George William Rutler, 36–8. Irondale, AL: Sophia Press, 2017.

BOETH. = Boethius (Anicius Manlius Severinus B-).

Boethius. *De differentiis topicis*. PL 64.

Boethius (pseudo). *De disciplina scholarium*. Edited by Olga Weijers. Leiden: Brill, 1976.

Breviarum Romanum ex Decreto Sacrosancti Concilii Tridentini restitutum. Rome, 1568. http://divinumofficium.com/.

CASS. = Cassiodorus Senator.

CHROM. = Chromatius Aquileiensis.

CHRYS. = Iohannes Chrysostomus. See below and also above, manuscript sources.

Clement VII. Bull of canonization *Rationi congruit*. 26 November 1523. In *Bullarium ordinis FF. Praedicatorum*, vol. 4, edited by F. Thomas Ripoll, 417–26. Rome, 1732.

Cod. = *Codex Iustinianus*. See: *Annotated Justinian Code*; *Corpus iuris civilis*; *Roman Law of Sale*.

Coluccio Salutati. "Letter to Giovanni Dominici." In *Humanism and Tyranny: Studies in the Italian Trecento*, by Ephraim Emerton, 341–77. Cambridge, MA: Harvard University Press, 1925.

Corpus iuris canonici. Edited by Emil Friedberg. 2 vols. Leipzig, 1879; repr. Graz: Akademische Druck und Verlaganstalt, 1959.

– Vol. 1: *Decretum magistri Gratiani*. http://geschichte.digitale-sammlungen.de/decretum-gratiani/online/angebot.

– Vol. 2: *Decretalium collectiones*.

Corpus iuris canonici cum glossis. 4 vols. Rome, 1582. http://digital.library.ucla.edu/canonlaw/.

Corpus iuris civilis. Edited by Theodor Mommsen et al. 3 vols. Berlin: Weidmann, 1915–28. Online version hosted by Université de Grenoble. https://droitromain.univ-grenoble-alpes.fr/.

Dante Alighieri. *The Divine Comedy: The Inferno, the Purgatorio, the Paradiso*. Translated by John Ciardi. New York: New American Library, 2003.

Decrees of the Ecumenical Councils. Edited by Norman P. Tanner. 2 vols. Washington, DC, 1990.

Dig. = *Digesta seu pandectae Iustiniani*. See: *Corpus iuris civilis*; *The Digest of Justinian*.

The Digest of Justinian. Edited and translated by Alan Watson et al. Revised ed. 2 vols. Philadelphia: University of Pennsylvania Press, 1998.

DUR. CAMP. = Durandus Campanus. See above, manuscript sources.

Francesco da Castiglione. *Vita Beati Antonini Archiepiscopi Florentini*. In *Acta Sanctorum*, May vol. 1, edited by P.D. Papebroch, 313–25. Antwerp, 1680. Facsimile ed. Brussels: Culture et Civilisation, 1968. http://visualiseur.bnf.fr/CadresFenetre?O=NUMM-6036&I=436&M=pagination.

Gaius. *The Institutes of Gaius*. Edited and translated by Francis de Zulueta. 2 vols. Oxford: Clarendon, 1946.

GAUF. TRAN. = Gaufridus de Trano.

Gaufridus de Trano. *Summa super titulis decretalium*. Lyon, 1519; repr. Aalen, 1968. https://works.bepress.com/david_freidenreich/17/.

Gelas. = Gelasius.

Ger. Odon. = Gerhardus Odonis. See above, manuscript sources.

Giorgio Vasari. *The Lives of the Artists*. Translated by Julia Conaway Bondanella and Peter Bondanella. Oxford World's Classics. Oxford: Oxford University Press, 1998. First published in 1991.

Giovanni Rucellai. *Zibaldone*. Edited by Alessandro Perosa. London, 1960.

Giuliano Lapaccini. *Annalia conventus sancti Marci de Florentia ....* Edited by Raoul Morçay: "La cronaca del convento fiorentino di San Marco: La parte più antica, dettata da Giulano Lapaccini." *Archivio Storico Italiano* 71, no. 1 (1913): 1–29.

Glossa ord. = *Glossa ordinaria*: *Bibliorum sacrorum glossa ordinaria*; *Corpus iuris canonici cum glossis*.

Gratianus. *Concord of Discordant Canons and the Ordinary Gloss*. Translated by Giulio Silano. Toronto: Pontifical Institute of Mediaeval Studies, forthcoming.

Greg. M. = Gregorius Magnus.

Gregorius Magnus. *Moralia in Iob*. PL 75.

– *Morals on the Book of Job*. Translated by J.H. Parker. 3 vols. Oxford, 1844. http://www.lectionarycentral.com/gregorymoraliaindex.html.

– *XL homiliarum in Evangelia*. PL 76.

Guido de Baysio (Archidiaconus). *Rosarium decretorum*. Lyon, 1497.

Guil. Red. = Guillelmus Redonensis. See below, Raymundus de Pennaforti.

Henricus de Segusio (Hostiensis). *In Decretalium libros commentaria*. 4 vols. Venice, 1581. http://amesfoundation.law.harvard.edu/digital/Hostiensis/HostiensisMetadataPrelim.html.

– *Summa aurea*. Venice, 1574. http://web.colby.edu/canonlaw/2009/09/24/liber-extra-decretalists/.

Hier. = Hieronymus Stridonensis.

The Holy Bible: Translated from the Latin Vulgate ... [Douay-Rheims Version]. Edited by Richard Challoner. Baltimore: John Murphy Company, 1899. http://www.drbo.org/drl/index.htm.

Hostien. = Henricus de Segusio (Hostiensis).

Hugo S. Vict. = Hugo de Sancto Victore.

Hugo de Sancto Victore. *In Salomonis Ecclesiastes*. PL 175: 113–256.

Inno. = Innocentius.

Innocentius III. *Die Register Innocenz' III*, edited by O. Hageneder, A. Sommerlechner et al., 13 vols. Graz: Verlag der Österreichischen Akademie der Wissenschaften, 1964–2001.

Innocentius IV. *Commentaria super libros quinque Decretalium*. Frankfurt, 1570. http://web.colby.edu/canonlaw/2009/09/24/liber-extra-decretalists/.

Io. Andr. = Iohannes Andreae.

Io. Dominici = Iohannes Dominici de Florentia.

Io. Lig. = Iohannes de Lignano. See above, manuscript sources.

Io. Reg. = Iohannes de Regina (de Neapoli). See above, manuscript sources.

Io. Scot. = Iohannes Duns Scotus.

Io. et Gasp. Cald. = Iohannes Calderinus et Gaspar Calderinus senior. See above, manuscript sources.

Iohannes Andreae. *Novella in Decretales*. 5 vols. Venice, 1581. http://amesfoundation.law.harvard.edu/digital/JohannesAndreae/JohannesAndreaeMetadata.html.

Iohannes Bodinus. *A Division of All Law: The "Iuris universi distributio" of Jean Bodin*. Translated by Jason Aaron Brown. Edited by Daniel Lee. History and Theory of International Law. Oxford: Oxford University Press, forthcoming.

Iohannes Caroli. *Liber dierum Lucensium*. Edited by Amos Edelheit: *Humanism, Theology, and Spiritual Crisis in Renaissance Florence: Giovanni Caroli's "Liber dierum Lucensium". A Critical Edition, English Translation, Commentary, and Introduction*. Renaissance Society of America 10. Boston: Brill, 2018.

Iohannes Chrysostomus. *Homilies on Matthew*. Translated by George Prevost, revised by M.B. Riddle. Nicene and Post-Nicene Fathers, First Series, 10. Buffalo: Christian Literature Publishing Co., 1888. https://www.newadvent.org/fathers/2001.htm.

Iohannes Dominici de Florentia. *Lucula noctis*. Edited by E. Hunt. Notre Dame: University of Notre Dame Press, 1940.

Iohannes Duns Scotus. *Political and Economic Philosophy: Latin Text and English Translation*. Edited by Allan B. Wolter. St. Bonaventure, NY: Franciscan Institute, 2001.

– *Quaestiones in librum quartum Sententiarum* (*Collationes Oxonienses*). Vol. 18 of *Opera omnia*. Paris: Vives, 1894.

Iustinianus. *The Institutes of Justinian: Text, Translation, and Commentary*. Edited and translated by J.A.C. Thomas. Amsterdam: North-Holland Publishing, 1975.

Lapo Mazzei. *Lettere d'un notaro a un mercante del secolo xiv*. Edited by Cesare Guasti. 2 vols. Florence, 1880.

Laur. Rod. = Laurentius de Rodulphis.

Laurentius de Rodulphis. *Tractatus de usuris*. Edited by Lawrin Armstrong. In *Usury and Public Debt in Early Renaissance Florence: Lorenzo Ridolfi on the "Monte Comune"*. Studies and Texts 144. Toronto: Pontifical Institute of Mediaeval Studies, 2003.

– *Tractatus de usuris*. In *Tractatus universi iuris …* Vol. 7. Venice, 1584. http://listview.lib.harvard.edu/lists/hollis-003538696.

Leonardo di ser Uberto Martini Berti. *Additiones ad Vitam, intra annum decimum a sancti obitu scriptae*. In *Acta Sanctorum* (see above, Francesco da Castiglione), 326–35.

Leon Battista Alberti. *Della famiglia*. In *Opere volgari*, vol. 1, edited by Cecil Grayson. Bari, 1960.

Luca Landucci. *A Florentine Diary from 1450 to 1516 by Luca Landucci continued by an anonymous writer till 1542 with notes by Iodoca del Badia*. Translated by Alice de Rosen Jervis. London: J.M. Dent & Sons; New York: E.P. Dutton, 1927.

Nic. IV = Nicolaus IV.

Nicolaus IV. *Les Registres de Nicolas IV: recueil des bulles de ce pape*. Edited by M. Ernest Langlois. 6 vols, bound in 2. Paris: Bibliothèque des écoles françaises d'Athènes et de Rome, 1886–93.

Nicolaus de Tudeschis (Panormitanus). *Commentaria in Decretales Gregorii IX et in Clementinas epistolas.* 5 vols. Venice, 1583. Reissued on CD-ROM with introduction by Kenneth Pennington: Il Cigno Galileo Galilei Edizioni Informatiche, 2000.

– *Commentaria in quinque Decretalium libros.* 4 vols. Venice, 1570–1. http://amesfoundation.law.harvard.edu/digital/Panormitanus/PanormitanusMetadata.html.

El Octàteuco. Vol. 2 of *La Vetus Latina Hispana.* Edited by Teófilo Ayuso. Madrid, 1967.

Panorm. = Nicolaus de Tudeschis (Panormitanus).

Paolo da Certaldo. "Book of Good Practices." In *Merchant Writers: Florentine Memoirs from the Middle Ages and Renaissance*, edited by Vittore Branca, translated by Murtha Baca, 41–97. Toronto: University of Toronto Press, 2015.

Petr. Abael. = Abaelardus Petrus.

Petr. Lomb. = Petrus Lombardus.

Petr. Olivi = Petrus Iohannis Olivi.

Petr. Pal. = Petrus de Palude.

Petr. Ques. = Petrus de Quesnell. See above, manuscript sources.

Petrus Iohannis Olivi. *Tractatus de contractibus (De emptionibus et venditionibus, de usuris, de restitutionibus).* In *Traité des contrats.*

– *Traité des contrats.* Edited by Sylvain Piron. Paris: Belles Lettres, 2012.

– *A Treatise on Contracts.* Translated by Ryan Thornton and Michael Cusato. St. Bonaventure, NY: Franciscan Institute Publications, 2016.

Petrus Lombardus. *The Sentences.* Translated by Giulio Silano. 4 vols. Medieval Sources in Translation 42, 43, 45, 48. Toronto: Pontifical Institute of Mediaeval Studies, 2007–10.

– *Sententiae in IV libris distinctae.* 3rd ed. 2 vols. Grottaferrata: Editiones Collegii S. Bonaventurae ad Claras Aquas, 1971–81.

Petrus de Palude. *Quartus sententiarum liber.* Paris, 1514.

Pius II. *Commentaries.* Edited by Margaret Meserve and Marcello Simonetta. 2 vols. I Tatti Renaissance Library 12. Cambridge, MA: Harvard University Press, 2007.

Poggio Bracciolini. *De avaricia.* Extracts in *Prosatori latini del Quattrocento*, edited by Eugenio Garin, 248–301. La letteratura italiana, storia e testi 13. Turin: G. Einaudi, 1976.

– *De avaritia (Dialogus contra avaritiam).* Edited by Giuseppe Germano. Livorno: Belforte, 1994.

– *On Avarice.* Translated by Benjamin G. Kohl and Elizabeth B. Welles. In *The Earthly Republic: Italian Humanists on Government and Society*, edited by Benjamin G. Kohl and Ronald G. Witt, 241–89. Philadelphia: University of Pennsylvania Press, 1978.

– *Opera Omnia.* Edited by F. Fubini. 4 vols. Turin, 1964–9.

Psalt. Rom. = *Psalterium Romanum.*

Raym. Penn. = Raymundus de Pennaforti.

Raymundus de Pennaforti. *Summa de paenitentia.* Edited by Xaviero Ochoa and Aloisio Diez. Universa Bibliotheca Iuris, vol. 1B. Rome: Instituto Iuridico Claretiano, 1976.

Raymundus de Pennaforti and Guillelmus Redonensis. *Summa sancti Raymundi de Peniafort … De poenitentia et matrimonio cum glossis Ioannis de Friburgo* (recte *Guillelmi Redonensis*). Rome, 1603.

Roberto Ubaldini da Gagliano. *Analecta ex summario Processuum impresso*. In *Acta Sanctorum* (see above, Francesco da Castiglione), 335–58.

Robertus Bellarminus. *The Eternal Happiness of the Saints*. Translated by John Dalton. London: Richardson and Son, 1847.

The Roman Law of Sale: Introduction and Select Texts. Edited and translated by Francis de Zulueta. Oxford: Clarendon, 1945.

SEN. = Seneca (Lucius Annaeus S-).

Seneca. *Moral Epistles*. Translated by Richard M. Gummere. Loeb Classical Library 75–7. 3 vols. Cambridge, MA: Harvard University Press, 1917–25. http://www.stoics.com/books.html.

THOM. AQ. = Thomas de Aquino.

Thomas de Aquino. *Corpus Thomisticum*. Fundación Thomás de Aquino. http://www.corpusthomisticum.org/.

– *New English Translation of St. Thomas Aquinas's Summa Theologiae (Summa Theologica)*. Translated by Alfred J. Freddoso. https://www3.nd.edu/~afreddos/summa-translation/TOC.htm.

– *Questiones disputatae de malo*. Turin, 1953. Accessed: Corpus Thomisticum.

– *Scriptum super libros Sententiarum magistri Petri Lombardi episcopi Parisiensis*. Vol. 1. Edited by P. Mandonnet. Paris: Lethielleux, 1929.

– *Summa theologiae: Latin Text and English Translation, Introductions, Notes, Appendices and Glossaries*. 61 vols. London: Blackfriars, 1964–81. Vol. 4: *Knowledge in God*. Translated by Thomas Gornall (1964); Vol. 18: *Principles of Morality*. Translated by Thomas Gilby (1966); Vol. 24: *The Gifts of the Spirit*. Translated by Edward D. O'Connor (1973); Vol. 38: *Injustice*. Translated by Marcus LeFébure (1975).

– *Summae theologiae pars prima*. Vol. 4–5 of *Opera omnia*. Rome: S.C. Propaganda Fide, 1888–9.

– *Summae theologiae prima secundae*. Vol. 6–7 of *Opera omnia*. Rome: S.C. Propaganda Fide, 1891–2.

– *Summae theologiae secunda secundae*. Vol. 8–10 of *Opera omnia*. Rome: S.C. Propaganda Fide, 1895–9.

– *The Summa Theologica*. Translated by Fathers of the English Dominican Province. 3 vols. New York: Benziger, 1947. http://dhspriory.org/thomas/summa/.

Thomas Waleys Anglicus. *De modo componendi sermones*. In *Artes praedicandi: Contribution à l'histoire de la rhétorique au Moyen Age*, edited by Th.-M. Charland. Publications de l'Institut d'Études Médiévales d'Ottawa 7. Paris-Ottawa, 1936.

VERG. = Vergilius (P. V- Maro).

Vergilius. *Eclogues. Georgics. Aeneid: Books 1–6*. Translated by H.R. Fairclough. Loeb Classical Library 63. Cambridge, MA: Harvard University Press, 1916.

– *Vergili Maronis Opera*. Edited by R.A.B. Mynors. Scriptorum classicorum bibliotheca Oxoniensis. Oxford: Clarendon, 1969.

Vespasiano da Bisticci. "Arcivescovo Antonino, Fiorentino." In *Vite di Uomini illustri del secolo* XV, edited by Ludovico Frati, 1:171–90. 3 vols. Collezione di opere inedite o rare dei primi tre secoli della lingua. Bologna: Romagnoli-dall'Acqua, 1892.

– *The Vespasiano Memoirs: Lives of Illustrious Men of the XV Century*. Translated by William George and Emily Waters. London: Routledge, 1926. Reprint ed. Renaissance Society of America Reprint Texts 7. Toronto: University of Toronto Press, 1997.

Vetus Latina: die Reste der altlateinischen Bibel. Edited by Roger Gryson. Vol. 12, *Esaias.* Freiburg: Verlag Herder, 1987.

Vitae Patrum de vita et verbis seniorum sive Historiae eremiticae libri X .... Edited by Heribert Rosweyde. Antwerp, 1628. Translated by Benedict Baker. http://www.vitae-patrum.org.uk/.

Vulg. = *Biblia Sacra iuxta Vulgatam versionem.*

Post-1600

D'Addario, Arnaldo. "Antonino, Pierozzi, santo." In *Dizionario biografico degli italiani*, edited by Alberto M. Ghisalberti. Rome: Istituto della Enciclopedia italiana, 1960–. Article published in 1961. http://www.treccani.it/enciclopedia/santo-antonino-pierozzi_%28Dizionario-Biografico%29/.

Amanieu, A. "Antonin (saint)." In *Dictionnaire de droit canonique*. Article published in 1935.

Anderson, Justin, and Atria Larson, eds. *Thomas Aquinas and Medieval Canon Law: Historical and Systematic Perspectives*. Turnhout: Brepols, forthcoming.

Andrée, Alexander. *Christopherus Laurentii de Holmis: Sermones, Disputatio in vesperiis et Recommendatio in aula. Academic Sermons and Exercises from the University of Leipzig, 1435–1438. Edition, Translation, and Introduction*. Runica et Mediaevalia, Editiones 4. Stockholm: Stockholm University, 2012.

"Antoninus Florentinus archiep." In *Compendium auctorum latinorum medii aevi (CALMA)*, edited by Michael Lapidge, Silvia Nocentini, Francesco Santi, and Claudio Leonardi. Bottai: SISMEL, Edizioni del Galluzzo, 2000–. Article published in 2001.

Aranci, Gilberto. "I 'confessionali' di s. Antonino Pierozzi e la tradizione catechistica del '400." *Vivens Homo* 3, no. 2 (1992): 273–92.

Armstrong, Lawrin. *The Idea of a Moral Economy: Gerard of Siena on Usury, Restitution, and Prescription*. Toronto Studies in Medieval Law 2. Toronto: University of Toronto Press, 2016.

– *Usury and Public Debt in Early Renaissance Florence: Lorenzo Ridolfi on the "Monte Comune"*. Studies and Texts 144. Toronto: Pontifical Institute of Mediaeval Studies, 2003.

– "Usury, Conscience, and Public Debt: Angelo Corbinelli's Testament of 1419." In *A Renaissance of Conflicts: Visions and Revisions of Law and Society in Italy and Spain*, edited by John A. Marino and Thomas Kuehn, 173–240. Toronto: Centre for Reformation and Renaissance Studies, 2004.

Aston, T.H., and C.H.E. Philpin, eds. *The Brenner Debate: Agrarian Class Structure and Economic Development in Pre-Industrial Europe*. Past and Present Publications. Cambridge: Cambridge University Press, 1985.

Baldwin, John W. "The Medieval Theories of the Just Price: Romanists, Canonists, and Theologians in the Twelfth and Thirteenth Centuries." *Transactions of the American Philosophical Society*, n.s., 49, no. 4 (1 January 1959): 1–92.

Baloup, Daniel. "Hermits of Saint Augustine, Order of." In Vauchez, *Encyclopedia of the Middle Ages*.

Balserak, Jon. "Review: Representing Avarice in Late Renaissance France by Jonathan Patterson." *Sixteenth Century Journal* 47, no. 4 (2016): 1076–8.

Baron, Hans. "Franciscan Poverty and Civic Wealth as Factors in the Rise of Humanistic Thought." *Speculum* 13 (1938): 1–37.

Barone, Giulia. "Conclusioni: Antonino Pierozzi, un vescovo esemplare." In Cinelli and Paoli, *Antonino Pierozzi*, 649–54.

Bazzichi, Oreste. "Antonino da Firenze." In *Il contributo italiano alla storia del Pensiero – Economia*. Rome: Treccani, 2012. http://www.treccani.it/enciclopedia/antonino-da-firenze_%28Il-Contributo-italiano-alla-storia-del-Pensiero:-Economia%29/.

Beattie, Blake. "A Lawyer's Florilegium: Gratian's *Decretum* in a Sermon from Fourteenth-Century Avignon." In *From Learning to Love: Schools, Law, and Pastoral Care in the Middle Ages: Essays in Honour of Joseph W. Goering*, edited by Tristan Sharp with Isabelle Cochelin, Greti Dinkova-Bruun, Abigail Firey, and Giulio Silano, 249–65. Papers in Mediaeval Studies 29. Toronto: Pontifical Institute of Mediaeval Studies, 2017.

Bec, Christian. *Les marchands écrivains: Affaires et humanisme à Florence, 1375–1434*. Paris: Mouton, 1967.

Beckert, Sven. *Empire of Cotton: A Global History*. New York: Vintage Books, 2015.

Berger, Adolf. *Encyclopedic Dictionary of Roman Law*. Transactions of the American Philosophical Society, n.s., 43, pt. 2. Philadelphia: American Philosophical Society, 1953.

Berlioz, Jacques. "Stephen of Bourbon." In Vauchez, *Encyclopedia of the Middle Ages*.

Bibliotheca Scriptorum Latinorum Medii Recentiorisque Aevi. Edited by Roberto Gamberini. Florence: SISMEL, Edizioni del Galluzzo, 2003. http://www.mirabileweb.it/ricerca_avanzata.aspx?cpage=ASP.ricerca_semplice_aspx.pinfo.

Bjork, Robert E. *The Oxford Dictionary of the Middle Ages*. Oxford: Oxford University Press, 2010.

Black, Christopher. *Church, Religion, and Society in Early Modern Italy*. New York: Palgrave Macmillan, 2004.

Bornstein, Daniel E. *The Bianchi of 1399: Popular Devotion in Late Medieval Italy*. Ithaca: Cornell University Press, 1993.

Boyle, Leonard E. *Pastoral Care, Clerical Education and Canon Law, 1200–1400*. London: Variorum Reprints, 1981.

– *The Setting of the* Summa theologiae *of Saint Thomas*. Etienne Gilson Series 5. Toronto: Pontifical Institute of Mediaeval Studies, 1982.

Brady, I.C., and J.E. Gurr. "Scholasticism." In *New Catholic Encyclopedia*, 2nd ed.

Braudel, Fernand. *Civilization and Capitalism, 15th–18th Century*. Vol. 2, *The Wheels of Commerce*, translated by Siân Reynolds. New York: Harper & Row, 1969.

Brentano, Lujo. *Der wirtschaftende Mensch in der Geschichte*. Leipzig, 1923.

Briquet, Charles-Moïse. *Les filigranes, dictionnaire historique des marques du papier jusqu'en 1660: a facsimile of the 1907 edition with supplementary material contributed by a number of scholars*. Edited by Allan Stevenson. 4 vols. Amsterdam: Paper Publications Society, 1968.

Brodrick, James. *Robert Bellarmine: Saint and Scholar*. Westminster, MD: Newman, 1961.

Brucker, Gene. *Florence: The Golden Age, 1138–1737*. Berkeley: University of California Press, 1998.

– *Giovanni and Lusanna: Love and Marriage in Renaissance Florence*. Berkeley: University of California Press, 1986.

– *Renaissance Florence*. 2nd ed. Berkeley: University of California Press, 1983. First published in 1969. http://hdl.handle.net.myaccess.library.utoronto.ca/2027/heb.02002.0001.001.

Brundage, James. "*Ius fori* and *Ius poli*: The Juridification of Classical Canon Law." In *On the Shoulders of Giants: Essays in Honor of Glenn Olsen*, edited by David F. Appleby and Teresa Olsen Pierre, 116–32. Papers in Mediaeval Studies 27. Toronto: Pontifical Institute of Mediaeval Studies, 2015.

– *Medieval Canon Law*. London: Longman/Routledge, 1995. https://www-taylorfrancis-com.myaccess.library.utoronto.ca/books/9781317895343.

– *The Medieval Origins of the Legal Profession: Canonists, Civilians, and Courts*. Chicago: University of Chicago Press, 2008.

Bryson, William H. *Dictionary of Sigla and Abbreviations to and in Law Books before 1607*. Charlottesville: University Press of Virginia, 1975.

Burckhardt, Jacob. *The Civilization of the Renaissance in Italy*. Translated by S.G.C. Middlemore. London, 1898. First published in 1860.

Butler, Alban. "St. Antoninus (May 10)." In *The Lives of the Fathers, Martyrs and Other Principal Saints*, edited by F.C. Husenbeth. 4 vols. London: Virtue, 1926–8.

Caferro, William. "Florence." In *The Oxford Encyclopedia of Economic History*, edited by Joel Mokyr. Oxford: Oxford University Press, 2003.

– "Premodern European Capitalism, Christianity, and Florence." *Business History Review* 94, no. 1 (2020): 39–72. https://doi.org/10.1017/S0007680520000045.

– "Tommaso Spinelli: The Soul of a Banker." *Journal of the Historical Society* 8, no. 2 (2008): 303–22.

Calzolai, Carlo Celso. *Frate Antonino Pierozzi dei domenicani, arcivescovo di Firenze*. Rome–Padua–Naples: Ars Graphica Editorialis Presbyterum, 1961.

Calzolari, Silvio, and Nino Giordano. *Antonino Pierozzi: un santo domenicano nella Firenze del Quattrocento*. Florence: Edizioni Polistampa, 2017.

Carmichael, Ann G. *Plague and the Poor in Renaissance Florence*. Cambridge History of Medicine. Cambridge: Cambridge University Press, 1986.

Cennini, Cennino. *Il Libro dell'Arte, o Trattato della Pittura*. Edited by Gaetano and Carlo Milanesi. Florence, 1859.

– *The Craftsman's Handbook: The Italian "Il Libro dell'Arte."* Translated by Daniel V. Thompson, Jr. New York: Dover, 1960.

Cessario, Romanus. *Introduction to Moral Theology*. Catholic Moral Thought 1. Washington, DC: Catholic University of America Press, 2001.

Cherubini, Paolo, and Alessandro Pratesi. *Palaeografia Latina: Tavole*. Littera Antiqua 10. Vatican City: Scuola Vaticana di Paleografia, Diplomatica e Archivistica, 2004.

Cinelli, Luciano, and Maria Pia Paoli, eds. *Antonino Pierozzi OP (1389–1459): La figura e l'opera di un santo arcivescovo nell'Europa del Quattrocento; Atti del Convegno internazionale di studi storici (Firenze, 25–28 novembre 2009)*. Memorie Domenicane, n.s., 43. Florence: Nerbini, 2012.

Clanchy, M.T. *From Memory to Written Record: England 1066–1307*. Cambridge, MA: Harvard University Press, 1979.

Clarence Smith, J.A. *Medieval Law Teachers and Writers: Civilian and Canonist*. Monographies juridiques 9. Ottawa: University of Ottawa Press, 1975.

Codex iuris canonici Pii X Pontificis Maximi iussu digestus, Benedicti Papae XV auctoritate promulgatus. Edited by Pietro Gasparri. New York: P.J. Kenedy & Sons, 1918.

Cohn, Samuel. "Florence (Firenze)." In Bjork, *Oxford Dictionary of the Middle Ages*.

Colosio, Innocenzo. "Prologus in novam editionem." In Antoninus Florentinus, *Sancti Antonini … Summa theologica* (see above, pre-1600 printed sources), 1:vii–x.

Comitato per le onoranze a S. Antonino nel 5. centenario della morte. *Settimana di studio sulla vita e le opere di S. Antonino Pierozzi: Firenze, 18–20 marzo 1960, Convento di S. Marco*. Florence: Giovacchini, 1960.

Cornelison, Sally J. *Art and the Relic Cult of St. Antoninus in Renaissance Florence*. Burlington, VT: Ashgate, 2012. See esp. ch. 1, "The Humblest of Men."

– "Tales of Two Bishop Saints: Zenobius and Antoninus in Florentine Renaissance Art and History." *Sixteenth Century Journal* 38, no. 3 (2007): 627–56.

"Coronati, Quattro Santi." In *The Oxford Dictionary of Christian Art and Architecture*, edited by Tom D. Jones, Linda Murray, and Peter Murray. 2nd ed. Oxford: Oxford University Press, 2013.

Crabb, Ann. *The Merchant of Prato's Wife: Margherita Datini and Her World, 1360–1423*. Ann Arbor: University of Michigan Press, 2015.

Cremona, Diego. *Carità e "interesse" in s. Antonino da Firenze (15o secolo). Il precapitalismo nella dottrina "De usura" di un economista santo*. Empoli: Aleph, 1991.

Creytens, R. "Les cas de conscience soumis à S. Antonin de Florence par Dominique de Catalogne, O.P." *Archivum Fratrum Praedicatorum* 28 (1958): 149–220.

Curran, Charles E. *Catholic Moral Theology in the United States: A History*. Washington, DC: Georgetown University Press, 2008.

Dahl, Gunnar. *Trade, Trust, and Networks: Commercial Culture in Late Medieval Italy*. Lund: Nordic Academic Press, 1998.

Davis, Henry. *Moral and Pastoral Theology*. 4th ed. 4 vols. London: Sheed and Ward, 1943.

Davis, James. "Economic History." *Oxford Bibliographies*. Online. Oxford University Press, last updated 25 June 2013.

– *Medieval Market Morality: Life, Law and Ethics in the English Marketplace, 1200–1500*. Cambridge: Cambridge University Press, 2012.

Debby, Nirit Ben-Aryeh. *Renaissance Florence in the Rhetoric of Two Popular Preachers: Giovanni Dominici (1356–1419) and Bernardino Da Siena (1380–1444)*. Late Medieval and Early Modern Studies 4. Turnhout: Brepols, 2001.

Decock, Wim. *Theologians and Contract Law: The Moral Transformation of the "Ius commune"*. Legal History Library vol. 9, Studies in the History of Private Law 4. Leiden: Nijhoff, 2013.

Deferrari, Roy J., and M. Inviolata Barry. *A Lexicon of St. Thomas Aquinas Based on the "Summa Theologica" and Selected Passages of His Other Works*. Washington, DC: Catholic University of America Press, 1948.

Delcorno, Pietro. "'Quomodo Discet Sine Docente?' Observant Efforts towards Education and Pastoral Care." In Roest and Mixson, *Companion to Observant Reform*, 145–84.

Derbes, Anne, and Mark Sandona. *The Usurer's Heart: Giotto, Enrico Scrovegni, and the Arena Chapel in Padua*. University Park: Pennsylvania State University Press, 2008.

Derolez, Albert. *The Palaeography of Gothic Manuscript Books: From the Twelfth to the Early Sixteenth Century*. Cambridge: Cambridge University Press, 2003.

de Roover, Raymond. "The Concept of the Just Price: Theory and Economic Policy." *Journal of Economic History* 18, no. 4 (1 December 1958): 418–34.

– "Monopoly Theory prior to Adam Smith: A Revision." In *Business, Banking, and Economic Thought in Late Medieval and Early Modern Europe: Selected Studies of Raymond de Roover*, edited by Julius Kirshner. Chicago: University of Chicago Press, 1974.

– "The Organization of Trade." In *Cambridge Economic History of Europe*, edited by M.M. Postan and E.E. Rich, vol. 3, *Economic Organization and Policies in the Middle Ages*, 42–118. Cambridge: Cambridge University Press, 1963.

– *The Rise and Decline of the Medici Bank, 1397–1494*. Cambridge, MA: Harvard University Press, 1963.

– *San Bernardino of Siena and Sant'Antonino of Florence: The Two Great Economic Thinkers of the Middle Ages*. Kress Library of Business and Economics 19. Cambridge, MA: Harvard University Press, 1967.

– "The Story of the Alberti Company of Florence, 1302–1348, As Revealed in Its Account Books." *Business History Review* 32, no. 1 (1958): 14–59.

Dessì, Rosa Maria. "John Dominici." In Vauchez, *Encyclopedia of the Middle Ages*.

Destrez, Jean. *La pecia dans les manuscrits universitaires du XIIIe et du XIVe siècle*. Paris: Éditions Jacques Vautrain, 1935.

Dictionnaire de droit canonique: contenant tous les termes du droit canonique avec un sommaire de l'histoire et des institutions et de l'état actuel de la discipline. Edited by R. Naz. Paris: Letouzey et Ané, 1935–65.

Dictionnaire d'histoire et de géographie ecclésiastiques. Paris: Letouzey et Ané, 1912–.

Dictionnaire de théologie catholique. Edited by A. Vacant and E. Mangenot. 15 vols. Paris: Letouzey et Ané, 1908–.

Dizionario biografico degli italiani. Edited by Alberto M. Ghisalberti. Rome: Istituto della Enciclopedia italiana, 1960–.

Dondaine, Antoine. *Secrétaires de Saint Thomas.* Rome: Commissio Leonina, 1956.

Drapeau, Thierry. "Review: Empire of Cotton by Sven Beckert." *Labour/Le Travail* 77 (Spring 2016): 329–31.

Du Cange et al. *Glossarium mediae et infimae latinitatis.* Niort: L. Favre, 1883–7.

du Plessis, Paul. *Borkowski's Textbook on Roman Law.* 5th ed. Oxford: Oxford University Press, 2015.

Edelheit, Amos. "A Discussion of Conscience, Cognition and Will." Ch. 4 in *Scholastic Florence: Moral Psychology in the Quattrocento*, 97–137. Brill's Studies in Intellectual History 230. Leiden–Boston: Brill, 2014. https://doi-org.myaccess.library.utoronto.ca/10.1163/9789004266285.

– "Introduction." In *Humanism, Theology, and Spiritual Crisis in Renaissance Florence: Giovanni Caroli's "Liber dierum Lucensium". A Critical Edition, English Translation, Commentary, and Introduction*, 1–44. Renaissance Society of America 10. Boston: Brill, 2018.

Edler (de Roover), Florence. *Glossary of Mediaeval Terms of Business: Italian Series 1200–1600.* Cambridge, MA: Mediaeval Academy of America, 1934.

Encyclopedia of Renaissance Philosophy, ed. Marco Sgarbi, living ed. (Springer, 2016–)

Faibisoff, Leah. "Chancery Officials and the Business of Communal Administration in Republican Florence: Ventura and Niccolò Monachi, Chancellors of Florence (1340–48/1348–75)." PhD diss., University of Toronto, 2018.

Fanfani, Amintore. *Catholicism, Protestantism and Capitalism.* New York: Sheed and Ward, 1935.

Field, Arthur. *The Intellectual Struggle for Florence: Humanists and the Beginning of the Medici Regime, 1420–1440.* Oxford: Oxford University Press, 2017.

Finucane, Ronald C. "The Reforming Friar-Archbishop: Antoninus of Florence (1389–1459, cd. 1523)." In *Contested Canonizations: The Last Medieval Saints, 1482–1523*, 167–206. Washington, DC: Catholic University of America Press, 2011.

Ford, John C., and Gerald Kelly. *Contemporary Moral Theology.* Vol. 1, *Questions in Fundamental Moral Theology.* Baltimore: Mercier, 1958.

Forte, S.L. "Dominici, John, Bl." in *New Catholic Encyclopedia*, 2nd ed., vol. 4, 855–6.

Fredona, Robert. "Review of *Come l'acqua e il sangue* by Giacomo Todeschini." *Business History Review* 96, no. 1 (2022): 208–11.

Fredona, Robert, and Sophus A. Reinert. "Italy and the Origins of Capitalism." *Business History Review* 94, no. 1 (2020): 5–38. https://doi.org/10.1017/S0007680520000057.

Frick, Carole Collier. *Dressing Renaissance Florence: Families, Fortunes, and Fine Clothing.* Baltimore: Johns Hopkins University Press, 2002.

Garin, Eugenio. *L'umanesimo italiano.* 2nd ed. Bari, 1965.

Gaughan, W.T. *Social Theories of Saint Antoninus from His Summa Theologica.* CUA Studies in Sociology 35. Washington, DC: Catholic University of America Press, 1950 [1951].

Gauthier, Albert. *Roman Law and Its Contribution to the Development of Canon Law.* Ottawa: Saint Paul University, 1996.

Germovnik, Francis. *Indices ad Corpus Iuris Canonici.* 2nd ed. Edited by Michaël Thériault. Ottawa: Saint Paul University, 2000.

Ghosh, Shami. "Rural Economies and Transitions to Capitalism: Germany and England Compared (c.1200–c.1800)." *Journal of Agrarian Change* 16, no. 2 (2016): 255–90.

Gilbert, Creighton. "The Archbishop on the Painters of Florence, 1450." *Art Bulletin*, 41 no. 1 (March 1959): 75–87.

Gleeson-White, Jane. *Double Entry: How the Merchants of Venice Created Modern Finance.* New York: Allen & Unwin, 2011.

Goering, Joseph. "The Internal Forum and the Literature of Penance and Confession." Ch. 12 in Hartmann and Pennington, *Medieval Canon Law in the Classical Period.*

Goldthwaite, Richard A. *The Economy of Renaissance Florence.* Baltimore: Johns Hopkins University Press, 2009.

Gordley, James. "*Ius quaerens intellectum*: The Method of the Medieval Civilians." In *The Creation of the Ius Commune: From Casus to Regula*, edited by John W. Cairns and Paul J. du Plessis, 77–101. Edinburgh Studies in Law 7. Edinburgh: Edinburgh University Press, 2010.

– *The Jurists: A Critical History.* Oxford: Oxford University Press, 2013.

Gordon, Barry. *Economic Analysis before Adam Smith: Hesiod to Lessius.* London: Macmillan, 1975.

Grande dizionario della lingua italiana. 21 vols. Turin: Unione tipografico-editrice torinese, 1961–2002. https://www.gdli.it/.

The Grove Encyclopedia of Medieval Art and Architecture. Edited by Colum P. Hourihane. Oxford: Oxford University Press, 2012.

Hartmann, Wilfried, and Kenneth Pennington, eds. *The History of Medieval Canon Law in the Classical Period, 1140–1234: From Gratian to the Decretals of Pope Gregory IX.* History of Medieval Canon Law. Washington, DC: Catholic University of America Press, 2008.

Haydock, George L. *Haydock's Catholic Bible Commentary.* New York: Dunigan and Bro., 1859.

Healy, James. *The Just Wage 1750–1890: A Study of Moralists from Saint Alphonsus to Leo XIII.* The Hague: Martin Nijhoff, 1966.

Heers, Jacques. *La Naissance du capitalisme au Moyen Âge: Changeurs, usuriers et grands financiers.* Paris: Perrin, 2012.

Herlihy, David, and Christiane Klapisch-Zuber. *Tuscans and Their Families: A Study of the Florentine Catasto of 1427.* New Haven: Yale University Press, 1985.

Hinnebusch, W.A., P. Philibert, and R.B. Williams. "Dominicans." In *New Catholic Encyclopedia*, 2nd ed., 848–55.

Holmes, George. *The Florentine Enlightenment 1400–50*. London: Weidenfeld and Nicolson, 1969.

Hoppenbrouwers, P.C.M., and J.L. van Zanden, eds. *Peasants into Farmers? The Transformation of Rural Economy and Society in the Low Countries (Middle Ages–19th Century) in Light of the Brenner Debate*. Turnhout: Brepols, 2001.

Howard, Peter F. "Antonino e la predicazione nella Firenze rinascimentale." In Cinelli and Paoli, *Antonino Pierozzi*, 333–46.

– *Aquinas and Antoninus: A Tale of Two Summae in Renaissance Florence*. Etienne Gilson Series 35. Toronto: Pontifical Institute of Mediaeval Studies, 2013.

– *Beyond the Written Word: Preaching and Theology in the Florence of Archbishop Antoninus, 1427–1459*. Istituto nazionale di studi sul rinascimento, quaderni di rinascimento 28. Florence: Olschki, 1995.

– *Creating Magnificence in Renaissance Florence*. Essays and Studies 29. Toronto: Centre for Reformation and Renaissance Studies, 2012.

– "Pierozzi, Antonino." In *Encyclopedia of Renaissance Philosophy*, edited by Marco Sgarbi. Living Edition. Springer, 2016–. Article published 2017. https://doi-org.myaccess.library.utoronto.ca/10.1007/978-3-319-02848-4_1121-1.

– "'Where the Poor of Christ Are Cherished': Poverty in the Preaching of Antoninus of Florence." In *Poverty and Devotion in Mendicant Cultures 1200–1450*, edited by Constant J. Mews and Anna Welch, 198–209. London: Routledge, 2016.

Huijbers, Anne. "'Observance' as Paradigm in Mendicant and Monastic Order Chronicles." In Roest and Mixson, *Companion to Observant Reform*, 111–43.

Hunt, Edwin S. *The Medieval Super-Companies: A Study of the Peruzzi Company of Florence*. Cambridge: Cambridge University Press, 1994.

Hunt, Edwin S., and James Murray. *A History of Business in Medieval Europe, 1200–1550*. Cambridge Medieval Textbooks. New York: Cambridge University Press, 1999.

Hwang, Alexander Y. "*Vitas* (*vitae*) *patrum*." In Bjork, *Oxford Dictionary of the Middle Ages*.

Ilgner, Carl. *In S. Antonini Archiepiscopi Florentini sententias de Valore et de Pecunia Commentarius*. Breslau: Typis Ephemerides "Schlesische Volkazeitung," 1902.

– *Die volkswirtschaftlichen Anschauungen Antonins von Florenz*. Paderborn, 1904.

Izbicki, Thomas M. "The Origins of the *De ornatu mulierum* of Antoninus of Florence." In *Reform, Ecclesiology, and the Christian Life in the Late Middle Ages*. Variorum Collected Studies Series 893. Aldershot: Ashgate, 2008. Reprinted with original pagination from *MLN* 119, no. 1, suppl. (2004).

Jamison, Daniel. "Fiscal Policy in an Italian Commune: A Study of the Lucchese *Gabella Maggiore*, 1373–1410." PhD diss., University of Toronto, 2017.

Jarrett, Bede. *St. Antonino and Mediaeval Economics*. London: Herder, 1914.

Jedin, Hubert. *Ecumenical Councils of the Catholic Church: An Historical Outline*. Translated by Ernest Graf. New York: Herder and Herder, 1960.

Jordan, Mark D. *Rewritten Theology: Aquinas after His Readers*. Challenges in Contemporary Theology. Oxford: Blackwell, 2006.

Jusztinger, Janos. "The Principle of *Laesio Enormis* in Sale and Purchase Contracts in Roman Law." *Studia iuridica auctoritate universitatis Pecs publicata* 149 (2011): 107–24.

Kaeppeli, Thomas, and Emilio Panella. *Scriptores ordinis praedicatorum medii aevi*. 4 vols. Rome: Istituto Storico Domenicano, 1970–93.

Kaye, Joel. *Economy and Nature in the Fourteenth Century: Money, Market Exchange, and the Emergence of Scientific Thought*. Cambridge: Cambridge University Press, 1998.

Kelly, J.N.D. *The Oxford Dictionary of Popes*. Oxford: Oxford University Press, 1986.

Kelly, J.N.D., and Michael Walsh. *A Dictionary of Popes*. 3rd ed. Oxford: Oxford University Press, 2015.

Kirsch, J.P. "Four Crowned Martyrs." In *The Catholic Encyclopedia*, vol. 6. New York: Robert Appleton, 1909.

Kirshner, Julius. "From Usury to Public Finance: The Ecclesiastical Controversy over the Public Debts of Florence, Genoa, and Venice (1300–1500)." PhD diss., Columbia University, 1970.

Klumpenhouwer, Samuel J. "The *Summa de penitencia* of John of Kent: Study and Critical Edition." PhD diss., University of Toronto, 2018.

Kristeller, Paul Oskar. *Renaissance Thought: The Classic, Scholastic, and Humanistic Strains*. New York: Harper, 1961.

Kuttner, Stephan. "Harmony from Dissonance: An Interpretation of Medieval Canon Law." In *The History of Ideas and Doctrines of Canon Law in the Middle Ages*, 1–16. London: Variorum, 1992.

– "Notes on the Presentation of Text and Apparatus in Editing Works of the Decretists and Decretalists." *Traditio* 15 (1959): 452–64.

Lane, Frederic C. "At the Roots of Republicanism." *American Historical Review* 71, no. 2 (1966): 403–20.

Langholm, Odd. *Economics in the Medieval Schools*. Leiden: Brill, 1992.

– *The Legacy of Scholasticism in Economic Thought: Antecedents of Choice and Power*. Cambridge: Cambridge University Press, 1998.

– "The Medieval Schoolmen (1200–1400)." In Lowry and Gordon, eds., *Ancient and Medieval Economic Ideas and Concepts of Social Justice*, 439–501.

– *The Merchant in the Confessional: Trade and Price in the Pre-Reformation Penitential Handbooks*. Studies in Medieval and Reformation Thought 93. Leiden: Brill, 2003.

– "Monopoly and Market Irregularities in Medieval Economic Thought: Traditions and Texts to A.D. 1500." *Journal of the History of Economic Thought* 28, no. 4 (2006): 395–411.

Latham, R.E., D.R. Howlett, and R.K. Ashdowne, eds. *Dictionary of Medieval Latin from British Sources*. Oxford: British Academy, 1975–2013.

Leinsle, Ulrich G. *Introduction to Scholastic Theology*. Translated by Michael J. Miller. Washington, DC: Catholic University of America Press, 2010.

Leo XIII. *Rerum Novarum: On Capital and Labor.* Encyclical letter, 15 May 1891. https://www.vatican.va/content/leo-xiii/en/encyclicals/documents/hf_l-xiii_enc_15051891_rerum-novarum.html.

Lesnick, Daniel R. *Preaching in Medieval Florence: The Social World of Franciscan and Dominican Spirituality.* Athens: University of Georgia Press, 1989.

Lewis, Charlton T., and Charles Short, eds. *A Latin Dictionary.* Oxford: Clarendon Press, 1879.

Lexikon des Mittelalters. 10 vols. 1977–99.

Little, Lester K. *Religious Poverty and the Profit Economy in Medieval Europe.* London: Cornell University Press, 1978.

Lopez, Robert S. *The Commercial Revolution of the Middle Ages, 950–1350.* Englewood Cliffs, NJ: Prentice-Hall, 1971.

Lowry, Todd S., and Barry Gordon, eds. *Ancient and Medieval Economic Ideas and Concepts of Social Justice.* Leiden: Brill, 1998.

Mahoney, John. *The Making of Moral Theology: A Study of the Roman Catholic Tradition (The Martin d'Arcy Memorial Lectures 1981–2).* Revised ed. Oxford: Clarendon, 1989.

Mandonnet, P. "Antonin (saint)." In *Dictionnaire de théologie catholique,* edited by A. Vacant and E. Mangenot. 15 vols. Paris: Letouzey et Ané, 1908–. Article published in 1909.

Marchetti, Leonardo. "Cronologia della vita e delle opere." In Cinelli and Paoli, *Antonino Pierozzi,* 9–17. Published in 2012.

Marichal, R. "Necrologie: Raoul Morçay." *Humanisme et Renaissance* 6, no. 1 (1939): 83–6.

Martines, Lauro. *The Social World of the Florentine Humanists 1390–1460.* Princeton: Princeton University Press, 1963.

Maurer, Karl. "Commonest Abbreviations, Signs, etc., Used in the Apparatus to a Classical Text." http://udallasclassics.org/maurer_files/APPARATUSABBREVIATIONS.pdf.

McClure, George W. *The Culture of Profession in Late Renaissance Italy.* Toronto: University of Toronto Press, 2004.

McHugh, John A., and Charles J. Callan. *Moral Theology: A Complete Course Based on St. Thomas Aquinas and the Best Modern Authorities.* Revised ed. 2 vols. New York: Joseph F. Wagner, 1958.

Melis, Federigo. *Aspetti della vita economica medievale (Studi nell'Archivio Datini di Prato).* Siena: Olschki, 1962.

– *Documenti per la storia economica dei secoli XIII–XVI.* Florence, 1972.

Michaud-Quantin, Pierre. *Sommes de casuistique et manuels de confession au Moyen Âge (XII–XVI siècles).* Analecta mediaevalia Namurcensia 13. Louvain: Éditions Nauwelaerts, 1962.

Mixson, James. "Introduction." In Roest and Mixson, *Companion to Observant Reform,* 1–20.

– "Observant Reform's Conceptual Frameworks between Principle and Practice." In Roest and Mixson, *Companion to Observant Reform,* 60–84.

Molho, Anthony. "The Italian Renaissance, Made in the USA." In *Imagined Histories: American Historians Interpret the Past,* edited by Anthony Molho and Gordon S. Wood, 263–94. Princeton: Princeton University Press, 2018.

Mormando, Franco. *The Preacher's Demons: Bernardino of Siena and the Social Underworld of Early Renaissance Italy*. Chicago: University of Chicago Press, 1999.

Morçay, Raoul. "Antonin (Saint)." In *Dictionnaire d'histoire et de géographie ecclésiastiques*. Paris: Letouzey et Ané, 1912–. Article published in 1924. http://apps.brepolis.net.myaccess.library.utoronto.ca/DHGE/test/Default2.aspx.

– *Saint Antonin: fondateur du couvent de Saint-Marc, archevêque de Florence, 1389–1459*. Tours: Mame et Fils, 1914.

More, Alison. "Dynamics of Regulation, Innovation, and Invention." In Roest and Mixson, *Companion to Observant Reform*, 85–110.

Mueller, John D. *Redeeming Economics: Rediscovering the Missing Element*. Wilmington, DE: ISI Books, 2010.

Mueller, Reinhold C. *The Venetian Money Market: Banks, Panics, and the Public Debt, 1200–1500*. Baltimore: Johns Hopkins University Press, 1997.

Muessig, Carolyn. "Bernardino da Siena and Observant Preaching as a Vehicle for Religious Transformation." In Roest and Mixson, *Companion to Observant Reform*, 185–203.

Muessig, Carolyn, George Ferzoco, and Beverly Mayne Kienzle, eds. *A Companion to Catherine of Siena*. Brill's Companions to the Christian Tradition 32. Leiden: Brill, 2012.

Mulchahey, M. Michèle. *"First the Bow Is Bent in Study ....": Dominican Education before 1350*. Studies and Texts 132. Toronto: Pontifical Institute of Mediaeval Studies, 1998.

Munro, John H. "The Medieval Origins of the Financial Revolution: Usury, Rentes, and Negotiability." *International History Review* 25, no. 3 (2003): 505–62.

Najemy, John M. *Corporatism and Consensus in Florentine Electoral Politics, 1280–1400*. Chapel Hill: University of North Carolina Press, 1982.

– *A History of Florence 1200–1575*. Malden, MA: Blackwell, 2006.

Neal, Larry, and Jeffrey G. Williamson, eds. *The Cambridge History of Capitalism*. Vol. 1, *The Rise of Capitalism: From Ancient Origins to 1848*. Cambridge: Cambridge University Press, 2014.

New Catholic Encyclopedia. 2nd ed. 15 vols. Detroit: Gale, 2003.

Noonan, John T., Jr. "Review: The Medieval Theories of the Just Price by John W. Baldwin." *Church History* 29, no. 2 (1960): 216.

– *The Scholastic Analysis of Usury*. Cambridge, MA: Harvard University Press, 1957.

Nuccio, Oscar. *La storia del pensiero economico italiano come storia della genesi dello spirito capitalistico*. Rome: LUISS University Press, 2008.

Nussbaum, F.L. "The Economic History of Renaissance Europe: Problems and Solutions during the Past Generation." *Journal of Modern History* 13, no. 4 (1941): 527–45.

Ochoa, Xaverio, and Aloisio Diez. *Index canonum et legum totius Corporis iuris canonici et civilis*. Universa bibliotheca iuris: subsidia 1–2. 2 vols. Rome: Institutum iuridicum Claretanum, 1964–5.

Oppel, John W. "Poggio, San Bernardino of Siena, and the Dialogue on Avarice." *Renaissance Quarterly* 30, no. 4 (1977): 564–87.

Origo, Iris. *The Merchant of Prato: Francesco di Marco Datini*. Harmondsworth: Penguin, 1963.

– *The World of San Bernardino*. New York: Harcourt, Brace & World, 1962.

Orlandi, Stefano. *Bibliografia antoniniana: descrizione dei manoscritti della vita e delle opere di S. Antonino O.P. Arcivescovo di Firenze, e degli studi stampati che lo riguardano*. Vatican City: Tipografia Poliglotta Vaticana, 1961.

– "La canonizzazione di S. Antonino nella relazione di Fra Roberto Ubaldini da Gagliano." *Memorie domenicane* 81 (1964): 85–115, 131–62.

– *S. Antonino, Arcivescovo di Firenze, Dottore della Chiesa: Studi bibliografici*. 2 vols. Florence: Edizioni "Il Rosario," 1959–60. Vol. 1: *La sua famiglia. Gli anni giovanili./I primi cinque anni di episcopato*; Vol. 2: *Il convento di S. Domenico di Fiesole./Gli ultimi otto anni di episcopato*.

The Oxford Classical Dictionary. Edited by Simon Hornblower, Antony Spawforth, and Esther Eidinow. 4th ed. Oxford: Oxford University Press, 2012.

The Oxford Companion to Classical Literature. Edited by M.C. Howatson. Oxford: Oxford University Press, 2011.

The Oxford Dictionary of the Christian Church. Edited by F.L. Cross and E.A. Livingstone. 3rd revised ed. Oxford: Oxford University Press, 2005.

The Oxford Dictionary of the Middle Ages. Edited by Robert E. Bjork. Oxford: Oxford University Press, 2010.

The Oxford Dictionary of the Renaissance. Edited by Gordon Campbell. Oxford: Oxford University Press, 2003.

The Oxford Encyclopedia of Ancient Greece and Rome. Edited by Michael Gagarin. Oxford University Press, 2010.

Oxford English Dictionary Online. Oxford: Oxford University Press. Last modified September 2017. http://www.oed.com/.

Oxford-Paravia Italian Dictionary. 2nd ed. Oxford: Oxford University Press, 2006.

Panella, Emilio. "Catalogo dell'Archivio di S. Maria Novella in Firenze." *Archivum Fratrum Praedicatorum* 70 (2000): 111–242. See esp. entry I.B.54 and I.B.55 (179–80).

Paoli, Maria Pia. "Sant'Antonino 'vere pastor et bonus pastor': storia e mito di un modello." In *Verso Savonarola: Misticismo, profezia, empiti riformistici fra Medioevo ed Età moderna*, edited by Gian Carlo Garfagnini and Giuseppe Picone, 83–139. Florence: Sismel, 1999.

Papi, Anna Venvenuti. "Florence." In Vauchez, *Encyclopedia of the Middle Ages*.

Patterson, Jonathan. *Representing Avarice in Late Renaissance France*. Oxford: Oxford University Press, 2015.

Pennington, Kenneth. "The 'Big Bang': Roman Law in the Early Twelfth Century." *Rivista internazionale di diritto comune* 18 (2007): 43–70.

– "Canon Law in the Late Middle Ages: The Need and the Opportunity." In *Proceedings of the Eleventh International Congress of Medieval Canon Law*, edited by Manlio Bellomo and Orazio Condorelli, 31–42. Vatican City: Biblioteca Apostolica Vaticana, 2006.

Pennington, Kenneth, Charles Donahue, Jr., Atria Larson, and Brandon Parlopiano. *Bio-Bibliographical Guide to Medieval and Early Modern Jurists*. Online: Harvard University and the Ames Foundation, 2011–17. Last updated online 27 May 2017.

Peters, Edward N. "*Ius decretalium*." Last modified 4 March 2017. http://www.canonlaw.info/canonlaw_IUSDECR.htm.

Peterson, David S. "Antoninus." In *Encyclopedia of the Renaissance*, edited by Paul F. Grendler. New York: Scribners with Renaissance Society of America, 1999.

– "Archbishop Antoninus: Florence and the Church in the Earlier Fifteenth Century." PhD diss., Cornell University, 1985.

– "An Episcopal Election in Quattrocento Florence." In *Popes, Teachers, and Canon Lawyers in the Middle Ages*, edited by James Ross Sweeney and Stanley Chodorow, 300–25. Ithaca: Cornell University Press, 1989.

– "Out of the Margins: Religion and the Church in Renaissance Italy." *Renaissance Quarterly* 53, no. 3 (2000): 835–79.

Pietschmann, Klaus. "Ablauf und Dimensionen der Heilgsprechung des Antoninus von Florenz (1523): Kanonisationspraxis im politischen und religiösen Umbruch." *Quellen und Forschungen aus italienischen Archiven und Bibliotheken* 78 (1998): 388–463.

– "The Sense of Hearing Politicized: Liturgical Polyphony and Political Ambition in Fifteenth-Century Florence." In *Religion and the Senses in Early Modern Europe*, edited by Wietse de Boer and Christine Göttler, 271–88. Intersections 26. Leiden: Brill, 2012.

Pirenne, Henri. *Economic and Social History of Medieval Europe*. Translated by I.E. Clegg. New York: Harcourt, Brace, & World, 1937.

– "The Stages in the Social History of Capitalism." *American Historical Review* 19, no. 3 (1914): 494–515. https://doi.org/10.2307/1835075.

Polecritti, Cynthia. *Preaching Peace in Renaissance Italy: Bernardino of Siena and His Audience*. Washington, DC: Catholic University of America Press, 2000.

Polizzotto, Lorenzo. "The Making of a Saint: The Canonization of S. Antonino 1516–1523." *Journal of Medieval and Renaissance Studies* 22 (1992): 353–81.

Pollick, Brian A. "The Merchant's Moral Eye: Money, Merchants, and the Visualization of Morality in Trecento Italy." PhD diss., University of Victoria, 2021.

Pomaro, G. "Censimento dei manoscritti della Biblioteca di S. Maria Novella, Parte II: Sec. XV–XVI." In *Libro e immagine*, edited by Eugenio Marino, 203–353. Memorie Domenicane, n.s., 13. Florence: Nerbini, 1982. See esp. 306–7.

Prümmer, Dominic M. *Handbook of Moral Theology*. Translated by Gerald W. Shelton. Cork: Mercier Press, 1956.

Resnick, Irven M., ed. *A Companion to Albert the Great: Theology, Philosophy, and the Sciences*. Leiden: Brill, 2013.

Robertson, H.M. *Aspects of the Rise of Economic Individualism: A Criticism of Max Weber and His School*. New York: Cambridge University Press, 1933.

Roest, Bert. "Observant Reform in Religious Orders." In *The Cambridge History of Christianity. Volume 4: Christianity in Western Europe, c.1100–c.1500*, edited by Miri Rubin and Walter Simons, 446–57. Cambridge: Cambridge University Press, 2009.

Roest, Bert, and James D. Mixson, eds. *A Companion to Observant Reform in the Late Middle Ages and Beyond*. Brill's Companions to the Christian Tradition 59. Leiden: Brill, 2015.

Rolfi, Gianfranco, Ludovica Sebregondi, and Paolo Viti, eds. *La Chiesa e la città a Firenze nel XV secolo: Firenze, Sotterranei di San Lorenzo, 6 giugno–6 settembre 1992*. Florence: Silvana Editoriale, 1992. See esp. tav. 2.3c (57–8).

Romano, Dennis. *Markets and Marketplaces in Medieval Italy, c. 1100 to c. 1440*. New Haven: Yale University Press, 2015.

Sanford, Eva Matthews. "*De disciplina scholarium*: A Medieval Handbook on the Care and Training of Scholars." *Classical Journal* 28:2 (November 1932): 82–95.

S. Antonino e la sua epoca. Atti del convegno tenutosi a Firenze 21–23 settembre 1989. Special issue of *Rivista di ascetica e mistica* 59, no. 3/4 (1990): 225–38.

Sapori, Armando. *The Italian Merchant in the Middle Ages*. Translated by Patricia Ann Kennen. New York: W.W. Norton & Co., 1970.

Schefold, Bertram."Thomas von Aquin, Petrus Johannes Olivi und Antoninus von Florenz. Mittelalterliche Kapitalkritik und die Weberthese." *Historisches Jahrbuch* 138 (2018): 92–118.

Schumpeter, Joseph A. *History of Economic Analysis*. Edited by E. Boody Schumpeter. New York: Oxford University Press, 1954.

Silano, Giulio. "The *Sentences* as a Medieval Casebook." In *Peter Lombard: The Sentences*, 1:xix–xxx. 4 vols. Medieval Sources in Translation 42, 43, 45, 48. Toronto: Pontifical Institute of Mediaeval Studies, 2007–10.

Slater, Thomas. *A Manual of Moral Theology for English-Speaking Countries*. 5th ed. 2 vols. London: Burns Oates & Washbourne, 1925.

– *A Short History of Moral Theology*. New York: Benziger, 1909.

Sombart, Werner. *Der moderne Kapitalismus*. Revised ed. 2 vols. Munich: Duncker and Humblot, 1919.

– *The Quintessence of Capitalism: A Study of the History and Psychology of the Modern Business Man*. Translated and edited by M. Epstein. New York: T.F. Unwin, 1915.

Spagnesi, Enrico. "Sant'Antonino e il diritto." In Cinelli and Paoli, *Antonino Pierozzi*, 427–48.

Spicciani, Amleto. *Capitale e interesse tra mercatura e povertà nei teologi e canonisti dei secoli XIII–XV*. Storia 24. Rome: Jouvence, 1990.

Spufford, Peter. *Handbook of Medieval Exchange*. London: Offices of the Royal Historical Society, 1986.

– *Money and Its Use in Medieval Europe*. Cambridge: Cambridge University Press, 1988.

Stansbury, Ronald, ed. *A Companion to Pastoral Care in the Late Middle Ages (1200–1500)*. Brill's Companions to the Christian Tradition 22. Leiden: Brill, 2010.

Stella, Alessandro. *La révolte des Ciompi: les hommes, les lieux, le travail*. Paris: EHESS, 1993.

Sullivan, Ezra. "Antonino Pierozzi: A *Locus* of Dominican Influence in Late Medieval and Early Renaissance Florence." *Angelicum* 93, no. 2 (2016): 345–58.

Supplemento alla posizione per il dottorato di Sant'Antonino, O.P., arcivescovo di Firenze. Rome: Sacra Congregazione per le cause dei Santi, 1983.

Thompson, Augustine. *Cities of God: The Religion of the Italian Communes, 1125–1325.* University Park: Pennsylvania State University Press, 2005.

– *Francis of Assisi: A New Biography.* Ithaca: Cornell University Press, 2012.

Todeschini, Giacomo. *Come l'acqua e il sangue: le origini medievali del pensiero economico.* Rome: Carocci editore, 2021.

– *Franciscan Wealth: From Voluntary Poverty to Market Society.* Translated by Michael Cusato. St. Bonaventure, NY: Franciscan Institute Publications, 2009.

– *Les marchands et le temple: la société chrétienne et le cercle vertueux de la richesse du Moyen Age à l'époque moderne.* Translated by Ida Giordano. Paris: Albin Michel, 2017.

– *I mercanti e il tempio: la società cristiana e il circolo virtuoso della ricchezza fra Medioevo ed età moderna.* Collana di storia dell'economia e del credito 11. Bologna: Il mulino, 2002.

– *Ricchezza francescana: dalla povertà volontaria alla società di mercato.* Intersezioni 268. Bologna: Il mulino, 2004.

Torrell, Jean-Pierre. *Saint Thomas Aquinas.* Vol. 1, *The Person and His Work.* Translated by Robert Royal. Washington, DC: Catholic University of America Press, 1996.

Trexler, Richard C. "The Episcopal Constitutions of Antoninus of Florence." *Quellen und Forschungen aus italienischen Archiven und Bibliotheken* 59 (1979): 244–72.

Trivellato, Francesca. "Renaissance Florence and the Origins of Capitalism: A Business History Perspective." *Business History Review* 94, no. 1 (2020): 229–51. https://doi.org/10.1017/S0007680520000033.

Tutino, Stefania. *Uncertainty in Post-Reformation Catholicism: A History of Probabilism.* New York: Oxford University Press, 2018.

Ullman, Berthold L., and Philip A. Stadter. *The Public Library of Renaissance Florence: Niccolò Niccoli, Cosimo de' Medici and the Library of San Marco.* Medioevo e Umanesimo 10. Padua: Editrice Antenore, 1972. https://quod-lib-umich-edu.myaccess.library.utoronto.ca/cgi/t/text/text-idx?c=acls;idno=heb01268.

University of Chicago. "Logeion." Last modified March 2017. http://logeion.uchicago.edu/about.html.

Van Engen, John. "The Church in the Fifteenth Century." In *Handbook of European History 1400–1600: Late Middle Ages, Renaissance and Reformation*, edited by Thomas A. Brady, Heiko A. Oberman, and James D. Tracy. Vol. 1, *Structures and Assertions*, 305–28. Leiden: E.J. Brill, 1994.

Vargas, Michael A. *Taming a Brood of Vipers: Conflict and Change in Fourteenth-Century Dominican Convents.* Medieval and Early Modern Iberian World 42. Boston: Brill, 2011.

Vauchez, André, ed. *Encyclopedia of the Middle Ages.* Cambridge: James Clarke, 2002.

von Heusinger, Sabine. "Catherine of Siena and the Dominican Order." In *Siena e il suo territorio in Rinascimento*, edited by Mario Ascheri, 3:43–51. Siena: Il leccio, 2000.

von Martin, Alfred. *Sociology of the Renaissance.* London: Oxford University Press, 1944.

von Schulte, J. Friedrich. "Antonius de Forciglione." In *Die Geschichte der Quellen und Literatur des Canonischen Rechts von Gratian bis auf die Gegenwart*, 2:444–5. 3 vols. Stuttgart: F. Enke, 1875–80.

Walker, J.B. "Antoninus, St." In *New Catholic Encyclopedia*, 2nd ed. https://link-galegroup-com.myaccess.library.utoronto.ca/apps/doc/CX3407700658/GVRL?u=utoronto_main&sid=GVRL&xid=61aecabd.

– *The "Chronicles" of Saint Antoninus: A Study in Historiography*. CUA Studies in Medieval History 6. Washington, DC: Catholic University of America, 1933.

Weber, Max. *The Protestant Ethic and the Spirit of Capitalism*. Translated by Talcott Parsons. London: Taylor & Francis, 2005.

Weinstein, Donald. *Savonarola: The Rise and Fall of a Renaissance Prophet*. New Haven: Yale University Press, 2011.

Wenzel, Siegfried. *Medieval Artes Praedicandi: A Synthesis of Scholastic Sermon Structure*. Medieval Academy Books 114. Toronto: University of Toronto Press, 2015.

Westbrook, Raymond. "The Origin of *Laesio Enormis*." *Revue internationale des droits de l'antiquité* ser. 3, no. 55 (2008): 39–52.

Whitaker, William. "Whitaker's Words." Version 1.97FC. Last modified December 2006. http://archives.nd.edu/whitaker/words.htm.

Wilms, H. "Das *Confessionale Defecerunt* des hl. Antoninus." *Divus Thomas* 24 (1946): 99–108.

Winroth, Anders. *The Making of Gratian's Decretum*. Cambridge Studies in Medieval Life and Thought 4. Cambridge: Cambridge University Press, 2000.

Wolter, H. "Antoninus, Ebf. v. Florenz." In *Lexikon des Mittelalters*. 10 vols., 1977–99. Article published in 1977. http://www.brepolis.net.myaccess.library.utoronto.ca/.

Wood, Diana. *Medieval Economic Thought*. Cambridge: Cambridge University Press, 2002.

Wood, Ellen Meiksins. *The Origin of Capitalism: A Longer View*. London: Verso, 2002.

Wranovix, Matthew. "Ulrich Pfeffel's Library: Parish Priests, Preachers, and Books in the Fifteenth Century." *Speculum* 87, no. 4 (2012): 1125–55.

Zarri, Gabrielle. "Ecclesiastical Institutions and Religious Life in the Observant Century." In Roest and Mixson, *Companion to Observant Reform*, 21–59.

Zimmermann, Reinhard. *The Law of Obligations: Roman Foundations of the Civilian Tradition*. Cape Town: Kluwer, 1992; reprint, New York: Oxford University Press, 1996.

Index

Note: Page numbers in *italics* refer to illustrations and tables. Page numbers in **bold** refer to the English translation of the *Summa*; these references may be used to find the corresponding material in the facing-page Latin text.

TORONTO STUDIES IN MEDIEVAL LAW

1. *The Politics of Law in Late Medieval and Renaissance Italy*, edited by Lawrin Armstrong and Julius Kirshner
2. *Marriage, Dowry, and Citizenship in Late Medieval and Renaissance Italy*, Julius Kirshner
3. *The Idea of a Moral Economy: Gerard of Siena on Usury, Restitution, and Prescription*, Lawrin Armstrong
4. *Jurists and Jurisprudence in Medieval Italy: Texts and Contexts*, Osvaldo Cavallar and Julius Kirshner
5. *St Antoninus of Florence on Trade, Merchants, and Workers*, Jason Aaron Brown

www.ingramcontent.com/pod-product-compliance
Ingram Content Group UK Ltd.
Pitfield, Milton Keynes, MK11 3LW, UK
UKHW022241150325
456187UK00012B/46/J